THE FILM HANDBOOK

G.K. HALL
PERFORMING
ARTS
HANDBOOKS

THE FILM HANDBOOK

Geoff Andrew

G.K. Hall & Co.
Boston

Acknowledgements

FOR MY PARENTS, AND MANDY AND CLINT, without whose forbearance on many fronts this book might never have been written.

Thanks also to David Thompson, Tony Rayns, Tom Milne, Wally Hammond, Brian Case, Nigel Floyd, Simon Field, Anne Billson, Paul Taylor, Kim Newman, Charles MacDonald, Patric Scott, Sue Blackmore, Adriana Capadose, Jo Lustig, Adrian Turner, Richard Combs, Graham Smith and Don Atyeo, who between them offered advice and understanding. Others, too many to mention, deserve gratitude for encouragement in times of darkness; it is to be hoped they know who they are. A special thank you, too, to Philip Dodd, who suggested the project to me and thus helped me to lose a year from my life; and to my publisher, Peter Zombory-Moldovan, who saw the whole thing through to final completion with patience and perceptive suggestions.

The picture on page 4 is from Martin Scorsese.
All other pictures are from the Joel Finler collection.

First published in 1989 by Longman Group UK Limited, Longman House, Burnt Mill, Harlow, Essex CM20 2JE, England and Associated Companies throughout the world.

Published in the United States by G.K. Hall & Co.,
70 Lincoln St., Boston, Massachusetts, 02111.

10 9 8 7 6 5 4 3

Library of Congress Cataloging-in-Publication Data

Andrew, Geoff.
The film handbook / Geoff Andrew.
p. cm.—(G.K. Hall performing arts series)
Includes bibliographical references.
ISBN 0-8161-9093-3 ISBN 0-8161-1830-2 (pbk)
1. Motion picture producers and directors—Biography—Dictionaries.
I. Title. II. Series.
PN1998.2.A64 1990
791.43'028'0922—dc20 89-77760
CIP

The paper used in this publication meets the minimum requirements of American National Standard for Information Sciences—Permanence of Paper for Printed Library Materials. ANSI Z39.48-1984. ∞™
MANUFACTURED IN THE UNITED STATES OF AMERICA

Contents

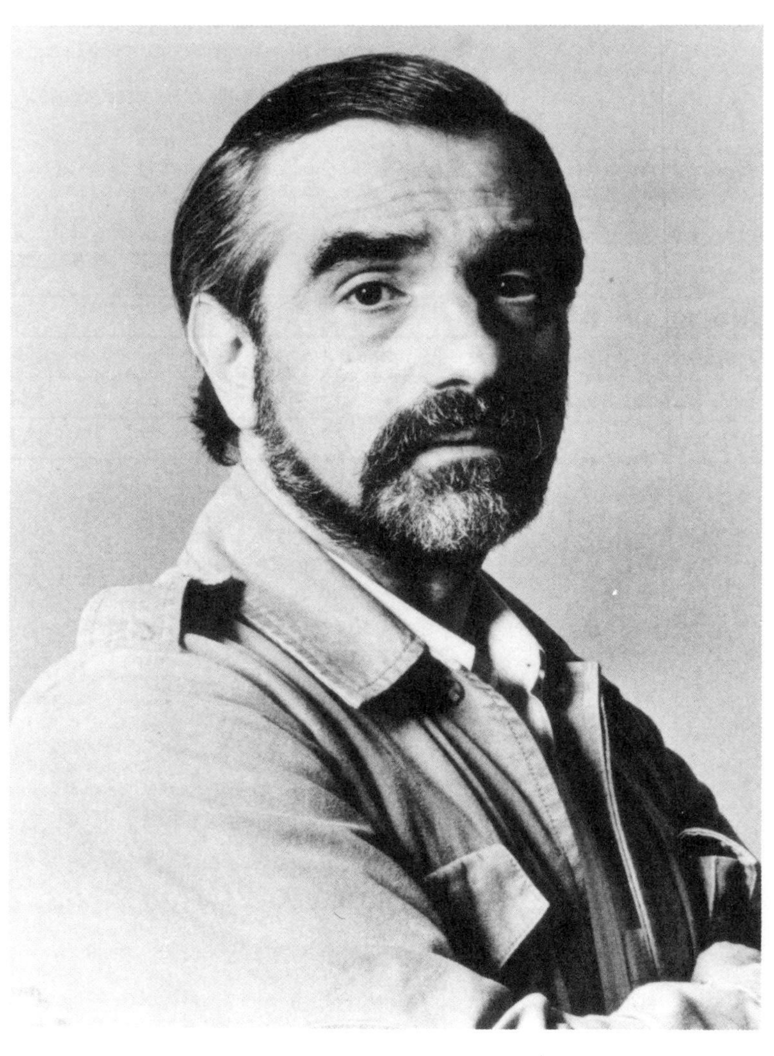

My earliest memory of a movie image is Roy Rogers riding Trigger. It was a preview of a feature that was coming soon. I was moved by the beautiful horse, and by the strange quality of the Trucolor process: the sky was aquamarine. And so my father took me to see Trigger in a theatre, and I became fascinated by Westerns. In this way, as a kid who was often ill, I also overcame my allergy to the outdoors and to animals.

I began seeing lots of movies. Around the age of five, I saw a film condemned by the Church, Vidor's *Duel in the Sun*. Since it was a Western, my mother was able to use me as an excuse to see it herself. I fell in love with the movie's sense of space, its vastness and its demonic hysteria, its story of two people so in love they kill each other. At that time I was not aware of who Vidor was or what he did, but by 1956 my friends and I had become familiar with the name John Ford. We saw *Fort Apache*, *She Wore a Yellow Ribbon* and *The Searchers* – featuring a more modern, neurotic John Wayne – and we knew Ford's name promised something special, beautiful, poetic.

Then came the pyrotechnics of Welles' *Citizen Kane*, which I first saw on TV. By studying Welles, I understood for the first time about camera style: I realised a director *chose* how to tell a story in images. Welles led to others: Minnelli, Reed, Powell/Pressburger and, again from TV, to Italians like De Sica and Rossellini. I remember my whole family reacted very strongly to the neo-realist films.

I love movies for the stories they tell, the way they affect our emotions. At times, it's not only possible to learn from them, but also to commiserate – to empathize with the characters. It's now constantly said that the film industry is ailing. But then, along comes Spielberg, pushing Hollywood into the megabucks territory and rejuvenating the entire industry. This rejuvenation creates activity – more films and different kinds of filmmakers appear. There is a little more room for everyone, especially with developments in video and cable. Nevertheless, despite all the technical advances and apparent commercial preference for Big Budget fantasy films, I do hope audiences will still want to see films that deal with character, where people communicate with each other.

Everyone enjoys movies, and a Film Handbook for laymen, with concise critical analyses of directors and lists of key films, is a fine idea. Very often I agree with Geoff Andrew; sometimes not. I certainly don't agree with his entries on David Lean and Elia Kazan, who both made films of the greatest importance to me. But I loved the piece on Michael Powell, and it was good to read the entries on people like Anthony Mann, Joseph H. Lewis and several of my friends. But, whether you agree with Andrew or not, it's encouraging that the book is provocative.

I myself first decided to become a filmmaker at the age of 18, when I took classes in film history. My teacher spoke even more quickly than I do. I was caught up in his ideas and his presentation of the panorama of film history. Before, I'd been interested in painting and the priesthood, but film was to be my vocation. And making movies has its own special challenge; you try to make your work grow, *and* you try to grow from your work. That, finally, is the battle.

Martin Scorsese

How to use The Film Handbook

The Film Handbook is a compact guide offering an alphabetical look at the extensive – and sometimes daunting – range of films that can now be seen in cinemas, film societies, on television and video. It approaches the medium by charting, chronologically and critically, the careers of the directors central to any serious study of cinema, and aims to encourage you, through a system of cross-references, to encounter as wide a variety of movies as possible.

The Handbook's purpose is to prepare the groundwork for building up an overall view of cinema, and to encourage you to develop your own personal tastes. In many cases, the writer has not been afraid to fly in the face of received critical opinion; in attempting to argue the case for his likes and dislikes, he hopes that he may provoke the reader into a thoughtful response. The different routes you can take are clearly marked; it is up to you whether or not you choose to pursue them.

The entries

At the core of the Handbook are a little over 200 main entries. The directors have been deliberately chosen to cover a wide and relevant spread of starting points, ranging from pioneers of the silent era (Griffith, Von Stroheim) to young, promising talents with only a few films to their name (Chen Kaige, Terence Davies). The Handbook is not a dictionary – it offers too personal a view for that – nor is it intended to be comprehensive, but a stimulus and springboard for further exploration. Omission by no means implies lack of importance; there will, however, still be those who wonder why, for example, John Farrow has been favoured over Jacques Rivette, or Paul Cox over Sylvester Stallone. Inevitably, any selection is to some extent arbitrary and therefore open to criticism but a number of criteria have been employed with regard to making the book as useful as possible. The work of the chosen directors should be easily available for viewing *at the time of writing*; the directors in question are widely considered, from the standpoint of the late 1980s, superior examples of their profession (though not necessarily by the writer); in some cases, figures are included whom the writer considers underrated and therefore deserving of re-appraisal; and in the case of some of the younger, less established directors, their inclusion derives from the writer's feeling that their work to date suggests that they may develop into important film-makers in years to come. The Handbook is as concerned with the future of cinema as it is with its past and present.

Inevitably, the Handbook has its limitations. In focussing, for example, on mainstream commercial cinema, it scarcely touches on documentary, experimental cinema, or the product of the lesser film-making nations. Moreover, in opting to approach its subject through directors, the Handbook is not proposing a simple-minded celebration of the solitary *auteur*; it is merely using a critical tool that seems to many, the writer included, to be the most logical, easily understood, and useful of the many methods available. It should be remembered, however, that film-making is collaborative, involving contributions from actors, writers, producers, cameramen, and countless other technicians and executives. Film, both art and industry, can be considered from many standpoints: social and political, technological, economic, historical, geographical, semiological and psychoanalytical, not to mention, in the case of Hollywood, the importance of both genre and studio 'house' style. Naturally, most of these elements are touched on within the pages of the Handbook but, in aiming to be of use to both the serious student of film and, more importantly, the ordinary enthusiastic movie-goer, the main approach is essentially one of aesthetics.

Main entries contain the following elements:

1 A block of **factual information**. This contains:
– Date and place of birth and death
– Directing career dates

2 The **main critique** sets the director in context, identifying what is important and/or interesting in his work, his impact on cinema, and what to look for in his films. Any references to other main entries are indicated in **bold**; films are usually mentioned in the order of their making/release; those films deemed of special interest (not all of a director's output will always be mentioned) are indicated by an arrow (>) and a number which refers to the Viewing section.

3 **Lineage**: the heart of the Handbook's network of connections, naming influences on the director and those whom the director in turn influenced, and suggesting – sometimes controversially – figures with whom the director might be compared or contrasted. Again, references to other main entries are indicated in **bold**.

4 **Further reading**: a selection for most entries of suggested books which focus on the director's work and/or life. In some cases, an autobiography may also be listed; or, where relevant, a collection of the director's own writings on film.

5 **Viewing**: the films themselves, often but not always the best by the director in question, and invariably those that are the most representative and illuminating with regard to style and thematic interest. An arrow (>) and number refer back to the main critique. Dates usually refer to the year of the film's initial release (although in some cases, where the film's release was delayed by several years, the year of completion is given). Nationality is largely a matter of common sense, and refers primarily not to the sources of finance but to the country in which the film was made. For Hollywood productions shot partly on location abroad, US is given). Cast members are those deemed central to the film's narrative, regardless of the actor's off-screen status. Where a film is known by more than one title, both are usually given, the name best known in the country of its production coming first. In the case of foreign movies, if a film is best known by its original, foreign-language title, for example *La Strada*, that is given, untranslated. If it is best known by its English title, that is used, followed by the foreign title if the English differs in meaning from the original, for example *Anne and Muriel (Les Deux Anglaises et le Continent)*. Titles in languages other than French, German and Italian are given in English unless they are known by their original title in Britain and the US.

The Databank

Following the main entries is a Databank of additional information, including:

- A **glossary**, which provides an outline of the thematic and stylistic characteristics of the main genres, including lists of directors who worked fruitfully in each; and brief summaries of four main styles, again with a list of relevant directors.
- **Film books**: a selection of general books that will increase the reader's knowledge of cinema, including reference books, books on genre, history, studios, theory, etc.
- A country-by-country **information source** section listing specialist magazines, institutes, archives, film-schools and major film festivals.
- **Index**: a comprehensive A-Z of all the people and films mentioned in the Handbook.

The Film Handbook is the fourth title in a series of Longman Handbooks on the arts: see the back cover for details.

Robert Aldrich

Born: 9th August 1918/Cranston, Rhode Island, USA
Died: 5th December 1983/Los Angeles, California, USA
Directing career: 1953-1981

While it is commonly held that Robert Aldrich was primarily an action director, a cynical purveyor of male violence whose movies diminished in value as he grew older, his career, like his films, is beset by contradictions; indeed, the abiding impression gained from an overview of his work is that of inconsistency.

After a series of jobs at RKO, Aldrich served as assistant to **Renoir**, **Ophüls**, **Chaplin**, **Losey**, **Polonsky** and Lewis Milestone. In 1953 he made his directing debut with *The Big Leaguer*, but it was only in his third film, *Apache* >**1**, that his assured grasp of genre and liberal sensibilities came to the fore in a sympathetic but never maudlin portrait of an Indian alienated from both white America and his own kind. But it was *Kiss Me Deadly* >**2** that first displayed the developed Aldrich style. Amidst a virtuoso array of Expressionist lighting effects, Mickey Spillane's private-eye was deglamorised to become a thug motivated by material self-interest and sadistic violence: a brutish incarnation of Cold War paranoia and McCarthyist bullying. The climactic explosive images push the Fascist allegory still further: when Hammer's investigation leads to a modern Pandora's Box, *film noir* enters the Nuclear Age.

Aldrich's characteristic combination of overheated imagery and polarised protagonists continued through a variety of genres. *The Big Knife* pitted an angst-ridden movie-star against a tyrant mogul (based, apparently, on Columbia's Harry Cohn) in a powerful one-set adaptation of Clifford Odets' Broadway play; Aldrich's choice and treatment of this material revealed his dislike of the Hollywood establishment. *Attack!* >**3** showed far less interest in America's war against Germany than in the fatal conflict between an embittered, idealist lieutenant and his cowardly superior; and *Whatever Happened to Baby Jane?* >**4** moved the battle to the female arena, with a wheelchair-bound cripple terrorised by her vengeful sister in a steamy atmosphere of mad melodrama and Gothic horror. Besides these riveting, mostly intelligent films, however, Aldrich also made several undistinguished flops, most depressingly of all the ludicrous epic, *Sodom and Gomorrah*.

As his career progressed, his work became increasingly erratic, alternating between muddy incoherence (*The Legend of Lylah Clare*, *Hustle*) and a rigorous, often disquieting depiction of humanity's excesses (*The Longest Yard*). In *The Dirty Dozen* >**5** he seemed torn between whether to mock American heroism (a troupe of psychopaths and convicts from Death Row conduct a suicide mission behind Nazi lines) or to indulge in a gung-ho celebration of violence; while the lesbian love triangle and TV 'soap' parody of *The Killing of Sister George* is fatally removed from reality. Conversely, *The Grissom Gang* (an inventive kidnapping thriller subverting James Hadley Chase's *No Orchids for Miss Blandish* to touching effect) and *Ulzana's Raid* >**6** provide taut and radical reworkings of genre stereotypes. In the latter, an ageing scout reluctantly aids West Point-trained cavalry officers in the self-destructive pursuit of renegade Indians: parallels with the Vietnam War are lucid and resonant, the atrocities committed by both sides never ignored.

In his final years, only the politically cynical *Twilight's Last Gleaming* >**7** – a chilling military-conspiracy thriller with a rebellious, retired general holding the President to ransom with threats of atomic warfare – showed Aldrich on peak form, whereas both *The Choirboys* and *The Frisco Kid* suffered from excessively broad comedy. Nevertheless, his final film *All the Marbles* (*The California Dolls*) treated the potentially disastrous subject of women's wrestling with moments of unexpected warmth and wit.

At his best, Aldrich employed vicious irony, muscular acting and vivid, sophisticated compositions to evoke a world divided by self-interest and forever on the verge of violent anarchy. At the same time those ingredients, when applied to an ill-focussed script, led to overstatement and vulgarity. Whatever, his signature is almost always discernible, if only through his repeated use of certain key actors – most notably Jack Palance and Burt Lancaster – and of the superb cameraman Joseph Biroc.

Lineage

Aldrich was one of many directors (**Losey**, **Ray**, **Fuller** and **Siegel** included) who in the late '40s and '50s used lowly, violent genres to make social statements about America. He may thus be seen as a precursor to **Peckinpah**, **Penn**, **Hopper** and **Scorsese**.

Further reading

Robert Aldrich, ed. Richard Combs (London, 1978).

Viewing

1 **Apache**
US 1954/ w Burt Lancaster, Jean Peters, John McIntire

2 **Kiss Me Deadly**
US 1955/ w Ralph Meeker, Albert Dekker, Paul Stewart

3 **Attack!**
US 1956/ w Jack Palance, Eddie Albert, Lee Marvin

4 **Whatever Happened to Baby Jane?**
US 1962/ w Bette Davis, Joan Crawford, Victor Buono

5 **The Dirty Dozen**
US/GB 1967/ w Lee Marvin, John Cassavetes, Ernest Borgnine

6 **Ulzana's Raid**
US 1972/ w Burt Lancaster, Bruce Davison, Richard Jaeckel

7 **Twilight's Last Gleaming**
US 1977/ w Burt Lancaster, Richard Widmark, Charles Durning

Woody Allen

Born: 1st December 1935/Brooklyn, New York, USA
Directing career: 1969-

While most other recent screen comics have aimed their lamebrain, slapdash spoofery at teenage audiences, Allen Stewart Konigsberg, as he was born, has alone been consistent in catering to more adult tastes. His is a comedy increasingly defined by character: notably, his own.

Like **Mel Brooks** and Carl Reiner, Allen worked in the '50s as a writer for Sid Caesar before taking up performing himself as a stand-up comic. In the mid-'60s, he diversified still further by contributing scripts and performances to *What's New Pussycat?* and *Casino Royale*. After adding absurd American dubbing to a Japanese spy-thriller for the sporadically funny *What's Up Tiger Lily?*, he made his directing debut proper with *Take the Money and Run*. This spoof crime-movie established the formula for his subsequent disjointed parodies – of South American revolution (*Bananas*), sex instruction (*Everything You Always Wanted to Know About Sex*), old Humphrey Bogart movies (*Play It Again, Sam*), science fiction (*Sleeper*) and Russian literature (*Love and Death* >**1**). The hero of these offerings was a little man in the **Chaplin** mould, a failure with women, cowardly, and bursting with modern neuroses about mortality, sex, and cosmic injustice. Artistically, the films were rag-bags of romance, gags and slapstick, unconcerned with any character but Allen's own. If *Love and Death* is by far the best of his early work, it is because the books and films that inspire his parody were topics he loved: **Eisenstein**'s montage of the stone lions aroused by revolution in *Battleship Potemkin* was neatly reversed to depict Woody's sexual prowess.

His first major critical and commercial success, *Annie Hall* >**2** entailed a change of style. Although it still lacked narrative coherence and relied too heavily on trick effects (split-screen, subtitled dialogue, direct-to-camera monologues), it was notably a more personal work. With Allen himself as Jewish comedian Alvie Singer and inspired by his off-screen relationship with co-star Diane Keaton, the comedy was imbued with a strained seriousness. For the

Human chameleon Leonard Zelig (Woody Allen) hobnobbing with Presidents Calvin Coolidge and Herbert Hoover, in *Zelig*.

first time, Allen examined themes that would recur in his later work, such as the moral conflict between a tortured intellect and a less meditative spontaneity, the transience of love, and the fragility of happiness.

The film's success encouraged him to experiment further. The sombre *Interiors* was a pretentious tribute to **Bergman**; *Manhattan* >**3** made fine use of Gordon Willis' black and white camerawork, Gershwin's music, and a wider range of characters as it worked gentle social satire into another failed romance; *Stardust Memories* gave an account of a film-maker's creative block in the face of public and critical hostility. It was both semi-autobiographical and a hackneyed tribute to **Fellini**'s *8½*. All displayed Allen's growing confidence and competence as a dramatic artist; all, however, still paraded his neurotic obsessions with a dismal, self-indulgent lack of irony.

The failure of *Stardust Memories* seemed to provoke a re-think. *A Midsummer Night's Sex Comedy*, although overshadowed by Allen's cultural heroes (Bergman, Shakespeare, **Renoir**, Chekov), exuded a warmth hitherto unseen. Then came several similarly 'small' films that, despite apparently limited ambitions, suggested a maturing of Allen's art. *Zelig* >**4**, an ingenious spoof documentary about a forgotten psychological freak whose entire appearance altered to match that of people he met, is not only hilarious (Allen's Zelig found hobnobbing with Hemingway, Hitler, the Pope) but a profound examination of issues of identity and performance; *Broadway Danny Rose* was a witty romance-cum-gangster parody; and *The Purple Rose of Cairo*, in which a '30s waitress falls for a fictional hero who steps out of the movie screen into real life, is a moving meditation on the relationship between experience and illusion, and on cinema's capacity to feed our need to dream.

Hannah and Her Sisters >**5** saw Allen return to a broad canvas (and upper-crust Manhattan) with a delicately romantic picture of the tensions and unwilling betrayals of family life. While Chekov and Lear's daughters hover in the wings, Allen's own style takes centre stage; even his now familiar invocation of the good things in life (art, comedy, friends, family parties) is integrated into the story instead of merely stated. Most impressively, the other characters are no less colourfully drawn than the director's own permanently hypochondriac court jester.

It was a pity then, that he resorted to Felliniesque fantasy and nostalgia in *Radio Days*, although the arty solemnity of *September* served to reveal his increasingly stylish, elegant direction. But *Another Woman*, a further exploration of mid-life melancholy among the wealthy and educated middle classes, was generally considered turgid, pretentious, even irrelevant. Nevertheless, Allen's career has always proceeded fitfully, and his body of work is one of the most inventive, enjoyable, and ambitious in recent years. Having built a career on the public's willingness to tolerate his personal anxieties – the films reek of the analyst's couch – Allen has, paradoxically, often seemed a strangely withdrawn artist. That, however, may prove to be the secret of his success.

Lineage

While Allen's early work is reminiscent of **Chaplin**, and New York Jewish humour defines much of his verbal felicity, he is also a self-confessed intellectual; references to **Bergman**, **Fellini** *et al* abound. His idiosyncratic style has few successful imitators.

Further reading

Douglas Brode's *Woody Allen: His Life and Career* (London, 1986) and Robert Beyanoun's *Woody Allen: Beyond Words* (London, 1986).

Viewing

1 **Love and Death**
US 1975/ w Allen, Diane Keaton, Harold Gould

2 **Annie Hall**
US 1977/ w Allen, Diane Keaton, Tony Roberts

3 **Manhattan**
US 1979/ w Allen, Diane Keaton, Mariel Hemingway

4 **Zelig**
US 1983/ w Allen, Mia Farrow, Stephanie Farrow

5 **Hannah and Her Sisters**
US 1986/ w Michael Caine, Barbara Hershey, Mia Farrow, Diane Wiest, Allen

Robert Altman

Born: **20th February 1925/Kansas City, Missouri, USA**
Directing career: 1957-

In the '70s, while the Hollywood mainstream foundered, the finest American films were made by Robert Altman. A natural outsider, he intuitively opposed the heroic traditions of Hollywood's seamless narratives to create a fresh, personal style and a consistently provocative critique of The American Dream.

Having served his apprenticeship in industrial documentary, Altman's first features proved inauspicious: *The Delinquents* and a documentary about James Dean – both made in the mid-'50s – are now all but forgotten. For a decade he then worked on television series such as *Bonanza* and *Alfred Hitchcock Presents*, before making, in 1967, *Countdown*, an intelligent, unusually humane space-race drama, notable partly for its low-key technical authenticity. Only with *M*A*S*H* >**1**, however, did his unique style first make itself felt. This seemingly chaotic black comedy, about a mobile army medical unit's anarchic adventures during the Korean War, made inventive use of a large cast, barely comprehensible multi-track dialogue and a spontaneity of performance verging on the improvisational. But for all its gleeful mockery of conventional war heroics, the film (clearly intended to evoke the Vietnam War) was flawed by cynical cliché; sadly, but perhaps not surprisingly, it remains Altman's greatest commercial success.

Thereafter, the director's prolific output soon reached maturity. After *Brewster McCloud* >**2**, an offbeat update of the Icarus story which introduced the archetypal, dreamy Altman protagonist, much of his '70s work played variations on long-nshrined genres: the Western (*McCabe and Mrs Miller* >**3**, *Buffalo Bill and the Indians*), *film noir* (*The Long Goodbye* >**4**), the rural gangster film (*Thieves Like Us*), the 'buddy' movie (*California Split*), the puttin'-on-a-show musical (*Nashville* >**5**), post-apocalyptic sci-fi (*Quintet*) and the meeting-cute romance (*A Perfect Couple*). Transcending satire and parody, Altman's semi-comic ruminations were critical dissections of American mythology, populated by deluded losers and loners in search of quick success. *McCabe and Mrs Miller*, pioneers planning to bring Civilisation and Capitalism to a frontier mining town, are a shy, unassuming gambler (mistaken for a hired gunman, thus prompting a superb shoot-out in the snow) and an opium-addicted brothel madame; in *The Long Goodbye*, Raymond Chandler's private-eye Marlowe becomes a shambling moral anachronism bewildered by the ruthless opportunism and deceit that defines upper-crust LA.

Altman's democratic style, whereby spectators 'take part' in the film by choosing from the garrulous soundtrack and widescreen gallery of characters whatever they want to hear and see, reached its zenith in *Nashville*. An epic account of a week in the lives of 24 musicians and fans attending a country music festival, its fragmented Impressionist observations retain an amazing emotional poignancy; its seething tapestry of contemporary American life is deceptively informal, its tightly-woven patterns deftly concealed beneath a veneer of naturalism. Disappointingly, the later *A Wedding and Health*, experiments along the same lines, were less successful.

Most bizarre of the genre-pieces, *Popeye* >**6**, with E.C. Segar's cartoon figures brought miraculously to life by real actors, was too anarchic, complex and profane for kids, and flopped; far less satisfactory an excursion into a comic-strip world was the later *O.C. & Stiggs*. Meanwhile a less ebullient side to Altman's personal vision periodically appeared in more intimate works, often sombre – even horrific – psychodramas about women redefining themselves under stress. *That Cold Day in the Park*, *Images* and *3 Women* thus presage *Come Back to the Five and Dime, Jimmy Dean, Jimmy Dean* >**7**, the first of several ambitious, profoundly cinematic adaptations of stage plays. In observing the revelatory reunion of a group of women – ageing members of a smalltown James Dean fan club – the camera, continually prowling a single bar-room set to alight on faces in close-up – illuminates the dark and hidden emotions that remain unexpressed by words. Such experiments (*Streamers*, *Fool for Love*, *Beyond Therapy*) peaked in *Secret Honor* >**8**, in which an astounding variety of sight-lines serve to explore the madness, mediocrity and delusions of one character: the ultimate Altman loser, Richard Milhous Nixon, in dialogue with his tape-recorder while he awaits and berates his pardon for the Watergate scandal.

Altman's recent stubborn focus on stage adaptations has lost him all but the most devout followers; he seems bent on single-handedly redefining the thin line between film and theatre. Gone are the genre variations and garrulous masses of characters, yet the director's taste for testing American myths, his sympathy for dreamers and underachievers, and his refusal to make compromises are still very evident. This is notably so in *Tanner '88*, a TV drama wittily using documentary methods to trace a fictional political campaign in contemporary America. The direction Altman will take in the future is anybody's guess: perhaps the greatest maverick in modern American cinema, he retains the capacity to disturb, provoke and surprise.

Lineage

Though Altman's style is unique, his use of overlapping dialogue was anticipated by **Hawks** while his critique of the American Dream through genre is perhaps most closely parallelled in the work of **Penn**. In the '70s, his seemingly chaotic spontaneity spawned many lesser imitators, though in producing films by **Rudolph** and **Benton** he

Robert Altman on the set of his widely acclaimed Bicentenary epic *Nashville.*

temporarily found two worthy disciples.

Further reading

Judith M. Kass's *Robert Altman: American Innovator* (New York, 1978).

Viewing

1 **M*A*S*H**
US 1970/ w Elliott Gould, Donald Sutherland, Robert Duvall

2 **Brewster McCloud**
US 1970/ w Bud Cort, Sally Kellerman, Shelley Duvall

3 **McCabe and Mrs Miller**
US 1971/ w Warren Beatty, Julie Christie, Keith Carradine

4 **The Long Goodbye**
US 1973/ w Elliott Gould, Nina Van Pallandt, Sterling Hayden

5 **Nashville**
US 1975/ w Lily Tomlin, Keith Carradine, Henry Gibson, Geraldine Chaplin

6 **Popeye**
US 1980/ w Robin Williams, Shelley Duvall, Paul Dooley

7 **Come Back to the Five and Dime, Jimmy Dean, Jimmy Dean**
US 1982/ w Karen Black, Cher, Sandy Dennis

8 **Secret Honor**
US 1984/ w Philip Baker Hall

Lindsay Anderson

Born: 17th April 1923/Bangalore, India
Directing career: 1948-

A progressive slackening, both in quality and quantity, in the work of Lindsay Gordon Anderson, belies the fact that of all the film-makers associated with Britain's Free Cinema movement in the late '50s, he was by far the most able. Since then, commitment seems to have calcified into self-righteous posturing, passion into bile.

As the young editor of the film journal 'Sequence', Anderson voiced polemical criticism of Britain's film industry (for its reliance on staid, bourgeois subjects). He endorsed his views by making documentary shorts on subjects as varied as factory workers, a school for the deaf, and the Covent Garden market. In 1963 he directed his first feature, *This Sporting Life* >**1**, based on David Storey's novel about a rugby player's doomed love for his widowed landlady. Marked by strong performances, it differs from other superficially similar British films of the time by introducing a great deal of poetry into its otherwise orthodox realist view of the Industrial North. Rugby games are shot in epic slow motion, linking actor Richard Harris' brute physicality to an almost primeval vision of humanity; while the spider he smashes against a white hospital wall as a black line of blood trickles from his beloved's corpse is a potent symbol both of death and of the character's own inability to communicate.

From the early '60s, Anderson spent a great deal of time working in the theatre, and another six years passed before his next feature, *If . . .* >**2**. While less coherent and compassionate than *This Sporting Life*, *If . . .* was far more ambitious. The violent eruption of emotions was again on display as public schoolboys – led by Malcolm McDowell's Mick Travis – rebel

against the constraints of a regimented life.
Openly inspired by **Vigo**'s *Zéro de Conduite*, it combined an accurate, realist depiction of the school's archaic rituals with a witty, surreal evocation of spiritual liberation and savagery: the school chaplain, bayonetted to death by the boys, is kept in a drawer in the headmaster's study to await an apology, and in an explosive, ambiguously fantastic finale, the rebels turn machine guns on teachers, governors, and parents.

These heady anti-authoritarian sentiments were revived in a loose sequel, *O Lucky Man!* McDowell's Travis reappears, in name if not character, as a Candide-figure whose picaresque progress towards winning an acting part in the film we are watching leads him through a strange, sinister version of modern Britain. A handful of images are arresting – notably a human head transplanted on to a pig's body – but the satire is too broad to be incisive. Ten years later, *Britannia Hospital*, another splenetic state-of-the-nation allegory, took aim at still easier targets by focussing on the microcosm of a run-down hospital beset by strikes and a royal visit. Widely dismissed by critics and public alike, its failure prompted a change of mood and style in *The Whales of August*, a tepid, stagey adaptation of a sentimental play about growing old. Despite able performances by veterans Lillian Gish, Bette Davis, Vincent Price and Ann Sothern, its lack of originality makes it unrecognisable as a work by Anderson.

Indeed, his future as a film-maker would seem to be uncertain, so at odds is he with both the establishment and with younger talents.

Lineage

Although Anderson's experiences as a documentarist with the Free Cinema movement (with which the Swiss directors Alain Tanner and Claude Goretta were briefly connected) inculcated a feeling for realism, other loves – **Ford**, **Vigo**, Humphrey Jennings – impelled him towards more poetic fantasy. In the '60s he turned his attention towards Eastern Europe, and **Milos Forman** has spoken of Anderson's encouragement.

Further reading

Elizabeth Sussex's *Lindsay Anderson* (London, 1969).

Viewing

1 **This Sporting Life**
GB 1963/ w Richard Harris, Rachel Roberts, Alan Badel
2 **If . . .**
GB 1969/ w Malcolm McDowell, Peter Jeffrey, Arthur Lowe

Michelangelo Antonioni

Born: **29th September 1912/Ferrara, Italy**
Directing career: 1943-

If the films of Michelangelo Antonioni reflect his own feelings on life, and there is little doubt that they do, it is curious that he makes them at all, since, although they attempt to express and illuminate human emotions, they simultaneously imply that human communication is futile, barren, even impossible.

The young Antonioni was involved in student drama and film criticism before working as a scriptwriter for **Rossellini** and as an assistant to **Carné**. After making a number of documentaries, he directed his first feature, *Cronaca di un Amore* (*Story of a Love Affair*) >**1** in 1950. A quiet study of the guilt felt by two lovers when the woman's husband, whom they have considered killing, dies in a car accident, it foreshadows the austere melancholy and lack of eventful narrative that would mark the director's later films. Indeed, throughout the '50s he refined his cool style to examine, repeatedly, the aftermath of love, the spiritual lassitude of the bourgeoisie, and the way environment affects and reflects mental states. In *Il Grido* (*The Cry*) >**2**, the protagonist – unusually, for Antonioni, from the working rather than middle class – is left by his lover and embarks upon an emotional and physical odyssey through a grey and rainy Po Valley, before finally returning to his home town, there apparently to commit suicide.

The circular story, the emphasis on isolation and futility, and the symbolic use of landscape recurred with greater force in *L'Avventura* >**3**, the first film in a loose trilogy (*La Notte* and *L'Eclisse* followed) about restless, disenchanted women and weak, unreliable men; it was, given Antonioni's dislike of conventional narrative, a surprising international success. Some way into the movie and without explanation, a central character vanishes from her holiday party. Few of the group – rich, chic, bored – appear bothered by what has happened, and while the girl's neglectful lover and her best friend (Monica Vitti, in the first of several roles for the director) conduct a half-hearted search around the barren island, they embark upon a desultory affair. Unconcerned himself with the reasons for the girl's sudden disappearance, Antonioni instead focusses on the moral malaise that impels her closest acquaintances to betray her memory.

If the film's slow pace and elliptical, enigmatic approach to character and situation alienated many, its detached, limpid visual style was perfectly in tune with '60s fashions. A first experiment with colour in *Red Desert* – with apples painted grey, a rubber-plant white, to convey the neurotic heroine's state of mind – was followed by a visit to 'Swinging London' to make *Blow Up* >**4**. Mixing mystery with metaphysics, the film was a bizarre, compelling riddle about visual perception and, thereby, about cinema itself: in an intriguing dark-room scene, a trendy photographer exposes film of a murder that may or may not have taken place, and Antonioni questions the dictum that the camera never lies.

From this less than convincing portrait of Carnaby Street culture, the director moved on to America and the disaffection of youth. Although *Zabriskie Point* >**5** was similarly naive in its analysis of a society on the brink of breakdown, Antonioni's eye for the American landscape – massive billboards, Death Valley – was as telling as ever. A long, lavish final shot of the exploded contents of an entire house, floating slowly through space, was a formally daring image of consumerism in chaos. More successfully, another English-language film, *The Passenger* >**6**, proved to be his finest work in years. Shot largely in North Africa and Spain, and about a disillusioned tele-journalist trading identity with a gun-runner he finds dead in a hotel room, it is a mesmerising account of one man's vain attempt to escape his destiny. The desert is a state of mind, the hero a burnt-out case, but the movie, with its quiet warmth and sporadic bursts of humour, is pleasingly free of the spiritual defeatism that marks Antonioni's earlier work.

In recent years, however, he has focussed on experiments with video. *The Oberwald Mystery* was a lame version of **Cocteau**'s *The Eagle Has Two Heads*, and the visually arresting *Identification of a Woman*, charting a director's futile search for the perfect actress for a new film, a return to the arid pessimism of earlier years. But Antonioni's reputation as a director of rare intellect remains intact: the visual precision with which he parallels his characters' emotions with the external world is flawed only by a philosophical inflexibility which often borders on mannerism.

Lineage

Despite his concern with the bourgeoisie, Antonioni's roots lie in neo-Realism and **Rossellini** would seem a special influence. Both his elliptical narratives and his semi-abstract visual style were influential on art cinema in the '60s; one may trace links with figures as diverse as **Bergman**, **Tarkovsky**, **Wenders**, and **Pakula**.

Further reading

Ian Cameron and Robin Wood's *Antonioni* (London, 1970).

Viewing

1 **Cronaca di un Amore (Story of a Love Affair)**
Italy 1950/ w Lucia Bose, Massimo Girotti, Ferdinando Sarmi

2 **Il Grido (The Cry)**
Italy 1957/ w Steve Cochran, Alida Valli, Betsy Blair

3 **L'Avventura**
Italy 1960/ w Monica Vitti, Gabriele Ferzetti, Lea Massari
4 **Blow Up**
GB 1966/ w David Hemmings, Vanessa Redgrave, Sarah Miles
5 **Zabriskie Point**
US 1969/ w Mark Frechette, Daria Halprin, Rod Taylor
6 **The Passenger (Professione: Reporter)**
Spain 1975/ w Jack Nicholson, Maria Schneider, Jenny Runacre

Jack Arnold

Born: 14th October 1916/New Haven, Connecticut, USA
Directing career: 1950-

In the '50s, low-budget sci-fi films were largely concerned with Cold War allegory: invading aliens threatening the American Way were brutally, unquestioningly destroyed. Into this atmosphere of gung-ho paranoia, Jack Arnold frequently injected a rare poetry. A former actor, and director of government and industrial documentaries, Arnold first gained attention with *It Came from Outer Space* >**1**. Shot in 3-D and adapted from a short story by Ray Bradbury, the film concerns a remote township whose population is steadily replaced by alien lookalikes. Though weakened by wooden acting, it benefits from Arnold's moody use of desert locations. Similarly, in *Creature from the Black Lagoon* >**2**, anthropologists in the Amazon jungle are menaced not only by the monstrous Gill Man but by the primeval nature of the world they have entered. The film's prologue quotes from Genesis, and its most lyrical scenes occur as the half-man half-fish swims through his oddly luminous aquatic paradise before erupting, as a deadly reminder of the crew's primitive origins, into the sunlit world above.

Arnold's pulp poetry connected with subconscious fears of uncontrollable forces – both violent and sexual – lying dormant beneath the surface of civilisation; indeed the Gill Man returned in *Revenge of the Creature* to haunt modern Miami from his prison at an oceanarium. *Tarantula*, a more conventional mutant-monster thriller, outlined the age-old problem of science outstripping more human concerns as a boffin's experiments inadvertently create a giant spider that goes on a murderous rampage. Again, desert locations ('Every beast that crawled or swam or flew began here') are used to create atmosphere, suspense and mystery. But Arnold's most memorable movie was *The Incredible Shrinking Man* >**3**, written by Richard Matheson from his own novel. The plot is simple: after being exposed to a mysterious, possibly radioactive mist, a man finds he is slowly but inexorably diminishing in size. His pride, job, marriage and, finally, his very life are threatened as his relation to the world about him changes daily. A cellar floor becomes a stark desert where giant insects hunt prey and the only food consists of rock-like crumbs of stale cheese left in mousetraps. Arnold's expert use of huge sets and props provides excitement, but it is the philosophical script that supplies its rare power: complacent modern man, forced back on his primitive wits simply to survive, finally discovers hope, peace and meaning in the realisation that everything in the cosmos, however small or insignificant, has its own place and worth.

Thereafter, Arnold's career went into decline. Unremarkable thrillers and comedies, of which *The Mouse That Roared* is the best known, gave way to television work. But, for a few brief years, his talent for evoking an unsettling world where irrational instinct reigns supreme put him in the vanguard of fantasy directors.

Lineage

Arnold's ability to invest mundane sci-fi with intelligence and imaginative visuals was equalled only by the team of George Pal and Byron Haskin. **Spielberg**'s *Jaws* was undoubtedly influenced by *Creature from the Black Lagoon*, while Arnold's small desert towns have their counterparts in countless modern horror/sci-fi films.

Further reading

John Baxter's *Science Fiction in the Cinema* (London, 1970).

Viewing

1 **It Came from Outer Space**
US 1953/ w Richard Carlson, Barbara Rush, Charles Drake
2 **Creature from the Black Lagoon**
US 1954/ w Richard Carlson, Julie Adams, Richard Denning
3 **The Incredible Shrinking Man**
US 1957/ w Grant Willams, Randy Stuart, April Kent

Dorothy Arzner

Born: 3rd January 1900/San Francisco, California, USA
Died: 1st October 1979/Los Angeles, California, USA
Directing career: 1927-1943

The only major woman director to work during Hollywood's 'Golden Age', Dorothy Arzner deserves reappraisal. Ignored for too long by film historians, she now risks over-enthusiastic re-evaluation by modern critics keen to appropriate her as an early feminist.

Arzner's father was a Hollywood restaurateur; as a girl she met many movie pioneers and later found work in Paramount's story department. Presently she turned to editing and writing, and her work on Valentino's *Blood and Sand* and James Cruze's epic Western *The Covered Wagon* was such that her desire to direct was granted. Her earliest films, beginning in 1927 with *Fashions for Women*, were conventional but charming comedies, and by the time she made the early Paramount talkie *The Wild Party*, starring 'It' girl Clara Bow, she was regarded as a top Hollywood director. As her subject matter increased in sophistication, so her interest in purposeful women and spineless, immature men became more evident. In *Merrily We Go to Hell* >**1**, a satire-cum-melodrama about the upper echelons of postwar society, an heiress is courted by a failed playwright given to bouts of alcoholic self-pity; in *Christopher Strong* >**2**, brave aviatrix Katharine Hepburn (in her first starring role) has an affair with selfish, married Colin Clive, but insistently pursues her career rather than be enslaved as 'the Other Woman'. Arzner had few delusions about double-standards: in a remarkably moving climax, Hepburn's suicide during a record-breaking flight becomes a castigation of contemporary society.

Brought in by Sam Goldwyn as replacement director, she could do little with *Nana* – a sanitised travesty of Zola, complete with a truncated, happy ending and miscast star Anna Sten – other than inject a few comments about the egoistic irresponsibility of men. The potentially bleak *The Bride Wore Red*, with Joan Crawford's gold-digger posing as a society woman to trap a millionaire, was similarly compromised by MGM's insistence on sumptuous sets and photography. *Dance, Girl, Dance* >**3**, however, was a superb blend of acid satire and backstage drama that contrasted both the attitudes and experiences of two rival dancers: Lucille Ball's sassy, pragmatic showgirl, and Maureen O'Hara's would-be ballerina, whose vehement accusatory speech to a leering burlesque audience gives the film its polemical bite.

Arzner's final feature, *First Comes Courage*, also concerned an independent woman, this time a Norwegian resistance fighter who prefers to fight the Nazis rather than flee with the man she loves. After a bout of pneumonia, Arzner retired from direction. During the '60s, however, she taught film at UCLA, and in 1975 she was the subject of a special tribute from the Directors' Guild of America.

While her films are stylistically conventional, the satire in her well-crafted comedies and melodramas was often at the expense of patriarchal tradition, and her many strong, determined, dignified heroines remain attractive and inspirational to this day.

Lineage

Arzner brought a personal touch to the glossily 'sophisticated' films of **Lubitsch**'s Paramount. Like Alice Guy and **Ida Lupino**, she has become something of a role model for women directors working in the commercial mainstream, of whom there are still sadly few;

nevertheless one might mention Susan Seidelman, Claudia Weill, Donna Deitch, Amy Jones, Marisa and Joan Micklin Silver.

Further reading

Dorothy Arzner: Towards a Feminist Cinema, ed. Pam Cook (London, 1975).

Viewing

1 **Merrily We Go to Hell**
US 1932/ w Sylvia Sidney, Fredric March

2 **Christopher Strong**
US 1933/ w Katharine Hepburn, Colin Clive, Billie Burke

3 **Dance, Girl, Dance**
US 1940/ w Maureen O'Hara, Lucille Ball, Louis Hayward

Hal Ashby

Born: 1936 (1932?)/Ogden, Utah, USA
Died: 27th December 1988
Directing career: 1970–1988

The films of William Hal Ashby exude a woolly liberalism that often counteracts their good intentions and manifest ambitions. He might be seen as an archetypal child of the idealistic '60s, sincere, naive, and ill-equipped to deal with the political and social realities on which he seemed so keen to pronounce.

Ashby's first important work in Hollywood was as editor for such strait-laced liberals as **William Wyler**, **George Stevens** and Norman Jewison. His own first feature, *The Landlord*, an engagingly characterised account of a rich white boy's relationship with his Harlem tenants, showed promise, but like the cult hit *Harold and Maude* >**1**, in which a death-obsessed teenager devises unsuccessful suicide attempts to attract the attention of his uncaring upper-class mother, it suffered from a stodgy, whimsical happy ending: through Maude, an innocuously eccentric crone devoted to visiting funerals and doing her own thing, Harold rediscovers the will to live, and cornball platonic romance wins out over black comedy.

Though emotionally manipulative, *The Last Detail* >**2** was an effectively bleak road-movie charting the anarchic journey of two seamen escorting a naive 18-year-old to the brig. As they educate the callow youth in the bawdy, boozy ways of adult life, a sense of waste is offset by the profane humour of Robert Towne's script and by authentically edgy performances, notably Jack Nicholson's foul-mouthed petty officer Buddusky. A further collaboration with Towne, *Shampoo*, dealt with a womanising Beverly Hills hairdresser who receives his come-uppance on the eve of Nixon's 1968 election victory. It failed dismally as socio-political comment, while Warren Beatty's narcissistic Don Juan was fatally indulged. Thereafter, Ashby's shallow radicalism produced increasingly portentous work. *Bound for Glory* was an inappropriately glossy, tedious biopic of Depression-era folksinger and unionist Woody Guthrie; *Coming Home* a shamelessly sentimental account of the Vietnam War's effect on serving soldiers, their wives and their wives' paraplegic lovers; *Being There* an inane, implausible satire, in which Peter Sellers' slow-witted gardener gains political power thanks to his mindless repetition of banal homilies gleaned from a lifetime watching TV.

Except for the Rolling Stones concert film, *Let's Spend the Night Together*, Ashby's last movies achieved only limited release; certainly, the thriller *Eight Million Ways to Die* reached a nadir of ineptitude. Seemingly unable to move with the times or progress beyond bland platitudes, Ashby lost his audience.

Lineage

Ashby's films seem a product of the anti-establishment sentiments of the late '60s and of the sanitised liberal humanism to which **Kramer**, **Zinnemann**, **Wyler** and **Stevens** ascribed a decade earlier.

Further reading

Diane Jacobs' *Hollywood Renaissance* (New York, 1980).

Viewing

1 **Harold and Maude**
US 1971/ w Bud Cort, Ruth Gordon, Vivian Pickles

2 **The Last Detail**
US 1973/ w Jack Nicholson, Otis Young, Randy Quaid

Richard Attenborough

Born: 29th August 1923/Cambridge, England
Directing career: 1969-

There is a sanctimonious air to the films of Sir Richard Samuel Attenborough: the earnest desire that fair play is *seen* to be done. Despite the publicity given to the 20 years taken to make *Gandhi*, the work for which he was knighted in 1976 may, as a whole, seem to lack genuine commitment.

How was it that, at the age of 40, the RADA-trained actor whose early career featured so many plucky little soldiers should make his directing debut with *Oh! What a Lovely War* >**1**? His adaptation of Joan Littlewood's anti-war stage musical was incoherent and laden with wasted British theatrical cameos. Indeed, it is tempting to view Attenborough as something of an opportunist; how else could he follow that supposedly radical movie with the patriotism of *Young Winston* - a lumbering, sepia-pink lump of cod-psychology, locating Churchill's greatness in an unhappy childhood – and the routine heroics of *A Bridge Too Far?*

A dull, derivative thriller about deadly power games between a ventriloquist and his dummy, *Magic* was less self-consciously epic than the early films, but *Gandhi* >**2** was touted as a *tour de force*. Still, while Attenborough's endless seas of extras testify to his ability to marshall crowds, the film was oddly hollow, a sprawling, reverential hagiography with scant insight either into its sublimely serene hero's mind or into the complex realities of Indian history and politics. Then, after the woeful, eminently forgettable glitz of *A Chorus Line*, he made a further misguided attempt at political film-making with *Cry Freedom* >**3**. Perversely focussing less on the martyred black South African activist Steve Biko than on the persecution of the white journalist Donald Woods (the film-maker's own surrogate spokesman for the anti-Apartheid cause), he again forsook ideological analysis for worthy sermons and visually spectacular set-pieces such as the Soweto Massacre.

As a director, Attenborough appears over-ambitious; his plans to make a film about **Chaplin** seem oddly appropriate. He is prone to stress his sincerity in addressing Big Subjects, but seems to lack the intellectual rigour and artistic gravity to produce anything more than simple-minded studies in hero worship. Indeed, his best creations are not his own Indian and South African epics, but two admirably plausible portraits of evil: his performances as Graham Greene's gangleader Pinkie in John Boulting's *Brighton Rock*, and as the mass sex-murderer Reginald John Christie in Richard Fleischer's *10 Rillington Place*.

Lineage

Attenborough derives from a strain of British social realism that takes itself all too seriously. Both **David Lean** and Bryan Forbes (a frequent Attenborough collaborator) may have influenced him.

Further reading

David Castell's *Richard Attenborough* (London, 1984).

Viewing

1 **Oh! What a Lovely War**
GB 1969/ w Laurence Olivier, John Mills, John Gielgud

2 **Gandhi**
GB 1982/ w Ben Kingsley, Martin Sheen, Candice Bergen

3 **Cry Freedom**
GB 1987/ w Kevin Kline, Denzil Washington, Penelope Wilton

Jacques Becker

Born: 15th September 1906/Paris, France
Died: 20th February 1960/Paris, France
Directing career: 1934-1960

Compared to many of his contemporaries, Jacques Becker is widely underrated. It is quite probably his very strengths – an elegant if unassertive visual style, an interest in characters rather than plot – that have brought about his critical neglect.

Becker drifted through a variety of jobs before his interest in cinema was aroused both by an encounter with **King Vidor** and by his friendship with **Renoir**, whose assistant he was throughout the '30s. After several false starts, Becker's directing career began with *Dernier Atout*, an engaging detective comedy-thriller. But it was *Goupi-Mains-Rouges*, a wittily black melodrama about poaching, that introduced his interest in groups of characters interacting within a carefully defined geographical and social milieu. Much of the director's subsequent work may be seen as a tribute to Paris itself: *Falbalas* concerns the world of fashion, *Antoine et Antoinette* is the first of several sprightly marital comedies; *Rendez-vous de Juillet* >**1**, partly set in the theatres and jazz clubs of the Left Bank, was an unusually sympathetic look at the disenchanted youth of postwar France; and *Edouard et Caroline* >**2**, an almost plotless comedy about a minor upset between newlyweds, impressed through its detailed evocation of their own humble flat and of a society salon they visit in an attempt to further the husband's career.

Casque d'Or >**3** again concerns Paris, this time the 'apache' underworld of the 1890s. But Becker's characteristic generosity towards his characters diverts attention away from violent crime towards a tragic, ill-starred romance that ends on the scaffold. In a warm, nostalgic evocation of the city painted by Renoir père the brief idyllic love between Serge Reggiani and Simone Signoret even survives, through the heroine's memories, Madame Guillotine. Crime figured again in *Touchez pas au Grisbi* >**4**, a moody gangster thriller concerning the plans made by Jean Gabin's ageing Max-le-Menteur to retire after one last heist. Once more, plot is rather less important than character: scenes of Max enjoying a dinner or a favourite record are central to the study of growing old, and almost take precedence over the taut, gripping action sequences.

Several disappointing projects – *Ali Baba*, *The Adventures of Arsène Lupin* and, inherited from **Max Ophüls**, *Montparnasse 19*, about Modigliani – ensued before Becker's last, greatest, film. In *Le Trou* >**5**, a spare, superbly detailed account of a prison escape doomed to failure, the director's interest lies, not in the misery of prison life, but in the unspoken camaraderie and mutual respect that grow between the men as they slowly tunnel their way towards freedom. The setting is claustrophobic but Becker's unsentimental observations – he likened himself to an entomologist – grow into a final statement of his abiding faith in human love and dignity.

All too often, Becker has been regarded as little more than an efficient craftsman. However, his excellence with actors, his preference for ordinary characters and plausible stories, and his continuing fascination with the themes of friendship, loyalty and betrayal mark him as a deeply appealing director.

Lineage

Becker's experiences with Renoir clearly influenced his own work, although his admiration for **Von Stroheim**'s *Greed* also suggests an interest in downbeat realism. *Grisbi* anticipated **Melville**'s terse, moody studies in thieves' honour, while Becker was one of the few older French directors admired by the New Wave film-makers. His son Jean is now a successful director, often of thrillers.

Further reading

Roy Armes' *French Cinema Since 1946*, Vol 1 (London, 1970).

Viewing

1 **Rendez-vous de Juillet**
France 1949/ w Daniel Gélin, Maurice Ronet, Bernard Lajarrige
2 **Edouard et Caroline**
France 1951/ w Anne Vernon, Daniel Gélin, Jacques François
3 **Casque d'Or**
France 1952/ w Simone Signoret, Serge Reggiani, Claude Dauphin
4 **Touchez pas au Grisbi (Honour Among Thieves)**
France 1954/ w Jean Gabin, René Dary, Paul Frankeur
5 **Le Trou (The Hole)**
France 1960/ w Michel Constantin, Jean Keraudy, Philippe Leroy

Robert Benton

Born: 29th September 1932/ Waxahachie, Texas, USA
Directing career: 1972-

In recent years, Robert Benton has exhibited a subtle capacity to manipulate audience emotions through an astute use of fashionable themes. In his more inventive films, however, his ear for witty, naturalistic dialogue and his expert handling of actors is allied with a perceptive, probing and quizzical attitude towards genre.

An ex-journalist, Benton first wrote films in collaboration with David Newman: *Bonnie and Clyde*, originally meant for **Godard** or **Truffaut**, gave **Arthur Penn** a huge hit, and the pair's success continued with scripts for *What's Up Doc?* and *Superman*. But Benton's most impressive work was his own directorial debut, *Bad Company* >**1**, a lyrical, funny Western about a group of young Civil War draft-dodgers seeking fame and fortune in the West as con-men outlaws. Clearly intended to strike an emotional chord in an America at war with Vietnam, the movie's strength lies in Benton's gentle, anti-romantic undermining of traditional pioneer myths: en route to a final encounter with death, the boys find themselves reduced to robbing infants of small change, while the 'heroes' they meet on the empty, dusty prairies are incompetent, braggart bullies. Equally affectionate was the *film noir* parody, *The Late Show* >**2**, with Benton eliciting superb performances from Art Carney as an elderly private eye plagued by deafness and a weak heart, and Lily Tomlin as his eccentric client-turned-assistant. Again, the satire is both sharp and delicate, but as betrayal and violence gradually supercede humour, Benton never loses sight of the fact that crime detection is dangerous, and ageing painful and lonely.

Altogether slicker, *Kramer vs Kramer* >**3** handled the thorny topic of divorce and child custody with kid gloves. Concealing a melodramatic core beneath a veneer of virtuoso acting, classical music and Nestor Almendros's immaculate photography, the film was finally little more than an above-par, up-market weepie. *Still of the Night*, although flawed by implausibility, was more ambitious, attempting to update the Hitchcockian psychoanalytical thriller, but the lachrymose *Places in the Heart* (based on Benton's great-grandmother's fight to preserve farm, faith and family in Texas during the Depression years) and the lively but uneven comedy-thriller *Nadine* both suffered from a certain predictability.

Benton's intelligence appears most fruitfully employed when gently mocking and demythologising traditional Hollywood heroics. Applied to subjects demanding a deeper emotional commitment, his cynicism may be submerged by a spurious accent on 'tastefulness'.

Lineage

Benton much admired **Joseph L. Mankiewicz**, fondly caricatured in *Bad Company*, and the French New Wave directors. His best work is distantly related to that of **Altman**, producer of *The Late Show*.

Viewing

1 **Bad Company**
US 1972/ w Jeff Bridges, Barry Brown, John Savage
2 **The Late Show**
US 1977/ w Art Carney, Lily Tomlin, Eugene Roche

3 **Kramer vs Kramer**
US 1979/ w Dustin Hoffman, Meryl Streep, Justin Henry

Ingmar Bergman

Born: 14th July 1918/Uppsala, Sweden
Directing career: 1945-1982

Ernst Ingmar Bergman's status as a master of cinema derives less from individual films than from his totally distinctive style and abiding preoccupations. Few directors have repeatedly given voice to such a deeply personal vision of human suffering and solitude.

The son of a Lutheran pastor, Bergman first made his mark as a theatre director, in which medium he has never ceased to work. After scripting Alf Sjöberg's cruelly impressive *Frenzy*, in 1945 he made his own feature debut with *Crisis*. His early movies were moody, quasi-realist investigations of male-female relationships, often flawed by a rather simplistic contrasting of innocent youth and corrupt adulthood. Nonetheless, by the time he had made *Summer Interlude* and *Summer with Monika* >**1** (both bitter-sweet studies of brief, doomed, youthful love affairs), and *Sawdust and Tinsel* >**2**, which uses a tatty travelling circus to symbolise man's capacity for cruelty, deceit and humiliation, his fertile invention, stark pessimism and sensitive handling of actors were well established.

His first international success was *Smiles of a Summer Night* >**3**. This elegant, sophisticated costume drama about assorted amorous intrigues at a *fin-de-siècle* houseparty revealed Bergman's comic sense of irony, but *The Seventh Seal* >**4** was more typically bleak. A medieval allegory in which a knight returns from the Crusades to challenge Death to a symbolic game of chess, the film evokes a plague-ridden world of suffering from which God is surely absent. Less contrived and altogether warmer was *Wild Strawberries* >**5**. Here, an elderly professor, affectingly played by veteran director **Victor Sjöström** travels across country to receive an award, visits the haunts of his youth, and belatedly recognises the arid sterility and loneliness of his life. Not all Bergman's work, however, is doom and gloom; in *The Face* >**6**, for example, macabre humour and Gothic horror create a thrilling, witty portrait of the artist as charlatan.

Bergman's mature style arose in a trilogy about lost faith which asks how God can exist if pain and evil are the inevitable attendants of human life. In *Through a Glass Darkly*, a young woman's madness leads her to imagine God as an obscene spider; in *Winter Light* >**7** a doubting pastor, faced with a lover's illness and the threat of the Bomb, finds the ritual of prayer increasingly meaningless; in *The Silence* >**8**, two sisters stranded in a foreign, war-torn city, yield, respectively, to desperate promiscuity and a lonely death.

In the early '60s, Bergman's visual and narrative style became ever more austere in focussing on tormented souls seeking guidance and comfort from an empty heaven, thus paving the way for a stark foray into extreme close-up in the enigmatic *Persona* >**9**. A modernist masterpiece, the film initiated an introspective trilogy about the ivory towers built by artists as a defence against the horror of existence. It was Bergman's first completely innovative work, acknowledging itself as artifice through the regular insertion of non-narrative images such as projectors burning, film breaking, snippets of silent movies). *Persona* depicts the vampiric relationship between a talkative nurse and an actress who refuses to speak or work after a traumatic realisation of the futility of creation in a loveless world beset by war. Psychology, philosophy and social comment are mixed to brilliant effect in a complex, lucid interrogation both of filmic illusion and of the illusory values of modern life.

After addressing problems of artistic doubt and suffering in *Hour of the Wolf* and *Shame*, Bergman once again focussed on simple human relationships in *A Passion*, *The Touch* and – most fruitfully –

Bibi Andersson and Liv Ullmann trapped in a tense, vampiric relationship in Bergman's *Persona.*

Cries and Whispers >**10**. Set in a country mansion largely silent except for the ticking of clocks, the film examines the effect of a woman's slow, painful death on her two sisters and her maid. Past and present, fantasy and reality are seamlessly interwoven to chart, with unsentimental clarity, the way humans inevitably protect themselves against the certainty of their own mortality.

Having dealt, at great length, with the anxieties resulting from failing relationships in two television series (*Scenes from a Marriage* and *Face to Face*), Bergman's career finally faltered. A battle with the Swedish government over tax payments drove him into temporary exile, and *The Serpent's Egg*, made in Munich, was a contrived account of the roots of Nazism, while the stale study of an emotionally fraught mother-daughter relationship in *Autumn Sonata* was notable only for the presence of Ingrid Bergman. But a sumptuous family saga, *Fanny and Alexander* >**11**, was seen by many as a return to form: both autobiography and a witty auto-critique explicitly reworking themes and scenes from his earlier work, it was, despite occasional longueurs, a fitting end to a remarkable, prolific career in cinema. He retired from film-making in 1982.

Both thematically and stylistically, Bergman's body of work is unusually coherent, partly due to his recurrent use of Gunnar Fischer and Sven Nykvist, two extremely fine cameramen, and of a close-knit family of actors among whom Bibi Andersson, Liv Ullmann, Ingrid Thulin, Harriet Andersson, Max Von Sydow and Gunnar Björnstrand are most memorable. Indeed, were it not for the intense power and naturalism elicited from these performers, Bergman's harrowingly personal accounts of doubt, suffering and solitude might never have won over so large an international audience. Finally, although he may be faulted for an occasional cold, humourless pessimism that may seem contrived, both his intellectual gravity and his uncompromising devotion to cinema as a serious art form are undeniable.

Lineage

Bergman is part of a Scandinavian tradition that stretches back, through Sjöberg and **Dreyer**, to **Sjöström** and Mauritz Stiller; the influence of Expressionism and horror films, not to say Mozart, Strindberg and Ibsen, may also be discerned. He has encouraged few true imitators, though directors as varied as **Woody Allen**, **Truffaut** and **Tarkovsky** have expressed their admiration.

Further reading

Robin Wood's *Ingmar Bergman* (London, 1969), Peter Cowie's *Ingmar Bergman: A Critical Biography* (New York, 1982). Stig Bjorkman's *Bergman on Bergman* (London, 1973) is interviews; Bergman's autobiography is *The Magic Lantern* (London, 1988)

Viewing

1 **Summer with Monika**
Sweden 1952/ w Harriet Andersson, Lars Ekborg, John Harryson
2 **Sawdust and Tinsel (The Naked Night)**
Sweden 1953/ w Harriet Andersson, Anders Ek, Hasse Ekman
3 **Smiles of a Summer Night**
Sweden 1955/ w Eva Dahlbeck, Ulla Jacobsson, Jarl Kulle
4 **The Seventh Seal**
Sweden 1957/ w Max Von Sydow, Gunnar Björnstrand, Bengt Ekerot
5 **Wild Strawberries**
Sweden 1957/ w Victor Sjöström, Bibi Andersson, Ingrid Thulin
6 **The Face (The Magician)**
Sweden 1958/ w Max Von Sydow, Ingrid Thulin, Gunnar Björnstrand
7 **Winter Light**
Sweden 1963/ w Gunner Björnstrand, Ingrid Thulin, Max Von Sydow
8 **The Silence**
Sweden 1963/ w Ingrid Thulin, Gunnel Lindblom, Jörgen Lindström
9 **Persona**
Sweden 1966/ w Bibi Andersson, Liv Ullmann
10 **Cries and Whispers**
Sweden 1973/ w Liv Ullmann, Ingrid Thulin, Harriet Andersson
11 **Fanny and Alexander**
Sweden 1982/ w Bertil Guve, Ewa Fröhling, Erland Josephson

Busby Berkeley

Born: 29th November 1895/Los Angeles, California, USA
Died: 14th March 1976/Los Angeles (New York?), USA
Directing career: 1930-1962

If William Berkeley Enos was not the best director of musicals in the '30s, he was certainly the most original director of musical sequences. For much of his career, his fantastic imagination was called upon simply to invent the more spectacular 'dance' numbers that would enliven or distract from a flagging, formulaic plot.

Born into a theatrical family – his mother went to work the night his father died, thus instilling him with the idea that 'the show must go on' – Berkeley spent much of World War I choreographing parade drills and stage shows for army camps. Peacetime found him producing Broadway musicals and, in 1930, Sam Goldwyn invited him to direct the musical scenes for *Whoopee*; besides promoting Eddie Cantor to star status, the film, featuring overhead shots of the Goldwyn Girls in kaleidoscopic, flower-like patterns, hinted at Berkeley's future style.

Nineteen thirty-three saw Berkeley at the height of his powers, contributing to the often surreal escapism of classics such as *42nd Street*, *Gold Diggers of 1933* >**1**, and *Footlight Parade* >**2**. Berkeley's talents were less choreographic – there was very little actual dancing – than cinematic. In visualising the onstage segments of backstage musical dramas, he abandoned the limited theatrical perspectives of the proscenium arch, freed his single camera to swoop, fly and observe from on high, and filled his 'stage' with exotically clad extras placed symmetrically in impossibly sumptuous sets. Absurd, abstract compositions, verbal and visual innuendo, and a superbly mobile camera together created images both sexually and formally daring. In the astonishing trilogy of numbers forming the climax of *Footlight*

Parade 'Honeymoon Hotel' is peopled solely by saucy, giggling newly-wed couples; 'By a Waterfall' features an aquacade of chorines, the camera swimming through a tunnel of parted legs; and 'Shanghai Lil' transforms a parade of marines and patriotic civilians into the American Eagle. *Gold Diggers*, meanwhile, drew on Expressionism to depict the desperate plight of unemployed war veterans in the oddly sombre finale 'Remember My Forgotten Man'.

Through the '30s, Berkeley's genius was most sympathetically fostered at Warner Bros., where the photographic wizardry of Sol Polito and the studio's taste for socially uplifting drama indulged his bizarre flights of fantasy. Moving in 1939 to MGM, he was reduced to embellishing the more prosaic teenage talents of Mickey Rooney and Judy Garland in films such as *Babes in Arms* and *Babes on Broadway*. His weird vision was not altogether neglected, however: his first full colour film, Fox's *The Gang's All Here* >**3** included Carmen Miranda in an outrageously suggestive tutti-frutti hat and 60 girls cavorting with giant bananas; the stylish *Take Me Out to the Ball Game* – the last film Berkeley directed in its entirety – heralded the teamwork of **Gene Kelly** and **Stanley Donen**; in *Million Dollar Mermaid*, he made much of Esther Williams' water ballets.

Berkeley's technical and visual flair and his blatant disregard for realism, place him among cinema's most formally ambitious visionaries. As a fitting postscript to his film career, in 1971 both he and Ruby Keeler (star of several of his '30s films) came out of retirement for a Broadway revival of *No, No, Nanette*.

Lineage

Though many musicals followed the **Mamoulian** and **Minnelli** example of integrating song and dance into the story, Berkeley's visual extravagance became a *sine qua non* of higher-budgeted musicals. Nevertheless, his virtually abstract sense of composition and camp sexual innuendo has closer parallels in the avant-garde; alternately, his formalism also calls to mind the work of Leni Riefenstahl.

Busby Berkeley's characteristically kaleidoscopic choreography for a shot cut from the 'By a Waterfall' sequence of *Footlight Parade*.

Further reading

The Busby Berkeley Book by Tony Thomas and Jim Terry (New York, 1973).

Viewing

1 **Gold Diggers of 1933**
US 1933/ w Ruby Keeler, Dick Powell, Warren William

2 **Footlight Parade**
US 1933/ w James Cagney, Joan Blondell, Ruby Keeler, Dick Powell

3 **The Gang's All Here**
US 1943/ w Alice Faye, Carmen Miranda, James Ellison

Bernardo Bertolucci

Born: 16th March 1940/Parma, Italy
Directing career: 1962-

The films of Bernardo Bertolucci seem simultaneously personal and strangely subject to swings in cinematic fashion, though there is no denying his work's thematic consistency nor, for that matter, certain quasi-autobiographical elements in much of his work.

The son of a successful poet and critic, Bertolucci himself wrote poetry in his early years. After making 16mm amateur films in his teens he worked as assistant to **Pasolini** on *Accattone*; in return he was allowed to direct the Pasolini-scripted *La Commare Secca* >**1**. Set, like *Accattone*, in Rome's working class suburbs, and charting a police investigation into the murder of a prostitute, the film mixes *film noir* photography, realistic characters, and a *Rashomon*-style narrative (the victim's final hours are described by various witnesses) to assured effect. More ambitiously, *Before the Revolution* >**2** revealed Bertolucci's interest in the effect of politics on everyday personal life; loosely inspired by *Stendhal*, it examines the psychology of a man torn between the security of a bourgeois marriage and a commitment to radical action. The same conflict between conformist and revolutionary attitudes recurred in *Partner*, an experimental, obscure reworking of Dostoevsky's *The Double*; far more successful were *The Spider's Stratagem* >**3**, taken from Borges, and *The Conformist* >**4**, from Alberto Moravia, both concerned with Fascism. The first is about Fascism's heritage, focussing on a young man who investigates the mystery of his Resistance-hero father's death, only to find he was a traitor working for Mussolini; the second deals with the ideology's roots by examining a coward who, afraid that he may be homosexual, proves his 'normality' by toeing the party line. In portraying protagonists torn by contradictory impulses, some of them Oedipal, Bertolucci seemed to draw on his experiences as an Italian Marxist; equally personal, however, was his increasingly confident visual style, a combination of flamboyant camera movements and lush, atmospheric colours, composed with painterly care by Vittorio Storaro.

Shot in altogether sparser fashion was *Last Tango in Paris* >**5**, an enormous *succés de scandale* in which politics gave way to brute, obsessive sex between strangers. Once again, however, the protagonists are tormented by inner conflict: Brando's Paul between self-hatred over his wife's suicide and his feelings for Maria Schneider's Jeanne, she between her adoring film-maker fiancé (based wittily on **Godard**) and the taboo-breaking Paul. The imagery – the stark, empty flat that is the lovers' retreat from conventional society, the cold, windy pavement where Paul screams his loathing for the world against the din of a passing train – exerts a raw power, but the film is flawed by Bertolucci's inability to create a rounded female character to counteract Brando's colossal, body-and-soul-baring performance.

By now regarded as one of the world's top directors, for the epic *1900* (*Novecento*) >**6** Bertolucci was able to command a cast of international stars. Nonetheless, in viewing Italian history from the turn of the century to the 1945 Liberation through the eyes of an aristocrat *padrone* (Robert De Niro) and his peasant friend-cum-nemesis (Gérard Depardieu), he endowed his politically naive pageant with absurdly stereotyped heroes and villains. *La Luna* >**7**, another Oedipal drama in which an opera singer, nursing near-incestuous feelings for her drug-addicted teenage son, effects an implausible reunion with his father, was high on style but short on substance. Conversely, *The Tragedy of a Ridiculous Man* >**8** was an intelligent, low-key return to political film-making, inverting the Oedipal theme as it followed a dairy farmer's search for his son, possibly the victim of a terrorist kidnapping.

Bertolucci's penchant for spectacle reached a peak in *The Last Emperor* >**9**, an epic account of the emperor Pu Yi's progress from a fatherless but spoilt childhood within the Imperial Palace to an old-age spent working as a gardener in Mao's China. Damagingly, the sumptuous exoticism of the early scenes (shot on location in and around Beijing's Forbidden City) tended to overshadow Pu Yi's later years, thus weakening the examination of how a man brought up to have total confidence in his own God-given superiority might possibly become a good Communist.

Bertolucci's career appears almost as schizophrenic as his protagonists: personal melodrama vies with political hypothesis, redundant stylistic flourishes with narrative and psychological complexity. Certainly, whenever he succumbs to epic spectacle, he seems to lose all perspective on his material. Sadly, but perhaps unsurprisingly, it is the less political, more conventional films which have ensured his now prestigious international reputation.

Lineage

A true *cinéaste*, Bertolucci has paid tribute to many influences – including **Vigo**, **Godard** and **Rossellini** – in films and interviews; neo-realists, **Buñuel**, **Welles** and **Ophüls** all cast shadows over his work, as do certain painters. His visual style would appear to have influenced **Coppola**, **Scorsese** and **Schrader**, amongst others.

Further reading

Robert Philip Kolker's *Bernardo Bertolucci* (London, 1984). Enzo Ungari and Don Ranvaud's *Bertolucci on Bertolucci* (London, 1988) is a collection of interviews.

Viewing

1 **La Commare Secca (The Grim Reaper)**
Italy 1962/ w Francesco Ruiu, Giancarlo De Rosa, Vincenzo Ciccora

2 **Before the Revolution**
Italy 1964/ w Adriana Asti, Francesco Barilli, Allen Midgette

3 **The Spider's Stratagem**
Italy 1969/ w Giulio Brogi, Alida Valli, Tino Scotti

4 **The Conformist**
Italy 1970/ w Jean-Louis Trintignant, Dominique Sanda, Stefania Sandrelli

5 **Last Tango in Paris**
France 1972/ w Marlon Brando, Maria Schneider, Jean-Pierre Léaud

6 **1900 (Novecento)**
Italy 1976/ w Robert De Niro, Gérard Depardieu, Burt Lancaster

7 **La Luna**
Italy 1979/ w Jill Clayburgh, Matthew Barry, Tomas Milian

8 **The Tragedy of a Ridiculous Man**
Italy 1982/ w Ugo Tognazzi, Anouk Aimée, Laura Morante

9 **The Last Emperor**
China/Italy/GB 1987/ w John Lone, Joan Chen, Peter O'Toole

Bertrand Blier

Born: 11 March 1939/Paris, France
Directing career: 1962-

Of the French directors who came to prominence during the '70s, Bertrand Blier is one of the most distinctive, his black humour and robust satirising of sexual anxieties placing him in direct, but often successful, opposition to the art-movie mainstream.

The son of veteran actor Bernard Blier, he first entered the movies as assistant to John Berry, Jean Delannoy and Christian-Jaque. After several *cinéma verité* documentaries he progressed to making his feature debut, *Hitler? Connais Pas!*, in 1962. But his first huge success was with *Les Valseuses* >**1**, a raw, deliberately offensive, road-movie about a pair of petty criminals. In their brutally determined but pathetically impotent efforts to satisfy the sexual needs of various women, the then unknown actors Gérard Depardieu and Patrick Dewaere typify Blier's future anti-heroes: boorish egotists pathologically unable to comprehend the opposite sex, often voicing their confusion through anarchic violence.

Less determinedly scandalous, the Oscar-winning *Preparez Vos Mouchoirs* (*Get Out Your Handkerchiefs*) offered a sly riposte to *Kramer vs Kramer*-style melodrama: worried by his wife's frequent depressions, Depardieu invites Dewaere (a total stranger) to try and 'cheer her up' by fathering a child; but she has other ideas, preferring a schoolboy lover. Even darker was Blier's best film, *Buffet Froid* >**2**, in which a psychotic (Depardieu), a mass killer, and an ageing, sadistic police inspector (Blier père) are united by their confused, callous impulses to murder; or is it by their dreams of killing? Structured according to a nightmare logic but shot in crisp tones suggestive of everyday reality, it is both a witty, surreal farce and a bizarre, very oblique examination of contemporary urban alienation.

After reworking 'Lolita' to engaging, even touching, effect in *Beau-Père*, Blier degenerated into safer, less misanthropic demonstrations of male obsession with both *My Best Friend's Girl* and *Our Story*. Next, however, *Tenue de Soirée (Evening Dress)* >**3** was clearly designed to offend everyone. Here, a burglar (Depardieu again) educates a bickering bankrupt couple in house-breaking, meanwhile falling passionately for the coy, mousey, apparently heterosexual husband. Decried by some as misogynist and homophobic, the film's fervent, relentless vigour was nevertheless undeniable.

If Blier's surreal anarchy has any 'meaning', it may be that men's maltreatment of women stems from a fear of impotence. That said, it is occasionally difficult to fathom whether the misogyny on view is really Blier's or that of his characters. Whatever, his black humour offers an intriguing alternative to the bland assumptions of conventional 'buddy' movies, while continually confounding our desire for easily explicable characters and stories.

Lineage

Blier's depiction of absurd, cruel obsession in a fundamentally realist visual style is occasionally reminiscent of late **Buñuel**; one might also compare him with the likes of Pedro Almodóvar, Paul Bartel, John Waters, and Paul Morrissey.

Viewing

1 **Les Valseuses (Making It)**
France 1973/ w Gérard Depardieu, Patrick Dewaere, Miou-Miou

2 **Buffet Froid**
France 1979/ w Gérard Depardieu, Jean Carmet, Bernard Blier

3 **Tenue de Sóiree (Evening Dress)**
France 1986/ w Gérard Depardieu, Michel Blanc, Miou-Miou

Budd Boetticher

Born: 29th July 1916/Chicago, Ohio, USA
Directing career: 1944-1969

Although the films of Oscar Boetticher Jr (familiarly known as Budd) never rose above the B-feature level, together with actor Randolph Scott, producer Harry Joe Brown and writer Burt Kennedy, he made some of the most perfectly realised, imaginative Westerns ever filmed.

Forsaking a career in football, the young Boetticher went to Mexico to become a professional matador before serving as advisor on **Mamoulian**'s *Blood and Sand*. He then progressed from assistant to directing low-budget thrillers and Westerns, although with the exception of two bullfighting pictures – *The Bullfighter and the Lady*, and *The Magnificent Matador* – most of his early movies were merely routine. Only in the mid-'50s did his talent for stark drama tinged with a dark, even comic sense of irony flourish.

A first Western made with Kennedy and Scott, *Seven Men from Now*, was instrumental in establishing the Scott persona of a loner, here obsessively determined to wreak vengeance on his wife's killer. More subtle however was *The Tall T* >**1**, which worked wonders with only a desert shack and a handful of actors as Scott embarked on a battle to the death with gangleader Richard Boone – the spoils being the lives of hostages held at a stagecoach station. The conflict, set characteristically in a parched, scrubby landscape that reflects the arid self-righteousness of the hero, takes on a bleak mythic austerity, while the deft characterisations (the lonely, homesick Boone is perhaps more truly human than Scott) add psychological and moral complexities that transcend B-Western conventions.

In *Buchanan Rides Alone* >**2** Boetticher's taste for the absurd produced a Western verging on parody; the corrupt town into which the innocent Scott wanders merely confuses him, while his enemies (three brothers) are too busy deceiving each other to do him much harm. Treachery and bluff form the core of Boetticher's world. In both *Ride Lonesome* >**3** and *Comanche Station* >**4** the villains, once more sympathetic, are forever boasting about how they will cheat Scott out of his just deserts, while he in turn hides his pride and his plans for vengeance behind a poker face.

Boetticher viewed his heroes, trapped in the past and doomed to wander, with no more sentimentality than his outlaws, who try, often hopelessly, to forget their criminal ways and settle down. His darkest film of all, however, was *The Rise and Fall of Legs Diamond* >**5**, in which the sun-baked desert is replaced by a dark, claustrophobic urban nightmare. Boetticher's psychopathic hood, played with relentless energy by Ray Danton, is a totally amoral figure whose lust for power leads him to destroy even his brother in order to protect himself. Fast, cruel and violent, the film is one of the cinema's bleakest visions of unbridled ambition.

Tired of Hollywood, Boetticher returned to Mexico where, for nearly a decade, he worked on a documentary about the bullfighter Carlos Arruza. In 1969, beset by disasters, he finally returned to America where he wrote the original story for **Don Siegel**'s *Two Mules for Sister Sara*, and directed one last Western, *A Time for Dying*.

Boetticher's forte during his most fertile period lay not in disrupting the Western genre, but in working intelligent, highly personal variations on a simple, repeated theme. Rarely have the limitations of low-budget productions, with their small casts, terse scripts and stark exteriors, been turned to advantage with such consistency.

Lineage

Boetticher's films steer clear of the poetry of **Ford**, their bleak settings, violence and doomed characters looking forwards to the work of **Peckinpah** and **Leone**. Interestingly, Burt Kennedy became a regular Western director in the '60s, although his taut scripts for Boetticher were replaced by a leisurely, good-natured humour. Lesser Western directors of the '50s included André De Toth, Hugo Fregonese, Delmer Daves and, best known, John Sturges.

Further reading

Jim Kitses' *Horizons West* (London, 1969).

Viewing

1 **The Tall T**
US 1957/ w Randolph Scott, Richard Boone, Maureen O'Sullivan

2 **Buchanan Rides Alone**
US 1958/ w Randolph Scott, Craig Stevens, Barry Kelley

3 **Ride Lonesome**
US 1959/ w Randolph Scott, Karen Steele, Pernell Roberts

4 **Comanche Station**
US 1960/ w Randolph Scott, Claude Akins, Nancy Gates

5 **The Rise and Fall of Legs Diamond**
US 1960/ w Ray Danton, Karen Steele, Warren Oates

Peter Bogdanovich

Born: 30th July 1939/Kingston, New York, USA
Directing career: 1967-

In his enthusiasm for classic American cinema, Peter Bogdanovich was one of the first young cinephile directors to take Hollywood by storm in the '70s. He differs from his successors, however, both in his lack of interest in flamboyant techniques, and in his increasing inability to find a wide audience.

The son of a Yugoslav painter, Bogdanovich's early interest in film and theatre led to a career as actor, off-Broadway stage director and film critic. Having written books on **Welles**, **Hawks**, **Hitchcock**, **Lang**, **Ford** and **Dwan**, he then began working for **Corman** at American International Pictures. A chance to direct arose when Corman offered the services of Boris Karloff, a two-week shooting schedule and footage from his horror film *The Terror*. The result, *Targets* >**1**, was a tense, inventive thriller in which a clean-cut middle-class youth turns into a psychopathic sniper; the contrast between real horror and its cinematic counterpart is vividly made plain when Karloff, virtually playing himself, confronts the boy in a climactic massacre at a drive-in cinema showing his films.

Shot in moody monochrome, Bogdanovich's first major hit, *The Last Picture Show* >**2**, also used film in symbolic terms, with a cinema's closure elegaically signifying the final passing of innocence in a claustrophobically small Texan town during the '50s. Besides allowing Bogdanovich to elicit vivid performances from both veteran actors and young unknowns, the film was a moving tribute to the likes of Hawks and Ford, as were the lively screwball caper *What's Up Doc?* and the Depression setting of *Paper Moon* >**3** (Ryan O'Neal's Bible-selling con-man meeting his match in a canny orphan played by his daughter Tatum). Further homages, however, in *At Long Last Love*, a Cole Porter musical in which none of the actors could sing or dance, and *Nickelodeon*, an affectionate but uneven comic salute to Hollywood's pioneers, proved extravagantly self-indulgent.

The critical and commercial failure of these films ensured a substantial re-think and a reduction in budget. Sadly, despite fine performances from Ben Gazzara, neither *Saint Jack* – based on Paul Theroux's novel about sordid, deadly intrigues in Singapore – nor the Lubitsch-style romantic comedy, *They All Laughed*, succeeded at the box-office. *Mask* >**4**, however, was a hit, largely because its story of a teenage boy's battle against a degenerative, deforming disease reeked of facile, smothering sentimentality.

Bogdanovich's decline in the mid-'70s derived, perhaps, from his inability to avoid the pitfalls of sudden success; certainly, a romance with Cybill Shepherd led him to miscast her in two of his worst films. At his best with a low budget and strong script, he would do well to remember the lessons of his early years.

Lineage

The example of Bogdanovich's initial homages to masters like **Hawks**, **Ford** and **Hitchcock** paved the way for subsequent 'Movie Brats' such as **Spielberg**, **De Palma**, **Scorsese** and **Carpenter**.

Further reading

Nothing to speak of, but some of his own work is still available.

Viewing

1 **Targets**
US 1967/ w Boris Karloff, Tim O'Kelly, Bogdanovich

2 **The Last Picture Show**
US 1971/ w Jeff Bridges, Timothy Bottoms, Ben Johnson

3 **Paper Moon**
US 1973/ w Ryan O'Neal, Tatum O'Neal, Madeleine Kahn

4 **Mask**
US 1985/ w Cher, Eric Stoltz, Sam Elliott

John Boorman

Born: **18th January 1933/London, England**
Directing career: 1965-

The films of John Boorman frequently concern contradictions and polarities: tensions between Nature and Civilisation, Dream and Reality. Equally, his career as a whole swings violently between success and failure, intelligent ambition and pretentiousness.

After a spell working as a film critic, Boorman made a name for himself making documentaries and current affairs programmes for TV. His feature debut, *Catch Us If You Can*, was a lively but derivative Swinging '60s vehicle for the Dave Clark Five, but two years later *Point Blank* >**1** revealed a more distinctive, ambitious talent at work. An enigmatic treatment of a conventional thriller plot, the film employed flashbacks, elliptical editing and remote performances to create a strangely compelling account of a dying gangster's dreams of entering his house justified. His fantasies, of wreaking violent revenge on the faceless criminal organisation responsible for his demise, gave rise to themes that would recur throughout Boorman's career – the quest for self-knowledge, the struggle of the individual against modern technological society.

The allegorical undercurrents coursing beneath *Point Blank*'s razor-sharp modernist veneer surfaced less subtly in *Hell in the Pacific*, about the absurd war waged by a Japanese soldier and an American GI stranded together on a remote desert island, and *Leo The Last*, about racism, inequality and alienation in a fantasised London. But *Deliverance* >**2** was a return to form, blending action with philosophical concerns to powerful and disturbing effect. In a gripping fable about complacency, four businessmen embark on an Appalachian canoeing trip and, partly through naivety and pride, fall prey to dark, primeval natural forces in the form of hostile hillbillies. Superbly shot, it effortlessly, and mercifully, avoided the woolly mysticism that would dog both the obscure sci-fi allegory *Zardoz*, and the ambitious but incoherent portrait of diabolical possession and shamanism in *Exorcist II: The Heretic*. Boorman's interest in the quest derived from his fascination with Arthurian legend; in 1981 in his adopted home of Ireland, he made *Excalibur* >**3**, a lavishly designed epic whose heady mixture of myth, dream and magic was undermined by fatally inappropriate elements of self-parody. Subsequently, *The Emerald Forest* used the tale of an American's 10-year odyssey in search of his lost son in the Amazon rain forests, to construct a worthy if naive thesis on ecology and anthropology; while the more modest *Hope and Glory* >**4** an autobiographical, child's view of the London Blitz was an often amusing, if excessively nostalgic, journey down Memory Lane.

However erratic Boorman's career, his finest work displays a passion, originality and consistency of vision all too rare among British directors. Despite his documentary origins, he has seldom felt restricted by his country's traditional demands for realism; his films are provocative, personal, and unusually unpredictable.

Lineage

Along with **Ken Russell** Boorman can be seen as a key figure in the modern British cinema. His interest in myth, dream, landscape and memory may be compared with that of **Resnais**, **Leone**, and **Roeg**.

Further reading

Michel Ciment's *John Boorman* (London, 1987).

Viewing

1 **Point Blank**
US 1967/ w Lee Marvin, Angie Dickinson, John Vernon

2 **Deliverance**
US 1972/ w Burt Reynolds, Jon Voight, Ned Beatty

3 **Excalibur**
Eire 1981/ w Nigel Terry, Nicol Williamson, Helen Mirren

4 **Hope and Glory**
GB 1987/ w Sebastian Rice-Edwards, Sarah Miles, Ian Bannen

Walerian Borowczyk

Born: 21st October 1923/Kwilicz, Poland
Directing career: 1953-

Along with **Tashlin** and Kon Ichikawa, Walerian Borowczyk is rare in having successfully proceeded from animation to live action. Given the excellence of his work in both media in the '60s and early '70s, his subsequent drift into soft-core pornography is especially disheartening.

After studying art, the young Borowczyk quickly established himself as a highly original animator. Frequently made with Jan Lenica, shorts like *Once Upon a Time* and *Dom* revealed not only an assured grasp of a variety of animation techniques (photomontage, collage, drawing), but also a dark, often violent vision of chaos and destruction akin to that of the Surrealists. Moving to France in 1959, he became even more adventurous. *Les Jeux des Anges* is a Kafkaesque portrait of torture and cruelty, while *Renaissance* >**1** uses reverse-motion camerawork to show a cosmos of broken objects – a doll, a stuffed owl, a prayer book, a trumpet – miraculously remaking themselves. His macabre wit, however, can be seen in the final moments, when the last object to reach completion, a hand-grenade, destroys the absurd, brave new world.

Made in 1969, Borowczyk's first live-action feature, *Goto, Isle of Love* >**2**, told a bizarre and highly imaginative story of love's brief bloom in a fascistic island prison colony, its grey decaying cells and passages a nightmarish distortion of a modern society. The director's methods derived from those in his earlier films, with the camera rarely moving, perspective flattened to stress the two-dimensional, and objects – notably the arcane paraphernalia of torture – imbued with as much significance as human characters. Similarly, in *Blanche* >**3**, a stylised version of the Mazeppa story, about tragic courtly intrigues in a 13th-century French château, Borowczyk's immaculate, restrained visual sense created a living tapestry of cruelty, betrayal and doomed love. A masterpiece, its cool, reserved camerawork is warmed by touching performances from the veteran Michel Simon as the jealous, ageing lord and by Ligia Branice (the director's wife) as his fragile young consort.

The success of his first two features established Borowczyk as something of an eroticist, and his subsequent films moved into the realms of the sexploitation genre. Although his distinctively elegant visuals could still be found in relatively sensationalist material such as *Immoral Tales*, *Story of Sin* (made during a brief return to Poland), *The Beast*, *Behind Convent Walls* and *Lulu*, the director's interest in narrative logic was vague and perfunctory, his once illuminating observations of inanimate objects now mere fetishism. Occasionally, his former ability to conjure up a world torn asunder by unbridled passions would re-emerge: in the black, sometimes brilliant *Blood of Doctor Jekyll* >**4**, Dr Hyde becomes an insatiable bisexual monster born of Victorian repression, and his fiancée, blinded by *amour fou*, elects to join him in a murderous, self-destructive quest for sensual transcendence. More frequently, however, titillation has taken precedence over subversive ambitions in films like *The Art of Love*, *Emmanuelle 5*, and *Rites of Love*.

Borowczyk nonetheless deserves praise for having viewed animation as a serious art-form, and for having broken down false barriers between live-action and techniques normally disparaged as 'cartoons'. It is a pity that he has become a marginal figure by repeatedly turning to material unworthy of his talents.

Lineage

Borowczyk's work derives less from earlier cinematic conventions than from modern painting, perhaps most notably Surrealism and Cubism. His work has been enormously influential on subsequent Eastern European animators, and one may compare it, perhaps, to the films of the Czech surrealist Jan Svankmajer.

Viewing

1 **Renaissance**
France 1963

2 **Goto, Isle of Love**
France 1969/ w Ligia Branice, Pierre Brasseur

3 **Blanche**
France 1972/ w Ligia Branice, Michel Simon

4 **Blood of Doctor Jekyll (Docteur Jekyll et les Femmes)**
France 1981/ w Udo Kier, Marina Pierro, Patrick Magee

Frank Borzage

Born: 23rd April 1893/Salt Lake City, Utah, USA
Died: 19th June 1962/Los Angeles, California, USA
Directing career: 1916-1961

With realism widely seen as a *sine qua non* of serious cinema, the work of Frank Borzage is frequently dismissed as melodrama marred by excessive sentimentality. Yet he was one of the cinema's greatest Romantics, his protagonists transcending the brutal circumstances of a modern, material world through a love verging on the divine.

Having paid for a correspondence course in acting by working in a silver mine, Borzage joined a touring theatre company and in 1912 embarked on an acting career in Hollywood. In 1916 he turned to directing, often playing the lead role in his own Westerns and comedies; by the end of the '20s, he was one of Hollywood's most successful directors. *Seventh Heaven* >**1**, which won an Oscar, and *Street Angel* were typical of his best work: both deal with lovers separated by forces beyond their control (respectively, war and poverty), and portray love as a spiritual state of being capable of overcoming those same forces.

Time and again, Borzage's lovers discover a heaven on earth in the cruellest of situations; indeed it is the struggle against war (*A Farewell to Arms* >**2**), Depression hardships (*Man's Castle*), or Fascism (*Little Man What Now?*, *Three Comrades* >**3**) that makes possible the characters' sublime faith in a union that transcends time and space. Even in the comedy *Desire*, Dietrich's jewel thief is rescued from her criminal ways by the purity of Gary Cooper's love. Bathing actors in a luminous soft-focus that contrasts with the grim darkness of their surroundings, Borzage invested his lovers with private, inner drives powerful enough to survive even death: At the end of the Hemingway adaptation, the deserter hero carries his wife's body to a window and murmurs 'Peace', while spiralling birds signify the end of war; in the F. Scott Fitzgerald-scripted *Three Comrades*, set in Germany after World War I, the shades of the dead accompany their living friends to a better life.

Borzage's fluid camera floated through spaces unoccupied by human characters to suggest mysterious, unseen forces that exist beyond the material world. At the same time, through a commitment to life, Borzage's tender, lyrical romances become political. In *The Mortal Storm* >**4**, Nazism is evil because its doctrine of hate threatens the bonds between people: families and lovers are torn apart when two sons turn to Hitler and denounce both their Jewish stepfather and their free-thinking friends. In other films love's power adopts a religious dimension. In *Strange Cargo* >**5**, escaped convicts attain true freedom only by coming to follow the example of self-sacrifice and tolerance set by one of their number who is explicitly compared, in several scenes, to God Himself.

From 1940 onwards, Borzage's work became more conventional. Only *Moonrise* >**6**, a *film noir* about an embittered killer redeemed when he comes to terms with his past and admits his love for the one person who still trusts him, reveals the emotional commitment to spiritual concerns found in the earlier films. Nonetheless, his finest work remains undiminished, for few directors have focussed on the regenerative strengths of love with such evident sincerity or with such an expressively appropriate visual style.

Lineage

Drawing on the melodramatic tradition of **Griffith**, Borzage's sympathy for outsiders predates the work of **Nicholas Ray**, while his interest in spiritual transcendence invites comparison with otherwise very different figures such as **Dreyer** and **Bresson**. Less interesting Hollywood romantics and melodramatists include John Cromwell, Clarence Brown, Edmund Goulding and Henry King.

Further reading

John Belton's *Hollywood Professionals*, Vol 3 (London, 1974).

Viewing

1 **Seventh Heaven**
US 1927/ w Janet Gaynor, Charles Farrell, Ben Bard

2 **A Farewell to Arms**
US 1932/ w Helen Hayes, Gary Cooper, Adolphe Menjou

3 **Three Comrades**
US 1938/ w Margaret Sullavan, Robert Taylor, Robert Young
4 **The Mortal Storm**
US 1940/ w Margaret Sullavan, James Stewart, Frank Morgan
5 **Strange Cargo**
US 1940/ w Clark Gable, Joan Crawford, Ian Hunter
6 **Moonrise**
US 1949/ w Dane Clark, Gail Russell, Rex Ingram

John Brahm

Born: 17th August 1893/Hamburg, Germany
Died: 11th October 1982/Malibu, California, USA
Directing career: 1936-1957

Although never a major director, during the '40s the underrated John (christened Hans) Brahm made several thrillers whose visual invention, vivid characters, and rich atmosphere remain effective to this day.

The son of a stage actor, Brahm directed in the Viennese and Berlin theatres until 1934, when the rise of the Nazis led him to emigrate to England. After working briefly as a screenwriter and production supervisor, he made his screen directing debut with a remake of **Griffith**'s *Broken Blossoms*, notable mainly for its evocation of London's seedy Limehouse area. In 1937 he left England for Hollywood and a career in routine B-movies such as *The Undying Monster* (a werewolf thriller) and *Guest in the House*, which were lent class by the moody, sinister camerawork of Lucien Ballard and Lee Garmes.

In the mid-'40s Brahm suddenly hit his stride. *The Lodger* >**1** was a surprisingly sympathetic portrait of Jack the Ripper, with corpulent Laird Cregar giving a marvellous melancholy performance as a quiet-spoken doctor with a psychopathic hatred of actresses. Even more impressive and, perhaps, influential, was Brahm's subtle vision of Victorian London as a schizophrenic city: the secure, comfortable middle-class household of the family with whom Cregar lodges astutely contrasted with the dark, foggy streets inhabited by the poor and stalked by the killer.

Although possessed of a ludicrous plot, *Hangover Square* >**2**, a second period thriller set in a studio-created London, may have been Brahm's finest hour. From a tale of a mad composer (Cregar in flamboyant form) driven to kill whenever he hears dissonance, the director fashioned a sumptuous psychodrama of epic lunacy but astonishing conviction. Visually bold (the symbolism climaxes with a deranged Cregar dumping his latest victim on top of a massive, blazing Guy Fawkes Night bonfire), the film also benefits from a thundering, impressively cacophonous Bernard Herrmann score.

The Locket >**3**, a Freudian *film noir* about a kleptomaniac who is also a compulsive liar, was more conventional, except that its Chinese-box structure, of flashbacks within flashbacks within flashbacks, is authentically and surreally dreamlike. *The Brasher Doubloon* (*The High Window*), conversely, abandons the hard-boiled tone of Chandler's novel for the Gothic trappings and upper-crust elegance of Brahm's London thrillers. Thereafter however, he sank into relative obscurity, finally working in television, where his prolific contributions to series like *The Outer Limits*, *Johnny Staccato*, *Alfred Hitchcock Presents* and *The Twilight Zone* allowed him to indulge his taste for the shadowy atmospherics by which he is best remembered.

Lineage

Brahm stands alongside German emigrés like **Lang** and **Siodmak** as an inventive visual artist, marked by the heritage of Expressionism and by a morbid interest in psychopathic behaviour.

Viewing

1 **The Lodger**
US 1944/ w Laird Cregar, Merle Oberon, George Sanders
2 **Hangover Square**
US 1945/ w Laird Cregar, Linda Darnell, George Sanders
3 **The Locket**
US 1946/ w Laraine Day, Brian Aherne, Robert Mitchum

Robert Bresson

Born: 25th September 1907/ Bromont-Lamothe, France
Directing career: 1934-

The films of Robert Bresson are quite unlike anything else in the cinema. In his disdainful determination to exclude elements often thought essential to the medium – spectacle, drama, performance – Bresson has followed a uniquely personal vision of the world that remains consistent whatever the nature of his subject matter.

Having abandoned plans to be a painter, Bresson directed an atypically comic short (*Les Affaires Publiques*) and wrote several screenplays for other directors. In 1943, after a year spent in a German prisoner-of-war camp, he directed his first feature, *Les Anges du Péché* >**1**. Although its concern with spiritual redemption (a young nun's attempts to save a murderess's soul succeed only through her own death) anticipates the themes of salvation in his later work, its professional actors and intentionally elegant and simple visual style would reappear only in *Les Dames du Bois du Boulogne*. For all their use of dialogue by Giraudoux and **Cocteau** (the director would henceforth be his own writer), these films are nonetheless recognisably Bressonian in their lack of naturalism.

Bresson's mature style was developed in his subsequent three films, all about the struggle to find spiritual peace. In *Diary of a Country Priest*, a parson comes to accept his imminent death through his conversion of others; in *A Man Escaped* >**2**, a prisoner of the Gestapo's flight is not only from the confines of his cell but from his own despair and isolation; in *Pickpocket* >**3**, an obsessive thief comprehends life's mystery only when his sense of his own superiority is broken and he discovers love for another. Most notable, however, is not the emphasis upon redemption achieved through communication and self-sacrifice, but the austere purity of Bresson's style. The non-professional performers remain flatly inexpressive, facially and verbally; the camera avoids pictorial beauty to create an abstract timeless world through the detached, detailed observation of hands, faces, and objects; natural sounds rather than music supply meaning; while the narrative is deprived of climaxes, and elliptically fragmented.

In thus rejecting conventional realism and characterisation, Bresson revealed a fascination not with human psychology but with the capacity of the soul to survive in a world of cruelty, doubt, and imprisonment. The perfunctory dialogue exchanges and repeated alternations between court and cell in *The Trial of Joan of Arc* stripped bare the story's historical and political elements, but foundered in having its heroine's saintly status already assured. *Au Hasard, Balthazar* >**4** and *Mouchette* >**5**, however, were convincing portraits of saintliness in the most unlikely of victims, an ass and a 14-year-old peasant girl, respectively. The beast of the first, bullied and exploited by its successive owners, and the sullen friendless child of the second, bear silent witness to mankind's vices and injustices; Balthazar, shot during a petty smuggling operation, breathes his last amidst a field of sheep; Mouchette drowns herself in a river. In escaping from the misery of existence, both ass and girl discover grace in a calm acceptance of death. Miraculously, such spiritual redemptions arise in a grimy material reality, a poverty-stricken rural France peopled by alcoholics, tramps, poachers, rapists and bike-gangs. And since Bresson finds an unsentimental, transcendent goodness in inarticulate figures doomed to seemingly meaningless lives, *Balthazar* and *Mouchette* are his most moving films.

With *Une Femme Douce*, a portrait of a failing marriage that ends in the wife taking her life, Bresson moved into colour and a series of films centred on suicide. Despite his evident sincerity and his assured style, however, both *Four Nights of a Dreamer* and *The Devil Probably* suffered from increasingly

A typical Bresson shot – de-dramatised to focus on essentials – in *Au Hasard, Balthazar.*

pessimistic, even unsympathetic characters, and the by-now veteran director's lack of understanding of Parisian youth. The long-planned *Lancelot du Lac* >**6** was an idiosyncratic study in transcendent love set at the end of the age of chivalry (Arthur's knights search for the Grail in a harsh world piled high with bloody corpses and echoing with the clash of sword against armour), but *L'Argent* >**7** was the film-maker's last masterpiece. A brilliant parable of corruption, with a counterfeit note passed from hand to hand as a symbol of evil, it climaxed in the admirably unsensationalist, but truly horrific depiction of a seemingly unmovitated mass axe-murder.

It is impossible to deny both the originality of Bresson's ascetic style and the power of his essentially Catholic vision of a sinful world offering perverse possibilities of redemption. His stubborn denial of conventional psychological realism may even be seen as overcoming the cinema's inability to probe beyond surface appearances; the blank faces, inanimate objects and narrative ellipses occasionally imply the mystery of the soul. Yet, in his later work, Bresson's tight control over the world he creates on film often seems oddly schematic, isolated from the joys that may accompany chance occurrences, in life as in film-making itself.

Lineage

Contemptuous of cinema in general, Bresson appears unsullied by filmic influences. Literature, however, is important, most notably Bernanos and Dostoevsky. He may be compared, tenuously, with **Bergman**, **Dreyer**, **Ozu** and **Terence Davies**, and has been a marginal influence on **Schrader** and **Scorsese**, amongst other admirers.

Further reading

The Films of Robert Bresson ed. Ian Cameron (London, 1969), Paul Schrader's *Transcendental Style in Film* (Los Angeles, 1972), Bresson's *Notes on Cinematography* (New York, 1977).

Viewing

1 **Les Anges du Péché**
France 1943/ w Renée Faure, Jany Holt, Sylvie
2 **A Man Escaped (Un Condamné à Mort s'est Échappé)**
France 1956/ w Francois Leterrier, Charles LeClainche, Roland Monod
3 **Pickpocket**
France 1959/ w Martin Lassalle, Pierre Leymarie, Marika Green
4 **Au Hasard, Balthazar**
France 1966/ w Anne Wiazemsky, François Lafarge, Philippe Asselin
5 **Mouchette**
France 1966/ w Nadine Nortier, Jean-Claude Guilbert, Paul Hebert
6 **Lancelot du Lac**
France 1974/ w Luc Simon, Laura Duke Condominas
7 **L'Argent**
France 1983/ w Christian Patey, Sylvie Van Den Elsen, Michel Briguet

James L. Brooks

Born: 9th May 1940/North Bergen, New Jersey, USA
Directing career: 1983-

The films of James L. Brooks are remarkable less for their inherent artistic qualities than for their virtually inexplicable success with both the public and most critics. After only two features, Brooks is widely seen as a major Hollywood director.

Having progressed from newsroom copyboy to writer-producer of some of American TV's finest sit-com series (*The Mary Tyler Moore Show*, *Lou Grant*, *Taxi*), Brooks made his directing debut in film, adapting a Larry McMurtry novel, purchasing the rights from former actress Shirley Jones, and engaging the talents of Shirley MacLaine, Debra Winger and Jack Nicholson. The result, the Oscar-winning *Terms of Endearment* >**1**, was a sprawling, semi-comic story of a possessive mother's fraught relationship with her daughter, resolved only by the latter's death from cancer. Its fundamental naturalism touched the hearts of millions, yet it was little more than a sloppily shot sit-com, bedecked with bravura performances, notably Nicholson's as a lecherous beer-bellied neighbour who finally overcomes the widow MacLaine's sense of propriety. The depiction of the emotionally and physically devastating effects of terminal illness was woefully soft-centred and manipulative, closer to the hackneyed clichés of soap opera than to the real onset of death.

The slow genesis of *Broadcast News* >**2** was attributed to the director's long, diligent research into the world of television newscasting, thus ascribing to the film the same 'realism' lauded in the earlier movie. Again, however, important ethical questions raised by the various promotions, ambitions and achievements of a news producer, a writer and a handsome, none-too-bright frontman were merely the pretext for a traditional romantic triangle; only Brooks' indecision over the triangle's final outcome was unusual. His ear for the inflections of everyday speech furnished dialogue of some wit, and Michael Balhaus' mobile camera, coupled with the fine performances, admirably captured the heady, hectic newsroom atmosphere. Still, beneath the deceptively topical veneer and the endless technical jargon, there was surely less than met the eye.

Brooks' work seems formular: a kiss, a laugh, a tear, and odd hints at a serious subtext. His facility with actors may be self-negating since, if forced to depend less on performances, he might perhaps examine his potentially controversial themes more thoroughly.

Lineage

Brooks' style reflects his history in 'quality' television sit-com; in cinema, his half-hearted treatment of Major Themes is a little reminiscent of **Capra**. Among modern directors, the work of Arthur Hiller and Jerry Schatzberg is not entirely dissimilar.

Viewing

1 **Terms of Endearment**
US 1983/ w Shirley MacLaine, Debra Winger, Jack Nicholson
2 **Broadcast News**
US 1988/ w William Hurt, Holly Hunter, Albert Brooks

Mel Brooks

Born: 6th July 1927/Brooklyn, New York, USA
Directing career: 1968-

During the '70s, the only writer-directors working consistently in comedy were Mel Brooks (born Melvin Kaminsky) and **Woody Allen**. If, at that time, the former's films were more popular than Allen's, in retrospect that may prove how obvious were Brooks' methods and targets.

Brooks entered show-business as a jazz drummer and stand-up comic in the late '40s. Graduating to writing scripts alongside Carl Reiner, Larry Gelbart and, later, Allen himself, for Sid Caesar's TV show, he subsequently moved into film with the Oscar-winning cartoon short *The Critic*, which he wrote and narrated. But it was his feature debut, *The Producers*, >**1** that finally converted him to the big screen. A black comedy about the efforts of two down-and-out, would-be Broadway tycoons to make a fortune by staging a sure-fire flop for insurance reasons, it remains his best film by far. Not only are its plot and characters unusually coherent, but its major set piece – the rehearsals and premiere of the obscure Nazi musical 'Springtime for Hitler', with the Fuehrer played by a demented, preening hippy – is gloriously, tastelessly inventive.

After *The Twelve Chairs* (a dull comedy-drama set in Czarist Russia), Brooks established the spoof formula that would become his trademark. *Blazing Saddles* >**2** was a flatulent, uneven ragbag of cowboy clichés, notable mainly for a chaotic finale when, with cinematic illusion tossed to the winds, a madcap chase breaks out of the cardboard Western sets. More appealing, *Young Frankenstein* >**3** gained comic mileage from Brooks' evident affection for the horror classics he was guying. With lavish sets and superb black-and-white photography, in a few scenes (the monster set alight by an unwittingly destructive blind hermit, or giving a top-hat-and-tie rendition of 'Puttin' on the Ritz' along with his maker), he even managed to evoke the bizarre, macabre wit of **Whale** himself.

Thereafter, sexual and scatological double-entendre set in as Brooks searched out further genres to plunder. Spoofing silent slapstick (*Silent Movie*), Hitchcockian thrillers (*High Anxiety*), historical epics (*The History of the World Part 1*) and *Star Wars*-style sci-fi (*Spaceballs*), his wit receded as his own flamboyant performances grew in size and vulgarity. What had once been, in *The Producers*, a sly satire on the conventions of good taste now declined into coarse stereotypes: camp gays, female sex-objects, and grotesque incompetents laden with loud neuroses. Worst, his remake of **Lubitsch**'s anti-Nazi *To Be Or Not To Be* replaced the original's truly black satire with aimless, indulgent mugging.

Brooks' dependence on broad, blunt parody has become ever more predictable and infantile; his scope and achievement seem woefully limited. Interestingly, however, his production company, Brooksfilms, also makes more serious, interesting fare like **David Lynch**'s *The Elephant Man* and David Jones' *84 Charing Cross Road*.

Lineage

Indelibly marked by the Jewish tradition, Brooks' inane spoofery also seems a direct successor of Abbott and Costello's comedies. His irreverent, brash style may be seen not only as an influence on former collaborators Gene Wilder and Marty Feldman, but as a precursor to the comedy of younger figures like Dan Aykroyd and Chevy Chase, not to mention the *Police Academy* films.

Viewing

1 **The Producers**
US 1968/ w Zero Mostel, Gene Wilder, Kenneth Mars

2 **Blazing Saddles**
US 1974/ w Cleavon Little, Gene Wilder, Brooks

3 **Young Frankenstein**
US 1974/ w Gene Wilder, Peter Boyle, Marty Feldman

Tod Browning

Born: 12th July 1882/Louisville, Kentucky, USA
Died: 6th October 1962/Santa Monica, California, USA
Directing career: 1913-1939

Best known for *Dracula*, Charles Albert Browning, to give him his full name, is often regarded primarily as a horror director; but he is more appropriately seen as a highly imaginative eccentric whose best work is typified by his continuing fascination with the grotesque and macabre.

Having left home in his late teens to join a carnival (where he appeared as The Living Hypnotic Corpse), in 1913 Browning went to Biograph Studios as an actor and met **D.W. Griffith** who, besides eventually letting him assist on *Intolerance*, encouraged him to write and direct. At first he made only routine adventure serials and melodramas but, in 1919, he directed Lon Chaney in *The Wicked Darling*, thus beginning a ten-film association that was to mark Browning's most creative period. Chaney – the Man of 1000 Faces — was already known as a performer dedicated to the grotesque, and Browning, with his obsessive interest in psychologically warped or murderous characters, was his ideal collaborator. Their first truly notable film together, *The Unholy Three* >**1**, charted a jewel heist by a bizarre trio of carnival performers – a strong man, a midget and a ventriloquist with a penchant for dressing as an old crone. Still more astonishing was *The Unknown* >**2** in which a circus knife-thrower plunges into masochism and murder when he becomes obsessed with Joan Crawford, who appears reluctant to accept the physical advances of men; to win her affections he has his arms amputated, only to discover her love for another. In Browning's world, physical deformity often reflects psychological torment, and a brutally ironic, savage justice holds sway.

The absurdly imaginative Chaney films, macabre accounts of frustration and revenge leavened by dark wit, came to an end with the actor's death in 1930, thwarting Browning's plans to cast him in *Dracula* >**3**. Bela Lugosi became the vampire Count, lending his slow, other-worldly diction to give the role an oddly sympathetic quality. The later London scenes betray Bram Stoker's novel, but the melancholy magic of the opening Transylvanian sequence – the gloomy castle laced with giant cobwebs, Lugosi's mesmeric tribute to the children of the night – ensured that Universal (makers of the film) embarked on an extensive, influential horror cycle.

Browning's masterpiece, however, was *Freaks* >**4**, made for the otherwise blandly wholesome MGM. A return to circus life, it told of the oppression and betrayal of a group of life's unfortunates by their more physically 'normal' colleagues. Although the freaks were real (to avoid sensationalism the pinheads, cretins, Siamese twins and a 'human torso' are introduced in lyrical long shots of a country idyll), Browning's sympathy for their wit, courage and camaraderie gives every frame a rare, non-voyeuristic integrity. The film was banned, however, and his career never recovered. He directed four more films of which only *The Devil Doll* >**5** remains notable. It is an ingenious thriller, co-scripted by **Erich von Stroheim**, which sees banker Lionel Barrymore, often in drag, use miniaturised humans to exact revenge on crooked partners. Thereafter the odd, shadowy cinematic world of Browning faded from view, though one last, suitably macabre event occurred during his long retirement: a very premature announcement by the press of his death in 1944.

Lineage

Browning's chiaroscuro visuals and concern with mutilation and madness parallel many German Expressionist films. Whereas the influence of *Dracula* on subsequent vampire films, and of *Freaks* on **Lynch**'s *The Elephant Man* and **Bogdanovich**'s *Mask* is undeniable, his sado-masochistic melodramas have few real progeny.

Further reading

The Hollywood Professionals, Vol 4 (London, 1975) by Stuart Rosenthal.

Viewing

1 **The Unholy Three**
US 1925/ w Lon Chaney, Harry Earles, Victor McLaglen
2 **The Unknown**
US 1927/ w Lon Chaney, Joan Crawford
3 **Dracula**
US 1931/ w Bela Lugosi, Helen Chandler, Edward Van Sloan
4 **Freaks**
US 1932/ w Harry Earles, Olga Baclanova
5 **The Devil Doll**
US 1936/ w Lionel Barrymore, Maureen O'Sullivan

Luis Buñuel

Born: **22nd February 1900/Calanda, Spain**
Died: **29th July 1983/Mexico City, Mexico**
Directing career: **1929-1977**

Atheist, Marxist, Freudian, Surrealist, anarchist, fetishist, satirist or Spaniard? Luis Buñuel Portoles was all these and more. One of the greatest of all film-makers, Buñuel expressed a uniquely personal vision of the world through a remarkably self-effacing cinematic style, producing a body of work unparalleled in its wealth of meaning and its ability to provoke and disturb.

After a Jesuit schooling, followed by studies at Madrid's Residencia where he befriended Salvador Dali and Garcia Lorca, Buñuel became a member of Spain's artistic avant-garde. Moving on to Paris, he fell in with the Surrealists and became assistant to Jean Epstein, before teaming up with Dali to write and direct *Un Chien Andalou* >**1**. Eschewing narrative continuity and filled with dreamlike images (Buñuel casually slicing a woman's eye with a razor, a man tethered to priests and a piano topped with rotting donkeys), this short, subversive cine-poem so impressed the Paris intellegentsia that in *L'Age d'Or* >**2**, commenced but not completed in collaboration with Dali, Buñuel with characteristic perversity intensified his attack on bourgeois sensibilities. The film concerns a couple constantly frustrated by Church and Establishment niceties, as well as their own sexual guilt. Such 'plot' as there is is structured according to the irrational dream-logic of fear and desire, starting with a 'documentary' on scorpions and working through a series of darkly comic, loosely connected scenes. The film climaxes in outrageous blasphemy, equating the meek figure of Christ with a participant in a murderous orgy in De Sade's *120 Days of Sodom*. Unsurprisingly, the work was widely banned.

After a superb, distinctly personal documentary, *Las Hurdes* (*Land Without Bread*) in which he observed the poverty of Northern Spanish peasants not with pity but with barely concealed contempt for the hypocrisy and wealth of the Catholic Church, Buñuel spent 15 years in obscurity, writing, producing, dubbing Spanish films in Paris, Madrid and America. In 1946, he moved to Mexico where, between more conventional assignments, he resumed his creativity with a vengeance. His first masterpiece of this prolific period, *Los Olvidados* (*The Young and the Damned*) >**3** was a savage response to the sentimental social comment of neo-realism. Portraying the plight of delinquents in Mexico City's slums, he acknowledged the effects of an atrocious environment but refused to glamorise his victim-heroes: the gang torments a blind beggar who is himself a cunning paedophile, while in Freudian dreams the most 'innocent' boy fights a friend for his mother's sexual favours.

In film after film, Buñuel's hatred of the Church and the bourgeoisie was expressed in imaginative, witty melodramas that focussed on the themes of male paranoia, sexual repression and impotence, and middle-class hypocrisy. In *El* >**4**, a respectable, foot-fetishist churchgoer becomes so jealous of his wife's (non-existent) infidelity

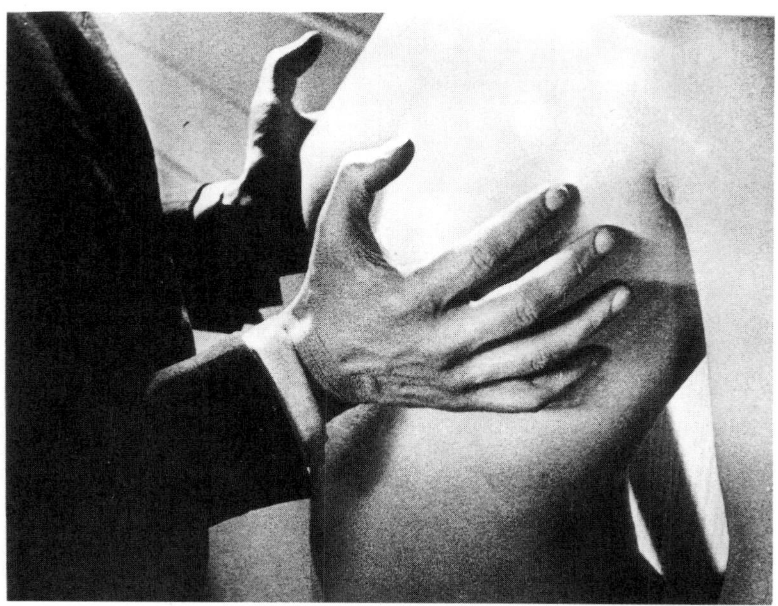

A none too obscure object of desire, in Buñuel and Dali's surreal, scandalous and still shocking *Un Chien Andalou.*

that, as she sleeps, he enters her room armed with a rope, scissors, needle and thread; in *The Criminal Life of Archibaldo de la Cruz*, the pathetically insecure hero fantasises about killing women to assert his superiority but ends up burning dummies; in *Viridiana* >**5** – which the Spanish government invited Buñuel to make in his home country, only to ban the finished film – a nun's self-regarding acts of charity climax in her hosting a beggars' banquet which becomes an obscene orgiastic parody of the Last Supper. Only in *Nazarin* is a well-doer deserving of Buñuel's full support, and he, a modest priest vainly attempting to follow Christ's teachings in a land tainted by sin, poverty, corruption and ingratitude, is excommunicated by the Church.

While Buñuel often rendered his characters' unconscious desires in visual terms, he never resorted to camera trickery and virtuoso technique; indeed, his cool, detached, rarely mobile camera stressed the clarity of his thinking. In *The Exterminating Angel* >**6**, a party of wealthy diners are strangely unable to leave their host's salon: as the outwardly respectable guests resort to increasingly 'uncivilised' and aggressive behaviour, Buñuel never rationalises their situation, nor explains the presence of a bear on the other side of the open doorway. The trapped sophisticates' spiritual paralysis merely signifies their moral ineffectuality.

In the '60s, Buñuel's reputation as a major film artist was assured, and he moved on to more polished productions, mainly in France. Established stars and colour camerawork were evidence of his increasingly acceptable status, but he remained true to his anarchic vision. In *Belle de Jour* >**7** he gleefully cast glamorous Catherine Deneuve as a masochistic middle-class housewife turning in secret to afternoon prostitution; *The Milky Way* was his most sustained attack on the oppressive absurdity of religious dogma; *Tristana*'s sardonic portrait of liberal hypocrisy had a paragon of bourgeois respectability ruthlessly seducing his virgin ward. But Buñuel was at his most subversively playful in *The Discreet Charm of the Bourgeoisie* >**8** (in which meals arranged by a group of wealthy gastronomes are repeatedly interrupted and abandoned) and *The Phantom of Liberty*, both of which made tantalising use of broken narratives – dreams within dreams, tales within unfinished tales – to spectacularly disorientating effect. The easy unforced Surrealism of these films, making no distinction between reality and fantasy, conscious and unconscious, was a glorious return to the narrative freedom and irrationality of the director's early work. Indeed, in his final film, *That Obscure Object of Desire* >**9**, his originality and fire were as strong as ever: the young woman who continually frustrates the desires of an ageing lecher is played, inspirationally, by two different actresses; while both the film and Buñuel's career end, appropriately, with a terrorist bombing.

Buñuel's own guerilla tactics were sustained throughout his lengthy, distinguished career; never yielding to the demands of fashion, he waged an unending one-man battle against all forms of hypocrisy, injustice and oppression, using as his weapons sly wit and Surreal images that were never gratuitous or amoral. It is in no way surprising that his films retain the power still to disturb, shock, offend and provoke.

Lineage

Buñuel's anti-clerical social satire has its roots in the Spanish picaresque novel, his interest in the unconscious in Surrealism. **Vigo**, **Renoir** and the Marx Brothers were similarly subversive; while **Saura**, **Blier**, **Bertolucci**, **Borowczyk**, Luis Berlanga and Jan Svankmajer, among many others, reveal his influence and/or admit to a great admiration for his work.

Further reading

Jose Francisco Aranda's *Luis Buñuel: a Critical Biography* (London, 1975), Raymond Durgnat's *Luis Buñuel* (Berkeley, 1978), *The World of Luis Buñuel* ed. Joan Mellen (New York, 1978). *My Last Breath* (New York, 1983) is Buñuel's autobiography.

Viewing

1 **Un Chien Andalou**
France 1928/ w Buñuel, Pierre Batcheff, Simone Mareuil

2 **L'Age d'Or**
France 1930/ w Gaston Modot, Lya Lys, Max Ernst

3 **Los Olvidados (The Young and the Damned)**
Mexico 1950/ w Alfonso Mejia, Roberto Cobo, Estela Inda

4 **El**
Mexico 1952/ w Arturo de Cordova, Delia Garces, Luis Beristein

5 **Viridiana**
Spain 1961/ w Silvia Pinal, Fernando Rey, Francisco Rabal

6 **The Exterminating Angel**
Mexico 1962/ w Silvia Pinal, Enrique Rambal, Jacqueline Andere

7 **Belle de Jour**
France 1966/ w Cathérine Deneuve, Jean Sorel, Michel Piccoli

8 **The Discreet Charm of the Bourgeoisie**
France 1972/ w Fernando Rey, Stéphane Audran, Delphine Seyrig

9 **That Obscure Object of Desire**
France 1977/ w Fernando Rey, Angela Molina, Carole Bouquet

Frank Capra

Born: 18th May 1897/Palermo, Sicily
Directing career: 1922-1961

Like **Chaplin**, Frank Capra began his film career as a simple, effective comic talent and progressed to 'message movies'. And, as with Chaplin, the populism of his later films demonstrated both a decline in humour and disturbing political ambiguities.

After emigrating to America at the age of six, the young Capra passed through a variety of jobs before becoming a prop-man, then an editor and gag writer for producers Hal Roach and Mack Sennett. Directing the baby-faced Harry Langdon in both *The Strong Man* and *Long Pants* – in which a doltish innocent triumphs over corrupt sophisticates – he established himself as a director of promise. Despite the films' success, however, Capra was fired by Langdon, and signed with Columbia, a Poverty

Row company that he would transform into a major studio almost single-handedly.

His films during the early '30s were likeable adventures and comedies notable for polish, pace and variety. *The Miracle Woman* – an exposé of evangelism, inspired by Aimee Semple Macpherson – and the witty *Platinum Blonde* were sparkling vehicles for Barbara Stanwyck and Jean Harlow, but it is *The Bitter Tea of General Yen* >**1** that remains Capra's finest film. This is an atypically exotic romance in which Stanwyck's prim American missionary is held hostage by a sinister but seductive Chinese warlord. Its story of a converter converted is not only erotic – a startling dream sequence reveals the woman's hesitant, nervous awakening to her physical desires – but a complex, tragic investigation of culture clash.

More conventional was the perky road comedy *It Happened One Night* >**2**, in which a sassy, fired journalist and a runaway heiress travel together through Depression America, put aside class differences and fall in love. Robert Riskin's predictable plot was enlivened by the sparkling vitality of Clark Gable and Claudette Colbert, while the mildly populist message struck a chord in the hearts of a troubled nation, won the film a fistful of Oscars, and put Columbia on the map. But Capra's longing to express his love for his adopted homeland resulted in a series of morally uplifting films, paying tribute to the archetypal WASP American. In *Mr Deeds Goes to Town* >**3**, Gary Cooper's smalltown simplicity overcomes city cynicism when his plans to donate an inherited fortune to the poor and needy land him in an insanity trial; in the turgid fantasy-allegory, *Lost Horizon*, the benevolent dictatorship of the High Lama's Shangri-La is piously devoted to peace; in *You Can't Take It With You*, a greedy munitions magnate is redeemed by a poor but happy family's folksy eccentricity; and in *Mr Smith Goes to Washington* >**4**, James Stewart's gangly country scoutmaster rids the Senate of corruption through his courage and faith in 'the little people'. Capra's well-meaning, emotionally manipulative (often Riskin-scripted) comedy-dramas suffer from a preachy sentimentality, and from a naive assertion that political and social evils can be dealt with by a lone patriot. He depicts corruption not as a complex, deep-rooted phenomenon but merely as a question of a few rotten apples; featuring a fickle populus easily swayed by a simpleton demagogue whose platitudes extol the virtues of anti-intellectual, humdrum conformism, Capra's view of New Deal democracy was complacent and reactionary. But jingoism and superb performances ensured critical and commercial success.

After making the *Why We Fight* series of wartime propaganda documentaries, Capra resumed his commercial career with a creaky black comedy, *Arsenic and Old Lace*, and another paean to small-town America in *It's a Wonderful Life* >**5**. Sensitively acted by Stewart, the film's first half is a surprisingly dark picture of the self-sacrificing compromises inevitable in a life devoted to goodness; sadly, the punches are pulled when the hero's suicide is averted by a cuddly, elderly angel's demonstration of how much worse his family and friends' lives would be had he never lived.

After the limp political satire of *State of the Union*, Capra muddled his way through a series of aborted projects, periods of inactivity, and tepid remakes. Times change, and his portentous pronouncements on the wonders of democracy appeared increasingly irrelevant. In retrospect, his much-vaunted didactic concern for 'the little people' seems both condescending and confused. Heroes and villains battle towards a contrived happy ending; his films have less to do with political realities than with fairy-tale.

Lineage

Capra's sentimental, socio-political satires – Capracorn – are reminiscent of **Chaplin** and early **Clair**. Indeed, his simplistic, vaguely liberal sermonising foreshadows that of **Stanley Kramer**.

Further reading

Frank Capra – The Man and His

Films (ed. Richard Glatzer and John Raeburn, Ann Arbor, 1975), Allen Estrin's *The Hollywood Professionals,* Vol 6 (London, 1980). *The Name Above the Title* (New York, 1971) is Capra's autobiography.

Viewing

1 **The Bitter Tea of General Yen**
US 1933/ w Barbara Stanwyck, Nils Asther, Walter Connolly
2 **It Happened One Night**
US 1934/ w Clark Gable, Claudette Colbert, Walter Connolly
3 **Mr Deeds Goes to Town**
US 1936/ w Gary Cooper, Jean Arthur, George Bancroft
4 **Mr Smith Goes to Washington**
US 1939/ w James Stewart, Jean Arthur, Edward Arnold
5 **It's a Wonderful Life**
US 1946/ w James Stewart, Donna Reed, Lionel Barrymore

Marcel Carné

Born: 18th August 1909/Paris, France
Directing career: 1929-1976

In the late '30s and early '40s, the films of Marcel Carné gave eloquent voice to a mood of fatalistic, romantic pessimism. After the war, however, his career was a sad shadow of its former self.

After working briefly as a film critic, Carné assisted both **René Clair** and Jacques Feyder; it was the latter's wife, actress Françoise Rosay, who proved most supportive to Carné's own debut, *Jenny*, by playing the title role of a nightclub owner whose lover falls for her daughter. A more fruitful collaboration, however, was with the poet and screenwriter Jacques Prévert, whose script for Carné's atypically ebullient *Drôle de Drame* >**1** concerned an absurd series of crimes committed, in a surreally evoked London, by eccentric characters brilliantly played by Rosay, Jean-Louis Barrault, Louis Jouvet and Michel Simon. Carné, in fact, always seemed unusually dependent on the talent of others: set-designer Alexandre Trauner, composer Maurice Jaubert and cameraman Eugen Schufftan also contributed to several of his finest films.

More characteristic than *Drôle de Drame* were three romantic, moody melodramas: *Quai des Brumes* >**2**, *Hôtel du Nord*, and *Le Jour se Lève* >**3**. Central to Carné and Prévert's conception of doomed love was Jean Gabin's proletarian anti-hero, trapped in darkened rooms and foggy streets while awaiting retribution for crimes he barely knew he might commit: in *Quai des Brumes*, Gabin's deserter comes violently up against local gangsters in a battle over the girl with whom he has fallen suddenly, passionately in love; in *Le Jour se Lève*, surrounded by police but unable to contemplate surrender, he recalls the events leading to his shooting of a girlfriend's seducer. Widely described as poetic realism, Carné's style is in fact anything but realist; the squalour, shadows, and smoky bars all externalise the hero's melancholy resignation to an unjust Destiny. Without Carné's expert control of atmosphere, the effect might seem merely picturesque, for rarely have solitude, alienation and death been imbued with such elegance and beauty.

During the Occupation, Carné and Prévert turned away from contemporary realities to historic fable. In *Les Visiteurs du Soir* (*The Devil's Envoys*), the triumph of love over Satan serves as an unconvincing medieval allegory on the German invasion. Far better was *Les Enfants du Paradis* >**4**, a lavish tragicomedy set in 1840s Paris and the world of the boulevard theatres. Mixing historical and fictional characters to probe the relationship between life and art, the film's epic crowd scenes and its flamboyant celebration of theatricality are offset by scenes of exquisite intimacy, notably between Barrault's mime Deburau and Arletty's Garance, lovers who are destined never to consummate their dreamlike passion. Running at three-and-a-quarter hours, Carné's masterpiece draws us into a vanished world through magnificent sets and virtuoso acting.

After the war Carné's work

became increasingly routine, even though occasionally he still managed to elicit fine performances: Gabin in *La Marie du Port*, Gérard Philipe in *Juliette ou la Clé des Songes*, Simone Signoret in *Thérèse Raquin*. Without, however, the collaborators of earlier years, he seemed to lose his way and made vain attempts to explore the subject of France's '50s youth culture; it is indeed ironic that he was one of the directors on whom the *Nouvelle Vague* film-makers heaped their scorn.

If Carné never fulfilled his early promise, his status as an accomplished craftsman remains assured. His most memorable work, made between the fall of the Popular Front and the Liberation, stands as a lasting testimony to the mood of France at that time.

Lineage

Carné's best work was indelibly influenced by **Renoir** and Feyder, and may be compared, perhaps, with that of **Julien Duvivier**; his films with Gabin foreshadow not only **Becker** and **Melville** but the doomed romanticism of American *film noir*; indeed Hollywood remade *Le Jour se Lève* as *The Long Night*, with Anatole Litvak directing.

Viewing

1 **Drôle de Drame (Bizarre, Bizarre)**
France 1937/ w Michel Simon, Louis Jouvet, Françoise Rosay
2 **Quai des Brumes (Port of Shadows)**
France 1938/ w Jean Gabin, Michèle Morgan, Michel Simon
3 **Le Jour se Lève (Daybreak)**
France 1939/ w Jean Gabin, Jules Berry, Arletty
4 **Les Enfants du Paradis**
France 1945/ w Jean-Louis Barrault, Arletty, Pierre Brasseur

John Carpenter

Born: **16th January 1948/Carthage, New York, USA**
Directing career: 1962-

Although John Carpenter's cine-literacy would seem to mark him as a 'movie brat', unlike many of his peers he seems happiest when working with low-budget, traditionally B-movie, genre material.

Even as a child, Carpenter wanted to make movies; by the age of eight he was shooting 8mm sci-fi shorts. As a film student, he wrote and directed several shorts, one of which (*The Resurrection of Bronco Billy*) won an Oscar. But it was his feature debut, *Dark Star* >**1**, that first achieved cult status. A cheap, very cheerful riposte to the lavish special effects and pompous intellectualism of *2001: A Space Odyssey*, it revelled in offbeat humour: a bouncing, bi-ped beach-ball serves as a troublesome alien, while **Kubrick**'s argumentative computer HAL 9000 is replaced by a witty talking bomb that spouts metaphysical philosophy before destroying the heroes' spaceship.

Assault on Precinct 13 >**2** enhanced Carpenter's international reputation while paying homage to **Howard Hawks**. About a motley crew of cops and cons besieged by terrorists in a disused police station, the film's blend of claustrophobic tension, low-key heroism and wry humour was reminiscent of *Rio Bravo*. Similarly, the huge hit, *Halloween* >**3**, in which baby-sitter Jamie Lee Curtis is menaced by a monstrous homicidal psychopath, used Hitchcockian shock-cuts, while making imaginative use of the wide CinemaScope screen, the killer appearing at the edges of the frame to devastating effect.

Hitchcock's *Rear Window* inspired the superior tele-thriller *High Rise*, but Carpenter's script – a further study in voyeurism – for *The Eyes of Laura Mars* was emasculated by director Irvin Kershner. *The Fog* >**4**, however, besides being an exemplary exercise in parallel narratives, was an atmospheric supernatural thriller reminiscent of **Jack Arnold**'s films, a subtly subversive tale of a quietly respectable coastal community celebrating its centennial anniversary and menaced by vengeful ghosts of lepers whose murder had made the town's growth possible. As with *Halloween* and *The Thing* – a witty but inevitably inferior remake of Hawks' sci-fi classic – *The*

Fog may be seen as an intelligent pulp movie about the eruption of a repressed, lethally destructive Id.

Sadly, Carpenter's recent films have been less interesting. While *Escape from New York* and *Christine* were visually inventive, they lacked the urgency of his best work. *Starman*'s touching mix of sci-fi and romantic comedy saw Jeff Bridges in excellent form as a humanoid alien whose encounter with a widow (whose husband's appearance he has adopted) enables him to experience emotion, but *Big Trouble in Little China* – a lame martial arts fantasy – was a distinct step backwards. Uneven and rather too verbose, but still clearly the work of a talented film-maker, *Prince of Darkness*, a Satanic thriller made in homage to the writer Nigel Kneale, once again suggested that Carpenter was stimulated rather than stunted by having to work within the confines of a low-budget. Certainly, at his best he is one of the most intelligently stylish craftsmen working within the once disreputable genres of horror and sci-fi.

Lineage

Despite his acknowledged debt to **Hawks**, Carpenter is a successor to genre-specialists such as **Arnold**, **Hitchcock** and Terence Fisher. Subtler than Tobe Hooper and Wes Craven, he has inspired many imitators.

Further reading

Peter Nicholls' *Fantastic Cinema* (London, 1984).

Viewing

1 **Dark Star**
US 1974/ w Brian Narelle, Dre Pahich, Dan O'Bannon

2 **Assault on Precinct 13**
US 1977/ w Austin Stoker, Darwin Joston, Laurie Zimmer

3 **Halloween**
US 1978/ w Jamie Lee Curtis, Donald Pleasence, Nancy Loomis

4 **The Fog**
US 1979/ w Jamie Lee Curtis, Tommy Atkins, Adrienne Barbeau

John Cassavetes

Born: 9th December 1929/New York, USA
Died: 3rd February 1989/New York, USA
Directing career: 1958-

The remarkable, sometimes infuriating, often brilliant films of John Cassavetes occupy a unique position in American cinema. Low-budget, partly improvised, inspired by *cinéma verité* documentary, and akin to underground film, they have nevertheless frequently managed to reach a wide and profoundly appreciative audience.

After drama studies, the young Cassavetes quickly made his name as an unusually raw, intense actor, often appearing in films about disaffected, rebellious youth such as *Crime in the Streets* and *Edge of the City*. Setting up an actors' workshop, he worked to transform an improvisational experiment into his feature debut. The result, *Shadows* >**1**, taking three years to complete and partly financed by his performances in TV's *Johnny Staccato*, was a breakthrough in American cinema. About the effect of racism on an already fraught relationship between two black men and their sister, two of whom pass for white, the film is impressive for its jagged, seemingly formless style and naturalistic performances. Plot was minimal, mood and emotional verisimilitude were everything.

Shadows' limited though prestigious success led to two relatively conventional studio films, *Too Late Blues* and *A Child Is Waiting*. While both exhibited excellent performances, Cassavetes himself found them frustrating experiences, and returned to acting (*The Killers*, *The Dirty Dozen*, and *Rosemary's Baby* are among his best performances of the '60s) as a means of funding the independently produced *Faces*. Here, hand-held camera, grainy stock, rough editing and lengthy scenes of semi-improvised, behaviourist performances embodied the writer-director's ideal of an actors' cinema;

at the same time, the nervy, close-up depiction of random events leading to marital crisis suggested an unsentimental view of family life.

Just as Cassavetes obsessively returned to the banal but often revelatory minutiae of friendship and family relationships, so he surrounded himself with a sympathetic, talented 'family' of performers: in *Husbands* >**2**, acting alongside friends Ben Gazzara and Peter Falk, he explored the neuroses of the menopausal male in a tale of three men who react to the death of a colleague by flying, impulsively, to London for an escapist weekend of boozy introspection; in *Woman Under the Influence* >**3**, a suburban wife driven slowly out of her mind by her routine existence is vividly incarnated by the director's own wife, Gena Rowlands. Conversely, *Minnie and Moskowitz* was a surprisingly upbeat, semi-comic look at the tortuous courtship of two eccentrics tired of solitude, but *The Killing of a Chinese Bookie* – a crazed flirtation with *film noir* complete with a riveting murder sequence – and *Opening Night* were more disturbing accounts of anxiety and self-doubt.

Still devoted to exploring the art of naturalistic acting, Cassavetes had simultaneously become increasingly concerned with theatricality. *Gloria* >**4**, however, was an atypically pacy crime thriller in which a gun-toting moll – Rowlands again – goes on the run to defend a dead friend's precocious son from the Mob. Full of sharp, subtle and idiosyncratic touches in conflating and confounding the movies' traditionally exclusive Mother/Whore female stereotypes, it was subversively feminist, while from its exhilarating opening aerial shots of New York to its poignant dreamlike ending in a cemetery, the film merged realism with fantasy to superbly stylish effect.

Strange and ambitious, *Love Streams* >**5** was a tale of sibling interdependence that only revealed its central characters to be brother and sister halfway through the film, and combined an edgy naturalism with opulent theatricality (notably a surreal operatic musical sequence) to summarise, in passing, the director's styles and thematic

John Cassavetes clearly exhilarated by Charles Mingus' music for *Shadows*, his debut as director and a milestone in modern American cinema.

obsessions. Still, however, it stressed psychology and relationships over narrative. Finally, plagued by illness, Cassavetes took over the direction of *Big Trouble*, a relatively commercial, comic pastiche of *Double Indemnity*, notable mainly for its strong performances and zany humour; even a chore for which he clearly felt little affection benefitted from his astute and challenging direction of actors, and from his refusal to conform.

Charges of indulgent amateurism miss the point: Cassavetes cherished his outsider status. His career was a relentless exploration of the ways in which acting, inspired by and based on everyday behaviour, might illuminate the darkest corners of human experience. To that end, uneventful stories and camerawork were placed entirely at the service of his actors, who, in turn, enabled the director to reveal his sympathy for loners and losers.

Lineage

Cassavetes' style emerged from the Method, from documentary and from that flowering of 'alternative' cinema that produced figures such as **Warhol**, **Godard**, and **Jacques Rivette**. His pessimism may be likened to that of **Bergman** and **Antonioni**; directors as diverse as **Altman**, **Loach** and **Scorsese** would seem marked by his naturalistic style. Interestingly, Cassavetes and Peter Falk starred in Elaine May's *Mikey and Nicky*, which looked very like a Cassavetes film.

Further reading

James Monaco's *American Film Now* (New York, 1979), Diane Jacobs' *Hollywood Renaissance* (New York, 1977).

Viewing

1 **Shadows**
US 1960/ w Lelia Goldoni, Ben Carruthers, Hugh Hurd

2 **Husbands**
US 1970/ w Ben Gazzara, Peter Falk, Cassavetes

3 **A Woman Under the Influence**
US 1974/ w Gena Rowlands, Peter Falk, Katherine Cassavetes

4 **Gloria**
US 1980/ w Gena Rowlands, John Adames, Buck Henry

5 **Love Streams**
US 1983/ w Gena Rowlands, Cassavetes, Seymour Cassel

Claude Chabrol

Born: 24th June 1930/Paris, France
Directing career: 1958-

While Claude Chabrol is certainly one of the most important film-makers to have emerged from the French New Wave, his consistency of theme and assured, expressive style are often betrayed by poor material, resulting in a career as uneven as it is prolific.

A cinephile in his teens, in the '50s Chabrol worked – along with **Godard**, **Truffaut** and Rivette – as a film critic for *Cahiers du Cinéma*. After writing, with **Eric Rohmer**, a book on Hitchcock, and producing a number of shorts, he turned to direction in 1958 with *Le Beau Serge*, now widely regarded as the first feature of the *Nouvelle Vague*. A bleak provincial drama of self-sacrifice and redemption, its somewhat schematic narrative structure and characterisation recurred more effectively in *Les Cousins* >**1**: clumsy country student Charles visits the brighter, seductively decadent Paul in Paris and, consumed by jealousy over a girl, contemplates killing his cousin; but it is Paul who accidentally shoots Charles, Chabrol subtly implying the victim's complicity.

This exchange of guilt – a Catholic motif he and Rohmer had identified in Hitchcock's films – would recur throughout Chabrol's career. In *Les Bonnes Femmes* >**2**, concerned with the banal romantic dreams of four bored Parisian shopgirls, the shyest of them lets herself be picked up by a biker who then strangles her. Equally, the director would often examine the theme of relationships disrupted by outsiders, with subsequent tensions climaxing in violence: *L'Oeil du Malin* >**3** depicted a journalist so jealous of a happily married couple that, when he learns of the woman's infidelity, he viciously tells the husband, who then kills his wife. Typically, Chabrol sees the intruder as guilty rather than the killer or the faithless woman.

Chabrol's cool, cynical examinations of contemporary mores and psychology have been distinguished by an expressive use of decor, movement, and geometrically conceived relationships. His initial success, however, was followed by a number of failures, and for several years he seemed content with commercial chores, mainly in the form of spoof spy-thrillers. Not until 1968 did he return to form with a series of mature, formalised variations on the theme of the bourgeois family and its capacity for criminal behaviour. In *Les Biches*, the 'family' consists of two bisexual women whose love is fatally destroyed by the deceit and jealousy prompted by a male lover; in *La Femme Infidèle* >**4**, a meek husband who murders his wife's paramour ironically wins her love when she perversely tries to protect him from prying police; and in *Que La Bête Meure* (*Killer!*), a hit-and-run victim's father plans vengeance against the driver, but wavers when he meets the killer's own son – who in turn, perhaps, murders his own father. The obsessive nature of Chabrol's examinations (through their reactions to murder) of the bourgeoisie's all-consuming desire to preserve respectability and the status quo was displayed in his repetitive use of a group of actors (Michel Bouquet, Jean Yanne, and his own wife Stéphane Audran) and of symbolic character-names: Héléne (aloof), Paul (hedonistic, threatening), and Charles (repressed, serious).

That the chaos-inducing intruder was an Id-symbol was clear in Chabrol's masterpiece, *Le Boucher* >**5**, where the extended family of a quiet Dordogne village is menaced by a child-killer. Though it includes several inventive, dramatic scenes (a body found when blood drips like ketchup on to a schoolgirl's picnic sandwich), the film's forte is its clear-eyed sympathy for the murderer, an Indo-China War veteran trained in killing, while shots of pre-historic cave-paintings evoke man's brute, primitive instincts.

Chabrol's growing confidence – *Ten Days' Wonder* was a weird, semi-comic Oedipal thriller-cum-theological allegory, *Nada*'s tale of terrorists besieged by boorish authority figures an attempt to deal with modern politics – finally deserted him in the mid '70s, when he turned increasingly to shaky international co-productions (*Blood Relatives*, *Innocents with Dirty Hands*) and tele-thrillers. More satisfyingly in recent years, *Violette Nozière* >**6**, based on a true story of a young woman driven by the deceptions of family life to poison her parents, was elegant, moody and beautifully acted; both *Poulet au Vinaigre* (*Cop au Vin*) >**7** and its sequel *Inspecteur Lavardin* were pleasantly grotesque detective thrillers, the first a witty tale of provincial corruption, the latter a bizarre study of a cop's attempts to play God in a paradise lost peopled by fallen angels; and *Une Affair des Femmes* an unusually touching and generous portrait of the last French woman to be guillotined (for performing abortions for soldiers' wives, a business that is anathema to the hypocritical puritanism of the Vichy government).

However intelligent or persuasive, Chabrol's examination of bourgeois morality is often weakened by his insistence on viewing characters with a Godlike detachment. A consummate craftsman, his interest in human emotions often seems intellectually motivated, which may explain the erratic, rather formal nature of his work.

Lineage

Chabrol's sour, fatalistic view of bourgeois criminality has its predecessors in **Lang**, **Hitchcock** and **Buñuel**, while his interest in disruptive intruders parallels **Losey**. The influence of his cool, aesthetic style on the contemporary French thriller is immense.

Further reading

Robin Wood's *Claude Chabrol* (London, 1970), James Monaco's *The New Wave* (New York, 1976).

Viewing

1 **Les Cousins**
France 1958/ w Gérard Blain, Jean-Claude Brialy, Juliette Mayniel
2 **Les Bonnes Femmes**
France 1960/ w Bernardette Lafont, Stéphane Audran, Mario David
3 **L'Oeil du Malin (The Third Lover)**
France 1962/ w Stéphane Audran, Jacques Charrier
4 **La Femme Infidèle**
France 1968/ w Michel Bouquet, Stéphane Audran, Maurice Ronet
5 **Le Boucher**
France 1969/ w Stéphane Audran, Jean Yanne
6 **Violette Nozière**
France 1978/ w Isabelle Huppert, Stéphane Audran, Jean Carmet
7 **Poulet au Vinaigre (Cop au Vin)**
France 1984/ w Jean Poiret, Stéphane Audran, Michel Bouquet

Charles Chaplin

Born: 16th April 1889/London, England
Died: 25th December 1977/Corsier sur Vevey, Switzerland
Directing career: 1914-1967

The once universal popularity of Charles Spencer Chaplin – during his lifetime one of the most famous men the world has ever known – is easily comprehended by a simple analysis of his films. Best known as 'the little tramp', he drew on his childhood experiences of poverty and loss to depict a quintessential underdog, a rather exquisite, sentimentalised vision of the Common Man eternally at odds with the strong and the rich, the powerful and unjust. For the huddled masses visiting movie houses in the early years of this century, Charlie was a moving, hilariously vengeful identification figure.

Having taken to the stage as a child, Chaplin became a major talent in Fred Karno's vaudeville troupe and, during the company's second American tour in 1913, he joined Mack Sennett at Keystone. Before two years had passed, he began directing his own one- and two-reeler comedies. In 1914, the Tramp made his first appearance (complete with cane, derby, baggy pants and winsome smile) in *Kid Auto Races at Venice*; by the end of the decade both the character and his popularity were overwhelmingly established, the secret of his success lying in pure slapstick mingled with a maudlin sentimentality. Only once, in the 1923 film *A Woman of Paris*, a sophisticated, elegant comedy of manners, would Chaplin completely depart from that formula.

In *The Kid* >**1**, Charlie's experience of a harsh Dickensian city is amplified through an almost maternal involvement with an orphaned street urchin. Already, the strands of straight humour and woolly social comment/satire are woven together to ingratiating effect.

As an actor, Chaplin has often been praised for his balletic grace, whereas in fact his mincing gait and simpering expressions are pure pantomime, a form used most effectively (since it is for once integrated into the story) in *The Pilgrim* >**2** when the Tramp, an escaped convict with an absurdly poor grasp of the Bible, is mistaken for a parson and forced to mime, to a bewildered flock, the story of David and Goliath. Elsewhere, the limitations of his style are more obvious, as is his lack of interest in using the camera as anything other than a simple recording device for his essentially vaudevillian comic routines.

By now, Chaplin's huge success had enabled him to become a founding member of United Artists. Nevertheless, as he moved into feature-length comedies, paranoia and self-pity were increasingly conspicuous in his vision of life. The Tramp, childishly spiteful but oddly gentlemanly in his manners, struggles against a hostile universe of brutal thugs and callous plutocrats; in *The Gold Rush* >**3**, he imagines himself as a chicken about to be devoured by the starving giant with whom he is trapped in a snowbound cabin; in *City Lights* >**4**, he is buffeted and betrayed by the fair-weather friendship of an alcoholic millionaire, whilst falling, somewhat bathetically, for a blind flower-seller; and in *Modern Times* >**5**, he is at the mercy of factory machinery, in danger of becoming a mindless cog in a mechanical world. By now – the mid-'30s, though Chaplin, resisting the coming of sound, was yet avoiding dialogue – simplistic social comment was beginning to dominate the comedy, and the Little Tramp had outstayed his welcome.

Nevertheless, certain elements of Chaplin's art would carry over into the most ambitious period of his career. For *The Great Dictator* >**6**, a brave but misbegotten attempt to warn America of the dangers of Nazism, he played two roles: the egomaniac tyrant Adenoid Hynkel (a vicious send-up of Hitler), and his double, a little Jewish barber whose life is threatened by the anti-Semitic dictatorship. An ingenious idea is wrecked not only by the film's essential similarity to the earlier films (with Hynkel replacing the bullying thugs and the barber the Tramp), but by the lengthy, politically naive, dramatically inept monologue that is its final call to arms. One sequence alone reveals any real cinematic verve – when Hynkel displays his desire for world domination by playing with a globe as if it were a balloon – and that, still, is mime.

Both the misogyny that had informed the Tramp's mawkish mooning over waifish women, and the effete, ingratiating glances at the camera that had become his means of securing an audience's sympathies, came to the fore in *Monsieur Verdoux* >**7**, an uneven if revealing black comedy about a mass wife-murderer with exquisite manners and dapper dress-sense. But the verbose and poorly staged *Limelight* >**8**, in which an ageing music-hall performer repeatedly bemoans his declining fortunes to anyone who will listen, was an unimaginative wallow in self-pity, complete with banal homespun philosophising on the nature of Art and the meaning of Life. But nothing had prepared the public for the embarrassment of *A King in New York* >**9**. Exiled in Europe, following marital scandals and troubles with the House UnAmerican Activities Committee over his alleged Communist sympathies, Chaplin indulged his resentment and bitterness to the full with an inane,

Chaplin – in typically sentimental mood – as the little tramp who adopts *The Kid*, played by Jackie Coogan.

unconvincing satire on the bigotry and commercialism of an America hypnotised by television and advertising. Openly autobiographical, the film suffered from wretched performances and direction, not to say undisguised bile.

One last film followed, the innocuous *A Countess from Hong Kong* >**10**. A limp romantic farce set on board an ocean liner and starring Marlon Brando and Sophia Loren (with Chaplin himself in a cameo role as a ship's steward), merely demonstrated how out of touch with the times Chaplin had become since taking up residence in Switzerland. Old age, however, brought both an accumulation of internationally conferred honours and a revival of his popularity in America; in 1972 he received an honorary Oscar, followed three years later by a knighthood. While the awards were in recognition of his genius, he should be remembered less as a great film-maker than as the man who was the first real icon of cinema. Whatever the worth of his films, Chaplin's importance lies in the way he embodied the movies' power to touch the world.

Lineage

The roots of Chaplin's art lie both in childhood experience and in the traditions of Victorian melodrama and music-hall. Sennett, **Clair** and the French silent comedian Max Linder also exerted an influence. His many imitators included Harold Lloyd and Harry Langdon, while his fascination for the underdog can be seen in later comedians like Jerry Lewis and early **Woody Allen**. In recent years his reputation as a film artist has been eclipsed by that of **Keaton**, who has a small but fascinating cameo in *Limelight*.

Further reading

David Robinson's *Chaplin: His Life and Art* (London, 1985), Walter Kerr's *The Silent Clowns* (New York, 1975), Chaplin's *My Autobiography* (London, 1964) and *My Life in Pictures* (London, 1974).

Viewing

1 **The Kid**
US 1921/ w Chaplin, Jackie Coogan, Edna Purviance
2 **The Pilgrim**
US 1923/ w Chaplin, Edna Purviance, Mack Swain
3 **The Gold Rush**
US 1925/ w Chaplin, Georgia Hale, Mack Swain
4 **City Lights**
US 1931/ w Chaplin, Virginia Cherrill, Harry Myers
5 **Modern Times**
US 1936/ w Chaplin, Paulette Goddard, Chester Conklin
6 **The Great Dictator**
US 1940/ w Chaplin, Paulette Goddard, Jack Oakie
7 **Monsieur Verdoux**
US 1947/ w Chaplin, Martha Raye, Marilyn Nash
8 **Limelight**
US 1952/ w Chaplin, Claire Bloom, Buster Keaton
9 **A King in New York**
GB 1957/ w Chaplin, Dawn Addams, Maxine Audley
10 **A Countess from Hong Kong**
GB 1967/ w Marlon Brando, Sophia Loren, Sydney Chaplin

Chen Kaige

Born: 12th August 1952/Beijing, China
Directing career: 1984-

Perhaps the best-known member of the 'fifth generation' of young directors to graduate from the Beijing Film Academy in 1982, Chen Kaige seems likely to become a challenging, innovative film-maker of international renown. Though working in a country noted for its aesthetic, economic and ideological conservatism, and in a film industry riven with dissent, he has so far managed to make deeply personal films of a wide moral and political relevance.

During the Cultural Revolution Chen (son of veteran director Chen Huai'ai) spent three years working, like so many of his age, in a remote rural region of China. Finally, in 1975 after a spell in the army, he returned to Beijing to work in a film laboratory, and in 1978 he was accepted for the directing course at the newly reopened Film Academy. Upon graduation he served for two years as assistant to Huang Jianzhong, before making his debut with *Yellow Earth* >**1**. Set in 1939 in the topographically dramatic, culturally backward province of Shaanxi, the film charts the brief encounter between a Communist soldier collecting folk songs and a family of villagers trapped by poverty and age-old feudal traditions. What distinguishes Chen's film, besides its oblique, metaphorical plot and Zhang Yimou's stunning, largely static landscape photography, is its acknowledgement of the gulf between peasants and outsider,of the difficulty, even impossibility, of enforcing political and social change. Thus both aesthetically (in terms of its poeticism and ambiguity) and ideologically, Chen was also acknowledging the chasm between 'official' history, as propagated by older Chinese film-makers, and his own less idealised account of culture-clash.

Also made with Zhang for the Guangxi Studio, *The Big Parade* >**2** concerned the training of military cadets for the National Day Parade. Again, Chen set himself apart from the gung-ho propaganda of most Chinese military films to focus on the personal sacrifice involved in allegiance to a regimented army (and, by implication, to China itself); again, his methods were inventive and original. Visually, military conformism was conveyed in static, formalised images of the trainees as an homogeneous mass, while more private emotions were evoked by the less abstract mobile shots of teeming barracks life; aurally too, frequent voice-overs testified to the soldiers' various inner doubts concerning the cost, and worth, of national unity. Indeed, the desire for independence and freedom of thought is central to Chen's work, both thematically and in terms of its uncompromising style. In *King of the Children* >**3**, made for the Xi'an Film Studio, the tale of a young man, exiled during the Cultural Revolution to Yunnan and chosen (despite his own minimal education) to teach a class of semi-literate peasant children who are accustomed to learning by rote, becomes a quiet but heartfelt portrait of the development of individual consciousness in a land stifled by economic, cultural and social poverty. The teacher, of course, is finally sacked for neglecting the official curriculum. But Chen's recognition of his country's need to revitalise itself through changes which still allow for the spiritual traditions of pre-Communist China, is gloriously manifested in the final liberating, dreamlike shots of a forest in flames, dead wood being destroyed to free an ancient and beautiful landscape.

Along with other young film-makers, Chen is instrumental in the creation of a new, politically and artistically invigorating Chinese cinema, far removed from simplistic agit-prop, melodrama and martial arts escapism. While he continually runs the risk of being marginalised, or even prevented from working, by pressures of censorship and bureaucracy, he has already proved himself a film-maker of great imagination, intelligence, courage, and influence.

Lineage

Perhaps influenced by the older Wu Tianming, Chen may be compared with his 'fifth generation' peers: Zhang Yimou, Zhang Zeming, Wu Ziniu and Tian Zhuangzhuang. These men may be seen as setting themselves in opposition to older more traditional figures like Xie Jin, and having themselves influenced 'fourth generation' directors like Huang Jianzhong, Zhang Nuanxin and Yan Xueshu. It is perhaps also worth noting in passing the progress of the New Taiwanese Cinema, perhaps best represented by Hou Xiaoxian and Edward Yang.

Viewing

1 **Yellow Earth**
China 1984/ w Xue Bai, Wang Xueqi, Liu Qiang, Tan Tuo

2 **The Big Parade**
China 1986/ w Wang Xueqi, Sun Chun, Lu Lei, Wu Ruofu

3 **King of the Children**
China 1987/ w Xie Yuan, Yang Xuewen, Chen Shaohua

Michael Cimino

Born: 1943/New York, USA
Directing career: 1974-

Since the much-publicised *Heaven's Gate* controversy, it has been difficult to view the films of Michael Cimino with any great objectivity. Certainly, he is an ambitious, troubling talent who remains on the fringes of Hollywood mainstream cinema.

A Yale graduate who went on to study ballet and acting, his entry into the film business was through industrial documentaries and television commercials. In 1971, he moved to Hollywood, and attracted attention by co-scripting the sci-fi thriller *Silent Running* and (with **Milius**) **Eastwood**'s *Dirty Harry* sequel, *Magnum Force*. Duly impressed, Eastwood invited him to write and direct *Thunderbolt and Lightfoot* >**1**. This low-key but gripping heist movie in the then fashionable 'buddy' vein is memorable for its playfully inventive tone – the star's customary tough-guy persona undercut by his initial appearance as a priest, Jeff Bridges seducing a security guard while in drag – and imaginative use of locations.

Far more audacious, *The Deer Hunter* >**2** was a long, episodic study of the traumatic effect of the Vietnam

War on three friends from an Ohio steel town. Its impressively detailed portrait of a Russian-American community preparing to send its sons to a war it barely comprehends was sadly overshadowed by the racist fiction of having sadistic Vietcong force American POWs to play Russian roulette. Nonetheless, Vilmos Zsigmond's spectacular photography – a wedding party, a hunting expedition, the fall of Saigon – and the vivid performances turned the rather contrived celebration of the capacity of America for survival into a very watchable film.

The film's success with critics and publics alike led United Artists to give Cimino carte-blanche on *Heaven's Gate* >**3**, an epic Western about the 1892 Johnson County Wars. The elliptical story, about the persecution of lowly European-born farmers by Wyoming's cattle-barons, was a muddled mixture of class-conflict, sumptuous pageant and underwritten, stereotypical characters. However, Cimino's fetish for authenticity and his sweeping sense of scale ensured that the film – running at nearly four hours – was rarely tedious. Its undeserved status as a *cause célèbre*, with critics divided as to whether it was a masterpiece or a fiasco, derived from its inflated budget. Blamed for the studio's financial problems, Cimino became a scapegoat for Hollywood's general decline, and the film, edited into an incomprehensible short version after its initial release, was a commercial disaster.

For a while it seemed that Cimino might never be allowed to direct again; he eventually returned to the fray with the **Oliver Stone**-scripted *Year of the Dragon*, in which a racist, Vietvet cop determines to clean up New York's Chinatown. Again, a few expertly handled set-pieces failed to offset the lack of critical distance from the protagonist's xenophobic hatred. Even more dismally, *The Sicilian* (a ludicrously hagiographic re-telling of the Salvatore Giuliano story which equated, through its narrative and elegantly composed visuals, the notorious bandit with Christ himself) was wrecked by portentous dialogue and inept performances.

It is perhaps strange that Cimino, clearly fascinated by the immigrant experience, should repeatedly invite charges of racism. Less surprisingly, his taste for visual spectacle and grandiose themes has led to narrative confusion and weak characterisation.

Lineage

In visual terms, Cimino may be seen as influenced by epic artists like **Ford**, **Visconti**, **Lean**, **Leone**, **Coppola** and **Spielberg**.

Further reading

Steven Bach's *Final Cut* (London, 1985) charts the history of *Heaven's Gate*.

Viewing

1 **Thunderbolt and Lightfoot**
US 1974/ w Clint Eastwood, Jeff Bridges, George Kennedy

2 **The Deer Hunter**
US 1977/ w Robert De Niro, Christopher Walken, John Savage

3 **Heaven's Gate**
US 1980/ w Kris Kristofferson, Isabelle Huppert, John Hurt

René Clair

Born: 11th November 1898/Paris, France
Died: 15th March 1981/Neuilly, France
Directing career: 1923-1965

During the '30s, René Chomette – his real name – was considered one of the cinema's most stylish innovators and satirists. Now, however, both the 'poetic realism' and the exuberant humour on which his reputation once rested seem shallow and dated.

A critic, and a poet and actor in the serials of Louis Feuillade, the young Clair aligned himself with the French avant-garde of the '20s. Indeed, his silent work may be seen as offshoots of the Dada movement: his debut, *Paris Qui Dort* (*The Crazy Ray*) >**1**, was a bizarre comic fantasy in which a mad scientist uses a magic ray to render the city immobile; only a group of strangers, safe atop the Eiffel Tower or in a plane, remain conscious to search for the culprit and bring Paris back to life. *Entr'acte*, shown during the intermission of Picabia's Dadaist ballet 'Relâche', was without meaning, a frivolous celebration of (slow and fast) motion, its cast including artists Marcel Duchamp and Man Ray, and composer Erik Satie; while the farce *The Italian Straw Hat*, merged gently mocking satire of the bourgeoisie with a hectic, Mack Sennett-style chase.

Even though Clair was initially scornful of sound, his first talkies brought him enormous success. Few directors used the new medium so enthusiastically: potentially realistic comedies and romances, *Sous Les Toits de Paris*, *Le Million* (which ends with an anarchic football match on an opera-stage), *A Nous la Liberté* >**2**, and *Le Quatorze Juillet* were transformed into lyrical operettas. Characters burst into song and strangely balletic movements while Georges Périnal's fluid camera explores the elaborate, *faux-naïf* studio sets of bustling streets and crowded tenements. Style, in fact, overshadows content; most notably in the fashionable satire on the dehumanising effects of factory technology that is *A Nous la Liberté*, artifice often renders the comedy toothless and fey.

After the failure of *Le Dernier Milliardaire*, Clair left for Britain and, for Alexander Korda, directed *The Ghost Goes West*, a witty, obvious jibe at material greed: shipping a Scottish castle to Florida, a tycoon is haunted by a resentful ancestral spectre. The director then spent the war years in Hollywood, where his taste for comedy, fantasy and romance thrived. *The Flame of New Orleans* was a lively, elegant Dietrich vehicle; more memorable, however, was *I Married a Witch* >**3**, about a witch, burnt at the stake 200 years previously, visiting contemporary America to wreak vengeance on her persecutor's descendant with deliciously malicious glee. But in *And Then There Were None*, a version of Agatha Christie's *Ten Little Niggers*, humour and suspense are more clumsily combined.

Clair's return to France found him in more sombre mood. *Le Silence est d'Or* paid nostalgic tribute to cinema's early years, while *La Beauté du Diable*'s turgid reworking of the Faust legend included concentration camp scenes, and the stilted *Porte des Lilas* was an examination of the doomed friendship between a lonely alcoholic and a young hoodlum. *Les Grandes Manoeuvres* >**4**, a tragi-comic romance set in a provincial garrison town in the summer of 1914, generates an emotional power rare in Clair, its portrait of love thwarted by bourgeois hypocrisy deepened by the acting of Michèle Morgan and Gérard Philipe. Thereafter, however, he sank further into forgettable comedies and portmanteau films.

Clair's penchant for studio-created elegance and whimsical gaiety was artistically limiting. His films seldom stimulate the emotions, so removed are they from reality. Indeed, their dated appearance derives from an excessive, hollow emphasis on style.

Lineage

Clair's mix of satire and fantasy influenced **Chaplin**, notably in *Modern Times*; *Le Million* influenced the Marx Brothers' *A Night At the Opera*. His later studio-bound 'poetic realism' parallels both **Carné** and French postwar cinema in general; indeed, it embodied the heritage so abhorrent to the *Nouvelle Vague*.

Further reading

Roy Armes' *French Cinema Since 1946, Vol 1* (London, 1966).

Viewing

1 **Paris Qui Dort (The Crazy Ray)**
France 1923/ w Henri Rollan, Albert Préjean, Marcel Vallée

2 **A Nous la Liberté**
France 1931/ w Raymond Cordy, Henri Marchand, Paul Oliver

3 **I Married a Witch**
US 1942/ w Fredric March, Veronica Lake, Susan Hayward

4 **Les Grandes Manoeuvres**
France 1955/ w Gérard Philipe, Michèle Morgan, Brigitte Bardot

Henri-Georges Clouzot

Born: 20th November 1907/Niort, France
Died: 12th January 1977/Paris, France
Directing career: 1942-1968

While several of Henri-Georges Clouzot's commercially successful films were festival prize-winners, he is often regarded as a mere technician, interested only in the mechanics of suspense. Yet his vision of humanity is more personal and consistent than that of many lesser directors who have been proclaimed as great artists.

A former film-critic, Clouzot entered the movie industry as scriptwriter and assistant on French-language versions of German films. His directing debut, *L'Assassin Habite au 21*, was a clever if relatively conventional semi-comic thriller, memorable chiefly for its atmospheric use of authentically seedy studio sets. His next film however, *Le Corbeau* (*The Raven*) >**1** was a masterpiece of misanthropy: dissecting the moral collapse of a small French town plagued by a wave of poison pen-letters, Clouzot revealed a sour, jaundiced vision of human motivation. Greed, envy, hypocrisy and hatred are his characters' primary instincts; cruelty and mutual suspicion inform every act of communication. Such was the power – and, perhaps, truth – of Clouzot's vision of provincial life that it was interpreted as an act of collaboration with the occupying Nazis; rumours suggested it was shown in Germany as anti-French propaganda. Clouzot found himself unemployable for several years.

The idiocy and falsity of the accusations were proven by his subsequent films. Even the relatively humorous *Quai des Orfèvres* >**2** revels in a bleak evocation of run-down music-halls, cramped apartments and gloomy police-stations, while its central couple, suspected of killing a lecherous pornographer, continually lie to each other as their marriage falters under pressure from poverty, police insinuation, possessiveness and infidelity. (Conversely, Louis Jouvet's tough, wisecracking cop, complete with much-loved black son, is depicted with rare, surprising warmth). In Clouzot, relationships are arenas of conflict: violent, callous, and often fated to sink into a maelstrom of deceit and destructive cruelty.

After a deglamorised, amoral update of *Manon Lescaut* and the inferior *Miquette et sa Mère*, Clouzot returned to form with *The Wages of Fear* >**3** in which four desperate European expatriates agree to drive two lorry-loads of nitro-glycerine across miles of rocky mountain tracks pitted with craters. An audaciously slow, atmospheric opening establishes both characters and the malignant influence of US oil interests in a dusty South American village, before the odyssey begins. The tension never falters: friendship falls prey to financial greed, honour to a sweaty fear of sudden death. Equally riveting in terms of suspense was *Les Diaboliques* (*The Fiends*) >**4**, a mystery set in a shabby boys' boarding school. The plot – a sadistic headmaster is murdered by his wife and his mistress; ominously and inexplicably, his corpse vanishes – is too contrived to survive repeated viewings, but the stark grey images emphasising physical decay offer a precise, grimly poetic visual correlative for the characters' warped emotions.

After an admirably lucid documentary showing Picasso at work and the uneven, farcical spy-thriller *Les Espions*, *La Verité* >**5** was a subtle picture of the events that lead to a young woman's murder of her lover, marked by Clouzot's evident distrust of the judicial system's attempt to explain away apparently unfathomable crimes. Analysis rather than condemnation of the perversities of human behaviour recurred in *La Prisonnière*, but – Clouzot having been ill for some time – the film was only marginally successful.

Clouzot is possibly the cinema's most devout pessimist: no other director has portrayed human vices so persuasively. If his bitter vision of the world is finally limited and unattractive, his status as a major film-maker, entertaining through suspense while simultaneously expressing his private dismay with cool and detached visual precision, remains intact.

Lineage

Clouzot's moral pessimism, shock tactics and readiness to display man's worst excesses suggest parallels with **Hitchcock** and **Fuller**, while his focus on cruelty, domination and decay may be compared with that of figures as diverse as **Leone**, **Blier** and **Fassbinder**.

Further reading

Roy Armes' *French Cinema since 1946, Vol 1* (London, 1976).

Viewing

1 **Le Corbeau (The Raven)**
France 1943/ w Pierre Fresnay, Pierre Larquey, Ginette Leclerc

2 **Quai des Orfèvres**
France 1947/ w Bernard Blier, Suzy Delair, Louis Jouvet

3 **Le Salaire de la Peur (The Wages of Fear)**
France 1953/ w Yves Montand, Charles Vanel, Peter van Eyck

4 **Les Diaboliques (The Fiends/ Diabolique)**
France 1955/ w Vera Clouzot, Simone Signoret, Paul Meurisse

5 **La Verité**
France 1960/ w Brigitte Bardot, Sami Frey, Charles Vanel

Jean Cocteau

Born: 5th July 1889/Maisons-Lafitte, France
Died: 11th October 1963/Milly la Forêt, France
Directing career: 1930-1960

In film, Jean Cocteau found the perfect medium to portray his own personal mythology. Though his involvement in cinema was uneven, spasmodic and largely undertaken during later life, his fantastic images, well-meaning amateurism and continuous self-preoccupation were inspirational to the avant-garde and underground.

By 1930, when Cocteau made his first film, he was already an established poet, novelist, dramatist and artist. *Le Sang d'un Poète* (*The Blood of a Poet*) >**1**, a 'realistic documentary of unreal events', was a characteristically romantic portrait of the artist structured as a surreal succession of images centred on a private mythology: desiring immortality, the poet, martyr to creativity, must first pass through a mirror into a deathly private dream-world. Financed, like *L'Age d'Or*, by the Viscomte de Noailles, its indulgent celebration of artists in general (and, therefore, Cocteau in particular) makes it inferior to **Buñuel**'s film, but its robust, bizarre symbolism is often startling.

Although Cocteau regularly collaborated with others as a scriptwriter (often adapting his own work), he did not direct again for many years. Nevertheless, *La Belle et la Bête* >**2**, an ornate version of the Beauty and the Beast story with decor and lighting inspired by Vermeer, confirmed his enthusiasm for film's illusionist properties. After committing to celluloid, mundanely, a pair of plays (*The Eagle with Two Heads*, *Les Parents Terribles*), he returned to the joys and agonies of artistic life examined in his debut. *Orphée* >**3** idiosyncratically updates the Greek myth: a poet falls for a beautiful Princess who it transpires is his own death; to recover his dead wife Euridice, he must travel through a mirror into the Zone, a bleak modern Hades reminiscent of Nazi-occupied Paris. Its various conceits are inventively appropriate – bizarre messages from the afterlife emanating from a car-radio, Death's cohorts as leather-clad bikers – and the film, though flawed by Cocteau's persistently pompous attitude towards creative genius, is an admirably accessible account of private concerns, its camera effects turning banal events into extraordinary dreamlike images.

After a droll, witty home-movie (*La Villa Santo-Sospir*), *Le Testament d'Orphée* >**4** elegaically confronted a lifetime's themes and obsessions, with Cocteau himself as the time-traveller poet who encounters friends and fictional characters before vanishing, disillusioned with modern society, into his own mythical world. Indulgence again prevails, while both images and 'narrative' are more obscurely private than ever.

Cocteau's obsession with creativity and mortality is finally self-celebratory and trite: artistic endeavour is a matter of fey posing while death, deprived of pain and decay, is prettified and romanticised. Indeed, better 'Cocteau films' were made by others: **Rossellini** (*La Voix Humaine*), **Franju** (*Thomas L'Imposteur*) and, most notably, **Melville** (*Les Enfants Terribles*). Nevertheless, Cocteau's indifference to cinematic convention and exuberant use of film as a means of self-expression counteract his precious aestheticism.

Lineage

Himself influenced (and reviled) by the Surrealists, Cocteau's independent, personal style of film-making was highly attractive to *Nouvelle Vague* directors; equally, very few experimental film-makers have not felt his influence. Indeed, one might compare him with Kenneth Anger.

Further reading

René Gilson's *Jean Cocteau* (New York, 1969). *Cocteau on the Film* (New York, 1954) is a selection of interviews.

Viewing

1 **Le Sang d'un Poète (The Blood of a Poet)**
France 1930/ w Lee Miller, Pauline Carton, Odette Talazac

2 **La Belle et la Bête (Beauty and the Beast)**
France 1946/ w Josette Day, Jean Marais, Mila Parely

3 **Orphée (Orpheus)**
France 1950/ w Jean Marais, Maria Casarès, François Perier

4 **Le Testament d'Orphée (Testament of Orpheus)**
France 1960/ w Cocteau, Edouard Dermithe, Maria Casarès

The Coen Brothers

Joel: **Born:** 29th November 1954/ Minneapolis, USA
Ethan: **Born:** 21st September 1957/ Minneapolis, USA
Directing career: 1984-

Though 'movie brats' (Joel studied film at New York University), Joel and Ethan Coen differ from their older counterparts in their apparent desire to work on relatively low budgets on the fringes of the Hollywood establishment. Like their predecessors, however – particularly the young **Spielberg** – they are inspired less by Hollywood's prestige productions than by B-movies and cartoons.

To date, the brothers have worked as a team: Joel directs, Ethan produces, both write. Their assured debut, *Blood Simple* >**1**, was a stylish *film noir*. The basic premise (a Texan bar-owner is betrayed by the private detective he hires to murder his faithless wife and her lover) is transformed by an imaginatively tortuous script into a subtle, almost farcical study of humans forever misinterpreting each other's actions: while the audience understands what is happening, the characters, their perceptions distorted by suspicion, fear and jealousy, flail in the dark and destroy friends, enemies and themselves. Murder, too, is a dirty, protracted business – one character is even buried alive – just as, in the Coens' irredeemably seedy Texas, the corrupt private eye (marvellously played by M. Emmett Walsh) sweats continuously.

If *Blood Simple* derived more from pulp fiction and B-movies than from real life, the brothers' scripts for Sam Raimi's quirky but undisciplined *Crime Wave* and for their own *Raising Arizona* >**2** were reminiscent of the spoofy two-dimensional anarchy of Warner Bros. cartoons. Opening with a brilliant pre-credits monologue, *Raising Arizona* tells of an incompetent, compulsive petty criminal's love for his prison warder: married but infertile, the couple abduct a baby, whose tycoon father hires a crazed biker to find and kill the culprits. A surreal, slapstick satire, it revels in hectic plotting, gaudy colours, and hilarious screwball characters.

For all the visual flair and deft performances on display in their films, the Coens' greatest virtue lies in writing. In terms of pacy stories, witty dialogue and the creation of a coherent, plausible fantasy world peopled by vivid characters, their ability to work original and entertaining variations on a genre bodes well for the future.

Lineage

While the Coens' visual bravura finds parallels in Jean-Jacques Beineix, Luc Besson and Raimi, their writing revives the fast, epigrammatic flair of earlier figures like **Wilder**, **Sturges** and **Tashlin**. Their closest contemporaries may be **Dante** and **Zemeckis**.

Viewing

1 **Blood Simple**
US 1984/ w Dan Hedaya, Frances McDormand, M. Emmett Walsh

2 **Raising Arizona**
US 1987/ w Nicolas Cage, Holly Hunter, John Goodman

Larry Cohen

Born: 20th April 1947/Chicago, Illinois, USA
Directing career: 1972–

Deprived of the benefits of expensive special effects, the low-budget films of Larry Cohen nevertheless remain notable for their wit, originality, and charming disregard for narrative logic.

After years spent writing for television, Cohen's first film work was in 'blaxploitation' with *Black Caesar* and *Hell Up in Harlem*, efficient thrillers, while *Bone* (*Dial Rat for Terror*) turned a black's menacing encounter with a bourgeois white couple into an almost Pinteresque attack on American values. *It's Alive* >**1** took Cohen's provocative style a stage further. In charting the blood-lust of a mutant baby (the product of pre-natal drugs), he guyed the then popular demonic-child horror genre (the infant massacres the hospital staff at birth) and probed the anti-social qualities of parenthood: the father abandons trying to kill his monstrous progeny to protect it against the police at all costs.

Demon >**2** was a similarly outrageous hybrid of cop thriller, sci-fi and religious allegory in which a guilt-ridden Catholic detective, investigating murders by snipers claiming God as the instigator, finds that the culprit – an androgyne Messiah sired by an alien father – is his brother. Equally subversive, *The Private Files of J. Edgar Hoover* >**3** located the seeds of US political chicanery in the hands of the sexually repressed, pathologically paranoid FBI chief. Indeed, much of Cohen's work concerns the desire for, and abuse of, power. In *Q – the Winged Serpent* >**4** a no-hope criminal holds New York hostage by concealing the whereabouts of a deadly reptile's nest; in *Special Effects* a director films the murders he commits, in an attempt to revive his flagging career with a sensationally realistic thriller; *The Stuff* wittily attacks the junk-food ethic of corporate America (responsible for selling a parasitic dessert that devours its consumers' innards).

Social satire aside, Cohen revels in absurd plot digressions and gags. *Q*'s tale of the lethal revival of the Aztec reptile-god Quetzalcoatl abounds in lunatic lines ('Maybe his head got loose and fell off'); *Full Moon High*, a time-warp werewolf comedy, guys movie lycanthropy; *The Stuff*'s hero proudly admits, '*Nobody* could be as dumb as I look'. Indeed, throwaway humour often wrecks the films' coherence; finally, they are too episodic and scattershot to warrant truly serious appraisal. Still, inventive eccentricity and a disregard for 'good taste' make Cohen a talent to cherish.

Lineage

Cohen works the B-movie vein once mined by Edgar G. Ulmer, William Beaudine and early **Lewis**; his wit renders his work more likeable than that of modern fantasy specialists like Wes Craven, Tobe Hooper, Abel Ferrara and the Italians Dario Argento and Lucio Fulci.

Viewing

1 **It's Alive**
US 1973/ w John Ryan, Sharon Farrell, Andrew Duggan
2 **Demon (God Told Me To)**
US 1976/ w Tony Lo Bianco, Deborah Raffin, Sandy Dennis
3 **The Private Files of J. Edgar Hoover**
US 1977/ w Broderick Crawford, Dan Dailey, Rip Torn
4 **Q – The Winged Serpent**
US 1982/ w Michael Moriarty, David Carradine, Candy Clark

Francis Coppola

Born: **7th April 1939/Detroit, Michigan USA**
Directing career: 1961-

The first, and initially the most successful, of the 'movie brat' directors who came to prominence during the '70s, Francis Ford Coppola now seems an erratic, troubled talent, restlessly torn between low and high budgets, popular and personal projects.

A UCLA film school graduate, Coppola made several 'nudie' shorts before becoming right-hand man to **Roger Corman**, for whom he worked in a variety of capacities. Allowed to direct *Dementia 13* (*The Haunted and the Hunted*), an atmospheric Gothic thriller set in Ireland, he then left Corman for a writing contract with Seven Arts (scripts included *This Property is Condemned*, *Patton* and *Reflections in a Golden Eye*). After directing a quirky '60s youth comedy (*You're a Big Boy Now*), he was invited to film the '40s musical *Finian's Rainbow*. Fey, dated and perversely wasteful of Fred Astaire, the film flopped, and Coppola returned to small-budget movie-making for the more personal *The Rain People* >**1**.

An arty, quasi-feminist road-movie, about a pregnant woman's efforts to change her claustrophobic life, it revealed Coppola's considerable expertise with actors and locations, but not even his audacious founding (along with **George Lucas**) of the American Zoetrope production company suggested that Coppola was the man to translate a best-selling novel about the Mafia on to film. But in adapting Mario Puzo's *The Godfather* >**2** his career was at once transformed. An audaciously slow dynastic melodrama focussing less on vice and violence than on the traditional codes of honour of the powerful Corleone family, this epic film deployed superb acting, sumptuous sets and lavish camerawork to distract attention from the basic superficiality of Coppola's premise, that Mafia business was only an offshoot of corporate free-enterprise America. Indeed, despite its dramatic coups (vendetta requested during a wedding party, a baptism intercut with scenes of brutal carnage) the film was none too authentic: Mafia violence is never presented as being harmful to innocent outsiders, while cops and politicians are portrayed, to a man, in a less honourable light than the Corleone clan.

Altogether more satisfying, *The Conversation* >**3**, about a bugging expert whose manic devotion to work and privacy leads to murder, reworked themes from **Antonioni**'s *Blow Up* while gaining mileage upon its release from the exposure of Watergate. A cool, modern horror movie about responsibility, voyeurism and paranoia, its abiding status as Coppola's masterpiece is rivalled only by *The Godfather Part II* >**4**, in which the '40s setting of the first movie is extended backwards and forwards to reveal the corrupting effect of power: in turn of the century New York, Vito Corleone's violence serves as the survival strategy of a young immigrant in a dangerous, hostile world, whereas his son Michael's dabbling in '60s politics and his methodical decimation of friends and family constitute a self-

Francis Ford Coppola with a bald-headed Brando on the set of his Vietnam epic, *Apocalypse Now!*

protective execution of power for power's sake.

By now, Coppola's popularity with critics and public seemed assured, and he spent some four years in the Philippines making the expensive *Apocalypse Now!* >**5**. A Vietnam War epic inspired by Conrad's *Heart of Darkness*, its characters were often poorly motivated, its story rambling, but Vittorio Storaro's images, so beautiful they appeared almost to glorify the napalm attacks upon civilian villages, were memorable indeed. The troubled production had proven exhausting, however, and Coppola returned to Zoetrope Studios for *One from the Heart*. A contemporary romantic musical whose songs and dancing were, sadly, of dismally low standard, its neon-lit Las Vegas sets and state-of-the-art video effects were a triumph of mind over emotional content; similarly, *Rumblefish* (an S.E. Hinton rites-of-passage teen movie, shot back to back with the comparatively conventional *The Outsiders*) paraded its black-and-white Expressionist photography and Camus-for-kids existentialism so rhetorically that the result was much ado about very little.

Coppola, by now forever on the brink of bankruptcy, sorely needed another hit. *The Cotton Club* >**6** was an often vivid blend of backstage musical and Prohibition gangster thriller, enlivened by a Duke Ellington score and superior dancing, but its story – a romantic triangle between a musician, a showgirl and manically violent gangster Dutch Schultz – and its treatment of the racial tension centred around the eponymous white-patronised Harlem jazz club were hackneyed and shallow. *Peggy Sue Got Married*, too, was derivative in its *Back to the Future*-style account of a woman driven into her own past in a dreamlike attempt either to abandon or come to terms with her failing marriage; next, *Gardens of Stone*'s low key study of the trauma of Vietnam as experienced by a veteran officer at Arlington military cemetery was muddled, and notable chiefly for James Caan's return to the screen. In *Tucker* >**7**, however, Coppola found a subject close to his heart (a visionary car designer of the '40s remaining true to his dreams in spite of crippling industrial sabotage by narrow-minded money men); if the film lacked emotional depth, it was a stylish, witty and entertaining paean to the razamatazz of American creativity.

Coppola's talents would seem to lie less in any intellectual or emotional profundity than in an ability to create convincing worlds through startling images and strong performances. Indeed, the contributions of actors like Brando, Duvall, Pacino and Caan, and cameramen Storaro and Gordon Willis seem crucial to his best work. Applied to mediocre material, his style – often grandiose, bombastic and extravagant – can seem hollow and inappropriate.

Lineage

Coppola's versatility may imply a lack of commitment to anything other than the desire to make films: his initial success helped to inspire a generation of directors, among them **Spielberg**, **Lucas**, **Scorsese**, **Bogdanovich** and **Dante**, many of whom were also given a start by Corman. He may also be compared with **Bertolucci**, **Leone** and **Cimino** and has been influential in producing, notably Lucas's *THX 1138* and *American Graffiti*, and **Wenders**' *Hammett*.

Further reading

Peter Cowie's *Coppola: The Man and His Dreams* (London, 1989). His wife Eleanor's *Notes* (New York, 1979) describes the making of *Apocalypse Now!*

Viewing

1 **The Rain People**
US 1969/ w Shirley Knight, James Caan, Robert Duvall
2 **The Godfather**
US 1972/ w Marlon Brando, Al Pacino, James Caan, Robert Duvall
3 **The Conversation**
US 1974/ w Gene Hackman, John Cazale, Allen Garfield
4 **The Godfather Part II**
US 1974/ w Robert De Niro, Al Pacino, Robert Duvall
5 **Apocalypse Now!**
US 1979/ w Martin Sheen, Marlon Brando, Robert Duvall
6 **The Cotton Club**
US 1984/ w Richard Gere, Diane Lane, James Remar, Gregory Hines
7 **Tucker**
US 1988/ w Jeff Bridges, Martin Landau, Joan Allen

Roger Corman

Born: 5th April 1926/Detroit, Michigan, USA
Directing career: 1955-

While the importance of Roger Corman may reside in his fostering of the young talent that would later define modern Hollywood, his prolific career and boundless enthusiasm for movie-making also resulted in many inventive, if inevitably flawed, films.

After studying English at Oxford, Corman entered the film industry via scriptwriting and producing. In 1955, he embarked on a directing career with the first of his countless B-movies, made on miniscule budgets at an average of five a year, usually for American International Pictures. Pulp sci-fi (*Not of this Earth*, *The Wasp Woman*), westerns (*Gunslinger*), and schlocky teen melodrama (*Rock All Night*) figured strongly, their non-existent production values enlivened by a sense of irony and the odd hint of satire on '50s America's tacky materialism. Occasionally, the mix of energetic hysteria and po-faced humour would result in an engagingly subversive genre-parody: *Sorority Girl* is an hilarious account of a warped, sadistic psychotic dominating a girls' dorm; in *Machine Gun Kelly* Charles Bronson features as a pathologically insecure hoodlum dominated by his moll; *Little Shop of Horrors* – reputedly shot over a rainy weekend – is a surreal comedy about a man-eating plant. Best of all, *A Bucket of Blood* >**1**, about a dumb waiter lionised as a great sculptor after he accidentally covers his pet cat with plaster, proffers both macabre horror-parody and a brilliant satire on the pretensions of the Beat Generation.

The diversity of Corman's films was countered by his growing dependence on a family of actors (Susan Cabot, Dick Miller *et al*) and technicians; the fertile invention of eight loose Edgar Allan Poe adaptations may even be attributed in part to cameraman Floyd Crosby, designer Daniel Haller, and star Vincent Price. More polished than his earlier work, Corman's Poe cycle passed through sinister psychological suspense (*The Pit and the Pendulum*), camp pastiche (*The Raven*), and arty seriousness (*Masque of the Red Death*); shot mainly in the studio, effectively using rich, gaudy colours, they culminated in *The Tomb of Ligeia* >**3**, a subtle tale of necrophile obsession, shot, for once, on location at a Norfolk abbey.

Now almost 'respectable', Corman entered the most ambitious phase of his career, alternating between topical, youth-oriented sensationalism (bikers in *The Wild Angels*, LSD in *The Trip*) and masterly variations on genre. The scientist's doomed experiments on his own sight in *The Man with the X-Ray Eyes* >**2** warn against an insatiable thirst for knowledge; *The St Valentine's Day Massacre* >**4** is a profane account of the Irish-Italian tensions that fuelled Prohibition Chicago's gang wars; *Bloody Mama* was an acerbic reply to *Bonnie and Clyde*'s romanticism, portraying the Ma Barker gang as an incestuous, self-destructive travesty of family life.

After the commercial failure of the incoherent apocalyptic satire *Gassss!* and the troubled aerial drama *The Red Baron* (*Von Richthofen and Brown*), Corman abandoned direction to focus on producing for his company, New World. Over the years he has given work to and encouraged many ambitious youngsters, including Paul Bartel, **Bogdanovich**, **Coppola**, **Dante**, **Demme**, De Niro, Peter Fonda, Monte Hellman, **Hopper**, Jonathan Kaplan, Jack Nicholson, **Sayles**, **Scorsese** and Penelope Spheeris. As the godfather of contemporary Hollywood, Corman's importance is undisputed; as an inspirational example of the ability to overcome absurdly minimal resources and intractable material through determination, enthusiasm, wit and – surprisingly frequently – intelligence, his reputation is unique.

Lineage

Corman may be seen as the '50s and '60s answer to B-movie figures like **Dwan**, **Lewis**, Edgar Ulmer, Edwin L. Marin and Joseph Kane. His artistic and financial nurturing of numerous untried talents has made his influence on modern American cinema almost incalculable.

Further reading

Roger Corman: The Millenic Vision (Cambridge, 1970) by David Pirie *et al*, Ed Naha's *Films of Roger Corman* (New York, 1982).

Viewing

1 **A Bucket of Blood**
US 1959/ w Dick Miller, Anthony Carbone, Barboura Morris

2 **The Man with the X-Ray Eyes (X – The Man with the X-Ray Eyes)**
US 1963/ w Ray Milland, Diana Van der Vlis, Harold J. Stone

3 **The Tomb of Ligeia**
US 1964/ w Vincent Price, Elizabeth Shepherd, John Westbrook

4 **The St Valentine's Day Massacre**
US 1967/ w Jason Robards, George Segal, Ralph Meeker

Constantin Costa-Gavras

Born: **12th February 1933/Athens, Greece**
Directing career: 1964-

Lauded as a political director, Costa-Gavras is of interest less for his finally unsophisticated analyses of government intrigue than for the way he manages to frame his impassioned polemics within a popular and entertaining format.

The son of a Greek bureaucrat deemed politically suspect, Konstantinos Gavras moved to Paris to study literature and film, before working as assistant to Yves Allégret, René Clément, **Clair** and **Demy**. After directing two conventional thrillers – the first the relatively polished mystery *The Sleeping Car Murders* – he set about establishing his future style with *Z* >**1**, which concerned a journalist's investigations into the officially accidental death of a pacifist. Based in fact, the film's uncovering of a right-wing conspiracy of terror was an attack on the Greek dictatorship of the '60s; with rapid editing, a gritty, forthright camera style and name stars, it favoured emotional manipulation over political objectivity, but there was no doubting the sincerity of Costa-Gavras' hatred of corruption and the erosion of human rights.

The abuse of power and its repressive, violent consequences became the themes of the director's subsequent work: *L'Aveu* (*The Confession*) dealt with the sinister Stalinist show-trials in '50s Czechoslovakia; *State of Siege* >**2** with US 'policing' procedure in Uruguay: a guerilla kidnapping of an American official leads to revelations that the CIA trains local police in torture-methods. *Section Speciale* was a caricature of Vichy France's collaboration with the Nazis, but Costa-Gavras' first Hollywood film, *Missing* >**3**, bravely examined the US role in Chile's fascist anti-Allende coup of 1973. Inspired by the disappearance of a young American during the coup, the film lacks moral complexity, but finds an admirable audience surrogate in the boy's Republican father, who is slowly educated in the imperialist hypocrisy of American foreign policy when he repeatedly encounters ambassadorial lies concerning his son's death. Most affecting is the evocation of a country under martial law falling apart at the seams: shots ring in the night, a white stallion gallops through the curfew pursued by a truck full of trigger-happy soldiers. Not surprisingly, Costa-Gavras' 'conjectural' film provoked the wrath of the US State Department.

Turning to the Palestinian question in *Hanna K*, Costa-Gavras unwisely abandoned the conspiracy thriller format for romance; *Betrayed*, a laudable expose of murderous white supremacist action against blacks and Jews in the American Midwest, fell prey to plot implausibilities and occasional overstatement. Still, his talent lies in his ability to attract wide audiences to bleak studies of socio-political problems using true stories, the emotional thrust of the thriller and a humanist stress on individual civil rights.

Lineage

Costa-Gavras' populist exposes of political corruption are paralleled in the work of Gillo Pontecorvo, **Rosi**, and **Güney**.

Viewing

1 **Z**
France/Algeria 1969/ w Yves Montand, Jean-Louis Trintignant

2 **State of Siege**
France 1972/ w Yves Montand, Renato Salvatori, O.E. Hasse

3 **Missing**
US 1982/ w Jack Lemmon, Sissy Spacek, Melanie Mayron, John Shea

Alex Cox

Born: **15th December 1954/ Bebington, The Wirral, England**
Directing career: 1984-

Given the discipline of a strong producer, Alex Cox might just become one of Britain's more distinctive directors. To date, he has revealed overwhelming ambition, a ferocious imagination, and, sadly, an erratic tendency towards premature self-parody.

After film studies at Bristol and UCLA, Cox made his feature debut with the anarchically inventive *Repo Man* >**1**. The tale of an LA punk's weird, comic and risky involvement in the world of car-repossessors, the film offered an authentically seedy but surreal vision of the underbelly of Reagan's America: characters included a lobotomised nuclear boffin, addled hippies, CIA clones and a repossessor who thrives on manic tension – all on the trail of a Chevrolet with a lethal cargo in the trunk – while Cox seamlessly combined grainy thriller iconography, sci-fi fantasy, and witty parodies of classic movies like *Psycho*, *Point Blank*, *ET* and *Kiss Me Deadly*. Best of all, the film exuded a fiery, relentless energy.

Sid and Nancy >**2** was equally impressive, turning the sordid and depressing true story of Sex Pistol Sid Vicious and his lover Nancy Spungeon into a surprisingly moving romance. Clear-eyed in his guarded celebration of the punk movement's rebellion against the harsh realities of Thatcher's Britain, and similarly lucid about the pitfalls of sudden fame, Cox never glamorised his drug-addict protagonists; nor, even more remarkably, did he condemn them for their idiotic, anti-social, frequently pathetic odyssey towards self-destruction in New York's Chelsea Hotel. Sadly, the film's taut, gripping authenticity of atmosphere and performance was to be repeated neither in the indulgent, unfunny spaghetti Western spoof *Straight to Hell*, nor in *Walker*, an uneven, ill-focussed allegorical satire on American imperialism in the form of a 19th-century colonialist who sets himself up as tyrant of Nicaragua.

Cox's intelligence and potential are evident from both his first two films and his articulacy in interviews. But his desire to be original and his taste for working with unusual, non-cinematic performers need to be tethered to a firmer, tighter grasp of the demands and advantages of dramatic convention.

Lineage

Cox's eccentric iconoclasm and punk ethos link him, loosely, with other young mavericks like Julien Temple and Penelope Spheeris.

Viewing

1 **Repo Man**
US 1984/ w Emilio Estevez, Harry Dean Stanton, Tracey Walter

2 **Sid and Nancy**
GB 1986/ w Gary Oldman, Chloe Webb, David Hayman

Paul Cox

Born: 16th April 1940/Venlo, Netherlands
Directing career: 1965-

While many Australian directors of the '70s and '80s repeatedly turned to period nostalgia, broad satire and Hollywood-derived thrillers, Paul Cox trod a more personal path, quietly exploring troubled romantic relationships in modern, middle-class suburbia.

After years of making (mostly short) experimental films, Cox attracted the attention of a wider public with *Kostas*, a touching account of a Greek-immigrant taxi-driver's love for an Australian divorcee. Flawed by obviousness in its portrait of class and racial prejudice, it nevertheless paved the way for *Lonely Hearts* >**1**. Again an ill-starred romance – this time between a middle-aged piano-tuner and a shy bank clerk, introduced by computer-dating – the film's emotional honesty was enhanced by subtle comedy and by an acute awareness of repressive parental pressures: exerting their right to live together, the lovers belatedly win their freedom.

Colder and more complex was *Man of Flowers*, a baroque, often pretentious study of a sexually insecure art-collector's bizarre, quasi-paternal encounter with a young artist's model. A wilfully oblique portrait of life imitating art, it was Cox's first major success, establishing a distinctive personal style. An elegantly mobile camera prowls immaculately lit interiors; flickery 16mm flashbacks denote both the fragility and importance of memory; quirky characters, classical music and flower symbolism feature. Far more powerful, however, was *My First Wife* >**2**, examining the collapse of a marriage and, temporarily, of the jealous, jilted husband's sanity. Again, Cox unravels the bonds between generations, with the parents of both wife and husband determined to gain influence over the on-off divorce, and the couple's child suffering her own lasting trauma. Crucially, Cox's refusal to judge his characters and the forceful performances held sentimentality at bay.

Though potentially an even more mawkish story (a girl semi-blinded in a car-crash comes to accept her disability through the love of a man sightless since childhood), *Cactus* >3 was impressive for its strangely becalmed tone and wry humour, but the premise that blindness provides a path to self-knowledge was romantic and patronising. *Vincent*, meanwhile, departed from Cox's customary preoccupations: a loving, low-key documentary tribute to Van Gogh with the artist's life and paintings seen by a subjective camera.

Cox's commitment to his characters' emotions and his ability to relate inner lives to external surroundings – often the quiet Edwardian suburbs of Melbourne – place him in the forefront of Australian cinema. Crucially, he avoids the melodrama inherent in his material by means of visual elegance and naturalistic acting.

Lineage

Cox's cool style, rare in Australian film, bears little relation to the genre movies of, say, **Weir** or George Miller; he is closer to European directors like Claude Goretta, **Truffaut** and **Malle**.

Further reading

Brian McFarlane's *Australian Cinema 1970-1985* (Secker and Warburg, 1987).

Viewing

1 **Lonely Hearts**
Australia 1982/ w Norman Kaye, Wendy Hughes, Jon Finlayson

2 **My First Wife**
Australia 1984/ w Wendy Hughes, John Hargreaves, Charlotte Angwin

3 **Cactus**
Australia 1986/ w Isabelle Huppert, Robert Menzies, Norman Kaye

David Cronenberg

Born: 15th May 1943/Toronto, Canada
Directing career: 1969-

Just as the films of David Cronenberg repeatedly take the fraught relationship between mind and body as their subject, so his work itself is defined both by intellectual complexity and by the gory and explicit depiction of physical decay, disease and mutilation.

After studying science then literature at university – where he made two surreal shorts – Cronenberg first attracted attention at a cult level with *Stereo* and *Crimes of the Future*, both highly experimental sci-fi films presaging his future obsessions. *Stereo* concerns the surgical induction of telepathy; *Crimes* deals with new genetic mutations resulting from cosmetics. The same subversive view of a recognisable society menaced by misguided experiments recurred in the more conventional *Shivers* (*The Parasite Murders*) >**1**: a luxury block of flats becomes an inferno of manic promiscuity when slug-like parasites pass from tenant to tenant. Intelligent, prescient even, in its exploration of primal fears to construct a brilliant allegory on venereal diseases that reach apocalyptic proportions, it is nonetheless gross – the black phallic slugs are repulsively realistic – and disturbing in its disgust at human physicality.

Possessed communities and the writer-director's puritanical if scatological interest in the perils of sexuality were central to *Rabid* (a girl with a penile sting in her armpit infects others with a virus that turns them into homicidal maniacs); *The Brood* (inspired by Cronenberg's divorce, it concerns a woman under the influence of a new form of psychotherapy who produces murderous, inhuman offspring as the organic manifestations of her own rage), and *Scanners* (two brothers, telepathic victims of institutionalised science, engage in a literally mind-blowing battle). Seen by some as Cronenberg's masterpiece, *Videodrome* >**2** was a complex media satire in which a cable-station producer – a video-freak literally intoxicated by sexual violence on television – develops a slit in his stomach to accept 'living' videos that programme his hallucinations. Partly social criticism, partly a wry response to accusations levelled against his own work, the film was horrific and inventively visionary.

Cronenberg's first American film, a relatively gore-free version of Stephen King's *The Dead Zone*, was followed by *The Fly* >**3**, in which genetic experiments fuse a scientist's own molecules with those of a fly; as he and his fiancee fight to come to terms with his changing, decaying body and character, repulsive visual effects are combined with a love story. Open to interpretation as an allegory on the harrowing emotional effects of the AIDS virus, it was followed by the similarly successful *Dead Ringers* in which identical twin brothers – gynaecologists at a fertility clinic – withdraw into a sinister, sadistic and insane world of their own after a woman with whom they have both slept (unbeknownst to her, naturally) provokes an unprecedented decline into jealousy.

Clearly imaginative in his attempts to invest the conventions of classic sci-fi (mad doctors, monsters, predatory, vampire-like women) with modernist elements of social and political criticism, Cronenberg still seems misanthropic and reactionary in his vision of the human anatomy as damned and dangerous. Indeed, despite his originality, intelligence and ambition – surely laudable in times of mindless spectacle and gratuitous massacres – there would seem a paradox, born of confusion, in his repeated and explicit focus on, and mutilation of, the physicality that so clearly disgusts him.

Lineage

Cronenberg's predecessors include the Gothic novelists, German Expressionists, **Browning**, Mario Bava, **Godard**, Dario Argento, **Romero**, and by his own admission, **Arnold**'s *Creature from the Black Lagoon*. His taste for explicit gore is paralleled in Tobe Hooper, Jeff Lieberman, Wes Craven, Sam Raimi and Lucio Fulci.

Further reading

The Shape of Rage: The Films of David Cronenberg (ed. Piers Handling, New York, 1983).

Viewing

1 **Shivers (The Parasite Murders/They Came from Within)**
Canada 1975/ w Paul Hampton, Joe Silver, Barbara Steele

2 **Videodrome**
Canada 1982/ w James Woods, Sonia Smits, Deborah Harry

3 **The Fly**
US 1986/ w Jeff Goldblum, Geena Davis, John Getz

George Cukor

Born: 7th July 1899/New York, USA
Died: 24th January 1983/Hollywood, California, USA
Directing career: 1930-1981

Though often seen as a mere adaptor of stage and literary works, and his sole value being his facility with actresses, George Dewey Cukor was one of Hollywood's finest directors. Never innovative, always faithful to his source-material, happy within the studio system, he created a body of work of enormous wit and elegance.

Already established as a talented director in the New York theatre, Cukor went to Hollywood in 1929 as dialogue director on Lewis Milestone's *All Quiet on the Western Front*. He began his directing career with film versions of plays, most notably *The Royal Family of Broadway*, a comedy based on the Barrymores. More memorably, two films made in 1932 – *What Price Hollywood?* >**1** and *A Bill of Divorcement* – established his future style: the first, about the sad human realities behind the movie industry's glossy facade, revealed his interest

The near-legendary Garbo in melancholy mood as Cukor's *Camille.*

in illusion and role-playing; the latter was the first of 10 films he made with Katharine Hepburn featuring unusually strong, intelligent and independent women.

In filmed classics like *Little Women*, *David Copperfield* (with W.C. Fields brilliantly cast as Micawber), and *Camille* (with Garbo), Cukor's visual sophistication, and his ease with actors and literate dialogue was at once evident. His obsession with various forms of theatricality was the focus of a number of more modern domestic comedy-dramas: *Sylvia Scarlett* >**2**, a beguiling romantic comedy about a group of Cockney con-artists, sees Hepburn spend half the film posing as a boy; *The Women* >**3** (made after Cukor was fired from *Gone with the Wind*) stars a superbly bitchy all-female cast deceiving each other as they set up ranch in response to one of the group's imminent divorce; *Holiday* and *The Philadelphia Story* >**4** depict the disruption of the stale illusions of upper-class families by the arrival of down-to-earth non-conformists. While retaining the sophisticated dialogue of the stage originals, Cukor avoids the effect of a proscenium arch with astute camera placement and long fluid takes; again he probes the gulf between private and public images. Yet in showing the delusions and lies of the world, he was never cynical: as with **Renoir**, his characters have their reasons, and are viewed with unsentimental sympathy.

The theme of pretence takes on more sinister connotations in *Keeper of the Flame* (a dead American hero is found to have been a fascist) and *Gaslight* >**5** (a woman is imperilled by her gem-thief husband's staging of events to suggest she is insane). After the war, however, a collaboration with writers Ruth Gordon and Garson Kanin led to a series of sparkling comedies about the deceptions and manipulations practised by the battling sexes. In *Adam's Rib* >**6**, married lawyers Hepburn and Tracy, opposing each other in a murder case, turn the courtroom into a theatre, while their home life witnesses a reversal of traditional roles; in *Born Yesterday* – an update of the Pygmalion story – Judy Holliday's re-educated 'dumb blonde' is so cunningly intelligent that she triumphs with ease over her hoodlum lover's boorish, chauvinist ways.

In the New York-based Kanin-Gordon films, Cukor had begun to combine studio scenes with location work; *A Star Is Born* >**7** was a move into colour and CinemaScope. His first musical (a full-blown melodrama not dissimilar in theme to *What Price Hollywood?*, and tracing the tragic demise of a matinee idol while his singer-wife rises to stardom), it confirmed Cukor's growing visual confidence. Working with photographer George Hoyningen-Heune, he subtly used colour to suggest mood and character, and broke the vast expanses of the wide screen with dramatic diagonals. Even more startling, in *Bhowani Junction* >**8**, about an Indian girl whose love-life is wrecked by confusion over her racial identity, he ventured into Expressionism (blood-red steam from a train fills the frame when she kills a drunk in self-defense) and expertly marshalled huge crowds to evoke a nation in turmoil as the British retreat.

Although diverging more and more from the domestic dramas that had made his reputation, Cukor remained true to his view of life as theatre. Even his one Western, *Heller In Pink Tights* >**9**, follows a theatrical troupe around the lawless West (the climax has life imitate art: a gunman makes his escape from the law by taking the role of Mazeppa). Nevertheless, during the '60s and '70s Cukor – a classical, old-fashioned director – was often ill at ease with unsuitable material. Miscasting, especially, flawed *My Fair Lady* (Audrey Hepburn as Eliza Dolittle), *Justine* (a film of Durrell's *The Alexandria Quartet* that Cukor took over from Joseph Strick) and *Travels with My Aunt*. Two television films with Hepburn (*Love Among the Ruins*, *The Corn Is Green*) showed his continuing mastery of more intimate pieces, but *Rich and Famous* – a remake of *Old Acquaintance* filmed when he was 82 – was an unworthy testament to a distinguished career.

For some years America's oldest working director, Cukor was noteworthy by his gentle sophistication, his direction of actors, and an ability to entertain without patronising the public. His view of life as the ultimate performance gave rise to a seamless merging of form and content, the mark of any major film-maker.

Lineage

Cukor's interest in theatricality and performance may be compared with that of **Renoir**, Jacques Rivette, **Kazan**, **Penn** and **Cassavetes**.

Further reading

Carlos Clarens' *George Cukor* (London, 1976); Gavin Lambert's *On Cukor* (New York, 1972) is a book-length interview.

Viewing

1 **What Price Hollywood?**
US 1932/ w Constance Bennett, Lowell Sherman, Gregory Ratoff
2 **Sylvia Scarlett**
US 1936/ w Cary Grant, Katharine Hepburn, Edmund Gwenn
3 **The Women**
US 1939/ w Norma Shearer, Joan Crawford, Rosalind Russell
4 **The Philadelphia Story**
US 1940/ w Katharine Hepburn, Cary Grant, James Stewart
5 **Gaslight (Murder in Thornton Square)**
US 1944/ w Ingrid Bergman, Charles Boyer, Joseph Cotten
6 **Adam's Rib**
US 1949/ w Spencer Tracy, Katharine Hepburn, Judy Holliday
7 **A Star Is Born**
US 1954/ w Judy Garland, James Mason, Jack Carson
8 **Bhowani Junction**
US 1956/ w Ava Gardner, Stewart Granger, Bill Travers
9 **Heller In Pink Tights**
US 1960/ w Sophia Loren, Anthony Quinn, Steve Forrest

Michael Curtiz

Born: 24th December 1888/ Budapest, Hungary
Died: 11th April 1962/Los Angeles, California, USA
Directing career: 1912-1962

While it is impossible to discover any thematic continuity in the prolific career of Mihaly Kertesz, to give him his Hungarian name, craftsmanship and versatility ensured his lasting reputation as a purveyor of classy escapism.

Curtiz' high standing in Hungary's nascent film industry (he is often credited as director of the first Hungarian feature) was followed by work in Scandinavia, France, Germany and Austria. In 1926, he was invited to America by Warner Brothers, the studio to which he would remain contracted until 1953. Of his early movies, the part-talkie *Noah's Ark* is the best known, largely because his staging of the flood scenes endangered hundreds of extras' lives. Consolidating his success with Expressionist fantasy – *Doctor X*, *The Mystery of the Wax Museum* (in lavish two-strip Technicolor) – and fast-paced thrillers like *20,000 Years in Sing-Sing* and *Front Page Woman*, Curtiz embarked upon the first of 12 films with the then unknown Errol Flynn (*Captain Blood*, *The Adventures of Robin Hood* >**1**, and *The Sea Hawk*), mixing action, tongue-in-cheek humour and epic sets to create genuinely dashing adventure. At the same time, he continued to work in other genres: the boxing film (*Kid Galahad*), gangster drama (*Angels With Dirty Faces* >**2**), Westerns (*Dodge City*, *Santa Fe Trail*), and a powerful version of *The Sea Wolf*, Jack London's tale of a sadistic, tyrannical sea-captain.

Thus far visual flair, a hectic work-rate (four films a year in the '30s) and a choice of contract actors – Robinson, Bogart, Cagney, and Bette Davis included – had ensured regular hits. In 1942, however, Curtiz surpassed expectations with *Yankee Doodle Dandy*, a patriotic musical about George M. Cohan, with Cagney displaying his remarkable dancing, and *Casablanca* >**3**. Originally a routine project for Ronald Reagan and Ann Sheridan, it was re-cast with Bogart and Ingrid Bergman to become a major triumph. Simply romanticised propaganda – a cynical expatriate cafe-owner abandons all hope of reuniting with an old flame when he discovers his own commitment to the Allies, represented by her current Resistance-hero husband – it is memorable for its sardonic script, ensemble acting (Claude Rains, Paul Henreid, Sidney Greenstreet and Peter Lorre add support) and glossy blend of exotica and fatalism. Neither emotionally nor morally profound, it reveals Curtiz' easy professionalism at its peak.

More artistically satisfying was a version of James M. Cain's *Mildred Pierce* >**4**, a tense hybrid of *film noir* and melodrama that depicts the folly of excessive maternal devotion; though Mildred (Joan Crawford, who won the Oscar for it) gains independence from men by working her way up from waitress to restaurateur, her lasting commitment to an ungrateful daughter leads only to murder. Not surprisingly, such subversive pessimism was balanced the same year by the poignant Americana of *Life with Father*, evidence of Curtiz' indifference to 'messages'.

In the '50s, his career went into decline with a variety of stale musicals (*White Christmas*, Elvis Presley's *Kid Creole*) and tepid biopics; away from Warners, his lack of originality and ambition came into sharper focus. In earlier years, however, when he was prepared to accept any studio chore, his clean, energetic narrative and visual style often made for polished entertainment.

Lineage

Curtiz' early films were vaguely influenced by the imagery of German Expressionism. His influence, besides the various homages to *Casablanca* (including Play It Again, Sam) is negligible; he may be compared to figures like Victor Fleming, George Marshall, Mervyn Leroy, Jean Negulesco and other versatile professionals.

Further reading

Kingsley Canham's *The Hollywood Professionals, Vol 1* (London, 1973).

Viewing

1 **The Adventures of Robin Hood**
US 1938/ w Errol Flynn, Olivia De Havilland, Basil Rathbone

2 **Angels with Dirty Faces**
US 1938/ w James Cagney, Pat O'Brien, Humphrey Bogart

3 **Casablanca**
US 1942/ w Humphrey Bogart, Ingrid Bergman, Paul Henreid

4 **Mildred Pierce**
US 1945/ w Joan Crawford, Zachary Scott, Ann Blyth

Joe Dante

Born: 28th November 1946/ Morristown, New Jersey, USA
Directing career: 1976-

Although his career has recently intersected with that of **Steven Spielberg**, Joe Dante's films are marked less by sentimentality than by anarchic black comedy and rampant cinephilia, typical of the **Corman** school of B-movies whence he originally emerged.

A keen fan of cartoons and sci-fi, Dante moved from cutting trailers for Corman's New World to directing (with Alan Arkush) *Hollywood Boulevard*. A self-consciously trashy, low-budget parody of New World's production methods, its endless in-jokes hinted at the spirit of Dante's later work. Also made for Corman, his solo debut *Piranha*, with man-eating monsters developed by the military wreaking havoc at a summer camp, featured a tongue-in-cheek **John Sayles** script parodying *Jaws*; *The Howling* (also Sayles-scripted) went even further, naming characters after horror-directors like Terence Fisher and Freddie Francis and littering its contemporary werewolf-thriller story with sly comic references to Little Red Riding Hood, Ginsberg's *Howl* and cult disc-jockey Wolfman Jack.

After contributing a genuinely inventive episode to *Twilight Zone The Movie* (significantly, a boy with miraculous telekinetic powers terrorises his family by conjuring up monsters inspired by his endless watching of cartoons), Dante had his first major hit with *Gremlins* >**1**. Produced by Spielberg, its beginning, with a boy given a cute furry pet for Christmas, is typically sugary in tone, but as the film progresses, so Dante's own anarchic humour takes over: the pet produces magnificently malevolent offspring that wreck the Spielbergian smalltown setting, and both **Capra**'s *It's a Wonderful Life* and Disney's *Snow White* are mercilessly mocked. But despite superb photography and special effects, the film's ethos is, in fact, disreputable: endless cartoon-style violence, diffident plotting, and gleefully amoral destruction constitute a full-scale onslaught on saccharine movie sentimentality.

Dante's fascination with the effects of film and television iconography peaked in *Explorers* >**2**, an initially traditional and charming kids fantasy that erupts into surreal humour when its boy-heroes encounter unforgettably ugly aliens whose knowledge of earth culture derives totally from television: communication is impossible with the monsters quoting random lines from W.C. Fields, Bugs Bunny, Marilyn Monroe and chat-show hosts. Less inventively, *Inner Space* turned the *Fantastic Voyage*-style story of a minute submersible floating around the bloodstream of a witless, nervous fool into slapstick spoof, its movie parodies too broad and brash to be incisive, its hectic pace finally growing wearisome. Tied to a strong script, Dante's anarchic black humour and subversive send-ups of movie stereotypes provide a delightfully imaginative alternative to Spielberg's manipulative mawkishness; *Inner Space*, however, exhibits the way his weak plot-sense can occasionally result in indulgent mayhem and irritating in-jokes.

Lineage

Dante's surreal celebrations of destruction are partly inspired by animator Chuck Jones (who appears in several cameos for Dante); his debt to Corman (seen in *The Howling*) is admitted in the frequent casting of Dick Miller. His comic sense bears comparison with Paul Bartel and the *Airplane* team of Jerry and David Zucker and Jim Abrahams, for whom Dante directed episodes of the TV spoof *Police Squad*.

Viewing

1 **Gremlins**
US 1984/ w Zach Galligan, Hoyt Axton, Phoebe Cates

2 **Explorers**
US 1985/ w Ethan Hawke, Jason Presson, River Phoenix

Jules Dassin

Born: 18th December 1911/ Middletown, Connecticut, USA
Directing career: 1941-1980

Ironically, the more artistic freedom Julius Dassin gained, the less satisfying his work became; much of it is pretentious, dull, even risible. But, for a brief period at the end of the '40s, he found his niche as a director of harsh, unsentimental thrillers.

After acting in the New York theatre (he would often appear in his own films under the pseudonym Perlo Vita) and writing for radio, Dassin was invited to Hollywood where he soon graduated to directing unremarkable thrillers and comedies. In 1947, however, for producer Mark Hellinger, he made *Brute Force* >**1**, followed by *The Naked City*, both lauded for a tendency towards gritty realism and extensive use of location shooting. *Brute Force* was the finer film. It was a stark prison drama, enhanced by a raw, unglamorous depiction of violence in which inmates drive an informer to his death with blow-lamps and a prison break-out ends in mass carnage. It was also an explicit allegory on the workings of Fascism (the sadistic, power-crazy head guard even listens to Wagner). In *The Naked City*, however, the supposed honesty of its account of a murder case investigated by a lovable Irish cop and his young assistant now seems contrived. Stressing not heroics but the hard graft of police teamwork, it was an often maudlin glorification of the common man, the wealthy being seen as wasteful, vain and criminal, and chiefly notable for a chase climaxing on the grey girders of New York's Williamsburg Bridge.

Dassin's blend of social criticism, muted realism and *film noir* again surfaced in *Thieves' Highway* (the tale of a lone truck driver's fight on behalf of free enterprise against gangster-like wholesalers), and in the more openly Expressionist *Night and the City* >**2**. Imaginatively transposing key *film noir* motifs – murder, betrayal, paranoia – to a London underworld of seedy nightclubs and wrestling joints, he peopled his urban hell with a gallery of moral and physical grotesques in thrall to dreams of easy money and a life of power. Sadly, however, in the HUAC hearings of the early '50s, **Edward Dmytryk** identified Dassin as a communist, and the insidious Hollywood blacklist rendered him unemployable.

Emigrating to Europe, he made the spasmodically impressive thriller *Rififi* (*Du Rififi Chez Les Hommes*) >**3**, celebrated for a soundless robbery sequence lasting almost 30 minutes. Thereafter, he moved to Greece where he met the actress Melina Mercouri (they married in 1966), who starred in most of his later films. Despite the success of *Never On Sunday* and *Topkapi* – the latter a semi-comic heist-movie modelled on *Rififi* – Dassin's European work was profoundly disappointing. His evident 'serious' pretensions – both *Phaedra* and *A Dream of Passion* are ludicrous updates of Greek tragedy – were ruined by a dependence on glossy, incoherent, fulsome melodrama.

Straining for significance, Dassin became an increasingly marginal figure, and retired from film-making in 1980. As with so many, the constrictions of Hollywood genre seem to have controlled his florid artistic ambitions, thus nurturing his most powerful work.

Lineage

In Dassin's best work, his social criticism and location shooting compares with early **Kazan**, **Polonsky**, **Rossen**, Henry Hathaway and Richard Brooks (who wrote *Brute Force*). *The Naked City* prompted a long-running television series of the same name.

Further reading

Colin McArthur's *Underworld USA* (London, 1972).

Viewing

1 **Brute Force**
US 1947/ w Burt Lancaster, Hume Cronyn, Charles Bickford

2 **Night and the City**
GB 1950/ w Richard Widmark, Googie Withers, Francis L. Sullivan

3 **Rififi (Du Rififi Chez Les Hommes)**
France 1954/ w Jean Servais, Magali Noel, Carl Mohner, Dassin

Terence Davies

Born: 10th November 1945/ Liverpool, England
Directing career: 1972-

While his films to date are few, and far from commercial, Terence Davies is arguably the most ambitious and most promising director currently working in Britain. With only a trilogy and a diptych to his name (each lasting under two hours) he has shown once and for all that British cinema may be poetic, personal and profound.

The Terence Davies Trilogy >1 (*Children, Madonna and Child, Death and Transfiguration*) was made over a period of ten years during and after time spent at drama and film school. Inspired by his own emotional experiences, the films follow a gay, Catholic Liverpudlian from a wretched, bullied childhood through a mother-dominated middle-age to a mute and painful death in hospital. The litany of cruelty and guilt is both honest and unsentimental, yet Davies' greatest achievement is the way he transcends the clichés of mere humanist realism through stylised black and white images, a taciturn script and a narrative that gradually forsakes linear progression for complex fragmentation as its hero ages. Memory, desire and fear create daring, original associations: shots of a church are overlaid with the man's voice phoning to enquire about the possibility of having his genitals tattooed; at the moment of death, he perceives the blinding light of a torch shone on to his face by a nurse as his entry into the kingdom of heaven. Wit and an unblinking focus on emotional and spiritual hardship combine to create a grave, intelligent and strangely uplifting account of the human soul's capacity to triumph over physical degradation.

Even more remarkable was *Distant Voices, Still Lives* >**2**, in which Davies again drew upon personal memories of family life in Liverpool in the '40s and '50s to devastating imaginative effect. Once more the situation is harsh, with a stern, brutal patriarch turning the lives of his wife and children into a bleak, endless nightmare; once more the film proceeds by memory-association as it moves back and forth between family gatherings (a christening, weddings, a funeral) at which renditions of popular songs of the period serve to stress the long-lost communal nature of working-class life, and to underline, embellish and counterpoint the emotions, situations and relationships of the story: a cinema audience listens rapt to the romantic theme tune from *Love is a Many-Splendoured Thing* after a woman has broken into tears in a pub at the thought of her ill-chosen husband; a girl is forced by her father to sing 'Roll Out the Barrel' in an air-raid shelter as bombs explode above. Equally notable is Davies' assured visual style, the rich, brown-tinted colour photography evoking a world of constraint and hardship, the surreal images (startlingly, two men falling in slow-motion away from the camera to plunge through glass) emphasising the interior, subjective nature of the 'plot'.

Made on low budgets provided by institutional resources, the films of Terence Davies reveal a highly original, audacious film-maker. Few contemporary figures match his ability or his interest in charting the dark recesses and haunts of the soul; fewer still do so with such sincerity and compassion. Indeed, he is that rarity: a British, but never parochial, director who views cinema seriously and passionately, thus fulfilling the loftiest demands of art.

Lineage

Davies' highly personal digressions from realism align him more closely with European directors like **Bresson**, **Bergman**, **Antonioni** and **Resnais** than with his compatriots. Though unique, his trilogy has often been compared, fatuously, with that of **Bill Douglas**.

Viewing

1 **The Terence Davies Trilogy (Children; Madonna and Child; Death and Transfiguration)**
GB 1976/80/83/ w Phillip Maudesley, Terry O'Sullivan, Wilfrid Brambell

2 **Distant Voices, Still Lives**
GB 1986/88/ w Freda Dowie, Pete Postlethwaite, Angela Walsh

Cecil B. DeMille

Born: 12th August 1881/Ashfield, Massachusetts, USA
Died: 21st January 1959/Hollywood, California, USA
Directing career: 1913-1956

In the spectacularly entertaining films of Cecil Blount DeMille, history is bunk. It seems as if, throughout his career, factual events, the classics,

Adopting a suitably Samsonesque pose, epic film-maker *par excellence* Cecil B. DeMille.

or even for that matter God, were repeatedly recruited merely to lend a bogus respectability to the display of sex, violence and generally libertine behaviour on screen.

DeMille followed his parents (his father was an Episcopalian minister) into the theatre, where he first met Jesse Lasky. In 1913, with Samuel Goldfish (later Goldwyn), the pair travelled to Hollywood, a then obscure Californian village, to shoot DeMille's first feature, *The Squaw Man*. A Western about an English lord who marries an Indian, its success helped put Hollywood on the film-making map, while in 1918 Lasky's company became Paramount, the studio for which DeMille would work for most of his career. At the same time, working in a number of genres, DeMille contributed to the development of film techniques, especially in the realm of exotic, atmospheric lighting and set-designs in costume pictures like *Carmen*, *Joan the Woman* and *The Woman God Forgot* >**1**. This last was a tale of romance and religious conflict between an Aztec warrior-tribe and the Spanish conquistadors, but all, though silent, starred the opera singer Geraldine Farrar.

DeMille's reputation as the creator of lurid, sensationalist epics often meant that his considerable story-telling talents were critically undervalued. Indeed, before embarking on the grandiose spectaculars that were to become his trademark, he made a series of witty marital comedies, often starring Gloria Swanson as their unusually independent heroine, and gently satirising the sexual mores of America's upper-crust society. Nonetheless, the sparkling brew of adultery, jealousy and generally flirtatious behaviour on view was offset not only by puritanical titles like *Don't Change Your Husband*, *Why Change Your Wife?* and *Forbidden Fruit*, but also by cautionary historical flashbacks. In *Male and Female* >**2**, for example, Swanson, infatuated by her butler, dreams she is in ancient Babylon, where she discovers – and here lies the moral uplift – that the position of faithless women was altogether more perilous in olden days.

For all the lavish detail of the gaudy sets and often scanty costumes in the ensuing pageants (including the first version of *The Ten Commandments*, and *King of Kings*), historical authenticity usually took second place to delirious spectacle, which was often accompanied by a last-minute moral warning. *The Sign of the Cross* >**3** is concerned less with the religious and political conflicts between Romans and Christians than with the splendiferous orgies hosted by **Charles Laughton**'s Nero; lions, too, rarely go hungry. But after the relative failure of *Cleopatra*, DeMille turned his attention to America's own past with a series of lusty Westerns; though the characters were sometimes taken from real life – Wild Bill Hickok and Calamity Jane in *The Plainsman* >**4** – romance and patriotic hokum take precedence over realism. In *Union Pacific*, *Northwest Mounted Police*, and *Unconquered*, his chief interest was in following the clean lines of a simple story, and celebrating the pioneer spirit that tamed the savages and won the West.

In the last years of his life DeMille worked less frequently and less imaginatively, though after the tedium of the circus epic *The Greatest Show on Earth*, the overblown hokum of *Samson and Delilah* came as a welcome relief. Most impressive, however, was his final *The Ten Commandments* >**5**, firmly materialist in its conception of God, who manifests Himself not through the salvation and guidance of human souls but through the vivid, miraculous manipulation of the physical world. Here, coloured smoke, a burning bush, parted seas, and – as Moses returns with the commandments carved in stone, by lightning, naturally, – Charlton Heston's shock of whitened hair offer tangible proof of His power. Old Testament values meet the Victorian melodrama and modern special effects. Indeed, DeMille was never a sophisticated film-maker, but his long, prolific and largely successful career is notable for the way he made both God and Mammon work to his very own advantage.

Lineage

DeMille was less interested in pictorial poetry, not to mention moral purity, than **Griffith**, while his love of lavish spectacle and simple plots is mirrored in virtually all subsequent epics, perhaps most notably in recent years in the movies of **Spielberg** and **Lucas**.

Further reading

DeMille's *Autobiography* (New Jersey, 1959); Charles Higham's *Cecil B. DeMille* (New York, 1973).

Viewing

1 **The Woman God Forgot**
US 1919/ w Geraldine Farrar, Wallace Reid, Theodore Kozloff

2 **Male and Female**
US 1919/ w Gloria Swanson, Bebe Daniels, Thomas Meighan

3 **The Sign of the Cross**
US 1932/ w Charles Laughton, Claudette Colbert, Fredric March

4 **The Plainsman**
US 1936/ w Gary Cooper, Jean Arthur, James Ellison

5 **The Ten Commandments**
US 1956/ w Charlton Heston, Yul Brynner, Edward G. Robinson

Jonathan Demme

Born: 22nd February 1944/Rockville Center, New York, USA
Directing career: 1974-

Of the directors who emerged from Corman's New World during the '70s, Jonathan Demme is the most talented and distinctive by far. While his apprenticeship was in exploitation films, his style and characters often hark back to earlier styles of film-making.

After working in film criticism and publicity, Demme served **Corman** as writer-producer on two thrillers by Joe Viola (*Angels Hard As They Come*, *The Hot Box*). Though unremarkable, they earned him the opportunity to direct *Caged Heat*, a witty women's-prison drama memorable for ambitious dream sequences, a rousing, quasi-feminist picture of solidarity, and a percussive John Cale score. *Crazy Mama* and *Fighting Mad* were equally offbeat action pictures; it was only, however, a departure from the exploitation format in *Handle with Care* (*Citizens Band*) >**1** that first attracted critical praise. Portraying a smalltown community of engaging eccentrics linked chiefly by their use of CB radio, his loosely structured narrative and understated sympathy for characters (including a bigamist trucker and his two wives) drew comparisons with **Renoir**, **Capra** and **Altman**. Then, after the stylish **Hitchcock** pastiche *Last Embrace* (which wisely avoided the voyeuristic sexual violence of **De Palma**'s homages), Demme painted a touching, witty picture of everyday working-class life in *Melvin and Howard* >**2**. Based partly in fact, this story of a milkman's meeting with mysterious tycoon Howard Hughes (leading to a controversial will greedily contested by Hughes' estate) is merely an excuse for a delicate comedy of manners. Ignoring Hughes for the most part, it focusses on Melvin, whose dreams of an easy life are doomed to founder in a cycle of divorce and debt. Crucially however, Demme neither patronises nor sentimentalises his beautiful losers, but gently satirises the absurd consumer culture endlessly promoted by the American media.

Avoiding easy formulas, Demme went on to direct a variety of hybrids: *Who Am I This Time?*, made for TV, depicts two shy amateur actors whose romance is facilitated and inflamed by role-playing; *Swingshift* examines women's increased independence through work during World War II; *Stop Making Sense* documents a Talking Heads concert with exemplary simplicity. If the stronger accent on sex and violence in *Something Wild* >**3** was a distant echo of earlier films, its fast, tortuous plot – strait-laced accountant yields to the advances of outrageous, unstable *femme fatale* (tellingly a lookalike of Louise Brooks in *Pandora's Box*) only to meet Nemesis in the form of a violently jealous ex-husband – provided another opportunity to explore an America rarely seen in film. Again, the characters – nervy Charlie, loopy Lulu, homicidal psycho Ray – are all allowed their 'reasons' by Demme's sympathetic direction, while the sudden, unpredictable shifts from comedy to suspense and back again are handled with breathless but impressive assurance.

Simplicity was the keynote of both *Swimming to Cambodia*, a record of Spalding Gray's witty monologue, and of a television documentary on Haiti, whereas *Married to the Mob* >**4** was a lively blend of black comedy and romance that revelled in the unexpected as it charted a mid-league Mafioso's widow's attempts to begin a new life while being amorously hunted by her late husband's boss. If the film was finally shallow, it was nevertheless fast, funny and gleefully imaginative in its depiction of underworld kitsch.

Although Demme's mix of social comedy, romance and suspense is difficult to categorise and has ranged over a wide variety of subjects, his unassuming visual elegance, unforced humanity, and detailed observation of daily life are impressive and consistent.

Lineage

Clearly indebted to Corman, Demme's simple, sweeping camera style and ingenious dramatic use of music occasionally draws comparison with **Scorsese**. His populism, reminiscent of Renoir, parallels the work of fellow Corman-graduates **John Sayles** and Jonathan Kaplan.

Viewing

1 **Handle With Care (Citizens Band)**
US 1977/Paul Le Mat, Candy Clark, Charles Napier

2 **Melvin and Howard**
US 1980/Paul Le Mat, Mary Steenburgen, Jason Robards

3 **Something Wild**
US 1986/Jeff Daniels, Melanie Griffith, Ray Liotta

4 **Married to the Mob**
US 1988/ w Michelle Pfeiffer, Matthew Modine, Dean Stockwell

Jacques Demy

Born: 5th June 1931/Pont Château, France
Directing career: 1955-

At his best, Jacques Demy is a true original, the creator of an enchanting, poignant fantasy world governed by chance, love and memory. Accusations that the sumptuous, sensuous surfaces of his films are merely decorative are misguided, since his modern-day fairy-tales are often rooted in the dark emotions of reality.

After film studies, Demy entered the industry as assistant to animator Paul Grimault, following which he directed several shorts. Not until 1960, however, with his first feature *Lola* >**1**, a love-story set in the provincial coastal town of Nantes, did his startling personal style mature. Its formal daring is evident in the opening shot of an American, garbed in white, driving his long white limousine across the 'Scope screen to the sound of jazz and Beethoven's 7th. The plot, about the man's belated return to his cabaret-singer lover of seven years earlier, is of scant interest in itself, but

Demy's style is remarkable. As the camera circles endlessly and elegantly around the carousel of characters who symbolise the central couple's past and future, the exhilarating celebration of love's rebirth is undercut by a sad awareness of love's transience and fragility. Indeed, the complex pattern of relationships is extended both within and without the film: *Lola* refers backwards to **Von Sternberg** (*The Blue Angel*) and **Ophüls** (*Lola Montes*), whose sophisticated bitter-sweet romances clearly influenced Demy's lavish black-and-white visuals and his themes.

Equally deceptive in its playful simplicity was *La Baie des Anges* (*Bay of Angels*) >**2** which gave added emphasis to the role of chance in love by having its protagonists fall prey to a gambling addiction; the Casino, tempting them away from the course of true romance with the prospect of easy money, is an elegant latter-day Hell. Then, in *The Umbrellas of Cherbourg* >**3**, Demy finally achieved his aim of mounting a musical in colour. His first movies had used Michel Legrand's music only to underline emotional content; here dialogue was sung throughout. Miraculously, the drab reality of a seaside town becomes a pastel fantasy world while, again, the romantic roundelay conceals a bitter pill inside a sugar coating, love being thwarted by endless coincidences involving such suitably banal phenomena as illegitimacy, military service and money. Even more intriguing is the way Demy subtly refers to figures from the earlier films: the hero admits to a past affair with Lola, thus extending the complex, fateful emotional tentacles of each movie.

After the success of *Umbrellas* Demy paid tribute to American musicals with *Les Demoiselles de Rochefort* by casting Gene Kelly and including dancing for the first time. Sadly, its choreography was only patchily inspired, but the film impressed for its audaciously contrived plotting, colour, and its use of yet another Atlantic town as an enormous set. Demy then went to America to make *Model Shop* >**4**, a decidedly darker, non-musical film which rediscovered Lola as a divorcee working none too profitably as a photographic model in a seedy Los Angeles suburb. Though its portrait of disenchanted youth was flawed, the evocation of rootless LA life, stranded in perpetual motion on and around the clogged freeways, was superb.

Back in Europe Demy's career went into inexplicable decline, with two merely decorative versions of classic fairy-tales (*Peau d'Ane*, *The Pied Piper*), a poor comedy (*A Slightly Pregnant Man*), and a French-Japanese co-production set during the French Revolution (*Lady Oscar*). Happily, *Une Chambre en Ville* (*A Room in Town*) >**5** saw him back on form with a return to Nantes and all-sung drama. The tone, however, was more sombre than ever: a tale of *amour fou* is set against the backdrop of a dockers' strike and Demy's formal invention reaches its zenith when a character slits his throat in mid-song. Sadly the film was not a success; nor, not surprisingly, was *Parking*, a misguided attempt to retell the story of Orpheus and Euridice within the format of a bland rock-opera. Next, hopes were raised and disappointed, by *Trois Places pour le 26*, a musical scored by Michel Legrand and starring Yves Montand.

Despite his mediocre output in recent years, Demy's surreal fantasies, often dismissed as whimsy, display an ambitious formal precision and elegance in their unique blend of dialogue, music, decor and movement. His finest films, consistently innovative and resolutely cinematic, confirm him as one of the most imaginative talents to have emerged from France during the late '50s and early '60s.

Lineage

Demy has admitted his admiration for Von Sternberg, **Vigo**, Ophüls, **Bresson**, **Cocteau**, and **Minnelli**, though his obsessive concern with patterns of courtship and memory suggests parallels in **Rohmer** and **Resnais**. One may also tentatively compare his use of music with **Terence Davies** and Julien Temple. He is married to Agnès Varda.

Further reading

Roy Armes' *French Cinema Since 1946, Vol 2* (London, 1976).

Viewing

1 **Lola**
France 1960/ w Anouk Aimée, Marc Michel, Alan Scott
2 **La Baie des Anges**
France 1963/ w Jeanne Moreau, Claude Mann, Paul Guers
3 **The Umbrellas of Cherbourg**
France 1964/ w Cathérine Deneuve, Anne Vernon, Marc Michel
4 **Model Shop**
US 1969/ w Anouk Aimée, Gary Lockwood, Alexandra Hay
5 **Une Chambre en Ville**
France 1982/ w Dominique Sanda, Danielle Darrieux, Michel Piccoli

Brian De Palma

Born: 11th September 1940/Newark, New Jersey, USA
Directing career: 1960-

Although Brian De Palma displays a firm grasp of film technology, of all the 'movie-brats' who rose to power in the '70s, he is the least emotionally satisfying; the abiding impression to be had from watching his films is of a sad waste of misapplied talent.

While still a student De Palma directed a number of vaguely underground shorts that anticipated the anti-establishment satire of his early features. In *The Wedding Party* improvised acting and frenetic editing exhibited the influence of **Godard**; *Murder à la Mod* imitated melodrama, **Hitchcock**'s thrillers and silent comedy; *Dionysus in '69* experimented with split-screen; *Greetings* and *Hi Mom!* were spasmodically funny revue-style comedies about draft-dodging and voyeurism, notable for their anarchic humour, *verité*-style camerawork and the presence of a young Robert De Niro.

After a first, unhappy brush with Hollywood while making the supposedly wacky youth satire *Get To Know Your Rabbit*, De Palma moved towards a more commercial style. A concise thriller about a journalist's investigations into a murder she alone believes in, *Sisters* opens with a scene derived from *Rear Window* and features a killer psychologically resembling *Psycho*'s Norman Bates. This homage to Hitchcock was enhanced by De Palma's inventive use of split-screen to embody the themes of voyeurism and schizophrenia. Even more imaginative, *Phantom of the Paradise* >**1**, a thematically rich update of the *Phantom of the Opera* story (with elements of *Faust* included for good measure), employed state-of-the-art video technology to embellish a black satire on the corruption, deceit and rampant egotism at the heart of the rock-music industry.

Thereafter, Hitchcock's shadow was cast over De Palma's ever more florid visual style and increasingly sensationalist subject matter. *Obsession* was a slow romance inspired by *Vertigo* and involving necrophilia and incest; *Carrie* >**2** evoked guilt and repression as it charted the traumatic effect of puberty on a shy schoolgirl with telekinetic powers; *The Fury* was a further flashy foray into paranormal psychology, wrecked by incoherence and arbitrary slow-motion effects. By now, the visual excess suggested the hollow triumph of style over content, serving to stress the voyeuristic, often misogynist, slant to De Palma's peculiar brand of suspense. *Dressed to Kill*'s leering depiction of violence against women, framed by stale tributes to *Psycho*'s shower-murder, angered many, while *Blow Out* brazenly plagiarised both **Antonioni**'s *Blow-Up* and **Coppola**'s *The Conversation* while delivering more of the same. The **Oliver Stone**-scripted *Scarface* >**3** was a change in genre, lifting scene after scene of **Hawks**' classic while updating the rise-and-fall gangster saga to modern, drug-infested Miami, but, as always, the focus was on decadence, profanity and violence – memorably a sickening chainsaw murder – rather than on the psychological and social reasons for the hoodlum's psychopathic behaviour.

Body Double, so gross and implausible in its absurd merging of the plots of *Rear Window* and *Vertigo* that it worked best as an unintentional black comedy, saw a return to misogynist violence, but *The Untouchables* >**4** was a refreshingly innocent retelling of

Elliott Ness's battles against Al Capone. Like a children's story written in blood, its disdain for historical fact and its simplistic heroics ensured that it was intellectually and emotionally empty. But the sterling performances and a slow-motion shoot-out finale stolen from the Odessa Steps sequence in **Eisenstein**'s *Battleship Potemkin* contrived to lend it a certain quasi-mythical naivety.

So preoccupied is De Palma with visual tricks and redundant homage that his films are fatally lacking in credible characters and real suspense. The calculating coldness smacks of the cynical hack who views both his work and his audience with contempt: sure proof that a glossy, fashionable stress on style for style's sake is no substitute for intelligence and emotional integrity.

Lineage

De Palma's interest in Godard having yielded to an obsession with Hitchcock, his own cine-literacy and gaudy visual style has been influential on any number of minor horror-directors seeking bogus respectability for their otherwise often widely discredited work.

Further reading

Lynda Myles and Michael Pye's *The Movie Brats* (New York, 1979).

Viewing

1 **Phantom of the Paradise**
US 1974/ w William Finley, Paul Williams, Jessica Harper

2 **Carrie**
US 1976/ w Sissy Spacek, Piper Laurie, Willam Katt

3 **Scarface**
US 1983/ w Al Pacino, Steven Bauer, Michelle Pfeiffer

4 **The Untouchables**
US 1987/ w Kevin Costner, Sean Connery, Robert De Niro

Vittorio De Sica

Born: 7th July 1902/Sora, Italy
Died: 17th November 1974/Paris, France
Directing career: 1940-1974

Long regarded as milestones of neo-realism, the films of Vittorio De Sica reveal a level of emotional manipulation that exposes the impossibility of achieving a single, all-embracing definition of Italy's postwar 'movement'. Their 'reality' is contrived, their tone poetic, their 'faith' in ordinary people often pessimistic.

A matinee idol in the '20s and '30s, De Sica was thus able, eventually, to finance his own films. Directing his first feature in 1940, he went on to make, with scriptwriter Cesare Zavattini, a number of Italy's best-known neo-realist films. Theme and style were established in their first collaboration; *The Children Are Watching Us*, a simple story concerning a woman's adultery and her husband's subsequent suicide, placed an emphasis on working-class characters, real locations, naturalistic performances and the vulnerability of children to the corruption of adults. All this was dealt with emotionally rather than analytically. Even more explicit in its critique of postwar Italy, *Shoeshine* >**1** saw the innocence and friendship of two homeless boys destroyed by an elder brother's involvement in the black market and by the authoritarianism of a reformatory for juvenile offenders. For all De Sica's use of non-professional actors, his taste for poetic symbolism was very much in evidence in the use of the boys' cherished horse to denote freedom.

Bicycle Thieves >**2** again used a child, this time to sentimentalise its examination of the humiliating effects of unemployment. Searching for a stolen bike, newly bought and crucial to his father's bill-posting job, a boy witnesses the injustice and despair in Rome's poorer suburbs. The deceptively simple plot leads to the father's own final, desperate act of theft, its supposed everyday realism scrupulously organised into bleakly poetic images suggesting the alienation of proletarian life. The boy alone offers a glimmer of hope, while the hostile Roman crowds continually serve to harass the man's struggle to regain his job and self-respect.

Miracle in Milan painted the plight of the poor and homeless in cloying, whimsically fantastic tones, its buffoon-like masses defeating capitalism with the aid of a symbolic dove and flying broomsticks. *Umberto D* >**3**, however, was a profoundly pessimistic account of the loneliness of a poverty-stricken old man, his only friends a dog and a young maid whose own suffering is barely felt by the grouchy protagonist. Noted for its use of real rather than filmic time to show the girl waking to go about her tedious daily tasks, it was the collaborators' last major neo-realist work.

During the '50s and '60s, the director moved away from real locations, non-professional actors and social comment into slick, studio-shot satirical farce and glossy melodrama; films such as *Two Women*, *Yesterday, Today and Tomorrow*, and *Marriage Italian Style*, often featuring established stars – notably Sophia Loren and Marcello Mastroianni – treated sexual issues with a shallow superficiality. As time passed, De Sica seemed an increasingly lightweight artist led by his sympathetic direction of actors and his astute comic timing towards ever more escapist material. Only in the '70s just before his death, did he return to more political subjects, depicting the incarceration of Jews in pre-war Fascist Italy in *The Garden of the Finzi-Continis* >**4**, and confronting the old problem of Italy's class and regional differences as revealed by a woman's visit to a sanatorium in *A Brief Vacation*. The first, however, was decorative in its rosy nostalgia and hazy elegance; the satire of the second was countered by the clichés of a romantic sub-plot.

In retrospect, even De Sica's neo-realist work was marred by melodrama; the authenticity of location-shooting is undermined by schematic plots and excessive heart-on-the-sleeve sentimentality. The superbly naturalistic, non-professional performances in his best work, however, do convey an overwhelming emotional power.

Lineage

De Sica's neo-realism is more simplistic than **Rossellini**'s; his visual sense anticipates many future Italian directors, notably **Antonioni** and **Rosi**. His later work may be compared with that of Dino Risi, Ettore Scola, Mario Monicelli and Luigi Comencini.

Further reading

Peter Bondanella's *Italian Cinema: From Neo-realism to the Present* (New York, 1983).

Viewing

1 **Shoeshine**
Italy 1946/ w Rinaldo Smordoni, Franco Interlenghi, Anielo Mele
2 **Bicycle Thieves**
Italy 1948/ w Enzo Staiola, Lamberto Maggioranni, Lianella Carell
3 **Umberto D**
Italy 1952/ w Carlo Battisti, Maria-Pia Casilio, Lina Gennari
4 **The Garden of the Finzi-Continis**
Italy 1970/ w Dominique Sanda, Lino Capolicchio, Helmut Berger

William Dieterle

Born: 15th July 1893/Ludwigshafen, Germany
Died: 9th December 1972/ Ottobrunn, W Germany
Directing career: 1923-1960

While there is no thematic or stylistic consistency in the films of Wilhelm (*sic*) Dieterle to suggest he was ever anything more than a proficient craftsman, the ambition, variety and intelligence of his finest work rewards any reappraisal of his neglected career.

An actor in German theatre and cinema, Dieterle worked for Max Reinhardt, **Murnau**, Paul Leni and E.A. Dupont before directing films himself, often choosing rather offbeat plots: *Sex in Chains* offended the censor with its look at love in prison. In 1930 he was invited by Warner Brothers to Hollywood; after playing Ahab in a German version of *Moby Dick*, he directed *The Last Flight* >**1**, an impressive, brittle comedy-drama about four ex-fliers, nerves and bodies shattered by The Great War, trying vainly to shrug off the shadow of death in a world that no longer cares. Profound and honest in suggesting the nihilism that underlied the joviality of the Jazz Age, it is a dark, touching but sadly neglected classic.

Several minor, expertly made films ensued – *Fog Over 'Frisco* is notable not only for its frantic pace and virtuoso editing but for the way it rids itself of its heroine, *Psycho*-style, after 20 minutes – before Dieterle collaborated once more with Reinhardt. Their *A Midsummer Night's Dream* >**2**, bizarrely cast with Mickey Rooney as Puck and James Cagney as Bottom, is inspired, while lavish sets and photography make for magical lyricism. He then alternated a series of plodding, reverential and clichéd biopics (Pasteur, Zola, Juarez) starring Paul Muni with more ambitious work. *Blockade* was a naive but controversial account of the Spanish Civil War, while an epic version of *The Hunchback of Nôtre Dame* created a definitive, grotesquely pathetic Quasimodo in the form of **Charles Laughton**, and memorably evoked an intolerant, cruel and ignorant medieval world on the brink of literacy and enlightenment.

Further biopics followed, of Reuter and Dr Erlich (inventor of the cure for syphilis) before the remarkable *All That Money Can Buy* >**3**. Relocating the Faust legend in New England, with an ambitious young farmer selling his soul to a mischievously evil hick named Mr Scratch, the film merged 1840s rural Americana with German Expressionism to witty, gripping effect. Then, having made one of Hollywood's more inventive attempts to deal with the jazz phenomenon (*Syncopation*), Dieterle signed with producer David O. Selznick and – besides shooting part of *Duel in the Sun* – made two swooning melodramas starring Jennifer Jones and Joseph Cotten: though burdened with ludicrous plots, both *Love Letters* (a girl's amnesia is cured by the love of her dead fiancé's friend) and *Portrait of Jennie* >**4** (an artist falls in love with the ghost of a dead girl) functioned as vivid, unashamed celebrations of *amour fou* through brooding camerawork (Jennie alternating between black and white, sepia and colour) and performances of rare conviction.

After suffering several attacks from the HUAC, Dieterle's American career ended with a number of uninspired romances, and he went back to Germany to direct a handful of films before returning to the theatre. If his track record was inevitably erratic, his talent with unusual projects, particularly those involving grotesque or supernatural elements, proved lively, original and intelligent.

Lineage

Dieterle's friendship with Reinhardt, Ludwig Berger, and numerous other German theatrical and film figures surely influenced his work; he was a close friend of Brecht, whose trip to America he partly financed and with whom he planned several (aborted) films.

Viewing

1 **The Last Flight**
US 1931/ w Richard Barthelmess, Helen Chandler, David Manners

2 **A Midsummer Night's Dream**
US 1935/ w James Cagney, Victor Jory, Olivia De Havilland

3 **All That Money Can Buy (The Devil and Daniel Webster)**
US 1940/ w Walter Huston, James Craig, Edward Arnold

4 **Portrait of Jennie**
US 1949/ w Jennifer Jones, Joseph Cotten, Lillian Gish

Walt Disney

Born: 5th December 1901/Chicago, USA
Died: 15th December 1966/Los Angeles, USA
Directing career: 1920-1966

While it is true that few of the many movies described as 'A Walt Disney film' were actually animated or directed by Walt himself, such was his creative vision and his control over the artists who worked for him that his claim to authorship would seem to extend even to Disney product released after his death. Though never a great artist, his business acumen and grasp of public tastes made him a major contributor to popular entertainment and folklore.

The young Walter Elias Disney delighted in drawing animals and, after serving as a commercial illustrator, he entered movies with the *Alice in Cartoonland* and *Oswald the Lucky Rabbit* series. But it was the *Silly Symphonies* and Mickey Mouse that set him on the road to fame and fortune: a technical innovator, he made the first cartoons to use sound (*Steamboat Willie* >**1**, *The Skeleton Dance*) and Technicolor (*Flowers and Trees*). Shortly afterwards, a mature style was very much in evidence, and cute animals (Mickey and Minnie, Donald Duck, the dogs Pluto and Goofy) were generally given human characteristics – Mickey's squeaky voice being supplied by Disney himself – and an all-American optimism. Indeed, unlike the more anarchic talents working at Warners and MGM (Tex Avery, Chuck Jones, Frank Tashlin, Friz Freleng and Bob Clampett), after a few early excursions into outright fantasy – *The Skeleton Dance* has skeletons playing music on each other's bones – Disney eschewed animation's potential for depicting the impossible to concentrate on an anthropomorphic, prettified form of everyday realism.

In 1934, work began on *Snow White and the Seven Dwarfs* >**2**, the first cartoon feature; reducing the fairy-tale's macabre tone to isolated moments of Expressionist terror, Disney located his wholesome, trilling heroine in a soft-focus world peopled by cute birds, bashful beasts and playful dwarfs. An enormously expensive technical tour-de-force, it was a massive success and encouraged Disney, after *Pinocchio*, to attempt something more artistic with *Fantasia* >**3**. But this creation of images and stories for much-loved pieces of classical music emerged as less a matter of high culture than kitsch. While the floating abstract shapes used to illustrate Bach, and a comically incompetent Mickey Mouse as 'The Sorcerer's Apprentice' were, respectively, pretty and amusing, Beethoven and Stravinsky suffered from a pretentious but irredeemably low-brow depiction of the usual anthropomorphised creatures in mythical landscapes.

The film was a relative failure, and Disney withdrew to the proven formula of children's stories, told in richly coloured and magically epic settings. His narrative talents and ability to draw pathos from a pantheistically-conceived universe contributed to the commercial success and predictable animation of films like *Dumbo* >**4** (big-eared baby elephant vanquishes bigotry by flying), *Bambi* (further fluttery-eyed forest folk), *Cinderella*, *Peter Pan*, *Alice in Wonderland*, *The Lady and the Tramp*, and *Sleeping Beauty* >**5** (squeaky-clean '50s teenagers menaced by an attractively evil and grotesque witch). Disney's perfectionism resulted in further sophisticated techniques, but his conservative WASP morality and mawkish sentimentality, resulting often in racist stereotypes, prevented his becoming a profound or truly innovative artist.

By now, Disney's hugely successful empire was making nature documentaries and live-action features characterised, like the cartoons, by an insipid populism promoting the glory of the American Way; while his canny business sense gleaned further profits from numerous non-filmic ventures such as television programmes, Mickey Mouse artifacts, and Disneyland. Efforts were made in the '60s to update the Disney image a little – the sugary *Mary Poppins* combined animation with live action, while *The Jungle Book* and *The Aristocats* were less sentimental and genuinely wittier than the earlier cartoons – but it was only years after Disney's own death that the studio finally managed to drag itself into the adult, contemporary world by producing, through its offshoot Touchstone Pictures, films like *Down and Out in Beverly Hills*, *The Color of Money* and *Tin Men*. Walt would probably not have approved.

Disney's reactionary ideology extended to his patriarchal control of the studio family, and key collaborators like Ub Iwerks and Ward Kimball were rarely given the credit they deserved. Indeed, his business practices and increasingly complacent approach to his chosen medium suggest both personal egotism and a timid and conservative indifference to the rich potential of animation.

Lineage

Disney, whose career in animation began shortly after those of Max and Dave Fleischer, rarely equalled the surreal anarchy of Avery, Jones or Clampett, nor did he take note of more experimental, non-American animation; his work is virtually a genre in itself. His influence is perhaps now most strongly felt in the live-action of **Spielberg** and the glossily sophisticated animation techniques of Don Bluth.

Further reading

Richard Schickel's *The Disney Version* (New York, 1968), Christopher Finch's *The Art of Walt Disney* (New York, 1973).

Viewing

1 **Steamboat Willie**
US 1928
2 **Snow White and the Seven Dwarfs**
US 1937
3 **Fantasia**
US 1940
4 **Dumbo**
US 1941
5 **Sleeping Beauty**
US 1958

Edward Dmytryk

Born: 4th September 1908/Grand Forks, British Columbia, Canada
Directing career: 1935-1976

In the mid-'40s, Edward Dmytryk made several superior B-movies that mixed suspense with social comment; but after a clash with the House UnAmerican Activities Committee, he went into artistic decline, ironically with more expensive, prestigious projects.

Having risen from studio messenger to editor, Dmytryk began directing with a number of programme fillers for Paramount and Columbia. Moving to RKO, he hit his stride with two propaganda films (*Hitler's Children*, and *Tender Comrade* which sees women working in wartime industry). A taut version of Raymond Chandler's *Farewell, My Lovely* >**1** helped both to define the shadowy visual style of *film noir* with a vivid Expressionist fantasy sequence, and to revive the flagging image of crooner Dick Powell, cast against type as a cynical and shabby Marlowe; whereas in *Cornered*, Powell's obsessive search for a man responsible for his wife's death uncovers a coven of Fascists disguised as respectable members of Buenos Aires' salon society. After *Till the End of Time*, a dramatisation of the disillusioning experiences of returning war-veterans, Dmytryk – a card-carrying Communist – went on to combine *noir* paranoia with a portrait of racism in *Crossfire* >**2**. A grim, investigative thriller about the murder of a Jew (the victim in Richard Brooks' original novel was homosexual), it benefitted from an atmospheric use of locations – seedy hotels, all-night cinemas, smoky bars – and Robert Ryan's frighteningly intense performance as the anti-Semitic psychopath.

Sadly, in 1947 Dmytryk's promising career was interrupted by his appearance before the HUAC as one of the 'Hollywood Ten'; his Communist connections led to imprisonment and exile, then to a second hearing in which he named names. Now off the blacklist, he made four movies for producer **Stanley Kramer**, the last a version of *The Caine Mutiny* with Bogart in tired form as the deranged Captain Queeg. The film's success led Dmytryk into sprawling, expensive projects (*Broken Lance*, *Raintree County*, *The Young Lions*, *Walk on the Wild Side*) in which glossy production values and unrestrained solemnity repeatedly swamped invention and vitality.

In the '60s, Dmytryk was a negligible director, reduced to fluff like *Shalako* (a British-produced Western starring Bardot and Connery); in 1976 he gave up directing to teach film. Perhaps the constraints of the B-movie (not to mention the collaboration of producer Adrian Scott and writer John Paxton on both *Cornered* and *Crossfire*) were crucial to his finest work; or, perhaps, the iniquities of the HUAC witchhunts simply sapped his confidence.

Lineage

Dmytryk's blend of social comment and *noir* suspense finds an echo in **Huston** and **Lang**, and prefigures **Kazan**, **Rossen** and **Losey**. His later work bears comparison with late **Stevens** and **Zinnemann**.

Further reading

It's a Hell of a Life But Not a Bad Living (New York, 1978), is Dmytryk's autobiography.

Viewing

1 **Farewell, My Lovely (Murder, My Sweet)**
US 1944/ w Dick Powell, Claire Trevor, Mike Mazurki

2 **Crossfire**
US 1947/ w Robert Young, Robert Mitchum, Robert Ryan

Stanley Donen

Born: **13th April 1924/Columbia, South Carolina, USA**
Directing career: **1949-**

If it is difficult to tell who did what in the films co-directed by Stanley Donen and Gene Kelly, one need only look at the work they undertook separately to realise that Donen surely supplied the films' visual elegance, while the dancer's ebullient balletic style was the perfect foil to Donen's taste for light romance.

A former Broadway dancer and choreographer, Donen's initial encounter with MGM was as choreographer on a number of musicals, including *Cover Girl*, *Anchors Aweigh* and *Take Me Out to the Ball Game*, the last of which he co-scripted and partly directed with Kelly. Their directing debut proper, however, was *On the Town* >**1**, a hectic 'sailors-on-leave' farce notable not only for a superb score but also for several musical numbers shot on location; few dance sequences in film are as exhilarating, fresh and purely imaginative as the ballet on top of the Empire State Building.

After making, without Kelly, *Royal Wedding* (in which Fred Astaire dances on the walls and ceiling of a hotel room), Donen re-united with him for *Singin' in the Rain* >**2**, a joyously funny and affectionate satire on the problems experienced by Hollywood as it made the transition from silent movies to sound. Again the film is infectiously lively and its eponymous set-piece a classic; most impressively, the craning camera frequently becomes both a choreographed participant in the film and a stylistic correlative to Kelly's weak-at-the-knees, heart-on-his-sleeve emotionalism.

While Kelly alone directed the experimental but pretentious all-ballet triptych *Welcome to the Dance*, Donen again displayed his visual originality with *Seven Brides for Seven Brothers*, an unusually muscular and acrobatic dance film set among mock Oregon mountains and meadows. *It's Always Fair Weather*, his final film with Kelly, about the awkward reunion of three soldiers who have drifted apart in the decade since the war, was an attempt to repeat the formula of *On the Town*, while *Funny Face* >**3** – his first film away from MGM – gently satirised the fashion business at the same time as charting a shy and serious Greenwich Village bookseller's reluctant transformation into a chic magazine model. If the dances lacked the energy of earlier films, there was no denying the success of Donen's collaboration with photographer Richard Avedon in numerous elegant experiments with ravishing colours, memorably in a subtly intimate dark-room sequence.

The musical's heyday was drawing to a close, however, and after two delightful versions of Broadway hits (*The Pajama Game*, *Damn Yankees*), Donen turned to comedy. *Indiscreet* and *The Grass Is Greener* were superficial cream puffs, enlivened only by fine acting, but *Charade* >**4**, a light blend of romantic comedy and mystery with Cary Grant protecting Audrey Hepburn from her husband's killers, occasionally approached Hitchcockian complexity. *Arabesque* was a less successful spy adventure in a similar vein, and *Bedazzled* a spasmodically funny update of the Faust legend. Thereafter, Donen lapsed into increasingly formulaic material: lame comic nostalgia (*Lucky Lady*), pointless '30s genre-parody (*Movie Movie*), vapid sci-fi (*Saturn 3*), and innuendo-laden farce (*Blame It on Rio*).

One of the finest dance-musical directors in the '50s, perhaps Donen needed both the genre and Kelly's uniquely relaxed romantic persona to inspire him. In that decade, his ability to merge comedy with romance, 'real' action with song and dance was almost unparalleled; the enduring popularity of his best-known films attests to his wit, intelligence and invention.

Lineage

Donen and Kelly worked for MGM's Freed unit (Arthur Freed being the studio's top musical producer), and thus bear comparison with **Vincente Minnelli** and the less gifted Charles Walters. Donen, who has expressed an admiration for **Fellini** and **Antonioni**, may in turn have influenced dance directors Bob Fosse (choreographer of *The Pajama Game* and *Damn Yankees*), Herbert Ross, and even Kelly himself.

Viewing

1 **On the Town**
US 1949/ w Kelly, Frank Sinatra, Vera-Ellen, Jules Munshin, Ann Miller

2 **Singin' in the Rain**
US 1952/ w Kelly, Debbie Reynolds, Donald O'Connor, Jean Hagen

3 **Funny Face**
US 1957/ w Audrey Hepburn, Fred Astaire, Kay Thompson

4 **Charade**
US 1963/ w Cary Grant, Audrey Hepburn, Walter Matthau

Bill Douglas

Born: 17th April 1937/Edinburgh, Scotland
Directing career: 1972-

While, paradoxically, British realism's focus on working-class life has traditionally been the preserve of middle-class, university-educated liberals, the films of Bill Douglas achieve a rare power and honesty by drawing on the deprivation of his own experiences.

After film studies, Douglas began an ambitious trilogy based on situations and relationships in his early life: *My Childhood*, *My Ain Folk* and *My Way Home* >**1** make no concessions to melodrama or sentimentality in following the harsh odyssey of a boy from virtually unwanted eight-year-old living with his grandmother in a poor Scottish mining village, through an unexpected meeting, as an adolescent, with his hitherto unknown father, to national service with the army in the Middle East. The poverty that limits his lonely life is economic, emotional and educational, and the sparse dialogue, narrative ellipses and austere documentary-style photography serve to stress cruelty, pain and misery throughout. Seven years in the making (the same boy plays the Douglas figure throughout), the trilogy is a bleakly cathartic labour of love.

Comrades >**2** was an equally impressive 'lanternist's account' of the Tolpuddle Martyrs, mixing politics, history, aesthetics and high adventure. Though shot in colour, it avoided the pitfalls of picturesque costume drama as it related the true story of Dorset farmers exiled to the Australian penal colony in the 1830s after forming a union in protest against subsistence wages. Douglas' realism provided the vehicle for an epic, humanist statement of faith in man's capacity to survive suffering, while his implicit call for working-class unity was framed in a wry, never dogmatic, portrait of class warfare and social injustice. Also intelligent was his integration into the narrative of numerous pre-cinematic devices – the panorama, rotoscope, shadow-play and thaumatrope – to reveal earlier methods of visual story-telling, and reflect on the history of film. But spectacle was paramount, with the beautiful evocation of the grey Dorset hills and the sun-baked expanses of the Australian outback lending the film a truly mythic poetry.

The emotional power of Douglas'

films may derive from his reluctance to compromise his vision of man's innate worth. Never patronising his characters, he has restored honesty and wit to a style – realism – long considered passé, simplistic and barren.

Lineage

Douglas' artistic ancestry includes the British realists, Mark Donskoi's *Maxim Gorki* trilogy and **Ray**'s *Apu* trilogy. **Terence Davies** is a still more original and audacious new British talent.

Viewing

1 **The Bill Douglas Trilogy (My Childhood; My Ain Folk; My Way Home)**
GB 1972-73-77/ w Stephen Archibald, Jean Taylor-Smith.

2 **Comrades**
GB 1987/ w Robin Soans, Alex Norton, Robert Stephens

Alexander Dovzhenko

Born: 12th September 1894 Sosnytsia, Ukraine, USSR
Died: 26th November 1956/Moscow, USSR
Directing career: 1926-1948

While inevitably marked by Soviet propaganda, the finest films of Alexander Dovzhenko are quite unlike those of his contemporaries. Where **Eisenstein**, **Vertov** and Pudovkin adhered to theories derived from Marxist dialectics and Constructivist art, Dovzhenko blended complex symbolism and pastoral lyricism into a personal poetry.

After a variety of occupations – clerk, teacher, artist and cartoonist – Dovzhenko began his film career making comparatively conventional comedies and thrillers. His fourth film, however, *Zvenigora* >**1**, was a weird taste of things to come. With a bizarre, highly complicated, elliptical story in which an old man tells his grandsons of an ancient treasure-mountain, before discovering the true treasure is the workers' revolution, it ranges through dreams and tales within tales, comedy, legend and history, past and present; even more significant, with regard to the director's future work, are the scenes depicting Ukrainian peasant life.

Dovzhenko's first major film was *Arsenal* >**2**, utilising a tortuous narrative moving from the carnage of World War I to the defeat of a Kiev workers' revolt by reactionary bureaucrats. This was traditional material for Soviet art, but Dovzhenko's methods were both original and often deeply moving. The work's visual adventurousness is evident from the long static opening shot of a battle trench suddenly exploded by an unseen mine, while its startling montage shifts from reality to satire to poetry: an old woman collapsing in grief and exhaustion in the fields is intercut with shots of a pensive Czar. He is not, however, concerned with the horrors of war, but simply writing a letter ('Today I shot a crow; weather fine'); his responsibility for the peasants' plight is then made plain as a crippled farmer beats a horse which replies, 'You're wasting your time, old man; it's not me you should strike at'.

This poignant, even pantheistic, sense of man's relation to nature is most touchingly evoked in *Earth* >**3**, which prefaces its thin tale, of a Ukrainian village's battle against the kulaks for a new tractor, with glowing close-ups of an old man dying happily and peacefully in a sunlit meadow full of ripe apples. Again, the remarkable opening shot of grain waving under a huge lowering sky establishes a quiet lyricism, which moves from stylised tableaux (loving couples staring at the moon) to slow-motion choreography (the hero shot while dancing joyously home) to an elaborate final sequence intercutting his funeral, his lover's hysterical grief, the flight of the killer through a graveyard, the birth of a new worker to take the hero's place and, once more, ripening apples. For Dovzhenko, death has meaning, not only in the context of the revolutionary struggle, but in

Answering the call of nature in Dovzhenko's lyrically poetic portrait of pastoral life, *Earth*.

nature's ceaseless, fertile cycle.

In *Ivan* and *Aerograd* (detailing the building, respectively, of a dam and a Siberian city), Dovzhenko further simplified his stories while enhancing his personal vision of man's place in the natural world through experiments with new techniques, notably in sound. In the mid-'30s, Stalin demanded that he make 'a Ukrainian *Chapayev*'. The result, *Shchors*, was a well-crafted but rhetorical propagandist portrait of a revolutionary intellectual. Thereafter, as head of Kiev studios, Dovzhenko's freedom and originality were eroded by bureaucracy; the ensuing war documentaries lacked the formal genius of his earlier work. Only in the '50s, when he wrote a number of scripts celebrating the life of a Ukraine village, did it seem as if he might regain his former artistic prominence; he died, however, just before shooting started, and *Poem of the Sea*, *The Flaming Years*, and *The Enchanted Desna* were completed by his widow, Yulia Solntseva. The last is noted for its rapturous use of colour and multi-track, non-synchronised sound.

While Dovzhenko's narrative intricacies and sophisticated use of symbols often make for somewhat demanding viewing, the simple, radiant visuals ensure an overwhelming emotional response. One of the great masters of early cinema, his love of nature and his poetic insistence on the value of human life effortlessly transcend the limiting propagandist ideology he was later required to promote.

Lineage

Barely influenced by Kuleshov, **Vertov**, **Eisenstein** and Pudovkin, Dovzhenko's films remain his own. His visual and narrative style, and faith in a pantheistic universe may be seen as an influence on **Tarkovsky** and **Paradjanov**; one might also tentatively compare his work with that of the **Taviani Brothers** and Tian Zhuangzhuang.

Further reading

Alexander Dovzhenko: The Poet as Film Maker ed. Marco Carynnyk (Cambridge Mass, 1974); Jay Leyda's *Kino* (London, 1973).

Viewing

1 **Zvenigora**
USSR 1928/ w Mikola Nademsky, Semyon Svashenko, Alexander Podorozhny
2 **Arsenal**
USSR 1929/ w Semyon Svashenko, Amvroziy Buchma, Mikola Nademsky
3 **Earth (Zemlya)**
USSR 1930/ w Stepon Shkurat, Semyon Svashenko, Mikola Nademsky

Carl Theodor Dreyer

Born: 3rd February 1889/ Copenhagen, Denmark
Died: 20th March 1968/Copenhagen, Denmark
Directing career: 1919-1964

Critical orthodoxy sees Carl Theodor Dreyer as a melancholy Dane, an austere Christian metaphysicist endlessly dealing with crises of faith and persecution. This, however, ignores the fundamental humanity of his work, not to mention his experimental style, his concern for the position of women in society, and his repeated examination of the joys and shortcomings of earthly love.

True, his upbringing was Lutheran, yet both his initial jobs (as café pianist, sports reporter, drama and film critic) and his early films, made after a scriptwriting apprenticeship, give the lie to the simplistic image of Christian commentator. Influenced by **Sjöström** and **Griffith** – the four-part *Leaves from Satan's Book* is a riposte to the latter's *Intolerance* – Dreyer hit his stride with *The Parson's Widow* >**1**, a moving, often bizarre comedy, about a young parson inheriting both his predecessor's living and his elderly widow to the dismay of himself and his fiancée. An almost farcical tale of frustrated young love, the film also anticipates Dreyer's future concerns: the old woman is in fact no harridan, but finally comes to happily sacrifice her own life in order that the couple's passion might be as fruitful as her own memories.

Similarly charming, *Mikael* and *Master of the House* focussed on love's pitfalls and pleasures with increasing assurance. It was, however, the French-produced *The Passion of Joan of Arc* >**2** that brought Dreyer to the attention of the international film world. An intense, profoundly moving account of the saint's suffering during the last hours of her life, the film deploys disjointed editing, luminous images and sweeping, virtuoso camera movements in an almost abstract contemplation of the conflict between good and evil. Yet for all its elevated spirituality and avant-garde technique, Dreyer's Joan remains a living, breathing country girl throughout; in a symphony of rapturous close-ups, the actress Falconetti reveals the entire range of human emotions.

Still more experimental was *Vampyr* >**3**, arguably the greatest of films about the supernatural. The narrative is elliptical and fragmented, even illogical; point of view is continually shifting or confounded; reality and fantasy, the normal and the extraordinary are barely differentiated as the hero is led into an increasingly dreamlike world of sinister, inexplicable forces. Its washed-out, misty images (like Joan, shot by Rudolph Mate) are unforgettable: the hero seeing his own premature burial through the glass window of a coffin; a doctor suffocating in a mountain of flour; an old man with a scythe waiting silently, like Death, for a ferry.

Too subtly inventive for a public enthralled by *Dracula* and *Frankenstein*, *Vampyr* was a commercial failure, and over the next 32 years Dreyer completed only four more features. Made after a gap of 11 years, his next, *Day of Wrath* >**4**, is stylistically far more conventional, its stately, linear narrative proceeding in images evocative of 17th-century painting. Thematically, however, it continues Dreyer's fascination with evil, the

The face of Falconetti in Dreyer's *The Passion of Joan of Arc.*

supernatural and passion, with an ageing parson's young wife hounded as a witch when an affair with her stepson leads to her husband's death. Again, in *Ordet* (*The Word*) >**5**, made after *Two People* in which Dreyer lost interest very early, the thin line between the power of love and seemingly divine (or diabolical) activity is investigated when a religious visionary, considered insane by family and villagers, performs the miracle of bringing back to life a sister-in-law who died in childbirth. But although the film concerns diverse crises of faith, it never degenerates into theological obscurity or speculation; as always, it was the variegated topography of the human soul that Dreyer wished to explore.

Ordet displayed Dreyer's return to a more radically formal style of film-making, the camera prowling stark grey interiors and moonlit pastures in long, elegant takes. But his final film, *Gertrud* >**6** (its two hours' duration consisting of only 89, largely interior, shots) proved too slow and static for many. Its Paris premiere was greeted with derisory howls of outrage; even today, when seen, it divides audiences. The portrait of an intellectually independent middle-aged woman who abandons husband and lovers to live alone in Paris, it concerns the desire (in her case unrequited) for love. Like, however, Joan, the parson's wife and the young women in *Day of Wrath* and *Ordet*, Gertrud is no mere victim; nourished by her memories and faith in love's power, she is confident, to the end, of the integrity of her own feelings.

After *Gertrud*, Dreyer spent the last four years of his life planning works on the life of Christ and Medea, further martyrs to passion; the films were never made, but the projects emphasise his continuing gravity, ambition and humanity even unto death. He was one of cinema's greatest directors; few others have rivalled his ability to imply, through a spare, ascetic style, the quality, or indeed the very existence, of the human soul, in a medium as fundamentally materialist and concerned with surfaces as film.

Lineage

The young Dreyer may be compared with Sjöström and Mauritz Stiller. Griffith, too, was an influence. His concerns and style are perhaps most clearly reflected in the films of **Bergman**, while **Paul Schrader** has traced parallels with **Bresson** and **Ozu**. **Godard** paid tribute to Dreyer's Joan in *Vivre Sa Vie*, while *Gertrud* compares interestingly with **Fassbinder**'s *Effi Briest*.

Further reading

Tom Milne's *The Cinema of Carl Dreyer* (London, 1971), Mark Nash's *Dreyer* (London, 1977), Schrader's *Transcendental Style in Film* (Los Angeles, 1972). *Dreyer in Double Reflection* (New York, 1973) features Dreyer's own writing on film.

Viewing

1 **The Parson's Widow**
Sweden 1920/ w Hildur Carlberg, Einar Rod, Greta Almroth

2 **The Passion of Joan of Arc**
France 1927/ w Falconetti, Michel Simon, Antonin Artaud

3 **Vampyr**
Germany 1932/ w Julian West, Sybille Schmitz, Rena Mandel

4 **Day of Wrath**
Denmark 1943/ w Thorkild Roose, Lisbeth Movin, Sigrid Neiiendam

5 **Ordet (The Word)**
Denmark 1954/ w Henrik Malberg, Birgitte Federspiel, Preben Lerdorff Rye

6 **Gertrud**
Denmark 1964/ w Nina Pens Rode, Bendt Rothe, Ebbe Rode

Allan Dwan

Born: 3rd April 1885/Toronto, Canada
Died: 21st December 1981/ Woodland Hills, California, USA
Directing career: 1911-1961

Widely acknowledged as one of the great movie pioneers, Allan (born Joseph Aloysius) Dwan has been called 'the last of the journeyman film-makers'. How far this perhaps less than enthusiastic verdict is true remains unclear, since of the 400 or more films he appears to have directed (not to mention the other 1,400 he claimed to have produced, written or cut), only a fraction remains extant. Admittedly, most of these were one or two-reel silents, made at the rate of two a week, but even later his output was prolific.

Dwan's entry into the film world, in 1909, came through his expertise in lighting. Soon he was writing stories to be turned into films; by 1911 he was directing. At first his work was fast, furious and routine, but he soon became known for his technical innovations: some hold that he invented the dolly shot in 1915; certainly he advised **Griffith** on mounting a moving camera to film the giant Babylonian set in *Intolerance*. By the early '20s he was promoted to making prestigious star vehicles. These included a group of comedies with Gloria Swanson (*Zaza*, *Manhandled*) and several lusty romps with Douglas Fairbanks. *Robin Hood* >**1**, besides being memorable for its massive sets, displays great narrative flair and a visual clarity that emphasises Fairbanks' apparently effortless athletic grace.

Dwan's transition to sound seems to have been painless; even so, on signing a long-term contract with Fox, he was relegated to B-features, highlights of the late '30s being two Shirley Temple vehicles, *Heidi* and *Rebecca of Sunnybrook Farm*. In the early '40s however, he left Fox to make four lively, intelligent comedies of which *Brewster's Millions* >**2** is especially charming, with Dennis O'Keefe forced to perform the almost impossible task of spending a million dollars in order to retain an even larger inheritance. Two years later, *Driftwood* >**3** made excellent use of child actress Natalie Wood as a war orphan experiencing death, dishonesty and neglect. Peppered with unusually pertinent biblical references as it follows the girl's troubled wanderings through the wilderness of smalltown America, the film is surprisingly unsentimental in its portrait of adult thoughtlessness, and stands alongside **Wise**'s *Curse of the Cat People* as one of the finest films about childhood.

The greatest success of Dwan's sound career came with *Sands of*

Iwo Jima >**4**, a rousing John Wayne war movie that embellished its patriotic message with a careful mixture of documentary and fiction footage. Rather more satisfying, however, was a group of Westerns made during the early '50s. *Silver Lode* >**5** is a taut and claustrophobic parable with an innocent John Payne hounded by Dan Duryea's charges of murder until he becomes prey to a town lynch mob; its intriguing flashbacks and expert action sequences never conceal the fact that it is Hollywood's most explicit attack on McCarthyism. Conversely, *Cattle Queen of Montana* >**6**, with Barbara Stanwyck protecting her murdered father's property from a greedy cattle baron, is a lyrical evocation of lost American innocence, symbolised by magnificent, sumptuously shot mountain scenery.

Dwan's final work lacks the Westerns' assurance and economy. *Enchanted Island* was an exotic but sluggish romance that betrayed its source in Melville's *Typee*, *The Most Dangerous Man Alive* a ludicrously low-budgeted sci-fi thriller with a vengeful convict turning into a man of steel after being exposed to a cobalt bomb explosion. A sad end to the career of a director admired for his no-nonsense narrative skills; but nothing could diminish the fact that he had survived so long in Hollywood's lower reaches without abandoning his sheer, unadulterated love of simply making movies.

Lineage

Dwan admitted to Griffith's influence. As a no-frills director of low-budget fare, his influence is hard to discern, but his early movie-making experiences inspired **Bogdanovich**'s *Nickelodeon*, and **Wenders**' *The State of Things* interestingly portrayed a film-crew attempting a remake of *The Most Dangerous Man Alive*.

Further reading

Peter Bogdanovich's *Allan Dwan: The Last Pioneer* (New York, 1971) is a book-length interview.

Viewing

1 **Robin Hood**
US 1922/ w Douglas Fairbanks, Wallace Beery, Enid Bennett

2 **Brewster's Millions**
US 1945/ w Dennis O'Keefe, Helen Walker, June Havoc

3 **Driftwood**
US 1947/ w Natalie Wood, Walter Brennan, Dean Jagger

4 **Sands of Iwo Jima**
US 1949/ w John Wayne, John Agar, Forrest Tucker

5 **Silver Lode**
US 1954/ w Dan Duryea, John Payne, Lizabeth Scott

6 **Cattle Queen of Montana**
US 1954/Barbara Stanwyck, Ronald Reagan, Gene Evans

Clint Eastwood

Born: **31st May 1930/San Francisco, California, USA**
Directing career: 1971-

For many years, Clinton Eastwood Jr has been one of the world's most popular box-office stars. He has also, however, established himself as a talented, if erratic, director, alternating between ambitious, seemingly personal projects and safer commercial fare.

Eastwood first came to fame as Rowdy Yates in TV's Western series *Rawhide*; his image as a tough, cool, laconic loner derives from his work in **Leone**'s 'Dollars' Westerns, while for **Siegel** his cops (*Coogan's Bluff*, *Dirty Harry*) and Western heroes (*Two Mules for Sister Sara*, *The Beguiled*) are troubled, respectively, by red tape and devious women. He was eager to direct, however, and his first two movies were made in the style of Siegel and Leone. Far subtler and less misogynist than the later *Fatal Attraction*, *Play Misty for Me* >**1** explores male paranoia as a radio DJ's one-night-stand pushes a pathologically jealous woman to pursue a murderous revenge, while *High Plains Drifter* is a stylish, baroque Western allegory about guilt: a reincarnated marshal returns to have the town that betrayed him painted red and renamed Hell before taking revenge on his killers and the cowardly, hypocritical townsfolk.

Breezy (in which he did not act) was totally unexpected: a sensitive, touching romance between a young hippy and a cynical middle-aged property developer. Indeed, while continuing to act in more conventional roles for others, in his own films Eastwood exposed his persona's more vulnerable aspects. After the routine spy-thriller *The Eiger Sanction*, *The Outlaw Josey Wales* >**2** – one of the great modern Westerns – saw a renegade Southern raider put aside the hatred he feels for his enemies and, acknowledging his need for others, begin a new life with a 'family' of misfits and outcasts. Eastwood's 'minimal' acting style was here balanced by admirably expressive direction; the lyrical landscape photography is psychologically evocative, the undermining of his character's heroism witty, the story's sweep both epic and moving. Next, *The Gauntlet* mocked the intelligence and moral fibre of Eastwood's cop persona, stressing the plot's fantasy elements, and turning the hero into an alcoholic puzzled by a fast-thinking hooker who repeatedly questions his virility. Even more ambitious was *Bronco Billy* >**3**, in which a failed shoe salesman takes to the road with a tatty Wild West show to live out his fantasies of the pioneering life. A gently comic jibe at the American Dream, the film's affectionate satire culminated in the replacement of his show's destroyed circus tent with a marquee – made out of American flags and sewn together by the inmates of an institution for the insane.

Since neither *Bronco Billy* nor *Honky Tonk Man* – a downbeat road-movie about a Country singer dying from consumption during the Depression – was very successful at the box-office, Eastwood cautiously reverted to more conventional heroics in *Firefox* and *Sudden Impact* (the most objectionable of the *Dirty Harry* films). He did, however, imprint his signature on both *Tightrope* (a cop hunting a sex-killer comes to confront his own insecure, sadistic masculinity) and *City Heat* (an engagingly absurd parody of crime movies), neither of which he directed. *Pale Rider*, a cheap, old-fashioned but stylish horse-opera in the *Shane* tradition, flew in the face of post-*Heaven's Gate* Hollywood's distrust of Westerns. *Heartbreak Ridge* countered an otherwise gung-ho account of marine training with a wry awareness of recent American defeats and widespread military ineptitude, and a climax that made the US invasion of Grenada look ludicrously like a boy-scouts' skirmish.

Before the disappointing *The Dead Pool*, Eastwood's willingness to take risks surfaced again in *Bird* >**4**, a supremely sensitive, unusually bleak account of the last debilitated, drug-dependent years of Charlie Parker. Arguably, this is not only the most authentic, least romanticised evocation of the jazz world ever seen in fiction films, but an unusually dignified, non-stereotypical depiction of blacks. Indeed, the variety Eastwood's audacity brings to his work is perhaps the most attractive aspect of his art: defined by an assured sense of pace, the uncluttered, stylish camerawork of regular collaborator Bruce Surtees, and his own effectively understated performances, Eastwood's best films remain fine examples of well-crafted, intelligent popular entertainment.

Lineage

While Eastwood's debt to Siegel is clear, he belongs to an action movie tradition that includes **Walsh**, **Mann**, **Boetticher** and **Hawks**. His success as an actor-turned-director may have led figures as diverse as Robert Redford and Sylvester Stallone to follow suit.

Further reading

David Downing and Gary Herman's *Clint Eastwood: All-American Anti-Hero* (London, 1977).

Viewing

1 **Play Misty for Me**
US 1971/ w Eastwood, Jessica Walter, John Larch, Donna Mills

2 **The Outlaw Josey Wales**
US 1976/ w Eastwood, Chief Dan George, John Vernon, Sondra Locke

3 **Bronco Billy**
US 1980/ w Eastwood, Sondra Locke, Geoffrey Lewis, Sam Bottoms

4 **Bird**
US 1988/ w Forest Whitaker, Diane Venora, Michael Zemiker

Blake Edwards

Born: 26th July 1922/Tulsa, Oklahoma, USA
Directing career: 1955-

Despite an abiding talent for imaginatively controlled slapstick, it seems as if William Blake McEdwards has in recent years lost the ability to tell a good story or create genuinely sympathetic characters. While his output is still prolific, his films' slick stylistic polish cannot conceal a basic dearth of invention.

A former actor, Edwards wrote several scripts for Richard Quine before turning to directing with a number of comedies and musicals. His first film of note, *Mister Corey*, a witty satire about a lowly young hustler breaking into society, was followed by *Operation Petticoat*, a cynical con-man comedy set on board a World War II submarine. With fine performances by Tony Curtis, these films, together with a bowdlerised version of Truman Capote's *Breakfast at Tiffany's*, established Edwards as a promising comic talent; meanwhile *Experiment in Terror* (a woman-in-peril thriller notable for its imaginative use of San Francisco locations) and a bleak, moving examination of alcoholism in *Days of Wine and Roses* revealed his abilities with serious drama. But it was *The Pink Panther* >**1** that transformed him into a major force. With Peter Sellers' bumbling French detective, Clouseau, continually prey to pratfalls, the elegant photography revealing a world of ludicrous sophistication, and characters knowingly derived from traditional stereotypes, the film's success as glossy, mindless entertainment was assured; indeed, numerous, increasingly routine sequels would bolster Edwards' flagging career during the doldrums of the '70s.

Though more ambitious and expensive, Edwards' ensuing films saw an almost immediate decline: *The Great Race*, only patchily funny, suffered from a sprawling plot and an hysterical cast; *The Party*, displaying the director's ability to create escalating disaster, sadly indulged Sellers' blackface performance as a clumsy Indian; *Darling Lili* was a disastrously extravagant period spy thriller-cum-musical romance. Surprisingly, Edwards' finest film in years was *The Wild Rovers* >**2**, an elegaic, semi-comic Western which pits two essentially harmless bank robbers against a violent society. Largely deprived of studio artifice and slapstick, Edwards was forced to rely on character, and William Holden and Ryan O'Neal as the ageing cowpoke and his young sidekick – doomed by their naïve desire to amount to something – responded magnificently.

Thereafter, Edwards found himself increasingly at odds with the Hollywood studios; flops were balanced by cynical rehashes of the *Pink Panther* series. Not until *10* >**3** did the writer-director find success without Clouseau; and that gave rise to a formula group of comedies depicting male sexual frustration. *10* itself concerns the problems faced by menopausal Dudley Moore when he momentarily betrays his wife for the vacuous girl of his dreams; likewise, *The Man Who Loved Women*, *Micki + Maude* and *That's Life!* portray male neuroses about age, fidelity and sexual potency, but ignore, for the most part, the emotions of wives and lovers. If their aimless plots can be said to be 'about' anything, many of Edwards' recent satires exude self-pity, none more so than *SOB*, a bilious attack on philistine Hollywood that substitutes vulgarity for wit. Only *Victor/Victoria* >**4**, elegantly mixing music, farce and sexual role-playing as a penniless singer (played by Edwards' wife Julie Andrews) takes to drag and becomes the toast of Paris as a supposed female impersonator, suggested that Edwards cared about anything other than his films' varnished visual surface.

It is sad that a director of Edwards' once evident talents should resort increasingly to stale, hackneyed, even offensive material. His recent work, however, offers ample proof that a sardonic tone, a clever compositional sense, and hectic pace are not sufficient to make moving, original or even successful films.

Lineage

A confessed devotee of Leo McCarey, Edwards may be seen as mining the same darkly comic vein as **Wilder**. His affection for physical comedy – slapstick and sight-gags – links him both to the silent comedians (his recent *A Fine Mess* was a hapless tribute to Laurel and Hardy, *Sunset* to the Westerns of Tom Mix) and to **Tati**.

Viewing

1 **The Pink Panther**
US 1963/ w Peter Sellers, David Niven, Capucine
2 **The Wild Rovers**
US 1971/ w William Holden, Ryan O'Neal, Karl Malden
3 **10**
US 1979/ w Dudley Moore, Julie Andrews, Bo Derek
4 **Victor/Victoria**
US 1982/ w Julie Andrews, Robert Preston, James Garner

Sergei Eisenstein

Born: 23rd January 1898/Riga, Latvia
Died: 11th February 1948/Moscow, USSR
Directing career: 1924-1946

Long regarded as one of the most important film artists the world has known, Sergei Mikhailovich Eisenstein was a giant among film-makers and theorists, his contributions to the cinema defined by his enormous intellect and his commitment to political art. Even so, his influence on the development of mainstream cinema seems ever more negligible with the passing years.

Eisenstein's life, films and thought are inextricably linked with the society in which he lived. As a young man, he seemed set to follow his father in a career as an architectural engineer, but after serving with the Red Army he found work as a scenic artist for the theatre. Studying under Meyerhold, he became increasingly interested in creating a revolutionary form of proletarian drama in which the masses, as opposed to the individual, were the hero. Presently, he found success as an adventurous, iconoclastic stage director, and in 1924 he moved into film with *Strike* >**1**. Already, inspired by the atmosphere of intellectual excitement ignited by the Soviet Revolution, he had worked out his own theory of film, drawn from various sources including Marxist dialectics, Pavlov's ideas about attraction and stimulation, Freud, and Constructivist art. His theory itself centred largely on a quasi-scientific idea of *montage*, according to which a film's meaning would arise, as in a mathematical equation, from the collision of images edited together. In *Strike*, the finale alternates shots of the massacre of striking workers by the Czarist police with documentary shots of a bull's death in an abattoir. The effect, while powerful in making its point, is weakened by the fact that the slaughterhouse is never integrated into the plot. Nevertheless, such contrivance is countered by the dynamism of the film's relentless pace, stark realist images and acerbic caricatures of the bourgeoisie; *Strike* is both rousing propaganda (Eisenstein's *kino-fist* serving as a riposte to **Vertov**'s objective *kino-eye*) and his finest film.

He next turned his attention, in *Battleship Potemkin* >**2**, to a re-creation of a Russian naval crew's 1905 mutiny against appalling conditions. Most famous for the 'Odessa Steps' sequence, in which innocent civilians are brutally mown down by the Czarist militia, the film offers evidence both of Eisenstein's continuing experiments with montage and of his interest in *typage*, according to which characters were represented not by professional actors but by amateurs, whose physical appearance he deemed appropriate to the archetype (rather than stereotype) they were playing. The film was a huge international success, and Eisenstein developed his art along similar lines in both *October* >**3**, an account of the 1917 revolution marked by an epic reconstruction of the storming of the Winter Palace, and *The General Line* (*The Old and the New*) >**4**, which deals with a peasant woman's struggles to establish a collective farm in her village. The theoretical underpinnings to each film, however, made them increasingly academic: in *October montage* effects, likening Kerensky to both Napoleon and a peacock to signify pride and vanity, are often simple-minded, while *The General Line* finds Eisenstein seemingly more interested in the glistening and virtually abstract visual qualities of agricultural machinery in motion, than in the people operating it.

In 1929 Eisenstein travelled to Europe and America where his plans to film Dreiser's *An American Tragedy* for Paramount never progressed beyond the script stage. Another project, entitled *Que Viva Mexico!*, remained unfinished, Upton Sinclair withdrawing his financial support and cancelling production. Dejected, Eisenstein returned home, only to experience further disappointments such as the abandonment of the production of his first sound film (*Bezhin Meadow*, based on a story by Turgenev) under the Stalinist regime. Only in 1938, 10 years after *October*, did he finally make another feature. But *Alexander Nevsky* >**5** saw a distinct change in his style. An historical epic serving as an allegory of Nazi aggression and Soviet heroism, it deployed professional actors, Prokofiev's music, significantly less 'intellectual' *montage* and a more conventional visual style. It was also largely dull, though a scene featuring Nevsky's battle against the invading Teutonic Knights on an ice-floe captured the world's imagination.

Eisenstein's final film, the two-part *Ivan the Terrible* >**6**, saw him move even farther away from his original methods. A slow, baroque account of the tyrant's long battle against betrayal and intrigue, its tone is ambiguous. While it may certainly be viewed as a comment on Stalin, are we to applaud his aim to unite Russia against enemies without and within, or to deplore the bloody means undertaken to achieve that end? Whichever, montage has given way to ornate pictorialism, and naturalistic typage is superseded by

An appropriately intense portrait of Sergei Eisenstein.

eye-rolling performances and operatically mannerised, even camp, postures; nevertheless, the monumental sets and a banquet scene which, for the only time in the director's career, explodes into garish colour with a Cossacks' dance, retain their fascination.

A third episode of *Ivan* was planned, but only a few scenes ever filmed; indeed, the second part was shelved by Stalin and released only 10 years after the director's death. Eisenstein's achievements are impressive and ambitious, but finally limited: as he discovered in his later years, *montage*, though interesting in theory, was too cerebral and repetitive a method in practice, while, for all the Revolution's initial devotion to the people, his films too often emerge as cold, soulless propaganda.

Lineage

A formidable intellectual, Eisenstein was influenced by all areas of human experience: cinematically, **Griffith**, Lev Kuleshov and **Dziga Vertov**. He also admired **Von Sternberg**, who took over *An American Tragedy*, and **Disney**. He influenced many Soviet Revolutionary film makers, notably Vsevolod Pudovkin, though **Dovzhenko's** poeticism now seems more attractive. The political/aesthetic ramifications of *montage* were taken up by certain members of the '60s Leftist avant-garde, **Godard** included; **Woody Allen** paid tribute in *Love and Death*, and **De Palma** plagiarised *Potemkin* in *The Untouchables*.

Further reading

Yon Barna's *Eisenstein* (London, 1973), Peter Wollen's *Signs and Meaning in the Cinema* (London, 1969); Eisenstein's writings can be found in *The Film Sense* (New York, 1942), *Film Form* (New York, 1949), *Film Essays* (London, 1968), and *Notes of a Film Director* (New York, 1970).

Viewing

1 **Strike**
USSR 1924/ w members of the Proletkult Theatre
2 **Battleship Potemkin**
USSR 1925/ w Alexander Antonov, Grigori Alexandrov, Proletkult Theatre
3 **October**
USSR 1928/ w V. Nikandrov, Boris Lipanov, N. Popov
4 **The General Line (The Old and The New)**
USSR 1927-29/ w Marfa Lapkina, Vasya Buzenkov, Kostya Vasiliev
5 **Alexander Nevsky**
USSR 1938/ w Nikolai Cherkassov, Nikolai Okhlopkov, Dmitri Orlov
6 **Ivan the Terrible (Parts 1 & 2)**
USSR 1944-46/ w Nikolai Cherkassov, Serafima Birman, Ludmila Tselikovskaya

John Farrow

Born: 10th February 1904/Sydney, Australia
Died: 28th January 1963/Beverly Hills, California, USA
Directing career: 1937-1959

Though a minor film-maker usually restrained by B-movie budgets, John Villiers Farrow often made stylish, inventive films. In the late '40s and early '50s, few directors depicted evil so subtly.

After a spell at sea, during which he wrote plays and short stories, Farrow arrived in Hollywood in the late '20s; initially an advisor on sea sequences, he soon progressed to scriptwriting. In the late '30s he began directing: both *The Invisible Menace* (a murder mystery set in a claustrophobic, foggy army barracks) and *Five Came Back* >**1** (a tense air-wreck drama with a desperate group of survivors bickering in the jungle, its emphasis on self-sacrifice and redemption anticipating the religious elements of his later films) display his control of atmosphere and his ability to draw fine performances from relatively unknown actors. But it was in the postwar era, after the impressively serious propaganda piece *The Hitler Gang*, that his quirky talent truly flourished.

Two Years Before the Mast was a reasonably authentic account of the intolerable working conditions of 19th-century seamen, *The Night Has a Thousand Eyes* an inventive psychological drama about a clairvoyant. But it was *The Big Clock* >**2** (later rehashed as *No Way Out*) that first established Farrow as a fascinating stylist in the *film noir* vein: **Charles Laughton**'s murderous, power-crazed tycoon is memorably evil, while the labyrinthine skyscraper that is his hellish domain serves as a bleak Expressionist symbol of fate. Still more persuasive as a portrait of corruption was *Alias Nick Beal* >**3**, an update of the Faust story that mixed political intrigue and hints of the supernatural in a witty *noir* framework; as it traces an honest politician's descent into corruption after selling his soul to a local 'fixer', Milland's dapper, diabolical gangster is never actually shown entering a scene: he is simply, suddenly *there*, discovered by the camera standing in the shadows. The director's fascination with evil, corruption, redemption and guilt perhaps derived from his devout Catholicism (besides novels he also wrote books on Thomas More and the Papacy); unusually, a number of his films include scenes involving prayer.

Where Danger Lives was a rather more conventional picture of temptation, with an innocent young doctor drawn into a fatal web of deceit and murder by a psychotic *femme fatale*, but *His Kind of Woman* >**4** was Farrow's most enjoyably bizarre film. Starting as a complex thriller (gambler Robert Mitchum involved with exiled US hoodlums down Mexico way), its harsh visuals, brutal violence and terse dialogue are increasingly intercut with hilarious, lunatic comedy, spoofing its own plot: while Mitchum is tortured aboard a yacht, Vincent Price – magnificently typecast as a ham actor – assembles a risibly incompetent posse and sallies forth spouting cod-Shakespearean dialogue. Such semi-improvised spontaneity, however, was replaced by taut plotting, solid characterisation and visual elegance in *Ride, Vaquero!* and *Hondo* (both superior Westerns), and *Back from Eternity* (a remake of *Five Came Back*).

Farrow's talent has been sadly overshadowed by the fact that he was Maureen O'Sullivan's husband and Mia Farrow's father. His films reveal a dark wit, an ability to create genuinely sinister moods and a readiness to experiment with genre often lacking in better known directors. His inventiveness deserves reappraisal.

Lineage

Farrow, like **Siodmak**, was most at home with *film noir*, though his versatility allowed him to work effectively in various genres. He may perhaps be compared with other minor, underrated figures like **John Brahm**, **Joseph H. Lewis**, **Jacques Tourneur**, and **Ida Lupino**.

Viewing

1 **Five Came Back**
US 1939/ w Lucille Ball, C. Aubrey Smith, Joseph Calleia

2 **The Big Clock**
US 1948/ w Charles Laughton, Ray Milland, Maureen O'Sullivan

3 **Alias Nick Beal**
US 1949/ w Ray Milland, Thomas Mitchell, Audrey Totter

4 **His Kind of Woman**
US 1951/ w Robert Mitchum, Jane Russell, Raymond Burr

Rainer Werner Fassbinder

Born: 31st May 1946/Bad Worishofen, W. Germany
Died: 10th June 1982/Munich, W. Germany
Directing career: 1965-1982

One of the finest directors working in the '70s, Rainer Werner Fassbinder ranged widely through genre and style, but consistent through his prolific career (he made over 40 films in 13 years) was an ironic approach towards often melodramatic subjects, and an abiding interest in the despair underlying the material affluence and bourgeois moral conformism of postwar German society.

After a lonely childhood which frequently drove him to the cinema, Fassbinder became deeply involved as an actor-director in Munich's fringe theatre where he met several of his future actors including Hanna Schygulla, Kurt Raab and Irm Hermann. Having made two shorts in 1965, he concentrated on work with his Anti-theatre group until his feature debut in 1969. As director, writer, actor and editor, he rapidly built up a body of films notable for their stark portrayal of the banality and cruelty of contemporary life, and for their rejection of traditional film style. *Katzelmacher* >**1** analyses everyday fascism through the experiences of a Greek immigrant worker whose mere presence provokes a group of bored middle-class couples to xenophobic envy, paranoia and violence; Fassbinder strips the story of drama, using long static takes of inexpressive characters intoning uninflected dialogue. A similar anti-style, stressing mood and social groupings, imbued most of his early films, from darkly comic gangster movies (*Gods of the Plague*, *The American Soldier*) through a bleak portrait of film-making (*Beware of a Holy Whore*) to the relatively realist *Why Does Herr R Run Amok?* >**2**, in which the casual humiliations and tedium of family life drive a seemingly happy, successful office worker to slaughter his neighbour, wife and son before hanging himself.

The Merchant of Four Seasons >**3** was warmer and more polished, though its account of the way in which a quiet fruit seller comes to feel increasingly irrelevant to his family, friends and former lover is equally bleak: the scene in which he drinks himself to death is observed sympathetically but unsentimentally. More and more, however, Fassbinder, inspired by American cinema's ability to reach a wide audience, turned to an increasingly stylised form of direction, adding to the flat pacing and performances a highly expressive use of decor, colour, lighting, and camera movements. The sado-masochistic power games defining the relationship of a lesbian fashion-designer, her lover and maid, in *The Bitter Tears of Petra Von Kant* take place in a sumptuously decadent apartment intended to inspire erotic pleasure; in *Fear Eats the Soul* >**4**, in which racism threatens the love of an elderly widow for a young, Arab guest-worker, gaudy primary colours are reminiscent of **Sirk** (whose *All That Heaven Allows* inspired the film); and *Effi Briest* >**5**, its monochrome images depicting a young girl's stale marriage to an old baron, explicitly alludes to Fontane's original 19th-century text, thus examining the relationship of film to words.

If *Petra Von Kant* provoked charges of misogyny, the portrait of male homosexual society in *Fox* proved that Fassbinder believed exploitation, prejudice, greed, and thoughtless cruelty to be the inevitable concomitants of any human relationship. He was himself bisexual, and many films reflect the constant tensions within his incestuous 'family' of collaborators, lovers and friends. Indeed, the enclosed group regularly served as a microcosm of society's failings: *Satan's Brew*, a relentless black comedy about artistic charlatanism, sees a failed writer move a coterie of gay admirers in with his obscene family to furnish an audience for readings of his poetry; *Chinese Roulette* >**6** assembles a wealthy couple, their lovers, their neglected crippled child and her nurse for a deadly truth game in which the players guess what others might have been in the Nazi era. The film's dazzling, complex visual sheen (with characters' reflections in glass caught by an endlessly circling camera) and its anxiety over the memory of Germany's fascist past proved to be the distinguishing marks of Fassbinder's last years.

After *Despair* >**7**, a riveting English-language version of Nabokov's novel in which a '30s Berliner kills a tramp he wrongly believes is his double, Fassbinder alternated a number of deeply personal projects – the account of the last days of a transsexual in *In a Year with 13 Moons* was his emotive response to a lover's recent suicide, *The Third Generation* an idiosyncratic analysis of contemporary German terrorism – with more commercial works that portrayed Germany's postwar 'economic miracle' in terms of sexual politics. *The Marriage of Maria Braun* >**8** has its upwardly mobile heroine sacrifice her body to men (an American GI, a rich German industrialist) in return for the money that will allow her to set up home with her husband; in *Lola* >**9** (a lavish Sirkian reworking of **Von Sternberg**'s *The Blue Angel*), a prostitute seduces corrupt city officials to gain power; in *Veronika Voss*, a has-been Third Reich film star slides into drug-addiction and despair. Here, and in *Lili Marleen* and *Querelle* – respectively a parodic wartime spy romance and a baroque studio version of Genet's play about sado-masochistic sailors – a garish anti-naturalistic style holds sway. For all the dense, complex, colourful fabric of verbose dialogue, movie references and glowing visuals, the moral remains constant: in an emotionally impoverished world marked by material greed and repressive bourgeois concepts of respectability, love is doomed.

Fassbinder's tragic death from a drink and drugs overdose robbed cinema (and television) of a brilliant artist. Though his methods were often provocative, his continuing insistence on the fragility of happiness, freedom and love in the face of political and economic, physical and psychological

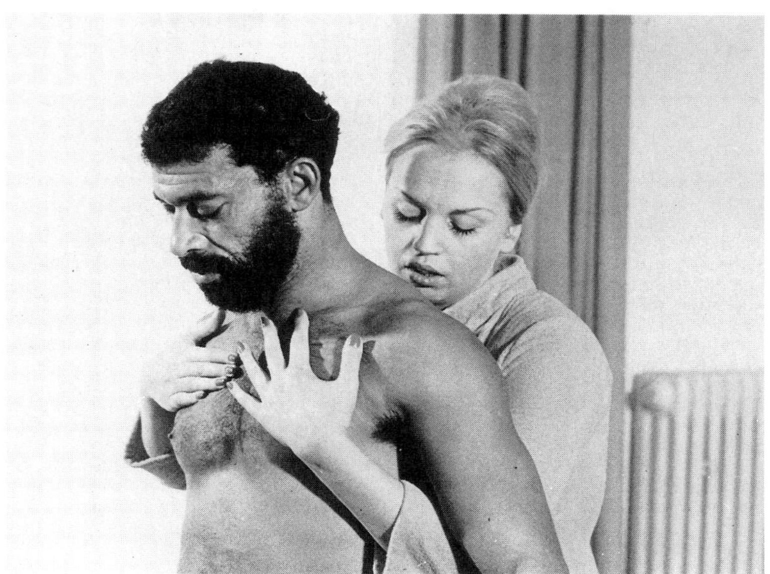

exploitation, identifies him as an unsentimentally pessimistic film-maker of great humanity. His hatred of spiritual and artistic complacency is evident both from his subjects and from the originality of his style; he set out neither to emulate not to challenge Hollywood, but to better it.

Lineage

Fassbinder's early works show the influence of Jean-Marie Straub, **Godard**, **Warhol** and Brecht, the more commercial later films that of Hollywood melodramatists like Sirk and **Wilder**. He confessed to an admiration for **Walsh**, **Rohmer** and **Chabrol**, and exerted a strong influence not only on all who worked with him but on other German directors, notably Edgar Reitz whose epic TV series *Heimat* is not a little reminiscent of Fassbinder's later work in both media.

Further reading

Fassbinder ed. Tony Rayns (London 1980); Ronald Hayman's *Fassbinder: Film Maker* (London 1984).

El Hedi Ben Salem and Barbara Valentin in *Fear Eats the Soul*, Fassbinder's loose 'remake' of Sirk's *All That Heaven Allows*.

Viewing

1 **Katzelmacher**
W. Ger 1969/ w Fassbinder, Hanna Schygulla, Harry Baer

2 **Why Does Herr R Run Amok?**
W. Ger 1969/ w Kurt Raab, Lilith Ungerer, Amadeus Fengler

3 **The Merchant of Four Seasons**
W. Ger 1971/ w Hans Hirschmuller, Irm Hermann, Hanna Schygulla

4 **Fear Eats the Soul**
W. Ger 1973/ w Brigitte Mira, El Hedi Ben Salem, Barbara Valentin

5 **Effi Briest**
W. Ger 1974/ w Hanna Schygulla, Wolfgang Schenck, Karlheinz Boehm

6 **Chinese Roulette**
W. Ger 1976/ w Margit Carstensen, Alexander Allerson, Anna Karina

7 **Despair (Eine Reise ins Licht)**
W. Ger 1977/ w Dirk Bogarde, Andrea Ferreol, Volker Spengler

8 **The Marriage of Maria Braun**
W. Ger 1978/ w Hanna Schygulla, Klaus Lowitsch, Ivan Desny

9 **Lola**
W. Ger 1981/ w Barbara Sukowa, Armin Mueller-Stahl, Mario Adorf

Federico Fellini

Born: 20th January 1920/Rimini, Italy
Directing career: 1950-

Long considered a major film-maker, Federico Fellini established his reputation through an insistence on the interest-value of his own fantastic and idiosyncratic vision of the world. In so doing, however, he repeatedly lays himself open to charges of egomania, self-indulgence and superficiality; certainly much of his work, if visually extraordinary, is hyperbolic, naive and incoherent.

After working as a comic-strip artist and a writer for radio, Fellini entered the movies by writing for various directors, most notably **Rossellini** for whom he co-scripted *Rome – Open City*, *Paisa* and 'The Miracle' sketch in *L'Amore*, in which he acted. He collaborated regularly with Alberto Lattuada, with whom he co-directed *Lights of Variety*, a gentle satire on the pretensions of a lowly touring theatrical troupe, notable for lively ensemble acting, a virtuoso party scene and a bleak evocation of the following dawn. His solo debut, *The White Sheik* >**1**, was a charming romantic comedy about a woman trapped in a boring marriage and ludicrously infatuated by the arrogant hero of a photo-strip adventure; a witty examination of the relationship between fiction and reality, it benefits from moody location work (windswept beaches, dark, lonely streets) and from Fellini's love-hate memories of the world of the *fumetti*. By now his position *vis-à-vis* neo-realism was already tangential: in both *I Vitelloni* >**2** (about five smalltown layabouts, only one of whom manages to fulfil his dream of leaving home) and *La Strada* >**3** (a trite and sentimental story of the relationship between a childishly naive waif, played by Fellini's wife Giulietta Masina, and her brutish strong-man boss), location work showing the seedy banality of everyday life is balanced by themes soon to become characteristic: the search for a moral identity, and the conflict between coarse, sexual physicality and a more cerebral innocence.

Il Bidone and *Nights of Cabiria* offered more of the same; in the first, a con-man comes to see the error of his ways when the colleagues he has betrayed beat him up; in the second, Masina is a tart-with-a-heart-of-gold whose childlike innocence renders her immune to cruel reality. But it was *La Dolce Vita* >**4** that brought Fellini international acclaim; a sprawling epic satire on what he considered the spiritual malaise of modern society, it followed a journalist employed by a scandal magazine around a Rome obsessed with orgiastic parties, voluptuous film stars and the commercial marketing of religion. While its images are flamboyant – a statue of Christ flying above the city suspended from a helicopter, Anita Ekberg dancing in the Trevi fountain, a kitten on her head - the film's despairing tone often rings hollow, even though Marcello Mastroianni's compulsive womaniser, never glamorised, fails to achieve redemption.

Mastroianni appeared again, as Fellini's alter-ego, in what is widely considered his masterpiece, *8½* >**5**. About a director lionised as a major artist but unable to complete a new film due to creative confusion and personal crisis, it is a voyage into an explicitly autobiographical world; its deeply personal symbolism, its gallery of grotesques and its blurring of reality and fantasy confirm Fellini's rejection of his neo-realist origins and anticipate the increasingly indulgent, sledge-hammer assertion of his own dubiously poetic way of presenting the world. *Juliet of the Spirits* was a tedious, overblown account of a woman virtually destroyed by a failing marriage and the ghosts of her conscience, couched in gaudily fantastic visuals; *Fellini Satyricon* a morbid, muddled portrait of sexual decadence in ancient Rome notable only for a handful of set-pieces involving extravagant, mythic imagery (a fight with a Minotaur, an anaemic hermaphrodite, a collapsing tenement) and for its homo-eroticism; *The Clowns* a vacuous essay on the director's love of the circus as a metaphor for the world and his own artistry; *Fellini*

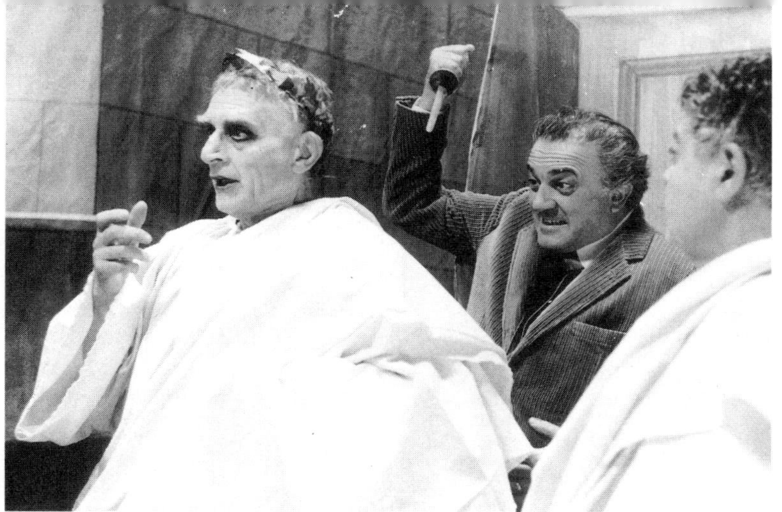

Et tu, Federico? Fellini demonstrates how to assassinate Caesar on the set of *Fellini's Roma.*

Roma a formless ramble around a surreal city existing in the director's imagination; *Amarcord* a nostalgic trip to the small coastal town of his youth, bereft of historical relevance (Mussolini's Fascists are woeful caricatures), and too reliant on vulgar humour, freakish characters and easy sentiment.

Though virtually disowned by the director, the surprisingly sombre *Fellini's Casanova* >**6** was a temporary return to form, its bleakly stylised portrait of the famous womaniser allowing for a quietly effective, self-reflexive meditation on impotence, love, failure and ageing; the lover, his powers spent, finds solace at last with a clockwork doll. Thereafter, however, Fellini focussed increasingly on bland, half-baked allegories. *Orchestra Rehearsal* attempted to comment on the directionless anarchy of contemporary Italy; *City of Women* (Mastroianni again serving as the director's alter-ego) countered charges of misogyny with a fantasy about a middle-aged man's confrontation with militant feminists; *And The Ship Sails On* peopled an ocean liner with complacent opera stars gathered for the funeral of a diva on the eve of World War I, their lives forever changed by a boatful of Serbian refugees; and *Ginger & Fred* >**7**, with Mastroianni and Masina as former dance-partners reunited in old age for a last grasp at fame in front of the television cameras, served as a satire on the small-screen's tendency towards transience, trivia, and advertising. Artifice is uppermost in these films: glitzy studio-sets lovingly exaggerate the tacky excesses of Italian culture, while the Maestro makes us continually aware of his enormous, indulgent, controlling presence.

Typically, *Intervista*, a documentary tribute to the fiftieth anniversary of Cinecittà studios, becomes another portrait of the director's own past, complete with clips from *La Dolce Vita* and appearances by Mastroianni and Ekberg. Indeed, Fellini has been described as 'a superlative artist with little to say', while his view of himself as a confused, deeply humane artist beset by a decadent, materialist world finally undercuts any claims to a generous tolerance of human weakness. If he revels in ugliness and folly, that may be because larger-than-life grotesques serve his taste for caricature and make for visually over-ripe fantasy. Certainly his earlier work offers ample evidence of a sharp eye for the absurd and atmospheric; his claims to artistic greatness, however, are severely limited by an insistence on the director's importance and by a weak grasp of character and narrative. One is left, finally, relating in an entirely subjective manner to the power and persuasiveness, or otherwise, of his private fantasies.

Lineage

While neo-realism clearly influenced Fellini's early films, it is likely that his work in comic-strips is just as relevant as **De Sica** and Rossellini. In making himself his own chief subject, he relates distantly to **Cocteau**, **Godard**, **Truffaut** and **Bergman**. His influence is widely acknowledged: **Mazursky** and **Woody Allen** paid tribute to *8½* in their own accounts of creative blockage, *Alex in Wonderland* (in which Fellini appeared), and *Stardust Memories*.

Further Reading

Suzanne Budgen's *Fellini* (London, 1966), Gilbert Sachalas' *Federico Fellini* (New York, 1969); *Fellini on Fellini* (ed. Christian Strich, New York, 1976) is a collection of interviews, and articles by the director.

Viewing

1 **The White Sheik (Lo Sciecco Bianco)**
Italy 1951/ w Alberto Sordi, Brunella Bova, Giulietta Masina
2 **I Vitelloni**
Italy 1953/ w Franco Interlenghi, Franco Fabrizi, Alberto Sordi
3 **La Strada**
Italy 1954/ w Giulietta Masina, Anthony Quinn, Richard Basehart
4 **La Dolce Vita**
Italy 1960/ w Marcello Mastroianni, Anita Ekberg, Anouk Aimée
5 **8½ (Otto e mezzo)**
Italy 1963/ w Marcello Mastroianni, Anouk Aimée, Claudia Cardinale
6 **Fellini's Casanova**
Italy 1976/ w Donald Sutherland, Tina Aumont, Olimpia Carlisi
7 **Ginger & Fred**
Italy 1986/ w Giulietta Masina, Marcello Mastroianni, Franco Fabrizi

Robert Flaherty

Born: 16th February 1884/Iron Mountain, Michigan, USA
Died: 23rd July 1951/Black Mountain, Vermont, USA
Directing career: 1913-1948

It is understandably common to regard Robert John Flaherty as the father of documentary; indeed, it was Flaherty's second film that prompted John Grierson to coin the very term. Yet, while the word is often used to denote an objective film record of an historical reality, Flaherty's work more frequently displayed the subjective vision of a poetic artist working, to some extent, in fiction.

The son of a miner-turned-prospector, Flaherty spent several years exploring the remoter reaches of Canada, where he developed a fascination with the daily rituals of Eskimo life. As early as 1913, he shot his first footage of the Eskimos, most of which was destroyed in a cutting-room fire. Undeterred, he returned several years later, financed by the Revillon Fur Company and equipped with more sophisticated cameras, to make *Nanook of the North* >**1**.

In recounting the tribulations facing Nanook and his family in their search for food and shelter in the Arctic wastes, Flaherty often deemed it necessary to modify reality. Inevitably, this was partly due to the eternally problematic relationship between the documentarist and his subject: how might human behaviour not be affected by the camera's gaze? Nevertheless, wishing to dramatise Man's conflict with Nature, the director also fell into the trap of transforming Nanook into a Noble Savage. The Eskimo was asked to dress in 'more genuine' costumes or to adopt more picturesque ways of seal-hunting to meet Flaherty's own conception of Truth.

Thanks, however, to Nanook's smiling charm and to Flaherty's own marvellously sharp photography, the film was a huge success; the result was that Paramount commissioned him to visit the South Seas to make another Nanook. Though flawed by the director's lush Romanticism, which envisaged Samoa as a paradise on the verge of extinction, *Moana* >**2** was a lyrically beautiful account of a young Polynesian's initiation into manhood, establishing its maker in the eyes of Hollywood's establishment as a specialist in exotica. He became involved in several abortive projects (including MGM's fictional *White Shadows in the South Seas*, and the collaboration with **Murnau** on *Tabu*) before travelling to Britain, in the early '30s, to make documentaries with Grierson, most notable of which was *Man of Aran* >**3**. A deliberately epic vision of the struggle of the island's handful of families to survive the harsh climate and seas of the North Atlantic, it suffered from the same faults as *Nanook*, with the islanders even being asked to hunt the basking shark in rough seas they would usually avoid – a form of fishing they had not, in fact, practised for some fifty years. Again, the film's abiding virtues were pictorial and emotional rather than anthropological, and the politically-minded Grierson was less than happy with Flaherty's total neglect of economic realities.

It is perhaps unsurprising then that much of his later work was even more closely bound to fiction. For Alexander Korda, he oversaw the exterior scenes of *Elephant Boy*, while the producer's brother Zoltan, directed the more narrative interior sequences. If *The Land* >**4** was an attempt to deal with more contemporary subject matter, its study of the many problems faced by America's migrant farmers was as resolutely apolitical as ever. Finally, *Louisiana Story* >**5**, financed by Standard Oil, featured real people acting out a fictional story designed partly to show the quality of life in the beauty of the bayous, partly to celebrate Man's ability to embrace the arrival of the oil derricks (surprisingly depicted as benign) with magnanimity. Again, while visually extraordinary, in terms of its theme it seemed to derive as much from Flaherty's inner longings as from the actualities of the outside world.

Whatever the drawbacks of his subjective, highly manipulative approach, Flaherty's importance as an innovator cannot be denied. If it is impossible to trust fully in his observation of cultures previously unseen in the cinema, it is difficult not to be moved by his naively idealistic vision and consummate artistry.

Lineage

While Flaherty's influence is huge, many (most notably Grierson and other British documentarists such as Harry Watt) rejected his apolitical stance, and *cinéma verité* and direct cinema adherents turned against his manipulation of actuality to tell a dramatic story. Given his achievements, one may compare him tenuously with Merian C. Cooper and Ernest B. Schoedsack (makers of *Grass*, *Chang* and *King Kong*), while his modern counterpart would seem to be **Herzog** whose films often function as records of their own making.

Further reading

Arthur Calder-Marshall's *The Innocent Eye: the Life of Robert J. Flaherty* (London, 1963), Richard Griffith's *The World of Robert Flaherty* (New York, 1970).

Viewing

1 **Nanook of the North**
Canada 1922
2 **Moana**
US 1926
3 **Man of Aran**
GB 1934
4 **The Land**
US 1947
5 **Louisiana Story**
US 1948

John Ford

Born: 1st February 1895/Cape Elizabeth, Maine, USA
Died: 13th August 1973/Palm Desert, California, USA
Directing career: 1917-1966

In portraying, throughout a long and prolific career, the history of the United States from the Revolutionary War to World War II, Sean Aloysius O'Feeney (his given name) continually resorted to a deeply personal, nostalgic form of legend. If there is no doubt of his importance to the development of the Western, his uniquely sentimental, poetic glorification of the white American's conquest of the wilderness is both picturesque and reactionary.

The son of Irish parents, Ford joined his Hollywood-director brother Francis in 1914, performing stunts, acting, and assisting figure like **Dwan** and **Griffith** (in whose *The Birth of a Nation* he appears as a Ku Klux Klan rider). In 1917 he began directing with several Westerns, one of which, *Straight Shooting*, about a gunman helping homesteaders in a war against cattlemen, was a five-reel feature. The genre served him well for the next six years, and in 1926 he made one of the finest silent, epic Westerns, *The Iron Horse*, concerning the race to complete a trans-American railroad.

Thereafter, the director forsook frontier life for a decade, focussing on war films, rural comedies and literary adaptations. *The Lost Patrol* was a bleak tale of a British platoon in the Mesopotamian desert being picked off by unseen Arab gunmen; *Judge Priest* >**1** – one of three films featuring cracker-barrel comic Will Rogers – a witty excursion into a Deep South riven by memories of the Civil War, was marred by its racist stereotyping of black actor Stepin Fetchit; *The Informer*, a sentimentalised version of Liam O'Flaherty's novel about a drunk betraying an IRA friend, revealed Ford's taste for Catholic religious allegory and for seldom appropriate but always arresting visual Expressionism. Only in 1939, however, did his talent fully mature with a return to the Western genre.

Lauded primarily for the editing of a final chase sequence, *Stagecoach* >**2** introduced several key Fordian motifs: shot beneath the stark, arid mesas of Monument Valley – henceforth a symbol of the primeval wilderness to be tamed by the white man – it starred for the first time John Wayne. While yet to embody the archetypal Ford hero – a laconic, self-sacrificing loner mystically devoted to WASP America and all it entailed (the family, madonna-women, a boisterous, *Boys' Own* sense of *bonhomie*) – Wayne's outlaw revealed Ford's nostalgic ambivalence towards progress: as the Ringo Kid and his tart-with-a-heart lover finally leave the hypocritical townsfolk he has rescued from marauding Indians, the observation is made that the pair is safe from the blessings of civilisation.

The invocation of an America unspoilt by cities, technology and business was most elegaic in *Young Mr Lincoln* >**3**. Armed with innate goodness and book-learnin', Godlike Abe quells a lynch mob and strides to a stormy Fate; as played by Henry Fonda, his meek idealism is a counterpart to the Wayne heroes' stoic pragmatism. As Ford's mythical America diminished in historical accuracy, so his films became mawkish: a travesty of Steinbeck's *The Grapes of Wrath* >**4** proposes a complacent faith in the land and the people; *How Green Was My Valley*, despite its loving studio re-creation of Welsh mining villages, founders in winsome, weepy emotionalism.

After war service Ford made *My Darling Clementine* >**5**, a fine account of Wyatt Earp and Doc Holliday's legendary defeat of the Clanton gang. By now, despite the film's climactic shoot-out at the OK Corral, Ford's talents lay less in action scenes than in playing endless variations on community rituals. Dances, church-meetings, saloon brawls and funerals were utilised to define social hierarchies and relationships, and to emphasise the role of tradition in the moulding of America's heroic culture. After *The Fugitive* – Graham Greene's *The Power and the Glory* piously turned into a naive and embarrassing defence of Latin America's Catholic Church – Ford filmed a loose 'cavalry trilogy' consisting of *Fort Apache*, *She Wore a Yellow Ribbon* and *Rio Grande*. Besides probing the gulf between born soldiers (Wayne) and by-the-book officers (Fonda in *Fort Apache*), these films managed to suggest that the heroes who died to make America safe from the Indians were virtually immortal. (Ever since Ford's early years, his protagonists had often spoken with the dead). Indeed, that sense of undying tradition was even more indulged in *The Quiet Man* >**6**, a fey romantic comedy painting Ireland as a green, leafy land of maudlin leprechaun-like morons, bellicose drunks and fiery colleens. *The Sun Shines Bright* >**7**, a touching, elegaic, witty but morally indefensible return to the smalltown Americana of *Judge Priest*, saw Ford in similar mood, while *Mr Roberts*, an unamusing, tedious adaptation of a theatrical success set aboard a warship, suggested that the director was beginning to run out of steam.

The Searchers >**8**, however, offered evidence that he was less certain of his faith than before: ambiguous in its harsh portrait of Wayne's eternal nomad, unbending in his bloodlust as he spends ten years trailing the Indian abductors of his niece, the film is either profoundly fascist or a disquieting attempt to examine the roots of xenophobic violence. While it remains unclear whether Ford condones or condemns Wayne's obsessive hatred, explicitly rooted in a fear of miscegenation, the film impresses by confronting its issues head on: hero or madman, Wayne is doomed to be a homeless loner. Less sentimental than Ford's earlier work, *The Searchers* presaged several attempts to make amends for past depictions of people low in Ford's social hierarchy: *Sergeant Routledge* showed the blacks' contribution to cavalry campaigns (admittedly in flashbacks used to affirm the good character of a black accused of raping a white woman), while *Cheyenne Autumn* accompanied an Indian tribe's troubled odyssey back to the reservation from which it had been evicted. Ford's finest film of this period, however, was *The Man Who Shot Liberty Valance* >**9**. This complex summation of past themes examined the truth behind a bandit's death in a town about to enter a new era: is the hero Wayne's gun-slinging rancher or James Stewart's pacifist lawyer, who brings education to the desert? Finally, for progress' sake, it is necessary to 'print the legend', but Ford insists that the facts, while less inspirational, be remembered as a monument to the pioneering purity of the Old West.

Finally, after the remarkably claustrophobic *Seven Women* >**10** – a far cry from the director's earlier sentimental piety in its depiction of the plight of a number of naive Western missionaries held hostage by a savage Chinese warlord – Ford retired. If his finest work was in the Western and its offshoots, he was not perhaps its greatest proponent, his flag-waving patriotism too often giving rise to simplistic heroism and the irritatingly tireless brawling of

Ok, sir?' Wyatt Earp (Henry Fonda) contemplates his tonsorial appearance before moseying along to the corral in Ford's *My Darling Clementine.*

his repertory group of actors. He was, however, a populist poet, despite insisting on the superiority of white military males over women, blacks and Indians, and his talent for creating mood and telling a story through purely visual means remains potent.

Lineage

Ford, himself possibly influenced by Griffith and Dwan, cast his shadow over all Westerns, most recently those of Andrew McLaglen, son of Victor (one of Ford's favourite actors). His visual poetry and sense of myth have been admired by many directors, including **Eisenstein**, **Welles**, **Kurosawa**, **Anderson**, and **Bogdanovich**.

Further reading

Andrew Sarris' *The John Ford Movie Mystery* (London, 1976), Joseph McBride and Michael Wilmington's *John Ford* (London, 1974), John Baxter's *The Cinema of John Ford* (London, 1971).

Viewing

1 **Judge Priest**
US 1934/ w Will Rogers, Tom Brown, Anita Louise

2 **Stagecoach**
US 1939/ w John Wayne, Claire Trevor, Thomas Mitchell
3 **Young Mr Lincoln**
US 1939/ w Henry Fonda, Alice Brady, Donald Meek
4 **The Grapes of Wrath**
US 1940/ w Henry Fonda, Jane Darwell, John Carradine
5 **My Darling Clementine**
US 1946/ w Henry Fonda, Victor Mature, Walter Brennan
6 **The Quiet Man**
US 1952/ w John Wayne, Maureen O'Hara, Barry Fitzgerald
7 **The Sun Shines Bright**
US 1953/ w Charles Winninger, Arleen Whelan, Stepin Fetchit
8 **The Searchers**
US 1956/ w John Wayne, Jeffrey Hunter, Ward Bond, Vera Miles
9 **The Man Who Shot Liberty Valance**
US 1962/ w John Wayne, James Stewart, Vera Miles, Lee Marvin
10 **Seven Women**
US 1966/ w Anne Bancroft, Sue Lyon, Margaret Leighton, Anna Lee

Milos Forman

Born: 18th February 1932/Caslav, Czechoslovakia
Directing career: 1963-

It is interesting that with greater political freedom and commercial viability, the films of Milos Forman have become increasingly conventional. The spontaneity of his early Czech work has sadly ossified into ostentatiously decorous middlebrow entertainment.

After film studies in Prague, Forman first entered the movie industry as a scriptwriter. A spell with the Magic Lantern multi-media group ensued before he directed two semi-documentary shorts released together as *Talent Competition*. Their focus on music and their concern with ordinary people anticipated his feature work. His debut feature, *Peter and Pavla*, established him as a major figure of the Czech New Wave. The slim plot deals with the relationships between a gauche young shop detective and a romantically disinterested girl, as well as his relationship with his parents. The semi-improvisational scenes, the mixture of non-professional and professional actors, and the gently ironic tone were amusingly fresh, and recurred in the even wittier *A Blonde in Love*, in which a one-night stand provokes a girl's visit to the home of her musician-lover's family, causing embarrassing confusion about sleeping arrangements. A slight, wry and non-ideological riposte to Czech cinema's dominant socialist realism, Forman's satires used a candid-camera style to achieve a sense of authenticity, while his characters were viewed with rare sympathy. *The Fireman's Ball* >**1**, however, is harsher in its account of bureaucratic intrigues at a beauty contest, and may be viewed as political allegory. The film was banned after the Soviet invasion and Forman, in Paris at the time, remained in exile in the West.

His first American film, *Taking Off* >**2** applied his customary methods to yet another look at the generation gap, intercutting a semi-improvised singing audition for young girls with scenes of a middle-class couple's search for their daughter; with characteristic irony, it is the adults whose morality lapses, as they enjoy marijuana at a meeting for the parents of runaway children. Similarly anti-establishment, *One Flew Over The Cuckoo's Nest* >**3** observed a rebel inmate's battle against the authoritarian rules of a hospital for the insane, but, despite formidable performances by Jack Nicholson and Louise Fletcher, it was flawed by overstatement, misogyny, and an alarming tendency towards facile emotional manipulation.

A film of the hippy musical *Hair* was woefully dated, while a version of E.L. Doctorow's novel *Ragtime* foundered on a simplistic reduction of the original's kaleidoscopic plot to a predictable, dimly liberal account of racial conflict in turn-of-the-century America. Lavish sets and costumes now seemed the norm; *Amadeus* >**4** furthered Forman's decline into respectably arty period drama: an adaptation of Peter Shaffer's play about the musically mediocre Salieri's murderous hatred for Mozart, it is flawed by a risible portrait of the famed composer as a flatulent, giggling youth and by redundant displays of virtuoso visual technique. It is perhaps no accident that Forman, whose early work was inspired by popular music, should turn to a genius of Western composition to make a movie so bereft of witty invention; in repeatedly resorting to literary and theatrical hits (he next set about making *Valmont*, based on *Les Liaisons Dangereuses*), he seems to have divorced himself from the genuine humanity and warmth of his Czech work.

Lineage

Like Ivan Passer (who co-wrote his early films) and Jiri Menzel, Forman was influenced by Czech writers (notably Josef Skvorecky) and Italian neo-realism; he has expressed an admiration for silent comedy and **Anderson**. The gently ironic humanism of his early work may be compared with that of **Truffaut** and early **Michael Ritchie**.

Further reading

Josef Skvorecky's *All the Bright Young Men and Women* (Toronto, 1971), Antonin Liehm's *Closely Watched Films* (New York, 1974), Liehm's *The Milos Forman Stories* (New York, 1976).

Viewing

1 **The Fireman's Ball**
Czech/It 1967/ w Jan Vostrcil, Josef Kolb, Josef Svet

2 **Taking Off**
US 1970/ w Buck Henry, Lynn Carlin, Linnea Heacock

3 **One Flew Over the Cuckoo's Nest**
US 1975/ w Jack Nicholson, Louise Fletcher, Brad Dourif

4 **Amadeus**
US 1983/ w F. Murray Abraham, Tom Hulce, Elizabeth Berridge

Bill Forsyth

Born: **29th July 1946/Glasgow, Scotland**
Directing career: 1979-

Despite their low-key naturalism, the most striking quality of the films of Bill Forsyth is his ability to invest gentle comedy, set in a recognisably modern everyday world, with beguiling and subtle intimations of an almost supernatural magic.

Having already directed documentaries and industrial films, in 1972 Forsyth began working with the Glasgow Youth Theatre, an experience that finally culminated in his making a feature debut with the low-budget *That Sinking Feeling*, in which unemployed and incompetent Glaswegian youths devise an ingenious plan to steal a hoard of bathroom fittings. At once streetwise and whimsical as it joyfully parodies/plagiarises scenes from **Cimino**'s *Thunderbolt and Lightfoot*, it reveals both the writer-director's sympathy for dreamers and his ability to elicit superb, comic ensemble playing from a young cast. Those qualities were again evident in the very successful *Gregory's Girl* >**1**, notable for fresh characterisation (a gawky schoolboy's dream-girl is a keen football player, while another's cooking obsession makes him a teachers' favourite), and for its sense of magic: when Gregory finally meets his true love (rather than the football star), they lie beneath a starry sky and talk of falling from the earth's spinning surface; in support of their theory, the camera tilts to show the pair defying gravity.

Even more ambitious, *Local Hero* >**2** combined gentle political satire with an understated, mystical sense of nature as the canny inhabitants of a small Scottish coastal village sabotage a Texan oilman's efforts to buy cheap land for a refinery. Avoiding easy sentimentality – the Scots do not refuse to sell their land, but simply demand a good price – Forsyth again allows celestial magic to hold sway, with the conflict resolved by the appearance of the Aurora Borealis. More mundanely, *Comfort and Joy* sees a radio DJ, suddenly deserted by his lover, regenerated by his arbitration of a Glasgow gang war between rival ice-cream companies; with the threat of violence muted, the film lacks genuine suspense but its dark wit, particularly the DJ's friends' absurd, tactless efforts to console him over his loss, is delightfully true-to-life.

Still more sombre, *Housekeeping* >**3**, Forsyth's first American film, featured two sisters burdened by a cruel family history, whose paths separate when they react differently to the eccentric ways of aunt Sylvie who looks after them. Avoiding cosy whimsy, Forsyth never hides the irresponsibility underlying Sylvie's non-conformism; reality is again offset by hints of the supernatural: a visit to a cottage in the forest (according to Sylvie, the home of invisible children) brings her closer to one niece, while the memory of a long-dead, visionary grandfather provides a spiritual precedent for the girl's dreams of expanding her horizons.

As Forsyth's career has advanced, his characters, situations and tone have grown more complex; what was once merely fresh, observational comedy has increasingly become emotionally mature. If his as yet undistinguished visual sense fails to bring to life the magic that punctuates his otherwise realist narratives, he is nevertheless an entertainer of originality, wit and charm.

Lineage

While realist settings suggest an influence in the Free Cinema of **Anderson**, Karel Reisz *et al*, Forsyth's light comic touch echoes early **Truffaut**, Olmi, and the Ealing comedies, his sense of a magic allied to nature the understated mysticism of **Powell** and Pressburger.

Viewing

1 **Gregory's Girl**
GB 1980/ w Gordon John Sinclair, Dee Hepburn, Jake D'Arcy

2 **Local Hero**
GB 1983/ w Peter Reigert, Dennis Lawson, Burt Lancaster

3 **Housekeeping**
US 1987/ w Christine Lahti, Sara Walker, Andrea Burchill

Georges Franju

Born: 12th April 1912/Fougères, France
Died: 5th November 1987/Paris, France
Directing career: 1934-1974

Georges Franju combined realism and fantasy, poetry and polemics, savagery and tenderness to unique effect. Imbuing his films with a surrealist's antipathy to established notions of normality, he was one of cinema's most fiercely independent visionaries.

Before directing full-time, Franju wrote criticism, worked on scientific documentaries and co-founded (with Henri Langlois, his partner on a 1934 16mm amateur short, *Le Métro*) the Cinémathèque Française. In 1949 the documentary short *Le Sang des Bêtes* >**1**, a cool, unflinching look at the brutal workings of a Paris slaughterhouse, established him as a moralist of rare integrity; its harrowing, unsentimental but beautifully composed images are less pro-vegetarian propaganda than a demand that we remember the victims of our desire for meat on our tables. Equally inventive in its blend of shock cutting and visual poetry was the anti-militarist *Hôtel des Invalides*, which mixed shots of the Paris soldiers' hospital – home of Napoleon's tomb and a national monument to the glory of war – with images of crippled veterans and, finally, a crocodile of visiting children, by implication the cannon fodder of the future.

Not all Franju's shorts were documentaries: *Le Grand Méliès* was a touching tribute to the pioneer of film fantasy, while *La Première Nuit* was a fictional account of a boy's escape from his chauffeur-driven prison into the dark, lonely world of the Metro, and his dreams of a strange sensuous vision of a small girl on a train. In both, Franju's transformation of reality into a lyrical poetry of unsettling intensity testified to his originality.

His first feature, *La Tête Contre Les Murs (The Keepers)* >**2**, revealed his continuing interest in victims. A delinquent biker from a well-to-do family is committed to a mental asylum by his father: unconcerned with the issue of whether he is sane or not, Franju focusses on the parental and medical ignorance that leads to his incarceration, while showing through visual symbols (caged doves, a miniature railway line) the doomed boy's often childlike irrationality. Even blacker, *Les Yeux Sans Visage* (*Eyes Without a Face*) >**3** turned to pulp conventions to create a superb study in obsession: guilty about his having destroyed his daughter's face in a car crash, a doctor transplants the flesh of abducted girls to restore, with his scalpel, her beauty. Franju combines horror and tenderness in startling images; the doctor's sadism is born of undying love, while the girl, still faceless, kills him out of sympathy for his other victims before wandering into the night surrounded by fluttering white doves, symbols simultaneously of her innocence, freedom, and (presumably) escalating madness.

After a comparatively conventional thriller (*Pleins Feux sur l'Assassin*) and a sensitive, austere, typically atheist version of Mauriac's Catholic novel *Thérèse Desqueyroux*, *Judex* >**4** paid tribute to Louis Feuillade's silent adventure serials. As a God-like master of disguise battles against an evil banker, Franju revels in absurd coincidences, impossible images (men walking up a vertical wall) and still more animal symbolism: Judex makes his first appearance at a costume ball, his head garbed in a superb bird mask, his hands conjuring a dead dove back to life, while his enemies include a woman eternally clad (except for one moment when she irreverently dresses as a nun to facilitate her crime) in a slinky black catsuit. Simultaneously nostalgic and surreal, restrained and joyful, the film attempts with total success to revive the early cinema's charming capacity for magical wonder.

A version of **Cocteau**'s *Thomas l'Imposteur* >**5** allowed Franju to return to the subject of the horrors of war: a young dreamer, serving in the ambulance corps in World War I, views trenches, corpses and explosions as a fantastic imaginary spectacle, his dreams coinciding with reality only at the moment of death. *The Sin of Father Mouret*, meanwhile, saw Zola's novel turned into yet another statement of Franju's anti-clericalism, with a country priest led by his excessive devotion to the Virgin Mary into erotic temptation. By now, however, Franju's film work was less frequent though he did sometimes direct for television; except for the *Judex*-like *Shadowman* (*L'Homme Sans Visage*), a rich pulp fantasy delighting in occult criminal organisations, moving waxworks and a mysterious hero, he made no more features but returned, in his last years, to preside over the Cinémathèque.

While Franju's films exhibit his dismay at various facets of humanity – hypocrisy, cruelty, piety and ignorance – at the same time they reveal his fascination with the mysterious poetry that lies behind surface reality. His surrealism was not a matter of artifice, but of a highly personal vision that was at once elegant, horrific, provocative, becalmed and nostalgic.

Lineage

Franju's poetic surrealism is related to that of **Vigo**, late **Buñuel** and even **Resnais**, while the verbal reticence of his films compares with **Bresson**'s. His love of silent cinema – most notably that of Feuillade – is everywhere evident in the elegance of his images.

Further reading

Raymond Durgnat's *Franju* (London, 1967), Roy Armes' *French Cinema since 1946, Vol II* (London, 1976).

Viewing

1 **Le Sang des Bêtes**
France 1949

2 **La Tête Contre Les Murs**
France 1958/ w Jean-Pierre Mocky, Pierre Brasseur, Anouk Aimée

3 **Les Yeux Sans Visage (Eyes Without a Face)**
France 1959/ w Pierre Brasseur, Alida Valli, Edith Scob

4 **Judex**
France 1963/ w Channing Pollock, Francine Berge, Edith Scob

5 **Thomas l'Imposteur (Thomas the Impostor)**
France 1965/ w Fabrice Rouleau, Emmanuelle Riva, Sophie Darès

John Frankenheimer

Born: 19th February 1930/Malba, New York, USA
Directing career: 1957-

It may now seem difficult to credit the praise once heaped upon John Frankenheimer. Claims that he was the most promising young American director of the '60s have been effectively disproven by the steady coarsening of his work during the last twenty years.

A successful director of television drama, Frankenheimer made his film debut with a version of the TV play *The Young Stranger*. A well-acted but routine generation-gap movie about a delinquent boy, its commercial failure ensured Frankenheimer's return to the small screen for three years. It was only after *The Young Savages* (much marred by special 'society-is-guilty' pleading as New York DA Burt Lancaster questions his motives in charging a delinquent from his own old neighbourhood with murder) that he hit his stride with three of the more adventurous films of 1962. *The Birdman of Alcatraz* >**1** – the true story of a killer whose passion for ornithology while serving a life sentence produces his moral regeneration – mixed fine performances, a leisurely narrative and an almost documentary realism to touching effect; *All Fall Down*, a melodrama about a teenager's growing disillusionment with his elder brother's selfish, philandering ways, featured impressively grotesque characters and an assured control of atmosphere; *The Manchurian Candidate* >**2**, a political conspiracy thriller about a Korean War veteran programmed through brainwashing to assassinate the president, skilfully combined taut suspense and black satire.

The last of these proved partly prophetic, of course; more notable, however, was Frankenheimer's complex use of frames within frames – often TV monitors in the foreground – to provide a wealth of information within a single image. Equally effective in creating a mood of widespread paranoia, *Seven Days in May* employed modern technology to evoke the labyrinthine channels of communication by which a military coup, following the US president's signing of a nuclear agreement with Russia, is planned and foiled. Thereafter, however, Frankenheimer's taste for visual flashiness and the cog-like mechanisms of a well-oiled plot led to sterile, pretentious and weakly characterised nonsense like *The Train*, *Seconds* (a grim satire on the perils of rejuvenation, steadily wrecked by rather self-conscious social comment), and *Grand Prix*.

Henceforth Frankenheimer seemed to lose his sense of direction and veered from glossy action movies to actorly adaptations (*The Fixer*, *The Iceman Cometh*). Two films written by Robert Dillon saw a brief return to form: *99 44/100% Dead* (*Call Harry Crown*) was an intermittently amusing crime-spoof, its black humour evident from the opening shot of countless corpses clad in concrete footwear on a river-bed, while *The French Connection II* >**3** was an enormous advance upon **Friedkin**'s original. Distancing itself from Doyle's bigotry as he trails a drugs ring in Marseilles, it simultaneously probed his insecurity during the harrowing scenes in which he suffers cold turkey after being injected with heroin. Since then, however, the director's career has declined further, encompassing routine, even risible thrillers (*Black Sunday*, *The Holcroft Covenant*, *52 Pick Up*), a disastrous excursion into Japanese martial arts (*The Challenge*), and an absurd ecological horror allegory (*Prophecy*).

In retrospect, Frankenheimer's adoption of an ever more busy visual surface in his early work may be seen as anticipating the hollow pyrotechnics of his later films, with style overshadowing content and commitment. He now seems an anonymous craftsman sadly unconcerned by the quality of the material with which he chooses to work.

Lineage

At his best Frankenheimer displayed greater ambitions regarding the visual quality of his work than fellow TV graduates such as **Lumet**, **Penn** and Norman Jewison; his rapid decline, however, has ensured that his influence on others has been negligible.

Further reading

Gerald Pratley's *The Cinema of John Frankenheimer* (London, 1969).

Viewing

1 **The Birdman of Alcatraz**
US 1962/ w Burt Lancaster, Karl Malden, Thelma Ritter
2 **The Manchurian Candidate**
US 1962/ w Frank Sinatra, Laurence Harvey, Angela Lansbury
3 **The French Connection II**
US 1975/ w Gene Hackman, Bernard Fresson, Fernando Rey

William Friedkin

Born: 29th August 1939/Chicago, USA
Directing career: 1967-

In many of the films of William Friedkin, there is an element of sensationalism that suggests not only the commercial sense of an opportunist but also the absence of artistic vision. Compared to the other 'whizzkids' who came to prominence in American cinema during the '70s, he seems singularly without personality.

A television director as early as his teens, Friedkin made his film debut with *Good Times*, a musical vehicle for the singing duo Sonny and Cher. Following *The Night They Raided Minsky*'s – a dull period drama set in the world of '20s vaudeville – and two stagey, redundant theatrical adaptations – Pinter's *The Birthday Party* and Mart Crowley's *The Boys in the Band* (another birthday gathering, this time attended by gays) – Friedkin had his first enormous hit with *The French Connection* >**1**. While authentically detailed in its depiction of New York's sleazier neighbourhoods, the film was flawed by a lack of critical perspective towards the foul-mouthed bigotry of its narcotics cop anti-hero Popeye Doyle. Nevertheless, as Doyle and his partner trail a heroin-smuggling ring around memorably vivid locations, Friedkin steps up the pace and distracts attention from the plot's incoherence: a celebrated car chase, with Doyle pursuing a fugitive riding the elevated railway above him, becomes a triumph of editing technique over content.

Likewise, *The Exorcist* >**2** neglected the implications of its bogus sub-plot about a crisis of faith, focussing instead on the grotesque physical transformations, verbal profanities and gory special effects that signify an innocent young girl's possession by Satan. Indeed, even as a horror movie, the film disappoints, the suspense built up by the camera's steady advance towards the child's bedroom door being repeatedly dissipated by the explicit nature of the violence on view: the bludgeoning effect of spewing bile, gyrating heads and a cacophonous soundtrack serves only to underline the fatuous conception of evil postulated by Friedkin's endlessly manipulative shock-cut editing.

Its sensationalist violence giving rise to promotional hype, the film was a worldwide success, winning its maker *carte blanche* for the filming of the deceptively titled *The Sorcerer*, an inept, unnecessary, and extravagantly expensive remake of **Clouzot**'s *The Wages of Fear*. Thanks to fine performances by Peter Falk, Warren Oates and others, the relatively modest *The Brink's Job* was a wry heist movie, but *Cruising* saw Friedkin at his most exploitative: an undercover cop's search for a killer psychopath in New York's gay bars sees him running the gauntlet of offensive homophobic stereotypes. *Deal of the Century*, a weakly characterised, ill-focussed satire on international arms trading, gained a limited release only, while *To Live and Die in*

LA >**3**, about two cops who investigate a gang of counterfeiters, diluted its occasionally efficient action scenes with an inappropriate emphasis on glossy style; it seemed as if Friedkin was trying to repeat the formula of *The French Connection* in a 'Miami Vice'-style milieu, with the cops virtually indistinguishable in their methods from the crooks they pursue, and the film's centre-piece an extended, destructive and barely relevant car chase through picturesque locations. No less half-baked was *Rampage*, a courtroom drama about a serial killer, with a muddled message about capital punishment.

Friedkin's dependence on violent physical action points up his poor sense of narrative and character. Any pretensions he has to seriousness are undermined by his films' repeated inability to transcend two-dimensional caricature and cliched situations.

Lineage

Friedkin's desire to manipulate audience emotions would seem to spring from an admiration for **Hitchcock** and **Clouzot**, both of whose talent and wit he lacks. The sledgehammer style of his two biggest hits has influenced many undistinguished thrillers and horror films.

Viewing

1 **The French Connection**
US 1971/ w Gene Hackman, Roy Scheider, Fernando Rey

2 **The Exorcist**
US 1973/ w Linda Blair, Ellen Burstyn, Max Von Sydow

3 **To Live and Die in LA**
US 1885/ w William L. Petersen, William Dafoe, John Pankow

Sam Fuller

Born: 12th August 1911/Worcester, Massachusetts, USA
Directing career: 1948-

Often accused of crudity and sensationalism, the films of Samuel Michael Fuller are in fact complex, powerfully dramatic analyses of American life. Whether arrived at consciously or not, the many ironies and contradictions which inform his tabloid journalist's vision of the violence and insanity that are the inevitable cost of the struggle for personal freedom, mark him as a major artist.

After a lengthy apprenticeship as a crime reporter and pulp novelist, Fuller entered the movies as a screenwriter, his finest script, for **Sirk**'s *Shockproof*, describing the doomed love of an ex-convict and her parole officer. Following distinguished army service in World War II, he embarked upon direction with *I Shot Jesse James* and *The Baron of Arizona*, inventive B-Westerns noted for their use of harsh close-ups and fast editing. Two war films, *The Steel Helmet* and *Fixed Bayonets*, confirmed Fuller as a tough, unsentimental patriot, their apparent anti-Communism masking raw observations on the troubled diversity of America and on the way courage is less a matter of heroism than of the will to survive. Similarly, *Park Row* >**1**, about a newspaper war in 1880s New York, is both a personal tribute to journalism's pioneering spirit and an ironic portrait of the deceptions and obstinacy needed to secure freedom of the press: a long, virtuoso tracking shot, moving from a saloon, down a street, into an office and out again, and coming to rest by a statue of Benjamin Franklin, vigorously exhibits the obsessive brawling mentality that underlies a glorious tradition.

While the Cold War was a backdrop to many of Fuller's films, few were simplistically anti-Red: *Pick Up on South Street*, about a petty, self-serving criminal dissuaded from selling micro-film to the enemy by a friend's death, is less anti-Commie propaganda than an unusually tough critique of the concept of honour among thieves; an undercover agent's investigations in *House of Bamboo* reveal American military strategies applied by crack veterans to postwar organised crime. Solitude, betrayal and violence are the ingredients of the American search for identity: *Run of the Arrow* >**2** sees a Southerner refusing to accept the Confederacy's defeat, and joining a tribe of Sioux Indians; only by turning against his own kind can he come to terms with the diversity and internecine conflict that define his nationality. America is threatened both from within and without, while individual torment mirrors that of society. With lines blurred and weapons drawn, film – to quote Fuller in **Godard**'s *Pierrot Le Fou* – becomes 'a battle-ground: love, hate, action, violence, death – in a word, emotion!'

The writer-director's insistence on forceful, even primitive, emotions was reflected in the directness of his visual style: the Freudian sexual passion between a cattle baroness and a marshal in *Forty Guns* is conveyed by thrusting camerawork and a swirling storm sequence; in *Verboten* the stark reality of race hatred that marks a Neo-Nazi threat to the reconstruction of postwar Germany is evoked in documentary footage of concentration camps; while in *The Crimson Kimono* >**3**, a ritualised kendo display goes violently out of control to give physical expression to a Japanese-American cop's sexual jealousy and paranoid fears of racial prejudice.

As Fuller's career progressed so his films became darker: in *Underworld USA* >**4**, to destroy a criminal empire operating beneath the stainless facade of a national business conglomerate, the FBI knowingly employs the services of a ruthless ex-convict obsessed by the need to avenge his father's murder. In *Shock Corridor* >**5**, a journalist's lust for recognition leads him to fake madness so that he might investigate corruption and cruelty in an asylum, a microcosm of American angst; inevitably his experiences drive him insane. *The Naked Kiss* sees a whore's plans to start life anew by helping handicapped children meet opposition from a small town's puritanical citizens; tellingly, it transpires that her fiancé – a rich, cultured, respected philanthropist – is a child-molester.

Sadly, Fuller's tabloid style exposés of the criminal under-currents accompanying America's competitive individualism proved ever less successful and he found it increasingly hard to finance films. *Dead Pigeon on Beethoven Street*, a complex, intentionally absurd thriller concerning political blackmail, prostitution and murder, was made for German television; only in 1980, when he had gained something of a cult reputation, was he able to film *The Big Red One* >**6**, based on his experiences in the Second World War. While the US platoon's contribution to the European cause is never less than courageous, flag-waving platitudes are ignored in favour of studies in both the camaraderie born of fear and the insanity of war: the film begins and ends with shots of a ravaged Christ upon a black, charred cross, while an attempt to wrest control of an asylum from the Nazis allows inmates to reassert their humanity and 'normality' by killing both Americans and Germans at random.

White Dog >**7** was a late masterwork, its narrative simplicity lending enormous emotional power as a girl tries to de-condition an attack-dog trained, by whites, to kill blacks. Precise in its colour symbolism, profoundly compassionate in its treatment both of the dog – a perfect cypher for racism as the product of social conditioning – and its victims, the film was widely ignored, its

Richard Widmark proffers his own ideas of cinematic punch in Fuller's *Pickup on South Street.*

unsentimental liberalism barely comprehended. Thereafter, Fuller went to Paris to make *Les Voleurs de la Nuit*, a film inspired by unemployment problems that found little critical favour.

The vitality and force of Fuller's work derive from his acute grasp of film's capacity to operate in the same way as newspaper headlines: script, performance, cutting, camera movement, close-ups all serve to ram points home with unerring accuracy. If his style lacks subtlety, his love for his medium (which incidentally he sees as educative) and his brash intelligence are undeniable. A genuine independent – his later films are credited as 'written, produced and directed by Samuel Fuller' – he is to be cherished for his distinctive, seamless integration of method and meaning.

Lineage

Fuller's treatment of American socio-political and moral issues through lowly genres aligns him with the likes of **Ray**, **Aldrich** and **Siegel** whose troubled relationship with Hollywood he shares. Admired by the French New Wave, he appears in Godard's *Pierrot Le Fou*, **Hopper**'s *The Last Movie*, **Wenders**' *The American Friend* and *The State of Things*, and (very briefly) **Spielberg**'s *1941*.

Further reading

Phil Hardy's *Samuel Fuller* (London 1970), Nicholas Garnham's *Samuel Fuller* (London 1971).

Viewing

1 **Park Row**
US 1952/ w Gene Evans, Mary Welch, Bela Kovacs

2 **Run of the Arrow**
US 1957/ w Rod Steiger, Ralph Meeker, Brian Keith

3 **The Crimson Kimono**
US 1959/ w James Shigeta, Glenn Corbett, Victoria Shaw

4 **Underworld USA**
US 1960/ w Cliff Robertson, Dolores Dorn, Beatrice Kay

5 **Shock Corridor**
US 1963/ w Peter Breck, Constance Towers, Gene Evans

6 **The Big Red One**
US 1980/ w Lee Marvin, Mark Hamill, Robert Carradine

7 **White Dog**
US 1982/ w Kristy McNichol, Paul Winfield, Burl Ives

Abel Gance

Born: 25th October 1889/Paris, France
Died: 10th November 1981/Paris, France
Directing career: 1911-1971

Despite his long career, it was only in the silent years that Abel Gance made films of any great importance. Very much a product of his times he reflects the interest in formal experimentation that swept the French intellegentsia in the 1910s and '20s. In terms of content, however, his films seem to spring directly from the Romantic novels of the 19th century.

Having acted in the theatre in Brussels, Gance began selling film scripts to Gaumont. Two years later he started directing, and quickly established himself as one of the brightest talents of his generation. The early films, often marked by Gance's respect for Culture (literary adaptations and historical/artistic heroes were common), display his increasing fascination with innovative techniques. In *La Folie du Docteur Tube*, Gance experimented with distorting lenses to convey a world of psychological fantasy; in other films, with ever faster and more varied editing patterns.

World War I, during which he was gassed, appeared at first to have affected Gance deeply. *J'Accuse!* >**1** is an explicit attack on the waste and insanity of war but, for all its grandiloquence, one is left suspecting its sensitivity, if not its sincerity: for an admittedly stirring climax, in which the dead return to ask if their lives were justifiably expendable, he cast French soldiers on leave from the War. It is as if the novelty of the cinematic effect were more important than the emotions that fuel the idea. Indeed, Gance's ambitions reached new heights with *La Roue* >**2**, an almost Zolaesque tale about the largely destructive passions that are aroused in an ageing train-driver and his son by the former's adopted daughter. If the old man, Sisif, was based on a combination of Sisyphus, Prometheus, Oedipus and Christ, the plot, running at about eight hours, is the stuff of pure melodrama. Most notable, however, were its innovative editing rhythms. In the more dramatic sequences, as when Sisif decides to wreck the train carrying the girl to her new husband, the intercutting between repeated shots accelerates to such a speed that the images themselves become virtually indecipherable, conveying meaning less by content than by form. The emotional effect is irresistible, the originality undeniable.

Gance developed these, and other, techniques still further in *Napoléon vu par Abel Gance* >**3**, a massive six-hour celebration of Bonaparte from visionary boyhood (commanding his schoolboy forces during a snowball fight) to the invasion of Italy. An astonishing technical *tour-de-force*, it features extravagant camera movement, frantic montage, magnificent period reconstruction and lighting effects and, for its finale with Napoléon advancing into Italy, a revolutionary wide-screen process – Polyvision – consisting of three images shown in counterpoint to one another. The bombastic display of form and symbolism, however, echoes the naive jingoistic adulation of Bonaparte as a near-divine embodiment of the French Revolutionary spirit; finally, the film is a technically avant-garde but morally reactionary work bordering on the fascistic.

Napoléon as it stands was originally planned as the first of six films recounting the life and achievements of Gance's godlike hero. But the advent of sound (for which he experimented with a form of stereophony) prevented the project from going further and his first talkie, *La Fin du Monde*, was poorly received. His career never recovered, although several melodramas made in the '30s and '40s still exhibited his desire to expand the language of cinema. *Un Grand Amour de Beethoven* >**4**, though hampered by a superficial conception of the Great Artist, made inventive use of cacophonous sound to illustrate the onset of the composer's deafness. At the same time, Gance would often return obsessively to earlier films, remaking *Mater Dolorosa* and *J'Accuse!*, and re-editing *Napoléon* into two new, shorter versions.

Gance's energetic enthusiasm survived into old age; the idea of becoming a great but neglected artist might even have appealed to his Romantic sensibilities. Shortly before his death, however, he was fortunate enough to witness the world's joyous rediscovery of a reconstructed version of *Napoléon*, complete with colour tints in the final triptych: a lasting testament both to his own visual inventiveness and to the pioneering spirit of silent cinema.

Lineage

As a member of the French avant-garde, Gance may be compared with Jean Epstein, Marcel L'Herbier, even **Clair**, **Renoir** and **Cocteau**. Inspired by **Griffith's** cross-cutting, his editing techniques are sometimes reminiscent of **Vertov**, **Eisenstein** and Pudovkin. Indeed, *Napoléon* (an epic hagiographic spectacle masquerading as populist drama) is not dissimilar from certain works of Soviet propaganda.

Further reading

Kevin Brownlow's *The Parade's Gone By* (London, 1968), Norman King's *Abel Gance* (London, 1984). Brownlow has written of how he restored *Napoléon, Abel Gance's classic film* (London, 1983).

Viewing

1 **J'Accuse!**
France 1919/ w Romuald Joube, Severin-Mars, Marise Dauvray

2 **La Roue**
France 1922/ w Severin-Mars, Ivy Close, Gabriel de Gavrone

3 **Napoléon vu par Abel Gance**
France 1926/ w Albert Dieudonné, Wladimir Roudenko, Gina Manes

4 **Un Grand Amour de Beethoven**
France 1936/ w Harry Baur, Jany Holt, Annie Ducaux

Terry Gilliam

Born: 22nd November 1940/ Minneapolis, Minnesota, USA
Directing career: 1974-

Previously the contributor of surreal animated scenes to the TV comedy series *Monty Python's Flying Circus*, Terry Gilliam seems likely to overshadow his ex-colleagues as a truly original film artist, an erratic, highly inventive director of fantasy movies.

Gilliam's feature debut was *Monty Python and the Holy Grail*, co-directed with fellow-Python Terry Jones, whose comparatively mundane directorial signature was later applied to *Monty Python's Life of Brian*, *Monty Python's the Meaning of Life* and the David Leland-scripted *Personal Services*. If Gilliam's hand in the funny but uneven Arthurian spoof was indistinguishable from that of his partner, *Jabberwocky*, a vaguely Pythonesque version of Lewis Carroll's poem about a dragon slaughtered by a cowardly innocent, contained its student humour within what would become a typically bizarre Gilliam world. The Middle Ages are viewed in a uniformly scatological light: a toothless king is dusty with debris falling from a palace ceiling; the hero's darling gives him a half-eaten, mouldering apple as a love token; filth and decay are ubiquitous.

Less Pythonesque was *Time Bandits* >**1**, a dreamlike lesson in living history taught to an incredulous schoolboy by six dwarfs and an immaculately English, headmasterly God. Patchily funny as its time travellers meet Robin Hood, Bonaparte, Agamemnon *et al*, it nevertheless benefitted from combining the visual splendour of a children's fairy tale with the irrational cruelty of nightmare. Even more imaginative was *Brazil* >**2**, a febrile, fertile satire on repressive, violent bureaucracy set in a grey future reminiscent of Orwell's 1984. A shy, well-intentioned clerk at the Ministry of Information dreams of flying to the rescue of a strange girl who, it transpires when he finally meets her, may be a terrorist; meanwhile complex problems with his eternally ineffective heating system lead to a session in the governmental torture-hall. Mixing myth and black comedy, surrealism and social caricature, the film is visually astonishing, both in its creation of epic landscapes (giant monoliths burst from the earth to block the hero's free-wheeling flights of desire) and in its grotesque details (faces obscenely misshapen by rejuvenation surgery, a crippled torturer garbed as Santa Claus). If the plot is often wayward – perhaps to be expected given its wealth of invention – the absurdly logical coherence of Gilliam's fantasy world, and the way it is rooted in a bleak reality not unlike that of postwar Britain, ensures that the plight of his hapless victims is finally tragic and touching.

In breaking free of Monty Python's brand of humour, Gilliam has proven an idiosyncratic visionary to rank alongside **Lynch**. If the much-publicised production problems on the hugely expensive *The Adventures of Baron Munchausen* >**3** – an extravagant costume fantasy about the triumph of Imagination over cool Reason, flawed by weak scripting but full of immaculately staged set-pieces – provoked fears that his inventiveness might be as undisciplined as it is vivid, *Brazil* provides ample evidence of a talent for creating impossible but nightmarishly familiar worlds.

Lineage

Gilliam's taste for the visually surreal and grotesque compares with **Borowczyk**, **Lynch** and **Tashlin**, also former animators.

Viewing

1 **Time Bandits**
GB 1981/ w David Rappaport, Kenny Baker, Ralph Richardson

2 **Brazil**
GB 1984/ w Jonathan Pryce, Kim Griest, Robert De Niro, Ian Holm

3 **The Adventures of Baron Munchausen**
GB/Italy 1988/ w John Neville, Eric Idle, Oliver Reed, Robin Williams

Jean-Luc Godard

Born: 3rd December 1930/Paris, France
Directing career: 1954-

Less about life itself than about how life is represented by film, Jean-Luc Godard's work is truly modernist. Packed with allusions, quotes and digressions, its blend of fiction and documentary is the equivalent of the critical essay rather than the novel; but as he repeatedly questions traditional film form and its relation to politics, Godard often lapses into wilful obscurity and half-baked pretensions. Nevertheless, his merging of the personal and political, and his quest for new meanings through new and complex juxtapositions of sound and image have ensured that his varied, prolific output has profoundly influenced post-'50s cinema.

An obsessive cinephile, the young Godard wrote criticism for *Cahiers du Cinéma* alongside **Truffaut**, **Rohmer** *et al.* While working as a film editor, publicist and journalist, he made five shorts – slight, witty, vaguely experimental – before directing his first feature, *A Bout de Souffle* (*Breathless*) >**1**. The story, written by Truffaut, is reminiscent of the Hollywood B-thriller, with an insolent Parisian picking up an American girl who finally betrays him to the police. What made it a key New Wave film was not plot but style: acknowledging its status as film throughout, it includes direct-to-camera monologues, an interview with **Melville**, and a hero who models himself on Bogart. While employing various realist methods, Godard never once pretends to realism; scenes are disjointed by a use of 'jump-cuts', and the killer's death is outrageously hammy.

Through the early '60s Godard laid siege to various genres, breaking down traditional form, confronting the process of filmic narration, creating a new hybrid style of cinema as he repeatedly turned to society's outcasts and problems of human communication. *Le Petit Soldat*'s portrait of an anti-terrorist assassin at once reflects on the Algerian War and moons over the face of Godard's wife Anna Karina. *Une Femme est une Femme*'s romantic triangle is framed in an engagingly silly tribute to American musicals. *Vivre Sa Vie* is twelve tableaux about a girl's slide into prostitution. *Les Carabiniers* >**2** guys war-movie heroism with two thuggish oafs whose battle spoils consist of a huge collection of postcards of places they have seen; carnage is evident in archive footage, but Godard's prime concern is still cinema itself, in parodies of the films of the Lumière Brothers, and in a scene in which one of his soldiers, bemused by the film-image, tries to climb into a cinema screen to inspect more closely a woman in a bath.

Arguably Godard's finest movie, *Le Mépris* (*Contempt*) >**3**, sees a writer, his wife, a director (played by **Lang**) and a philistine producer fall out over a film of The Odyssey: sombre, beautiful, it parallels the writer's artistic humiliation with the seduction of his wife by the producer, while stressing the lack of contact between humans by having the international crew continually speak to one another through an interpreter. Indeed, after the gangster spoof *Bande à Part* (largely made up of lively irrelevances like a record-breaking sprint through the Louvre), Godard became more and more pessimistic in his concern with exploitation, isolation and prostitution. *Une Femme Mariée* depicts a day in the life of an adulterous wife. *Alphaville* >**4** draws on myth, *film noir* and pulp sci-fi to chart a detective's war against the inhuman logic of a computerised city where women are paid seductresses and emotions banned. In *Pierrot le Fou* >**5**, about a couple's doomed flight away from a murder in the city to a brief romantic idyll on a deserted island, an intellectual writer's love for an intuitive woman ends in the man's suicide. Typically Godard saw his wayward film, shot in lush primary colours, as concerning the space between things; it endlessly refers to writers and artists, notably Velasquez.

With the end of his marriage to

Part *enfant terrible*, part cigar-chewing movie mogul: Jean-Luc Godard.

Karina, whose presence had inspired his films' witty romanticism, Godard's work became more explicitly political: *Masculin-Feminin* offers '15 precise facts' about the children of Marx and Coca-Cola to convey the confusion of contemporary youth; *Made in USA* is an impenetrable allegorical thriller (with characters named **Siegel**, **Aldrich** and **Mizoguchi**) on the Left's similarity to the Right; *Two or Three Things I Know About Her* >**6** is a fragmented account of the everyday prostitution both of a bourgeois housewife (actress Marina Vlady speaking both in character and as herself) and of Paris itself, where adverts, consumerism and industrialisation are rampant. It was, however, *La Chinoise* that cannily predicted the unrest of May '68, depicting in barely narrative form the endless ideological discussions of five young revolutionaries planning a political assassination. If prophetic, the film remains woefully verbose, its Maoist slogans simplistic and wearisome. Far more involving was the anarchically satirical *Weekend* >**7**. Here, a bourgeois couple travels through the bloody carnage of a traffic jam to kill the wife's mother for her money before meeting up with hippy cannibals, who first eat an English tourist and then the husband – to the wife's total lack of concern. Thereafter, Godard abandoned narrative cinema for years to focus on committed analyses of the political and semiological significance of words and images. In *Le Gai Savoir*, two militants in a darkened film studio discuss the (de)construction of filmic meaning; *One Plus One* (*Sympathy for the Devil*) alternates shots of the Rolling Stones in rehearsal with laconic interviews with 'Eve Democracy' and scenes of a Black Power group; *British Sounds* lends support to workers at a Ford plant; *Vent d'Est* distorts the imagery of the Western to paint a Marxist picture of a strike; *Pravda* concerns Czechoslovakia, *Vladimir and Rosa* the trial of the Chicago Eight. If Godard's rejection of mainstream film forms was revolutionary, his politics were not, and his pessimism led him to attack existing society without proposing an alternative; his dense visual and verbal dialectics were accessible only to a converted intellectual elite, rendering his status as a committed socialist artist (he had forsaken bourgeois notions of authorship to work with Jean-Pierre Gorin under the name of the **Dziga Vertov** group) profoundly problematic.

Tout Va Bien >**8** was an attempt to renew contact with a wider audience, with Jane Fonda and Yves Montand as, respectively, a US telejournalist and a film-director, musing on their involvement in a workers' sit-down strike; fiction, documentary, even humour are combined as in the early films, but here the actors serve both to attract a general public and to add their own real-life political backgrounds to the film's complexity. Then a break with Gorin saw Godard move into television and video; not until *Numero Deux*, an analysis of the exploitation of women (presumably a reply to the many charges of misogyny made against Godard's earlier work), did he make another feature; the small screen's influence is evident throughout, however, the frame frequently divided into separate video images that obscure rather than clarify the film's thesis.

In 1980 Godard returned to cinema with a vengeance, using established stars, lyrical camerawork and occasional vestiges of a plot to create a synthesis of his early, witty genre pieces and his later, more iconoclastic work. *Slow Motion* (*Sauve Qui Peut . . . La Vie*) and *Passion* were lavish but muddled, their depictions of labour/sexual relations and the problems of film-making being too piece-meal to add up to anything more than anti-realist doodles; but *First Name: Carmen* >**9** was a funny, imaginative, lively update of the famed romance, with Bizet replaced by Beethoven, the cigar-rolling heroine by a barely competent terrorist, and Spain by a seedily grandiose hotel. Similarly straightforward was *Hail Mary* >**10**, a profane Nativity tale, with Joseph deeply suspicious of Mary's fidelity and Gabriel performing the Annunciation at a gas station. *Detective* was an elegant if uneven parody of the B-movie thriller, but *King Lear* was a messy, indulgent and opaque gloss on Shakespeare and, yet again, on the problems of film-making.

While there is no denying either Godard's importance as an influence on others or his probing intelligence, his films often suffer from emotional coldness and an apparent determination to preserve his image as cinema's *enfant terrible*. An extension of his criticism, already notable for its contempt for '*le cinéma du papa*', his innovative work is often conceived as diaries or films in progress: accordingly they may be chaotic, obsessively private or infuriatingly pretentious. At his most playful, he is genuinely witty and offers surprisingly fresh ways of seeing the world. His view, however, is coloured by his love-hate relationship to film; in transforming that abiding passion into a framework for political hypothesis he often seems out of his depth. Fatally for a self-confessed intellectual, his free-wheeling style tends to militate against thorough, lucid and rational argument.

Lineage

Godard's magpie mind tends to turn everyone into a figure whose influence is to be accepted or rejected. While admiring **Nicholas Ray**, **Sirk**, **Fuller**, **Lang**, **Minnelli** and many more, his tributes to the American cinema were European in mood, relating more closely to French genre specialists like **Melville**; **Rossellini**, **Vigo**, **Renoir**, **Bresson** and documentarists Chris Marker and Jean Rouch were also an influence. His own contributions to modern cinema affected such diverse figures as **Makavejev**, **Bertolucci**, **Fassbinder**, **Cronenberg**, **Oshima**, Jean-Marie Straub, and countless others; of the latest wave of French directors, Léos Carax (who appears in *King Lear*) seems closer to Godard than Jean-Jacques Beineix or Luc Besson.

Further reading

Richard Roud's *Godard* (London, 1970), James Monaco's *The New Wave* (New York, 1977). Godard's own writings are available in *Godard on Godard*, ed. Tom Milne (London, 1972).

Viewing

1 **A Bout de Souffle (Breathless)**
France 1959/ w Jean-Paul Belmondo, Jean Seberg, Daniel Boulanger

2 **Les Carabiniers**
France 1963/ w Marino Masè, Albert Juross, Geneviève Galéa

3 **Le Mépris (Contempt)**
France 1963/ w Brigitte Bardot, Michel Piccoli, Jack Palance

4 **Alphaville (A Strange Adventure of Lemmy Caution)**
France 1965/ w Eddie Constantine, Anna Karina, Howard Vernon

5 **Pierrot le Fou**
France 1965/ w Jean-Paul Belmondo, Anna Karina, Dirk Sanders

6 **Two or Three Things I Know About Her**
France 1967/ w Marina Vlady, Anny Duperey, Roger Monsoret

7 **Weekend**
France 1967/ w Mireille Darc, Jean Yanne, Jean-Pierre Kalfon

8 **Tout Va Bien**
France 1971/ w Jane Fonda, Yves Montand, Vittorio Caprioli

9 **First Name: Carmen (Prénom Carmen)**
France 1983/ w Marushka Detmers, Jacques Bonnaffe, Godard

10 **Hail Mary (Je vous salue, Marie)**
France 1984/ w Myriem Roussel, Thierry Rode, Philippe Lacoste

Peter Greenaway

Born: 5th April 1942/London, England
Directing career: 1973-

The eccentric Peter Greenaway began his career making low-budget experimental shorts revealing an erudite obsession with taxonomy, numerology, natural history and apocryphal anecdote. It is, then, perhaps surprising that his graduation to features, made with little evidence of artistic compromise, has been so successful.

Greenaway's early films were at once formally ambitious and unusually witty satires of documentary film styles. *Windows* tells of 37 people who died falling from windows. *Water Wrackets* merges lyrical shots of streams with a dry narration about a forgotten, inhuman dynasty. *A Walk Though H* pans over weird maps to explain the work of fictional ornithologist Tulse Luper. And in *Vertical Features Remake* >**1**, various hypothetical reconstructions of a film from fragments showing upright objects in a landscape serve to parody, hilariously, academic pedantry, while the epic *The Falls* offers brief biographies of 92 victims (whose names begin with FALL) of a Violent Unknown Event involving birds.

The Draughtsman's Contract >**2** introduced Greenaway's unique, quizzical talent to a wider public. A labyrinthine 17th-century mystery (about a painter who, paid in sexual kind to commemorate a country house, believes his pictures have uncovered a murder), it is a punning portrait of patronage and class warfare between the artist and the nobility. Rather more typical of the writer-director was *A Zed & Two Noughts* >**3**, in which twins, their wives killed in a car crash caused by a flying swan, take consolation by studying biological decay, making love to the accident's sole surviving, amputee victim, and indulging a wish to become Siamese twins. Plotless, but packed with unlikely anecdote, the film, with its characters derived from Roman Gods, is a surreal black comedy about grief, loss and evolution, viewing the world as a perverse human zoo; crucially, its many intersecting ideas were lent unity by the taut symmetries of Sacha Vierny's Vermeer-inspired camera-work and by Michael Nyman's baroque music. Indeed, Greenaway's interest in visual and aural art was confirmed in television work such as the series *Four American Composers*, and a short version of *Dante's Inferno* made in collaboration with painter Tom Phillips.

Greenaway's intellectual originality is undeniable, but many felt his work lacked emotional depth. In *The Belly of an Architect*, a harrowing performance by Brian Dennehy as an American architect dying of cancer almost tears the film to shreds. Nevertheless, as the architect's life falls apart, his wife deserting him for an Italian who plans to take control of the exhibition he has planned in tribute to the unsung visionary Boullée, the film displays Greenaway's abiding reluctance merely to tell a story: Roman history and architecture, New World innocence and Old World decadence, and endless visual and verbal rhymes and allusions are interwoven in a complex configuration as intriguing as an unsolved crossword. Likewise, *Drowning By Numbers* >**4** sees a naive coroner exploited and destroyed by a friend, her daughter and grand-daughter, all three bearing the same name, all guilty of killing their husbands. Again, barbed dialogue and surrealistic imagery evoke odd, unseen bonds between primaeval game-playing and numbers, humanity and nature; again, a tall tale is invested with philosophical hypothesis, bogus statistics and magical metaphor.

If Greenaway's self-conscious excursions into private myth seem emotionally cold and so removed from everyday reality that they verge on self-parody, he remains an imaginative, provocative director. His obsession with wordplay, lists, and archival arcana might seem literary, but his eye for visual patterns and the grim beauty of nature ensure his status as a unique cinematic artist.

Lineage

While Greenaway would seem to have no real antecedents in cinema, literature supplies a parallel in the writings of Borges, and the importance of the regular contributions of Vierny and Nyman must not be underestimated. It is, however, interesting to compare his surreal/mythic tendencies with those of **Buñuel**, **Demy**, **Fellini**, **Gilliam**, **Lynch**, **Resnais**, **Syberberg**, Michel Deville and Raul Ruiz.

Viewing

1 **Vertical Features Remake**
GB 1979
2 **The Draughtsman's Contract**
GB 1982/ w Anthony Higgins, Janet Suzman, Anne Louise Lambert
3 **A Zed & Two Noughts**
GB/Ned 1985/ w Brian & Eric Deacon, Andrea Ferreol, Joss Ackland
4 **Drowning By Numbers**
GB 1988/ w Bernard Hill, Joan Plowright, Juliet Stevenson

D.W. Griffith

Born: 23rd January 1875/La Grange, Kentucky, USA
Died: 23rd July 1948/Los Angeles, California, USA
Directing career: 1908-1931

Very often, hindsight may be a distinct advantage in the attempt to evaluate the artistic status of a once popular creator; but in the case of David Wark Griffith, it is perhaps a hindrance. Considered a great innovator who towered above other directors of the silent years, many of his best-known films nevertheless now seem maudlin, dated and even, in several cases, offensive.

Raised on a Kentucky farm, Griffith was an almost archetypal Southern gentleman, courteous, determined and liberal, but marked by the experiences of slavery and the Civil War. After spending his formative years acting with touring theatrical troupes, he began work as a writer and director for Biograph Studios where, over the next five years, he made almost 500 one and two-reel films. It was at this time that Griffith (with cameraman Billy Bitzer and a group of actors that included Mary Pickford, Bobby Harron and the Gish sisters) set about exploring and expanding the language of film. Close-ups, cross-cutting and other techniques now taken for granted had in many cases already been 'invented', but it was Griffith who learned how to use them to best express emotion.

His early films are often charming, lyrical and inventive. Westerns and romances abounded, though other genres were explored in works such as *An Unseen Enemy* (a simple but effective thriller that saw the debut film appearance of Dorothy and Lillian Gish) and *The Musketeers of Pig Alley* (arguably the first gangster film). After seeing the Italian epic *Quo Vadis?*, however, Griffith ambitiously made the four-reel feature *Judith of Bethulia* >**1**. Its combination of extravagant historical reconstruction with relatively intimate scenes concerning the love-hate relationship between Judith and Holofernes, set the pattern for many of his later triumphs. But Biograph baulked at the expense of the production, and Griffith left to set up his own company with Mack Sennett and Thomas Ince.

In 1915 Griffith's most successful and controversial film, *The Birth of a Nation* >**2**, was released. Following the fortunes of two families – one Southern, one Northern – during and after the Civil War, he drew upon both his personal love for the South and the technical lessons of the Biograph years. An astounding three-hour epic, its battle scenes seem even now powerfully real, while a last-minute rescue – a regular climactic finale in his shorts – is a model of fast, exciting cross-cutting. But Griffith's film, while grieving over the futility of war and the death of Lincoln, was also racist in its portrayal of irresponsible and treacherous blacks who challenge white supremacy during the Reconstruction of the South; its heroes are the Ku Klux Klan. Understandably, its status as the first genuine masterpiece of the American cinema was fiercely

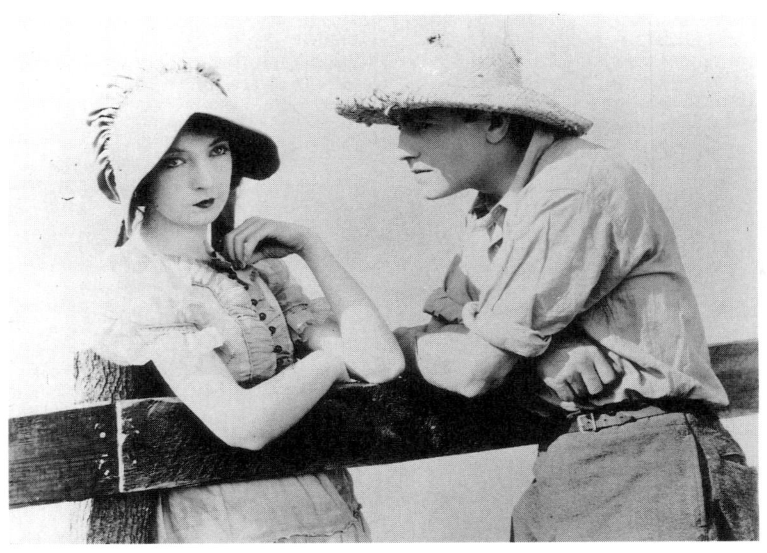

Lillian Gish and Richard Barthelmess in Griffith's *Way Down East.*

questioned by blacks and civil rights groups.

As if in reply to his critics, Griffith's following film was called *Intolerance* >**3**. Another truly gargantuan epic, it paints a picture of cruelty and injustice through the ages by intercutting four thematically linked stories: the crucifixion of Christ, the fall of Babylon, the St Bartholomew's Day Massacre, and a modern story concerning strike-breaking, reform movements, and a young husband wrongly accused of murder. Again, the scale is vast and the technique formidable, most notably in the scenes of thousands of extras cavorting around the monumental Babylonian set. Again too, however, the message was blurred by frequent lapses into maudlin, portentous moralising.

Contemporary audiences found *Intolerance* long and hard to understand; its immense ambitions were its commercial downfall. Wisely if, perhaps, reluctantly, Griffith began making simpler, less expensive pastoral romances and lyrical melodramas in which Bitzer's shimmering camerawork and Lillian Gish's increasingly subtle performances held sway. *Hearts of the World* >**4** was a love story set against the backdrop of the Great War; *True Heart Susie* >**5** a tender account of rural life and emotional self-sacrifice; *Broken Blossoms* >**6** a magnificently atmospheric studio recreation of London's Limehouse, the setting for a tragic friendship between a poverty-stricken waif and a gentle Chinaman. Notably, though the plot suggests that Griffith was horrified by the very prospect of miscegenation, he allows his Oriental hero a far greater dignity than the blacks in *The Birth of a Nation*.

In 1920, together with **Chaplin**, Douglas Fairbanks and Mary Pickford, he formed United Artists, and built his own studio. His star was on the wane, however, even if *Way Down East* >**7** (a turgid tale of an innocent girl tricked into a false marriage, redeemed by a stirring climax in which Richard Barthelmess rescues Lillian Gish from an ice floe) was a substantial hit. *Orphans of the Storm* >**8** – impressive in its portrayal of hardship and poverty, and featuring the storming of the Bastille, duels, abductions and a rescue from the guillotine – reunited the Gish sisters; but this tale of the French Revolution failed to find the audience it deserved. Griffith's Victorian values and lofty sermonising were becoming increasingly unfashionable in an age more concerned with vamps and gangsters; as his films became more conventional, so his audiences and financiers deserted him. Indeed, after making just two talkies (the first, *Abraham Lincoln* >**9**, featuring a very effective performance by Walter Huston), he faded from view.

Griffith, finally, was a man of contradictions. Forever tied to the morality and, to some extent, the dramatic conventions of the 19th century and the Old South, he was nevertheless a crucial figure in the development of a film language during the medium's infancy. For the director, preachy messages often took precedence over technique; whereas for modern audiences, his narrative flair and originality would seem to be of far greater importance.

Lineage

Griffith's influence is immense. Interestingly, many important early Hollywood directors – **Browning**, **Dwan**, **Ford**, **Walsh** and **Von Stroheim** among them – worked as actors or assistants on *The Birth of a Nation* and *Intolerance*; his editing style, pictorial realism and conception of film as a pedagogic medium for the masses were greatly admired by Soviet film-makers. More recently, the **Taviani Brothers** paid tribute to Griffith in *Good Morning, Babylon*.

Further reading

Anthony Slide and Edward Wagenknecht *The Films of D.W. Griffith* (New York, 1975), Lillian Gish's *The Movies, Mr Griffith and Me* (New Jersey, 1969), Karl Brown's *Adventures with D.W. Griffith* (New York, 1973).

Viewing

1 **Judith of Bethulia**
US 1914/ w Blanche Sweet, Henry B. Walthall, Mae Marsh
2 **The Birth of a Nation**
US 1915/ w Mae Marsh, Lillian Gish, Robert Harron
3 **Intolerance**
US 1916/ w Mae Marsh, Robert Harron, Constance Talmadge
4 **Hearts of the World**
US 1918/ w Lillian Gish, Dorothy Gish, Noel Coward
5 **True Heart Susie**
US 1919/ w Lillian Gish, Robert Harron, Clarine Seymour
6 **Broken Blossoms**
US 1919/ w Lillian Gish, Richard Barthelmess, Donald Crisp
7 **Way Down East**
US 1920/ w Lillian Gish, Richard Barthelmess, Lowell Sherman
8 **Orphans of the Storm**
US 1921/ w Lillian Gish, Dorothy Gish, Joseph Schildkraut
9 **Abraham Lincoln**
US 1930/ w Walter Huston, Una Merkel

Yilmaz Güney

Born: 1st April 1937/near Adana, Turkey
Died: 9th September 1984/Paris, France
Directing career: 1966-1982

The production methods and, indeed, the meaning of the films for which Yilmaz Güney (born Putun) remains best known are inextricably connected to the troubled circumstances of their making. Such was Güney's talent as a writer-director, however, that a knowledge of Turkish political history is not necessary to appreciate his work.

After studies in law and economics, Güney entered the movies in the late '50s as a writer and assistant director. Following a prison sentence for writing a novel deemed pro-Communist, he then established himself as a matinee-idol ('the Ugly King') in heroic adventures he had written himself. In 1966 he made his directing debut with *The Horse, The Woman, the Gun*; not until 1970, however, did he develop a mature style of his own. In *Hope* (*Umut*) a down-at-heel cab-driver dreams of finding hidden treasure, leaves his family and embarks upon a search that ends in madness; in *Elegy* (*Ağit*), a rural bandit-smuggler is betrayed by the treacherous, middle-class entrepreneurs for whom he takes risks, having been hounded (in starkly dramatic images sometimes reminiscent of the Westerns of **Leone**) by a faceless, gun-toting militia. Conversely, *The Friend* (*Arkadas*), made after Güney's further imprisonment for sheltering militants, transfers its ironic gaze from the poor and needy to the bourgeoisie: a former political activist's visit to the home of a now wealthy old friend provokes tensions within the latter's family, while driving the protagonist to suicide. The bleak realism of Güney's films was so at odds with the bland melodrama favoured by the authorities that it was not unexpected when, in 1974, he was sentenced to 24 years for the alleged murder of a judge.

Due both to his national popularity and to the comparatively liberal tendencies of the short-lived Ecevit government, Güney was allowed to make, as it were by proxy, several more films from prison, sending highly detailed scripts to Serif Gören and Zeki Ökten, directors he trusted to abide by his instructions. *The Herd* (*Sürü*) >**1** took an unsentimental look at the patriarchal, superstitious lives of peasants and the corruption of the bureaucracy as a sheep-farming family disintegrates during its epic overland journey to the city of Ankara; *The Enemy* examines the destructive effect of poverty and ignorance upon a marriage. Most impressively, *Yol* (*The Way*) >**2** viewed the entire country as a prison: five convicts discover, during a week-long parole that Turkey is chained by feudal poverty, hatred and bigotry to a violent medieval morality; adulterous women are caged like animals or even killed, Kurdish peasants are repressed and massacred by the militia. Güney's stories, bleak, simple and powerful, never glorify the traditions of the peasant life, but display the way they have been stunted by an uncaring government.

In 1981, a year after martial law was established, the director escaped to Switzerland while, in Turkey, *The Friend*, *The Herd* and *The Enemy* were banned. With French finance, he then made *The Wall* >**3**, a dramatic reconstruction of events leading up to an Ankara prison revolt in 1976. Even though most of the violence was kept offscreen, the sheer repetition of scenes showing aggression and suffering tends to dissipate the film's power. Nonetheless, in stressing the very tedium that defines the humiliation and repression of prison life, Güney avoided melodramatic cliche to create a plausible microcosm of a society engineered and immured by the powers of Fascism.

Tragically, Güney died from cancer shortly after the release of the film, the first he had directed himself since *The Friend*, eight years earlier. That he could ever have returned to Turkey is unlikely; but his sense of socio-political injustice, and his ability to express it lucidly in images of stark beauty, suggest that in exile he might still have become a major director.

Lineage

Güney was a revolutionary force in Turkish cinema, bringing realism to a country weaned on routine fantasies, even though he had seen very little Western cinema; even so, he may be compared to figures such as **Rosi**, Gillo Pontecorvo, and (visually) **Leone**.

Viewing

1 **The Herd (Sürü)**
Turkey 1979/ w Tarik Aken, Melika Deminag
2 **Yol (The Way)**
Turkey 1981/ w Tarik Aken, Halil Eergun
3 **The Wall**
France 1982/ w Saban, Sisko, Ziya

Robert Hamer

Born: **31st March 1911/ Kidderminster, England**
Died: **4th December 1963/London?, England**
Directing career: **1945-1960**

Briefly, Robert Hamer introduced psychological sophistication and bleak pessimism to the largely cheery portraits of British life perpetrated by Michael Balcon's Ealing Studios. Alas, however, increasing alcoholism had a detrimental effect on his later work.

A former editor and scriptwriter, Hamer's directing debut was the impressive 'Haunted Mirror' episode in Ealing's compendium horror film *Dead of Night*; interestingly, its disturbing tale of a complacent young couple whose purchase of an antique mirror gives rise to murderous sexual jealousies, foreshadows the themes of his finest work. *Pink String and Sealing Wax* >**1**, in which a young man yields to adulterous lust and becomes involved in a murder after entering a pub against his strait-laced father's orders, is a vivid portrait of the traumatic effects of repressive patriarchy and obsessive conformism. It was lent power by an elegant, unsentimental presentation of Victorian Brighton and by superb acting, most notably by Googie Withers as the bored, voluptuous barmaid who exploits the boy to gain the poison that will kill her husband. She starred again in *It Always Rains on Sunday* >**2**, a taut contemporary thriller set in an authentically evoked East End of London, as a housewife whose past erupts into her routine, stultifying life in the form of her ex-lover – an escaped convict who persuades her to hide him in the bedroom while her family waits, as ever, for the Sunday lunch. Once more the threat to the status quo is sexual, but the sympathy for Withers in each film suggests Hamer's hatred for the suppression of passion that the conformist discipline of family life can entail.

Class, too, was seen, as a constricting force, nowhere more so than in *Kind Hearts and Coronets* >**3**, a Wildean masterpiece of dark wit. Again the theme is subversive: determined to avenge the insults paid his mother after she eloped with a lowly Italian, a young haberdasher decides to lay claim to his rightful Dukedom by murdering the entire D'Ascoyne family (all eight members of which are played by Alec Guinness). The vision of Britain as a haven of snobbery and tradition makes for powerful satire, but the greatest *coup* lies in Hamer's marriage of highly literary dialogue to a pictorial style that is both elegant and comic, and in his use of typically English *sang froid* to express outrageous moral values.

Thereafter, the director's career went into steep decline. While retaining visual and verbal felicities, his work displayed a lack of energy and discipline. *The Spider and the Fly* was a spasmodically intriguing mystery set in World War I France, *The Long Memory* a dull revenge drama, *Father Brown* a meandering and strangely dour, though finely acted, adaptation of G.K. Chesterton's detective stories, and *The Scapegoat* a stylish murder thriller often rendered incoherent by re-editing demanded by Hollywood. Finally, Hamer suffered the indignity of being removed from directing the limp, episodic one-upmanship satire, *School for Scoundrels*, before its completion.

In mapping out the dark currents of sexuality, violence and class conflict lying beneath the apparently unruffled waters of British society, Hamer proved one of the most fascinating and provocative of postwar British directors. Without resort to cosily parochial comedy or documentary realism, his work was, for a few short years, defined by an unusually subtle, tough and subversive romanticism.

Lineage

Of regular Ealing directors (Charles Crichton, Charles Frend, Basil Dearden, Henry Cornelius *et al*), Hamer is rivalled only by **Alexander Mackendrick** as a fiercely individual, pessimistic talent. He may be compared tentatively with **Carné**, **Siodmak**, and early **Mankiewicz**.

Further reading

Charles Barr's *Ealing Studios* (London, 1977).

Viewing

1 **Pink String and Sealing Wax**
GB 1945/ w Gordon Jackson, Googie Withers, Mervyn Johns

2 **It Always Rains on Sunday**
GB 1947/ w Googie Withers, Edward Chapman, John McCallum

3 **Kind Hearts and Coronets**
GB 1949/ w Dennis Price, Alec Guinness, Joan Greenwood

Howard Hawks

Born: 30th May 1896/Goshen, Indiana, USA
Died: 26th December 1977/Palm Springs, California, USA
Directing career: 1926-1967

Howard Winchester Hawks, by his own confession a storyteller only interested in 'fun and business', was one of the finest directors cinema has known. An unassuming entertainer working in almost all the traditional Hollywood genres, he brought a personal style and vision intuitively to bear on a startling diversity of material. Indeed, it may be argued that his Westerns, war movies, screwball comedies, his contributions to the private eye and gangster thriller, and to the sci-fi genre have rarely been surpassed.

Hawks' first encounter with the movies was as a prop-boy but, after the First World War, during which he served in the US Army Air Corps, he worked as editor and assistant to directors like **Dwan** and Marshall Neilan. By 1924 he was head of the Paramount story department, and two years later he made his directing debut with *The Road to Glory*. His silent work was routine, but mostly but efficiently crafted, and *A Girl in Every Port* >**1**, starring Louise Brooks, introduced the enduring Hawksian theme of male friendship threatened by a strong female. With sound, however, the director came into his own, using fast, often overlapping, dialogue to create tension, while gesture and action defined character. His first talkie, *The Dawn Patrol* >**2**, established an archetypal Hawks situation: during the First World War fliers overcome their fear of death through professionalism and a mutual respect barely expressed in words. Male groups, stoically coping with danger, appear repeatedly in Hawks' adventure films, allowing for subtle variations on themes of courage, integration, failure and responsibility. *The Criminal Code* concerns a prison revolt, *The Crowd Roars* is about motor-racing, *Tiger Shark* deals with tuna-fishermen. Throughout, heroic action was balanced by dark wit, and *Scarface* >**3**, by far the best of early gangster movies, depicts its Capone-like protagonist as a bestial moron plagued by an incestuous jealousy towards his sister, his sole redeeming feature his love of opera.

Indeed, besides his action films, Hawks also proved himself a superb director of comedy, often about the battle of the sexes. One of the greatest screwball comedies, *Twentieth Century* >**4**, pits a ruthlessly manipulative Svengali against his cunning protegée, an ingenue-turned-star; a hilarious satire on unbridled theatrical habits, its use of John Barrymore's famed hamminess is inspired. *Bringing Up Baby* >**5** throws together a drab palaeontologist and a madcap socialite in a romantic farce to portray the attraction of insanity; interestingly, the insecurity about women implicit in the male groups of the adventure films becomes, in the comedies, a total paranoia and impotence. In fact, by the time of *Only Angels Have Wings* >**6**, a flying drama in which Cary Grant struggles to keep afloat an airline carrying mail over the Andes, comedy is inseparable from tragedy and the platonic love between men explicit: a pilot's sudden death is remembered in jokes and songs that hide his colleagues' grief; the women, whose presence first threatens the group's unity, simultaneously prove themselves by acting like the men, serving to expose the fliers' unspoken, tender emotions.

Increasingly, Hawks played against sexual stereotypes and genre conventions. *His Girl Friday*, >**7** perhaps the fastest-talking comedy ever, derives humour from macabre situations (ruthlessly self-centred, a newspaper editor fights to prevent his wife/star reporter from leaving him in order to scoop a witless innocent's execution for murder); while *Ball of Fire* translates the story of Snow White into a gangster comedy about a burlesque dancer and seven childlike professors researching a lexicon of slang. At the same time *Sergeant York* weaves pacifist sentiments into the tale of a war hero, and the thrillers *To Have*

Howard Hawks (right) prepares to go ape with Cary Grant, chimp and Henri Letondal, on the set of *Monkey Business*.

and Have Not and *The Big Sleep* >**8** become, primarily, witty romances fired by the sparring between Bogart and Hawks' discovery, Lauren Bacall. Dialogue, insolent and laden with innuendo, suggests the unseen barriers characters build against each other; deeper emotions are conveyed through a dazzling, often ironic array of subtle gestures, notably centred around the communal ritual of lighting cigarettes. Effectively, Hawks was now less interested in story than characters, proudly admitting that neither he nor Raymond Chandler knew who killed the chauffeur in the labyrinthine *noir* plotting of *The Big Sleep*.

The director's art had reached the point where he no longer felt the need to conceal his abiding preoccupations. Recurring in film after film, scenes and even lines of dialogue used in varied contexts, supply endless emotional nuances; Hawks even remade *Ball of Fire* as the musical *A Song Is Born*. *Red River* >**9** was the first of four Westerns with John Wayne; typically, the actor's heroic, determined persona is turned into a portrait of warped patriarchy as he obsessively leads an epic cattle drive that results in both his cowhands and his surrogate son losing faith in him. *The Thing From Another World* >**10**, too, while credited as directed by Hawks' editor Christian Nyby, is clearly the work of the master: again, amid hectic dialogue and witty asides, an isolated group (boffins in the Arctic) threatens to fall apart with an outsider's arrival (not, this time, a woman but an alien 'intellectual carrot'). But the sex war continued in comedies laced with dark hints of insanity and humiliation: *I Was a Male War Bride* (*You Can't Sleep Here*), *Monkey Business*, and the lavish musical *Gentlemen Prefer Blondes* >**11**, which effortlessly turns a farce about gold-diggers into both a tribute to female guile and a jibe at infantile male lechery.

Towards the end of his career, Hawks' films became ever more leisurely in style, the hectic dialogue yielding to a relaxed and contemplative summation of themes. *Rio Bravo* >**12**, besides being a witty riposte to *High Noon* (the sheriff rejects, rather than asks for, the help he desperately needs against the villains), becomes a moving portrait of redemption through self-respect, its drunken deputy reprised in barely different form in the later, very similar *El Dorado*. Indeed, almost all of Hawks' last films may be viewed as variations on earlier work. The safari group of *Hatari!* >**13** combines aspects of *Only Angels Have Wings*, *Red River* and *Rio Bravo*; *Man's Favourite Sport*, which wittily equates fishing with courtship strategies, brazenly quotes from *Bringing Up Baby*; the often stilted *Red Line 7000* returns to car-racing; while one last Western, *Rio Lobo*, adds (perhaps appropriately) the problem of ageing to the clutch of motifs that had consistently been refined throughout Hawks' work for some three-and-a-half decades.

In moving increasingly further from plot towards characters concerned with basic moral and social issues, Hawks proved himself a great humanist. His unassertive style (eye-level medium shots, unobtrusive editing, linear narratives that observe the dramatic unities) avoided self-consciousness, reflecting not the gaze of a lofty artist, but the essential worth of his characters (and, by implication, his audience), while the full rein he allowed actors ensured a rare spontaneity. In adapting genre to his own purposes, Hawks displayed an unpatronising attitude to popular entertainment and transformed a personal world-view into universal myth.

Lineage

Less maudlin and determinedly poetic than **Ford**, with whom he is often compared, Hawks' portrait of humans defined by action has a parallel in **Walsh**, while his generosity towards their inner lives echoes **Renoir**. The diversity of his work ensures his wide-ranging influence; recently, on **Bogdanovich**, **Hill** and **Carpenter**.

Further reading

Robin Wood's *Howard Hawks* (London, 1977), Gerald Mast's *Howard Hawks, Storyteller* (New York, 1982); Peter Bogdanovich's *The Cinema of Howard Hawks* (New York, 1962) features an interview.

Viewing

1 **A Girl in Every Port**
US 1928/ w Victor McLaglen, Robert Armstrong, Louise Brooks

2 **The Dawn Patrol**
US 1930/ w Richard Barthelmess, Douglas Fairbanks Jr, Clyde Cook

3 **Scarface (Shame of a Nation)**
US 1932/ w Paul Muni, Ann Dvorak, Boris Karloff, George Raft

4 **Twentieth Century**
US 1934/ w John Barrymore, Carole Lombard, Walter Connolly

5 **Bringing Up Baby**
US 1938/ w Cary Grant, Katharine Hepburn, Charles Ruggles

6 **Only Angels Have Wings**
US 1939/ w Cary Grant, Jean Arthur, Richard Barthelmess

7 **His Girl Friday**
US 1940/ w Cary Grant, Rosalind Russell, Ralph Bellamy

8 **The Big Sleep**
US 1946/ w Humphrey Bogart, Lauren Bacall, John Ridgely

9 **Red River**
US 1948/ w John Wayne, Montgomery Clift, Joanne Dru

10 **The Thing (from Another World)**
US 1951/ w Kenneth Tobey, Robert Cornthwaite, Margaret Sheridan

11 **Gentlemen Prefer Blondes**
US 1953/ w Marilyn Monroe, Jane Russell, Charles Coburn

12 **Rio Bravo**
US 1959/ w John Wayne, Dean Martin, Angie Dickinson

13 **Hatari!**
US 1962/ w John Wayne, Elsa Martinelli, Red Buttons

Werner Herzog

Born: 5th September 1942/Munich, West Germany
Directing career: 1962-

The sensation of *déjà vu* that may accompany viewings of the more recent films of Werner Herzog – born Werner Stipetic – cannot obscure his status as an eccentric original of enormous talent. Eclectically drawing style and subject from a diversity of sources – German Romanticism and Expressionism, surrealism, ethnology, his own travels around the world – he has created a body of work almost unique in its epic ambitions and its despair at the banality of human aspirations.

After studying history, literature and drama, Herzog taught himself film-making with a number of shorts financed by his work as a welder. An ostensibly realist feature debut, *Signs of Life*, anticipated later motifs: as a German soldier, bored at a useless munitions dump in Crete during World War II, slowly goes insane, man's smallness in relation to nature is shown through intensely lyrical landscape photography, and his madness provides visionary epiphanies (the hero cracks at the sight of a plain dappled with countless windmills). Even more bizarre, both *Fata Morgana* >**1** and *Even Dwarfs Started Small* also took Herzog to strange landscapes: the first, set amid debris left by humanity on the Sahara's edge, is a surreal, plotless, ironic parody of creation myths, with the Gods' arrival on Earth implied by repeated shots of a jet spewing fumes as it lands; the second, made on the arid volcanic island of Lanzarotte, satirises the futility of human activity in its account of a revolt by inmates at a dwarfs' penal institution that climaxes in wanton destruction and a driverless truck endlessly circling.

Conversely, the documentary *Land of Silence and Darkness* >**2** – arguably Herzog's finest film – is a deeply moving portrait of an elderly woman deaf and blind since childhood. As she takes her first ride in a plane, overjoyed by interior emotions rather than the things we see but she cannot, Herzog shows that life, however difficult, is immensely valuable. Indeed, his sympathy has often gone out to outcasts usually deemed abnormal, mad, or grotesque. *Aguirre, Wrath of God* >**3** examines the megalomaniac defiance of God by the Spanish conquistador leading a doomed exhibition up the Amazon in search of the mythical El Dorado; a documentary on a champion ski jumper, *The Great Ecstasy of Woodcarver Steiner*, becomes a tribute to fearless obsession; and *The Enigma of Kaspar Hauser* >**4** (*Every Man for Himself and God Against All*) insists on the dignity and truth of the dreams of a middle-aged foundling discovered, as if newly born, in a town square in the 1820s. For Herzog, there is beauty in madness: Aguirre asserts his godliness over a stranded raft peopled only by monkeys; Kaspar's lack of 'civilisation' is infinitely worthier than the pedantry of the scientists and the dogmatic obstinacy of the pastors who try to explain his origins and save his soul. Normal society is perceived as cruel, blinkered and hampered by empiricism, and only the eternal elements – portrayed in lavish, lingering shots of streaming clouds, billowing meadows, rippling rivers, craggy cliffs – are untainted, unless by man.

Werner Herzog ponders the Herculean task of hauling a ship over a mountain for *Fitzcarraldo.*

Herzog's nostalgic romanticism has led him to ever more extreme celebrations of seers and noble savages: in *Heart of Glass*, the coming of the Industrial Revolution is viewed as the apocalyptic end of an Arcadian era, while the film's prophetic intensity is increased by the director's hypnotising of his cast throughout; in *Stroszek* >**5**, a trio of outcasts leave Germany for the promised land of America, where their dreams of a better life founder in a morass of credit cards, repossession and desperate armed robbery; and in *Nosferatu the Vampyre*, a tribute to and remake of Murnau's horror classic, Dracula is not only a threat to bourgeois society but the sorrowing victim of his own immortal misery. Central to the success of this last film, which stressed beauty and pathos over horror, was the performance of Klaus Kinski, who had played Aguirre and would come increasingly to represent, in Herzog's future work, the obsessive underdog at the end of his tether.

Woyzeck was a moving, relatively straightforward and small-scale adaptation of Buchner's play about a quiet soldier impelled by the hideous scientific experiments of the military authorities to murder his wife, but *Fitzcarraldo* >**6** offered evidence that the writer-director was in decline. About an Irish plantation owner's efforts to build an opera house deep in the Amazon jungle in the last century, it is wilfully epic, and its overblown treatment of typically bizarre material often seems suspiciously like self-parody. Irony is sadly absent, and despite the often impressive visual audacity – notably the scenes of a paddle-steamer being dragged over a mountain from one river to another – the film remains oddly hollow, working most fruitfully as a surreal documentary on its own hazardous making. The same may be said of Herzog's subsequent films. Shot in the Australian outback, *Where the Green Ants Dream* weakened its pro-Aborigine message by applying a muddled mystical gloss to the story of a fight for land rights, while *Cobra Verde*, admirable in its sumptuous but never sentimental evocation of the trappings of a West African dynasty, was an inept and incoherent account of the mentality of colonialism and slavery. Except ~~for~~ Herzog's regular documentary work (*Ballad of the Little Soldier*'s moving examination of the training of Nicaraguan children for war proved his non-fictional films to be as sceptical as the features of accepted versions of reality), it has seemed increasingly as if the director was finally running out of imaginative steam.

Herzog is a poet of the apocalypse, and yet the images that accompany his tales of man's folly reveal the harsh beauty and permanence of the universe. Full of such contradictions (his work is simultaneously ecstatic and despairing, contemptuous of and sympathetic to others), he seems unconcerned by commercial cinema; the medium is a channel for his private dreams, and his finest films revel in irrationality, imbued with a power that defies common logic.

Lineage

Unlike most directors of the New German Cinema, Herzog prefers the personal and epic to the political and realist; he has described himself as a Bavarian in the style of castle-building Ludwig II, and his work compares to the art of Caspar David Friedrich. **Paul Cox** and documentarist Errol Morris are admirers. He is in two Les Blank documentaries, *Burden of Dreams* (on making *Fitzcarraldo*), and *Werner Herzog Eats His Shoe* – a gambling debt paid to Morris.

Further reading

John Sandford's *The New German Cinema* (London, 1980).

Viewing

1 **Fata Morgana**
W. Germany 1970

2 **Land of Silence and Darkness**
W. Germany 1971

3 **Aguirre, Wrath of God**
W. Germany 1972/ w Klaus Kinski, Cecilia Rivera, Ruy Guerra

4 **The Enigma of Kaspar Hauser (Jeder Für Sich und Gott Gegen Alle)**
W. Germany 1974/ w Bruno S, Walter Ladengast, Brigitte Mira

5 **Stroszek (The Ballad of Bruno S)**
W. Germany 1977/ w Bruno S, Eva Mattes, Clemens Scheitz

6 **Fitzcarraldo**
W. Germany 1982/ w Klaus Kinski, Claudia Cardinale, Paul Hiltscher

Walter Hill

Born: 10th January 1942/Long Beach, California, USA
Directing career: 1975-

In the early years of his career, Walter Hill was one of the most promising young Hollywood directors. But, after the disappointing box-offices of his best work, he appears to have been seduced by the success of *48 HRS* into more conventional, anonymous material.

A former assistant to Norman Jewison and **Woody Allen**, Hill made a name for himself in the early '70s writing action movies; **Peckinpah**'s *The Getaway* remains by far the most notable. In 1975 he made his directing debut with *Hard Times*

(*The Streetfighter*), an atmospheric bare-knuckle boxing exploiter set in New Orleans during the Depression. More ambitiously, *The Driver* >**1** not only proved Hill's abilities in the action arena (the car chases are expertly staged) but revealed his interest in the mythic elements of traditional Hollywood genres: the central characters – simply called the Driver, the Detective, the Girl – are taciturn cyphers in a moody, almost abstractly formalised game of double-cross, their laconic exchanges reluctantly acknowledging their rivals' professionalism. Similarly, *The Warriors* >**2** explicitly drew from myth – Xenophon's *Anabasis* – to portray a street gang's perilous journey home to Coney Island during one long dark night of brutal teenage warfare. Hill's punchy editing and lurid, neon-lit images transform New York into a fantastic urban desert while the gangs, equipped with bizarre uniforms and weapons, are reminiscent of futuristic tribes, each defined by its own idiosyncratic powers.

Pursuit and conflict were essential elements in these quirky distillations of action-movie conventions; but far more important was the accent on ritual and the delineation of character through deeds rather than words. In *The Long Riders* >**3**, a fine account of the James-Younger gang's bank raid at Northfield, Minnesota, the theme of kinship that underlies its study in loyalty and betrayal is emphasised by the casting of three sets of real-life brothers (Stacey and James Keach, Randy and Dennis Quaid, David, Keith and Robert Carradine) as the outlaws, while stark, lyrical images of funerals, dances and other family gatherings pay tribute to older Westerns; indeed, the film is not 'about' individuals at all but about the genre itself. Equally unconcerned with psychological realism, *Southern Comfort* >**4** transforms a battle in the Louisiana bayoux, between part-time National Guardsmen and barely seen Cajuns, into an allegory on America's doomed war against Vietnamese guerillas.

48 HRS, an efficient cop-thriller with witty buddy-routines between shamblng Nick Nolte and supercool Eddie Murphy, was far more conventional, the oppressive silences and bleak austerity of the early films replaced by hip backchat and slick urban glamour. In *Streets of Fire*, a thudding return to gang warfare, myth gives way to comic-strip caricature and rock 'n 'roll cliches. *Brewster's Millions* was a bland remake of the old comedy chestnut in which a man has to spend an entire fortune in a month in order to inherit ten times that amount; *Crossroads*, a misbegotten tribute to black blues artists, featured a white teenage hero; *Extreme Prejudice* was an irrelevant, hollow update of Peckinpah's *The Wild Bunch* with a Texas ranger, aided by Vietnam veterans, conducting a bloody, hi-tech campaign against a drugs ring on the Mexican border.

Though *Red Heat* (a culture-clash cop-thriller set in Chicago and Moscow) was seen by many as something of a return to form, in abandoning his mythic tone for a more traditional and glossy slant on genre, Hill has exposed an uneasiness in dealing with human emotion; characters now seem mere macho clichés, plots contrived; his more adventurous early work, however, remains impressive for its stark visual simplicity, taut pacing and the director's ability to revitalise and comment on Hollywood conventions without sliding into parody.

Lineage

The laconic understatement of Hill's finest work has its ancestry in **Hawks**, **Melville**, **Peckinpah** and **Leone**. Tentative comparisons may be made with **Carpenter**, **Malick**, **Michael Mann** and **Milius**.

Viewing

1 **The Driver**
US 1978/ w Ryan O'Neal, Isabelle Adjani, Bruce Dern

2 **The Warriors**
US 1979/ w Michael Beck, James Remar, Deborah Van Valkenburgh

3 **The Long Riders**
US 1980/ w the Keach, Carradine, Quaid and Guest brothers.

4 **Southern Comfort**
US 1981/ w Keith Carradine, Powers Boothe, Fred Ward

Alfred Hitchcock

Born: **13th August 1899/Leytonstone, London, England**
Died: **29th April 1980/Los Angeles, California, USA**
Directing career: 1926-76

The self-styled 'master of suspense', Alfred Joseph Hitchcock has been described as a Catholic theologian, as a formalist important for his manipulative use of narrative and as an austere moralist. But such claims seem at odds with the actual experience of seeing his work: primarily concerned with the psychology of fear, he was forever devising new ways to frighten both his characters and the audience. Thematic consistency, apart from several motifs common to most thrillers (guilt, hounded innocents, *femmes fatales* and death), is conspicuous by its absence from his work. Rather, his greatness lies in his development of a homogeneous style which he applied to various genres, transforming them all into suspense.

Hitchcock's first employment in the film industry was as the designer of title-cards for Famous Players-Lasky movies at their Islington studios in London. Soon, encouraged by Michael Balcon, he progressed via writing to directing, and made his first feature, *The Pleasure Garden*. But it was *The Lodger*, also made in 1926, that established him as a promising talent. About a man suspected of being Jack the Ripper, it made fresh use of Expressionist visuals, while featuring the director himself in a brief cameo appearance – something that would recur, with increasingly jokey cleverness, in his every film. At this time, in fact, his admiration for the German and Soviet cinemas was clear and, in his best silent, *The Ring* >**1** (a pun on a love triangle set in the boxing world), a drunk's vision as he passes out is conveyed by an image that 'melts' and slides off-screen; similarly, *Blackmail* >**2**, both Hitchcock's and Britain's first talkie, not only bathes its story (a policeman's girlfriend is blackmailed after she kills a lecherous assailant) in shadows but reveals an inventive enthusiasm for sound – as the guilt-ridden girl listens to a conversation, she hears only the word 'knife', which steadily grows louder on the soundtrack until it finally blots out all other noise.

But it was not until 1934 after several melodramas, comedies and musicals, that Hitchcock became a regular thriller-director with *The Man Who Knew Too Much*, followed by *The 39 Steps* >**3**, *Secret Agent*, *Sabotage*, *Young and Innocent* and *The Lady Vanishes* >**4**. Fast-paced, and notable for virtuoso set-pieces, vivid characters, colourful, witty dialogue and a preference for dramatic, familiar locations, the films often hinged on a MacGuffin: something that is purely a plot motor, so irrelevant to the film's theme that its exact nature is never divulged. In *The 39 Steps*, for example, the stolen plans serve merely to endanger the hero, forcing him to live on his wits as he comes up against police, enemy agents and a woman who wrongly suspects him of murder. Even more irrelevant was the female spy who goes mysteriously missing from a European train in *The Lady Vanishes*, an adroit and dazzling comedy-thriller set on the eve of war; her real function was to unite an apparently mismatched couple, amidst pleas to stay alert against the Nazis (even two cricket-mad Englishmen finally take up weapons and forget their ludicrously isolationist disdain for those who don't share their obsession).

Hitchcock's ability to capitalise on almost any genre for his own dark and comic form of suspense became even more apparent when he went to Hollywood to take advantage of more sophisticated technology. *Rebecca* >**5** (a Gothic romance laced with a morbid fear of death) and *Suspicion* (in which a woman comes to believe that her husband plans to murder her) turn novelettish material into nightmare; in *Foreign Correspondent*, *Saboteur* and *Lifeboat*, thrills combine with wartime propaganda; *Shadow of a Doubt* >**6** lends a dark, diabolical dimension to the low-key realism of a smalltown domestic drama as a bored young girl's dreams of an exciting family life are answered by the arrival of a favourite uncle. He, it turns out, is a wife-murderer. By the time of *Spellbound*, Hitchcock's taste for 'pure cinema' (the telling of a story through purely visual means) had led to formal experimentation, with Salvador Dali hired to design a surreal dream scene to embellish the psychoanalytical theme. Indeed, after *Notorious* >**7**, a bitter-sweet blend of lush romance and spy thriller which presented an unusually mature male-female love relationship, both *Rope* and *Under Capricorn* consisted of very long takes and complex camera movements. The first, about two killers who conceal a corpse in a trunk from which their dinner guests – including the victim's parents – will serve themselves with food, was constructed from shots lasting an entire 10-minute reel. Cutting, however, was central to the creation of tension, and thereafter Hitchcock would alternate slow tracking shots with rapid montage.

Frequently he focussed on psychopaths, seen as more charming and intelligent than their victims, to define a world where order and chaos, the normal and the abnormal, coexist in precarious balance. *Strangers on a Train* >**8**, in which a sportsman jokingly agrees to exchange murders with a fellow passenger who then proceeds to put their 'plan' into practice, creates patterns of light and shadow to paint a picture of the two men as mirror-images of each other. *I Confess* (a killer confesses his guilt to a priest who is bound to silence) was worthy but dull, *Dial M for Murder* an unusually stagey experiment with 3D, before Hitchcock regained his stride with a series of films that included his finest work. *Rear Window* >**9** was a witty, amoral and complex study of voyeurism, its camera confined, along with the crippled photojournalist hero, to one room, the apartments he watches providing stories in which he becomes increasingly involved, as if watching a film; like us, he is both excited and disturbed by his belief that he may have been a witness to murder. *Vertigo* >**10** was a slow, bleak romance about a detective, deranged by guilt and necrophile obsession, trying to turn a girl into

On the set of *Psycho*, Alfred Hitchcock prepares Janet Leigh for what would become the most famous shower-scene of all time; 45 seconds long, it was pieced together from some 70 separate shots.

his ideal woman; Hitchcock's lack of interest in conventional suspense was evident from the way he 'explained' his mystery halfway through the movie. Indeed, that such films had an altogether stronger emotional force than those made earlier, may be attributed to the focus on character rather than simple thriller mechanisms: though glossy and full of action (a hero menaced by a plane in an empty landscape, an escape across the stern faces of Mt Rushmore), *North By Northwest* >**11** is affecting because the threat to a man's very identity teaches him to care for his reluctant betrayer.

While all Hitchcock's best work concerns ordinary people suddenly plunged into chaos, few films were as extreme in voicing such fears as *Psycho* >**12** and *The Birds* >**13** . The first, famous for its shower-murder, is at once a scream of terror at the very idea of insanity and a relentlessly black comedy that plays havoc with audience sympathies, killing the heroine after 30 minutes and coming to focus on a shy homicidal psychopath who both controls and is controlled by a dead mother ('Mother's not quite *herself* today'), while spoofing Hollywood horror clichés. Even more complex was *The Birds*, an apocalyptic sci-fi thriller notable for an audaciously slow prologue to the birds' violent attack on a small sea resort; tossing out various red-herrings as possible explanations for the sudden onslaught, Hitchcock finally allows his birds to be simply that. Concerned with fear itself rather than its cause, he offers no answer to his ecological mystery; the creatures are terrifying *because* they are normally taken for granted as friendly, familiar and innocent. More relevant to the director's purpose is the way their onslaught first exposes and then destroys human prejudice.

After *Marnie*, a lavish melodrama about the love of a wealthy playboy for a sexually disturbed kleptomaniac, Hitchcock's career took a downward turn with two banal spy thrillers (*Torn Curtain*, *Topaz*), reminiscent of the many lesser movies littered throughout his career and redeemed only by occasional set-pieces. *Frenzy* was an intriguing but dated portrait of a sex-killer, but *Family Plot* >**14**, a lively comedy-thriller with an ironic kidnapping plot, was something of a belated return to form. Poor health prevented the completion of further projects but finally, in 1980, months before his death, the world's best-known director was knighted.

Since Hitchcock's finest films are less concerned with 'pure cinema' (ie the manipulative and sadistic mechanics of suspense) than with theme and character, it is perhaps regrettable that he restricted himself to the thriller form. If his sly black humour suggests a subversive artist, his fear of disorder (as seen both in the films' content and in his working methods, which precluded improvisation at all costs) suggests great caution. Nevertheless, despite the presence of several dull, plodding, even wooden films during a long and prolific career, his most complex work ensures him an enduring status as a major director with a unique visual style and a remarkably intuitive, suspenseful sense of pace.

Lineage

Himself influenced by German Expressionism and Soviet montage, Hitchcock managed virtually to create a genre of his own. Much admired by **Truffaut** and **Chabrol**, he has also been paid homage in endless thrillers, most notably by **De Palma** and Richard Franklin.
His suspense style compares interestingly with that of **Clouzot**.

Further reading

Robin Wood's *Hitchcock's Films* (London, 1965), Raymond Durgnat's *The Strange Case of Alfred Hitchcock* (London, 1974). Truffaut's *Hitchcock* (London, 1978) is a definitive interview, Donald Spoto's *The Dark Side of Genius: The Life of Alfred Hitchcock* (New York, 1982) a detailed, controversial, biography.

Viewing

1 **The Ring**
GB 1927/ w Carl Brisson, Lillian Hall-Davies, Ian Hunter

2 **Blackmail**
GB 1929/ w Anny Ondra, John Longden, Sara Allgood

3 **The 39 Steps**
GB 1935/ w Robert Donat, Madeleine Carroll, Godfrey Tearle

4 **The Lady Vanishes**
GB 1938/ w Margaret Lockwood, Michael Redgrave, Paul Lukas

5 **Rebecca**
US 1940/ w Joan Fontaine, Laurence Olivier, Judith Anderson

6 **Shadow of a Doubt**
US 1943/ w Joseph Cotten, Teresa Wright, Patricia Collinge

7 **Notorious**
US 1946/ w Cary Grant, Ingrid Bergman, Claude Rains

8 **Strangers on a Train**
US 1951/ w Farley Granger, Robert Walker, Ruth Roman

9 **Rear Window**
US 1954/ w James Stewart, Grace Kelly, Raymond Burr

10 **Vertigo**
US 1957/ w James Stewart, Kim Novak, Barbara Bel Geddes

11 **North By Northwest**
US 1959/ w Cary Grant, Eva Marie-Saint, James Mason

12 **Psycho**
US 1960/ w Anthony Perkins, Janet Leigh, Vera Miles

13 **The Birds**
US 1963/ w Tippi Hedren, Rod Taylor, Jessica Tandy

14 **Family Plot**
US 1976/ w Barbara Harris, Bruce Dern, Karen Black

Dennis Hopper

Born: 17th May 1936/Dodge City, Kansas, USA
Directing career: 1969-

By the mid-'70s, it seemed that Dennis Hopper's directing career was over; drugs and indulgence had taken their toll and the sole outlet for his unique talent appeared to be as an actor in cheap offbeat movies. In the '80s, however, he has become an inventive and influential figure in both the acting and directing fields.

Hopper made his film acting debut as an unruly teenager in **Nicholas Ray**'s *Rebel Without a Cause*, an experience that cast a long shadow over his future work. During the late '50s and '60s, he alternated between mainstream Hollywood fare (*Giant*, *Gunfight at the OK Corral*, several films for Henry Hathaway) and offbeat, often disreputable movies made by Curtis Harrington, **Warhol** and **Corman** (*The Trip*). His potent presence as a young, often violent and rebellious, outsider finally made possible his directing debut with *Easy Rider* >**1**, a bikers' odyssey perfectly tuned to the spiritual disenchantment and drug-based hedonism of contemporary youth. As Hopper and Peter Fonda (the film's producer) ride on the proceeds of a drugs deal down to New Orleans' Mardi Gras, their voyage in search of freedom in the backroads of the American South takes on the mythic dimensions of a Western; if, however, the rednecks who persecute them for their hippy appearance display complacency and bigotry in response to the heroes' pioneering spirit, the film is nevertheless both celebration and elegy, with the bikers depicted as inarticulate, naive and, finally, doomed. Minutes before dying in a shooting incident at first intended merely as a joke by two trigger-happy truckers, they belatedly realise, 'We blew it'.

The enormous success of Hopper's low-budget movie surprised the Hollywood moguls, who not only attempted to follow suit with a series of lame road- and youth-movies but virtually gave Hopper *carte blanche* for his next film, *The Last Movie*. Though typically imaginative, it was both pretentious and messy. The central character, a stunt-man working on a Western in Peru, becomes fatally embroiled in the Indians' ritual recreation of cinema when the film crew leaves for home; the Peruvians' wicker-work cameras are artificial, the violence all too real. Fragmented, incoherent, obscure, the film was never properly released, and Hopper spent the next decade acting for others, his romantic vulnerability and manic, volatile energy lending a dark power to low-budget delights like James Frawley's *Kid Blue*, Philippe Mora's *Mad Dog Morgan*, Henry Jaglom's *Tracks*, and, most memorably, as Ripley in **Wenders**' *The American Friend*.

A cameo appearance in Coppola's *Apocalypse Now* brought him back to the attention of a wider public, and in 1980 he made *Out of the Blue* >**2**. Again, the film focusses on the generation gap but this time Hopper played the drunken father who lands in jail after crashing into a school bus, and who entertains incestuous feelings for his nihilistic punk daughter. Both an acid portrait of smalltown values and an oddly moving analysis of the roots of delinquency, the film exudes an edgy sense of danger through harsh visuals and raw performances that forever threaten to spiral into hysterical excess. Often, the paranoia and confusion on screen seem to mirror the director's off-screen personality, just as later performances in **Coppola**'s *Rumblefish*, Tim Hunter's *River's Edge*, and **Lynch**'s *Blue Velvet* (where his mad, menacing and sexually demented sadist dominates the film) testify to his ability to draw upon his inner demons to create characters of extreme and remarkable intensity.

In 1988, Hopper's continuing importance as a provocative and unorthodox artist was made plain by the controversial success of *Colors* >**3**, an admirably self-disciplined if episodic cop-thriller about the horrific violence of Los Angeles' notorious gang wars. The film is memorable for its authentically colloquial dialogue and for a superbly sensitive performance by Robert Duvall. Although now in his 50s, the actor-director retains an unusual and impressive understanding of youth; his unsentimental sympathy for idealistic outsiders, deranged dreamers, and rebels with no cause other than sheer survival has not diminished. Indeed, as time passes, Hopper's lucid work seems ever braver and more relevant.

Lineage

Hopper's experiences with **Ray**, James Dean and **Corman** have clearly marked his maverick career; the casting of **Sam Fuller** in *The Last Movie* is possibly a tribute to a further influence, while Hopper's increasingly frequent appearances in the films of others suggest, in turn, his immense standing among many younger directors.

Viewing

1 **Easy Rider**
US 1969/ w Hopper, Peter Fonda, Jack Nicholson, Karen Black

2 **Out of the Blue**
US 1980/ w Hopper, Linda Manz, Sharon Farrell, Raymond Burr

3 **Colors**
US 1988/ w Robert Duvall, Sean Penn, Maria Conchita Alonso

John Huston

Born: 5th August 1906/Nevada, Missouri, USA
Died: 28th August 1987/Middletown, Rhode Island, USA
Directing career: 1941-1987

By repeatedly emphasising the importance of remaining faithful to literary sources, John Marcellus Huston inadvertently highlighted not only his lack of artistic personality but the probable reason for the variability of his film-making career. Much of his work is eminently forgettable; his best films appear to stem from a fortuitous combination of a fine script, well-chosen cast and, in the finest examples, a rare emotional commitment to his subject.

The son of actor Walter Huston, the young John dabbled in acting, boxing, riding, writing and painting before settling in Hollywood, where his scripts for Warner Bros. films like *Jezebel*, *Juarez*, *High Sierra* and *Sergeant York* won him an opportunity to direct. His debut, *The Maltese Falcon* >**1**, one of the first *films noirs*, would be a merely competent thriller were it not for the performers, who include Bogart (as Hammett's private-eye Sam Spade), Mary Astor, Sidney Greenstreet and Peter Lorre; indeed, Huston's first few films were by and large unremarkable genre pieces. Only after World War II (during which he directed documentaries) was his work of real note: *The Treasure of Sierra Madre* >**2**, despite a clutch of hammy performances, is a bleak allegory on the futility of greed, the dreams, deceits and deaths of prospectors observed with withering cynicism. The stagey *Key Largo*, a claustrophobic gangster thriller about the need for moral commitment, was again redeemed by an excellent cast (Bogart, Bacall, Robinson), while *The Asphalt Jungle* >**3** (a heist-thriller that locates the reasons for a failed robbery in impotent masculine pride) was the first film to suggest that the director might have a distinctive visual style; its opening shots of a virtually deserted, seedy cityscape established a tangible atmosphere of pessimistic fatalism.

Throughout the '50s, however, Huston opted increasingly for arty respectability. The rather strained seriousness of literary adaptations and biopics (*The Red Badge of Courage*, *Moulin Rouge* – with Jose Ferrer on his knees as the diminutive Toulouse Lautrec – and *Moby Dick*) alternated with lazy comedies, both sentimental (*The African Queen*, *Heaven Knows, Mr Allison*) and cynical (*Beat the Devil*). The hollow emphasis on vulnerable non-conformists was often couched in a prettified veneer: picturesque imitations of old engravings, Impressionist paintings and whaling prints in *Red Badge*, *Moulin Rouge*, and *Moby Dick* added little or nothing to the films' meaning. Less portentous was *The Unforgiven*, an unusually sensitive Western about racism, but *The Misfits* >**4** (a rodeo-epic with an obvious, rather leaden ecological message) was a muddled, self-important fable on male impotence and destructiveness tamed by creative feminine vitality, that gained its power incidentally by featuring the last appearances of the ailing Gable and Monroe.

Huston's erratic nature became even more evident in the next three decades. A Freud biopic and literary adaptations like *Night of the Iguana*, *The Bible* and *Reflections in a Golden Eye* ranged from worthy but dull to frankly embarrassing; *The List of Adrian Messenger* presaged the inconsequentiality of later works like *The Mackintosh Man*, *Escape to Victory* and *Annie*. *The Kremlin Letter* was a fashionably cynical but confusing spy thriller; *The Life of Judge Roy Bean* a lively but messy Western, its debunking of myths undermined by sentimentality; and *Wise Blood* a clever but finally shallow account of religious fanaticism and hypocrisy. By far his best films were *Fat City* >**5**, a convincingly low-key and unusually compassionate tale of smalltime boxers vainly hoping for success, and *The Man Who Would Be King* >**6**, a warm, humorous and visually exciting adventure taken from Kipling's tale of British trickery in 1880s India. In both, as in all Huston's most enjoyable work, casting was crucial, while his evident delight in story-telling suggested that he was personally engaged with his material, thereby deepening his emotional and psychological insights.

In his final years, after a decade of unworthy films that climaxed in a misbegotten adaptation of Malcolm Lowry's *Under the Volcano*, all too indulgent of Albert Finney's drunk-act, Huston partly redeemed his reputation with *Prizzi's Honor*, a camp, romantic black comedy about Mafia assassins, memorable mainly for wildly undisciplined acting and a tediously flat visual style. Far more heartfelt was *The Dead* >**7**, adapted from Joyce's story by Huston's son Tony, and featuring his daughter Anjelica as a woman who, one dark Dublin night after a happy New Year's Eve family gathering, confesses to her husband that, years ago, a young boy died out of love for her. Almost plotless, and unassertive in its vivid evocation of turn-of-the-century Irish society, Huston's film is an elegant meditation on mortality, memory, and the transience of happiness. It is a moving testament both to a veteran film-maker and to his beloved Ireland, his adopted home for many years.

As in his performances (**Polanski**'s *Chinatown*, **Milius**' *The Wind and the Lion* and William Richert's *Winter Kills*), Huston's films veer between shallow bombast and a lively enjoyment in the telling of a good yarn. Usually at his best when dealing in genre rather than Great Art, he sometimes leavened thriller conventions with quirky wit; elsewhere, reverence for a literary text tended to drain his more ambitious films of humour, irony and vitality.

Lineage

Though Huston was clearly interested in literature (Hemingway and W.R. Burnett are likely influences), his earlier genre films may be compared with those of **Hawks** and **Walsh**. His son Danny directed *Mr North*, which John co-produced just before his death.

Further reading

Stuart Kaminsky's *John Huston: Maker of Magic* (London, 1978).

Viewing

1 **The Maltese Falcon**
US 1941/ w Humphrey Bogart, Mary Astor, Sidney Greenstreet

2 **The Treasure of Sierra Madre**
US 1948/ w Humphrey Bogart, Walter Huston, Tim Holt

3 **The Asphalt Jungle**
US 1950/ w Sterling Hayden, Sam Jaffe, Louis Calhern, Jean Hagen

4 **The Misfits**
US 1961/ w Clark Gable, Marilyn Monroe, Montgomery Clift

5 **Fat City**
US 1972/ w Stacy Keach, Jeff Bridges, Susan Tyrell

6 **The Man Who Would Be King**
US 1975/ w Sean Connery, Michael Caine, Christopher Plummer

7 **The Dead**
GB 1987/ w Anjelica Huston, Donal McCann, Dan O'Herlihy

James Ivory

Born: 7th June 1928/Berkeley, California, USA
Directing career: 1963-

Early in his career James Ivory gained a reputation as a director of low-budget independent films of rare sensitivity. But as time has passed, his emphasis on tasteful discretion and his penchant for literary quality have ossified into dullness and predictability.

After making a number of student works during the '50s Ivory developed a passion for India, a country embodying the culture-clash that would become his abiding theme; indeed, since 1963 he has worked consistently with producer Ismail Merchant and, almost as often, with the Polish-Indian novelist Ruth Prawer Jhabvala. His first film of note, *Shakespeare Wallah* >**1**, examining British imperialism through the travels of an English acting troupe, was lauded for its low-key, carefully balanced account of an inter-racial romance and its quietly eccentric characters; less impressive and assured was *The Guru* (about a British pop star in India for sitar lessons), while *Bombay Talkie*, in which an American writer has an affair with an Indian film actress, was an awkward mixture of Ivory's customary concerns and the populist Indian musical. A first American feature, *Savages* >**2**, was a portentous, simplistic allegory of primitive jungle folk taking over a deserted country house and imitating the decadence of '30s socialites before they regress to their former ways; *The Wild Party*, on the other hand, was unusually lively as it followed a silent comedian's come-back celebrations along a tortuous path towards murder. By now Ivory's dominant quality seemed to be either quirky versatility or a lack of commitment, according to point of view; in hindsight, the facile and detached irony and emphasis on glossy decoration in the later films, may suggest the latter, although *Roseland* >**3**, a trilogy of tales revealing the forlorn hopes of ageing loners frequenting a famous New York ballroom, is at times surprisingly touching.

Thereafter, Merchant-Ivory turned increasingly to novels for inspiration – Jean Rhys (*Quartet*) and, rather more notably, Henry James (*The Europeans*, *The Bostonians*) and E.M. Forster (*A Room with a View* >**4**, *Maurice*), both of whom had anticipated the director's obsessively intimate depiction of class and culture conflict. This theme perhaps reached its nadir in the naive *Heat and Dust*, about a woman tempted to follow in the footsteps of a great-aunt whose '20s romance with an Indian prince led to scandalous exile. All these films, however, though distinguished by efficient acting, were languid and bland, their immaculately polished veneers failing to illuminate the complex psychological subtleties of the originals. The accent on tastefulness and pointed ironies resulted in a lack of passion (fatal in studies of human emotions), while the verbose tableaux set in glowingly nostalgic landscapes echoed TV costume drama at its most literal-minded. Indeed, the growing popularity of Ivory's recent work suggests a capacity for turning literature into classics for beginners: *A Room with a View* betrays Forster's wry satirical wit by means of excessively broad comedy, while the increasingly repetitive similarity of the films implies either a dearth of imagination or a manipulative commercial cynicism.

Lineage

Ivory has expressed his admiration for **Satyajit Ray**; his literary bent allies him more closely with British directors than with his American compatriots, though he may be seen as a lesser, latter-day **Wyler**. Comparison with late **Visconti** is also interesting.

Further reading

John Pym's *The Wandering Company* (London, 1983).

Viewing

1 **Shakespeare Wallah**
India 1965/ w Shashi Kapoor, Felicity Kendal, Geoffrey Kendal

2 **Savages**
US 1972/ w Louis Stadlen, Thayer David, Anne Francine
3 **Roseland**
US 1977/ w Teresa Wright, Geraldine Chaplin, Christopher Walken
4 **A Room with a View**
GB 1985/ w Helena Bonham-Carter, Maggie Smith, Julian Sands

Miklós Jancsó

Born: 27th September 1921/Vác, Hungary
Directing career: 1954-

One of the most distinctive stylists to win international acclaim in the '60s, Miklós Jancsó may be seen both as a highly personal director and as an artist whose roots lie firmly in his country's history, geography and culture. In reinterpreting Hungary's past, he has developed a form of cinema that correlates, poetically and politically, to his conception of revolutionary class warfare.

Jancsó's early career was spent making documentary shorts on ethnographical subjects. In 1958 he made his feature debut, *The Bells Have Gone to Rome*, but only after *Cantata* and *My Way Home* – slices of social realism with conventional characters – did he develop his own personal style. Based in historical events of the mid-19th century, *The Round-Up* >**1** concerns the capture, torture and murder of peasant partisans by the Austrian authorities, and abandons psychologically rounded heroes for lengthy shots of mass activity exposing the mechanics by which power is sustained. Even more remarkable was *The Red and the White* >**2**, set in the Russian Civil War of 1917: across the wide plains – the beautiful, bleak theatre of many of Jancsó's conflicts – soldiers and horses sweep endlessly as one side then the other gains temporary ascendancy in a hollow ritual of triumph and defeat. The fluid camera swoops and zooms, dialogue is sparse, characters are nameless pawns. Highly formalised, even abstract, Jancsó's style serves both to portray war's futility – the armies simply reflect each other's violence – and to offer a visual equivalent of dialectical theory.

Revolutionary conflict lay at the heart of all Jancsó's work; only his methods grew in complexity. Naked bodies become symbolic of humiliation and of defiant, liberating impulses; both pagan and Christian mythical motifs are pressed into the service of the revolutionary cause; song and dance take on an increasing importance as expressions of unity and insurrection. After *The Confrontation*, in which the confusions and ambitions of postwar Hungarian youth are based on the director's own past, he returned to the plains for the largely incomprehensible *Agnus Dei*, about a clash between rebels and religious fanatics in 1919. By contrast, *Red Psalm* >**3** was admirably lucid: dealing with the struggles of farmers and unemployed against aristocratic landlords, Church and army in only 27 shots, its intricate, fluent camera movements and balletically conceived characters are both politically meaningful and visually sensuous, their significance universal yet Hungarian to the core. Indeed, by now the prolific Jancsó was also filming in Italy (*The Pacifist*, *Rome Wants Another Caesar*), but his work abroad lacked the dimension of the films that dealt with his own country's history. Likewise, *Elektreia* lacked the requisite power to transform the Greek myth into a plausible revolutionary tract; and *Private Vices and Public Virtues* (a version of the Mayerling story that employs a young man's scandalous pan-sexual debauchery to symbolise anti-patriarchal rebellion) is flawed by lingering, lavish and repetitive scenes of naked youth. Thereafter, Jancso's career faltered, and since the epic *Hungarian Rhapsody*, he appears to have worked with less frequency. He now attracts scant attention in the West, his reputation overtaken by compatriots like **Szabó**, Pál Gábor, Pál Sándor, and his own former wife Márta Mészarós. Indeed, it may be appropriate that *Season of Monsters* (a study of a contemporary group of successful academics in self-destructive crisis, seen variously as a promising new departure or as virtual self-parody) was his bleakest, most pessimistic film to date.

It is perhaps easy to fault even Jancsó's best work for its stress on style at the expense of content; certainly his remote, detached choreography of human conflict often seems designed to impress through elegance, rather than stir the emotions with his vision of persecutors and victims. Nevertheless, his finest films have a formal beauty and intelligence rarely found in traditional historical drama, while his interest in massed forces rather than individual romantic heroes remains true to the spirit of Marxism.

Lineage

Initially influenced by social realism, Jancsó has spoken of his admiration for **Godard**, **Bergman** and **Antonioni**. Understandably, his style has influenced few, but comparison with **Visconti**, **Pasolini**, the **Tavianis**, and Theodoros Angelopoulos is not fruitless.

Further reading

John Russell-Taylor's *Directors and Directions* (London, 1975), Graham Petrie's *History Must Answer to Man: The Contemporary Hungarian Cinema* (London, 1978).

Viewing

1 **The Round-Up**
Hungary 1975/ w Janos Gorbe, Tibor Molnar, Andras Kozak

2 **The Red and the White**
Hungary/USSR 1967/ w Tatyana Konyukova, Krystyna Mikolaiewska

3 **Red Psalm (People Still Ask)**
Hungary 1971/Andrea Drahota, Lajos Balazsovits, Andras Balint

Derek Jarman

Born: 31st January 1942/Northwood, Middlesex, England
Directing career: 1971–

At odds with British mainstream cinema (not only because of his abiding aversion to realism but also due to a profoundly personal vision rooted in his open, unselfconscious homosexuality), Derek Jarman paradoxically remains a very English Romantic. Avant-garde in method but largely nostalgic in temperament, his low-budget films intertwine politics, sex and art in highly poetic fashion.

With a background in fine art, Jarman began making shorts in Super-8 while working as art director on **Russell**'s *The Devils* and *Savage Messiah*: non-narrative, they were mysterious evocations of arcane rituals, as passionate and private as a diary. His feature debut, *Sebastiane* >**1**, was equally personal, the saint's martyrdom brought about by the sexual jealousies of Roman soldiers manning a remote Sicilian garrison. With Latin dialogue often translated into irreverent English subtitles (Oedipus = mother-fucker), and lyrical shots infused with homoerotic tenderness, the film was a provocative combination of camp wit, visual bravura, and original variations on the themes of sexuality and power. Also imaginative, but far less disciplined, was *Jubilee*, in which Elizabeth I is led by a court seer through the anarchic, violent and bleak wasteland of a vaguely futuristic England; unfortunately, its startling imagery was wrecked by the punkish posturing of a fashionable but talentless cast and by a script that settled for obvious satirical targets.

The Tempest, a typically playful condensation of the classic text, replaced Shakespeare's island with a decaying Gothic manse, high on camp and fanciful decor, with the acting again amateurish. *The Angelic Conversation*, however, in which readings of 14 of the Bard's sonnets were accompanied (but not illustrated) by tableaux of young men bathing, washing and making love in romantic natural locations, was both a return to the plotless formal experiments of Jarman's earlier work and a stylish meditation on desire. (He has never abandoned his work in Super 8, 16mm and video, often making iconoclastic pop-promos.) But it was the studio-shot, long planned *Caravaggio* >**2** that revealed Jarman at his most mature. An elegant biopic of the Renaissance painter, reminded on his death-bed of his volatile relationships with two models that led to artistic triumphs and to his arrest for murder, the film is simultaneously accessible and highly personal. For once, close engagement with the characters makes for a strong emotional pull, while the quiet, painterly style, reminiscent of Caravaggio's own *chiaroscuro*, renders various deliberate anachronisms in dialogue and decor (typewriters, motor-bikes) oddly plausible.

The Last of England >3 was altogether more controversial. A fragmented essay on England past, present and future, it combined old family home-movies, with scenes of Jarman himself and facile references to the Falklands, the flag and royalty. Presented in an urban landscape of decay and violence, the film was over-emphatic, indulgently bitter, and littered with leaden symbolism. It was followed by *War Requiem*, in which Benjamin Britten's mass, inspired by the poems of Wilfred Owen, was accompanied by often powerful images – fictional and documentary – illustrating the brutal waste of war. Again, its uncompromising tone confirmed Jarman as a maverick whose self-confidence may verge on arrogance, but whose commitment to cinema as an art-form, however lowly or private, is unshakeable.

Lineage

Jarman's use of film for homo-erotic self-expression, influenced by **Cocteau**, **Warhol**, **Pasolini** and Kenneth Anger, compares with **Terence Davies**; his Romanticism echoes **Powell** and **Russell**, while his experimentalism may be contrasted with the more cerebral work of **Greenaway**, and that of Peter Wollen and Laura Mulvey.

Further reading

Jarman's autobiography *Dancing Ledge* (London, 1984).

Viewing

1 **Sebastiane**
GB 1976/ w Leonardo Treviglio, Barney James, Richard Warwick

2 **Caravaggio**
GB 1986/ w Nigel Terry, Sean Bean, Tilda Swinton

3 **The Last of England**
GB 1988/ w Spring, Gerrard McArthur, Tilda Swinton

Jim Jarmusch

Born: 22nd January 1954/Akron, Ohio, USA
Directing career: 1979-

Rarely do underground or experimental films reach beyond a small specialist audience. Happily, the cult surrounding the work of Jim Jarmusch may increase in size; wit and warmth are on his side.

Former film student Jarmusch's feature debut was *Permanent Vacation*, a loosely structured account of an alienated teenager drifting dejectedly around New York and memorable mainly for its stylish location photography. But it was with *Stranger Than Paradise* >1 that the writer-director first won wider public attention. About two hilariously inert friends – laconic, self-obsessed, addicted to sleaze – whose fashionably apathetic lives are transformed by the unexpected arrival of a young Hungarian girl (cousin to one of the pair), the film, shot in stark black and white, consists entirely of brief, action-free scenes, each a single static shot. Minimalist in style, it impresses through hip but notably trivial dialogue, bleached landscape photography (which manages to make a snowy Cleveland and a sunny Florida beach look equally bleak and poetic) and gently absurdist humour. Originally a short anecdote about the girl's arrival in New York but expanded by the addition of two further segments in which the trio travels around a dreamlike, depopulated America, the film is an offbeat, original examination of concepts of home, belonging, solitude and strangeness.

Down By Law >2 was another tale of posturing deadbeats whose self-regarding complacency is transformed – if only temporarily – by the advent of an outsider: when two small-time hoods from New Orleans, framed and jailed, find themselves sharing a cell, their mutual animosity is deflected by an apparently idiotic, garrulous Italian whose pidgin-English asserts a faith in life that enables them to escape to the Louisiana bayoux. Ultra-cool behaviour again yields to a realisation of basic human needs; again, the film, in lustrous black and white, comprises three acts, centred on wilful inertia, enforced imprisonment, freedom of movement; once more banal conversations are imbued with poetry and humour. Part fairy-tale, part-*noir* mood-piece, *Down by Law* both celebrates and derives comedy from its characters' eccentricities. If humour plays a greater part in counteracting the tendency towards trendiness than in the earlier film, Jarmusch nonetheless remains true to a vaguely experimental aesthetic, with elliptical editing, a story deprived of climactic action, and moody mannerisms that continually undercut 'realism'.

Jarmusch should beware of placing too much emphasis on static scenes depicting terminally bored hipsters. However, he shows great promise as the quirky creator of credible characters who are usually relegated to the margins of mainstream movies, and of refreshingly hybrid movies that resist conventional categorisation. His visual sense is superb, his control of atmosphere strong; one only hopes that success will not compromise his highly individual style.

Lineage

Jarmusch compares with New York independents like Eric Mitchell, Amos Poe, Michael Oblowitz, Spike Lee and Lizzie Borden, while **Warhol**, **Cassavetes** and Shirley Clarke are among his artistic ancestors. He studied film under **Nicholas Ray**, and *Stranger Than Paradise* was completed with film stock donated by **Wenders**. He has also spoken of his admiration for **Godard**, **Antonioni**, **Bresson**, **Ozu** and **Dreyer**.

Viewing

1 **Stranger Than Paradise**
US/W. Germany 1984/ w John Lurie, Richard Edson, Eszter Balint

2 **Down By Law**
US 1986/ w John Lurie, Tom Waits, Roberto Benigni

Neil Jordan

Born: 1950/County Sligo, Eire
Directing career: 1982-

Already an established writer, Neil Jordan seems one of Britain's more promising young directors. Though beset by flaws, his first three films were engagingly difficult to categorise, while revealing a distinctly cinematic sensibility.

Set in his native Ireland, Jordan's debut film, *Angel* was an impressive thriller about a showband saxophonist who witnesses a murder and, in trailing the culprit, discovers that he too has a frightening capacity for violence. Deceptively realist in tone, the film may be more fruitfully seen as fantasy: beginning and ending in the Dreamland dance-hall, the musician's search progresses through a series of coincidences as unlikely as they are frustrating. Far more assured was *The Company of Wolves* >**1**, a delirious, sensuous fantasy comprising tales within tales, dreams within dreams. Part symbolic allegory on the awakening of pubescent sexuality (a girl is both fascinated by, and fearful of, adult warnings of men who turn into wolves), part fairy-tale (the stories often echo Little Red Riding Hood), part horror-movie, it is memorable not only for its rich narrative invention but for its lavish, studio-shot Arcadian forest whose shadows contain a myriad of sinister creatures. Most impressive, however, was its subtle ambivalence (the werewolves, at once dangerous, beautiful and pitiable, symbolise adolescent confusion about the onset of physical maturity) and the fact that the film, though rooted in dream-logic, remains lucid throughout.

In *Mona Lisa* >**2**, Bob Hoskins gave one of his most touching performances to date as the ex-con who, as chauffeur to a high-class black prostitute, proceeds from racist prejudice to an absurd romantic obsession with the girl; as a result, he descends into a garish underworld of pornographic cinemas and sex-parlours in search of the girl's drug-addicted lesbian lover. Occasionally violent, the film nevertheless steers clear of sensationalism and constructs instead a contemporary *noir*-inflected variation on the theme of Beauty and the Beast: realism is again counterpointed by frequent allusions to the surreal crime fiction of John Franklin Bardin, and an Expressionist evocation of London's red-light areas; there is also an imaginative plethora of references that reinforce the themes of innocence and obsession – these range from the song of the title, through an aria from Puccini's *Madam Butterfly*, to a scene from **Nicholas Ray**'s *They Live By Night*. The film's success led to *High Spirits*, a supernatural comedy all too clearly aimed at the international market, in which frantic farcical performances simply revealed the director's poor sense of comic timing.

Jordan's stress on visual pleasures and his tendency towards fantasy rather than realism mark him as a talent to watch. If he often signposts themes too bluntly, instead of letting them arise naturally from the narrative, he remains inventive and ambitious.

Lineage

Powell, **Boorman** (who produced *Angel*), **Laughton** and **Cocteau** may be seen as having influenced Jordan's films, while literary figures, especially perhaps his collaborators Angela Carter (*The Company of Wolves*) and David Leland (*Mona Lisa*), are also significant. His distaste for realism may be compared with that of contemporaries such as Julien Temple, **Jarman**, and Stephen Frears.

Viewing

1 **The Company of Wolves**
GB 1984/ w Sarah Patterson, Angela Lansbury, David Warner

2 **Mona Lisa**
GB 1986/ w Bob Hoskins, Cathy Tyson, Michael Caine

Philip Kaufman

Born: 23rd October 1936/Chicago, USA
Directing career: 1963-

While it is difficult to argue for the existence of any thematic or stylistic consistency in the films of Philip Kaufman, his very eclecticism makes him one of the more intriguing American film-makers of recent years. His originality stems from the unusually adult nature of his projects and his oblique approach to genre.

After law-studies and a spell teaching in Europe, Kaufman returned to Chicago to make two low-budget independent films, the Cannes prize-winning *Goldstein* (a surreal, episodic parable about a prophet unrecognised in Chicago) and *Frank's Greatest Adventure* (*Fearless Frank*), a satire on politics and urban crime. But Hollywood beckoned and, in 1972, Kaufman made *The Great Northfield Minnesota Raid* >**1**, a witty, demythologising Western which portrayed the folk-hero outlaw, Jesse James, as a psychopathic mystic forced into ever more criminal ways by capitalism; genre clichés are overturned with subversive glee, the vision of an America riven by exploitation serving both as socio-political analysis and as a springboard for delightful black humour. Similarly eccentric and intelligent, *The White Dawn*, set at the turn of the century, uses the exploitation of Eskimos by three marooned American sailors as a vivid, persuasive allegory on the evils of US imperialism.

A remake of **Siegel**'s *Invasion of the Bodysnatchers*, updating the story of human beings replaced by emotionless alien 'pods' to '70s San Francisco, ingeniously blurred the lines between 'real' people, continually spouting Me-generation psychobabble, and the invading look a likes, to create a powerful atmosphere of paranoia. *The Wanderers*, set in the Bronx in 1963, was a superior gang movie notable for its excellent use of rock 'n' roll, comic-strip colours, and lively performances. Kaufman had already made a name for himself as the co-writer of **Eastwood**'s *The Outlaw Josey Wales* and **Spielberg**'s *Raiders of the Lost Ark* (which he had originally been slated to direct), but his first major critical success came with his truly epic adaptation of Tom Wolfe's *The Right Stuff* >**2**, in which the quiet heroism of test pilot Chuck Yeager, who broke the sound barrier in the late '40s, both inspires and overshadows the more famous achievements of the seven astronauts of America's pioneering Mercury programme. A tribute to courage, common sense and professionalism, the film is a modern Western with scenes and images reminiscent of **Ford** at his most laconically poetic; at the same time, Kaufman avoids the pitfalls of sentimental patriotism, and exposes the publicity machine driven by politicians and the Press as a ludicrous mechanism fuelled by manipulative self-interest.

The director's adventurousness was once again evident in his sensitive, faithful version of Milan Kundera's 'unfilmable' novel *The Unbearable Lightness of Being* >**3**. It deals with a womanising Czech doctor's irresponsibility, born of the liberation of the 'Prague Spring', which is finally cured by the love of an innocent country girl and by the universal paranoia and betrayal that follow the Soviet invasion of 1968. Slow, elegant, beautifully performed, the film, though occasionally marred by the voyeuristic misogyny present in the book, was a superb example of literary adaptation, its lucid, carefully composed images effortlessly accommodating, and lending immediacy to, the often opaque philosophising of the original.

Something of a maverick, Kaufman remains true to his hatred of commercial compromise, applying a distinctive blend of ironic wit, stylish visuals and historical authenticity to a variety of subjects. In treating serious social and political themes through the medium of popular entertainment, he has proved to be a film-maker of intelligence, integrity and imagination.

Lineage

Kaufman has spoken of his admiration for **Welles**, **Bergman** and the French New Wave; like **Altman**, **Penn** and **Rafelson**, his sensibility would seem to be at once American (in style) and European (in its quizzical, critical attitude to American institutions).

Viewing

1 **The Great Northfield Minnesota Raid**
US 1971/ w Cliff Robertson, Robert Duvall, R.G. Armstrong

2 **The Right Stuff**
US 1982/ w Sam Shepard, Ed Harris, Dennis Quaid, Scott Glenn

3 **The Unbearable Lightness of Being**
US 1987/ w Daniel Day-Lewis, Juliette Binoche, Lena Olin

Elia Kazan

Born: **7th September 1909/Instanbul, Turkey**
Directing career: **1937-**

The co-founder, in 1948, of the Actors' Studio, Elia Kazan (a short form of Kazanjoglou) will be remembered as the director of some of the most vivid film performances of the '50s. His work, however, is variable, veering from low-key lyricism to hysterical melodrama, from embarrassing self-justification to naive and didactic social comment.

Brought to America at the age of four, Kazan later became one of the finest theatrical directors of his generation, working with New York's Group Theatre in the '30s and making his name in the next decade with productions of plays by Thornton Wilder, Arthur Miller and Tennessee Williams. Expanding his range to film, he made a couple of shorts before his feature debut with *A Tree Grows in Brooklyn*, one of several early films applauded for the naturalism of their performances. *Gentleman's Agreement* and *Pinky* confronted anti-Semitism and racism, but with scripts both obvious and contrived; *Boomerang* and *Panic in the Streets* >**1** were taut thrillers, the latter shot on New Orleans locations and following a police-hunt for two minor gangsters who might be plague-carriers. But it was a film of Williams' *A Streetcar Named Desire* >**2** that introduced the 'Method' style of acting to the screen and displayed the Kazan aesthetic in full flow: studio-shot and steamily atmospheric, it opts for all-out emotionalism, with Brando's mumbling sweaty Kowalski imported intact from Kazan's earlier stage production; Vivien Leigh's mannered Blanche, in contrast, derives from a more pedantic and classical accent on technique. The clash is clumsy but frequently riveting.

In *Viva Zapata*, the Method was applied to Steinbeck's thesis that power inevitably corrupts, with Brando again charismatic as the doomed Mexican revolutionary. But in 1952, Kazan's career hit a crisis: as a 'friendly' witness before the HUAC he confessed to past membership of the Communist Party; less attractively, in an artist widely supposed radical, he named names. Interestingly his next film, *On The Waterfront* >**3**, may be seen as an act of self-justification on the part of Kazan and writer Budd Schulberg (who had also cooperated with the Commie-bashers): a docker, persuaded by a priest to inform on old friends (union-controlling mobsters responsible for his brother's death), becomes by the film's melodramatic end a Christ-like martyr, saviour of longshoremen and defender of the right to work. While didactic, even meretricious, the film remains memorable for its earlier, quieter, scenes between Brando, Steiger and Eva Marie-Saint, lent conviction by the grey, steely location photography on New York's wharfs and roof-tops.

East of Eden >**4** also depended on performances to enliven a rather bland Cain-and-Abel story, taken from Steinbeck, about the rivalry of two brothers for their father's love. While place and period (California on the eve of World War I) are well evoked, Kazan's frequently tilted camera turns a potentially subtle story of family tension into overblown melodrama; still, James Dean (in his first major role) and Raymond Massey are magnificent as love-hungry son and repressive father, the tense mannerisms of the one contrasting fruitfully with the stern tranquillity of the other. Less portentous, the dark humour derived from Williams' *Baby Doll* saw the director relaxing with scenes of virtuoso acting shot in long, revealing takes, but *A Face in the Crowd* was a rather naive Schulberg-scripted satire on TV culture, with a hillbilly rising to stardom thanks to the banality of his homespun philosophising. *Wild River* >**5** was Kazan's best film. A lovingly shot drama set in the '30s, it concerns the attempts of an engineer to buy land for a dam from an old woman bent on resistance. As usual, the acting is superb and once more

Elia Kazan with Karl Malden during the shooting of *Baby Doll*.

the theme explores the clash between individual integrity and the prevailing wishes of society, but the tone is gentler; meaning arises from setting and character rather than from bludgeoning theatrical rhetoric. But *Splendor in the Grass* (about teenage love during the late '20s, frustrated by parental pressure and ending in self-denial, separation and insanity) yields to silly symbolism, becoming an uneven, spasmodically moving elegy to natural sexuality.

Thereafter, Kazan directed less frequently as he turned increasingly to writing. His subsequent films, and the books on which they were based, were semi-autobiographical: *America, America* (*The Anatolian Smile*) >**6** reflected on his own career and his family's life in Turkey, acknowledging the compromises a boy makes in order to fulfil his dream of reaching America; epic, intimate and realist, it is a far – and moving – cry from the sophisticated dramatic structure and Method acting of his earlier films. Less successfully, *The Arrangement*, about a wealthy, ageing advertising executive who drops out and finds himself, was transformed into glossy soap-opera clichés. Finally, the starry cast – De Niro, Nicholson, Mitchum, Milland, Moreau *et al* – gathered for a film of Scott Fitzgerald's *The Last Tycoon* could do little to alleviate the tedious burden of Kazan's pedantic direction and Harold Pinter's leaden script.

Kazan's retirement from film, if such it be, went almost unnoticed; he was long past his peak. While it is impossible to deny his talent for discovering and nurturing actors, with hindsight much of his work appears manipulative and contrived. He was, finally, a director of memorable scenes rather than fully realised films: the cost of focussing on performance at the expense of everything else.

Lineage

Influenced by Stanislavsky, Lee Strasberg and Harold Clurman in the theatre, Kazan may to some extent be likened to the Italian neo-realists, **Nicholas Ray**, **Aldrich** and **Polonsky**. His influence on screen acting is huge: **Penn**, **Cassavetes**, **Lumet**, **Scorsese**, Paul Newman and Ulu Grosbard are worthy successors. Kazan's former wife Barbara Loden took naturalism to the limit in *Wanda*.

Further reading

Michel Ciment's *Kazan on Kazan* (London, 1973) is an interview, *Elia Kazan: A Life* (London, 1988) an exhaustive autobiography.

Viewing

1 **Panic in the Streets**
US 1950/ w Richard Widmark, Jack Palance, Zero Mostel

2 **A Streetcar Named Desire**
US 1951/ w Marlon Brando, Vivien Leigh, Kim Hunter

3 **On the Waterfront**
US 1954/ w Marlon Brando, Eva Marie Saint, Karl Malden

4 **East of Eden**
US 1955/ w James Dean, Raymond Massey, Julie Harris

5 **Wild River**
US 1960/ w Montgomery Clift, Jo Van Fleet, Lee Remick

6 **America, America (The Anatolian Smile)**
US 1963/ w Stathis Giallelis, Frank Wolff, Harry Davis

Buster Keaton

Born: 4th October 1895/Piqua, Kansas, USA
Died: 31st January 1966/Woodland Hills, California, USA
Directing career: 1920-1929

Joseph Francis Keaton is arguably the greatest film comedian the world has ever known. What is perhaps less commonly recognised is that he was also one of cinema's greatest directors: unlike most comics, he displayed a masterly, apparently intuitive grasp of the possibilities of film, both before and behind the camera.

Born into a vaudeville family, the young Keaton learned the physical aspects of his art from an early age, an education that served him well when he came to appear in several Roscoe 'Fatty' Arbuckle shorts in the late 1910s. But for all his expert comic timing, Keaton's apparently joyless figure often seemed at odds with the frantic slapstick surrounding him and, within a couple of years, he began directing his own two-reelers in which a far more subtle comic style and vision held sway. Strangely, Buster's persona was born fully developed: where **Chaplin** and his countless imitators portrayed 'little men' harassed by bullying giants and class prejudice, Buster was an altogether less maudlin creation. Eternally unsmiling, quietly dignified, profoundly pragmatic in his efforts simply to survive in an absurd and chaotic universe, Buster rarely resorted to petulant childlike malice, one-off gags or contrived heroic fantasy for effect. Instead, the humour arose from character, situation and a wry acknowledgement of life's futility. Keaton's comedy, despite its bright invention, is often extremely dark: *The Goat* ends with Buster on the run for a crime he did not commit; *Cops* goes even further as Buster, for no good reason, finds himself hunted by a city's entire police force and ends up in jail. Little wonder that he never smiled.

But it was in his features that Keaton's dramatic genius came to full fruition. The stories, unlike those of most of his contemporaries, were emotionally complex and credible, while Buster's character, though consistently imbued with intelligence, resilience, and a dignity that was never contrived, underwent an imaginative series of variations. Most impressive, perhaps, was his unceasing exploration of, and commentary on, his own medium: his first feature, *The Three Ages* >**1** saw him parodying **Griffith**'s *Intolerance* with an absurdly anachronistic view of Stone Age and Roman life in which cavemen play golf with brutal clubs, Buster's chariot is drawn through a snowy arena by huskies, and slaves gamble with a soothsayer's dice.

Our Hospitality >**2**, on the other hand, was a satire on the ludicrous hypocrisy of Old Southern manners, with city-slicker Buster the innocent victim of a rural family's lust for revenge in a long-standing feud. Honour forbids that they murder a

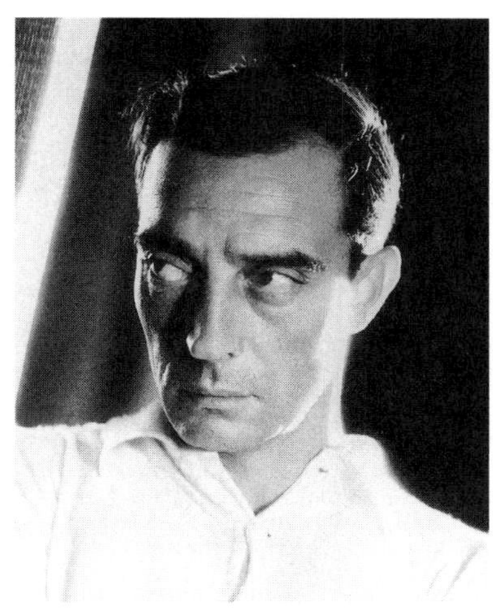

Buster Keaton: according to actress Louise Brooks, 'the most beautiful face of any man I have ever seen'.

house-guest and Buster, aware of their plans, forces himself to stay with his enemies; a bleak conceit, but Keaton's performance and direction are superb. His mask-like face becomes an exquisitely expressive instrument of bluff in a game of death; pre-Industrial America is evoked through lyrical photography; the danger that underlies his hilarious predicament is conveyed in an unforgettable finale when he saves his beloved from plummeting over a waterfall. Except for one scene (in *College*), Keaton always performed his own stunts, shot in long continuous takes that emphasised their actuality and feasability.

Visual authenticity was but one facet of Keaton's style. In the spoof detective thriller, *Sherlock Junior* >**3**, he revealed his complete understanding of film as a plastic medium: when Buster's projectionist dreams himself into a movie, he is both menaced and confounded by the very editing. Striving to gain his bearings in cinematic time and space, he is transported within a fraction of a second from a quiet garden to a busy street, from a desert to an island. A philosophical, side-splitting examination of filmic illusion, the sequence foreshadows **Godard** by some 40 years.

Further comic masterpieces followed: the shipboard scenes in *The Navigator* >**4**, the boulder-hopping finale of *Seven Chances*, the splendidly inept boxing-training sessions in *Battling Butler*, and a surreal chase at the end of the spoof, Western *Go West*, are particularly notable. Whether parodying dramatic conventions or opting for suspense, Keaton's work was consistent in offering a plausible world, totally unlike the unreal studio concoctions of his peers. Perhaps his best film in terms of historical accuracy was *The General* >**5**, a tautly structured chase picture set during the Civil War. Here, as train driver Buster embarks on an epic journey to retrieve his engine stolen by the enemy, the superb location photography and highly detailed period reconstruction repeatedly threaten to distract us (but never, amazingly, succeed) from his comic purpose. The result is beautiful, exciting and very funny.

Unlike Chaplin, Keaton's battle is not against other people but against himself; his initial, alienating incompetence is time and again transformed through determination and common sense into nothing more than an ability to take part in society. Notably, in Keaton's work, women are never patronisingly deified but viewed as another symptom of Buster's desire to make contact with humanity. In *College* >**6**, bookworm Buster wins the girl by playing the jocks at their own game and discovering his own physical nature. And in *Steamboat Bill Junior* >**7**, the psychological confusion that arises from the effete Buster's struggles to live up to the expectations of a stern, macho father is brilliantly symbolised by a cyclone; in an astoundingly inventive and dangerous gag, he comes out of a building and an entire wall is blown down on top of him. He survives, a door having cleared his head and shoulders by inches.

For all his genius, Keaton's career took a downward turn. A move to MGM curtailed his creative freedom, though *The Cameraman* >**8**, with its hilarious compendium of deliberate cinematic errors, frequently reveals the same fertile invention as *Sherlock Junior*, and *Spite Marriage* is scattered with moments of brilliant comedic wit. Nevertheless, a broken marriage, alcoholism and poor business sense ensured that Keaton was later reduced to decades of dismal appearances and gag-writing chores for other, lesser talents. This tragically wasteful situation lasted until a few years before his death when, much to Keaton's evident bemusement, his masterworks were revived to universal public and critical acclaim.

Keaton is widely remembered as the Great Stone Face, a sadly inadequate description of his thoughtful, expressive eyes. But an altogether greater achievement was his ability, as a director, to transcend the traditions of filmed vaudeville and slapstick. His appeal to modern audiences may lie in his bleak, absurdist vision of the world, but his artistry and humour remain timeless.

Lineage

While other silent comedians followed **Chaplin** (in whose *Limelight* Buster had a cameo role), Keaton influenced later comics, notably **Tati** and **Woody Allen**. He took the central role in Samuel Beckett's *Film* as a symbolic embodiment of existential consciousness, while **Wilder** and **Lester** paid tribute by casting him in, respectively, *Sunset Boulevard* and *A Funny Thing Happened on the Way to the Forum*.

Further reading

David Robinson's *Buster Keaton* (London, 1969), Walter Kerr's *The Silent Clowns* (New York, 1975). Rudi Blesh's *Keaton* (New York, 1966) and Tom Dardis' *Keaton: The Man Who Wouldn't Lie Down* (New York, 1979) are biographies.

Viewing

1 **The Three Ages**
US 1923/ w Keaton, Wallace Beery, Margaret Leahy

2 **Our Hospitality**
US 1923/ w Keaton, Joe Roberts, Natalie Talmadge

3 **Sherlock Junior**
US 1924/ w Keaton, Kathryn McGuire, Joe Keaton

4 **The Navigator**
US 1924/ w Keaton, Kathryn McGuire, Frederick Vroom

5 **The General**
US 1926/ w Keaton, Marian Mack, Glen Cavender

6 **College**
US 1927/ w Keaton, Ann Cornwall, Harold Goodwin

7 **Steamboat Bill Junior**
US 1928/ w Keaton, Ernest Torrence, Marion Byron

8 **The Cameraman**
US 1928/ w Keaton, Marceline Day, Harold Goodwin

Elem Klimov

Born: 9th July 1933/Volgograd, USSR
Directing career: 1964-

With the advent of *glasnost* it is now possible to see the work of Elim Germanovich Klimov in the West. The change in Soviet policy has also affected his career: at odds with repressive authorities for many years, his uncompromising integrity finally brought about his promotion to First Secretary of the Film Makers' Union.

A former aviation engineer, Klimov ran into trouble with his first three films – spritely satires little seen in the West – which make original use of fantasy. His film-school graduation feature, *Welcome, or No Unauthorised Admittance*, concerns a rebellious boy causing havoc at a holiday camp; *Adventures of a Dentist* portrays the initial celebration and subsequent disrepute of a dentist who is able to pull teeth painlessly without anaesthetic; and *Sport Sport Sport* merges documentary, dreamlike tall tales, and parody to create a surreal collage depicting international competition. Clearly allegorical (with the second reflecting on the situation of Soviet artists), the films were deemed subversive and briefly shelved after completion; indeed, his next film, *And Nonetheless I Believe* became a Klimov project only halfway through production when its original director, the veteran Mikhail Romm, died.

Several years passed before he completed, in 1975, *Agony*, a chaotic epic about Rasputin's dealings with the Romanov family in the last years before the Bolshevik revolution. Again, fantasy, in the form of the peasant-monk's hallucinatory visions, disrupts the taboo-breaking narrative (Rasputin had never before been seen in Soviet film, while Tsar Nikolas was shown in a semi-favourable light), but the film is wearisome and incoherent; unsurprisingly, perhaps, the emphasis on sex, violence and religion ensured that it remained unreleased for almost a decade. Moreover, until the tragic death of his wife, the director Larisa Shepitko, in a car crash in 1979, Klimov was unable to continue making films.

After the short, touching, photo-montage *Larisa*, Klimov took over a project instigated by his wife: ironically, *Farewell* >**1** is by far the finest of his films released in the West, a powerfully elegaic account of the death-rites of a remote Siberian village about to be flooded by a government hydro-electric project. The elegant images linger lovingly on the ancient inhabitants, proudly protecting their home against the destructive forces of progress, and evoke an almost pantheistic sense of Nature; the land is both the *raison d'être* of the conflict between past and future and the force that governs the islanders' simple, dignified lives. At the same time, the film – a poetically simple, hypnotically beautiful meditation on death – is a moving testament to Klimov's wife.

Come and See >**2**, loosely shaped by the director's memory of war and set in Byelorussia in 1943, follows a young partisan into the brutal, bloody carnage of the Nazi invasion; after witnessing the annihilation of an entire village the boy emerges aged beyond belief. Driven by a rare emotional intensity, the film returns to the excessive style of *Agony*, wallowing in surreal juxtapositions and expressionist effects to create a lurid, numbing portrait of the horrors of Fascism. While the film is manipulative, however, Klimov's craftsmanship is evident in every painstakingly composed scene.

In rejecting the tenets of socialist realism Klimov, like many of his contemporaries, has opted for a blurring of the lines between naturalism, fantasy and documentary. An overblown stress on style as opposed to meaning is the occasional result; equally, however, ambition and imagination are allowed full rein.

Lineage

One may compare Klimov with other modern Soviet film-makers: **Tarkovsky**, **Paradjanov**, **Konchalovsky**, Nikita Mikhalkov, Tengiz Abuladze, Alexei Gherman, Otar Iosseliani, Gleb Panfilov, Vadim Abdrashitov and Alexander Mindadze, and, of course, Shepitko.

Viewing

1 **Farewell**
USSR 1981/ w Stefaniya Stayuta, Lev Durov, Alexei Petrenko

2 **Come and See**
USSR 1985/ w Alexei Kravchenko, Olga Mironova, Vladas Bagdonas

Andrei Konchalovsky

Born: 20th August, 1937/Moscow, USSR
Directing career: 1961-

Considered, in the early '60s, a promising young Soviet director, Andrei Mikhalkov-Konchalovsky seemed to lose momentum after the end of the relatively liberal Kruschev era; similarly his move to America has failed to sustain the interest it initially aroused.

He was born into a highly talented family of artists, writers and musicians. His brother is actor-director Nikita Mikhalkov, widely regarded as the maker of cinema's best ever Chekov adaptations, including *Unfinished Piece for Mechanical Piano*, and *Dark Eyes*. Konchalovsky himself studied film under Mikhail Romm, before going on to write screenplays for **Tarkovsky**'s *The Steamroller and the Violin* and *Andrei Rublev*. In 1965 he made his own feature debut with *The First Teacher*: set in the Asian steppes after the Revolution, it deals with a young soldier's attempts to educate the local peasants in a new way of life. Lyrically shot and low on didacticism, the film was followed by *Asya's Happiness*, a partly improvised rural romance featuring members of a peasant collective. Like a number of other Soviet films of the time, it was banned, and thereafter the director drifted into sensitive, non-controversial literary adaptations of Turgenev (*A Nest of Gentlefolk*) and Chekov (*Uncle Vanya*). His originality thus muted, he moved into syrupy melodrama (*The Romance of Lovers*) before following the fates of two Siberian families after the Revolution in *Siberiade*, the epic scale of which brought its maker to the attention of the Western world.

Moving to America at the invitation of actor Jon Voight, the director made *Maria's Lovers* >**1**, a gently elegaic romance in which a World War II soldier of Slav descent returns home to the Pennsylvania farmlands and a childhood sweetheart: but reality fails to live up to his dreams and the marriage is not consummated. Though unremarkable in its examination of the traumas that face homecoming veterans, the film features an immaculate recreation of period and lush landscape photography; with its immigrant community, the pastures and hills are quietly reminiscent of Konchalovsky's early work. Similarly, *Runaway Train* >**2**, taken from an idea by **Kurosawa**, might just as easily have been shot in Siberia as Alaska, while the symbols that colour the fast-moving story of a convict's escape from a top-security prison seem oddly Russian: in the last shot the violent anti-hero, redeemed when he sacrifices himself to dissuade a young disciple from the criminal life, hurtles on the driverless train towards certain death, his arms defiantly outstretched, Christ-like, to meet his maker.

If *Runaway Train* was a superior thriller lent distinction by

Konchalovsky's powerfully imaginative visual sense, *Duet for One* was a disastrous 'opening-out' of a theatrical success in which a violinist comes to terms with her imminent death from multiple sclerosis: mawkish and bereft of any real sense of pain, its soap-opera sentiments were totally lacking in insight or originality. *Shy People* was no better, with its initial, simplistic culture clash, between a rich, pretentious New York journalist and her unsophisticated, superstitious cousins living deep in the Louisiana bayoux, quickly succumbing to trite clichés involving attempted rape, capsized boats, marauding crocs and ghosts. Again, thanks to Chris Menges' lustrous photography, the film looked superb, but its sociological, psychological and philosophical pretensions were laughably melodramatic.

Perhaps, in working for Cannon producers Golan and Globus, Konchalovsky has dealt himself a poor hand: often, Cannon's idea of 'art' is irredeemably bound up with cheap, formular notions of commercialism. *Runaway Train* proved the director capable of making a fine if derivative genre-film; mostly however, he seems to be burdened by a fruitlessly middle-brow concept of 'quality entertainment'.

Lineage

While Konchalovsky's early works may be seen as part of a series of imaginative Soviet debuts (including films by Otar Iosseliani, **Tarkovsky**, **Shepitko** and **Paradjanov**), he himself has expressed his admiration for **Woody Allen** and **Scorsese**.

Viewing

1 **Maria's Lovers**
US 1984/ w Nastassja Kinski, John Savage, Robert Mitchum

2 **Runaway Train**
US 1985/ w Jon Voight, Eric Roberts, Rebecca De Mornay

Grigori Kozintsev

Born: 22nd March 1905/Kiev, USSR
Died: 11th May 1973/Leningrad, USSR
Directing career: 1924-1971

Along with regular collaborator Leonid Trauberg, Grigori Kozintsev was one of the most inventively versatile of Soviet revolutionary film-makers. In addition, his later, solo work revealed him as an unrivalled master of the literary adaptation.

Swept along by the energy of the 1917 Revolution, the young Kozintsev involved himself in experimental theatre, founding with Trauberg the Factory of the Eccentric Actor. The pair made their film debut in 1924 with *The Adventures of Oktyabrina* (now lost), in which propagandistic slogans and elliptical editing reputedly told a fast, fragmented story of a girl's determined, triumphant struggle against capitalism. Indicative of their methods is the surviving *The Devil's Wheel* >**1**, which couches its moral message – a call for slum-clearance in Leningrad – within a pacy adventure about a sailor who, missing his boat after falling for a girl at a fair, finds himself immersed in a murky underworld of grotesque criminal types. The film's vivid, deft characterisations and its delight in virtuoso visual effects recur in *The Cloak* (based on two Gogol stories), and in *The New Babylon* >**2**, an account of the fall of the Paris Commune in 1870, seen through the militant eyes of a department-store salesgirl. The latter, clearly inspired by the 1905 Revolution, merges sardonic wit with heroic drama, and sees the pair, at the peak of their powers, working with a highly sympathetic team: cameraman Andrei Moskvin, set-designer Yevgeni Yenei and brilliant young composer Dmitri Shostakovich, who would continue to work with Kozintsev to the end of his career.

In 1931 Kozintsev and Trauberg

made their first sound film, *Alone*, about a woman teacher learning to enjoy a new life in the snowy countryside. Their finest talkies, however, were the films comprising *The Maxim Trilogy* >**3** (*The Youth of Maxim*, *The Return of Maxim*, *The Vyborg Side*), which delineated, in unusually humorous detail, the gradual genesis of a revolutionary hero from 1910 to 1918. Its epic scale notwithstanding, what most impresses is the unromantic conception of the decidedly ordinary Maxim (political virtually by accident), a refreshingly non-didactic alternative to the manipulative, orthodox ideologies of socialist realism.

After one last film together (*Plain People*, an account of the wartime evacuation of factory workers, banned until 1956 when it was re-edited in a version Kozintsev disowned), Trauberg and Kozintsev went their separate ways, the latter to a successful solo career. Following two reputedly stolid Stalinist biopics, he embarked upon three literary adaptations, exemplary for their subtle, sensitive reinterpretation of notoriously difficult texts. *Don Quixote* is a marvellous feat of condensation, a touching picture of Cervantes' naive, idealist knight errant brought vividly to life by Nikolai Cherkassov's dignified performance and Moskvin's masterly 'Scope camerawork; *Hamlet* takes its inspiration from a notion of Denmark as a prison and, through Pasternak's poetic translation, offers a mesmerising portrait of a non-conformist destroyed by a rigid and hostile world; while *King Lear* >**4** becomes a universal rather than an individual tragedy, and a tale of redemption: in his madness, the once arrogant ruler finally assumes his rightful place among the crippled, ragged victims of a cruel feudal society. *Lear* is a Marxist, and a profoundly humane, reading of Shakespeare's masterpiece. An imaginative, powerful visualisation of a poetic text, its brooding atmosphere is effortlessly conveyed by the grey camerawork that captures bleak, windswept mudflats and unwelcoming rocky plains.

To the end, Kozintsev remained an artist of rare energy and invention, seldom allowing ideological concerns to dictate either the form or the content of his work. If many of his films revolve around political themes, that is not to deny his fascination with colourful, credible characters, nor his sense of humour and his desire to use the visual qualities of his chosen medium to the full.

Lineage

Influenced by Mayakovsky, Meyerhold and **Eisenstein**, Kozintsev and Trauberg may be seen as part of a Russian eccentric movement that included Lev Kuleshov and Boris Barnet. Colleagues during their early years also included Sergei Yutkevich and Sergei Gerasimov.

Further reading

Jay Leyda's *Kino* (London, 1960).

Viewing

1 **The Devil's Wheel**
USSR 1926/ w Pyotr Sobolevsky, Lyudmila Semyenova, Gerasimov

2 **The New Babylon**
USSR 1929/ w Yelena Kuzmina, Pyotr Sobolevsky, Gerasimov

3 **The Maxim Trilogy**
USSR 1935/37/39/ w Boris Chirkov, Valentina Kibardina

4 **King Lear**
USSR 1971/ w Yuri Yarvet, Oleg Dal, Elsa Radzinya

Stanley Kramer

Born: 29th September 1913/New York, USA
Directing career: 1955-

Extremely successful during the late '50s and early '60s, Stanley Earl Kramer is both proponent and victim of the misguided belief that 'message-movies' might change the world. Alas, however good his intentions, his films reek of complacency, their preachiness as formulaic as their maker's systematic sifting through 'topical' issues.

A former editor and writer, Kramer first made his name as an independent producer working with

Mark Robson, Richard Fleischer, Laslo Benedek, **Zinnemann** and **Dmytryk**: his first film, **Albert Lewin**'s *The Moon and Sixpence*, is by far his best; *The Men*, *High Noon* and *The Caine Mutiny* his best known. In 1955, he turned to direction with *Not as a Stranger*, a mediocre but sensitively performed melodrama about the sacrifices made by medical students in the pursuit of a successful career. Then, after the ludicrous Napoleonic War epic *The Pride and the Passion*, Kramer found his calling with a series of turgid social-conscience dramas given to simplistic moralising and stereotypical characters. Racism (*The Defiant Ones*, *Guess Who's Coming to Dinner?)*, nuclear war (*On the Beach*) and Fascism (*Judgement at Nuremberg*) ran the gamut of Kramer's heart-on-his-sleeve liberalism; only *Inherit the Wind* >**1**, in which a teacher is arrested and tried for teaching Darwin's evolution theory in a Deep South populated by fundamentalist bigots, remains diverting, thanks to superior acting and a genuinely claustrophobic, sweaty atmosphere. Even here, however, action is swamped by extended and verbose courtroom sermonising, the arguments loaded and contrived.

As Kramer moved into the '60s he tried to dilute seriousness with lighter fare, but both *It's a Mad, Mad, Mad, Mad, World* >**2** (an epic slapstick farce) and *Ship of Fools* (a *Grand Hotel*-style melodrama set on the eve of World War II) displayed a lumbering, humourless dramatic sense and a desperate dependence on redundant cameo appearances by famous faces. Inevitably, as society became both more permissive and more complex with the advent of the hippy era and the escalation of the Vietnam War, so Kramer's woolly liberal platitudes seemed increasingly irrelevant: *R.P.M.* was a woefully inadequate examination of student unrest, *Oklahoma Crude* a trite castigation of big-business practices, and *The Runner Stumbles* a risible crisis-of-faith drama with Dick Van Dyke absurdly miscast as a priest tormented by his physical longings for a nun.

Unsurprisingly, Kramer's later films achieved only a limited release; the best that might be said of his early work is that it seemed to strike a chord in audiences eager to have films flatter their sense of their own self-righteous, patronising tolerance.

Lineage

Kramer belongs to a liberal tradition that embraces **Zinnemann**, **Dmytryk** and Richard Brooks; his taste for the 'issue-movie' finds later parallels in the work of **Attenborough** and Martin Ritt.

Further reading

Donald Spoto's *Stanley Kramer: Film Maker* (New York, 1978).

Viewing

1 **Inherit the Wind**
US 1960/ w Spencer Tracy, Fredric March, Gene Kelly

2 **It's A Mad, Mad, Mad, Mad World**
US 1963/ w Spencer Tracy, Sid Caesar, Ethel Merman, Edie Adams

Stanley Kubrick

Born: 26th July 1928/New York, USA
Directing career: 1950-

Widely acclaimed for his serious ambitions and his uncompromising perfectionism, Stanley Kubrick has won for himself a unique degree of artistic freedom. Paradoxically, while his films have repeatedly dealt with the threat of dehumanisation (with man in thrall to war, the machine, or his own unbridled ambitions), he himself has increasingly displayed an obsession with technique at the expense of character.

After working successfully as a photojournalist for *Look* magazine, Kubrick made his film debut with two documentary shorts, *Day of the Fight* and *Flying Padre*; in 1953, he made the feature *Fear and Desire*, followed two years later by *Killer's Kiss*. Both – the first a virtually abstract war story, the second a stylish *noir* thriller – were made on miniscule budgets, with the director also acting as producer, writer,

Stanley Kubrick on location for *Dr Strangelove.*

editor and cameraman. Not until *The Killing* >**1** – a heist movie about a racetrack robbery notable for a rather pretentious and redundant use of temporal flashbacks and for an excellent cast of B-movie character actors – was there any real suggestion that Kubrick might become a major talent; its cold, oddly remote style reappeared to devastating effect in *Paths of Glory* >**2**. An anti-war film based in historical fact, it exposes the corrupt mechanisms by which three French soldiers, in World War I, come to be executed as an example to their peers, after refusing orders to march to certain death; fuelled by anger rather than compassion, Kubrick's fluid camera prowls the trenches and explores the officers' quarters to paint a powerful, precise portrait of callous Machiavellian intrigue.

The success of *Paths of Glory* led Kirk Douglas – in the film the personification of cool reason – to employ Kubrick to replace Anthony Mann on *Spartacus*: while superior to most epic spectacles, the film nevertheless suffered from miscasting and a seeming lack of concern for the rebel slaves. A version of Nabokov's *Lolita* >**3** was rather more affecting, with the obsessively jealous paedophile hero lent sad dignity by James Mason's quietly mocking but moving performance; Kubrick's own obsession for visual authenticity was also much in evidence, with the cheerless highways and motels of Middle America carefully evoked on English locations (by now the director had opted to work in Britain). Equally, in the supremely black comedy *Dr Strangelove* >**4**, he relished the re-creation of an American air-base, the Pentagon war-room and the cockpit of a jet bomber: a visually ornate account of the ultimate military error, with an insane, sexually paranoid general pushing the button to send a convoy of nuclear warheads flying towards Russia, the film is simultaneously painfully pessimistic, hilarious, and beady-eyed in its gloating over human hypocrisy, stupidity and failure.

Kubrick's insistent emphasis on style and his cool attitude towards characters came to a head in *2001: A Space Odyssey* >**5**, a pretentious and overblown hypothetical history of mankind, raised from ape-status, via the present, to divine rebirth by the obscure intervention of alien black monoliths. Revelling in the slow, stately progress of spaceships through the heavens, and reserving his greatest sympathies for a talking computer, Kubrick turned his human characters into faceless automatons, the film's polished veneer barely concealing the hollow, muddled Nietzschean borrowings within. Similarly, an adaptation of Anthony Burgess's *A Clockwork Orange* >**6**, in which the criminal brutality of a gang of futuristic punks is met by the punitive, dehumanising brain-washing deemed legal by a repressive government, was excessively concerned with bludgeoning visual effects (fish-eye lenses, fast motion, decadent set-design), and a bombastic display of violence verging throughout on the voyeuristic. Again, it was hard to feel sympathy for any of Kubrick's deliberately grotesque characters.

By now the director, lionised as a great, provocative artist, appeared to view his work as unusually sacrosanct, spending years on each film, brooding over redundant questions of technique and authenticity, while straining for thematic respectability. *Barry Lyndon*, a three-hour adaptation of Thackeray's ironic novel about an

18th-century rake's brief, fatal passage through high society, was notable chiefly for its lush, painstakingly painterly images, its characters unusually two-dimensional for a comedy of manners. Conversely, *The Shining* was an inflated version of a Stephen King thriller in which a writer's growing insanity leads him to try to kill his wife and son at a remote, out-of-season hotel (explored with characteristic baroque bravura by Kubrick's roving camera). Finally, following seven years' work, the director completed *Full Metal Jacket* >**7**, an efficient if unremarkable and rather academic account of the dehumanising effects of military training on young Americans sent to fight in an absurd, chaotic Vietnam War. Again, the accent is on human weakness: one grunt, driven insane by his foul-mouthed sergeant's orders that he become a killing machine, turns his gun on his superior before splattering his own brains against a wall; another, a pacifist, inevitably learns to kill. Again, set pieces are handled with enormous visual panache but, again, Kubrick's dry manipulation of characters and audience implies a condescending attitude towards humanity that prevents our understanding, or sympathising with, his deadly victims.

The lack of warmth in Kubrick's later work is fatal to his claim to be a great artist; few directors take either technique or themselves so seriously. While his early work tends to suggest the controlling intelligence of an ambitious maverick, his recent films smack of self-indulgent egotism and a heartless obsession with style for style's sake; indeed, he seems guilty of the very qualities in mankind against which he repeatedly rails.

Lineage

Perhaps initially influenced by *film noir*, Kubrick has expressed an admiration for the films of **Fellini**, **Chaplin**, **Bergman**, **Welles** and **Antonioni**: all directors with a distinctive artistic vision, some prey to the same indulgence, pessimism and egotism as he.

Further reading

Michel Ciment's *Kubrick* (New York, 1983), Alexander Walker's *Stanley Kubrick Directs* (London, 1972).

Viewing

1 **The Killing**
US 1956/ w Sterling Hayden, Vince Edwards, Ted De Corsia

2 **Paths of Glory**
US 1957/ w Kirk Douglas, Ralph Meeker, Adolphe Menjou

3 **Lolita**
GB 1962/ w James Mason, Sue Lyon, Shelley Winters, Peter Sellers

4 **Dr Strangelove**
GB 1964/ w Peter Sellers, George C. Scott, Sterling Hayden

5 **2001: A Space Odyssey**
GB 1971/ w Keir Dullea, Gary Lockwood, William Sylvester

6 **A Clockwork Orange**
GB 1971/ w Malcolm McDowell, Patrick Magee, Michael Bates

7 **Full Metal Jacket**
GB 1987/ w Matthew Modine, Vincent d'Onofrio, Lee Ermey

Akira Kurosawa

Born: 23rd March 1910/Tokyo, Japan
Directing career: 1943-

Ever since *Rashomon* introduced Japanese film to Western audiences at the 1951 Venice Film Festival, Akira Kurosawa's status as that country's most famous director has been secure. His success stems from the fact that his work, unusually accessible, is imbued with a humanism that, albeit sometimes trite, is often profoundly emotionally affecting.

Trained as a painter in the Western style, Kurosawa entered the film industry as writer and assistant director for the Toho company. In 1943 he made his own directing debut with *Judo Saga*, memorable mainly for focussing on a master-pupil relationship, a motif that would recur throughout his long career. For the rest of the decade the distinguishing characteristic of his work was its variety, both in choice of subject (a Noh theatre classic in

They Who Step on the Tiger's Tail, the clash between a wounded gangster and an alcoholic doctor in *Drunken Angel*, police work in the thriller *Stray Dog*) and in his visual technique: wipes, rapid editing and an array of dramatic angles and lighting effects all revealed the director's confident command of his medium. But it was *Rashomon* >**1** that first won the attention of foreign audiences: a somewhat simple- and single-minded thesis about the relativity of truth, its tale of rape and murder as seen by various witnesses, their conflicting accounts coloured by greed and pride, becomes a rather weak assertion of faith in human nature. It is remarkable mainly for sumptuous camerawork and its clear delight in the relentless, animalistic energy of Toshiro Mifune, Kurosawa's favourite actor.

Through the '50s, Kurosawa alternated period films with more provocative contemporary subjects, at the same time refining his already considerable technique and acknowledging his debt to both Russian literature and the films of John **Ford**. *The Idiot* and *The Lower Depths* were sensitive adaptations of Dostoevsky and Gorky, transposed to modern Japan; far more assured, however, were *Ikiru* (*Living*) >**2** and *Seven Samurai* >**3**. The first, the slow, affecting story of a lowly clerk's attempt to give meaning to his life (he is dying of cancer) by turning a city wasteland into a children's playground, sees Kurosawa at his most impeccably liberal; the mix of social realism and humanist poetry serves to castigate modern bureaucracy and to stress the importance of modest, everyday acts of heroism. Similarly elegaic but altogether different in subject matter, *Seven Samurai* is a genuine epic both in its scale and characterisation, with an ill-assorted collection of samurai – a doomed warrior-class – sacrificing their lives in a final battle to defend a peasant village from marauding bandits. Inspired by a respect for traditional Japanese concepts of honour and for the Western, Kurosawa combines melancholy, meditative scenes with bursts of enthralling, violent action, his visual mannerisms (the repeated use of the telephoto lens and rapid tracking and panning shots) and expert control of mood climaxing in a long, powerfully authentic fight to the death in pouring rain and splattering mud.

After the bleak *I Live in Fear* (a melodrama in which a man's paranoia about atomic warfare leads to his family dismissing him as insane), *Throne of Blood* >**4** transposed *Macbeth* to feudal Japan to striking effect. Drawing upon Noh traditions (white mask-like faces, stylised gestures), it climaxed in the samurai warlord's visually astonishing death, his flailing armoured body an obscene human pincushion pierced by countless arrows. Indeed, thereafter, with the exception of *The Bad Sleep Well* (about corruption in the world of big business) and *High and Low* (about the kidnapping of a tycoon's son) – both contemporary thrillers with a liberal bent – Kurosawa largely restricted himself to period thrillers, often distinguished by a refreshing, amoral sense of humour. *The Hidden Fortress* introduced elements of parody into the samurai genre, a development repeated in *Yojimbo* >**5** and *Sanjuro*, in which Mifune's lazy mercenary displays a cool cynicism (in the first film he is hired by two rival families in a village feud, but simply allows them to destroy each other) with such style that **Leone** stole both the basic characterisation and the plot for the first film of his 'Dollars' trilogy. While *Red Beard* >**6** was also historical, its long, complex, finally moving portrait of a feisty young doctor's education in humility and self-sacrifice at the hands of an aged superior saw a return to the self-consciously humanist themes of earlier years. By now however, compared to younger Japanese film-makers, Kurosawa was beginning to seem quite out of touch with contemporary realities, and it was some years before he made his next film, the flawed, fascinating *Dodeskaden* >**7**. This *Lower Depths*-style drama about the dreams and disappointments of the poverty- and disease-stricken inhabitants of a garbage-dump shanty town, is memorable for its clumsy but ambitiously surreal experiments with colour and symbolism. Shortly afterwards, in 1971, Kurosawa made an unsuccessful attempt to end his life.

Made a few years later in the USSR, *Derzu Uzala* >**8** evidenced a return to form: while old-fashioned, its account of a Siberian trapper's determination to survive the ravages of old age and an often hostile natural world, was exciting, epic adventure and an unusually plausible portrait of human goodness; certainly its action scenes (notably the building of a shelter during an Arctic blizzard) reveal Kurosawa's sense of composition and pace working at full stretch. A return to Japan, however, was artistically less successful: *Kagemusha*, a lavish costume drama in which a thief is forced to take the place of the dead warrior-king whose double he is, only to become embroiled in the horrors of war, was marred by a rather formulaic manipulation of the audience's emotions, while *Ran* >**9**, a visually splendid but otherwise unremarkable adaptation of *King Lear*, impressed more by its scale (a whole nation plunged into chaos by the samurai warlord's folly) than by any insight or originality (even if some saw it as partly autobiographical).

Thanks to a painterly eye and an ability to extract powerful performances from actors (especially Mifune and Takashi Shimura), Kurosawa's reputation as one of Japan's finest directors remains assured; moreover, in assimilating Western genres and styles, he has achieved a rare success as a universally popular entertainer. If in the more deliberately humanist dramas his sentimentality seems sometimes contrived and maudlin, his feel for action and his concern for historical authenticity reveal a talent that both delights in and transcends genre limitations. Certainly, his best work merges psychological precision, narrative subtlety and visual bravura to extraordinary effect.

Lineage

Usually working within traditional Japanese genres, Kurosawa has also been influenced by the Russian novel and by Ford and **Renoir**; his acknowledged favourite among Japanese directors is **Mizoguchi**. In turn, he deeply influenced the modern Western; John Sturges' *The Magnificent Seven* was a remake of *The Seven Samurai*, while **Leone** and **Eastwood** drew upon his work of the early '60s. Other Japanese directors of note during the '50s and '60s include Kon Ichikawa, Masaki Kobayashi, Kaneto Shindo and Tadashi Imai.

Further reading

Donald Richie's *The Films of Akira Kurosawa* (Berkeley, 1970).

Viewing

1 **Rashomon**
Japan 1950/ w Toshiro Mifune, Masayuki Mori, Machiko Kyo

2 **Ikiru (Living)**
Japan 1952/ w Takashi Shimura, Nobuo Kaneko, Kyoko Seki

3 **Seven Samurai**
Japan 1954/ w Takashi Shimura, Toshiro Mifune, Yoshio Inaba

4 **Throne of Blood**
Japan 1957/ w Toshiro Mifune, Isuzu Yamada, Minoru Chiaki

5 **Yojimbo**
Japan 1961/ w Toshiro Mifune, Eijiro Tono, Takashi Shimura

6 **Red Beard**
Japan 1965/ w Toshiro Mifune, Yuzo Kayama, Yoshio Tsuchiya

7 **Dodeskaden**
Japan 1970/ w Yoskitaka Zushi, Noboru Mitani, Tomoko Yamazaki

8 **Derzu Uzala**
USSR 1975/ w Maxim Munzuk, Yuri Solomine

9 **Ran (Chaos)**
Japan 1985/ w Tatsuya Nakadai, Satoshi Terao, Peter

John Landis

Born: **30th August 1950/Chicago, Illinois, USA**
Directing career: 1971-

One of the more successful comedy directors of recent years, John Landis has spawned numerous imitators, proffering a lazy blend of spoof and slapstick aimed at a predominantly young audience. His is an erratic talent, most rewarding on the rare occasions when it is applied to a polished script and disciplined performers.

Landis directed his first film as early as 1971: *Schlock*, in which he himself took the title role, was a cheap, rather obvious and only spasmodically funny monster-movie spoof about a 'missing link' on the rampage in contemporary California. It was, however, six years before he scored a hit with *Kentucky Fried Movie*, a coarse, chaotic but lively spoof of various movies and television programmes (most notably of the kung-fu thriller *Enter the Dragon* and of a charity appeal for the dead); equally episodic and brash was *National Lampoon's Animal House*, a raucous, nostalgic campus-comedy set in 1962 and featuring the anarchic antics of John Belushi, who went on to star with Dan Aykroyd in the extravagantly mounted *The Blues Brothers*. A disastrous flop, the latter was an indulgent, patronising rock 'n' roll epic, with the pair converting countless black musicians and singers to their cause in a crazed attempt to raise funds for an orphanage. More successful on both an artistic and commercial level was *An American Werewolf in London* >**1**, about a young hitcher whose travels in Britain turn into a lycanthropic nightmare after he is attacked one night on the moors. Mixing in-jokes with gory suspense, Landis for once concerned himself with plausible characters and narrative structure and logic, while a clever use of songs (*Blue Moon*, *Bad Moon Rising*) and an inventive choice of locations (a Soho sex-cinema, Piccadilly Circus) served both to establish atmosphere and lend dark comic colour.

After contributing a none-too-coherent episode to the sci-fi compendium *The Twilight Zone* (the shooting of which involved a fatal accident and prompted a controversial court case), Landis made *Trading Places*, a sloppy satire on financial intrigue and racial inequality, with a canny black hustler taking the place of a smug yuppie broker when two ageing tycoons make a bet on the effects of breeding and conditioning. Rather less obvious, *Into the Night* >**2** was a likeable caper-movie, gleefully plundering movie cliches and visiting picturesque LA locations as it followed an insomniac suburbanite's descent into a strange, menacing world of smugglers and hit-men after he encounters a mysterious blonde. Occasionally too knowing for its own good, and full of rather indulgent cameos from Landis' director friends (an in-joke he would repeat in the rather dismal parody *Spies Like Us*), the film is nevertheless a stylish comic-strip thriller executed with verve and sometimes effective intimations of violent paranoia. Subsequently, however, Landis has regressed to clumsy if amiable parody: *Three Amigos!* made too-frequent recourse to slapstick as it guyed the cliches of the low-budget, singing-cowboy Western, while the compendium spoof, *Amazon Women on the Moon* (with segments directed by **Dante**, among others), was a patchily amusing return to the absurdity and gross tastelessness of late night television, ads and old movies. Most successful commercially, *Coming to America* was a slick Eddie Murphy vehicle, notable only for the star's talent for mimicry.

Given Landis' erratic comic timing and unimaginative sense of visual composition, it is hardly surprising that slapstick and parody have been the mainstays of his humour; if he is ever to be a great comic director, he should try to temper his cinephile's love of movie lore with a firmer grasp of plot and character.

Lineage

While Landis may be seen as a modern, lesser **Tashlin** or **Edwards**, he more closely parallels figures from TV's *Saturday Night Live*: Belushi, Aykroyd, Eddie Murphy, Steve Martin, Chevy Chase, Bill Murray, Ivan Reitman and Harold Ramis. Comparison with Dante, the **Coen brothers** and the Zucker brothers of *Airplane* fame (with whom he worked on *Kentucky Fried Movie*) is also illuminating.

Viewing

1 **An American Werewolf in London**
US 1981/ w David Naughton, Jenny Agutter, Griffin Dunne

2 **Into the Night**
US 1984/ w Jeff Goldblum, Michelle Pfeiffer, Richard Farnsworth

Fritz Lang

Born: 5th December 1890/Vienna, Austria
Died: 2nd August 1976/Los Angeles, California, USA
Directing career: 1919-1960

The economy, austerity and directness of the films of Fritz Lang make him one of the most profound, precise and perennially modern of directors. Remarkably, when he left Europe for America, the constraints of the Hollywood studio system, and its adherence to genre and taut narrative structures, brought about a distillation of the themes and style he had already established in Germany.

The son of an architect, Lang spent his early years studying engineering, travelling and painting. Wounded in World War I he turned to writing while convalescing; in 1918, he moved to Berlin where he became regular scriptwriter and assistant to Joe May at Ufa studios. He directed his first feature, *Halbblut* (*Halfbreed*), in 1919; later that year he embarked upon the two-part adventure serial *Die Spinnen* (*The Spiders*), whose lively, fluent narrative marked the arrival of a promising talent. But it was *Der Müde Tod* (*Destiny*) >**1** that first suggested an interest in serious abstract ideas: as a girl tries to avert her lover's demise, she is led by Death through three historical eras in which he demonstrates the inevitability of his work. Monumental sets, sober photography and unusually restrained acting show Lang's distance from the baroque tendencies of Expressionism, but the humour that runs through a Chinese fantasy sequence would be eradicated in future films.

Lang's silent work is notable for its sheer variety: *Doctor Mabuse the Gambler* >**2** and its sequel, (*Inferno*), concern a criminal mastermind; the two-part *Die Nibelungen* is an epic account of the death of Siegfried and Kriemhild's revenge; *Metropolis* >**3** sets an ambivalent allegory on the relationship of Capital to Labour in a partly sinister, partly Utopian subterranean city of the future; *Spione* (*Spies*) is a complex espionage adventure, *The Woman in the Moon* mundane sci-fi about space travel. But despite the diversity in genre, Lang's work repeatedly focussed on key motifs of revenge, violence, the abuse of power, dark cities populated by alienated innocents and psychopathic-criminal types. The finest expression of this pessimistic vision of the world came in his first sound film, *M* >**4**, a virtuoso, virtually Brechtian thriller in which a paedophile sex-killer (Peter Lorre, in a wonderfully sympathetic performance) is brought to trial and sentenced, not by the police, but by the united forces of a criminal underworld. Notable for an inventive, non-naturalistic use of sound and of visual rhymes and symbols, it is Lang's best German film, although *The Testament of Dr Mabuse* impresses with its thinly disguised portrait of Nazism.

Invited by Goebbels to head the Nazi film industry, Lang at once left Germany for France where he directed one film, *Liliom*, before proceeding to America. After two years of extensive travel and abandoned projects, he made *Fury* >**5**, an intense, provocative thriller in which the innocent victim of a lynch mob survives to bring the culprits to justice; unsentimentally portraying a good man warped by revenge, the film is the first of many stark dramas to reflect the injustice, violence and psychotic criminality of modern America; next, *You Only Live Once* and *You and Me* proceeded to reveal the problems of rehabilitation facing convicts within a bigoted society. Similarly, Lang's stark war-propaganda films are framed by the conventions of the crime-thriller: in *Man Hunt*, an apolitical marksman, stalked through a shadowy London by Gestapo assassins, finally develops a commitment to the anti-Nazi cause in his desire to avenge the death of a young girl; while *Hangmen Also Die!*, made in collaboration with Brecht, couches the tale of the Czech Resistance's assassination of the Nazi

Peter Lorre as the doomed child-murderer – based on the real-life killer Peter Kurten – in Lang's *M*.

tyrant Heydrich within a bleak contemplation of human brutality and betrayal.

In 1944, Lang embarked upon a series of nightmarish *films noirs* in which innocent heroes find themselves battling against psychological, social and political forces beyond their control. Graham Greene's *Ministry of Fear* evokes a wartime Britain where nothing and nobody are as they seem; both *The Woman in the Window* >**6** and *Scarlet Street* envisage quiet, ordinary Americans whose subconscious desires (both sexual and murderous) lead them into terrifying worlds of humiliation, guilt and criminality; while *Secret Beyond the Door* >**7**, a perverse variation on the wife-in-peril melodrama, sees a woman who longs for excitement marry a psychopathic architect whose secret hobby is collecting rooms in which gruesome murders have been committed. By now, Lang's films had achieved an admirable economy of execution, their complex plots developed through unusually exact visual information; detached and unsentimental in their analysis of their protagonists' moral weaknesses, they were bleak, fatalistic acknowledgements of the destructive mechanisms of Sex, the Law and Society, pressurising isolated individuals to conform. Indeed, the architecturally straight narrative lines and precisely framed images suggest a philosophical syllogism: if X desires this, and Y is the world in which he lives, then Z will become his inexorable tragic destiny.

In the '50s Lang's work became even darker: *Rancho Notorious* and *Clash By Night* transcended the conventions of the Western and romantic melodrama, respectively; they examined the self-destructive violence of love, a theme that would recur in two of his bleakest thrillers – *The Big Heat* >**8** (in which a cop's desire to destroy a criminal empire takes him far beyond the realms of duty, when he is consumed by a need to avenge the death of his wife) – and *Human Desire*. *Moonfleet* was an unusually black account, seen through a child's eyes, of smugglers in 18th-century Devon, *While the City Sleeps* a return to the psychopathic sexuality of *M*. Best of all, *Beyond a Reasonable Doubt* >**9**, Lang's last American film, was also his final word on the thin line between law and justice: keen to prove the fallibility of the jury system, and thus the iniquity of capital punishment, Dana Andrews frames himself for a murder, only to find his life endangered when a friend, who possesses the photos that will prove his innocence, is suddenly killed in a car crash that also destroys the evidence; only after he has been sentenced to death and subsequently pardoned does Andrews' actual guilt come ironically to light. Again, the tortuous complexity of the plot, coupled with Lang's minimally decorative images, lends the film the clarity and depth of a scientific theorem.

Tired of Hollywood producers, Lang returned to Germany where his first production was an adventure he had written in the '20s with his then collaborator and wife Thea Von Harbou; shot partly on location, partly in the studio, *The Tiger of Eschnapur* and *The Indian*

Tomb are a return to the serial-style of the silent years, played without a hint of camp or parody. Similarly, *The Thousand Eyes of Dr Mabuse* >**10** revives the master criminal, dead but still influential through disciples; characteristically, the seemingly old fashioned and unsophisticated style conceals a rare seriousness of subject matter: political assassinations, surveillance techniques and the nuclear threat. The tragedy, once personal, is now universal.

In film after film, Lang deployed studio artifice to create an austerely stylised world in which socio-political forces and psychological impulses entrap ordinary individuals, isolating them and pushing them towards violence and death; it is a vision indelibly marked by the director's youthful experiences, notably his hatred of Nazism. Crime, whether derived from passion or from careful planning, is endemic in Lang's world, never glorified but analysed and understood. The complexity of his thought is belied by the simplicity of his style; in comparison, other film-makers often seem to indulge in irrelevant embellishment. His pessimism may be daunting, but his artistic rigour is rare and admirable.

Lineage

Like many German emigré directors (**Siodmak**, **Murnau**, **Wilder**, **Brahm** and Edgar Ulmer included), Lang was shaped by the bleak ideology (less so the style) of Expressionism; in turn he may perhaps have influenced **Hitchcock**, **Nicholas Ray**, and others; certainly he was admired by **Godard** (who cast him in *Contempt*) and Jacques Rivette.

Further reading

Lotte Eisner's *Fritz Lang* (New York, 1977), Bogdanovich's *Fritz Lang in America* (New York, 1969).

Viewing

1 **Der Müde Tod (Destiny)**
Germany 1921/ w Lil Dagover, Bernhard Goetzke, Walter Janssen
2 **Dr Mabuse the Gambler (The Great Gambler/Inferno)**
Germany 1922/ w Rudolf Klein-Rogge, Gertrude Welcker, Alfred Abel
3 **Metropolis**
Germany 1926/ w Alfred Abel, Brigitte Helm, Gustav Fröhlich
4 **M**
Germany 1931/ w Peter Lorre, Gustav Gründgens, Ellen Widmann
5 **Fury**
US 1936/ w Spencer Tracy, Sylvia Sidney, Walter Abel
6 **The Woman in the Window**
US 1944/ w Edward G. Robinson, Joan Bennett, Raymond Massey
7 **Secret Beyond the Door**
US 1948/ w Joan Bennett, Michael Redgrave, Ann Revere
8 **The Big Heat**
US 1953/ w Glenn Ford, Gloria Grahame, Lee Marvin
9 **Beyond a Reasonable Doubt**
US 1956/ w Dana Andrews, Joan Fontaine, Sidney Blackmer
10 **The Thousand Eyes of Dr Mabuse**
Germany 1960/ w Peter van Eyck, Dawn Addams, Wolfgang Preiss

Charles Laughton

Born: 1st July 1899/Scarborough, England
Died: 15th December 1962/ Hollywood, California, USA

Famous as a stage and film actor, Charles Laughton directed one film only, *Night of the Hunter* >**1**. Grievously for Laughton, at the time of release it was a critical and commercial failure; with the passing years, however, it has come to be regarded as one of the finest, indeed one of the strangest, films ever to have emerged from Hollywood.

Laughton's enormous talent, distinctive appearance (which he himself regarded with revulsion), and often flamboyant style ensured his early success in the theatre and the cinema: his most impressive film performances include his work in **Whale**'s *The Old Dark House*, Korda's *The Private Life of Henry VIII* and *Rembrandt*, his Bligh in *Mutiny on the Bounty*, Quasimodo in **Dieterle**'s *The Hunchback of Nôtre Dame*, **Renoir**'s *This Land of Mine*,

Siodmak's *The Suspect* and **Preminger**'s *Advise and Consent*. In the '40s, for the theatre, he collaborated with Brecht on *Galileo*, but *Night of the Hunter*, in which he does not appear, remains perhaps his most enduring and remarkable achievement. Magnificently shot in black and white by Stanley Cortez, the film is a nightmarish fairy-tale taken, via a script by James Agee, from a bizarre but impressive novel by Davis Grubb. The story itself is simple enough: two children live happily with their mother until a preacher arrives to woo her, in the hope of finding the money their late father stole and hid; unable to learn of its whereabouts from the woman, he kills her. When the children, scared for their lives, escape down river, he follows, and a final battle for their souls is waged when he is forced to confront an old woman – a true Christian – who takes in the children to live with her adopted family of stray orphans.

Laughton's parable of good and evil derives its power from a deceptively naive tone; amidst a plethora of deliberately archaic visual coups recalling both German Expressionism and the pastoral melodramas of **Griffith** (reinforced by the casting of Lillian Gish as the children's protector), he creates a dreamlike landscape of epic simplicity and startling beauty. Their mother embalmed on a river bed, throat slit and hair floating frond-like in the water, the boy and girl flee their deadly pursuer in a skiff, watched by toads, rabbits and foxes, shot in enormous close-ups reminiscent of the paintings of Douanier Rousseau. Artifice, indeed, is evident throughout: the performances of Robert Mitchum (as knife-wielding preacher Harry Powell, his knuckles tattooed with the words LOVE and HATE), Shelley Winters (the guilt-ridden mother), and Gish all evincing a stylised intensity that transcends naturalism. If the film may be seen partly as Biblical allegory (Mitchum as serpent, Winters as Eve; the children's experiences compared to those of the infant Moses), it nevertheless functions most effectively as a determinedly poetic child's-eye view of the hardship and moral uncertainties that swept rural America during the Depression; few films have matched its strange merging of beauty and horror, fear and desire, fairy-tale fantasy and psychological reality. It is, perhaps, the most remarkable portrait of childhood (a combination of terror, innocence and courageous adventure) in cinema; and it is only regrettable that Laughton's next project, *The Naked and the Dead* – to be shot again by Cortez – never came to fruition.

Lineage

Laughton took his inspiration from **Griffith** and early German cinema. The best example of a one-off excursion into directing by an actor, it is perhaps interesting to compare with *The Lost One* and *One Eyed Jacks*, the only films made by equally flamboyant and original performers, respectively, Peter Lorre and Marlon Brando.

Further reading

Charles Laughton and I (New York, 1968) by Laughton's wife Elsa Lanchester; Simon Callow's *Charles Laughton: A Difficult Actor* (London, 1987).

Viewing

1 **Night of the Hunter**
US 1955/ w Robert Mitchum, Shelley Winters, Lillian Gish

David Lean

Born: 25th March 1908/Croydon, England
Directing career: 1942-

Claims that David Lean is Britain's greatest Romantic director sit awkwardly with his pedantic attention to detail and his overwhelmingly middle-class, middlebrow conception of Art. A superior technician, he is too fastidious and restrained a film-maker to be seen as anything more than an able literary adaptor with an abiding if misguided taste for the

epic mode.
After a Quaker childhood which forbade his seeing films, Lean steadily worked his way up through the film industry from tea-boy to editor, in which capacity he worked for Paul Czinner, Anthony Asquith, Gabriel Pascal and **Michael Powell**. His directorial debut was made in collaboration with Noel Coward with a version of the playwright's *In Which We Serve*, patriotic propaganda about seamen survivors of a wartime torpedo attack. The film's success led the pair to work together on three further films: *This Happy Breed*, an account of a South London working-class family's life between the wars which now seems patronising; *Blithe Spirit*, a whimsical supernatural comedy; and *Brief Encounter* >**1**, about adultery contemplated and renounced by two awfully decent married types whose furtive meetings occur in archetypally suburban locations of tea-shop, cinema, and a railway-station cafe (watering hole for lower-class gossips and a symbol of life's transient joys and tearful separations). Despite the Rachmaninov piano concerto endlessly heard on the soundtrack, the film seems strangely academic, its cosiness afflicted by the same repressed, stiff-upper-lip fear of passion as its self-denying central pair. (It was, and is, immensely popular, enshrining Trevor Howard and Celia Johnson forever in the public memory).

Versions of Dickens' *Great Expectations* >**2** and *Oliver Twist* were rather more satisfying. The first was a genuinely affecting and visually imaginative melodrama about the cruelty and deception of love, the second was marred only by an offensively stereotyped Fagin, which justifiably drew charges of anti-Semitism in America. Lean then made a trio of films starring his then wife Ann Todd (*The Passionate Friends*, *Madeleine*, *The Sound Barrier*) and the actorly comedy *Hobson's Choice*, dismally indulgent of **Charles Laughton**.

By now Lean had acquired a taste for picturesque imagery and location work; his next film, *Summer Madness*, took him to Venice for the first of several extravagant international productions; not surprisingly, the city's beauty outshone the story's mundane romance between an American tourist and an Italian. His first, and best, epic, *The Bridge on the River Kwai* >**3** was an intelligent if over-long tale of obsessive professionalism, set in a Burmese POW camp during the Second World War and centring on the conflict between the Japanese CO and his British counterpart who, against the wishes of his men, agrees to build the eponymous bridge for the enemy. The film impresses through its performances, authenticity, and clear sense of irony; alas, that last quality was lacking in Lean's subsequent works (*Lawrence of Arabia*, *Doctor Zhivago*, and *Ryan's Daughter*) where the director's quest for the perfect image and a stress on lavish spectacle sapped story and characters of energy. *Ryan's Daughter* especially was a redundantly massive treatment of an essentially small-scale subject (the adultery of an Irish wife and a British officer in a remote Irish coastal village in 1916), with Lean giving most of his attention to earth, water and wind.

The film was savaged by many critics and the director absented himself from film-making for over a decade; he returned, after a projected film of *The Bounty* had failed to materialise, to make a version of Forster's *A Passage to India* >**4**. As ever, the film displayed his expert handling of crowd scenes and love of exotic landscapes, but the detailed script and strong performances were not able to conceal a fundamental misconception of the novelist's portrait of the English adrift in India; indeed, the use of Alec Guinness in blackface only underlined suspicions that the film's attitude towards dusky foreigners was, at heart, condescending.

Lean's work is suffused with overtly respectable ambitions; he tends to illustrate Great Works with a pictorial literalness that has little to do with cinema's capacity to express emotion through motion. Worse, he seems to have fallen prey to the idea that big is better, failing to appreciate that economy is an enduring filmic virtue.

Lineage

Lean's experiences with Czinner, Pascal and Asquith seem to have fostered his taste for literary values and discreet opulence; he may be seen as an influence on Ronald Neame (with whom he worked on the Dickens films) and **Attenborough**. Lean himself credits the relatively unknown Bernard Vorhaus as an influence, while **Steven Spielberg** has spoken of his admiration for Lean's epics.

Further reading

Gerard Pratley's *The Cinema of David Lean* (New York, 1974), Alain Silver and James Ursini's *David Lean and His Films* (London, 1974).

Viewing

1 **Brief Encounter**
GB 1945/ w Celia Johnson, Trevor Howard, Stanley Holloway
2 **Great Expectations**
GB 1946/ w John Mills, Valerie Hobson, Alec Guinness
3 **The Bridge on the River Kwai**
GB 1957/ w Alec Guinness, William Holden, Sessue Hayakawa
4 **A Passage to India**
GB 1984/ w Judy Davis, Peggy Ashcroft, Victor Banerjee

Mitchell Leisen

Born: 6th October 1898/Menominee, Michigan, USA
Died: September 1972/Los Angeles, California, USA
Directing career: 1933-1963

Often regarded as a sub-Lubitsch Paramount contract director of variable material, James Mitchell Leisen has been widely, indeed shamefully neglected. The fabled **Lubitsch** 'touch' may seem heavy-handed compared to Leisen's unassertively stylish and intricate handling of comedy and melodrama, which repeatedly treated themes of sex, money and class with delicate irony and emotional depth.

Educated in art and architecture, Leisen entered Hollywood as costume designer then as art director for **DeMille** and others: his early credits include *Male and Female*, *The King of Kings*, and the Fairbanks epics *Robin Hood* and *The Thief of Bagdad*. His directorial debut came in 1933 with *Cradle Song*; the following year, *Death Takes a Holiday* and *Murder at the Vanities* (a bizarre backstage-musical-cum-comedy-thriller noted for exotic chorine routines and the song *Sweet Marijuana*) established him as a talent to watch. A series of glamorous, sophisticated comedies ensued, revealing his fine handling of actors (MacMurray, Milland, Lombard and Goddard, amongst others, would prove particularly responsive) and his love of lavish, elegant sets: indeed, after the charming *Hands Across the Table* (a comic romance deepened by scenes of real emotional pain) Leisen was able to work with Hollywood's most promising writers. **Wilder** and Charles Brackett scripted the sparkling *Midnight* >**1** in which a gold-digging American finds herself up to her neck in a mire of deception and jealousy when she poses as the mistress of a wealthy French aristocrat bent on winning back the affections of a faithless wife. They were also responsible for two superior melodramas: *Arise My Love*, its propaganda leavened with wit as it charts the troubled love of two Americans in war-torn Spain, and *Hold Back the Dawn*, an achingly moving account of the passionless union of a stateless refugee and the woman he weds to obtain US citizenship.

During the same fertile period, Leisen also benefitted from **Preston Sturges**' writing talents. *Easy Living* was a mordant Wall Street satire, while *Remember the Night* >**2** merged gentle comedy, poignant romance and a hint of social comment: a tale of a successful attorney whose career falters when he falls for a shoplifter he is prosecuting but has released on bail for Christmas. But Leisen was not simply a sensitive interpreter of others' scripts – pace, warmth and a commitment to the emotional undercurrents of occasionally contrived plots lent grace and power to his consistently entertaining work.

Despite a recurring interest in the absurdities and problems raised by societies obsessed with sex, status and class, Leisen's directing style was essentially 'invisible', eschewing virtuoso visual effects to focus on credible characters and smooth-running narratives. *Lady in the Dark* >**3**, however, based on the Moss Hart-Kurt Weill musical, saw the director's taste for design taken to an extreme. About a fashion-magazine editor who undergoes psycho-analysis to unravel her feelings about the three men in her life, it makes lurid use of ludicrously extravagant sets and costumes to create a Freudian fantasy that is inadvertently a masterpiece of Technicolor kitsch. Lavish designs also enlivened *Frenchman's Creek* (a superior swashbuckler) and the *Pygmalion*-like *Kitty* >**4**, an elegant, witty and unusually authentic Hollywood re-creation of Regency England, with Paulette Goddard in superb form as the street urchin whose life is dramatically transformed when she is painted in aristocratic garb by Sir Joshua Reynolds. Thereafter, however, Leisen's lush sophistication was at odds with the dominant postwar penchant for dour realism, and his career went steadily into decline, although original and entertaining films still surfaced at regular intervals: *To Each His Own* was a sensitive tale of the heartaches of maternal love, *Golden Earrings* an exotic Dietrich vehicle, *No Man of Her Own* >**5** an impressively moody thriller with Barbara Stanwyck blackmailed by an old flame when she assumes the identity of a soldier's widow to inherit the fortune of a family. *The Mating Season* used Thelma Ritter's garrulous talents to fine comic effect, and *The Girl Most Likely* was a perky musical notable for the bright, expressive colours of its sets and costumes. By now, however, Leisen's film career was virtually over: after directing a documentary about Las Vegas and several television assignments, he retired to concentrate on his Beverly Hills tailor's business and interior design.

At his frequent best, Leisen was the archetypal director of light but unfailingly intelligent entertainment with performance, plot and visual organisation honed to glossy perfection. While he rarely dealt with 'important' subjects, an assured sense of tone and taste, an ability to blend comedy and drama without creating jolts in mood, and a willingness to confront human emotions with honesty rather than indulgence, mark him as a film-maker deserving of greater critical attention than he has hitherto received.

Lineage

Perhaps even more than **Lubitsch** the ultimate Paramount director, Leisen may be seen as a less theatrical counterpart to **Cukor** and as anticipating both **Wilder** and **Sirk**; his sense of design, itself possibly derived from figures like **DeMille**, **Von Stroheim** and **Von Sternberg**, looks forward to the work of **Minnelli**.

Further reading

David Chierichetti's *Hollywood Director* (New York, 1973).

Viewing

1 **Midnight**
US 1939/ w Claudette Colbert, John Barrymore, Don Ameche

2 **Remember the Night**
US 1940/ w Barbara Stanwyck, Fred MacMurray, Beulah Bondi

3 **Lady in the Dark**
US 1944/ w Ginger Rogers, Ray Milland, Warner Baxter

4 **Kitty**
US 1945/ w Claudette Colbert, Ray Milland, Constance Collier

5 **No Man of Her Own**
US 1950/ w Barbara Stanwyck, John Lund, Jane Cowl

Sergio Leone

Born: 3rd January 1929/Rome, Italy
Died: 30th April 1989/Rome, Italy
Directing career: 1959-1989

Often viewed as an opportunist who plagiarised American genres to cynical, sensationalist effect, Sergio Leone was in fact a highly personal film-maker. At once pessimistic and romantic, he was a European fascinated by and critical of the heroic mythology perpetrated by

America. In the '60s he breathed new life into the ailing Western and in the '80s directed the definitive modern gangster movie.

Leone served his apprenticeship in film by assisting various Italian directors as well as **Walsh**, **Wyler** and Mervyn LeRoy. By the late '50s he was writing scripts for gladiatorial epics, the genre in which he first gained directing experience, and took over *The Last Days of Pompeii* when the director fell ill before helming solo on *The Colossus of Rhodes*. Not until 1964, however, did he establish himself as a true original with the first film in what would come to be known as the *Man With No Name* trilogy, *A Fistful of Dollars* >**1**. With a young and barely known **Clint Eastwood** as the laconic, ultra-cool, amoral hero, and a plot based on **Kurosawa**'s *Yojimbo*, Leone's stark, darkly comic tale of a nameless gunfighter hiring his services to two rival factions, deeply influenced the future of the Western in general and the Italian 'spaghetti' Western in particular. Plot would become a series of ritualised set-pieces, dialogue minimal, characters a bundle of elemental emotions: greed, the desire for revenge, and the need simply to survive in an arid, desolate world of horrific, seemingly random violence. Similarly in his next two films (which made Eastwood a star), *For a Few Dollars More* and *The Good, the Bad and the Ugly* >**2**, the hero was morally little better than the villains: only his deadly professionalism and taciturn, cunning intelligence differentiated him from the sadistic killers who were his prey and rivals. This nihilistic view of civilisation was framed in Leone's voluptuous, formalised visuals; shoot-outs became extended, geometric dances of death, faces were shot in huge close-up and extreme deep focus in impossibly magnificent and primeval landscapes, accompanied by the harsh, bestial howls of Ennio Morricone's inimitable music.

But Leone's Western masterpiece was *Once Upon a Time in the West* >**3**, an operatic, mythical epic rhyming the introduction of Civilisation to the Wilderness with a tale of murder and revenge as monolithically insistent as a Greek tragedy. Capitalism – in the form of a railway tycoon and his hired gunman – is ruthlessly evil; the romantic frontier ethos is doomed, its adherents haunted by a past seen in wordless flashback. Macho violence is inevitable but futile: the gunmen die and a stoic woman's determination to build a town around the railroad in the desert offers society its only hope. Equally stylish but less resonantly mythic was *A Fistful of Dynamite*, an account of the uneasy partnership formed by a bandit and an expatriate IRA terrorist during the Mexican revolution. Leone reluctantly agreed to direct, rather than produce this one, at the insistence of stars Rod Steiger and James Coburn.

After a lengthy period of apparent inactivity, Leone finally managed to film the long-planned *Once Upon a Time in America* >**4**, a complex, epic tale of the lives and times of four Jewish street urchins-turned-gangsters from the years before Prohibition to the mid-'60s. While drawing upon both historical fact and memories of classic gangster movies, Leone never glamorised his 'heroes' but showed them in an authentically unflattering light as misogynist, psychotically violent, irredeemably petty-minded and proud. Still more remarkably, the film's mosaic-like structure of emotionally associative jumps in time transforms a virtuoso genre-piece – all speakeasy parties, robberies, shoot-outs – into an examination of guilt, loyalty, betrayal and the subjectivity of truth, mirroring its protagonist's attempts to discover the link between a corrupt politician and a partner-in-crime whose death he thinks he caused decades earlier. Steadily progressing from explicit violence to a surprisingly introspective tranquillity, the film comments both on the dog-eat-dog morality that mars the American Dream, and on one man's belated ability to discover dignity and peace through self-knowledge and the rejection of a desire to take deadly revenge.

Leone's work steadily grew in emotional profundity and intellectual sophistication. No longer is he regarded as a mere genre-innovator with a caustic view of American history, he is now recognized as a director of huge international importance whose love of cinema was clear in his every frame; few directors indeed are blessed with such a rich and readily recognisable style.

Lineage

While it is interesting to compare Leone with Western specialists like **Ford**, **Mann**, **Boetticher** and **Peckinpah**, it is equally fertile to parallel his distinctly European attitude towards America and its films with that of **Melville**. In his apparent indifference to neo-realism he may seem the least Italian of his country's directors, although comparisons with **Bertolucci**, who worked on the original story of *Once Upon a Time in America*, may be illuminating.

Further reading

Christopher Frayling's *Spaghetti Westerns* (London, 1981).

Viewing

1 **A Fistful of Dollars (Per un Pugno di Dollari)**
Italy 1964/ w Clint Eastwood, Gian Maria Volonte, Marianne Koch
2 **The Good, The Bad and The Ugly (Il Buono, Il Brutto, Il Cattivo)**
Italy 1966/ w Clint Eastwood, Lee Van Cleef, Eli Wallach
3 **Once Upon a Time in the West (C'era una Volta il West)**
Italy 1968/ w Henry Fonda, Charles Bronson, Claudia Cardinale
4 **Once Upon a Time in America**
Italy 1983/ w Robert De Niro, James Woods, Elizabeth McGovern

Richard Lester

Born: **19th January 1932/ Philadelphia, Pennsylvania, USA**
Directing career: 1959-

The fast, flashy, fragmented cutting and light, wacky satire that brought Richard Lester widespread acclaim in the Swinging '60s now seem the product of a mind caught up in inconsequentiality and incoherence. Indeed, the vigour of his early work would seem to have ossified into redundant mannerisms and bland hack-work.

After directing for American television, Lester went to Europe where he made a living as a musician before finding work in British television, notably in advertising and with the Goons comedy team. In 1959, with Peter Sellers and Spike Milligan, he made the short, surreal and now badly dated *The Running, Jumping and Standing Still Film* before making his feature debut two years later with the pop vehicle *It's Trad Dad!* A dim comedy, *The Mouse on the Moon*, followed; it was only with the Beatles film, *A Hard Day's Night* >**1**, that he had his first significant success. Using improvisation, hectic action, music, documentary footage of fans, and a slim plot about life on the road, he elicited the essentially amiable 'mop-top' image of the group. Thereafter Lester stuck to the same basic formula – physical and verbal slapstick, frantic editing and zany but innocuous satire coupled with semi-documentary realism – whether adapting a theatrical comedy of sexual manners (*The Knack*), enlivening a Beatles spy-spoof (*Help!*) or turning to Broadway musical comedy (*A Funny Thing Happened on the Way to the Forum*). With *How I Won the War* he embarked upon a more portentous and didactic phase, employing bizarre colours and a rather forced surreal anarchy to underline a trite anti-war message; similarly pretentious and patchily effective were *Petulia* >**2** (a relatively serene but heartlessly modish romantic melodrama set in chic San Francisco) and the Goonish post-apocalypse comedy *The Bed-Sitting Room*. Whatever their ambitions they flopped, and as the '60s drew to a close Lester found himself unable to make another film.

It was five years before he returned to the fray with *The Three Musketeers*, an unusually straightforward adventure with a sly, dry sense of humour and a visual elegance derived from fine location photography in Spain. *Juggernaut*, too, was a routine but taut thriller. Lester soft-pedalled on hints that the luxury ocean liner, laden with a bomb about to explode, might symbolise contemporary Britain and focussed instead on formulaic suspense.

Henceforth his career has been alarmingly variable: *Royal Flash*, the gay farce *The Ritz*, and the comedy thriller *Finders Keepers* were all unmitigated disasters; *The Four Musketeers*, *Superman II* and *Superman III* efficient but unremarkable sequels, enlivened by occasional moments of carefully choreographed, disarmingly casual visual slapstick. Only *Robin and Marian* >**3**, *Butch and Sundance – The Early Days*, and *Cuba* suggested any real flair: the last two -a 'prequel' Western and an often tongue-in-cheek, glossy romantic thriller set in Batista's Cuba – merged engagingly offbeat humour with a jaunty, deftly devil-may-care approach towards narrative logic, while an account of the love of an ageing Robin Hood (Sean Connery in charismatic, docile mood) for an equally elderly Maid Marian (Audrey Hepburn) was more tranquil and elegaically moving than anything the director made before or since.

When Lester concentrates on people rather than technique he reveals a likeable if none too demanding talent for adventure and comedy; however, a penchant for gimmicky trickery, redolent of television advertising, works against the proper development of character and theme, and too often results in shallow spoofery.

Lineage

Lester seems a child of the early '60s, and may be tentatively compared to directors of the French New Wave, although silent comedy – most notably **Keaton**, who appears in *A Funny Thing. . .* – has influenced him a great deal. *Petulia* anticipates much of the work of **Roeg**, who served as cameraman on the film.

Further reading

Joseph Gelmis' *The Film Director as Superstar* (London 1970).

Viewing

1 **A Hard Day's Night**
GB 1964/ w The Beatles, Wilfrid Brambell, Victor Spinetti

2 **Petulia**
US 1968/ w Julie Christie, George C. Scott, Richard Chamberlain

3 **Robin and Marian**
US 1976/ w Sean Connery, Audrey Hepburn, Robert Shaw

Barry Levinson

Born: 2nd June 1932/Baltimore, Maryland, USA
Directing career: 1982-

Though Barry Levinson has yet to fulfil the promise of his debut, he is one of the more intriguing mainstream Hollywood film-makers to emerge in recent years. Unlike many of the post-Spielberg generation, he seems happier with words than visual effects, and is more adept at making films for adults than for teenagers.

Levinson first made an impression as a writer of comedy for film and television – his scripts included **Mel Brooks**' *Silent Movie* and *High Anxiety* and Norman Jewison's *And Justice for All*, co-written with Valerie Curtin – then broke into directing with *Diner* >**1**. Based partly on his own youth and set in Baltimore in 1959, the movie recounts the experiences of a group of late-teenagers whose favourite and persistent pastime is discussing sport, rock 'n'roll and dating in the late-night eaterie of the title. The film's plot is thin and muddled, but the characterisations, fleshed out by the superb ensemble acting of a virtually unknown young cast, are vivid; and Levinson's ear for witty, obsessive and plausibly inconsequential dialogue – one character intones record-label serial numbers like some inspirational litany, another lines from **Mackendrick**'s *Sweet Smell of Success* – enhance his assured sense of period detail.

The Natural was an overstated, glossy adaptation of Bernard Malamud's baseball novel, occasionally moving in a syrupy way but too emphatically mythical, and mired in Robert Redford's wholesome all-American image; worse, *Young Sherlock Holmes and the Pyramid of Fear*, made for **Spielberg**, undermined its portrait of a school-boy sleuth's precociousness with excessive special effects and a frantic plot. *Tin Men* >**2**, however, a black comedy about the insane rivalries arising between two aluminium-sidings salesmen after a minor car-accident, was something of a return to form. Though the plot finally sinks into sentimentality, with one character's vengeful seduction of his enemy's wife producing unlikely mutual love, its view of human pettiness and pride is largely astringent and Levinson's discreet evocation of time and place – Baltimore, again, in 1963 – gives rise to fine gags and an effortless air of authenticity. Again anecdote and performance take precedence over plot, qualities that also dominate *Good Morning, Vietnam*, where Robin Williams' virtuoso, fast-talking portrait of an irreverent, iconoclastic and anti-authoritarian American air-force DJ is ill-served by a plot that both sentimentalises relations between US servicemen and the Vietnamese in 1965 Saigon, and slides into a suspect, facile heroism in its assessment of the DJ's importance to air force morale. Nevertheless, the dialogue is often a witty delight – nostalgic, knowing, but never archaic or mannered. Less typical, perhaps, was *Rain Man*; Dustin Hoffman's highly acclaimed performance as an autistic numerical wizard, whose basic goodness helps to redeem his younger, con-man brother, is the only element of note in an otherwise dull, if worthy, film.

Levinson's love of words, gags and anecdote is symptomatic of his origins as a writer; by the same token his films' visuals are often flat and banal. While he may need to develop his sense of plotting, his characters are credible, lively, and amusing in their unselfconscious displays of monomaniacal obsession and attachment to ephemera. An alternative to the current prevailing interest in mindless adventure and tepid remakes and sequels, his work – mature and offbeat – deserves attention.

Lineage

Levinson would seem to belong to a tradition of dialogue-oriented writer-directors that includes **Sturges**, **Wilder** and **Mankiewicz**. Of younger directors, he may perhaps be compared with the **Coens**.

Viewing

1 **Diner**
US 1982/ w Daniel Stern, Mickey Rourke, Steve Guttenberg

2 **Tin Men**
US 1987/ w Richard Dreyfuss, Danny DeVito, Barbara Hershey

Albert Lewin

Born: 23rd September 1894/New York, USA
Died: 5th April 1968/New York, USA
Directing career: 1942-1956

At the time of their making the films of Albert Lewin were widely dismissed as the products of a pretentious cultural dilletante given to verbose and vulgar literary adaptations. With the passing of the years, however, he has come to be regarded (in a few critical circles, at least) as a remarkably modern film-maker whose love of words in no way impeded the cinematic potential of his work.

A former student and teacher of English, Lewin first came to prominence in Hollywood in the late '20s and '30s as the head of the script department, then producer, for MGM's Irving Thalberg; most notable among his productions were Jacques Feyder's *The Kiss* (with Garbo), *Mutiny on the Bounty*, and (for Paramount) **Cukor**'s *Zaza*. In 1942 he directed his first film, a sensitive, verbally witty and immaculately performed version of Somerset Maugham's *The Moon and Sixpence*. George Sanders, admirably lacking in sentimentality, starred as the Gauguin-like artist whose selfish obsession with painting leads him to abandon his family and clerical job to work in Paris and the South Seas. Sanders' articulate and amoral cynicism was put to even better use by Lewin in a film of Wilde's Faustian cautionary tale *The Picture of Dorian Gray* >**1**. As the epigram-spouting Lord Henry Wotton, he serves as a perfect foil and mentor to Hurd Hatfield's bland, malleable Dorian, whose soul is debauched and corrupted by a desire for eternal youth and beauty. Lewin's sophisticated, densely allusive dialogue is savoured throughout, though the film's visual qualities are never neglected: both the cluttered *fin-de-siècle* elegance of Mayfair and the seedy netherworld of Blue Gate Fields, visited by Dorian in search of depravity, are rendered in authentic and atmospheric detail, while the Technicolor inserts of the painting that reflects the degradation of his inner self are appropriately hideous.

Equally intelligent, a version of Maupassant's *The Private Affairs of Bel Ami* >2 outshone the original source in its subtle and generous understanding of the emotions of an ambitious young journalist whose social climbing is facilitated by an opportunist and destructive disregard for lovers and friends. *Pandora and the Flying Dutchman* >3 was similarly literary and allusive, though in a more self-consciously mythic vein: in a Spanish coastal village in the '30s, an expatriate American singer – likened to her Greek namesake for the lethal effect she seems to have upon her suitors - falls in love with a mysterious yacht-owner who turns out to be a ghost doomed to eternal misery until he meets a woman ready to sacrifice her life for him. Logically absurd, the film benefits from a complex web of literary and legendary references, powerful performances and virtually surreal Technicolor images, which lend the tale of *amour fou* both emotional poignancy and a stormy, lush romanticism. But the film's unusual plot and elevated dialogue proved unattractive to audiences and, in the next seven years, the writer-director made only two more films – *Saadia*, in which a young European doctor in the Sahara falls foul of local superstition, and *The Living Idol*, about a Mexican girl believed to be possessed by the spirit of an ancient jaguar. Thereafter, following medical advice, Lewin retired from directing.

With hindsight, Lewin's widely decried artiness seems the hallmark of a perennially adventurous, unusually literate and independent director. Nor was his personality totally subservient to the writers to whose works he turned; the Maugham, Wilde and Maupassant adaptations also reveal his own interest in characters trapped and destroyed by an idealistic dream of winning a better life for themselves. The elaborate visual and verbal patterns and allusions of Lewin's best work may be seen as his own idealistic attempts to provide a complex, subtle alternative to the escapist and decidedly low- and middle-brow fare promoted by Hollywood.

Lineage

Lewin himself cited Robert Wiene's *The Cabinet of Dr Caligari* as having inspired him to enter film; Thalberg, too, was clearly an influence. To some extent, he may be compared with **Cukor**, though his taste for refined verbal delicacies perhaps places him closer to the likes of **Mankiewicz**, **Rohmer**, or even **Greenaway**.

Further reading

Lewin's *The Unaltered Cat* (New York, 1967) is a novel. There is little of substance written about his work.

Viewing

1 **The Picture of Dorian Gray**
US 1945/ w Hurd Hatfield, George Sanders, Angela Lansbury

2 **The Private Affairs of Bel Ami**
US 1947/ w George Sanders, Angela Lansbury, Ann Dvorak

3 **Pandora and the Flying Dutchman**
GB 1951/ w Ava Gardner, James Mason, Nigel Patrick

Joseph H. Lewis

Born: 6th April 1900/New York, USA
Directing career: 1937-1958

One of the finest B-movie makers, Joseph H. Lewis regularly proved himself superior to the formular nature (or, sometimes, sheer lunacy) of his low-budget assignments, through daring, inventive visuals, intense performances and an assured grasp of genre. Indeed, such was his ability to turn economic shortcomings to his advantage that his finest work rivals that of many better-known directors.

Having worked his way up from MGM camera-loader to head the editing department at Republic, Lewis started directing in 1937. The early films are lowly indeed: Bowery Boys dramas, inept horror thrillers, singing Westerns. And yet, despite appalling scripts and next-to-non-existent budgets, time and again Lewis enlivens a scene with uncommon visual flair: a cowboy brawl may benefit from an imaginative placing of props, boring dialogue may be shot from above; *Secrets of a Co-Ed* ends with a ten-minute courtroom scene constructed astonishingly from a single take. After years of such work, urged on by Columbia's Harry Cohn, he made a bid for higher budgets with the moody, elegantly shot psychological thriller *My Name Is Julia Ross*; less polished but more quirkily adventurous was *So Dark the Night* >**1**, in which his penchant for shadows and reflections was given full rein as a detective investigating a series of murders discovers that he is the amnesiac culprit.

In the late '40s Lewis hit his stride with an intermittent series of superior crime-thrillers: *Undercover Man* combined an almost documentary evocation of law-enforcement procedures with a strong sympathy for crime's victims; *Gun Crazy* >**2** told a fast, dark *Bonnie and Clyde*-style tale of a couple whose obsession for firearms verges on the sexual. It was memorable for virtuoso visuals (a daring bank raid shot from start to end in one long, complex take from the back of a car) and subversively sympathetic but entirely unsentimental performances. The elegant *A Lady Without Passport* concerned refugees attempting illegal entry into America from an atmospherically evoked Havana; *Cry of the Hunted* – like several other Lewis films – featured a superb climax in a swamp. Best of all, however, was *The Big Combo* >**3**, a relentlessly imaginative *noir* thriller about organised crime in which the cop-hero, callously using those around him in his efforts to nail the gang-boss lover of the woman for whom he himself harbours a psychotic passion, is no less ruthlessly self-obsessed than the villain. Lewis is again on top, inventive form, squeezing into his taut narrative bizarre scenes involving a pair of gay gunmen, torture by deaf-aid and a thinly-disguised hint of oral sex, while presenting a disturbing, dark portrait of assorted perverse relationships and obsessions.

Lewis' last four films were solid Westerns. *Seventh Cavalry* was notable for its unusually critical attitude towards Custer's role in the Little Big Horn massacre and a virtually supernatural finale, in which the General's horse appears, ghost-like, to settle a confrontation between Indians and Army. *Lawless Street* and *The Halliday Brand*, while less nonsensical, were more conventional, but *Terror in a Texas Town* >**4**, shot in ten days, was remarkable both because many involved in the production were HUAC blacklist victims, and because the climax saw a Swedish immigrant farmer avenge his father's death by killing the villain with a harpoon.

Thereafter Lewis turned to television before retiring. Never a major film-maker, he was nonetheless a spirited talent of great intelligence and enormous resourcefulness. Given fine actors and sufficient finance, his sense of composition and pace enabled him to transcend script limitations; with a good script, however, his ambitions and talent could produce memorable, if minor, classics.

Lineage

Lewis' early career in Poverty Row studios provokes comparisons with figures such as Edgar Ulmer, William Beaudine and Joseph Kane. In later years, at his best and given a larger budget, he might have aspired to the ranks of a **Siegel**, **Fuller** or **Tourneur**. *Gun Crazy* has many admirers among film-makers, notably **Schrader**, while **Penn** 'remade' *My Name Is Julia Ross* as *Dead of Winter*.

Further reading

Kings of the Bs, ed. Todd McCarthy and Charles Flynn (1975, New York).

Viewing

1 **So Dark the Night**
US 1946/ w Steven Geray, Micheline Cheirel, Eugene Borden
2 **Gun Crazy (Deadly is the Female)**
US 1949/ w John Dall, Peggy Cummins, Berry Kroeger
3 **The Big Combo**
US 1954/ w Cornell Wilde, Richard Conte, Jean Wallace
4 **Terror in a Texas Town**
US 1958/ w Sterling Hayden, Ned Young, Sebastian Cabot

Ken Loach

Born: 17th June 1936/Nuneaton, England
Directing career: 1967-

While firmly entrenched in the British realist tradition, Kenneth Loach's films transcend the limitations common to such methods by means of a rich combination of politics, poetry and pathos. Unfortunately, his rigorous naturalism and left-wing sympathies have effectively confined his more recent work to television, although his imagery seems equally authentic on both the large and small screens.

Developing an interest in theatre while studying law, Loach went on to direct for television, where the power and accuracy of his portraits of contemporary British working-class life in plays such as *Up the Junction*, *Cathy Come Home* and *In Two Minds* singled him out as an exciting new talent. In 1967, with long-term collaborator and producer Tony Garnett, he made his feature debut, *Poor Cow*, in which a young wife's adultery with her criminal husband's closest friend gave rise to a somewhat schematic evocation of the poverty and banality of working-class experience. *Kes* >**1**, however, was altogether more affecting. It is naturalistic portrait of a young delinquent, whose feelings for a kestrel he finds and trains are symbolic of a doomed attempt to escape the stultifying, limited opportunities offered school-leavers in the industrial North. The dialogue (delivered in broad dialect) and profoundly truthful performances lend the film an air of documentary, but the use of the bird as a poetic metaphor for freedom and dignity, and the lucid analysis of the pressures to conform brought to

Sandy Ratcliffe as a girl on the brink of a mental breakdown, in Ken Loach's indictment of the pressures of *Family Life*.

bear on the boy by the adult world, transcend objective realism and push the film into the realm of moving, low-key political melodrama.

Equally devastating in its emotional sway, and sharp in its comprehension of the destructive demands for obedience necessary to the preservation of familial stability and complacency, *Family Life* >**2** was a dramatic example of R.D. Laing's then controversial theories on the social origins of schizophrenia. Thereafter, for most of the '70s, Loach worked mainly in television, the four-part *Days of Hope* (a family saga from the start of the Great War to the 1926 General Strike) being a highlight. In 1979 he returned to features with *Black Jack*, a children's film about pre-industrial Britain, while the television film, *The Gamekeeper* was a superb, deeply ironic analysis of its hero's relationship to his family and his dog, the land itself, the poachers who are his friends, and his country-aristocrat employers. No less clear-eyed was *Looks and Smiles* >**3**, a remarkably plausible account of a teenage romance blighted by the frustration and despair that accompany unemployment in Thatcher's Britain. Loach's sympathies for his young working-class victims were as strong as ever, while unsentimental performances gave evidence of the integrity of his approach. Equally balanced but rather more simplistic, *Fatherland* saw him widen his horizons with a bleak, sceptical account of the differences and similarities between East and West as experienced by an East German protest-singer in exile; while the thesis that Western capitalism is just as oppressive as Communist dogmatism was well handled, its gradual progress into conspiracy-thriller territory, though ambitious, saw the drama fall uneasily between bland genre conventions and Loach's customary realist style.

The most politically committed of British film-makers, Loach is to be valued for his imaginative exploration of the thin line separating fiction and documentary. Carefully wrought scripts and grainy location shooting provide an astute, authentic analysis of society at large, while his excellent handling of actors lends the films an often deeply moving human dimension.

Lineage

Loach is perhaps the most distinguished successor to the British Free Cinema of the '50s and '60s (Karel Reisz, Tony Richardson, **Anderson**). While similarities with the work of **Bill Douglas** and even **Terence Davies** exist, comparison with the rather more politically oriented Barney Platts-Mills and Maurice Hatton is also worthwhile.

Viewing

1 **Kes**
GB 1969/ w David Bradley, Colin Welland, Lynne Perrie

2 **Family Life**
GB 1971/ w Sandy Ratcliffe, Bill Dean, Grace Cave

3 **Looks and Smiles**
GB 1981/ w Graham Green, Carolyn Nicholson, Phil Askham

Joseph Losey

Born: **14th January 1909/La Crosse, Wisconsin, USA**
Died: **22nd June 1984/London, England**
Directing career: **1939-1984**

Joseph Losey was a director of unusual intellectual ambitions and abilities. It is perhaps salutary that his best work emerged from the confines of traditional genres, whereas his films of the '60s and early '70s, when his artistic freedom was greater, often seem pretentious, over-emphatic, studied and stale.

Losey began his artistic career in theatre and radio, where an interest in experimental and politically committed work led to a successful collaboration with Brecht on the play *Galileo*. Film, however, attracted him and, after making several educational shorts, he turned in 1949 to directing features with *The Boy With Green Hair*, an adventurous if uneven fantasy with an anti-war and anti-racism message. Allegory, in fact, would be a common element in Losey's later work, but for the next two years he concentrated on taut, economic thrillers, often set against a backdrop of moral and social unrest: in *The Lawless*, Mexican-American fruit-pickers suffer racist violence; in *The Prowler* >**1**, a policeman's love for a married woman leads him to murder; *M* was an unexpectedly strong remake of Lang's classic about a child-murderer; *The Big Night* an effectively melodramatic study of teenage crime. Losey's keen eye for detail and social environment created intelligent, gripping entertainment. Then, after making *Stranger on the Prowl* in Italy, he became a victim of the McCarthy blacklist and moved to Britain where, for some years, he worked under a pseudonym.

Although his early British work was largely undistinguished, films like *The Sleeping Tiger* (about a psychopathic gunman), *Time Without Pity* (about an alcoholic) and *The Gypsy and The Gentleman*, revealed his continuing interest in outsider-figures who, by their very presence, inflame the latent tensions already existing within an enclosed society or relationship; at the same time, his visual style became steadily more baroque. After two straightforward but superior crime thrillers starring Stanley Baker (*Blind Date*, and *The Criminal* >**2**, a perceptive study of the betrayals and loyalties of prison life), he embarked upon a series of films more notable for an evocative use of landscape and interiors than for their rather schematic, sour view of human aspirations. *Eve* charted the lethal obsession of a married Welsh writer for a cool, classy temptress in a lavishly shot, wintry Venice; *The Damned*, an apocalyptic sci-fi film, featured teddy-boys, an American tourist and a visionary sculptress in the Victorian coastal town of Weymouth; *The Servant* >**3** (the first of several Losey collaborations with Harold Pinter, and the first, since *The Sleeping Tiger*, to feature Dirk Bogarde, whose reputation would benefit by becoming a Losey regular) embellished its role-reversal tale of a spineless upper-class man ruined by his scheming butler with a portentously symbolic use of mirrors and staircases. Awkwardly balanced between cool restraint and overheated excess, Losey's style often hinted at allegory and opted for meticulous design at the expense of true vitality.

As the director gained something of a cult reputation so his films became more waywardly uneven. *King and Country*, in which a World War I soldier is executed for desertion, was predictable anti-war pleading; the spoof comic-strip thriller, *Modesty Blaise*, only confirmed Losey's lack of humour; *Accident* >**4** was a crisply shot, needlessly complicated drama about adulterous Oxford dons; *Boom!* and *Secret Ceremony* were risible variations on the theme of claustrophobic relationships intruded on by an outsider; *Figures in a Landscape* a banal allegory about two fugitives searching for freedom. Time and again Losey's detached direction drew attention to itself, resulting less in clarity than in a coldly mechanistic view of character. Even the sumptuous *The Go-Between* >**5**, about a young boy traumatised by the part he unwittingly plays in an Edwardian farmer's clandestine romance with an aristocratic girl, founders on portentous flashes to the future and a sense of class conflict that is as simplistic as it is emotionally uninvolving.

Through the '70s Losey seemed to lose his way still further; arty, precious, sometimes disastrously dull, *The Assassination of Trotsky*, versions of *A Doll's House* and *Galileo*, and *The Romantic Englishwoman* did little to improve his status. Moving to France, he temporarily revived his reputation with *Mr Klein*, a disturbing if contrived account of a man in Nazi-occupied Paris who becomes self-destructively obsessed with his Jewish namesake, and with a visually elegant version of Mozart's *Don Giovanni*; but *The Trout*, *Les Routes du Sud*, and the exceedingly theatrical *Steaming* (made in England and released posthumously) were generally dismissed as negligible by all but the director's most fervent admirers.

Too often, Losey's taste for allegory and his over-elaborate use of symbolism and metaphor resulted in turgid narratives and a strained seriousness. As an exile, he occasionally managed to see British and European life from a fresh perspective; nevertheless, his drily intellectual and schematic approach to art often meant that his films were woefully lifeless and academic.

Lineage

Losey's early genre-films bear comparison with the social-minded works of directors like **Kazan**, **Ray** and **Fuller**, while his English films are rather closer to European art-movies. A devout admirer of Brecht, he may be compared to figures like **Resnais**, **Chabrol**, **Antonioni**, **Visconti**, **Bertolucci**, and **Roeg**.

Further reading

James Leahy's *The Cinema of Joseph Losey* (New York, 1967). Tom Milne's *Losey on Losey* (London, 1967) and Michel Ciment's *Conversations with Losey* (London, 1985) offer long interviews.

Viewing

1 **The Prowler**
US 1951/ w Van Heflin, Evelyn Keyes, John Maxwell

2 **The Criminal**
GB 1962/ w Stanley Baker, Sam Wanamaker, Margit Saad

3 **The Servant**
GB 1963/ w Dirk Bogarde, James Fox, Sarah Miles, Wendy Craig

4 **Accident**
GB 1967/ w Dirk Bogarde, Michael York, Stanley Baker, Jacqueline Sassard

5 **The Go-Between**
GB 1970/ w Julie Christie, Alan Bates, Dominic Guard, Margaret Leighton

Ernst Lubitsch

Born: 28th January 1892/Berlin, Germany
Died: 29th November 1947/ Hollywood, California, USA
Directing career: 1914-1947

Much praised for the veneer of smart European sophistication he brought to American musicals and comedy, Ernst Lubitsch became a major force in Hollywood during the '30s. It is arguable, however, that the films of that decade, praised as displaying the finest examples of the 'Lubitsch touch', are ultimately shallow in their cynicism and urbane innuendo, whereas his later work, often seen as relatively coarse, exhibits a rather more affecting poignancy.

In Germany, Lubitsch moved from acting for Max Reinhardt to directing himself in several slapstick shorts as a Chaplinesque hero. In 1918 he embarked upon a series of features that offered evidence of a more ambitious talent, combining romantic comedies highlighting intimate intrigue with extravagant historical dramas (*Madame DuBarry*, *Anna Boleyn*) noted for lavish sets, and a rather more human, small-scale sense of character than was usual at the time. Such was his success that in 1922 he emigrated to Hollywood at the behest of Mary Pickford to direct her in *Rosita*. This was followed by a number of uncommonly refined comedies (*The Marriage Circle*, *Lady Windermere's Fan*) that established him as an urbane, witty commentator on sexual mores and as a visually imaginative adaptor of literary sources. But it was the coming of sound that saw Lubitsch, by now one of Paramount's most important directors, really come into his own; indeed by 1935 he was promoted, for one year only, to the position of studio production head.

His first talkie, *The Love Parade* >**1**, was a Maurice Chevalier-Jeanette MacDonald operetta set among the royalty of a Ruritanian country and distinguished from other musicals of the time by its integration of songs into the plot and by its risqué sense of humour. Indeed, except for the turgidly anti-war *The Man I Killed* (*Broken Lullaby*), throughout the early and mid-'30s the director, both in musicals (*Monte Carlo*, *The Smiling Lieutenant*, *The Merry Widow*) and romantic comedies (*Trouble in Paradise* >**2**, *Design for Living*, *Angel*), combined elegant costumes and sets with a knowing amorality embodied in suggestive dialogue, raised eyebrows and a hint of sexual intimacies behind closed doors. Frequently, as in *Trouble in Paradise* (in which a suave jewel thief is torn between his female partner in crime and the heiress they plan to swindle) and *Design for*

Living (a *ménage-à-trois* is threatened when the woman leaves her lovers to marry a wealthier older man), comedy is derived from deception, suspicion and incessant role-playing; infidelity is a constant element, often serving to bring a couple closer together. For all the films' cynicism, however, the smart modernity often seems contrived, forced, hollow; style becomes an end in itself rather than a means of describing the world. Indeed, the insistent trivialising of emotions for the sake of elegantly delivered innuendo, means that many of the films now seem dated.

After two comparatively harsh comedies written by **Wilder** and Charles Brackett (*Bluebeard's Eighth Wife*, and *Ninotchka* >**3**, which was most notable for casting Garbo in an unusually light role as the gloomy Soviet commissar whose icy ideology is melted by love, Paris, and Melvyn Douglas's smug hedonist), Lubitsch, who by now had severed his connections with Paramount, began producing the most mature works of his career. *The Shop Around the Corner* >**4**, set in a nostalgically evoked Budapest, is genuinely moving as it charts the complex courtship of two shop assistants who hate each other, even as they unwittingly conduct an anonymous, romantic correspondence with one another. This new-found willingness to confront real pain was even more evident in *To Be Or Not To Be* >**5**, a truly astonishing black comedy set in war-torn Warsaw where a troupe of incompetent Polish actors triumph over the occupying Nazis through mimicry and a cunning manipulation of the enemy's appalling bad manners. The farce, full of brilliant and outrageous dialogue, is frantic, but its power derives from the danger and seriousness of its situation, thus ensuring our emotional involvement. If *Heaven Can Wait* (in which a man's philandering life is seen to be motivated by goodness when he is turned away by Satan) and *Cluny Brown* (about a working-class romance blooming in the stuffy upper echelons of English society) are gentler and less inventive, they still provide ample evidence of Lubitsch's ability to touch the heart whenever he resisted the temptation to indulge in cynicism.

Sadly, just when he seemed to have achieved a real artistic maturity, Lubitsch died from a heart attack, having spent only a few days filming *That Lady in Ermine*. (It was completed by **Preminger**.) In retrospect, his celebrated 'touch', once considered subtle, even subversive, appears dated, theatrical, heavy-handed. Conversely, the work of his last years has gained in stature, its unreserved commitment to its characters' emotional lives lending it a belated but enduring and affecting profundity.

Lineage

Lighter in tone than his German contemporaries, Lubitsch compares more closely with figures like **Mamoulian**, **Von Sternberg**, **Arzner**, **Cukor** and **Leisen**; he himself admitted to admiring **Chaplin**'s *A Woman of Paris*. He may be seen as an influence on **Wilder**.

Further reading

Herman G. Weinberg's *The Lubitsch Touch* (New York, 1977).

Viewing

1 **The Love Parade**
US 1929/ w Maurice Chevalier, Jeanette MacDonald, Lupino Lane

2 **Trouble in Paradise**
US 1932/ w Herbert Marshall, Miriam Hopkins, Kay Francis

3 **Ninotchka**
US 1939/ w Greta Garbo, Melvyn Douglas, Sig Rumann

4 **The Shop Around the Corner**
US 1940/ w James Stewart, Margaret Sullavan, Frank Morgan

5 **To Be Or Not To Be**
US 1942/ w Jack Benny, Carole Lombard, Sig Rumann, Felix Bressart

George Lucas

Born: 14th May 1944/Modesto, California, USA
Directing career: 1965-

Along with **Steven Spielberg**, with whom he regularly collaborates,

George Lucas is financially the most successful of the Hollywood 'movie-brats'. Revealingly, after three features he seems to have forsaken directing for producing; indeed, his importance lies less in his films themselves than in his influence on various current tendencies – including marketing – in American cinema.

Lucas studied film at the University of Southern California where his shorts (including the prize-winning satire on a robot-controlled future, *THX 1138: 4EB*) promised a future in relatively experimental cinema. Thanks to his friendship with **Coppola** (whose assistant he was on *Finian's Rainbow* and *The Rain People*), he was able to expand the cybernetics film into the feature *THX 1138* >**1**, a rather conventional *1984*-style tale of an individual who rebels against the drug-induced, sex-free conformism of the subterranean society in which he lives, and escapes in search of freedom. What distinguishes an otherwise hackneyed, predictable movie is Lucas' use of sound (supplied by Walter Murch) and image to establish a sinister world, where every action is seen and heard by invisible policing authorities: video screens proliferate, and incidentally lend the plot a fragmented, spurious air of complexity. Similarly imaginative, however, was the film's overall design, with shaven-headed actors merging into the blinding whiteness of their stark surroundings to reinforce the theme of universal conformism.

The film was not a success, but for *American Graffiti* >**2** the young director drew upon his nostalgic memories of adolescence to create a witty and colourful, if finally soft-centred, entertainment about the music, mating and driving rituals of Californian youth in the early '60s. Emphasising the innocence of a mythical past, Lucas neglected painful reality to paint an often sexist, teeming portrait of strutting rockers, feeble wimps, complacent girls and cruising cars, engaged one long night in an absurdly event-filled search for thrills and self-awareness. Despite its relentless pace, excellent rock soundtrack and superb ensemble playing from a then unfamiliar cast, the film is finally shallow – a quality even more conspicuous in the enormously successful space fantasy *Star Wars* >**3**, which single-handedly turned back the clock for adult sci-fi by decades. A mindless light-show with virtuoso special effects, cardboard characters and a formulaic adventure plot, *Star Wars* drew on sources as diverse as **Ford**'s *The Searchers*, Arthurian legend and the *Buck Rogers* serials to create a tale of Good vs Evil as cold and calculated as it was brazenly insubstantial. Again, nostalgia, for simpler black-and-white moralities and untroubled heroes, lay at the film's heart: indeed, both its message and its promotion, which made much of tie-in toys, T-shirts and other ephemera, may be seen as the ultimate expression of the classic American Dream.

With his fame and fortune secure, Lucas has since concentrated on the production (and occasional co-writing) of similar adventures aimed at children and undemanding teenagers: two *Star Wars* sequels (*The Empire Strikes Back*, *The Return of the Jedi*), not to mention an involvement in Spielberg's *Indiana Jones* films, have made him one of the most powerful moguls in Hollywood. It is a pity then, that he seems uninterested in making films with anything more than the most fantastic of stories or sketchiest of characters. As such, it may be argued that his influence on recent developments in cinema – notably its single-minded focus on the teenage audience – is unhealthy; his productions are pure merchandise rather than art.

Lineage

Even more than **Spielberg**, Lucas adheres to a bland, childlike and Disneyesque concept of entertainment; many younger directors, few talented, have followed his example, but former colleagues Murch, **Coppola**, **Milius** and Haskell Wexler seem adult in comparison. His special effects company, Industrial Light and Magic, is highly influential on technical developments in film.

Further reading

Skywalking by Dave Pollock (London, 1983); Linda Myles and Michael Pye's *The Movie Brats* (New York, 1979).

Viewing

1 **THX 1138**
US 1971/ w Robert Duvall, Donald Pleasence, Maggie McOmie
2 **American Graffiti**
US 1973/ w Richard Dreyfuss, Ron Howard, Candy Clark, Paul Le Mat
3 **Star Wars**
US 1977/ w Mark Hamill, Harrison Ford, Carrie Fisher

Sidney Lumet

Born: 25th June 1924/Philadelphia, Pennsylvania, USA
Directing career: 1957-

A prolific director of varied and variable material, Sidney Lumet all too often displays the thumping theatricality and half-baked seriousness of his origins in television drama. But occasionally, especially when dealing with the subject of urban crime, he has created a chilling, corrupt and seemingly chaotic world, notable for convincing characters and the detail of his observations.

A child actor from the age of four, Lumet gradually moved towards directing, making his name in television during the '50s. His film debut, *Twelve Angry Men* >1 (from a stage play by Reginald Rose), was a somewhat contrived but remarkably well acted one-set drama with archetypal liberal Henry Fonda slowly but surely persuading his fellow jurors to pronounce innocent a boy accused of murder; while the characters are drawn in vivid detail, it is Lumet's claustrophobic evocation of a hot summer's evening in the stuffy jury room that lends the film its relentless tension. For the next decade, he continued to focus mainly on similarly theatrical or worthy subjects, filming Williams (*The* Fugitive Kind), Miller (*A View from the Bridge*), O'Neill (*Long Day's Journey Into Night*) and Chekov (*The Sea Gull*), and treating nuclear apocalypse (*Fail Safe*), the legacy of the Nazi Holocaust (*The Pawnbroker*), and modern espionage (*The Deadly Affair*). *Bye Bye Braverman*, in which four friends get drunk searching for the funeral of a friend, was a rare, often witty foray into comedy, but the strongest elements of his stolid direction in his early career were his excellence with actors and his fidelity to source.

In the '70s he interspersed misbegotten projects like *Murder on the Orient Express*, the over-emphatic satire about TV, Network, an absurdly realist version of Peter Shaffer's *Equus*, and the black musical *The Wiz*, with a number of increasingly ambitious accounts of crime and police work. *The Offence*, in which a detective beats to death a man suspected of child molestation, and *Serpico*, about an honest cop who exposes corruption in the force, were intensely felt but slightly simplistic portraits of obsession leading good men into a world of unexpected violence; *Dog Day Afternoon* >**2**, a tragicomic, loosely structured tale of a disastrous bank hold-up committed by a married bisexual to finance his gay lover's sex-change operation, benefitted from superb performances, a strong feel for the absurdities of city life and of media coverage, and a sense of good intentions wrecked by innocence. Most impressive, however, was *Prince of the City* >**3**, a long, complex blend of taut action and legal speculation that reworked the police-corruption theme of *Serpico* to infinitely more sophisticated effect. Here, a sprawling, impressionistic and fragmented narrative slowly closes like a spider's web around its hero, who is both honest and stubborn, an example to the force but a Judas to his friends.

In recent years, Lumet has continued to treat serious themes (the law and medical negligence in *The Verdict*, political protest and capital punishment in *Daniel*, manipulative election marketing in *Power*, teenage unrest and disillusionment in *Running on Empty*) with variable success, while *The Morning After* was a beautifully performed if strangely suspenseless psychological thriller. Lumet warrants attention, in fact, for his ability with actors. But the sheer inconsistency of his work and a curious lack of commitment to much of his material suggest that he is unusually dependent upon a strong script and a sympathetic cast to achieve his best.

Lineage

Lumet's style, derived from years in television, and his liberal sensibility provoke comparison with figures like **Frankenheimer**, Robert Mulligan, Martin Ritt, Franklin Schaffner, Norman Jewison and Sidney Pollack; sadly, he lacks **Penn**'s quirky intelligence.

Viewing

1 **Twelve Angry Men**
US 1957/ w Henry Fonda, Lee J. Cobb, Ed Begley, Jack Warden
2 **Dog Day Afternoon**
US 1975/ w Al Pacino, John Cazale, Charles Durning
3 **Prince of the City**
US 1981/ w Treat Williams, Jerry Orbach, Richard Foronjy

Ida Lupino

Born: 4th February 1918/London, England
Directing career: 1950-1966

Best known as a versatile actress who was often cast as a tough, outspoken, unusually independent woman, Ida Lupino was the only female director of note to work in Hollywood in the years between **Dorothy Arzner**'s heyday in the '30s, and the '70s when a handful of women, presumably inspired by feminism, turned to directing.

The daughter of comedian Stanley Lupino and actress Connie Emerald, Lupino first appeared in films in her teens while studying acting at London's RADA. In 1933 she gained a Hollywood contract with Paramount, though she came to prominence at Warners. Unforgettable in **Walsh**'s *High Sierra*, **Nicholas Ray**'s *On Dangerous Ground* and **Aldrich**'s *The Big Knife*, in 1949, with her then husband Collier Young, she formed her own production company and turned to writing and directing, often dealing with the plight of women.

After writing and taking over the direction of *Not Wanted* – about the experiences of an unmarried mother – when Elmer Clifton fell ill, she made her debut proper with *Never Fear*, the tale of a dancer's battle against polio. More controversially, in *Outrage* she examined the devastating psychological and emotional effects of rape, while *Hard, Fast and Beautiful* zoned in on the relationship of a girl and her ambitious, domineering mother who pushes her to compete on the tennis circuit. Such melodramas, notable for their unusual subject matter and good intentions, were followed, rather surprisingly, by *The Hitch Hiker* >**1**, a remarkably tense and atmospheric B-thriller in which a pair of complacent businessmen, returning from a hunting trip, find that the man they have picked up in the desert is a homicidal psychopath. Lupino milks the plot for all it is worth, deftly fleshes out the characters, and makes superb use of the stark locations, preying on agoraphobic fears, and transforming the hapless drivers' predicament into a primeval struggle for survival. This minor masterpiece of economy (both in terms of budget and length) was followed by the very different but equally impressive *The Bigamist* >**2**, a sensitive account of how a travelling salesman comes to marry twice. What distinguishes the film, beyond the fine performances and unglamorous evocation of working-class life, is the compassion with which Lupino views her characters: the man is no callous skirt-chaser but a troubled and foolish individual whose actions stem from loneliness. Crucially, Lupino casts the wives against type, with the usually mousey Joan Fontaine as a tough, go-getter career-woman, and herself as a shy homebody. Indeed, the treatment of a profoundly emotional, often taboo issue is notable both for its balance and for its awareness that to love more than one person is at once painful and common.

In later years, Lupino focussed on directing for television and acting, making only one more film – the 1966 convent comedy *The Trouble with Angels*, memorable solely for its oddly-assembled all-woman cast with Rosalind Russell as the Mother Superior. Several of her performances, such as that in **Peckinpah**'s *Junior Bonner*, displayed the independent spirit that was hers in real life. The films she made are minor, but distinguished by intelligence, courage, and a sensitivity to people's emotional lives; now rarely seen, they deserve re-appraisal – particularly in the light of recent feminist theory.

Lineage

It is tempting if obvious to compare Lupino's films with those of **Dorothy Arzner**: Lupino, perhaps due to her work with the likes of **Walsh** and **Wellman**, seems tougher. Modern women directors who seem equally determined to work in commercial rather than avant-garde cinema include Amy Jones, Susan Seidelman, Martha Coolidge, Donna Dietch, Marisa and Joan Micklin Silver, and Penelope Spheeris.

Viewing

1 **The Hitch Hiker**
US 1953/ w Edmond O'Brien, Frank Lovejoy, William Talman

2 **The Bigamist**
US 1953/ w Edmond O'Brien, Joan Fontaine, Lupino

David Lynch

Born: 20th January 1946/Missoula, Montana, USA
Directing career: 1967-

Perhaps the most original and imaginative director to emerge from America in recent years, David Lynch reveals an uncanny ability to draw upon his own inner fantasies and create strange, sinister worlds at once unreal and oddly familiar. If the films' precise meaning is sometimes less than clear, their power and invention remain virtually unparalleled in contemporary mainstream cinema.

Lynch worked in film while studying painting in art school, making a one-minute animated loop before filming two shorts in which painted animation, modelling and live action are mixed to original effect: both *The Alphabet* (a parable on the horrors of education) and *The Grandmother* (a bizarre portrait of childhood) display a grotesque visual sense and dark wit. But it was his debut feature that first attracted cult audiences: *Eraserhead* >**1**, a low budget experimental fantasy shot in murky, moody black and white, was both an authentically nightmarish cinepoem filled with castration symbols, and a stark comic parody of family life, with a hapless innocent deserted by his wife to nurse a mewling mutant baby. Most remarkable of all was Lynch's evocation of threatening urban decay through sets (crumbling factories, mouldering rooms), sound (hissing, dripping, roaring), and mysterious characters.

In the rather more conventional *The Elephant Man* >**2**, based on the true story of celebrated Victorian 'freak' John Merrick, Lynch applied his idiosyncratic vision and style to melodrama, couching his profoundly moving tale of suffering and dignity in an authentically Dickensian portrait of London where, beneath a civilised, elegant surface, lies a seething subterranean city of grimy architecture and grotesque bullies; still more impressive, Lynch's non-sensationalist approach to his physically malformed but otherwise refined hero investigated voyeurism but never fell prey to it. A version of the cult sci-fi novel *Dune*, however, was largely incoherent (partly due to producer interference); only the extravagantly bizarre imagery suggested its maker's identity.

Blue Velvet >**3** was a triumphant return to form, merging the private symbolism of *Eraserhead* with a plot that straddled small-town romance, *film noir* and fairy tale. A shy adolescent unearths a severed ear in an overgrown meadow and – determined to find its owner – stumbles into a terrifying, sado-masochistic relationship between a psychotic hoodlum and a distressed singer whose child he holds hostage. Again, Lynch explores a violent netherworld of unspeakable

Isabella Rossellini – daughter of Roberto and Ingrid Bergman – as the *femme fatale*-cum-damsel in distress in Lynch's extraordinary *Blue Velvet.*

horror, an obscene, absurd reflection of the homely suburban society that fosters the hero's vanishing innocence; again, too, Freudian symbols (the plot is clearly Oedipal) merge with a heightened, artificial sense of everyday 'reality' in this vision of a world both stunningly beautiful and ineffably cruel. Images, sound, performance, and deliberately naive dialogue create both a non-naturalistic atmosphere and a uniquely *cinematic* work; rarely in recent years has anybody deployed the full potential of film techniques with such assurance, wit and unbridled invention.

In moving from his avant-garde origins to commercial cinema, Lynch has thankfully remained true to his distinctly personal and corrosively humorous vision of a world cracking apart at the seams. Crucially, his partly surreal, partly Expressionist style is not a matter of affectation but seems to derive from an inborn way of seeing things. Film, after all, depends partly on the creation of coherent, mesmerising and meaningful textures – both visual and aural – for effect: a condition Lynch fulfils with apparent ease.

Lineage

While Lynch's debt to both German Expressionism and Surrealism is clear, the shadow of such diverse American directors as **Griffith**, **Browning** and **Corman** may also be discerned. Of his contemporaries, the Czech animator Jan Svankmajer perhaps comes closest to Lynch's blend of fantasy, grotesque visuals, and piercing black comedy.

Viewing

1 **Eraserhead**
US 1976/ w Jack Nance, Charlotte Stewart, Jeanne Bates

2 **The Elephant Man**
GB 1980/ w John Hurt, Anthony Hopkins, Freddie Jones

3 **Blue Velvet**
US 1987/ w Kyle MacLachlan, Isabella Rossellini, Dennis Hopper

Alexander Mackendrick

Born: **1912/Boston, Massachusetts, USA**
Directing career: **1949-1967**

Like **Robert Hamer**, Alexander Mackendrick was one of the finest and the least typical directors at Ealing Studios. Perhaps best known for the four comedies he made there, he nonetheless created films of a rare blackness, marked by a pessimistic – albeit witty – vision of human cruelty, corruptibility, and self-obsession.

Born during a visit by his parents to America, Mackendrick grew up in Scotland and studied at the Glasgow School of Art. His first film work was as an animator in advertising; having spent the war working in documentary and propaganda, he was taken on at Ealing as a scriptwriter. After two years he made his directorial debut with *Whisky Galore*, seemingly a characteristically whimsical Ealing comic fantasy: Scottish islanders unite in battle against English authoritarianism to obtain an illegal shipload of whisky marooned on the shore. Mackendrick, however, avoided Ealing's usual sentimental populism by stressing the cruelty of the humiliation suffered by the pompous but honest Home Guard bureaucrat. He thus achieved a rare balance of sympathies that would recur in *The Man in the White Suit*, a caustic satire on industrial relations that catalogued the self-interested objections brought by bosses and workers alike against the naive, idealistic inventor of a fabric that repels dirt and never wears out. Indeed, Mackendrick revealed British society as apathetic, reactionary and stuffily class-conscious – qualities that attain tragically destructive dimensions in *Mandy* >**1**, a serious, sensitive and overwhelmingly moving drama about a small girl's deafness and its effects on her parents' marriage. Superficially about physical disability, the film is in fact a study of alienation and stifling patriarchy: the father's refusal to face up to his daughter's needs are a sign of his own immaturity which threatens both the girl's education and an entire family's unity.

Mackendrick's finest Ealing work was *The Ladykillers* >**2**, a macabre comedy in which four villains fall to killing each other when they find themselves unable to murder a kindly old landlady whose house is their hideout. The acting is marvellously subtle, the timing superb, but most memorable of all is the cool assessment of corrupt experience inadvertently defeated by casual innocence. This theme was repeated in Mackendrick's masterpiece and first American film, *Sweet Smell of Success* >**3**, a dazzlingly cynical exploration of opportunist ambition, betrayal and everyday evil in New York's newspaper world. Burt Lancaster and Tony Curtis gave their finest performances ever as, respectively, a power-crazed gossip columnist and a fawning publicity agent; the latter's ruthless hypocrisy extends to framing the lover of the former's sister in a drugs offence, and the film painted a relentlessly acerbic picture of greed and dog-eat-dog intrigue through vividly stylised dialogue, dark glistening camerawork and a bleak insistence on human foibles.

The director's work never again seemed so assured, though his next two films displayed a similarly acute awareness of mankind's propensity for cruelty and self-preservation. Paradoxically, both concerned children: in *Sammy Going South* a young boy, orphaned by the war in Egypt, makes a long, lonely odyssey to Durban in search of his aunt, while in *A High Wind in Jamaica*, a group of children are captured by pirates. Avoiding kids-movie clichés, Mackendrick demonstrates not only the children's ability to survive, transcend, and even ignore, danger and death, but also their capacity to inflict pain and violence, whether accidentally or for spite. It is the adults who suffer most; selfish, blinkered innocence protects the children.

After gently satirising Californian high-life in the uneven *Don't Make Waves*, Mackendrick retired from directing to teach film. While *Sweet Smell of Success* has an all-embracing cynicism lacking in the rest of his work, his career is remarkable for its consistently unsentimental investigation of the darker corners of the human psyche. His precise visual sense not only marked him as an excellent craftsman but was the perfect stylistic correlative to his coolly analytical, morally corrosive vision of the world.

Lineage

If Mackendrick provokes mention of **Hamer**, it might also be useful to compare him – distantly – with figures like **Hawks**, **Sturges** and **Wilder**. If anybody may be said to be following in his footsteps it is **Forsyth**, although his films are both gentler and warmer.

Further reading

Charles Barr's *Ealing Studios* (London, 1979).

Viewing

1 **Mandy**
GB 1952/ w Mandy Miller, Jack Hawkins, Phyllis Calvert

2 **The Ladykillers**
GB 1955/ w Alec Guinness, Katie Johnson, Cecil Parker

3 **Sweet Smell of Success**
US 1957/ w Burt Lancaster, Tony Curtis, Susan Harrison

Dušan Makavejev

Born: 13th October 1932/Belgrade, Yugoslavia
Directing career: 1953-

In the '60s, Dušan Makavejev, one of Europe's most original and provocative film-makers, seemed set for a distinguished career. Failing to fulfil his initial promise, however, his quirky sense of humour and interest in the relationship between sexuality and politics have been undermined by an increasing self-indulgence.

After studying psychology and film, Makavejev spent over a decade making shorts and documentaries, often experimental in form. In 1966 his feature debut, *Man Is Not a Bird*, announced an audacious new talent to the world. Its loose, elliptical plot (a factory worker falls for a girl who finally betrays him with a lorry driver) was full of ambiguities, contrasting the man's old-fashioned concept of love with the girl's more liberated views, within a clearly defined social milieu that lent the fiction an air of documentary. Even more novel and effective was *Switchboard Operator* >**1**, which again used the tale of a doomed relationship (between the girl of the title and a rat-killer) to construct a multi-faceted picture of contemporary Yugoslavia. Fragmenting the narrative into brief non-chronological episodes, intercut with all kinds of witty, seemingly irrelevant but in fact highly pertinent digressions (lectures on sex, sanitation and crime; archive film of demonstrations and church demolition), Makavejev constructed a free-wheeling essay on questions of oppression and freedom, the State and the individual, the past and the future. The result, at once moving, thought-provoking and funny, also displays an unusually generous tolerance for different ways of life.

Innocence Unprotected abandoned plot altogether, consisting of footage from Serbia's first (disarmingly naive) talkie, shot during the Nazi occupation by a daredevil strongman; interviews with surviving members of the film's cast and crew; and archive footage of the conflict between the Communists and Nazis. More a dazzling formal exercise in collage and montage than a full-blown portrait of various forms of innocence, its extreme methods gave rise to the complex dialectics of the now-dated *WR: Mysteries of the Organism* >**2**. Shot partly in America, partly in Yugoslavia, it rhymed various non-fictional scenes that explain and illustrate the ideas of psychologist Wilhelm Reich (who saw sexual freedom as Communism's true aim) with the tale of a Reich-spouting girl's seduction of a repressed Russian skater. Again, interviews, stock footage, fiction, slogans and so forth are intercut to diverting effect, though the use of hippies and explicit physicality tends to detract from the film's underlying seriousness of purpose.

Since taking to working abroad with *WR*, Makavejev's talent has dissipated somewhat. After the widely banned *Sweet Movie* (which contrasted a sexually and mentally traumatised Miss World with a plainly allegorical whore, who captains a boat with Marx as its masthead between killing her lovers), he was unable to make another film for over half a decade. Happily, *Montenegro* >**3**, though slight and more conventional than his early work, was a sly, imaginative and amusingly amoral comedy of manners, set in Sweden, with a wealthy but bored housewife rediscovering sexual passion at a gaudily disreputable bar used by immigrant workers. Thereafter, however, the director seems to have lost his sense of direction, with both *The Coca-Cola Kid* (about an American drinks salesman's disastrous attempts to eliminate local competition in Australia) and the political satire/sex romp, *Manifesto*, ruined by meandering plots, uneven acting and overall inconsequentiality.

For all the charm of his still off-beat sense of humour, it may be that Makavejev, stimulated by the rebellious spirit of the '60s, is now stranded by widespread sexual and political apathy. Nonetheless, as one of the more accessible and witty experimental film-makers of that decade, he deserves serious consideration.

Lineage

Similarities between Makavejev and **Godard** are superficial, faint and uninformative; as in Brecht, the Yugoslav's use of distancing strategies serve to elucidate rather than mystify. **Eisenstein** may be seen as an influence on his montage, Chris Marker and **Oshima** as distant relations in the development of the film essay form.

Further reading

Second Wave, ed. Ian Cameron (London, 1970), John Russell Taylor's *Directors and Directions* (London, 1975).

Viewing

1 **Switchboard Operator (An Affair of the Heart)**
Yugo 1967/ w Eva Ras, Ruzica Sokic, Slobodan Aligrudic
2 **WR: Mysteries of the Organism**
Yugo 1971/ w Milena Dravic, Jagoda Kaloper, Ivica Vidovic
3 **Montenegro**
Sweden 1981/ w Susan Anspach, Erland Josephson, Per Oscarsson

Terrence Malick

Born: 30th November 1943/Waco, Texas, USA
Directing career: 1973-

Despite having directed only two features (and it is questionable whether he will ever direct again), Terrence Malick remains one of the most idiosyncratic American film-makers to have worked in recent years. Possessed of a sensibility that is at once literary and intensely visual, and seemingly dismissive of the conventions of commercial Hollywood, he employs an oblique, ironic approach to narrative and character that is reminiscent of European art-movies.

A former Rhodes scholar and journalist, Malick lectured in philosophy before studying film. After scripting *Pocket Money* (a semi-comic contemporary Western directed by Stuart Rosenberg), he made his directing debut with *Badlands* >**1**, a factually-based tale of a delinquent couple who go on a senseless killing spree in the Midwest during the '50s. Crisply shot by Tak Fujimoto and using a music score that ranges from Carl Orff to Nat King Cole, the film differs from *Bonnie and Clyde* (and other similar films) in the tone it adopts towards the young killers, whose dreams of fame and love are fuelled by the films of James Dean and the mindless magazines of the era. Dialogue reveals little in the way of motivation, but Malick includes a narration – taken from the girl's diary – which testifies to the couple's warped, misguided romanticism, written as it is in the vacuous hyperbolic style of '50s fan journals and comics. Image, plot, conversation and commentary are set in sharp and ironic counterpoint to show the impenetrable mystery of human actions and thought: murder remains unexplained by mere facts.

Malick revived and expanded on these methods in the visually stunning *Days of Heaven* >**2**, the tale of a love triangle that ends in tragedy during World War I. Again, the director filters perceptions of character and events through the naive, inarticulate but oddly poetic narration of a small girl, in the form of a commentary – on the actions of her elder sister, torn between her lover and the wealthy farm-owner he has persuaded her to marry for money – that only serves to mystify matters. Motivation is further obscured by the acting, with the performers' faces inscrutably mask-like; indeed, the elements – caught in all their primeval power by Nestor Almendros' camera, most notably during a locust storm – are equally important to the unfolding of the drama, their purity and magnificence standing in stark contrast to the petty intrigues and social injustices that define human ambition. Rarely has an American film been so coolly abstract, so lavishly beautiful in its attention to the shifts in meaning created by the collision of sound and image. The film's plot bears some similarity to that of **Murnau**'s *City Girl*; certainly Malick's poetic images recall the simplicity and power of silent classics like *Sunrise*.

Reputedly disappointed by the film's box-office performance, Malick withdrew to Paris where he regularly receives scripts for potential projects, none of which have yet come to fruition. It is to be hoped that he may be coaxed out of retirement, since, however cold, detached or precious his detractors may find his work, he is a film-maker of rare intelligence and originality.

Lineage

If Malick's small output makes it impossible to suggest general influences, visually *Badlands* may recall **Nicholas Ray** and **Penn**, *Days of Heaven* the silent cinema. His idiosyncratic narrative style provokes comparison with figures as diverse as **Welles**, **Lewin**, **Mankiewicz**, **Kubrick**, **Bresson**, **Godard** and **Rohmer**.

Viewing

1 **Badlands**
US 1973/ w Martin Sheen, Sissy Spacek, Warren Oates

2 **Days of Heaven**
US 1979/ w Richard Gere, Brooke Adams, Linda Manz, Sam Shepard

Louis Malle

Born: **30th October 1932/Thumeries, France**
Directing career: **1956-**

The diversity and stylistic restraint of the films of Louis Malle have led some critics to dismiss him as an opportunistic director with little to say. Yet versatility may be a virtue, discretion a strength, and Malle's unsentimental sympathies for his characters and his feel for the apparently banal but quietly meaningful details of everyday life have established him as an imaginative, if erratic, talent.

After film studies Malle worked as assistant to **Bresson** and the marine documentarist Jacques-Yves Cousteau, with whom he co-directed *The Silent World*. His solo debut, *Lift to the Scaffold*, was an impressively shot and structured thriller whose precision plotting and pacing failed to conceal a cold heart. *The Lovers*, in which Jeanne Moreau abandons the boring life of a bourgeois wife for a young lover, was notable for its lyrical yet controversial depiction of sexual passion, while the frenetic farce, *Zazie dans le Métro*, about a foul-mouthed teenage girl let loose in Paris, was less witty than abrasive. Unlike his New Wave contemporaries, Malle seemed bent on unpredictability: *Vie Privée* (*A Very Private Affair*) featured Bardot in a movie-star character study inspired, loosely, by her own life; *Le Feu Follet* (*A Time to Live, a Time to Die*) >**1**, was a sombre, subtle and movingly authentic portrait of an alcoholic on the verge of suicide; *Viva Maria* was a gaudy Western comedy pairing Moreau and Bardot; *Le Voleur* (*The Thief of Paris*) clothed its study of kleptomania as revenge on society in an immaculate evocation of late 19th-century Paris. Uniting such diverse material were Malle's old-fashioned emphasis on sumptuous camerawork (by Henri Decaë), a sensual rather than sensationalist eroticism and a tendency to focus on lonely, isolated individuals.

In 1967 he visited India where he shot the highly subjective and engrossing documentaries *Calcutta* and *Phantom India*, in which questions asked about the director's relationship to what he sees gave evidence of a new seriousness of purpose that would attach to and deepen much of Malle's future work. *Le Souffle au Coeur* (*Dearest Love*), a light-hearted and semi-autobiographical look at a boy's adolescence in the '50s, mixes comedy with a discreet insistence on its protagonist's confusion, that culminates in incest with his mother; while *Lacombe, Lucien* >**2** calmly explored the psychic and emotional alienation that pushes a peasant boy into collaboration with the Nazis, without once falling into the trap of simplistic moralising. Even *Black Moon*, a bizarre, sometimes obscure fantasy inspired by Lewis Carroll, was notable for its lack of whimsy as it conjured up, without dialogue, a bleak post-apocalyptic world.

In the mid-'70s Malle embarked upon a decade-long visit to America where, after *Pretty Baby* (a glossy, sensitive but finally tedious look at child prostitution in 1917 New Orleans), he made *Atlantic City* >**3**, in which an ageing small-time mobster sees his romanticised memories of villainy become reality when he acts as father confessor, protector and, finally, lover to a lonely young croupier. Part romantic comedy, part thriller, part fairy-tale, the film is simultaneously mythic and rooted in reality, and charms through its wry ackowledgement of human delusions and its tender portrait of passion and dignity regained. Fantasy was also crucial to the surprisingly captivating conversation-piece, *My Dinner with André*, and to the lacklustre *Crackers* (a remake of the classic Italian caper-comedy *Big Deal on Madonna Street*). But *Alamo Bay* >**4** an intelligent and gripping thriller concerning racist violence perpetrated by Texan fishermen against Vietnamese immigrants, was distinguished by its low-key, essentially realist approach to the rhythm and nuances of working-class life. At the same time, Malle returned to his documentary beginnings with *God's Country* (about the dreams and disappointments of the inhabitants of a small town in Minnesota, consisting of interviews conducted six years apart) and *And the Pursuit of Happiness* (about immigrant life in modern America). In both, Malle's deeply humane, but never sentimental, respect for his subjects makes for provocative, gripping cinema.

In 1987 the director returned to France to plunder his own personal memories in *Au Revoir Les Enfants* >**5**, in which the friendship of two Jesuit schoolboys in 1944 comes to a tragic end when betrayal results in the capture and killing of one – a Jew – by the Gestapo. As ever, performances and evocation of time and place are superb; most remarkable, however, is the way maudlin melodrama is avoided by stressing the boys' selfishness and arrogant immaturity. The final result is honest, compassionate, and quietly affecting.

Fascinated by the effects of loneliness (thus the frequent return to adolescents and outsiders), Malle has ignored fashionable trends to create a personal, varied – and variable – body of work that reveals, but rarely passes judgement on, the complex emotions that lead humans towards self-delusion, treachery, taboo-breaking or criminal behaviour. Never as innovative as the finest New Wave directors, wary of imposing himself on a subject, he nevertheless deserves acclaim for his unassuming integrity and humanity.

Lineage

Malle's versatility and sensitivity suggest comparisons less with **Godard**, **Truffaut**, **Rohmer**, **Chabrol** and Jacques Rivette than with earlier figures like **Becker**, even occasionally **Renoir**, with whom he shares a rare tolerance for human foibles. In his rather old-fashioned concern for craftsmanship and characterisation, he may be compared – albeit superficially – with **Tavernier**.

Further reading

Roy Armes' *French Cinema Since 1946, Vol II* (London 1970).

Viewing

1 **Le Feu Follet (A Time to Live, a Time to Die)**
France 1963/ w Maurice Ronet, Léna Skerla, Jeanne Moreau

2 **Lacombe, Lucien**
France 1973/ w Pierre Blaise, Aurore Clément, Gilberte Rivet

3 **Atlantic City**
US 1980/ w Burt Lancaster, Susan Sarandon, Kate Reid

4 **Alamo Bay**
US 1984/ w Amy Madigan, Ed Harris, Ho Nguyen

5 **Au Revoir Les Enfants**
France 1987/ w Gaspard Manesse, Raphael Fejto, Francine Racette

Rouben Mamoulian

Born: 8th October 1898/Tiflis, Georgia, Russia.
Died: 4th December 1987/Woodland Hills, California, USA
Directing career: 1929-1957

Often grudgingly admired as an innovator whose career went into a steep decline after the early '30s, Rouben Mamoulian was one of Hollywood's most consistently imaginative and rewarding directors for over two decades. If his work lacks thematic unity, its sheer elegance and wit, and his intelligent use of film's full potential make his versatility both startling and stylistically unique.

Mamoulian arrived in America (by way of London) in the '20s, having worked in the Moscow Art Theatre where he was a disciple of the late Stanislavsky. By the time he became a successful opera and theatre director in New York, however, he had already forsaken naturalism for a more experimentally poetic stylisation, based on the ideal of achieving dramatic expression by carefully blending action, dance, music, dialogue, decor, colour and performance. In 1929 he directed his first film for Paramount: *Applause*, the tale of an ageing burlesque dancer's self-sacrificing love for her daughter, became one of the finest early talkies, with Mamoulian using complex camera movements, sound effects and Expressionist composition to lend pace and force to a potentially mawkish plot. Even better was *City Streets* >**1**, a gangster-cum-love story noted for a novel use of subjective sound to suggest inner torment, and for a remarkably elliptical narrative that suggested rather than showed killings and the plans made to carry them out. But it was in *Dr Jekyll and Mr Hyde* >**2** that Mamoulian first employed sound, camerawork and editing to create a masterpiece of social and psychological insight. Hyde's monstrosity is clearly sexual, the result of Jekyll's already existing frustration and contempt for the repressive mores of Victorian England, while the first reel's use of subjective camera and the explicit contrast between London's staid aristocracy and its more voluptuous lower-classes serve to reveal individual and universal schizophrenia.

Very different but equally effective, *Love Me Tonight* >**3** was a superbly witty musical comedy. It outshone **Lubitsch**'s work in the same field through a relentlessly inventive blend of rhyming dialogue, sound montage, special camera effects, bright innuendo and the unlikely but charming ploy of having all the actors (even stately toff C. Aubrey Smith) sing in their own voices. Thereafter, Mamoulian made several intelligent costume dramas that revealed his talent for directing actresses: Dietrich in *Song of Songs*, Garbo at her best in *Queen Christina*, Anna Sten in *We Live Again* (well adapted from Tolstoy's *Resurrection*) and, most delightful of all, Miriam Hopkins in *Becky Sharp* >**4**, the first ever feature made in full, three-strip Technicolor. A fluid, funny and elegant version of Thackeray's *Vanity Fair*, it saw Mamoulian use his palette for dramatic rather than decorative purposes, delineating character through costume, and signifying news of the Battle of Waterloo in a ballroom scene in which bright dance gowns are suddenly swamped by soldiers' blood-red cloaks. By now, however, he was once again working regularly in the theatre – often directing musicals – and his films became less frequent and more uneven. *The Gay Desperado* and *High, Wide and Handsome* were musical fantasies, the one lively but shallow, the other an ambitious epic set in the Pennsylvania oilfields in 1859; *Golden Boy* was a well-cast version of Clifford Odets' play about a penniless youth torn between the boxing ring and the violin, and *Rings on Her Fingers* an unusually anonymous, patchily amusing con-artist comedy.

The Mask of Zorro and *Blood and Sand* >**5**, however, confirmed Mamoulian's abiding concern with drama conveyed through movement

'The son of a gun is nothing but a tailor': Maurice Chevalier sizes up Jeanette MacDonald in Mamoulian's delightful musical, *Love Me Tonight.*

of characters and camera. The former was a rousing, deliciously ironic swashbuckler; the latter an adaptation of Ibañez's story about a simple country boy whose success as a matador leads him into temptation and towards a violent, early death; colour, and Mamoulian's almost choreographic direction, turned the whole into exquisite, subtle melodrama. Finally, though made ten years apart, two fine musicals exhibited his still consummate artistry: *Summer Holiday*, adapted from O'Neill's *Ah! Wilderness*, combined smalltown nostalgia with an acute rites-of-passage story, while *Silk Stockings* >**6**, a remake of Lubitsch's *Ninotchka* with a witty Cole Porter score, alternated some of the most engaging, intimate dance sequences ever filmed with a brash satire on the philistine mentality of contemporary Hollywood. Alas, Mamoulian was to direct no more films. In 1944 he had already resigned from what was to become **Preminger**'s *Laura*; in 1949 he was replaced on *Porgy and Bess* by the same director and, over a decade later, he resigned from directing *Cleopatra*, which was taken over by **Mankiewicz**.

It may seem suprising that a director whose background (and continuing livelihood) was the theatre should tell filmic stories so adeptly, never depending on realistic dialogue for effect. But Mamoulian's sense of composition, movement, music and colour signify a major stylist, just as irony – never cynical – ensures a comic touch more delicate than that of Lubitsch. Taste, technique, and an intelligent interest in form are the hallmarks of his art.

Lineage

While it is common to compare Mamoulian's early work with that of **Lubitsch**, **Clair**, **Cukor**, **Whale**, **Ophüls**, **Powell** (whose *Gone to Earth* Mamoulian reworked for American release) and **Minnelli** seem equally relevant. Charles Lederer's *Never Steal Anything Small*, a 1958 musical, was taken from *The Devil's Hornpipe*, a play written by Mamoulian with Maxwell Anderson.

Further reading

Tom Milne's *Mamoulian* (London, 1969).

Viewing

1 **City Streets**
US 1931/ w Gary Cooper, Sylvia Sidney, Paul Lukas

2 **Dr Jekyll and Mr Hyde**
US 1931/ w Fredric March, Miriam Hopkins, Rose Hobart

3 **Love Me Tonight**
US 1932/ w Jeanette MacDonald, Maurice Chevalier, Charles Ruggles

4 **Becky Sharp**
US 1935/ w Miriam Hopkins, Sir Cedric Hardwicke, Nigel Bruce
5 **Blood and Sand**
US 1941/ w Tyrone Power, Linda Darnell, Rita Hayworth
6 **Silk Stockings**
US 1957/ w Fred Astaire, Cyd Charisse, Janis Paige, Peter Lorre

Joseph L. Mankiewicz

Born: 11th February 1909/Wilkes-Barre, Pennsylvania, USA
Directing career: 1946-1972

The incessant talkiness that clutters many of the films of Joseph Leo Mankiewicz has led to accusations that his work is theatrical rather than cinematic. At his peak, however, he managed to couch his distinctly literary narratives and dialogue in appropriately elegant visuals, producing unusually civilised entertainment.

The younger brother of Herman J. Mankiewicz (best known for his scripting of *Citizen Kane*), Joe Mankiewicz came to film after working in journalism in Berlin. Initially a writer at Paramount and MGM, in 1935 he turned to production; **Lang**'s *Fury*, **Borzage**'s *Three Comrades* and *Strange Cargo*, **Cukor**'s *The Philadelphia Story* were the finest of the films he oversaw. Finally, in 1946, he was allowed to direct: his debut, *Dragonwyck*, was an intelligent and exquisitely mounted Gothic melodrama, *The Ghost and Mrs Muir* >**1** (the best of his admittedly humble early films) a very poignant, atmospheric supernatural romance, in which a widow's life is oddly transformed by the ghost of a sea-captain who may in fact be her conscience. In 1948, *A Letter to Three Wives* >**2** introduced the mature Mankiewicz style with the eponymous epistle, sent somewhat maliciously by an unseen female narrator, serving to point up, in deliciously ironic tones, the smug complacency of married life in contemporary country-club America. *House of Strangers*, a *noir*ish, impressively brooding drama about a banking family dominated by a scheming patriarch, was unusual in highlighting visual qualities, but *All About Eve* >**3** was triumphantly literary in tone. Its dense multiple narration and mordant wit were a perfect stylistic framework for its cynical story of overweening ambition and bitchy pretence in the world of theatre; revelling in artifice, relentless in its parade of pithy epigrams, the film not only concerns, but displays to the full, the joys of performance. Similarly verbose and almost as impressive were the romantic comedy *People Will Talk*, the subtle spy thriller *Five Fingers*, a sensitive and imaginatively cast *Julius Caesar* (with Brando as Mark Antony), and *The Barefoot Contessa* >**4**. This last, a lavish melodrama about a gypsy-turned-film star's troubled love-life, was distinguished by the writer-director's articulate wit and his fascination with role-playing, flashbacks, and structure.

A musical deliriously appreciative of gaudily stylised '50s design, *Guys and Dolls* >**5** revealed both Mankiewicz's versatility and his abiding love of vividly non-naturalistic language, here derived from Damon Runyon; while *The Quiet American*, adapted from Graham Greene's tale of expatriates in wartorn Saigon, abandoned the book's anti-American bias, but created a superbly dark, moody picture of treachery and cowardice through sharp performances and evocative location camerawork. Henceforth, however, Mankiewicz's films became increasingly uneven. Tennessee Williams' *Suddenly Last Summer* was excessively, tediously wordy; *Cleopatra* a turgid epic wrecked by production problems; *The Honey Pot* an intriguing, only spasmodically comic thriller based on Ben Jonson's *Volpone*. Indeed, for his last two films, the director worked not from his own scripts but from **Robert Benton** and David Newman (the Western *There Was a Crooked Man*) and Anthony Shaffer (the theatrical two-hander *Sleuth*, which once again allowed Mankiewicz to indulge his interest in the complexities of role-playing and performance).

While Mankiewicz's erratic later work may support the thesis that he was a minor cinematic talent, more concerned with verbal than visual style, articulacy and irony have always been notable for their rarity in mainstream Hollywood. Thus, however removed from everyday reality, his finest films deserve acclaim for their formal precision, smart sardonic humour and adult sophistication.

Lineage

Mankiewicz's eloquent, elevated comic sense bears comparison with figures as diverse as **Cukor**, **Mamoulian**, and **Lewin**; among modern directors, **Benton**, **Levinson**, even **Rohmer**, **Greenaway** and **Woody Allen** may be seen as sharing his love of the spoken word.

Further reading

Gary Carey's *More About All About Eve* (New York, 1972) is an interview; Kenneth Greist's *Pictures Will Talk* (New York, 1978) a biography.

Viewing

1 **The Ghost and Mrs Muir**
US 1947/ w Gene Tierney, Rex Harrison, George Sanders

2 **A Letter to Three Wives**
US 1948/ w Jeanne Crain, Linda Darnell, Ann Sothern, Kirk Douglas

3 **All About Eve**
US 1950/ w Bette Davis, Anne Baxter, George Sanders, Gary Merrill

4 **The Barefoot Contessa**
US 1954/ w Humphrey Bogart, Ava Gardner, Edmond O'Brien

5 **Guys and Dolls**
US 1955/ w Marlon Brando, Frank Sinatra, Jean Simmons

Anthony Mann

Born: 30th June 1906/San Diego, California, USA
Died: 29th April 1967/Berlin, Germany
Directing career: 1942-1967

Though he worked in a variety of genres, the reputation of the director born Emil Anton Bundsmann rests firmly on a series of classic Westerns made in the '50s, many starring James Stewart. Their use of landscape, emotional and psychological intensity, and structural complexity signal his contribution to the genre as crucial to its development.

Having worked in various capacities in the New York theatre, Mann first entered the movies as talent scout for producer David O. Selznick and assistant to **Sturges**. In 1942, with *Dr Broadway*, he began directing a series of lowly musicals and melodramas; it was only in the late '40s with *films noirs* like *Desperate*, *T-Men*, *Raw Deal* and *Border Incident* that his eye for dramatic visuals, and his expertise in scenes of brutal violence came to the fore. In 1950, the Westerns *Devil's Doorway* >**1**, *The Furies* and *Winchester '73* presaged his finest work of the coming decade: the first, with an Indian Civil War hero divided between his tribe and the white men who refuse him his own ancestral farmlands, introduces the theme of a hero torn and haunted by the past; the second displays Mann's classical interest in the evils of patriarchy; the third, with Stewart bent on recovering a rifle stolen by his patricidal brother, embraces the destructive power of revenge.

After *The Tall Target*, an impressively *noir*-inflected period thriller about an attempt to murder Abe Lincoln on the eve of his inauguration, Mann alternated several efficient but routine films (*Thunder Bay*, *The Glenn Miller Story*, *Strategic Air Command*, *Men in War*, and *God's Little Acre*) with the Westerns that reveal him at his most engaged and imaginative. *Bend of the River* >**2** rhymes and conflates the tale of pioneers seeking a home in a mountain wilderness with ex-outlaw Stewart's desperate efforts to escape his past – embodied by his troubled friendship with vicious opportunist and alter ego Arthur Kennedy; *The Naked Spur* >**3** deals with the corrosive effects of a lust for revenge, with Stewart's bounty hunter portrayed as no less violent and neurotic than his murderous prey. In both films,

Arthur Kennedy in a moment of typically well-staged violence in Anthony Mann's *Bend of the River (Where the River Bends).*

geographical odysseys reflect the hero's spiritual struggles, with landscape – lush or bleakly hostile – serving as an elemental symbol of his emotions; only by coming to terms with, rather than repressing, his own violence may he find redemption and exorcise the lethal influence of the past.

The Far Country was a relatively lacklustre variation on the same themes, *The Tin Star* (with the obsessive, haunted persona of Stewart replaced by the less troubled Henry Fonda) a conventional 'apprenticeship' Western about a young sheriff learning his trade from an older bounty hunter. Far better were *The Man from Laramie* (Stewart infiltrating a cattle baron's family in order to avenge his brother's death) and *Man of the West* >**4** (Gary Cooper ridding himself of his criminal past in the shape of a psychotic gang of which he was once a member). Both evoked *King Lear* through an array of Freudian father-figures, jealous siblings, and brutal plots that embraced patricide, fratricide, and scenes of violence suggesting castration and humiliation. While landscape and the revenge motif tethered the drama firmly to Western conventions, the monstrous family rivalries lent these films a complexity and power largely missing from Mann's earlier work. Regrettably, a final Western, *Cimarron*, was so mutilated that the director disowned it.

In the '60s Mann made two superior epics for producer Samuel Bronston: *El Cid* >**5**, about the Spanish lord's dreams of and fight for a Moorless Spain, was memorable both for its visually elegant evocation of medieval life and for its truly epic simplicity; *The Fall of the Roman Empire* >**6** was notable for its sobriety, period authenticity and unusually intelligent analysis of corruption born of power. After *The Heroes of Telemark*, a routine war thriller, but boasting characteristically fine landscape photography, he began work on the spy film *A Dandy in Aspic*, but died before its completion.

Mann's greatest talent was his ability to transcend the often limiting conventions of genres, while never displaying a contempt for the structural strengths they provided. He did so through astute psychological details, themes judiciously plundered from the classics, and an externalisation of inner emotions. His career was highly variable, but his achievements within the B-thriller, the Western and the epic reveal a consistently probing intelligence at work.

Lineage

Mann adopted an altogether tougher approach to Western mythology than **Ford**, his obsessive, neurotic characters and his emphasis on violence presaging the work of **Peckinpah**, **Leone** and **Eastwood**. His unusually adult epics are rivalled only by those of **Nicholas Ray**.

Further reading

Jim Kitses' *Horizons West* (London, 1970), Derek Elley's *The Epic Film* (London, 1984).

Viewing

1 **Devil's Doorway**
US 1950/ w Robert Taylor, Louis Calhern, Paula Raymond

2 **Bend of the River (Where the River Bends)**
US 1952/ w James Stewart, Arthur Kennedy, Rock Hudson

3 **The Naked Spur**
US 1953/ w James Stewart, Robert Ryan, Janet Leigh, Ralph Meeker

4 **Man of the West**
US 1958/ w Gary Cooper, Lee J. Cobb, Julie London, Jack Lord

5 **El Cid**
Spain 1961/ w Charlton Heston, Sophia Loren, Raf Vallone

6 **The Fall of the Roman Empire**
Spain 1964/ w Stephen Boyd, Sophia Loren, James Mason

Michael Mann

Born: 5th February 1943/Chicago, Illinois, USA
Directing career: 1979-

Although Michael Mann's film output is small in comparison to his work for television (as writer, director and producer), so strong has been his influence on recent styles in both media that, provided his film career escapes the marketing problems that have blighted it so far, future recognition of his importance seems assured.

While studying film-making in London, Mann gained experience directing commercials and documentaries for television, then returned to America to make a name for himself writing for series like *Starsky and Hutch* and *Police Story*. After working uncredited on the script of Ulu Grosbard's *Straight Time*, he directed his first feature, *The Jericho Mile*; made for television but released in cinemas outside America, it was a taut, intelligent prison-thriller in which an inmate averts boredom and beats the system by training to become a runner of Olympic standard. Far more impressive, however, was Mann's first genuinely theatrical release, *Thief* (*Violent Streets*) >**1**: as it coolly observes an ex-con's attempts to improve his life through professional expertise as a safe-cracker, the film's terse dialogue, understated acting, and crisp, almost abstract photography of modern architecture and hi-tech machinery, emphasise the protagonist's emotionally burnt-out condition. Indeed, so anti-realist is Mann's style that the film, while it includes admirably gripping set-pieces, is less a thriller than a moody, modernist meditation on the thriller form.

Still more ambitious, *The Keep* was an attempt to combine the conventions of the German Expressionist cinema with a story that rather uneasily straddled both war- and horror-genres: unfortunately, the film (in which Nazi soldiers occupying a mysterious Gothic pile in Romania meet their destiny in the shape of a primeval monster) suffered from incoherence; but its gloomy grey-green visuals and Mann's unusual perspective on a conflict between Evil and Evil – the script is designed to depict the psychopathological allure of fascism – made for fascinating viewing. Unsurprisingly, with distributors unsure how to promote this hybrid, it flopped disastrously and Mann returned to television. He became known as the creator and executive producer of the highly successful and self-consciously stylish series *Miami Vice* and *Crime Story*.

Happily, Mann's absence from the large screen was temporary, and *Manhunter* >**2** is perhaps his best film to date. About a former FBI forensics expert brought back from retirement to use his psychological skills (he is able to enter the criminal mind and duplicate its thought patterns) in the tracking down of a manic serial murderer, it once again employs complex camera movements, startling Expressionist compositions and colour, and a brooding score to create a mood of unbearable violence. Never an end in itself, the stylistic excess reflects the cop's tormented mentality and the nightmarish world in which he operates. Indeed, Mann's direction is both powerful and surprisingly subtle: until the climax, violence is suggested rather than shown, evoked by stains left on walls and floors, so that we, like the cop, are left to imagine unspeakable horror.

Production company complications barely relevant to the film effectively limited its release; it is to be hoped that in future Mann's career will be less troubled. Certainly, his ability to create and maintain a palpably sinister atmosphere, and to tell a story in images rather than words, suggest a talent of rare promise.

Lineage

While *The Keep* vaguely recalled **Lang**'s early German films, the modernist veneer of *Thief* and *Manhunter* may be compared to the work of **Melville**, **Boorman** and early **Walter Hill**. Mann's influence on film (**Friedkin**'s *To Live and Die in LA*, for example) and, even more especially, television is not to be underestimated.

Viewing

1 **Thief (Violent Streets)**
US 1981/ w James Caan, Tuesday Weld, Willie Nelson, James Belushi

2 **Manhunter**
US 1986/ w William L. Petersen, Kim Greist, Brian Cox, Joan Allen

Paul Mazursky

Born: 25th April 1930/Brooklyn, New York, USA
Directing career: 1969-

Superficially, the films of Paul (originally Irwin) Mazurksy seem to operate firmly within the Hollywood commercial mainstream: light satires with no discernibly personal visual style, they nonetheless reveal a rare affection for their characters and a delicate awareness of the need for companionship in a world obsessed by status and independence.

After starting out as an actor (appearing in **Kubrick**'s *Fear and Desire* and Richard Brooks' *The Blackboard Jungle*), Mazursky became first a nightclub comic and then a writer of television comedy. Despairing of the way his script for the hippy satire *I Love You Alice B. Toklas* had been treated, he turned to directing his own scripts with *Bob & Carol & Ted & Alice* >**1**, a satire on Esalen-inspired attempts at sexual liberation amongst the wealthy denizens of contemporary California. Topicality, and a final scene depicting a *ménage-à-quatre* may have ensured the film's huge box-office success, but Mazursky's subtle investigation of deception, gullibility and guilt transcended fashion, refusing to condemn or condone his absurdly serious, well-meaning consciousness-raisers, and finally favouring monogamous marriage over infidelity without ever falling prey to bland moralising. Genuinely funny, and more concerned with character than plot, the film marked Mazursky as an unusually sensitive if old-fashioned observer of modern mores.

Somewhat indulgent, the ambitious, partly autobiographical *Alex in Wonderland* (about a **Fellini**-obsessed film-maker suffering from a creative block) was a total flop, and Mazursky returned to examine human relationships in *Blume in Love*, about an incurable romantic desperate to win back the wife who has left him for another man. Still more affecting was *Harry and Tonto* >**2**, in which an old man, evicted from his New York home, travels with his cat across country to visit his children and grandchildren; a poignant, ironic study of solitude, shattered dreams and the joys and pains of family life, the film's gentle power stemmed from an unsentimental observation of the minutiae of everyday behaviour, and from a deft merging of humorous and serious scenes. Again, despite the communication breakdowns on view, Mazursky's tone was affirmative, a celebration of companionship and private dignity.

In film after film the writer-director revealed his ability to view a relationship or conflict from all sides. Following *Next Stop Greenwich Village* (an account of the Boho posing that had marked his late teens), he dealt with the after-effects of divorce in *An Unmarried Woman* >**3**, which, despite a weak ending, is an honest and affecting picture of a woman's enforced loneliness leading to independence. Mazursky never sidesteps her pain, nor is she indulged: the film throughout admits to her obstinacy and brittleness. Rather more offbeat but less successful were *Willie and Phil* (a whimsical *ménage-à-trois* inspired by **Truffaut**'s *Jules et Jim*) and *Tempest*, an updating of Shakespeare's classic in which a New York architect retreats to a Greek island to face a mid-life crisis.

Mazursky's even-handed attitude embraced politics in *Moscow on the Hudson* >**4**: a Russian saxophonist, tired of food queues and bureaucracy, defects in Bloomingdale's, only to find that American life involves racial inequality, rampant consumerism and muggers. In a finale mistakenly seen by some critics as Reaganite, with a despondent and battered hero revived by fellow non-WASP Americans voicing their faith in the US constitution (rather than reality), Mazursky proclaims his own belief in the worth and unity of man. Equally misunderstood but broader in its satire, was *Down and Out in Beverly Hills*, a remake of **Renoir**'s *Boudu Saved From Drowning* in which a tramp spreads chaos among a *nouveau-riche* family that shelters him. Swiping at fairly obvious targets (obsessions with sex, money, status), it differs from the original in having the tramp yield to, rather than abandon, seductive wealth: typically Mazursky neither condones nor condemns his once subversive hero's choice, but recognises it as inevitable in contemporary America.

Moon Over Parador, however, about an actor persuaded to double for the dead dictator of a South American state, was too broadly farcical to amuse. But Mazursky's unassuming directorial style, his bemused affection for his creations and his reluctance to allow plot to dominate character, all identify him as a modern comedy director of rare warmth. Artistically conservative, he is nevertheless to be valued for both his humanity and his ability to treat serious subjects with a wit that is uplifting but rarely sentimental.

Lineage

Mazursky's gentle satires on contemporary lifestyles sound faint echoes of **Lubitsch**, **Leisen**, **Renoir**, **Rohmer**, **Forman**, **Woody Allen**, and early **Ritchie**. He himself has paid tribute to Fellini (who appeared in *Alex in Wonderland*) and **Truffaut** (*Willie and Phil*).

Further reading

James Monaco's *American Film Now* (New York, 1979), Diane Jacobs' *Hollywood Renaissance* (New York, 1977).

Viewing

1 **Bob & Carol & Ted & Alice**
US 1969/ w Robert Culp, Natalie Wood, Elliott Gould, Dyan Cannon

2 **Harry and Tonto**
US 1974/ w Art Carney, Ellen Burstyn, Larry Hagman

3 **An Unmarried Woman**
US 1978/ w Jill Clayburgh, Michael Murphy, Alan Bates

4 **Moscow on the Hudson**
US 1984/ w Robin Williams, Maria Conchita Alonso, Cleavant Derricks

Jean-Pierre Melville

Born: 20th October 1917/Paris, France
Died: 2nd August 1973/Paris, France
Directing career: 1946-1972

Although the career of Jean-Pierre Grumbach – an obsessive Americanophile who renamed himself after his favourite novelist – was dominated by his interest in the gangster-thriller (widely considered an American and highly commercial genre), he was in fact a profoundly personal and an essentially European artist. Proudly independent, he used the ritualised situations and traditional iconography of the genre to create a stylised, near-mythical world through which he addressed questions of honour, loyalty, friendship and faith.

After fighting for the Free French cause in World War II, Melville set up his own production company to make the now lost short, *24 Hours in the Life of a Clown*. His first feature, *Le Silence de la Mer*, suggested an almost Bressonian talent, with a German officer (cultured and musicianly) ostracised by the old Frenchman and his niece with whom he is billeted; perversely, the girl comes to love him. Made on a low budget and notable for its counterpointing of image and text, the film reveals a poetic bent that was given full rein in *Les Enfants Terribles* >1. This superb adaptation of **Cocteau**'s novel about the claustrophobic and quasi-incestuous relationship of a brother and sister introduced Melville's abiding interest in fidelity and betrayal. But it was only after the comparatively routine melodrama, *Quand Tu Liras Cette Lettre*, that his mature style first made itself felt, in *Bob Le Flambeur* >**2**, a light-hearted, loosely structured, partly location-shot gangster thriller in which an ageing criminal, having carefully planned a casino robbery, allows the heist to go wrong when his passion for gambling sees him break the bank. The film's gentle irony, casual approach to narrative and atmospheric evocation of Paris by night greatly influenced the New Wave directors; equally idiosyncratic and offbeat was *Deux Hommes dans Manhattan*, in which fiction (two journalists search for a missing diplomat) and non-fiction merge to produce a Frenchman's freewheeling love letter to New York.

Although Melville's early work had already manifested his concern for the ethics of professionalism, it was only after *Léon Morin, Priest* (in which a young priest plays upon the love a girl feels for him in the hope of converting her) that he achieved the heightened stylisation that marked his most rigorous examinations of dignity, honour, courage and loyalty. *Le Doulos*, in which an informer is torn between his feelings for a cop and a crook, and *L'Ainé des Ferchaux*, about an ageing absconding banker and his strong-arm man who take refuge in America, both brought the theme of friendship to the fore; *Le Deuxième Souffle* (*Second Breath*) >**3** brought it centre-screen. About an escaped convict who plans one last job before leaving the country and becomes trapped in a dark, treacherous underworld of shifting loyalties, corrupt cops, and deadly rivals, the film adopts a measured pace, laconic dialogue and an array of emblematic gestures and images: trench coats, guns, limousines and bars serve to construct a seemingly timeless, abstract universe in which faith in oneself and one's peers is the sole defence against betrayal, violence, failure and death. Ritual actions (observed in minute, telling detail) become symbolic of spiritual worth, death the only possible escape after a momentary lapse from grace. In *Le Samourai* >**4**, where Melville's taste for visual austerity led him to a subtly stylised muting of colours, the self-enforced solitude that guarantees a hired gun's invulnerability is threatened when he falls for the woman who can provide his alibi in a murder case; thus doomed, he faces the cops with an empty gun. Similarly, *Army in the Shadows* >**5** portrays the struggles of the French Resistance in images and situations that recall the director's crime films, with courage, professionalism and profound camaraderie constituting the Underground's only weapons in the fight against the occupying Nazis and their collaborators.

If Melville's style and themes remained the same in his last films – *The Red Circle* and *Un Flic* (*Dirty Money*) >**6** – the tender romanticism of his best work gave way to bleak, abstract accounts of solitude, treachery and futile action; in the latter film, loyalty and friendship are conspicuous by their absence, the opening shots of a desolate rain-soaked sea-front evoking a bank robbery's doomed outcome. Melville's work had always been notable for its pared-down style and its focus on how men prepare to meet death; but at its most optimistic, the self-knowledge and companionship, the purity and dignity which counterpoint the

The moody, mythic gangster iconography of Melville, in *Le Deuxième Souffle (Second Breath)*.

world's capacity for betrayal lent his films a gentle emotional power, remarkable for the very fact that it arose from a genre noted for its celebration of violence.

Lineage

It is possible to compare Melville's austere visuals and laconic dialogue with **Bresson**, although he himself (a devotee of pre-war Hollywood) expressed his greatest admiration for **Becker** (*Le Trou*) and **Huston** (*The Asphalt Jungle*). His influence on New Wave film-makers was acknowledged by **Godard**, who cast him in a cameo role in *Breathless*, while **Leone**, **Hill** and **Michael Mann** may be seen as having adopted Melville's rigorously stylised approach to genre.

Further reading

Roy Armes' *The French Cinema Since 1946, Vol. II* (London, 1970), Colin McArthur's *Underworld USA* (London, 1972). Rui Noguiera's *Melville* (London, 1971) is a lengthy interview.

Viewing

1 **Les Enfants Terribles**
France 1949/ w Nicole Stéphane, Edouard Dhermitte, Renée Cosima

2 **Bob le Flambeur**
France 1955/ w Roger Duchesne, Isabelle Corey, Daniel Cauchy

3 **Le Deuxième Souffle (Second Breath)**
France 1966/ w Lino Ventura, Paul Meurisse, Michael Constantin

4 **Le Samourai**
France 1967/ w Alain Delon, Nathalie Delon, François Périer

5 **L'Armée des Ombres (Army in the Shadows)**
France 1969/ w Lino Ventura, Simone Signoret, Paul Meurisse

6 **Un Flic (Dirty Money)**
France 1972/ w Alain Delon, Richard Crenna, Cathérine Deneuve

John Milius

Born: 1944/St Louis, Missouri, USA
Directing career: 1973-

The films of self-styled 'Zen anarchist' John Milius are amongst the most brazenly personal to emerge from Hollywood in the last two decades, drawing, as they do, on the director's own obsessions (violence, weaponry, surfing, American legend) and heroes. While potentially fruitful, this approach has led, in recent years, to self-indulgent nonsense and a simplistic endorsement of gung-ho patriotism.

After film studies at the University of Southern California, where he befriended **George Lucas**, Milius was denied entry to the US Marines on grounds of health and turned to scriptwriting. His work included *Apocalypse Now* (made years after it was written), *Dirty Harry*, Sydney Pollack's *Jeremiah Johnson*, **Huston**'s *The Life and Times of Judge Roy Bean*, and the first *Dirty Harry* follow-up, *Magnum Force*. In 1973 he made his directing debut with *Dillinger*, a simultaneously tongue-in-cheek and mythical gangster thriller that played fast and loose with historical facts to present the notorious bank-robber and his nemesis, federal agent Purvis, as deadly enemies who both view their mission in life as the ticket to a place in the hall of fame. Even more appealing was *The Wind and the Lion* >**1**, a witty, dashing and often nostalgic desert epic in which Milius' hero, Teddy Roosevelt, sends the US militia to rescue an American woman and her two children kidnapped by a courageous, respectful and thoroughly civilised Arab chieftain. Milius' use of the Panavision screen ensured excellent action sequences, but what distinguished the film was its blend of epic heroism with a wry, gently self-mocking humour. Similarly romantic and elegaic but rather more sentimental, was *Big Wednesday* >**2**, a tribute to the surfing heroes of the director's youth that spanned the years from the naivety of the early '60s to the post-Vietnam confusion and bitterness of the mid-'70s. Conservative, macho, overblown in its use of the Californian waves as a symbol for the vicissitudes of growing up, the film – shot and performed with great expertise – manages nonetheless to be funny, intensely moving and an oddly plausible meditation on the courage needed to face everyday life.

Apparently in awe of his own reputation as Hollywood's most reactionary young director, Milius then fell prey to archaic and relatively witless will-to-power fantasy in the visually splendid but dimly dramatised comic-strip adaptation, *Conan the Barbarian*, with Arnold Schwarzenegger cast as the legendary hero. Far worse, however, was *Red Dawn*, a risible Reaganite war thriller in which a massive airborne Russian invasion of the American Midwest finds itself up against a determined, strangely adept group of teenage guerillas. (The youngsters' strength stems partly from drinking the blood of slain beasts in the woods that constitute their last refuge from the stereotypically sadistic Commie enemy.) Milius' earlier sense of irony was here conspicuous by its absence, and sentimentality was allowed to overshadow the few efficiently shot action scenes.

His next film, *Farewell to The King*, about a US marine who becomes chief of a tropical island's head-hunting tribe towards the end of World War II, raised, and at least partly satisfied, hopes that the writer-director might have exorcised his political demons sufficiently to return to an idiosyncratic blend of romanticised mythical action, ironic wit and elegaic pathos. Few modern directors celebrate the ethos of individualism with such eloquent fervour; few, too, seem so consumed by adolescent fantasies of heroic masculinity.

Lineage

Milius, friend and colleague of **Lucas**, **Coppola** and **Spielberg** (to whose *Jaws* he contributed the superb 'Wreck of the Indianapolis' monologue), has cited as influential both **Ford** and **Kurosawa**.

Further reading

Lynda Myles and Michael Pye's *The Movie Brats* (New York, 1979).

Viewing

1 **The Wind and the Lion**
US 1975/ w Sean Connery, Candice Bergen, Brian Keith, John Huston

2 **Big Wednesday**
US 1978/ w Jan-Michael Vincent, William Katt, Gary Busey

Vincente Minnelli

Born: 28th February 1913/Chicago, Illinois, USA
Died: 21st July 1986/Los Angeles, California, USA
Directing career: 1942-1976

Best known for his MGM musicals (which in fact constituted less than a third of his output), Vincente Minnelli also worked with variable success in comedy and melodrama. A flamboyant stylist, whose interest in dreams and the imaginary led to many startling fantasy sequences, at his worst he was merely a decorative, even kitschy illustrator; but at his best, form and content combined to produce cinema of great dramatic power and originality.

A child actor who grew up to become a highly successful set and costume designer and director on the Broadway stage, Minnelli was invited to Hollywood in 1940 by Arthur Freed, innovative head of MGM's musicals unit. In 1943, having shot isolated scenes for several musicals, he directed his feature debut, *Cabin in the Sky*, a witty all-negro musical fantasy largely set in Heaven. *Meet Me in St Louis* >**1** evidenced his growing assurance, integrating songs into the nostalgic plot (about a family's joys and sorrows at the turn of the century) with dramatic ease and revealing an ability to evoke mood through colour, costume and sets that would serve him well in his later, often increasingly ambitious musicals: the extravagantly dreamlike *Yolanda and the Thief*, the hilarious and gaudy *The Pirate*, *An American in Paris* >**3** (memorable for a final ballet inspired by Impressionist paintings), and *The Band Wagon*, a one-off return to the backstage-musical format parodying, with Jack Buchanan's director figure bent on staging a song-and-dance version of Goethe's *Faust*, Minnelli's own tendencies towards high-flown artiness.

Between musicals, Minnelli regularly turned to melodrama and comedy with variable success. *The Clock* was a poignant if stilted romantic comedy starring, like a number of his films, Minnelli's then wife Judy Garland; *Undercurrent* a middling thriller; *Madame Bovary* a lavish literary adaptation; and *Father of the Bride* >**2** a superbly performed comedy, its dark core (a father's anxieties over losing his daughter to another man) momentarily exposed in a beautifully imaginative nightmare sequence. But it was melodrama that proved Minnelli's strongest asset in the '50s as his musicals steadily became more whimsically fantastic (*Brigadoon*) or redundantly ornamental (*Kismet*, *Gigi*). The sardonically comic *The Bad and the Beautiful* >**4** used a *Citizen Kane*-style flashback structure to analyse the combination of talent and exploitative ambition required to ensure a Hollywood producer's success; *The Cobweb* deployed a daring dramatic conceit (an on-going argument about a mental hospital's curtains) to expose the staff's rather than the patients' neuroses; *Lust for Life* >**5** was an emotionally powerful biopic of Van Gogh, partly shot on European locations, unusually respectful of the painter's work, and acutely aware of the dark psychological undercurrents that made his art possible.

Indeed, Minnelli seemed more comfortable in the hysterical register than with quieter material, such as *Tea and Sympathy*, which he often appeared to treat with dull indifference. Expressionist colours, fluid camera movements, and emotional excess verging on the absurd made his finest melodramas as compulsive and affecting as his early musicals: in *Some Came Running* >**6**, caustic satire on the blinkered hypocrisy of smalltown America merges with scenes that alternate between lyrical introspection and dreamlike delirium, reflecting the schizophrenic sensibility of a writer-turned-drunken gambler; *Home from the Hill* is a powerhouse exposé of the malignant influence of patriarchal tyranny; *Two Weeks in Another Town* >**7** a virtual follow-up to *The Bad and the Beautiful*, with a has-been actor and a megalomaniac movie-director waging a bitter, private war against the gloriously orgiastic backdrop of the jet-set decadents whose lives centre around Rome's Cinecittà studios.

After the charming domestic comedy, *The Courtship of Eddie's Father*, Minnelli finally left MGM and faltered. *Goodbye Charlie* was dim farce, *The Sandpiper* portentous soap, *On a Clear Day You Can See Forever* an uneven, belated return to the musical, and *A Matter of Time* an indulgent and maudlin vehicle for Minnelli's daughter Liza. These films were a sad postscript to the remarkable if erratic career of a man who, at his peak, had shown that escapism need be neither mindless nor cautious, and that a profound love of colour, motion and music might produce intelligent entertainment.

Lineage

Influenced by Freed, Minnelli's style can also perhaps be traced to **Mamoulian**. His melodramas may be compared to those of **Sirk**; his musicals probably influenced **Donen**, Gene Kelly and **Demy**, not to mention lesser figures like Charles Vidor, Charles Walters and Walter Lang. **Godard** paid homage to *Some Came Running* in *Le Mépris*, while the casting of Liza Minnelli in Scorsese's *New York, New York* may also be taken as a respectful tribute.

Further reading

Minnelli's autobiography *I Remember It Well* (New York, 1974).

Viewing

1 **Meet Me in St Louis**
US 1944/ w Judy Garland, Margaret O'Brien, Mary Astor, Leon Ames

2 **Father of the Bride**
US 1950/ w Spencer Tracy, Joan Bennett, Elizabeth Taylor

3 **An American in Paris**
US 1951/ w Gene Kelly, Leslie Caron, Oscar Levant, Nina Foch

4 **The Bad and the Beautiful**
US 1952/ w Kirk Douglas, Lana Turner, Dick Powell, Gloria Grahame

5 **Lust for Life**
US 1956/ w Kirk Douglas, Anthony Quinn, James Donald

6 **Some Came Running**
US 1958/ w Frank Sinatra, Shirley MacLaine, Dean Martin

7 **Two Weeks in Another Town**
US 1962/ w Kirk Douglas, Edward G. Robinson, Cyd Charisse

Kenji Mizoguchi

Born: 16th May 1898/Tokyo, Japan
Died: 24th August 1956/Kyoto, Japan
Directing career: 1923-1956

Although only a fraction of the total output of Kenji Mizoguchi remains extant (with almost two thirds of his 80 to 90 films – including nearly all of the 55 made before 1936 – now missing), it is clear from the dozen or so films seen commercially in the West that he was a major director, remarkable not only for his sympathetic, even radical appraisal of the position of women in Japan, but for his uniquely graceful visual style.

Mizoguchi came to films after studying Western painting and illustrating newspaper advertisements. After a year as assistant to Osamu Wakayama, he embarked upon his prolific directing career with *The Resurrection of Love*. For the most part his early films were melodramas, thrillers, and adaptations of literary and stage successes, and it was not until 1936 that he achieved a genuinely mature style in *Osaka Elegy* and *Sisters of the Gion*, the first a moving account of a woman forced into prostitution to support her family (a symbol and victim of 20th-century Japanese capitalism). Also relevant to the plight of Japanese women were *The Story of the Late Chrysanthemums* >**1** (in which a woman from a lower class than her weak, Kabuki-actor lover, sacrifices their relationship to ensure the success of his future career); *Five Women Around Utamaro* (with the

The exquisite artistry of Mizoguchi, as evidenced in a scene from *Five Women Around Utamaro.*

18th-century artist's models serving as a multi-faceted mirror of the oppression of women in Edo Japan); and *My Love Has Been Burning*, about a women's rights pioneer who finds that Japan's late 19th-century struggle for democracy takes account of only one half of the population. Besides the wealth of historical detail on view (one of Mizoguchi's greatest strengths was his perfectionist recreation of the past), what distinguishes such films is the way both script (often written by regular collaborator Yoshitaka Yoda) and direction illuminate the injustices of the world without falling prey to easy sermonising.

But it was *The Life of Oharu* >**2** which revealed Mizoguchi at the peak of his powers, won the International Prize at Venice, and ensured that Dahei Films would allow him virtual *carte blanche* in the future. Based on a 17th-century classic, the story of an imperial courtesan's fall from favour after responding to a lowly page's love, and her slow, inexorable descent into prostitution, poverty and old age, would seem ripe for melodrama: so sympathetic, however, is Mizoguchi's insistence on the woman's brave dignity in the face of cruel betrayal and exploitation, so tranquil his treatment of passion, that Oharu's predicament becomes tragic and universal. An unobtrusively fluid camera, coupled with long takes and precise, painterly compositions often seen from a distance at once remote and discreet, lends the film both beauty and emotional integrity, and we are never pummelled into a point of view. Similarly, in *Ugetsu Monogatari* >**3**, the ghost with whom a potter falls in love is barely differentiated visually from the film's other characters, while the dreadful, barbaric sufferings of a family in feudal 11th-century Japan, in *Sansho the Bailiff*, are viewed with a contemplative, rather than a voyeuristic, eye.

Perhaps Mizoguchi's greatest film, *Chikamatsu Monogatari* >**4** again treated the oppression of women and the lower-classes, with a merchant's wife forced to flee death (the penalty for adultery, of which she is wrongly accused) with an employee of her husband. Notable for its stunning cinematography (most especially when the woman's planned suicide in a tiny rowing boat on a becalmed lake is averted by her fellow-fugitive's final declaration of love), the film also climaxes with Mizoguchi's most hauntingly defiant image as the bound pair are slowly driven to the site of their crucifixion, now serene and happily assured of their mutual love.

Yang Kwei Fei, the first of the director's two colour films, was a rather more mundane variation on a similar theme, but *Shin Heike Monogatari* >**5** was a complex 12th-century historical epic in which internecine intrigues and battles subtly portray the shift in power from repressive dynastic lords and lackey monks to a new warrior class. The use of colour is exemplary, both astonishingly elegant in itself and dramatically significant; but typical also is the elegaic tone with which Mizoguchi evokes a long vanished world, while simultaneously questioning the Japanese taste for elitist, oppressive, archaic traditions. This radical outlook, that had informed his continued interest in the position of women, inspired his last completed film, *Street of Shame*, which treated the plight of modern-day prostitutes with characteristic sympathy.

The historical settings, fragile grace and quiet lyricism of Mizoguchi's films cannot conceal their carefully controlled anger, and their pertinence to 20th-century life. It is to his eternal credit, however, that they emerge less as socio-political tracts than as emotionally moving, dramatically refined works of art: so much so that they have won universal recognition as magnificent cinema.

Lineage

Since few of Mizoguchi's early films are extant and most Japanese movies are made according to strict genre conventions, to discern influences on his work is difficult. He himself, on the other hand, is thought to have influenced, among others, Masahiro Shinoda and, to a lesser extent, **Kurosawa**, a self-confessed admirer.

Further reading

Donald Richie and Joseph Anderson's *The Japanese Cinema* (New York, 1960), Joan Mellen's *The Waves at Genji's Door* (New York, 1976), Noel Burch's *To the Distant Observer* (London, 1979).

Viewing

1 **The Story of the Late Chrysanthemums**
Japan 1939/ w Shotaro Hanayagi, Kakuko Mori, Gonjuro Kawarazaki
2 **The Life of Oharu**
Japan 1952/ w Kinuyo Tanaka, Toshiro Mifune, Hisako Yamane
3 **Ugetsu Monogatari**
Japan 1953/ w Machiko Kyo, Kinuyo Tanaka, Masayuki Mori
4 **Chikamatsu Monogatari (The Crucified Lovers)**
Japan 1954/ w Kazuo Hasegawa, Kyoko Kagawa, Yoko Minamida
5 **Shin Heike Monogatari (New Tales of the Taira Clan)**
Japan 1955/ w Raizo Ichikawa, Ichijiro Oya

F.W. Murnau

Born: 28th December 1888/Bielefeld, Germany
Died: 11th March 1931/Santa Barbara, California, USA
Directing career: 1919-31

Of the 21 films made by Friedrich Wilhelm Murnau (born Plumpe), almost half are now lost, while several that remain are incomplete, mutilated, or rarely seen. On the evidence, however, of a handful of films, his tragically early death robbed the world of a major poetic talent.

Educated in art history and literature, Murnau first gained experience in the theatre under Reinhardt. After World War I, during which he edited propaganda films, he turned to directing with *The Boy in Blue*. The next few years were prolific, but the earliest surviving film of note is *Nosferatu* >**1**, a vampire film based on Bram Stoker's classic *Dracula* and remarkable, not only for its truly subhuman and cadaverous conception of the Count, but for its ingenious blending of fantasy and reality, the latter evoked through superb location photography. Indeed, Murnau's greatest strength was his eclectic visual style, which combined the Expressionist tendencies of contemporary German cinema with a quieter, lyrical naturalism familiar from Swedish and American films. *The Last Laugh* >**2**, for instance, remains impressive less for its typically Teutonic plot (about a hotel commissionaire who, demoted to lavatory attendant, sinks so low that he is led to try and steal back his beloved uniform) than for its eternally mobile camera. While Emil Jannings' overblown acting, and a happy ending tacked on by the Ufa studios against Murnau's wishes, serve only to highlight the fable's gloomy bathos, the camera swoops, tracks and prowls to suggest a vibrant world existing outside the film frame. Indeed, so expressive were Murnau's fluid visuals that he abandoned the usual device of intertitles to develop the story.

Tartuffe, an elegant version of Molière's comedy, and *Faust* both displayed Murnau's painterly sense of composition, although the latter's startlingly beautiful supernatural scenes (including a soaring aerial voyage) were let down by the poorly judged farce of a tedious central section. In 1926, however, Murnau was invited by William Fox to Hollywood, where he made what is arguably his masterpiece, *Sunrise* >**3**. Again, the story itself is unremarkable: an affair with a city vamp leads an innocent country fellow to plot his wife's murder, but a change of heart brings about the rebirth of their love. Again, however, the camera captures in detail both the simple purity of rural life and the bustling night-time world of the neon-lit city, supplying the film's emotional power, its poetically unreal *chiaroscuro* textures, and its identification with the central characters, suspending all disbelief in the potentially risible romance. The film, unfortunately, fared badly with audiences despite critical acclaim, and both *Four Devils* (now lost) and *Our Daily Bread* were subject to studio interference, the latter – a still sporadically moving, visually lush tale of a young farmer's wife rejected by her father-in-law – partly reshot, recut and retitled *City Girl*.

In 1929, Murnau travelled to the South Seas with **Flaherty** to make what would be his last picture. Though a sound film, *Tabu* >**4** is

Max Schreck as the cadaverous vampire count in Murnau's classic *Nosferatu*.

neither talkie nor documentary but a fictional cinepoem that uses real Polynesians, on location, to tell a story (of young love, an ancient tribal curse, and death) through music and images of a hitherto unbroached homo-eroticism (giving rise to disagreement over the director's own sexuality). Flaherty left the production after differences of opinion; happily, however, Murnau's simple, dreamy conception of a cruel island paradise on the verge of extinction was both a unique, lyrical masterpiece in its own right and a sad but glorious epitaph. In 1931, with a contract with Paramount (a studio unusually sympathetic to 'arty' European directors) now in his sights, he was killed in a car accident.

Murnau's visual style unites the diverse themes and stories that constitute his best work; his fluently moving camera implies an openness of attitude that transcends both the rigid schematics of Expressionism and the limiting conventions of genre. His films are difficult to categorise (*Nosferatu* is too lyrical to be seen as mere horror, while many of his other works suggest an interest in metaphysics rather than simple story telling), but they retain an ability to touch the heart and stimulate both mind and eye.

Lineage

Murnau's blend of realist detail and emotional poeticism, not to mention a taste for elaborate camera movements as opposed to the montage practices developed by **Eisenstein**, may suggest comparison with **Von Stroheim**, **Von Sternberg**, **Renoir**, **Mizoguchi**, **Ophüls**, even perhaps **Welles**, **Minnelli** and **Altman**. Interestingly, though **Herzog** paid tribute by remaking *Nosferatu*, among modern German directors perhaps **Wenders**' visual methods most closely resemble Murnau's.

Further reading

Lotte H. Eisner's *The Haunted Screen* (London, 1969) and *Murnau* (London, 1973).

Viewing

1 **Nosferatu (A Symphony of Horror)**
Germany 1922/ w Max Schreck, Alexander Granach, Greta Schroeder

2 **The Last Laugh (Der Letzte Mann)**
Germany 1924/ w Emil Jannings, Maly Delschaft, Max Hiller

3 **Sunrise**
US 1927/ w Janet Gaynor, George O'Brien, Margaret Livingstone

4 **Tabu**
US 1931/ w Reri, Matahi, Hitu, Jean, Jules, Kong Ah

Max Ophüls

Born: **6th May 1902/Saarbrucken, Germany**
Died: **26th March 1957/Hamburg, West Germany**
Directing career: 1930-1955

Having concentrated throughout his career on the theme of love's impermanence, Max Oppenheimer, later Ophüls, was often dismissed by contemporary critics as a frivolous talent with an uncommonly elaborate visual style. More recently, however, his reputation has been subject to drastic reassessment, partly because of his abiding interest in the fate of women living in an oppressively patriarchal society.

Having made his name as an actor-turned-director in theatre, Ophüls was invited in 1930 to try his hand with film; his debut, *Rather Cod Liver Oil*, was co-scripted with Emeric Pressburger from a story by children's writer Erich Kästner. The best of his early films, *Liebelei* >**1**, already reveals the Ophüls style in relatively developed form: a portrait of the doomed love of a shy young girl for a lieutenant haunted by his past, it uses music (the sinister opening chords of Beethoven's 5th Symphony), oppressively lavish decor and a bleak view of Hapsburg Empire notions of propriety to stress the constricting forces that render innocence and passion transient. Similarly (having fled the rise of Nazism – to work in France, Holland and Italy), in *La Signora di Tutti* Ophüls examined the gulf between romantic fantasy and harsh reality through a dying actress' memories of lost love. Time, absence and death are set in constant counterpoint to the endless roundelay of seduction, love and betrayal.

With the fall of France, Ophüls left Europe for Hollywood where, for several years, he remained without work. In 1947, **Robert Siodmak** finally brought him to the attention of Douglas Fairbanks Jr, who employed him to direct *The Exile*, a stylish swashbuckler about Charles II notable for the graceful acrobatic mobility with which the camera follows its star's movements. More reminiscent of Ophüls' early work, however, was *Letter From an Unknown Woman* >**2**, a potentially novelettish tale of a girl nursing a crush on a pianist, only to be treated in later years, as his mistress, with tragically callous disregard. Again, the director transformed his material by visual means, the immaculate recreation of late 1800s Vienna (a favourite Ophüls setting) and the roving camera serving to trap the heroine both in an uncaring male world and in her own romantic fantasies. *Caught* >**3** (a fashion-model weds the tycoon of her dreams, before finding that he is psychotically incapable of real love) and *The Reckless Moment* (a woman is blackmailed after concealing a man's death to protect her daughter from charges of murder) were even more remarkable, adapting Ophüls' distinctively mobile visual style and his sympathetic view of beleaguered women to the taut, suspenseful and fatalistic conventions of *film noir*.

The films made upon Ophüls' return to France are, if anything, even more heavily stylised and disdainful of realism than before, relishing period decor, costume and absurd narrative coincidence. The chain of interlinked episodes examining the joys and pains of seduction and separation in *La Ronde* becomes a formal exercise in circularity, its motifs (a carousel, a waltz) drawn attention to by an omniscient narrator who edits the story together, explains and wanders through the action, and comments on the theme of love with suave, ironic wit. *Le Plaisir*'s omnibus of three Maupassant stories is yet another meditation on the various options open to women, while in *Madame De . . .* >**4**, arguably Ophüls' finest film, a pair of earrings passed from hand to hand simultaneously provides a daring plot-device, and illuminates the economic nature of the heroine's dependence on a rich spouse and involvement in a tragic affair; rarely had the director's focus on the implacable passage of time (signified as always by the restlessly circling, tracking camera) and his acknowledgement of the power of material wealth and bourgeois morality been employed to such dark and moving effect.

Ophüls' last film is at once his most famous, ambitious and, finally, most disappointing. *Lola Montès* >**5**, shot flamboyantly in 'Scope and colour, is his definitive account of a woman trapped. It outlines, through flashbacks announced by circus ringmaster-cum-narrator Peter Ustinov, the notorious past of the celebrated adventuress who is now reduced to posing (woman as exploitable spectacle) for a public weaned on scandal. Noted for its equation of style and meaning (never did Ophüls' taste for circular motion trap a character so incessantly), the film is nevertheless too explicit (Lola tells us that 'life is movement'), too insistently virtuoso in its baroque visual *coups*; surface becomes everything, and our emotional involvement is accordingly limited.

Ophüls died all too soon after seeing *Lola Montès* released in a cut and re-edited version; only years later was it shown as originally intended. His work remains impressive, partly for his use of space and motion to elaborate on theme, partly for his ironic, poignant but never maudlin explorations of the chasm between romantic fantasies of idealised love and the sad, treacherous and ephemeral realities of human passion.

Lineage

Ophüls himself expressed a deep admiration for **Murnau** and **Renoir**, with whom he may be compared. Further parallels may be found in figures as diverse as **Von Stroheim**, **Von Sternberg**, **Borzage**, **Sirk**, **Minnelli** and **Truffaut**. He was much admired by the *Nouvelle Vague*. His son is the excellent documentarist, Marcel Ophüls.

Charles Boyer (left) and actor-director Vittorio De Sica (right) in a typically ornate Ophüls scene from *Madame De . . . .*

Further reading

Ophüls ed. Paul Willemen (London, 1978), Alan Williams' *Max Ophüls and the Cinema of Desire* (New York, 1980).

Viewing

1 **Liebelei**
Germany 1932/ w Wolfgang Liebeneiner, Magda Schneider
2 **Letter from an Unknown Woman**
US 1948/ w Joan Fontaine, Louis Jourdan, Mady Christians
3 **Caught**
US 1949/ w Barbara Bel Geddes, Robert Ryan, James Mason
4 **Madame De . . .**
France 1953/ w Danielle Darrieux, Charles Boyer, Vittorio De Sica
5 **Lola Montès**
France 1955/ w Martine Carol, Peter Ustinov, Anton Walbrook

Nagisa Oshima

Born: 31st March 1932/Kyoto, Japan
Directing career: 1959-

The most original and important Japanese film-maker to emerge on to the international scene since **Kurosawa**, Nagisa Oshima is both stylistically versatile and politically astute. Many of his films treat the problems facing postwar Japan with a blend of political commitment and brilliant formal inventivenesss virtually unknown either in his own country or in the West.

After studying political history, Oshima joined the Shochiku studios, first as assistant then as scriptwriter. After five years he made his directing debut with *A Town of Love and Hope*, notable for a hostile attitude towards the traditional codes of behaviour governing contemporary Japan. Indeed, Oshima's early work, often in genres depicting sex and violence, was distinguished by a sympathetic, rarely sentimental, understanding of the rebellious disillusionment of youth, coupled with an awareness of the hypocrisy and corruption underlying much of Japan's recent history: *The Catch*, for example, uses the device of a black American prisoner of war murdered by the inhabitants of a mountain village to examine both inter-generational tensions and Japan's attitudes towards its own violently xenophobic past. Stylistically, most of Oshima's early work reveals a preference for long-shot and long takes (although *Violence at Noon* and the comic-strip *Band of Ninja* are noted for rapid editing); but only with *Death By Hanging* >**1** did the director come to be universally recognised as a major innovative movie-maker.

A *tour-de-force* on every level, *Death by Hanging* tells of the chaos that follows the failed execution, for the rape and murder of two Japanese girls, of a young Korean. Simultaneously operating as an argument against capital punishment, as an inquiry into Japan's treatment of minorities as second-class citizens, and as a witty black comedy on the relation of reality to illusion, it couches a sharp satire on absurd bureaucratic incompetence and corruption in an imaginative array of Brechtian effects. Questions are addressed to the audience, austere realism spirals into surreal fantasy, there are repeated acknowledgements that what we are watching is, like the theories on the cause of the crime put forward by the officials, not real but invented artifice. Even more formally daring, if less rigorously argued, was *Diary of a Shinjuku Thief*, in which street theatre, documentary, and a fictional couple's search for sexual fulfilment against a backdrop of student riots, form an allusive collage illustrating struggles for freedom and self-expression in a society consumed by materialism and conformist codes of conduct.

In *Boy* >**2** and *The Ceremony* >**3**, Oshima adopted a rather less experimental, more linear narrative style to equally successful effect. The first, about a family who make a living by faking car accidents and then blackmailing drivers into paying compensation for the son's non-existent wounds, was both an unusually touching portrait of the boy's gradual retreat from reality into mournful fantasy, and a further example of Oshima's interest in society's outsiders; while the second, a subtle allegory on Japan's post-war history as symbolised by a family's ritual gatherings, was a superbly crafted demonstration of the hollow absurdity of many of his country's traditions (convention demanding, for instance, that a wedding go ahead as planned even though the bride is absent). Likewise, *Dear Summer Sister* steadily proceeds from a light drama about teenage holiday romance to a darker portrait of the effects of Japan's record of wartime atrocities in Okinawa.

In 1976, Oshima achieved a *succès de scandale* with *Empire of the Senses* (*Ai No Corrida*) >**4**, an elegantly stylised, physically explicit account of an obsessive sexual relationship climaxing in death and castration. Remarkably, despite its repeated images of the sex act, the film displayed an unprecedented warmth in its awareness of the tender emotional undercurrents that lead the protagonists to retreat into an isolated world of private fantasy. Subsequent films, however, with their more conventional narrative style have seemed more opportunistic in their accent on eroticism. *Empire of Passion* was a glossy, shallow story of adulterous lovers haunted by the ghost of the woman's husband; *Merry Christmas Mr Lawrence* >**5** an intriguing, if finally mundane, war movie in which a Japanese concentration camp officer's homosexual love for an English major does little to deepen an investigation of culture clash; *Max My Love*, a sly, strangely unsensational, almost Buñuelesque satire on bourgeois mores, set in Paris and about an adulterous affair between the wife of a respectable diplomat and a chimpanzee.

If Oshima's recent films lack the energy, subversive power, and innovative originality of his finest work, he remains a major director who avoids the facile and obvious. His early, political films were lucid, invigorating and intelligent attempts to create new forms of cinematic narrative, while his more visually elegant later work represents a sometimes delicately oblique, even subversive, contribution to the conventions of the international art movie.

Lineage

Belonging to the generation of Japanese film-makers that includes Hiroshi Teshigahara, Yoshishige Yoshida, Masahiro Shinoda and Shohei Imamura, Oshima displays an emotional and political profundity lacking in **Godard**, with whom he is often compared. His more Brechtian work more closely resembles that of **Makavejev**; and he may have influenced the late Shuji Terayama.

Further reading

Ian Cameron's *Second Wave* (London, 1970), Audie Bock's *Japanese Film Directors* (New York, 1978).

Viewing

1 **Death By Hanging**
Japan 1968/ w Yun-Do Dun, Kei Sato, Fumio Watanabe
2 **Boy**
Japan 1969/ w Tetsuo Abe, Fumio Watanabe, Akiko Koyama
3 **The Ceremony**
Japan 1971/ w Kenzo Kawarazaki, Atsuo Nakamura
4 **Empire of the Senses (Ai No Corrida)**
Japan/France 1976/ w Tatsuya Fuji, Eiko Matsuda
5 **Merry Christmas Mr Lawrence**
Japan/GB 1983/ w David Bowie, Ryuichi Sakamoto, Tom Conti

Yasujiro Ozu

Born: 12th December 1903/Tokyo, Japan
Died: 12th December 1963/ Kamakura, Japan
Directing career: 1927-1962

Though Yasujiro Ozu spent his entire film-making career working in the commercial mainstream, his uniquely contemplative style is perhaps the most inimitably personal in the history of film. Even more importantly, his greatness was assured by the way that style reflected meaning, its rigour and richness finally amounting to a vision of life as becalmed and poignant as it was profound.

A film fan from childhood, Ozu first entered the movies as assistant cameraman and assistant director at Shochiku studios. In 1927 he made his directing debut with *Sword of Penitence*, and over the next three years proved himself as an able director of light comedy-dramas about college life and office workers. His first film of real note was *Tokyo Chorus*, made in the home-drama genre in which he would increasingly specialise and reflecting on the depression then currently afflicting Japan through its tale of an office worker suddenly made redundant. In the years that followed, Ozu steadily refined his art, coming to focus more and more on a handful of domestic situations (the generation gap, death in the family, marital strife, unemployment, wedding plans), all set in a subtly evoked contemporary Japan coping with industrialisation, Westernisation and capitalism. *I Was Born But...* >1 starts out as comedy and gradually takes on darker overtones as two young boys, bemused by the absurdities of the adult world, come to lose faith in their father; *Passing Fancy* focusses on a son's confusion when his widowed father neglects him to woo a homeless girl.

Spurning sound until 1935, Ozu opted instead for a wealth of observational details and a gentle balance of surprisingly physical comedy and sombre lyricism to create a unique form of stylised realism; even more crucial to the development of his style was a steady paring down of plot and visual syntax. Narrative is drained of eventful drama, dissolves and fades are replaced by the simple cut or (to signify a change of place or time) a sequence of shots of nearby buildings or landscape; still more remarkably, the camera almost never moves or pans, always observing characters from a position lower than they. Far from being limiting, however, this rigorous asceticism, coupled with the repeated use of a repertory troupe of actors (notably Chishu Ryu), enabled Ozu to perform endless delicate, even playful, variations on theme, motifs, and style.

Time and again the director turned to the same situations, occasionally even remaking his own films. Thus *Late Spring* >**2** – a tale of cross-purposes with a father wanting to see his daughter wed before he dies and the girl, not wanting to leave him alone, resisting – is both a reversal of *Passing Fancy* and a precursor to Ozu's final film, *An Autumn Afternoon*. Similarly, *Tokyo Story* >**3** echoes various extended-family sagas, including *Brothers and Sisters of the Toda Family* and *Early Summer*, while yet existing as a masterpiece in its own right: about an old couple making one last visit to their children and grandchildren in Tokyo, it slowly but inexorably builds, through dialogue as deceptively trivial as the gestures are delicate, to a lucid awareness of the inevitability of humans growing apart as they grow older. The film's

Chishu Ryu and Shima Iwashita, shot from a characteristically low angle, in Ozu's final film, *An Autumn Afternoon.*

emotional power is devastating but never maudlin, Ozu's stoic acceptance of human nature reflected in the tranquil restraint of his camera's gaze. 'Isn't life disappointing?' asks a girl of her war-widowed sister-in-law, after her mother's funeral; 'Yes' comes the reply, with a smile. It is indeed arguable that Ozu, by this late stage in his career, was the most profoundly humane and philosophical of all directors to work in an intellectually accessible genre.

Even to the end, however sombre many of his later films, Ozu never entirely abandoned humour, and *Good Morning!* (*Ohayo*) >**4** was a gloriously funny reworking of *I Was Born But . . .*, its tale (two boys refuse to speak until their parents buy a television) giving rise to gags about flatulence, inane gossip, and the consumerism of modern Japan, even as it addresses, with a deceptively playful wit, complex questions about the nature of human communication.

After the aching lyricism and sublime colour camerawork of *An Autumn Afternoon*, Ozu died of cancer on his sixtieth birthday. He left behind him a body of work so consistently understated, so unpatronisingly generous in its perception of human foibles, and so idiosyncratically homogeneous, that it could never be mistaken for the work of any other film-maker. Ozu's quiet strength lay in his knowledge that film need not be dramatically contrived to move an audience; that closely observed actors, situations and landscapes might, if organised with intelligence and integrity, reveal the mysterious, infinitely varied joys and sadnesses of life itself.

Lineage

So personal was Ozu's mature style that it is hard to compare him with contemporaries such as **Mizoguchi**, Heinosuke Gosho, Mikio Naruse and Sadao Yamanaka. His asceticism has encouraged comparison with **Dreyer** and **Bresson**. Among modern directors, **Eric Rohmer** exhibits a similarly detailed, obsessive, steadily refined low-key style, while the Taiwanese director Hou Xiaoxian echoes Ozu's tranquil and unassertive observations of everyday life. **Wenders**, **Jarmusch** and João Botelho (whose *A*

Portuguese Farewell was an inventive reworking of *Tokyo Story*) have professed themselves admirers.

Further reading

David Bordwell's *Ozu and the Poetics of Cinema* (London, 1988), Donald Richie's *Ozu* (Berkeley, 1974), Schrader's *Transcendental Style in Film* (Berkeley, 1972).

Viewing

1 **I Was Born But . . .**
Japan 1932/ w Tatsuo Saito, Mitsuko Yoshikawa, Hideo Sugawara
2 **Late Spring**
Japan 1949/ w Chishu Ryu, Setsuko Hara, Yumeji Tsukioka
3 **Tokyo Story**
Japan 1953/ w Chishu Ryu, Chieko Higashiyama, Setsuko Hara
4 **Good Morning! (Ohayo)**
Japan 1959/ w Keiji Sata, Kuniko Miyake, Haruko Sugimura

G.W. Pabst

Born: 27th August 1885/Raudnitz, Czechoslovakia
Died: 29th May 1967/Vienna, Austria
Directing career: 1923-1956

Worthy, ambitious and solidly crafted, the early German films of Georg Wilhelm Pabst seem less impressive with the passing years, while his later work is largely negligible. Though once acclaimed for their psychological insights and humanist commitment, many of his films now appear merely proficient, notable mainly for strong performances and an assured creation of atmosphere.

Pabst spent some 15 years acting and directing for the stage before turning to film as an assistant director and scriptwriter. His feature debut, *The Treasure*, was an exercise in Expressionism, while *The Joyless Street* >**1**, made two years later starring Greta Garbo and Asta Nielsen, was lauded for its comparatively realist depiction of the moral and economic crises afflicting a Europe in the throes of postwar inflation; but despite dark, moody photography reflecting the film's basic pessimism, Pabst's treatment frequently lapsed into melodrama. *Secrets of a Soul*, drawing upon Freudian psychoanalytic theory to illustrate a man's anxieties by means of symbolic dream images, was ambitious and intelligent but flawed by what appears to be a sense of its own importance, while *The Love of Jeanne Ney*, set against a backdrop of revolution and exile, impresses less for its contrived romance between a Russian communist and a French *bourgeoise* than for the precisely detailed performance Pabst elicited from Brigitte Helm. Indeed, he was an adept director of actresses, *Pandora's Box* >**2** remaining his most powerful film thanks to the inspired casting of Louise Brooks as Wedekind's Lulu, whose unabashed sexuality inadvertently entraps and destroys men before resulting in her own death at the hands of Jack the Ripper. Pabst's skilful delineation of the decadence and hypocrisy surrounding his free-spirited heroine is masterly, the richly textured photography creating a convincingly corrupt world of irresponsible pleasures; but it is Brooks, vital, amoral and spontaneously sensuous, who supplies an emotional complexity often absent from the director's other work.

Brooks appeared again in the rather more plodding *Diary of a Lost Girl* >**3**, a schematic and predictable story of a pharmacist's daughter's odyssey from shop to reform school to brothel; despite drawing another fine performance from the actress, Pabst's moral perspective on his material was muddled, divided between a rather voyeuristic interest in all things sordid and sadistic and a more humane sympathy for the girl's predicament. Deprived of Brooks' animated presence, however, his first sound film, *Westfront 1918*, demonstrated a return to a somewhat academic liberalism, its pacifist sentiments verging on the portentous. In contrast, *The Threepenny Opera* >**4** was an effectively atmospheric adaptation of Brecht and Weill's musical, although Brecht, unhappy with the way his anti-capitalist satire had been blunted, brought an unsuccessful court case against the film's producers. Nevertheless, Pabst's sense of decor and his ability with actors ensured a distinctly cinematic vision of the original's London underworld of pimps, prostitutes, and corrupt politicians. More simplistically anti-establishment was *Kameradschaft* >**5**, a tense but risibly idealistic call for the unification of the workers of all countries, with German miners burrowing under the national border (against the bosses' wishes) to rescue their French counterparts trapped below. Pabst's subtle use of sound and superb studio evocation of the dark subterranean tunnels make for taut suspense, but his political message is naive and facile in its black-and-white oppositions.

After leaving Germany during the rise of Hitler, Pabst failed to regain his momentum; the films he made in France (not to mention A *Modern Hero*, his one Hollywood production) are uneven and forgettable. In World War II, for reasons that remain unclear, he returned to Germany, making three films for the Nazis; ironically, his first postwar project, *The Trial*, attacked anti-Semitism while, of his later films, *The Last Ten Days* dealt with Hitler's final downfall, and *The Jackboot Mutiny* with a 1944 plot against the Fuehrer's life led by German army officers. Such was Pabst's wavering 'commitment' in the latter stages of his career. Finally, after suffering a stroke in 1956, he retired from film-making.

At his best, Pabst was able to depict, in convincing detail, a society in moral turmoil, although his ambition frequently exceeded his ability, and the results were merely decorative. His early work – revealing him as very much a product of his times – will be best remembered for the opportunities it offered actresses such as Garbo, Asta Nielsen, Brigitte Helm and Louise Brooks.

Lineage

Pabst's achievements seem distinctly limited when compared with those of **Murnau** and **Lang**. Any lasting influence on the development of cinema would seem to be minimal, while his taste for sordid psychological realism compares poorly with that of **Von Stroheim**.

Further reading

Lotte H. Eisner's *The Haunted Screen* (London, 1969).

Viewing

1 **The Joyless Street**
Germany 1925/ w Asta Nielsen, Greta Garbo, Werner Krauss

2 **Pandora's Box**
Germany 1929/ w Louise Brooks, Fritz Kortner, Franz Lederer

3 **Diary of a Lost Girl**
Germany 1929/ w Louise Brooks, Fritz Rasp, Josef Rovensky

4 **The Threepenny Opera**
Germany 1931/ w Rudolf Forster, Carola Neher, Lotte Lenya

5 **Kameradschaft**
Germany 1931/ w Ernst Busch, Alexander Granach, Fritz Kampers

Alan J. Pakula

Born: 7th April 1928/Bronx, New York, USA
Directing career: 1969-

A producer successfully turned director, Alan Jay Pakula was one of the most promising talents to emerge in Hollyood in the '70s, displaying a keen eye and a strong sense of character arising from an interest in psychology. Recently, however, his career seems to have entered the doldrums; while his films reveal a continuing flair for directing actors, they lack pace, tension and originality.

A former drama student with some experience in the animation department at Warner Bros., Pakula first made his name as producer of several sensitive, well-crafted, and somewhat middlebrow films directed by Robert Mulligan, collaborating between 1957 and 1968 on movies that included *Fear Strikes Out*, *To Kill a Mockingbird*, *Love with the Proper Stranger* and *The Stalking Moon*. In 1969, he turned to direction with *Pookie* (*The Sterile*

Cuckoo), quietly observing the brief romance of a college girl with a fellow student. Far more indicative of Pakula's strengths was *Klute* >**1**, in which a shy detective's search for a missing friend leads to a hesitant relationship with a highly-paid New York hooker who herself becomes a murderer's next intended victim. Sympathetic, but self-conscious in its de-sensationalised portrait of a prostitute's working day, the film worked fruitfully as a study of voyeurism (the killer as the cop's alter ego) and as a visually claustrophobic account of urban paranoia. Even better, after the slight but well-acted *Love and Pain and the Whole Damn Thing*, *The Parallax View* >**2** saw Pakula's camera explore the menacing nature of empty, wide open spaces: as a journalist investigates a series of deaths that follow a political murder and discovers the existence of a secret organisation recruiting psychotically insecure assassins, Pakula employs virtually abstract compositions and an artfully elliptical narrative to create a world both unsettling and oddly familiar.

Equally intelligent in its visual organisation was *All The President's Men* >**3**, transforming the real-life story of two lowly journalists uncovering the truth behind Watergate into effective *film noir*; if its final outcome could be seen as a tribute to the pioneering spirit of the American press, its images – the two men viewed from overhead and engulfed in the concentric circles of a library as they laboriously sort through documents; the informer Deep Throat shrouded in the sinister darkness of an underground car park – suggested that political corruption was deeply rooted indeed. Less compelling, though similarly ambitious, was *Comes a Horseman*, a visually sumptuous Western set in the 1940s in which lyrical understatement gave way to overblown Gothic melodrama.

Thereafter Pakula seemed to lose his way. In *Starting Over*, about a man's post-divorce confusion, poor casting highlighted the director's uncertain comic sensibility; in *Rollover*, a brave stab at an apocalyptic thriller about economics, financial jargon rendered an uneven script largely incomprehensible; both *Sophie's Choice*, about a Polish refugee in postwar America unable to come to terms with having survived the holocaust, and the Hitchcockian thriller *Dream Lover*, about a young girl traumatised by murderous nightmares, revealed Pakula's abiding interest in psychology, but were spoilt, respectively, by a sluggish pace that indulged Meryl Streep's every mannerism, and by a meandering, implausible plot.

The sentimental *Orphans*, adapted from a stage-play, in which a pair of delinquent brothers find salvation through a brief encounter with a fatherly gangster, only emphasised Pakula's continuing downward slide, accelerated by increasingly unsuitable material. At his best with relatively straightforward genre thrillers dependent on the creation of atmosphere by purely visual means, he clearly has the potential to provide entertainment of a rare intelligence; recent films, however, suggest a rather limited and variable talent.

Lineage

Pakula's finest work reveals a feel for landscape and environment akin to that of **Lang**, **Antonioni** and **Boorman**. Indeed his often oblique approach to genre suggests that European rather than American directors may have influenced him most strongly.

Viewing

1 **Klute**
US 1971/ w Jane Fonda, Donald Sutherland, Charles Cioffi

2 **The Parallax View**
US 1974/ w Warren Beatty, Hume Cronyn, William Daniels

3 **All the President's Men**
US 1976/ w Robert Redford, Dustin Hoffman, Jason Robards

Sergo Paradjanov

Born: 9th January 1924/Tiflis, Georgia, USSR
Directing career: 1954-

Though very few films by Sarkis Paradjanian have been seen in the West, his best-known work signals a profoundly original (if difficult) talent. His idiosyncratic blending of medieval folk-lore with cinematic modernism makes for movies as challenging and obscure as they are sensually poetic.

Born in Georgia of Armenian parents, Paradjanov studied film and music before becoming an assistant director at the Dovzhenko studios in Kiev. His 1954 debut, *Andriesh*, co-directed with Yakov Bazelian, was followed by several shorts and features, shot in the Ukraine and dismissed by the director as 'failures' (they are as yet unseen in the West). In 1964, however, he made *Shadows of our Forgotten Ancestors* >**1**, a Romeo and Juliet-style tale of love transcending a tragic family feud. Set in Carpathia, the film's flamboyant style (fluid camera movements, a narrative punctuated by folk music and dancing, and bizarre non-naturalistic colours) announced a visionary talent seemingly more in tune with a pagan past than with the socialist realism adopted by his peers. Indeed, his poetic sensibility found little favour with the authorities, who rejected no less than 10 scripts during the next five years. Finally, in 1969, he was able to make *The Colour of Pomegranates* >**2**, a life of the 18th-century poet Sayat Nova told, not through a conventional linear narrative, but through sequences of highly stylised, often static, icon-like tableaux. These are notable for their surreal beauty and an arcane, nationalist symbolism largely impenetrable to Western audiences – the poet, for example, is played by a man *and* a woman. The film, however, met with official disapproval as being 'hermetic and obscure'; it was cut, re-edited and given only limited release five years after completion. Still worse, in 1973 Paradjanov was charged with various crimes, including homosexuality and speculation in art objects, and sentenced to six years hard labour. Only in 1978, after protests both within Russia and from abroad, was he released.

The director's eventual return to film-making, in 1984, was characteristically defiant: *The Legend of the Suram Fortress* >**3**, while rather easier to follow than his previous feature, was an equally dense celebration of a mythic Georgia, telling the story of a couple who become the parents of their nation's saviour, a youth who gives up his life to be buried as part of the walls of a strategic fortress that keeps collapsing. Again, the treatment is ritualised, poetic and painterly, at once cinematically modern and imbued with a love of the archaic and pagan. With the advent of a political and cultural climate more sympathetic to non-orthodox Soviet art, Paradjanov's film was allowed a release in the West; he next made the short *Arabesques on the Pirosmani Theme*, a tribute to the Georgian folk painter, and *Ashik Kerib*, the third part of the trilogy of tableaux films that began with *Pomegranates* and continued with *Legend*. It is to be hoped that the long planned epic, *The Lay of Igor*, will also come to fruition.

While Paradjanov's films are perhaps inevitably obscure for Western audiences, his originality is striking, and the sheer sensuality of his imagery remains both powerful and startling.

Lineage

It is possible to place Paradjanov's poeticism in a tradition stretching back as far as **Dovzhenko**. He himself has spoken of his admiration for **Pasolini** and the Armenian film-maker, Arthur Pelechian.

Viewing

1 **Shadows of Our Forgotten Ancestors**
USSR 1964/ w Ivan Nikolaichuk, Larissa Kadochnikova

2 **The Colour of Pomegranates (Sayat Nova)**
USSR 1969/ w Sofiko Chiarelli, M. Aleksanian, V. Galstian

3 **The Legend of the Suram Fortress**
USSR 1985/ w Dodo Abashidze, Veneriko Andzhaparidze, Sofiko Chiarelli

Alan Parker

Born: 14th February 1944/London, England
Directing career: 1976-

Though obvious, it is nevertheless true to say that the films of Alan Parker betray his origins in TV and film commercials. Style tends to dominate content, with plot-logic, characters and moral consistency forsaken in favour of facile emotional effects.

An outspoken critic of the British tradition of polite, grey social realism, Parker made his feature debut with the innocuous, eminently forgettable spoof gangster epic *Bugsy Malone*, in which children in '30s garb gleefully fired guns loaded with ice-cream at each other. More seriously, the **Oliver Stone**-scripted *Midnight Express* >**1** portrayed the horrendous, brutal tribulations suffered by an American drugs-smuggler in a Turkish jail: Parker's pacing and flashily lit camerawork marked him as a superior technician, but his manipulation of the essentially melodramatic script laid him open to justifiable charges of racism, with every single Turk on view depicted as sweaty, sadistic and irredeemably corrupt. Less inflammatory but similarly overblown were *Fame* (a tiresome, vacuous dance-musical that inspired a TV series), *Shoot the Moon* (an inadequately motivated tale of the collapse of a novelist's marriage), and *Pink Floyd: The Wall*, a ludicrously naive account of a rock star's breakdown, which used Gerald Scarfe's grotesque animation to reinforce its vision of an insane, unjust and cruel world. Perhaps not surprisingly, given Parker's background, the result was rather like an over-extended, pretentious rock video.

Parker's distaste for realism and love of fantastic effects next led him to film William Wharton's allegorical novel *Birdy*, in which a Vietnam veteran reluctantly tries to help a childhood friend, mutely thinking himself a bird, regain his sanity. Again, an emphasis on glossy images drained the film of subtlety, though the performances were sometimes forceful enough to counteract the bombast. Likewise, *Angel Heart* >**2**, despite being unusually well suited to the overheated Parker style (a down-at-heel detective is hired by a literally diabolical stranger to find a missing singer, only to find himself involved in a series of brutal ritual killings), relied on clichéd religious symbolism and hackneyed sensuality to embellish its Faustian examination of guilt and corruption. Then, still with the thriller form, he made the gripping, emotionally effective but controversial *Mississippi Burning* >**3**, about FBI agents investigating the murder of three civil rights workers in Mississippi in 1964. As with *Midnight Express*, its very fine muscular performances and its justifiably hostile attitude to the extremist activities of the Ku Klux Klan were undermined by its perverse neglect of the crucial part played by blacks in the civil rights movement.

Parker has often attacked arty pretentiousness but his work, characterised by heavy-handed visuals and a taste for controversial or sensationalist subjects, seems to suggest a desire for artistic and intellectual recognition. Facile moralising, allegories and symbolism ensure that his work discloses less than meets the eye.

Lineage

Parker may be compared to **Ridley Scott** and Tony Scott, Adrian Lyne and Hugh Hudson, all of whom emerged from advertising.

Viewing

1 **Midnight Express**
GB 1978/ w Brad Davis, John Hurt, Bo Hopkins, Randy Quaid

2 **Angel Heart**
US 1987/ w Mickey Rourke, Robert De Niro, Lisa Bonet

3 **Mississippi Burning**
US 1988/ w Gene Hackman, Willem Dafoe, Brad Dourif

Pier Paolo Pasolini

Born: 5th March 1922/Bologna, Italy
Died: 2nd November 1975/Ostia, Italy
Directing career: 1961-1975

The films of Pier Paolo Pasolini – film-maker, poet, novelist, theorist, painter and Communist – reveal an artist beset by many contradictions. At once concerned with the real and the poetic, and influenced by ideologies as seemingly polarised as Marxism and Christianity, he remained a restlessly iconoclastic talent throughout his eclectic, troubled and controversial career.

By the time he began directing movies, Pasolini had already made a name for himself as a poet, novelist and scriptwriter on various films, including **Fellini**'s *Nights of Cabiria*. His natural sympathy for the sub-proletariat and peasantry (reinforced by his intellectual attraction to the political ideas of Gramsci) was at once evident in both *La Commare Secca* (which **Bertolucci** directed from a Pasolini script) and *Accattone* >**1**, a seedily romantic view of pimps, prostitutes and petty thieves in the squalid suburbs of modern Rome. Clearly influenced by neo-realism in its use of non-professional actors and location shooting, the film is likewise notable for its perverse application of Christian symbolism and classical music to suggest the spiritual redemption of its doomed layabout hero. Less assured, thanks to a maudlin performance by Anna Magnani, was *Mamma Roma*, also dealing with urban poverty and crime; *The Gospel According to Matthew* >**2**, however, was a superb combination of Pasolini's realist methods, semi-Marxist ideology, and nostalgia for pre-capitalist societies. Here, Christ is envisioned as a rebel battling against inequality in an arid landscape (Southern Italy), populated by heroically primitive peasants; the atheist director, while never going so far as to show miracles, revealed his awareness of the Christian tradition through music (from Bach to Billie Holliday), and images inspired by religious paintings.

Thereafter, Pasolini moved further from his realist origins to a more stylised and ambitiously poetic mythography: after the whimsical fantasy, *Hawks and Sparrows* (a double parable about two peasants encountering a Marxist intellectual crow, and being told by St Francis in the second story to convert birds to Christianity), he framed an exotic, Morocco-located, virtually silent version of Sophocles' *Oedipus Rex*, within a semi-autobiographical prologue and epilogue, set in '30s Italy and stressing Freudian aspects of the myth. With little more than impressive landscape photography added to the original story, the film smacks of indulgence. Altogether more rigorous was *Theorem* >**3**, a myth of the director's own making in which a mysterious, God-like visitor wreaks havoc on a wealthy bourgeois family by seducing its male and female members alike. Though rather contrived, often pretentious and politically naive, the film – an expression of Pasolini's hatred for bourgeois values – remains haunting as a coolly provocative, surprisingly coherent account of divine possession in contemporary capitalist society, and as an explicitly erotic admission of Pasolini's own homosexuality.

Pigsty >**4** was even more ambitious, rhyming the execution, by the church, of a nomadic cannibal in medieval times with a story about an ex-Nazi industrialist's revolutionary son who is himself finally eaten by the pigs that provide his sole source of sexual satisfaction. If Pasolini's precise meaning is obscure (although, given his nostalgic preference for pre-capitalist, pre-Christian societies, one may infer his belief that morality has degenerated since medieval times), his delight in exposing the hypocrisy that underlies modern business practices is both clear and very funny, while the volcanic desert that is the cannibal's hunting ground provides him with some of his most austerely poetic images.

After another redundant foray into Greek myth with *Medea*, he embarked upon his 'trilogy of life': coarse, bawdy adaptations of *The Decameron*, *The Canterbury Tales* and *The Arabian Nights*. If his intention was to celebrate the sexual and moral innocence of the peasantry in times past (and to make films to appeal to the masses rather than the critics and art-movie elite), his actual achievement was to create artless sex-romps memorable mainly for their adolescent scatological humour and the frequency with which the characters' period costumes were removed. Worse, however, was *Salò, or the 120 Days of Sodom*: De Sade's story is transposed to Mussolini's Italy, where the wealthy and powerful inflict upon imprisoned teenagers a series of humiliating, increasingly cruel sexual tortures ending in death. As a purported analysis of the workings of Fascism the film is woefully shallow; as voyeuristic spectacle, it suffers from the same sickeningly sadistic impulses as the bourgeoisie it purports to indict; as an expression of its maker's disillusionment with humanity, it is indeed salutary. It was therefore perhaps not surprising to learn of Pasolini's brutal death shortly after the film's completion; it is widely supposed that the fatal beating he received was somehow connected with his sex life, which often involved sado-masochists and criminals; another theory, however, links his death with the fact that he had long been an outspoken, profoundly unpopular critic of the corruption that, he alleged, tainted Italy's government, church and police.

Many of Pasolini's films are marked by self-indulgence, not to mention a simplistic antagonism towards the bourgeoisie and a romanticised celebration of the poor. As an attempt, however, to examine the contradictions both within Italian society and within the director himself, they remain fascinating; as explorations of cinema's capacity for poetic myth-making, they are uneven but ambitious.

Lineage

If many of Pasolini's influences were non-filmic (Gramsci, Marx, Freud, Roland Barthes, painters), **Buñuel**, **Rossellini**, **Mizoguchi** and **Godard** also figure. Among Italian directors, **Bertolucci**, the **Taviani** brothers and Marco Bellochio provide possible comparisons.

Further reading

Peter Bondanella's *Italian Cinema* (New York, 1983). Oswald Stack's *Pasolini on Pasolini* (London, 1969) is an interview, Pasolini's *A Violent Life* (Manchester, 1985) a novel.

Viewing

1 **Accattone**
Italy 1961/ w Franco Citti, Franca Pasut, Silvana Corsini

2 **The Gospel According to Matthew (Il Vangelo secondo Matteo)**
Italy 1964/ w Enrique Irazoqui, Margherita Caruso, Mario Socrate

3 **Theorem**
Italy 1968/ w Terence Stamp, Silvana Mangano, Massimo Girotti

4 **Pigsty**
Italy 1969/ w Pierre Clementi, Jean-Pierre Léaud, Ugo Tognazzi

Sam Peckinpah

Born: 21st February 1925/Fresno, California, USA
Died: 28th December 1984/ Inglewood, California, USA
Directing career: 1961-1983

Although less than half of his films were Westerns proper, David Samuel Peckinpah is widely recognised as the most important film-maker to work in that genre in the '60s. Unhappily, his complex, deeply elegaic explorations of frontier values were often overshadowed by his controversially graphic use of violence; more disturbing, however, is the way his vision of virile independence besieged by a changing, industrial society gave rise to rampant misogyny.

Having grown up on a ranch, Peckinpah worked in a variety of

Sam Peckinpah (in open truck, with earphones) shooting a scene from *Convoy*.

capacities in theatre and television before becoming assistant to **Don Siegel**. In the late '50s he established himself as writer and director on classic Western TV series like *Gunsmoke*, *The Rifleman* and *The Westerner*, and in 1961 he made his feature debut with *The Deadly Companions*. A quirkily observed, if unremarkable, picaresque Western, it told of a widow journeying with her son's coffin, escorted through Apache territory by three none too respectable gunmen. Far better was *Guns in the Afternoon* (*Ride the High Country*) >**1**, in which two ageing cowboys, old friends but now on opposing sides of the law, rediscover their self-respect while falling out over a gold shipment and defending a young girl from a villainous gang. The plot allows Peckinpah to compose a moving, wittily mythic variation on traditional Western ideas of courage, loyalty and duty within a landscape marked by the advent of the modern world. Even more ambitious, though savagely cut by the studio, *Major Dundee* >**2** was an epic account of a punitive raid by reluctant Confederate criminals against Apaches, led by a Union officer driven by race hatred and a fear of failure. Indeed, the strengths of Peckinpah's Westerns were his acknowledgement of the psychotic insecurities that produce violence (to which he had an extremely ambivalent attitude, seeing it also as an expression of man's need for freedom) and his refusal to view ethical issues in simplistic, conventionally black-and-white terms.

After the failure of *Major Dundee*, Peckinpah's career entered the doldrums; only five years later did he complete another film. *The Wild Bunch* >**3**, however, was a superb consummation of his work to date. Here, he employed the doomed exploits of an outlaw gang, pursued by bounty hunters and betrayed by a ruthless Mexican dictator, to paint a rich, brutal portrait of a male group consciously meeting with death in a last act of defiance against a world where money buys honour and the machine gun is ousting the rifle. Criticised for its final, bloody, slow-motion climax, it was nevertheless merely the other side of the coin to *The Ballad of Cable Hogue*, a tender, lyrical comedy Western in which the hero finally forsakes his desire for revenge, only to die beneath the wheels of the car in which his long absent lover has returned. *Straw Dogs*, however, was a return to violence, its plot (a liberal intellectual responds with murderous rage to the rape of his wife and the invasion of his home by Cornish oafs) executed with a meticulous narrative logic that failed to conceal both its basic misogyny and its glee in celebrating the triumph of primitive hatred over rationality.

Junior Bonner was again gentler, although its quiet portrait of a rootless, middle-aged rodeo-rider seemed a shallow update of **Ray**'s *The Lusty Men*. *The Getaway* (scripted by **Walter Hill**) was a slick contemporary thriller ruined by a vulgar, semi-comic sub-plot, while *Pat Garrett and Billy the Kid* (again re-cut by producers, and Peckinpah's last Western) was an uneven and dismally underwritten elegy for a once heroic friendship now fated to end in death and self-contempt. Far more original was the Gothic *Bring Me The Head of Alfredo Garcia* >**4**, in which a down-and-out American pianist in Mexico (Peckinpah's favoured landscape, symbolising freedom and an acceptance of death), paid to hunt down the seducer of a wealthy farmer's daughter, slowly and painfully rediscovers both his self respect and his purpose in life. While resolutely macho, the film benefits from tough characterisation, discreet symbolism, and the director's evident commitment to his hero's spiritual redemption.

In the last decade of his life, however, Peckinpah seemed to lose interest in his subjects (possibly due to the decline of the Hollywood Western). *The Killer Elite* was a polished, complex but unremarkable CIA thriller, its initial focus on themes of trust, betrayal and revenge yielding to expertly shot, undemanding set-pieces; *Cross of Iron* was a brave but muddled attempt to examine the courage, cruelty and suffering of war; *Convoy* a coarsely comic CB-radio adventure, with anti-establishment truckers taking the place of existentialist cowboy heroes; *The Osterman Weekend*, his last – and once-again troubled – production, a routine spy thriller memorable only for its inventive use of surveillance equipment to embellish the film's otherwise undistinguished visual style.

An uncompromising film-maker whose battles with the studios often led to his films appearing in forms other than he intended, Peckinpah was at his best when probing the psychological and spiritual pain of violent men at odds with the 'civilised' world. At once harsh in his assessment of America and sentimental in his nostalgia for simpler times, he was a romantic, paradoxically committed to an ideal of self-expression through violent death.

Lineage

Peckinpah himself greatly admired **Ford**, though his lonely, brutal and troubled heroes are perhaps closer to those of **Walsh**, **Siegel**, **Mann**, **Aldrich** and **Penn**. It is also fruitful to compare him with **Leone** and **Eastwood**, while he may be seen as an influence on **Hill**.

Further reading

Jim Kitses' *Horizons West* (London, 1970), Terence Butler's *Crucified Heroes: The Films of Sam Peckinpah* (London, 1979).

Viewing

1 **Guns in the Afternoon (Ride the High Country)**
US 1962/ w Joel McCrea, Randolph Scott, Mariette Hartley

2 **Major Dundee**
US 1965/ w Charlton Heston, Richard Harris, Jim Hutton

3 **The Wild Bunch**
US 1969/ w William Holden, Robert Ryan, Ernest Borgnine

4 **Bring Me the Head of Alfredo Garcia**
US 1974/ w Warren Oates, Gig Young, Isela Vega, Robert Webber

Arthur Penn

Born: 27th September 1922/ Philadelphia, Pennsylvania, USA
Directing career: 1958-

One of the most distinctive and intelligent directors to emerge from television in the late '50s, Arthur Penn has created a body of work that focusses, for the most part, on the violent conflict between authorities and outcasts: a violence viewed as endemic in American society. Indeed, in the '60s and '70s, he pin-pointed the changing moods of contemporary America with unerring accuracy.

In the '50s, Penn established himself as a leading director of serious drama both on television and on the stage. In 1958 he made his film debut with *The Left-Handed Gun*, a version of Gore Vidal's play about Billy the Kid,

'We rob banks': Faye Dunaway and Warren Beatty put in a little shooting practice in Penn's *Bonnie and Clyde.*

characterising him as a mentally unstable youth whose need to avenge the death of a friend finally provokes the law-abiding Pat Garrett (the first of Penn's several threatening father-figures) to action. Psychologically astute, the film was also notable for its performances and its unusually physical depiction of violence – strengths that would recur still more rewardingly in *The Miracle Worker* >**1**, a tough and affecting account of Annie Sullivan's emotionally devastating struggles to teach the deaf, mute and blind Helen Keller to react to the world about her in a 'civilised' manner. Long takes ensure the intensity of the film's mood, just as a variety of jump-cuts, rapid editing and unusual camera angles serve to increase the air of mystery and paranoia in *Mickey One*, a sometimes pretentiously arty thriller influenced by the French New Wave, in which a night-club comic's anxieties about a faceless 'organisation' mirror the mood of suspicion and betrayal of the McCarthy 'witchhunt' years.

But it was in *The Chase* >**2** that Penn analysed the roots of American violence most powerfully. A dark melodrama, re-cut by the studio, it employs a ruthless logic to chart the gradual descent into lynch-mob anarchy of an apparently respectable community in Texas, fired by the news of an escaped convict's unexpected return to town: financial greed, petty ambition, racism and family bonds are instrumental in fermenting a mass hysteria that climaxes in a killing reminiscent of Jack Ruby's shooting of Lee Harvey Oswald. Equally disenchanted with conventional society was *Bonnie and Clyde* >**3**. This hugely influential rural gangster thriller combined black comedy, graphic violence, and a sense of the spiritual boredom and moral confusion induced by the cultural and economic poverty of the '30s Depression, to evoke the anti-establishment rebellion of the late '60s. Crucially, Penn's sympathetic view of the Barrow gang was not clouded by sentimentality, and the film's initially jokey tone steadily darkens to end in chaotic, bloody carnage.

Alice's Restaurant was an altogether gentler expression of disillusionment, employing a rambling, ballad-like form to depict the doomed attempts of idealist hippies to set up an alternative society of their own; *Little Big Man* >**4**, however, was a ferocious debunking of Western myths, with a 121-year-old man (product of a childhood divided between whites and Indians) recalling the folly of frontier life in a sprawling shaggy-dog saga. It provided a corrective to traditional notions of Indian life, while telling a tale of American imperialism that clearly echoed the Vietnam war.

During the '70s, Penn – still active in the theatre – worked far less regularly in film. Both *Night Moves* >**5** and *The Missouri Breaks* >**6**, however, were remarkably fine movies, the first a taut and elliptical modern *film-noir* in which a private-eye's failure (both to solve a case and to come to terms with his own voyeurist impulses) is simply part and parcel of a subtly suggested post-Watergate mood of apathy, deceit and cynicism affecting America at large; the second is an outrageous, discursive semi-comic Western which gleefully overturns genre clichés (stock detective Brando in countless absurd disguises, his boss reading *Tristram Shandy*) and revels in dialogue at once poetic and vividly colloquial. The film, alas, was widely neglected and Penn (replaced by **Ken Russell** on *Altered States*) took five years to return to the fray with the uneven but highly intelligent *Four Friends* (*Georgia*, *Georgia's Friends*), a panorama of America from the '50s to the '70s, seen through the eyes of a young Yugoslav immigrant.

The director's most recent work suggests an unexpected slackening: *Target* was a relatively conventional spy thriller, mainly notable for its sensitive portrait of a troubled father-son relationship and a teasing investigation of various conceptions of 'family' (the CIA, the Communist spy network, the threatened central characters themselves); while *Dead of Winter*, inspired by **Lewis**' *My Name Is Julia Ross*, was a proficient, old-fashioned but finally formulaic thriller about a woman abducted for sinister purposes. Both films provided Penn with material unworthy of his considerable talents: he is at his best when adopting a more oblique, even iconoclastic approach to genre, and focussing his attentions on the rebellious outsiders who illuminate, by their very opposition, the dark undercurrents of a society devoted to conformism and repression.

Lineage

Though his background encourages comparison with **Frankenheimer**, **Lumet** and other television graduates, Penn himself has spoken of his admiration for the *Nouvelle Vague*, especially **Truffaut** and **Godard**. His fascination with outsiders and American violence is reminiscent of **Nicholas Ray**, while *Bonnie and Clyde* was immensely influential on younger American film-makers.

Further reading

Robin Wood's *Arthur Penn* (New York, 1969).

Viewing

1 **The Miracle Worker**
US 1962/ w Anne Bancroft, Patty Duke, Victor Jory

2 **The Chase**
US 1966/ w Marlon Brando, Robert Redford, Jane Fonda, E.G. Marshall

3 **Bonnie and Clyde**
US 1967/ w Warren Beatty, Faye Dunaway, Michael J. Pollard

4 **Little Big Man**
US 1970/ w Dustin Hoffman, Faye Dunaway, Chief Dan George

5 **Night Moves**
US 1975/ w Gene Hackman, Susan Clark, Jennifer Warren

6 **The Missouri Breaks**
US 1976/ w Marlon Brando, Jack Nicholson, Kathleen Lloyd

D.A. Pennebaker

Born: 1930/Evanston, Illinois, USA
Directing career: 1953-

The importance of Don Alan Pennebaker rests not in the actual quality of his films, but in his contribution to developments in new forms of documentary film-making in the late '50s and '60s. A founding member of the movement known as Direct Cinema, he helped to pioneer methods of reportage that would exert a huge influence on non-fiction work in both television and film.

Trained as an engineer, Pennebaker made his film debut with *Daybreak Express*, a delightfully atmospheric, sometimes abstract collage of images of New York set to music by Duke Ellington. But it was his work in the early '60s with the Drew Associates group of film-makers (Richard Leacock and Albert Maysles included) that brought him to the forefront of American documentary. Employing recent technical developments like lightweight cameras, fast film stock and better sound-recording equipment, the group was able to steer away from the polished, highly structured, usually narrated style hitherto the norm in documentary, towards a more objective, fly-on-the-wall observation of events and people, with the camera unobtrusively recording rather than creating images. Thus *Primary* (about the election campaigns of rivals John F. Kennedy and Hubert Humphrey), *Eddie* (a portrait of racing driver Eddie Sachs), and *The Chair* (about lawyers' attempts to commute a convict's death-sentence to life imprisonment) never adopt an explicit attitude towards their subjects, who simply speak for themselves.

Pennebaker's interest in the performing arts was already to be seen in both *Jane* (with Jane Fonda preparing for a new play) and *Lambert and Co*, a record of an audition given by jazz singer Dave Lambert; and with *Don't Look Back* >**1**, he first embarked upon a series of films intended to capture the spirit of rock music in both concert and backstage footage. *Don't Look Back*, a record of Bob Dylan's 1965 tour of Britain, is a raw, grainy, but witty and perceptive portrait of a leading cult-figure's dealings with the press, his fans and his management; while *Monterey Pop* >**2** – first and best of rock festival films – gloriously captured the peace and love ethos of the hippy movement (as well as numerous fine performances with expertly placed cameras), without ever relying on the propagandist pleading that wrecked *Woodstock*, or the hindsight that marked the Maysles brothers' *Gimme Shelter*. Pennebaker's subsequent concert films (*Keep on Rockin'* with Chuck Berry, Little Richard, Bo Diddley *et al*; *Ziggy Stardust and the Spiders from Mars*, with David Bowie) are notable mainly for their simplicity; more ambitious and cinematically rewarding are *One PM* (which successfully combines American footage shot and abandoned by **Godard** for a film called *One AM*, with Pennebaker's own footage of the Frenchman at work), and *Town Bloody Hall* >**3**, an hilarious, intelligently shot and edited record of a heated public debate on feminism featuring figures such as Norman Mailer, Germaine Greer and Susan Sontag, and an enthusiastically participatory audience.

That Pennebaker eschews analysis may be limiting, as may his focus on music; but an ability to capture and preserve the spirit of an event through careful camera placement and editing marks him as a superior, if self-effacing, chronicler of popular entertainment and public figures. His greatest virtue is clarity.

Lineage

Along with Leacock and David and Albert Maysles, Pennebaker has influenced such documentarists as Fred **Wiseman** and Robert Mugge (also a music specialist) and the rather more politically-oriented Emile de Antonio and Haskell Wexler. Direct Cinema differs from *cinéma verité* in that it adopts as its ideal an invisible camera, while the ethnographer Jean Rouch, for example, regards the camera as a catalyst between the film-maker and his subject.

Further reading

Richard Meran Barsam's *Non-Fiction Film* (London, 1974).

Viewing

1 **Don't Look Back**
US 1966/ w Bob Dylan, Joan Baez, Donovan, Albert Grossman

2 **Monterey Pop**
US 1968/ w Jimi Hendrix, Otis Redding, Ravi Shankar, The Who etc

3 **Town Bloody Hall**
US 1979/ w Norman Mailer, Germaine Greer, Diana Trilling

Maurice Pialat

Born: 21st August 1925/Puy-de-Dôme, France
Directing career: 1958-

Although he became a film-maker relatively late in life, in the last few years Maurice Pialat has established himself as one of France's leading directors. Intriguingly, his films have become increasingly bleak while he himself has steadily risen from comparative obscurity to international renown.

A former painter and occasional actor (he still sometimes appears in his own films), Pialat first became interested in film in the late '50s, when he made a number of shorts (including the award-winning *L'Amour Existe*). His first feature, however, was not made until 1968, after extensive work in television: already establishing a basically realist style (through the use of non-professional actors, a penetrating observation of everyday banalities, and discreet editing techniques), *L'Enfance Nue* (*Naked Childhood*) was a gentle account of a boy's drift into delinquency when he is sent to live with foster-parents. Similarly unassertive examinations of common emotional crises were *Nous Ne Vieillirons Pas Ensemble* (*We Won't Grow Old Together*), about a relationship's traumatic break-up; *La Gueule Ouverte* (*A Mouth Agape*) in which a woman's cancer forces a family painfully to come to terms with death; and the relatively lighter but equally perceptive *Passe Ton Bac D'Abord* >**1**, in which the hopes, anxieties and tedious existences of a group of teenage schoolchildren are viewed with a beguilingly low-key honesty that never falls prey to easy moralising or maudlin sentimentality.

With the added star-power of Gérard Depardieu and Isabelle Huppert as a slobbish working-class drunk and his bored bourgeois lover, *Loulou* >**2** brought Pialat international acclaim, even though its portrait of a troubled, down-market love-affair, grounded in unrepentant physicality, was relentlessly sordid. *A Nos Amours* (*To Our Loves*) >**3** was still more pessimistic – a rambling story of a promiscuous 15-year-old girl turning to a loveless marriage to escape from a family home-life in which mutual misunderstandings and violent recrimination are the everyday norm. Indeed, Pialat's films – often partly improvised, and notable for their unglamorous settings – now seemed to thrive on conflict. *Police*, which ambitiously attempted to deal with a cop's obsessive love for an attractive young criminal within the format of the modern thriller, was an indulgent, controversial portrait of an utterly sexist and racist hero; while *Under Satan's Sun* >**4** focussed its attention on spiritual self-loathing, presenting in austere images a world of poverty, random evil and blind faith. In this milieu a priest, believing that life is ruled by the Devil rather than God, comes to chastise himself with such vehement passion that he is seen as a divinely inspired saint with miraculous powers. Again, despite the film's interior, religious subject matter, Pialat's style is ruthlessly realist, thus allowing for genuine ambiguities.

While the director's talent for portraying psychological reality through detailed observation of the material world is undeniable, there are, in his recent films, elements of misanthropy that smack of a coolly superior, even contemptuous intelligence. His finest early work, however, is distinguished by a restrained tenderness.

Lineage

Pialat's realism has led to (often inappropriate) comparison with **Loach**, Ermanno Olmi, **Forman** and **Truffaut**'s *400 Blows*. Morally, he may perhaps be compared with figures like **Clouzot** and **Franju**.

Viewing

1 **Passe Ton Bac D'Abord**
France 1976/ w Sabine Haudepin, Philippe Marlaud, Bernard Tronczyk

2 **Loulou**
France 1980/ w Gérard Depardieu, Isabelle Huppert, Guy Marchand

3 **A Nos Amours (To Our Loves)**
France 1984/ w Sandrine Bonnaire, Pialat, Dominique Besnehard

4 **Under Satan's Sun**
France 1987/ w Gérard Depardieu, Sandrine Bonnaire, Pialat

Roman Polanski

Born: 18th August 1933/Paris, France
Directing career: 1955-

It is arguable that the violence, evil and sense of dislocation prevalent in the films of Roman Polanski is directly derived from the dramatic, even horrendous details of his life. Nevertheless, such is his talent that his work transcends mere autobiographical considerations, standing in its own right as a pessimistic but compelling vision of contemporary existence.

Polanski's parents returned to Poland two years before World War II broke out; both were later taken to concentration camps (his mother dying at Auschwitz), while the boy's strategy for survival in the ghetto included frequent visits to cinemas. In the '50s he took up acting, appearing in **Wajda**'s *A Generation* amongst other films, before studying at the Lodz Film School. His early work – shorts such as *Two Men and a Wardrobe*, *The Fat and the Lean*, and *Mammals* – displayed a taste for absurdist black humour and a fascination with bizarre relationships involving dominance and submission. In his feature debut, *Knife in the Water* >**1**, strange power games were again to the fore, with ridiculous macho rivalries arising when a young man hitches a lift with a sportswriter and his wife. Though the plot itself is slim, the film is distinguished by Polanski's precise visuals, which point the shifts in allegiance between the three characters through subtle groupings; impressively, although almost the whole film is situated on a small yacht, the effect is always cinematic rather than theatrical. Indeed, locations are of prime importance in Polanski's finest work: made in Britain, his next two features, *Repulsion* >**2** and *Cul-de-Sac*, respectively took place largely within a London bedsit and in a crumbling castle on Holy Island. The first, about the murderous mental breakdown of a sexually disturbed Belgian girl left alone when her sister leaves to go on holiday, is remarkable for the way Polanski uses objects and shapes (decaying food, cracks in walls) to convey the state of his heroine's disintegrating mind; the second, about a hoodlum invading the privacy of a rich, highly eccentric couple, impresses with its darkly comic account of power games and communication breakdown.

After the elegant but often predictable horror-spoof, *Dance of the Vampires*, Polanski went to Hollywood to make *Rosemary's Baby* >**3**, a chilling supernatural thriller (from a novel by Ira Levin) in which a mother-to-be comes to fear that she is pregnant with Satan's child. As before, location (a rambling old New York apartment), psychological angst and a protagonist isolated from a treacherous outside world are central, although Polanski's hitherto almost abstract visuals are here replaced by images of a more classical nature. Precision was still his trademark, however, and the move to more commercial film-making had entailed no artistic compromises. Thus, even when he made a version of *Macbeth* (whose explicit violence was thought by many to be inspired by the appalling murder of the director's wife Sharon Tate by the Manson 'family'), it was as much a Polanski film as an intelligent, faithful Shakespeare adaptation.

Made in Italy, *What?* was a dismal, disappointing sex-comedy, offering only a playfully illogical narrative; far better was *Chinatown* >**4**, in which the director effortlessly revealed that he could cope both with a complex, labyrinthine thriller script (set in '30s LA, and concerning murder, incest and political corruption), and with the detailed, credible re-creation of a vanished world: again, an acute awareness of the human capacity for evil combined with black comedy to mesmerising effect. *The Tenant*, in which the director played a foreigner in Paris whose sanity cracks when he rents an apartment previously inhabited by a suicide, seemed less restrained than *Repulsion*, making overblown use of surreal visual effects. However, *Tess* >**5** – made in France, whither the director fled after being convicted in America of having sex with a 13-year-old girl – was a surprisingly effective adaptation of Hardy's classic novel, benefitting from strong performances and an admirable use of landscape to mirror its doomed heroine's mood and predicament.

By now resident in France, Polanski stretched his talents to include occasional work in the theatre; sadly, his next film, the spoof swashbuckler *Pirates*, was woefully unamusing. *Frantic*, though, showed a partial return to form, its thriller plot allowing for a homage to Hitchcock, and once again sprinkled

with moments of dark wit as it followed an American around Paris, confounded, isolated and menaced by the sudden, mysterious disappearance of his wife.

While Polanski seems unable to manage outright comedy, his best work treats events and relationships of an often nightmarish nature with sharp irony and an engaging sense of the absurd. Even though he adapts his style to the material at hand, his camera is consistent in framing people and places with economic precision.

Lineage

Though Polanski's first experiences in film were with **Wajda** and Andrzej Munk, he is closer in tone to **Skolimowski**, who worked on the script of *Knife in the Water*. Playwrights Beckett and Ionesco may also be seen as influences; his versatility and idiosyncratic vision are such that his own influence on Western directors may be minimal.

Further reading

Ivan Butler's *The Cinema of Roman Polanski* (London, 1970). *Roman* (London, 1984) is an autobiography.

Jack Nicholson, John Huston, and Roman Polanski – actor-directors all – on the set of *Chinatown.*

Viewing

1 **Knife in the Water**
Poland 1962/ w Leon Niemczyk, Jolanta Umecka, Zygmunt Malanowicz

2 **Repulsion**
GB 1965/ w Cathérine Deneuve, Yvonne Furneaux, John Fraser

3 **Rosemary's Baby**
US 1968/ w Mia Farrow, John Cassavetes, Ruth Gordon

4 **Chinatown**
US 1974/ w Jack Nicholson, Faye Dunaway, John Huston

5 **Tess**
France 1979/ w Nastassia Kinski, Peter Firth, Leigh Lawson

Abraham Polonsky

Born: 5th December 1910/New York, USA
Directing career: 1948-1971

Abraham Lincoln Polonsky warrants attention as probably the most extreme example of a talented film-maker whose career was ruined by the pernicious McCarthyite blacklist that followed the anti-Communist witch hunts of the early '50s. Indeed, he spent most of his working life in enforced obscurity, anonymously writing film and television scripts.

After a variety of jobs, Polonsky – who had already written for radio, not to mention several novels – was hired by Paramount as a screenwriter. His work for **Leisen**'s *Golden Earrings* was re-written to the point of extinction, but *Body and Soul*, directed by **Robert Rossen**, was an unusually cynical boxing saga, in which the slum-boy hero's dreams of success lead him not only to reject the clean-living ways of his family, friends and lover, but to throw fights in return for fame and fortune. An even more acerbic view of integrity destroyed by the lure of the dollar was evident in Polonsky's directing debut, *Force of Evil* >**1**. A taut *film noir*, shot partly on location in New York, it is about a lawyer working for a numbers racket who justifies his criminal activities by reference to filthy lucre – until his small-time bookie brother, resolutely independent of the Mob is murdered by hoodlums. Though a revenge thriller, the emphasis on greed and corruption suggests Polonsky also intended to attack the internecine, self-seeking ambitions fostered by the capitalist optimism of the American Dream.

After writing *I Can Get It For You Wholesale*, in which the American obsession with money served as the basis for a satire on garment industry intrigues, Polonsky was called before the HUAC, and took the Fifth Amendment, thus effectively sacrificing a career as a visible writer-director. Indeed, until 1968, when he was at last credited with writing **Siegel**'s impressively ambiguous police thriller *Madigan*, he was in constant remunerative work; his name, however, never appeared on the credits, so long was the shadow of the blacklist. Finally, 21 years after *Force of Evil*, he directed a second film, *Tell Them Willie Boy Is Here*, a liberal but bitter Western about an Indian (read: Polonsky) mercilessly hunted by a WASP sheriff, symbol of an unforgiving and callous white society. Sadly, the film was predictable, its shaky narrative and visuals providing evidence of its maker's long absence from behind the camera. The following year he made *Romance of a Horse Thief*, set in 1904 near the Polish border; reputedly undistinguished, it has hardly ever been seen.

Polonsky will almost certainly never direct again, although there are hopes that **Bertrand Tavernier** (an expert on the McCarthy years) will direct a script Polonsky has himself adapted from his semi-autobiographical novel, *Season of Fear*, dealing with a director called to testify before the HUAC. Both his desire to provide a caustic alternative to conventional Hollywood homilies, and his fine ear for stylised but colloquial dialogue are evident in *Body and Soul* and *Force of Evil*, suggesting that he might have become a major film-maker had not McCarthy's acolytes interfered.

Lineage

One can compare Polonsky's use of genre to address social issues with that of **Losey**, **Rossen**, **Fuller**, **Dassin**, early **Kazan**, **Dmytryk** and Richard Brooks.

Viewing

1 **Force of Evil**
US 1948/ w John Garfield, Thomas Gomez, Beatrice Pearson

Michael Powell

Born: 30th September 1905/ Bekesbourne, Kent, England
Directing career: 1931-

Together with Hungarian-born writer Emeric Pressburger, Michael Powell formed one of the most inventive and ambitious film-making partnerships in the history of cinema. Though much of their work incidentally concerns what it means to be British, this is incidental to his flamboyance, mysticism, passion, and disdain for realism, non-existent

The machine that kills: Carl Boehm watches as the police examine his lethal camera in Powell's study in sadistic voyeurism, *Peeping Tom.*

in the films of Powell's contemporary compatriots.

Powell's first experience of film-making was as an actor and assistant to Rex Ingram on *The Magician* and *The Garden of Allah*, both made in the South of France. Returning to London, he worked in various capacities at Elstree before directing his first film, *Two Crowded Hours*, in 1931; it was the first of many lowly 'quota quickies' – often comedy thrillers – on which he would expend his unpretentious skills during the early and mid-'30s. Only with *The Edge of The World* >**1**, a factually-based drama made in 1937 about the evacuation of a remote barren island in the Shetlands, did he finally reveal his distinctly romantic, almost supernatural, feel for landscape; the film led to a contract with producer Alexander Korda and a crucial meeting with Pressburger, with whom he wrote the script of the thriller *The Spy in Black*. The film was notable both for its atmospheric Expressionist images and for an unusually sympathetic treatment of the German villain. Even more indicative of Powell's increased confidence was his contribution to *The Thief of Bagdad*, in which he indulged his penchant for exoticism and the rich hues of Technicolor to create a witty, magical, full-blown fantasy.

After sealing their partnership with a further war thriller (*Contrabande*), Powell and Pressburger embarked upon a propaganda film for the Ministry of Information: the result, *49th Parallel*, called for an end to American isolationism with an intelligently dramatised story of German U-Boat sailors stranded in Canada and meeting with various vividly drawn representatives of democracy. *One of Our Aircraft is Missing* reversed the situation, detailing the plight of British pilots in Nazi-occupied Holland, but it was *The Life and Death of Colonel Blimp* >**2** which served as P and P's most complex and moving meditation on the ethics of war. A warm portrait of a British army officer whose career, from the Boer War to World War II, comes to mirror the sad but inevitable changes in military ideals (from gamesmanship to beneath-the-belt ruthlessness), the film is a deeply personal tribute to England, to friendship (between Blimp and yet another 'good' German), and to the endurance of love (three women who inspire Blimp's youth, middle- and old-age all played by Deborah Kerr). Even more lyrical in its response to issues of propaganda was *A Canterbury Tale* >**3**, which merged a bizarre thriller plot (a man pours glue into the hair of local girls who date US soldiers) with a contemporary version of Chaucer's pilgrimage; while *I Know Where I'm Going* portrayed a love affair inspired by the supernatural forces of sea and land.

By now at the peak of their powers, P and P embarked on some of their most inventive, ambitiously anti-realist works. In *A Matter of Life and Death* >**4** a crashed pilot's fight against brain-damage is presented as a logical but extravagantly fantastic courtroom drama, with Heaven and its inhabitants (shot in black and white) arguing for his death against the airman's friends and lover on earth (in sumptuous Technicolor); in-jokes, literary references, propaganda and impassioned romance are mixed to moving and often astonishingly original effect. Equally memorably, *Black Narcissus* >**5**, concerning the emotional, sexual and cultural frustrations of English nuns high in the Himalayas, recreated India in the studio to paint, with Expressionist colours and compositions, an exotic, erotic landscape of the mind. And *The Red Shoes* >**6**, arguably the finest dance film ever, was not only a superb example of Powell's desire to create new forms of drama through music, dance, colour, acting and camera technique, but an inspired combination of fairy tale, fact (the plot was loosely based on Diaghilev and Nijinsky) and feminism (the ballerina's career, desires and life are destroyed by the manipulations of a jealous husband and a demonic mentor).

Never again would P and P's collaborations be as fruitful, even though *The Small Back Room*, an intelligent study of an alcoholic bomb-disposal expert's self-loathing, was scattered with moments of eccentric Expressionism (a giant whisky bottle included), and *The Tales of Hoffman* and *Oh Rosalinda!* attempted, not altogether successfully, to repeat the visually lavish experiments with non-filmic art-forms of *The Red Shoes*. *Gone to Earth* was intelligent, if occasionally overblown, 19th-century melodrama, distinguished by its fine landscape photography and complex animal symbolism, but *The Battle of the River Plate* was a relatively routine wartime naval drama, marking the end of Powell's partnership with Pressburger.

The Hungarian would never equal the brilliance he had achieved in The Archers (the company they had formed together in 1942), while Powell's films would become noticeably more uneven. Nevertheless, in 1960, he made one last masterpiece, *Peeping Tom* >**7**, a dark but sensitive study of a cameraman-killer, who films the faces of his victims as he stabs them with a blade hidden in his tripod. A wry acknowledgement of the sadistic impulses of voyeurism (especially the making and watching of movies), Powell's film gains in power by making the murderer the shy, gentle victim of his own father's interest in the psychology of fear, traumatised by a past seen in morbid home-movies, in which Powell himself plays the father and his own son the infant killer-to-be. Both profoundly disturbing and intellectually brilliant, the film was badly misunderstood at the time; blinkered, puritanical critics ruined Powell's career.

Forced to alternate comparatively minor work with television chores, Powell went to Australia in 1966, where he made *They're a Weird Mob*, a zesty comedy of manners about an Italian immigrant's confusion in a strange land, and *Age of Consent*, a perceptive but unfocussed account of a painter revitalised by his obsession with a young model. Subsequently, he reunited with Pressburger on the charming children's fantasy *The Boy Who Turned Yellow*, since when (despite plans for a version of *The Tempest* and the encouragement of younger directors like **Scorsese**) he has failed to find finance to complete another film. He has not, however, given up hope.

Powell's originality lies in his refusal to surrender to the limitations of genre: while highly personal both in style (lavish visuals) and theme (the demonic nature of creativity; irrational, elemental powers; England), his work resists categorisation. Few British directors have been so ready to portray emotions and the effect of their repression; fewer still do so with such a sense of cinema's ability to liberate and inspire the imagination.

Lineage

Powell was clearly influenced by Ingram and German Expressionism, while Pressburger started out writing for **Ophüls** and **Siodmak**. One can make hesitant comparisons with **Mamoulian**, Ophüls, even late **Renoir**; among modern directors, **Scorsese** is a fervent admirer.

Further reading

Ian Christie's *Arrows of Desire* (London, 1985); Powell's *A Life in Movies* (London, 1986) is a first autobiography.

Viewing

1 **The Edge of the World**
GB 1937/ w Niall McGinnis, John Laurie, Finlay Currie
2 **The Life and Death of Colonel Blimp**
GB 1943/ w Roger Livesey, Anton Walbrook, Deborah Kerr
3 **A Canterbury Tale**
GB 1944/ w Eric Portman, Sheila Sim, Dennis Price
4 **A Matter of Life and Death (Stairway to Heaven)**
GB 1946/ w David Niven, Kim Hunter, Roger Livesey
5 **Black Narcissus**
GB 1947/ w Deborah Kerr, Kathleen Byron, David Farrar, Sabu
6 **The Red Shoes**
GB 1948/ w Moira Shearer, Anton Walbrook, Marius Goring
7 **Peeping Tom**
GB 1960/ w Carl Boehm, Anna Massey, Maxine Audley, Esmond Knight

Otto Preminger

Born: 5th December 1906/Vienna, Austria
Died: 23rd April 1986/New York, USA
Directing career: 1931-1980

Though the films of Otto Preminger are both varied and variable, they share for the most part a detached objectivity in their attitudes to character and moral issues. Even in several films deemed controversial at the time of release, the director's matter-of-fact, observational tone deflated tendencies towards melodrama.

A lawyer's son, Preminger studied acting under Max Reinhardt before becoming a successful director in the Austrian theatre. He also made one film, *Die Grosse Liebe*, in his home country, but it was only after moving to America in 1935 that his film career got firmly under way. A handful of films made at Fox in the late '30s – negligible B-comedies and musicals – did little to enhance his reputation, but in 1944 he took over *Laura* >**1** from **Mamoulian**, and enjoyed his first major hit. A murder mystery, in which the detective falls for a portrait of the presumed victim, only to have her suddenly turn up alive and well, the film is a subtle study of vividly drawn characters, seen from a variety of shifting perspectives: Laura herself exists primarily in the minds of both the investigator and the witnesses he interrogates. Equally, the finest of Preminger's subsequent thrillers for Fox (*Fallen Angel*, *Whirlpool*, *Where the Sidewalk Ends*) were concerned with obsession and neurosis, culminating in the RKO-made *Angel Face* >**2**, in which a girl's innocent demeanour conceals a murderous Elektra complex that results in the death of her parents, her lover and herself.

In 1953, Preminger turned to independent production with *The Moon Is Blue*, a lame romantic comedy, imported from Broadway, that stirred up controversy with its use of then-censorable words like virgin and pregnant. After an amiable Western (*River of No Return*), Preminger's taste for provocative material manifested itself in the black musicals *Carmen Jones* and *Porgy and Bess*; *The Man with the Golden Arm* (in which a drummer struggles with drug addiction); and *The Court Martial of Billy Mitchell* (about military incompetence). Equally ambitious but less satisfactorily realised were his adaptations of Shaw's *Saint Joan* and Sagan's *Bonjour Tristesse* (another study in a teenage girl's destructive dislike for her widowed father's lover), both starring the director's gamine *protégé* Jean Seberg. Preminger's cool style, however, was seen at its best in *Anatomy of a Murder* >**3**, a superbly detailed, suspenseful courtroom drama in which smalltown lawyer

Dana Andrews, Clifton Webb, and Gene Tierney in Preminger's cool and witty *film noir, Laura.*

James Stewart defends a soldier charged with murdering a man who, he alleges, raped his wife. Preminger's penchant for long takes and a mobile camera (rather than cuts and conversational reaction shots) here served both to illuminate the crucial ambiguities in the characters, and to facilitate an objective appraisal of the mechanics of the legal process. It was the first and finest of four epic investigations of serious socio-political issues: *Exodus*, recounting the struggle to establish Palestine as a home for the Jews, focussed on nationalism; *Advise and Consent* >**4**, about the intrigues and smear-campaigns aroused by the need for a new Secretary of State, examined the elective processes of democracy; *The Cardinal* dealt with the possibilities of religious faith in a world beset by Nazis, the Ku Klux Klan, death and intolerance. Sombre, balanced, intelligent, the films occasionally reveal a cautiously middle-brow mentality; nevertheless, they possess a clarity sadly lacking in most of Preminger's work after the lengthy but largely routine war-drama *In Harm's Way*. *Bunny Lake Is Missing* was a none too credible kidnapping mystery; *Hurry Sundown* an overheated Deep South drama about racism; *Skidoo* a dim hippy satire; *Tell Me That You Love Me Junie Moon* a winsome account of three emotionally and physically scarred misfits; *Such Good Friends* a blackish comedy about illness and adultery; *Rosebud* a risibly inept spy thriller; *The Human Factor* >**5** an uneven but sometimes oddly moving version of Graham Greene's novel about a British intelligence agent whose treasonable activities result in his defection to Russia.

In the last years of his career, Preminger often indulged in modish attitudes and strident outbursts of stylised fantasy; even though the former might also be said of his controversial earlier work, for the most part contrived hysteria was held at bay by the cool restraint and visual balance he brought to the screen.

Lineage

While Preminger crossed paths with **Lubitsch** (two of whose films he took over), **Mamoulian** and **Wilder** (in whose *Stalag 17* he acts), the trajectory of his eclectic career and the occasional flatness of his style may suggest a more fruitful comparison with **Huston**. His detached objectivity finds a parallel in **Buñuel**; his sense of everyone having their reasons is not unlike **Renoir**'s.

Further reading

Gerard Pratley's *The Cinema of Otto Preminger* (London, 1971). *Preminger* (New York, 1977) is an autobiography.

Viewing

1 **Laura**
US 1944/ w Dana Andrews, Gene Tierney, Clifton Webb
2 **Angel Face**
US 1952/ w Jean Simmons, Robert Mitchum, Herbert Marshall
3 **Anatomy of a Murder**
US 1959/ w James Stewart, Lee Remick, Ben Gazzara, George C. Scott
4 **Advise and Consent**
US 1962/ w Henry Fonda, Charles Laughton, Don Murray, Lew Ayres
5 **The Human Factor**
GB 1979/ w Nicol Williamson, Iman, Richard Attenborough

Bob Rafelson

Born: 1935/New York, USA
Directing career: 1968-

One of the most eloquent cinematic talents to treat the themes of disillusionment and alienation so fashionable in the early '70s, Bob Rafelson has recently fallen back on hollow, arty variations on traditional thriller motifs. His early work, however, is noted for its laconic humour and its oblique approach to narrative.

Rafelson spent much of his youth travelling in America and Europe before embarking on a philosophy degree. Dropping out, he gained work as a writer in television, where he became famous as the creator (along with producer Bert Schneider) of The Monkees pop group. After co-producing and writing the hugely successful series starring the band, he made his film debut directing them in *Head*, a typically psychedelic and wacky blend of music, comedy and archive footage, perhaps most memorable for its gentle parody of genres like the musical and the war movie. The film was the first project of BBS Productions, formed by Rafelson with Schneider and Steve Blauner, which went on to produce *Easy Rider*, *The Last Picture Show* and Jack Nicholson's *Drive He Said*, not to mention Rafelson's first major feature *Five Easy Pieces* >**1**. About a young loner torn between the crippling cultural aspirations of his bourgeois family and a more anarchic working-class life with his none-too-bright waitress girlfriend, the film was a wry look at failure, self-pity and futile rebellion, its sparse and moody images enriched by a gallery of superbly natural performances. As a portrait, moreover, of class differences in an America hitherto rarely seen in the cinema, it remains unrivalled in its subtlety.

Still more offbeat was *The King of Marvin Gardens* >**2**, again using family tension to evoke the sadness and banality underlying the American Dream: in a windswept Atlantic City, two brothers – one a depressive late-night radio DJ, the other a petty criminal out on bail – join together in an absurd scheme to get rich quick from a Hawaiian gambling concession. Their plans end in domestic murder, but Rafelson offsets tragedy with scenes of dark, laconic wit; the result is admittedly uneven but tantalisingly believable. *Stay Hungry* >**3** was yet another portrait of disenchantment, though the plot was more accessible. Here, the young black sheep of a rich Alabama family turns against the crooked property developers, for whom he works, to save a local gym which has revitalised his interest in life. Less melancholy than earlier Rafelson films, it left room for inconsequential but uplifting scenes (a country dance, a Mr Universe contest that suddenly erupts on to a city's streets) that constitute an offbeat, affirmative celebration of community.

In 1981, after being sacked from the prison-movie *Brubaker*, Rafelson collaborated with playwright David

Mamet on a remake of James M. Cain's classic thriller *The Postman Always Rings Twice*; while the film was able to restore the explicit, sordid sexuality absent in earlier versions, and effectively demonstrated the desperate emotions of a couple led by adulterous passion to commit murder, its sombre tone left it fatally stranded between conventional thriller and art-movie. Equally, the role-reversals at the heart of *Black Widow* (in which a federal agent becomes obsessed with the power and independence of the psychopathic husband-murderer she tracks down) were insufficiently complex to suggest anything more than a pleasingly tortuous homage to '40s style *noir* melodrama.

Rafelson is at his best portraying disenchanted losers and loners in stories that are less a matter of suspense than of digression. Character study, the creation of mood, and an ability to evoke emotions through intimate observation are his strengths; his quirky talent would seem uncomfortably constricted by genre.

Lineage

BBS's brief success linked Rafelson's career with Jack Nicholson, **Hopper**, **Bogdanovich** and Henry Jaglom; he may be compared, for different reasons, to such diverse figures as **Antonioni**, **Bergman**, **Penn**, **Altman** and Monte Hellman.

Viewing

1 **Five Easy Pieces**
US 1970/ w Jack Nicholson, Karen Black, Susan Anspach

2 **The King of Marvin Gardens**
US 1972/ w Jack Nicholson, Bruce Dern, Ellen Burstyn

3 **Stay Hungry**
US 1977/ w Jeff Bridges, Sally Field, Arnold Schwarzenegger

Nicholas Ray

Born: 7th August 1911/La Crosse, Wisconsin, USA
Died: 16th June 1979/New York, USA
Directing career: 1948-1979

One of the finest directors of the '50s, originally christened Raymond Nicholas Kienzle, Nicholas Ray transcended the limitations of genre to create movies of a highly personal nature. Imbued with an intense, romantic pessimism and photographed with a rare feel for the emotional resonance of colour and space, Ray's films are distinguished by a passionate identification with society's outsiders, his sympathies possibly arising from his own troubled relationship with the film-making establishment.

Before entering movies as **Kazan**'s assistant on *A Tree Grows in Brooklyn*, Ray studied architecture under Frank Lloyd Wright and worked extensively in theatre and radio. In 1948, for producer John Houseman, he made his directing debut with *They Live By Night* >**1**, a rural gangster thriller notable for the tenderness displayed towards its young, innocent and doomed fugitive lovers, and for the assurance of Ray's visuals, announced in the opening credits sequence by a dramatic helicopter shot of a speeding car driven by escaped convicts. Rather less successful, although made with evident skill, were the melodrama *A Woman's Secret*, the first of several studio chores (*Born to Be Bad*, *Flying Leathernecks*) made for RKO, and *Knock on Any Door*, a sturdy, if predictable, liberal account of juvenile delinquency. At the same time, however, Ray's special talent for undermining genre conventions could be seen in *In a Lonely Place* >**2** (a cynical Hollywood screenwriter's violent temper leads to his being suspected of murder and to the eventual destruction of a fragile love affair), *On Dangerous Ground* (about a psychotically brutal city cop exiled upstate, where nature and a blind woman's love bring about his spiritual regeneration), and *The Lusty Men* >**3** (a melancholy rodeo epic that explores the folly of masculine pride and obstinacy). In all three, Ray's ability to create emotional intensity through characters both vulnerable and violent, and through vividly shot landscapes and interiors, serves to portray a world of lonely alienated dreamers unable

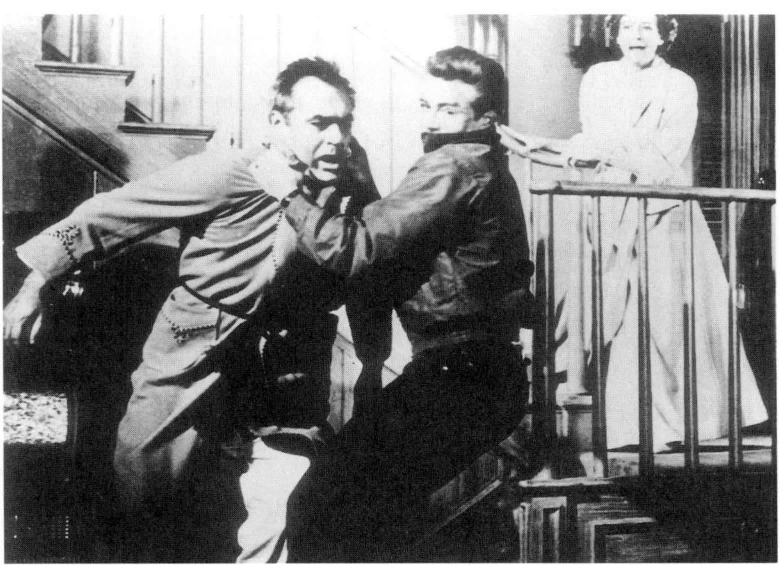

Family life: Jim Backus, James Dean and Ann Doran in Nicholas Ray's seminal teenage-angst drama, *Rebel Without a Cause.*

to conform to the destructively competitive ethos of the American Dream.

A bizarre, baroque and allegorical Western in which two gun-toting women battle to the death over men and land, *Johnny Guitar* >**4** was also Ray's first film in colour, which he used to poetic, symbolic effect to heighten the drama and lend his characters an almost mythic dimension. Two further Westerns (*Run for Cover*, *The True Story of Jesse James*) portrayed the outlaw-hero as an idealist embittered by society's injustices, but it was *Rebel Without a Cause* >**5** that spoke for the massive disillusionment of an entire generation. In James Dean, playing the middle-class adolescent torn apart by his presumed duties to family, friends, and the adult world at large, Ray found the perfect embodiment of neurotic, confused youth; but it was the director's expert, virtually Expressionist handling of composition, colour and camera movement that lent the film its raw, burning power. Indeed, no other director made so much of the wide expanses of the 'Scope frame: tense emotions erupting in violent diagonal lines (staircases, especially, signify moments of crisis and transition), character conflict conveyed by clashing colours. *Bigger Than Life* >**6**, made after the boldly flamboyant gypsy saga *Hot Blood*, may thus be seen as Ray's masterpiece, its vivid reds, looming shadows and immaculate sense of decor exactly evoking the nightmarish, cortisone-induced transformation of a quiet suburban teacher into a murderous megalomaniac who comes to believe that, in preventing Abraham from killing Isaac, 'God was wrong!' Rarely have the frustrations, conformities and petty ambitions of American family life been subject to such a devastating critique.

In the late '50s, Ray's dissatisfaction with the conventions of genre became increasingly apparent: *Bitter Victory* ignores the usual war heroics to focus on the acid rivalry between a cowardly commanding officer and an idealistic captain, whose sense of war's absurdity leads to futile death; *Wind Across the Everglades* >**7**, set in turn-of-the-century Miami and charting a game-warden's battle against bird-killing poachers, merges Western-style stand-offs with ecological and ethnological themes to paint a picture, poetic but brutal, of mortals proudly firing guns at the face of God; and the lavish gangster thriller, *Party Girl* >**8**, repeatedly threatens to turn into a stylised musical, while using a story of gangland violence as a backdrop to the romance of two emotionally crippled, self-loathing social outcasts. Still more ambitious was *Savage Innocents*, in which an Eskimo's battles to survive against nature come to a tragic end when he takes on the additional force of Civilisation, embodied by Christianity, capitalism and rock'n' roll. A troubled international co-production, the film is largely intelligent, often visually stunning, but uneven – qualities also to be found in *King of Kings* >**9**, the first of two epics Ray made for Samuel Bronston, which elevates Barrabas in the tale of Christ in order to explore the twin forces of Judaean revolt (both pacifist and violent) against Roman oppression. Finally, *55 Days at Peking* blended a spectacular re-creation of the Boxer rebellion with more intimate scenes questioning the worth of heroism and pride; alas, Ray, often ill, and disheartened by the film industry in general, walked off the film, never to work in commercial cinema again.

His career was not altogether over, however; as a teacher of film, he made with his students *We Can't Go Home Again*, an avant-garde split-screen mosaic of images evoking the political, sexual and spiritual unrest of America in the early '70s. More agonising still, he collaborated with **Wenders** on the documentary *Lightning Over Water (Nick's Movie)* in which his last, brave but frequently confused efforts to remain creative despite the ravages of cancer are evident with an honesty verging on the morbidly voyeuristic.

Ray's work was largely devoted to exploring cinematic means of expressing the inner torment of lonely individuals hoping for a way to integrate themselves within a society that cares little for the weak and different; the result was frequently remarkably moving in its empathetic depiction of conflict, pain and despair. Ray's importance lies in his innate grasp of film: his talent was visual rather than literary, and colour, composition, gesture and movement repeatedly combine to reveal thoughts and emotions.

Lineage

Of the same socially-conscious generation of directors as **Fuller**, **Losey**, **Kazan**, **Polonsky** and **Aldrich**, Ray became the hero of French New Wave directors, especially **Godard**. His influence can be seen in the work of **Hopper** (who appeared in *Rebel Without a Cause*) and **Wenders** (Ray had a cameo role in *The American Friend*). **Jarmusch** studied under and assisted Ray at New York University.

Further reading

John Kriedl's *Nicholas Ray* (Boston, 1977).

Viewing

1 **They Live By Night**
US 1948/ w Farley Granger, Cathy O'Donnell, Howard Da Silva

2 **In a Lonely Place**
US 1950/ w Humphrey Bogart, Gloria Grahame, Frank Lovejoy

3 **The Lusty Men**
US 1952/ w Robert Mitchum, Susan Hayward, Arthur Kennedy

4 **Johnny Guitar**
US 1953/ w Joan Crawford, Mercedes McCambridge, Sterling Hayden

5 **Rebel Without a Cause**
US 1955/ w James Dean, Natalie Wood, Sal Mineo

6 **Bigger Than Life**
US 1956/ w James Mason, Barbara Rush, Walter Matthau

7 **Wind Across the Everglades**
US 1958/ w Christopher Plummer, Burl Ives, Gypsy Rose Lee

8 **Party Girl**
US 1958/ w Robert Taylor, Cyd Charisse, Lee J. Cobb

9 **King of Kings**
Spain 1961/ w Jeffrey Hunter, Robert Ryan, Siobhan McKenna

Satyajit Ray

Born: 2nd May 1921/Calcutta, India
Directing career: 1951-

Almost single-handedly, Satyajit Ray brought Indian cinema to the attention of the West. In adopting a realist, even literary, style, far removed from the exotic musical fantasies that have been the staple diet of Indian audiences, he established himself both as Bengal's leading director and as an artist of great international stature, his ability to touch upon complex human emotions rivalled by few.

Born into an artistically distinguished Bengali family, Ray worked as a commercial illustrator after studies in economics and painting. At the same time, however, he developed a keen interest in film and, after a visit to London during which he went to the cinema frequently, he began shooting *Pather Panchali*, the first part of what would finally become *The Apu Trilogy* >**1**. The film, four years in the making, portrayed the harsh existence of a village family, its central figure a small boy. Basically realist in tone, with everyday events enacted on authentic locations by a largely non-professional cast, it transcended mere observation through a superb use of symbolic motifs (trains, water, eyes), composition, music and gesture. The result offered a richly moving and poetic account of a boy's progress through a childhood marked by poverty and family death. The subsequent parts of the trilogy (*Aparajito*, *The World of Apu*), taking the hero from adolescence to marriage, fatherhood and the death of his wife, were no less remarkable or touching.

Ray avoided, however, being typecast as a realist chronicler of peasant life with the fantasy-satire *The Philosopher's Stone*, and *The Music Room* >**2**, a vivid, immaculately detailed portrait of an ageing aristocrat who, as a defiant stand against his family's decline, re-opens a crumbling, once magnificent room for one last *soirée* of dance and song; again characters and environment supply a wealth of social resonance, but Ray's finest achievement lies in his reluctance to judge his protagonist, a doomed member of an oppressive elite. Likewise, after examining fanatical religious obsession in *Devi* (*The Goddess*), and showing his talent for

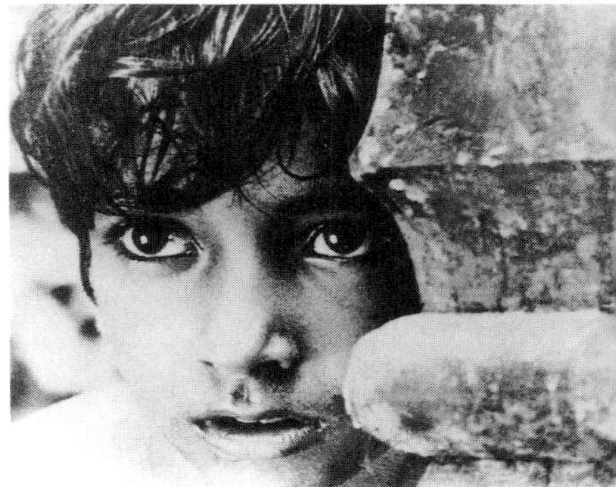

The infant Apu's eyes are opened to the ways of the adult world, in Satyajit Ray's acclaimed directing debut, *Pather Panchali*.

comedy and horror in *Three Daughters*, Ray revealed his balanced sympathy for no less than 10 characters in his first colour film, *Kanchenjunga* >**3** which, in mapping patterns of marital dissatisfaction affecting a family on vacation in the Himalayas, effortlessly observes the classical unities, using a single main location and depicting 100 real-time minutes in equal film-time.

Ray's finest films at this time were masterpieces of nuance, exploring individual emotions in order to suggest the wider dynamics of society. *Mahanagar* (*The Big City*), for example, uses a wife's experiences of finding and keeping a job to reflect on the oppressed position of women in contemporary India; *Charulata* >**4**, set in the late 1870s and about a woman's confusion when she falls in love with her neglectful husband's poet cousin, is similarly tender and sympathetic; and *Days and Nights in the Forest* >**5**, in which four young city businessmen are given an insight into their own complacency, snobbery and childishness by various women they meet on holiday, subtly comments on double standards, class differences and petty corruption. Although Ray's style was still grounded in realist, humanist observation, by now his films, laced with droll satire, were becoming rather tougher: his long takes and stately, elegant camera movements were now often broken by brief but expressive moments of dramatic, even violent action. Indeed, at the start of the '70s, Ray tried to deal more directly and explicitly with India's pressing socio-political problems. *The Adversary*, *Company Limited* and *The Middle Man* focussed on various forms of unrest arising from inequality, unemployment, capitalist greed and corruption; the shift in thematic perspective, appropriately, was accompanied by scenes of rapid montage that satirised the absurdity and harshness of modern life. Ray's most effective political film, however, was *Distant Thunder* >**6**, about a Brahmin family coming slowly but surely to feel the effects of the 1942 famine caused by India's involvement in World War II; the number of resulting deaths becomes apparent only in the final credits, but Ray's profoundly humane drama, revealing the way in which the caste system enlarges the tragedy, is darkly moving.

In recent years, the director has worked less fruitfully. His first Hindi film, *The Chess Players* rhymed two stories about the danger of becoming fatally obsessed (with either chess or art) to convey a simplistic symbolic parable on colonialism; while the made-for-TV *Sadgati* (*Deliverance*) was an altogether predictable and coarse, albeit deeply felt, critique of a society that allows humans to be designated as untouchables. Happily, *Home and the World* >**7**, adapted from a novel by Ray's long-term inspiration, Rabindranath Tagore, was a return to form, merging the personal and political as, in 1908 Bengal, a woman is seduced both by the passion and by the anti-British revolutionary sentiments of a friend of her husband; Ray's treatment of his characters was as balanced, lucid and warm as in his earlier work, the film's pace measured and graceful.

Since suffering a heart attack, Ray has virtually retired, returning only to directing with a studio-shot version of Ibsen's *Enemy of the People*. His reputation, however, rests firmly on his detached, unsentimental humanism, and on an ability to derive subtle emotional nuances and ironies from a simple but effective marshalling of performance, dialogue, decor and composition. He has been his own scriptwriter, designer, composer and cameraman on many of his films; he is a consummate artist whose faith in the cinema as a medium to rank alongside the other art forms remains undimmed.

Lineage

Ray may be compared with **Renoir** (whom he met during the filming of *The River*), **Rossellini**, even **Welles**, **Bergman** and **Visconti**; he himself claimed **De Sica**'s *Bicycle Thieves*, not to mention Tagore, as a major inspiration. His own influence on younger Indian film-makers such as Shyam Benegal and Mrinal Sen is inestimable.

Further reading

Robin Wood's *The Apu Trilogy* (London, 1972), John Russell Taylor's *Directors and Directions* (London, 1975), Marie Seton's *Portrait of a Director* (Bloomington, 1970).

Viewing

1 **The Apu Trilogy (Pather Panchali; Aparajito (The Unvanquished); The World of Apu)**
India 1955/6/9/ w Karuna Bannerjee, Kanu Bannerjee, Soumitra Chatterjee

2 **The Music Room (Jalsaghar)**
India 1958/ w Chabbi Biswas, Ganga Pada Basu, Kali Sarkar

3 **Kanchenjunga**
India 1962/ w Chabbi Biswas, Alakananda Ray, Anuba Gupta

4 **Charulata**
India 1964/ w Madhabi Mukkerjee, Soumitra Chatterjee, Sailen Mukherjee

5 **Days and Nights in the Forest**
India 1969/ w Soumitra Chatterjee, Sharmila Tagore, Samit Bhanja

6 **Distant Thunder**
India 1973/ w Soumitra Chatterjee, Babita, Sandhya Roy

7 **Home and the World**
India 1982/ w Soumitra Chatterjee, Swatilekha Chatterjee, Victor Bannerjee

Carol Reed

Born: 30th December 1906/London, England
Died: 1976/London, England
Directing career: 1933-1972

Once deemed a major British director, Sir Carol Reed was in fact a competent craftsman who hit his peak during a brief period at the end of the '40s with three consecutive literary adaptations. Even in his best work, however, his penchant for unusually angled shots and Expressionist lighting can seem studied and irrelevant.

After working as a stage actor and director (including a few years with mystery writer Edgar Wallace), Reed entered the movies as a dialogue director. In 1933 his directing debut, *Midshipman Easy*, began a series of modest, if technically solid, films that steadily established his reputation as a reliable director of actors. *Bank Holiday*, a well-intentioned but patronising view of the working-classes, now looks woefully dated, as does *The Stars Look Down*, a sympathetic account of the hardships suffered by a Welsh mining community; more rousing was *Night Train to Munich*, a wartime spy thriller, clearly intended by its writers, Frank Launder and Sidney Gilliat, to repeat their earlier success with **Hitchcock**'s *The Lady Vanishes*. But it was only after the war, during which Reed worked on propaganda films such as *The Way Ahead* and the documentary *The True Glory*, that the director finally found a suitable outlet for his rather uneasy blend of melancholy melodrama and dour realism.

The first film of his most fertile period was *Odd Man Out* >**1**, a dark, moody thriller in which a wounded IRA gunman hides out in a menacing Dublin, populated by vivid but stereotypical characters; unusually tough for its time, the film only flags towards its end which is both predictable and sentimental. Equally well acted and blessed with a more consistent tone, was *The Fallen Idol* >**2**, the first of his three collaborations with Graham Greene. A subtle account of an ambassador's small son's companionship with a butler, whose love for a young girl leads him to consider killing his wife, the film effectively evokes the deceitful manipulations of the adult world as seen through the innocent eyes of a child, and treads a careful path between ironic humour and more affecting pathos. It was a second Greene adaptation, however, that became Reed's best-loved film: *The Third Man* >**3**, a cynical thriller about the black market in penicillin set in a largely devastated postwar Vienna, benefitted enormously from the presence, as drug-trafficker Harry Lime, of **Orson Welles**, who himself invented the film's wittiest, most sinister speech, contrasting the artistic achievements of corrupt, wartorn Renaissance Italy with that of neutral, pacifist Switzerland, home of the cuckoo-clock. Indeed, though his role is small, Welles overshadows the entire film, with Reed indulging in a turgid array of tilted angles, reminiscent of Welles' own early work, but fatally lacking both real meaning and emotional power.

Reed had now become eminently respectable; in 1952, after a tepid but expertly acted version of Conrad's *Outcast of the Islands*, he was knighted. Despite, however, increasingly generous budgets (many of them Hollywood-financed), his career went into artistic decline: *The Man Between* unimaginatively reworked themes from *The Third Man*; *A Kid for Two Farthings* was sentimental whimsy set in London's East End; *Trapeze*, *The Agony and the Ecstasy* and *Oliver!* (a musical version of *Oliver Twist*) were glossy and vacuous. Only a last Greene adaptation, the spy-thriller, *Our Man In Havana*, was distinguished by true wit; even so, Reed's unnecessarily frequent dependence on tilted shots made for irritating viewing. Finally, after the forgettable *The Last Warrior* and *Follow Me*, he retired.

For the most part, Reed seems a shallow director, content to rely on strong performances and a sense of detail that suggests only a superficial interest in atmosphere. Even his best work has been somewhat overrated; its elaborate embellishment of genre academic and contrived; only *The Fallen Idol* shows emotional conviction.

Lineage

Though probably influenced by Hitchcock's English films, Reed is more closely aligned with the equally craftsmanlike **Lean**. One may say that figures like **Parker** and **Scott**, known for facile visuals, are his modern British equivalents.

Viewing

1 **Odd Man Out**
GB 1947/ w James Mason, Kathleen Ryan, Robert Newton
2 **The Fallen Idol**
GB 1948/ w Ralph Richardson, Michèle Morgan, Bobby Henrey
3 **The Third Man**
GB 1949/ w Joseph Cotten, Valli, Trevor Howard, Orson Welles

Rob Reiner

Born: 6th March 1945/New York, USA
Directing career: 1984-

Yet to establish a consistent style, Robert Reiner is nonetheless one of the most promising directors of film comedy to emerge from America in recent years. Son of comic actor-writer-director Carl Reiner, he first became known for his regular appearances in the TV series *All in the Family*, but it was his feature debut, *This is Spinal Tap* >**1**, that revealed a gifted new directing talent. A spoof 'rockumentary' following the less than illustrious American tour of a fictional (but entirely credible) British Heavy Metal band, the film is remarkable both for the precision of its parody of *cinéma-verité* documentary methods and for its affectionate but sharp satire on the excesses of the music business: the phoniness of promotional parties, the vulgar, sexist lyrics and pretentious posing of performance, the internecine intrigues between band and management, all observed in *bona fide* fly-on-the-wall style. Less original and amusing, but again notable for a skilful handling of actors, was *The Sure Thing*, a road-movie comedy admirably free of the gross, innuendo-laden pitfalls of most teen-dream romances.

Reiner's most affecting work to date, however, was *Stand By Me* >**2**, a gentle rites-of-passage comedy, based on a short story by Stephen King, in which four 12-year-old boys spend a long, hot summer weekend in 1959 searching for another boy's dead body. Wit remains the dominant force as the film follows their adventures – a meeting with a ferocious dog, deep discussions about why *Wagon Train* never gets anywhere, sinister animal noises in a forest at night – but Reiner subtly, unsentimentally transforms the odyssey into an elegy to youthful friendship, shaded by mortality (one of the four's own brother has recently died) and confusion about the sins of adult life (the victim of a teacher's deceit, another is wrongly considered a delinquent). Vividly characterised, poignant and nostalgic, foul-mouthed and funny, the film is a small gem. Disappointingly, however, *The Princess Bride*, an engagingly far-fetched but uneven fairy tale about pirates, monsters and wizards, was caught between knowing parody and straightforward children's fantasy.

Despite the modest nature of his films to date, Reiner has established himself both as an expert director of actors, and as a comic artist whose attitude towards his characters is warm but never patronising. His touch is unusually light and unassertive – qualities too often absent from contemporary mainstream comedy.

Lineage

Reiner's films are generally less brash than those of his father, long a collaborator of **Mel Brooks**. Indeed, it may be more relevant to compare his old-fashioned humanism with, say, **Ritchie** or **Demme**.

Viewing

1 **This is Spinal Tap**
US 1984/ w Christopher Guest, Michael McKean, Harry Shearer
2 **Stand By Me**
US 1986/ w Wil Wheaton, River Phoenix, Corey Feldman, Jerry O'Connell

Jean Renoir

Born: 15th September 1894/Paris, France
Died: 12th February 1979/Beverly Hills, California, USA
Directing career: 1925-1970

If only for the rich variety of his work Jean Renoir would remain one of the finest film-makers ever. His greatness, however, lies also in his willingness to experiment, in his effortless blending of realism and artifice, and in his profound, unsentimental view that everybody, good or bad, has his reasons. In Renoir's films, form and content combine to create a coherent but multi-faceted portrait of the chaos, absurdity and transience of human life.

The son of the Impressionist painter Auguste Renoir, Jean abandoned pottery for cinema in 1924, when he produced a film to star his wife Catherine Hessling, a former model for his father and actress in several of his own silent films. The same year he made his directing debut with *La Fille de l'Eau*, the lyrical riverbank photography of which looked forward to the almost pantheist sense of nature that would recur throughout his career. The variety of his silent films, in fact, anticipated aspects of his later work: brooding Zolaesque realism in *Nana*; surreal, whimsical fantasy in *Charleston*; dramatic poignancy in *The Little Match Girl*; historic pageant and an expert handling of a large cast in *The Tournament*. It was with the advent of sound, however, that he achieved a real maturity, synthesising these various elements into a cohesive and original whole. After adapting a Feydeau farce (*On Purge Bébé*) he made two superior thrillers, *La Chienne* and *La Nuit du Carrefour*, notable, respectively, for authentic location shooting and superb studio atmospherics. Then Renoir directed *Boudu Saved From Drowning* >**1**, the first of several masterpieces he made during the '30s.

A subversive comedy of manners about the anarchic power a tramp exerts over a bourgeois family that rescues him from the Seine, the film is notable for Renoir's unobtrusive, brilliant techniques, with deep focus and long takes effortlessly evoking the geography of the family's apartment. Remarkable, too, is his free-wheeling approach to narrative, allowing for numerous incidental, even documentary-like pleasures, and an open, unresolved ending in which Boudu, without explanation, suddenly returns to the freedom of the river – a persistent Renoir symbol for life, fertility and transience. Equally splendid were *Toni*, a location-shot thriller anticipating neo-realism, and *The Crime of Monsieur Lange* >**2**, an offbeat comic fantasy in which the murder of a greedy, lecherous publisher by his employees serves as a celebration of collective action in general and of the leftist Popular Front in particular. Indeed, many of Renoir's '30s films are concerned with social and political issues: *La Vie est à Nous* and *La Marseillaise* were made for the Communist Party and a trades union organisation, while in the lyrically beautiful, never completed *Partie de Campagne* >**3**, a romance is quashed by class differences. Despite Renoir's leftist leanings, however, he was too much the humanist to think in black and white terms: in *La Grande Illusion* >**4**, where the friendship that arises between prisoners-of-war and commanders transcends divisions wrought by class, creed and nationality, each character is seen as a living, feeling, thinking being; and in *La Bête Humaine*, Renoir examines each psychological corner of a murderous romantic triangle with an equal awareness of frailty and passion.

The finest of his films, however, was *La Règle du Jeu* >**5**, a supremely touching, complex farce charting the romantic intrigues of a decadent *haute bourgeoisie* weekending in a country château. In no other film did his flexible, semi-improvisational shooting methods attain such an immediate sense of time and space, lending the intricate plot and characters a documentary feel; and yet, at the same time, it is the director's first great meditation on how life may become a form of theatre, his own buffoon-like, genial, lovelorn Octave becoming an unwitting orchestrator of the frantic, chaotic party that ends in tragic death. Unbelievably, Renoir's blend of satire and nostalgia proved too heady for contemporary audiences, and was cut then banned. Next, war interrupted his filming, in Italy, of *Tosca*; he left the work to his assistant and departed for Hollywood.

While *Swamp Water* and *The Southerner* >**6** (the stark tale of a Texan farming family's efforts to work their own land in the face of poverty, jealous neighbours and a hostile nature) were basically realist works shot on location, for his other American films Renoir made use of studio resources to conjure up an artificial, fantastic world distilled from reality: *This Land Is Mine* (a moving tribute to the Resistance in Occupied France), *The Diary of a Chambermaid* (a bizarre black comedy at times reminiscent of *La Règle du Jeu*), and *Woman on the Beach* (a broodingly atmospheric *noir* melodrama) saw the director progressing towards a more abstractly formalised contemplation of human relationships. Made in India, *The River* >**7** went still further in this direction; though shot on location and featuring sequences more reminiscent of documentary than fiction, its story – of an English family's experiences of death, birth and the disillusionment of transition from adolescence to adulthood – was drained of dramatic climaxes; its supremely poetic serenity reflected on the theme of life as an endless stream, a fertile cycle of regeneration that transcends individual tragedy.

The luminous natural hues that distinguished *The River*, his first colour film, were replaced in *The Golden Coach* >**8**, *French Cancan* >**9**, and *Eléna et les Hommes* >**10** by a painterly palette, designed to blur the lines dividing life from theatre. In all three films (the first about a *commedia dell'arte* troupe in Peru, the second set in the 1890s Paris of his father, the third in the same city a decade earlier), the heroine must finally choose not only from various lovers, but between hopes and reality. Elegant, nostalgic, and wittily revelling in studio artifice, the loose romantic trilogy astonishes with its sense of life as theatre, of human action as performance, and of love itself as life's greatest drama.

Renoir's last films were no less restlessly experimental. In *The Testament of Dr Cordelier* and *Le Déjeuner sur l'Herbe*, multi-camera techniques adopted from television caught performances of a rare spontaneity, while *The Vanishing Corporal* reworked themes from *La Grande Illusion* to dark comic effect. Finally, *The Little Theatre of Jean Renoir* employed three episodes to reflect back on the preoccupations of his long career. He retired in 1970.

Renoir may be praised for his warm humanism; for his love of nature, the permanence and beauty of which stands in contrast to the comparatively petty, ephemeral passions of mankind; for his ability to see characters within a clearly defined sociopolitical milieu; for his free-wheeling, adventurous and ultimately realist attitude towards narrative. Finally however, his importance rests in the way these and other qualities interact with each other to create a wide range of films of unparalleled wit and immediacy.

Lineage

Himself an admirer of **Chaplin** and **Von Stroheim**, Renoir exerted an enormous influence on various directors, most notably **Becker**, **Rossellini**, **Visconti**, **Satyajit Ray**, **Truffaut** and **Godard**. One may perhaps compare him most closely with **Vigo**, **Buñuel** and **Ophüls**.

Further reading

Leo Braudy's *Jean Renoir: The World of His Films* (New York, 1972), Raymond Durgnat's *Jean Renoir* (London, 1975), André Bazin's *Jean Renoir* (Paris, 1973). *My Life and My Films* (London, 1974) is an autobiography.

Viewing

1 **Boudu Saved From Drowning**
France 1932/ w Michel Simon, Charles Granval, Marcelle Hainia

2 **The Crime of Monsieur Lange**
France 1936/ w René Lefèvre, Jules Berry, Florelle

3 **Partie de Campagne (A Day in the Country)**
France 1936/ w Sylvia Bataille, Georges Darnoux, Jacques Brunius

4 **La Grande Illusion**
France 1937/ w Jean Gabin, Pierre Fresnay, Erich Von Stroheim

5 **La Règle du Jeu (The Rules of the Game)**
France 1939/ w Nora Gregor, Marcel Dalio, Renoir, Gaston Modot

Jean Renoir and Julien Carette, shocked by how quickly tragedy can strike, at the end of Renoir's *La Regle du Jeu (The Rules of the Game).*

6 **The Southerner**
US 1945/ w Zachary Scott, Betty Field, J. Carroll Naish
7 **The River**
India 1950/ w Patricia Walters, Esmond Knight, Nora Swinburne
8 **The Golden Coach**
Italy 1953/ w Anna Magnani, Duncan Lamont, Paul Campbell
9 **French Cancan**
France 1955/ w Jean Gabin, Françoise Arnoul, Maria Félix
10 **Eléna et les Hommes (Paris Does Strange Things)**
France 1956/ w Ingrid Bergman, Jean Marais, Mel Ferrer

Alain Resnais

Born: 3rd June 1922/Vannes, Brittany, France
Directing career: 1946-

A leading figure in the development of a modernist cinema, Alain Resnais seems recently to have retreated further into an hermetic artiness that takes little account of the demands of the popular audience. In dealing repeatedly with the effect of memory and the imagination upon human passions, his intellectual, near-abstract approach to plot and character counteracts emotional involvement.

Having already made 8mm films as a child, Resnais graduated from film school and turned to 16mm amateur films, many of them documentary portraits of artists. His first professional work was in the same field, including documentaries on Van Gogh, Gauguin and Picasso's *Guernica*; more indicative of his later development, however, were *Night and Fog* (which counterpointed shots, past and present, of concentration camps, with a narration, warning against forgetfulness, by novelist Jean Cayrol), and *Toute la Mémoire du Monde*, which prowled Paris' Bibliothèque Nationale to present the massive archive as a repository for collective cultural memory.

But it was Resnais' first feature, *Hiroshima Mon Amour* >**1**, that established him as an original new talent. Though the film coincided with the early successes of the New Wave, it evidenced his allegiance to the more intellectual and avant-garde Left Bank artists, comprising Chris Marker, Agnès Varda, and the novelists Marguerite Duras, Alain Robbe-Grillet, and Cayrol who scripted his first three features. About the way memories of her wartime love for a German soldier are revived in a woman having an affair with a Japanese architect in postwar Hiroshima, the film introduced Resnais' abiding themes (the complex interaction between past, present and future; the reality of memory, dream and the imagination) and his elaborate style of editing – fragmenting 'story' into sequences of temporally disparate shots, linked by emotional import rather than linear narrative logic. *Last Year in Marienbad* >**2** took this anti-naturalistic style even further, its stately tracking shots around the maze of rooms, corridors and gardens of a château mirroring a labyrinthine mystery in which a man claims, perhaps untruthfully, that he had an affair the year before with a woman who denies all knowledge of their liaison. Time is jumbled, scenes are repeated, the acting is highly theatrical; relishing ambiguity to the end, the film remains too coldly cerebral to involve us fully in the attraction, doubts, passion and fears that cloud the minds of its characters.

Time and again, despite working with a variety of writers, Resnais returned to similar themes: in *Muriel* >**3**, a woman hopes an old love affair might be revived, only to be disillusioned by the falsifications of memory; in *La Guerre est Finie*, an exiled Spanish revolutionary is haunted by reminiscences and hopes that undermine his sense of identity; and in *Je t'Aime, Je t'Aime*, a time traveller is trapped in a troubled romance from his past.

At the end of the '60s, Resnais entered a fallow period in his career, which finally ended in 1974 with *Stavisky*, a stylish but academic attempt to link the story of a 1930s French swindler with that of Trotsky. Rather more satisfying was *Providence* >**4**, scripted by David Mercer. This portrait of an elderly, sickly writer whose ideas for a novel become inextricably tangled with his apparently embittered feelings towards his family – who become the characters populating his drunken dreams of the book – is acerbic, witty and, on occasion, quite horrific (shots of an autopsy, a city patrolled by totalitarian troops). The film nevertheless fails to convince as a mosaic-study of repressed emotions or of the creative process. Far more effective, thanks to a quietly touching Gérard Depardieu as a workaholic businessman driven to suicide, was *Mon Oncle d'Amerique* >**5**, in which three barely intersecting tales of people suffering from stress are linked by a lecture, given by a behavioural scientist, on the effects of frustration and anxiety on rats. The equation between humans and animals is illuminating and witty, situating the film between fiction and documentary.

Since then, however, Resnais has opted for ever more obscure or slight subjects: *La Vie est un Roman* interlinked three stories of Utopian folly and fell foul of obvious satire; *L'Amour à Mort* mixed religious theorising with a romantic tale of a man recalled from death by his wife's love; *Mélo* was a deliberately theatrical return to the haunted triangular relationships of his early work. Though still visually lavish and determinedly anti-naturalistic, Resnais' recent work seems increasingly redundant in its endless emphasis on ambiguity. For a director concerned with the doubts, delusions and anxieties of the human mind, he appears strangely lacking in warmth and compassion for his puppet-like creations.

Lineage

Though Resnais' contemporaries were Marker and Varda, he admires silent director Louis Feuillade. Early avant-garde figures like Marcel L'Herbier and Jean Epstein may also have been influential. One may compare Resnais' taste for ambiguity with that of **Buñuel**, **Welles**, André Delvaux and **Roeg**.

Further reading

Roy Armes' *The Cinema of Alain Resnais* (London, 1968), James Monaco's *Alain Resnais* (London, 1978).

Viewing

1 **Hiroshima Mon Amour**
France 1959/ w Emmanuelle Riva, Eiji Okada, Bernard Fresson
2 **Last Year in Marienbad**
France 1961/ w Delphine Seyrig, Giorgio Albertazzi, Sacha Pitoeff
3 **Muriel**
France 1963/ w Delphine Seyrig, Jean-Pierre Kerien, Nita Klein
4 **Providence**
France 1977/ w John Gielgud, Dirk Bogarde, Ellen Burstyn
5 **Mon Oncle d'Amerique**
France 1980/ w Gérard Depardieu, Nicole Garcia, Roger Pierre

Michael Ritchie

Born: 28th November 1938/ Waukesha, Wisconsin, USA
Directing career: 1969-

Just as Michael Ritchie's recent films have met with a commercial success denied his early work, so they have become increasingly anonymous and less artistically rewarding. In the early '70s, his career showed great promise, which now seems disappointingly unfulfilled.

After involving himself in theatre while at Harvard, Ritchie found work in television on series such as *The Man from UNCLE* and *Dr Kildare*; at the same time he worked on several documentaries with the Maysles brothers. The latter experience served him especially well on his feature debut, *Downhill Racer*, an incisive portrait of a champion skier (played by Robert Redford), impressive not only for the authenticity of its superbly shot and edited skiing sequences, but for its unsentimental account of the way a surly, selfish and inarticulate sportsman is transformed by the media into a popular hero. Indeed, the ethics of competition were a constant theme of Ritchie's early work after the outrageously inventive and blackly comic *Prime Cut* >**1**. This *noir* fantasy gangster thriller merged Hitchcockian homage and a surreal, telling equation of attitudes towards women and meat, with wicked, irreverent satire on rural Americana. *The Candidate* >**2**, however, was a wry, *verité*-style parable about political compromise, in which an idealistic young lawyer succumbs to inevitable demands that he adopt a marketable media image; *Smile* >**3**, conversely, was a gently comic dig at the absurd illusions that fuel the American Dream as embodied by the contestants and the smalltown organisers of a Young American Miss beauty competition. What distinguished this, and the two comedies that followed, was an ear for funny but naturalistic dialogue, and Ritchie's genuine affection for his flawed but invariably well-meaning characters. Thus, *The Bad News Bears* offers a surprisingly credible collection of kids training for Little League baseball, while *Semi-Tough* portrays a bizarre *ménage-à-trois* with a benign awareness of the deceit involved, at the same time revealing, hilariously, the baleful commercialisation of football and the delirious double-speak of certain consciousness-raising groups.

Perhaps Ritchie's last, and most personal, word on playing fair, winning and losing, the charming but uneven sentimental comedy *An Almost Perfect Affair* (about an ex-movie actress forced to choose between a producer-husband and a naive director-lover) was shot on location at the Cannes Film Festival. Alas, the film's failure to find an audience seems to have encouraged Ritchie to follow a more conventionally commercial path. An adaptation of Peter Benchley's horrific tale of contemporary pirates, *The Island*; the Bette Midler concert documentary *Divine Madness*; the black comedy thriller *The Survivors*; and efficient but derivative comic vehicles for Chevy Chase (*Fletch*), Eddie Murphy (*The Golden Child*), and Dan Aykroyd (*The Couch Trip*) manifest little or nothing of the director's earlier quirky irony and warmth. Apparently no longer keen to examine the way American life is shaped and distorted by institutions and the media, he now regurgitates the bland formulas of the mainstream. His artistic decline has been one of the major disappointments of Hollywood in the '80s.

Lineage

Ritchie's early films reflect his former interest in documentary, while his satirising of American life may recall both **Mazursky** and the admittedly far tougher, more iconoclastic **Altman**.

Further reading

James Monaco's *American Film Now* (New York, 1979), Diane Jacobs' *Hollywood Renaissance* (New York, 1977).

Viewing

1 **Prime Cut**
US 1972/ w Lee Marvin, Gene Hackman, Sissy Spacek
2 **The Candidate**
US 1972/ w Robert Redford, Peter Boyle, Allen Garfield
3 **Smile**
US 1975/ w Bruce Dern, Barbara Feldon, Geoffrey Lewis

Nicolas Roeg

Born: 15th August 1928/London, England
Directing career: 1970-

One of the most ambitious and idiosyncratic film-makers to emerge from Britain in the '70s, Nicolas Jack Roeg is most notable for his total rejection of the realist tradition and his Resnais-like interest in fragmented narrative. His recent work, however, shows signs of stale repetition; what once seemed a significant stylistic strategy now looks more like mannerist affectation.

Before directing, Roeg slowly worked his way up from clapper boy to become cameraman on films that included **Corman**'s *The Masque of the Red Death*, **Truffaut**'s *Fahrenheit 451*, **Schlesinger**'s *Far From the Madding Crowd* and **Lester**'s *Petulia*. Finally, together with writer Donald Cammell, he co-directed *Performance* >**1**, in which a fugitive London hoodlum hides out in the druggy home of a rock star, where he is forced to participate in bizarre power games that culminate in the annihilation of his personality. Violent and full of verbal and visual riddles, the film, for all its originality, was marred by the undisciplined, half-baked nature of its pretensions. Far more coherent were his solo debut, *Walkabout* >**2** (in which two children, deserted by their suicidal father in the Australian outback, meet an aborigine boy who is subsequently destroyed by the encounter), and *Don't Look Now* >**3**, a supernatural thriller set in Venice, in which a man haunted by his daughter's death unwittingly foresees his own murder. Both benefitted from atmospheric camerawork; more crucially, Roeg's complex cross-cutting between past, present and future to evoke a *psychological* reality was unusually appropriate to the films' themes of culture clash and psychic prescience.

Similar ideas lay at the heart of *The Man Who Fell to Earth* (a sci-fi epic about a benign alien visitor to Earth destroyed by the human behaviour patterns he adopts) and *Bad Timing* >**4**, a love story ending tormentedly in a suicide attempt and near-necrophiliac rape. Both films were strikingly unconventional, but the first suffered from an increasingly incoherent script, the second from an inappropriately fragmented narrative that weakened the subversive emotional effect of its study in *amour fou*. *Eureka*, a dense and often overblown portrait of a Klondike prospector whose discovery of gold brings him not only wealth but trouble with family and rivals, was flawed by poor performances and portentous symbolism, and gained only limited release. Subsequently Roeg has restricted himself to smaller-scale works, often set in one or two locations, but still uncompromising in their blurring of the line between psychic and objective reality, and in their non-linear narratives. Nevertheless, *Insignificance* (about a meeting between Einstein, Marilyn Monroe, Joe DiMaggio and Joe McCarthy in a New York hotel), *Castaway* (an ill-matched couple alone together on a desert island run the gamut of heterosexual courtship and hostility), and *Track 29* (the mysterious arrival of a stranger claiming to be a woman's long lost son drives her to madness and, perhaps, murder) seemed slight in comparison to Roeg's earlier achievements, their uneven performances and visual trickery amounting to little more than a redundant modernist embellishment of hackneyed themes.

As Roeg's recent work has grown increasingly theatrical, so it has underlined his need for greater discipline: his one genre film, *Don't Look Now*, also seems the most adequately realised. At the same time, however, in stressing the need for a visual rather than literary mode of story-telling, Roeg remains one of the most individualistic, provocative, and promising of British directors.

Lineage

Roeg's fragmented style inevitably recalls that of **Resnais** and **Lester**'s *Petulia*. It is also interesting to compare his work with that of former collaborators Donald Cammell and Paul Mayersberg.

Viewing

1 **Performance**
GB 1970/ w Mick Jagger, James Fox, Anita Pallenberg

2 **Walkabout**
Australia 1971/ w Jenny Agutter, Lucien John, David Gumpilil

3 **Don't Look Now**
GB 1973/ w Donald Sutherland, Julie Christie, Hilary Mason

4 **Bad Timing**
GB 1980/ w Art Garfunkel, Theresa Russell, Harvey Keitel

Eric Rohmer

Born: 21st March (or 4th April), 1920/Tulle, France
Directing career: 1951-

In remaining true to his style and preoccupations, and resisting the vicissitudes of fashion, Eric Rohmer (born Jean-Marie Maurice Scherer) has built up a unique, consistently magnificent body of work, almost unrivalled for its psychological insights. It is ironic that through an emphasis on the spoken word and with a formal sensibility partly derived from literature, he has become one of cinema's greatest realists.

After teaching literature throughout the '40s, Rohmer took up film criticism and eventually became editor of *Cahiers du Cinéma*. At the same time, starting with *Charlotte et son Steak* (featuring **Godard** as its sole actor), he began directing short films. It was not until 1959, however, that he made his first feature, *Le Signe du Lion* >**1**, an immaculately observed parable in which a musician, misguidedly depending on an inheritance, finds himself by chance penniless, friendless, and reduced to tramping the hostile streets of Paris in August. More traditionally realist than the movies of his New Wave colleagues, the film was largely neglected, and only in 1963 was he able to resume directing with two delightful short features made in 16mm, *La Boulangère de Monceau* and *La Carrière de Suzanne*. These began a series of six 'Moral Tales': lucid, ironic, but unmoralising meditations on the minutiae of human behaviour. In each film, such plot as there is concerns a male, committed or about to commit himself to one woman, who is temporarily drawn to another before returning to the first. In *La Carrière de Suzanne*, the hero only becomes interested in a girl when another boy shows interest; in *La Collectioneuse*, two friends decide not to sleep with a promiscuous girl who virtually ignores them anyway; and in *My Night with Maud* >**2**, a Catholic, having already determined to wed a total stranger who attends the same church as he, spends an entire night with a free-spirited divorcée, indecisively resisting seduction. Avoiding melodramatic cliché, Rohmer simply observes, in precise and witty detail, the emotional and intellectual paths by which his characters arrive at a choice: words, actions and gestures expose the gulf between impulse and reason, idealism and pragmatism, determinism and free will, and Rohmer's images, accurately nailing particulars of time and place, turn what might otherwise seem mere literary exercises into touching cinematic revelations of rare intelligence. Equally remarkably, as his characters talk about a myriad of

The brief, discreet, sidelong glance: a key element in Rohmer's precise filmic vocabulary, as seen in *The Aviator's Wife*.

topics during their complex courtship rituals, he constructs a multi-levelled inquisition on such thorny questions as the nature of love, beauty, happiness, truth and life.

The almost neo-classical formalism and literary allusions of *Claire's Knee* >**3** (which featured a hero confronted by a veritable trinity of women) and *Love in the Afternoon*, the last of the six 'Moral Tales', again appeared in both *Die Marquise von O . . .* >**4**, and *Perceval Le Gallois* >**5**. Once more, although Rohmer was working from a novella by the German writer Heinrich von Kleist (about a 19th-century noblewoman, ravished in her sleep, who advertises for the unknown father of her child to present himself) and from the 12th-century epic by Chrétien de Troyes, he remained faithful to himself (Perceval, in his search for the Grail, even discovers the perils of too much conversation) as well as to his sources; and, as if to rebut those blind to his visual talents, he lit and designed these films to evoke, respectively, German Romantic and medieval paintings.

With the start of the '80s and *The Aviator's Wife*, Rohmer began a second series of films ('Comédies et Proverbes'). As before he concentrated on words, thoughts and emotions rather than plot, but his attention now focussed on groups of characters, often in their late teens or early 20s, played by a semi-regular troupe of largely unknown actors. Basic common themes again ran through the series: the unattainability of perfect love, and the way average human capabilities tend to be outstripped by hopes and ambitions. In *The Aviator's Wife* >**6**, a young postman, enlisting a schoolgirl to help spy on the girlfriend he suspects of infidelity, belatedy realises that his self-centred obsession has cost him his relationship with both; in *A Good Marriage*, a girl decides to marry a man whom she later learns is already engaged. Ironically, delusions often shatter due to deception or mere chance: in *Pauline at the Beach* >**7**, a teenage girl, emotionally more mature and truthful than her elders, comes to understand the ways of the adult world after she suffers, thanks to a hypocritical lover's lie, pangs of jealousy; and in *Les Nuits de la Pleine Lune* (*Full Moon in Paris*), a girl's one-sided desire for independence backfires when her lover reacts to her moving out by taking a new girlfriend. This pessimism was countered by Rohmer's affection for his characters, a compassion most evident in the largely improvised *The Green Ray* >**8**, in which a shy girl, deserted by friends for the summer and full of self-pity, travels alone around France in the forlorn hope of meeting the perfect boyfriend. Stunningly performed (by a partly amateur cast), featuring subtle colour symbolism, and filled with scenes of captivating, deceptively inconsequential authenticity (a meal-time discussion of the girl's vegetarianism, a lonely walk along a crowded holiday beach), the film ends with a moving, virtually imperceptible miracle: the ray's appearance over the sinking sun, ambiguously implying the heroine's faith in her future happiness.

Before *My Girlfriend's Boyfriend*, a deliciously complicated quadrangular romance and the sixth of the 'Comédies et Proverbes', Rohmer made *Four Adventures of Reinette and Mirabelle* >**9**. Another exercise in improvisation, it explored the gradual development of a friendship between a Parisian student and a girl she meets in the country. Typically credible and psychologically astute, the film confirmed Rohmer's abiding youthfulness (its subtle, offbeat wit, quirky narrative and low budget reminiscent of New Wave methods), and displayed his fascination with the joys of *seeing*: the effect of a scene taut with suspense as the pair stand immobile in a field at dawn, hoping to experience total silence, is entirely, purely cinematic.

Rohmer reveals a rare ability to merge simple observation with psychological precision and philosophical discussion; words, images and performance combine to create a distinctive style of cinema as sensual as it is intelligent. His achievement, however, would be less profound were his attitude towards his characters less generous; and it is that unsentimental warmth that makes his countless obsessive variations on a theme so endlessly watchable.

Lineage

Although Rohmer co-wrote a book with **Chabrol** about **Hitchcock**, his own films are probably more influenced by **Mankiewicz** (in their love of the spoken word) and **Renoir** (in their humanism and poetic realism). His style is now so assured and unique that comparisons with his contemporaries are inevitably inexact. His films bear no resemblance to those of his long term producer-associate Barbet Schroeder, who acted in *La Boulangère de Monceau*.

Further reading

James Monaco's *The New Wave* (New York, 1976). Rohmer's *Six Moral Tales* (London, 1976) are available in translation.

Viewing

1 **Le Signe du Lion (The Sign of Leo)**
France 1959/ w Jess Hahn, Van Doude, Michéle Girardon

2 **My Night with Maud**
France 1969/ w Jean-Louis Trintignant, Françoise Fabian, Marie-Christine Barrault

3 **Claire's Knee**
France 1970/ w Jean-Claude Brialy, Beatrice Romand, Aurora Cornu

4 **Die Marquise von O . . .**
Germany 1976/ w Edith Clever, Bruno Ganz, Peter Luhr

5 **Perceval le Gallois**
France 1978/ w Fabrice Luchini, André Dussolier, Arielle Dombasle

6 **The Aviator's Wife**
France 1980/ w Philippe Marlaud, Marie Rivière, Anne-Laure Meury

7 **Pauline at the Beach**
France 1982/ w Amanda Langlet, Arielle Dombasle, Pascal Gregory

8 **The Green Ray**
France 1986/ w Marie Rivière, Rosette, Carita, Vincent Gauthier

9 **Four Adventures of Reinette and Mirabelle**
France 1987/ w Jessica Forde, Joelle Miquel, Marie Rivière

George A. Romero

Born: 4th February 1940/New York, USA
Directing career: 1968-

Although an erratic talent, George Andrew Romero remains important for his virtually single-handed development of the horror film from a form where menace was suggested and shadowy to a newly visceral genre in which gore and violence are largely explicit.

An ex-actor who had made films in 8mm, Romero's debut feature was with *Night of the Living Dead* >**1**, a low-budget thriller in which, for reasons unexplained, the dead return to life as zombies with an insatiable hunger for human flesh. Besides its stark and moody monochrome camerawork and its gruesome focus on physical gore, it was notable both for its bleak pessimism (the potential heroes, a brother and sister, are respectively slain and driven insane by a zombie's attack in the opening scene, while the most sympathetic character, mistaken for a zombie, is killed by redneck vigilantes at the film's climax) and for its cynical attitude towards family and authority figures. Less genuinely terrifying were *Jack's Wife* (*Season of the Witch*), about a bored suburban housewife taking an interest in the occult, and *The Crazies*, in which an epidemic of homicidal maniacs caused by a secret biological weapon produces a ruling militia as lethal as the menace it seeks to confine. But with *Martin* >**2**, Romero returned to form: a contemporary vampire thriller, it concerns a sexually insecure, emotionally disturbed teenager haunted by the fear that his aged cousin's superstitious claims – that he is cursed to thirst for human blood – are true. Intriguingly, the boy is viewed sympathetically, while the outside world, especially his family, is seen as largely oppressive. Even more imaginative and condemnatory of modern America was *Zombies – Dawn of the Dead* >**3**, the wittily satirical and gripping sequel to *Night of the Living Dead* in which the by now numerically superior dead wander the land searching for shopping malls, in remembrance of old habits; the living, however, are no better, as consumer greed leads them to fight each other over luxury goods that are essentially worthless in an apocalyptic, primitive world.

In recent years Romero's taste for violent comic strip-style action has resulted in less subversive, more conventional fantasy films: *Knight Riders*, about jousting bikers, was an ambitious but self-indulgent update of Arthurian legend, and *Creepshow* an anthology of uninspired horror stories written by Stephen King in homage to EC comics. A third instalment in the zombie saga, *Day of the Dead*, in which largely unsympathetic survivors argue over whether or not to try and domesticate the living dead as slaves, was suitably gory, but offered little advance on the witheringly caustic assessment of human aspiration in the earlier films; nor could *Monkey Shine* – an often ludicrously predictable account of a paralysed man cared for, then endangered, by trained monkeys – reverse the general decline in Romero's critical standing.

Visually gruesome, Romero's finest work nevertheless evinces a sharp intelligence. At the same time, his decision to remain a low-budget independent film-maker in Pittsburgh (location of many of his films) has allowed him to avoid the compromises likely had he moved to Hollywood. He may be in danger, however, of simply reworking his most successful films *ad nauseam* and with diminishing results.

Lineage

In breaking from the suggestive tradition of horror pioneered by figures like **Whale** and producer Val Lewton, not to mention the lurid but innocuous style of the Hammer films, Romero may be seen to have taken up where **Hitchcock**'s *Psycho* and the Italian Mario Bava left off. His influence is seen in figures like **Carpenter**, **Cronenberg**, **De Palma**, Wes Craven, Tobe Hooper, Sam Raimi, Dario Argento and Lucio Fulci.

Further reading

Peter Nicholls' *Fantastic Cinema* (London, 1984).

Viewing

1 **Night of the Living Dead**
US 1968/ w Duane Jones, Judith O'Dea, Russell Streiner

2 **Martin**
US 1976/ w John Amplas, Lincoln Maazel, Christine Forrest

3 Zombies – Dawn of the Dead
US 1977/ w David Emge, Ken Foree, Gaylen Ross

Francesco Rosi

Born: **15th November 1922/Naples, Italy**
Directing career: 1956-

Adapting neo-realist methods to his own purposes, Francesco Rosi became a leading figure in political cinema during the '60s. While his more recent films have tended toward less controversial, art-house subjects, his finest work remains provocative and gripping.

After working in radio journalism and the theatre, Rosi made his entry into movies as assistant to directors such as **Visconti** and **Antonioni**. Having co-directed, in 1956, Vittorio Gassman's *Kean*, he at once revealed a concern for contemporary social problems in *La Sfida* and *I Magliari*, dealing with corrupt business practices in Naples and Germany. But it was in *Salvatore Giuliano* >**1**, about the notorious Sicilian bandit found shot dead in 1950, that Rosi first displayed his distinctive style: location-shot and using a large cast of non-professional actors, flashing back and forth in time to amass a wealth of facts pertaining to the life, deeds and times of Giuliano (who is himself barely shown), the film traces a web of connections between the Mafia and the State to portray a country riven by a North-South divide and steeped in violence and corruption. Similarly straddling the gulf between documentary and drama, and concerned with criminal conspiracy and cover-up, *Hands Across The City* was a controversial look at property speculation in Naples, while *The Moment of Truth*, shot in Spain, set a *Blood and Sand*-style bullfighting saga against a backdrop of financial exploitation and bourgeois contempt for its matador protagonist.

After a less than successful excursion into comedy with the fanciful *C'era una Volta* (*Cinderella Italian Style*) and an exposé of military incompetence in *Uomini Contri*, *The Mattei Affair* and *Lucky Luciano* >**2** saw Rosi return to an examination of the hidden bonds between politics, commerce and the underworld. The first is a complex, fragmented hypothesis on the reasons for the mysterious death of a petroleum tycoon, the second a stylish and subversive variation on the gangster genre, linking the hoodlum's return to Italy with narcotics and America's involvement in postwar Italian politics. In the latter, and still more in *Illustrious Corpses* >**3** – a fictional thriller about a detective who, while investigating the deaths of several leaders of the judiciary, unmasks a massive political conspiracy involving both Left and Right – Rosi moved away from docu-drama forms to create visually lavish but forceful studies of paranoia and the abuse of institutionalised power. In subsequent films, however, his hard-hitting, anti-establishment tone has steadily diminished: *Christ Stopped at Eboli*, in which a writer, exiled by the Fascists, lives among the poverty-stricken peasants of the South, tends towards picturesque pastoral; *Three Brothers* >**4**, about three men (symptomatic of contemporary Italian fears of terrorism, delinquency, etc) called home by their father to their mother's funeral, is an affecting if uneven tribute to a vanishing way of rural life. Glossier and more conventional still were a relatively realist version of Bizet's *Carmen*, and a miscast but visually splendid adaptation of Gabriel Garcia Marquez' novel *Chronicle of a Death Foretold*, about an entire Colombian village keeping a conspiracy of silence over a mysterious revenge murder.

Although Rosi's work has declined in the last decade, he is important for his use of certain elements of neo-realism to forge an original form of investigative journalism in film. Questioning and criticising official positions on crime, politics and social problems, he has merged the didactic qualities of documentary realism with the accessibility of traditional fictional genres.

Lineage

Rosi may be seen as influenced by **Rossellini** and, perhaps, **Eisenstein**. It is useful to compare him with Gillo Pontecorvo, Elio Petri, and **Costa-Gavras**.

Further reading

Peter Bondanella's *Italian Cinema: From Neo-Realism to the Present* (New York, 1983).

Viewing

1 **Salvatore Giuliano**
Italy 1961/ w Frank Wolff, Salvo Randone, Pietro Camarata
2 **Lucky Luciano**
Italy 1974/ w Gian Maria Volonte, Edmond O'Brien, Rod Steiger
3 **Illustrious Corpses (Cadaveri Eccellenti)**
Italy 1976/ w Lino Ventura, Fernando Rey, Max Von Sydow
4 **Three Brothers**
Italy 1981/ w Charles Vanel, Philippe Noiret, Michèle Placido

Roberto Rossellini

Born: 8th May 1906/Rome, Italy
Died: 3rd June 1977/Rome, Italy
Directing career: 1936-1977

Often dismissed as a founder of Italian neo-realism whose career degenerated either at the start or the end of his much publicised relationship with Ingrid Bergman, Roberto Rossellini remains one of the most underrated directors in cinema history. Exploring the links between fiction and documentary, observation and education, and the individual and society, he was an important figure in the development of the cinema.

Born to a wealthy family, Rossellini shot several faintly experimental shorts (largely concerned with nature) before making his feature debut in 1940 with *The White Ship*, a polished account of life aboard an Italian hospital ship during World War II. Two further features were completed, however, before *Rome, Open City* >**1**, made under difficult and penurious circumstances towards the war's end, established him as a leading figure in the neo-realist movement. A tough, sometimes melodramatic account of the struggle of the Resistance against the occupying Nazis, the film's use of grainy, newsreel-like images, real locations and a number of non-professional actors gave it a rare force and immediacy. Even more impressive, however, was *Paisa* >**2**, whose six, often barely dramatic 'stories' of part-comic, part-tragic encounters between Italians, Germans and liberating Americans (several centred on the theme of the inability to communicate through a common language) were rooted in specific locations (the Po Valley, the Uffizi Gallery), but were universal in their portrait of an entire nation destroyed and divided by war. Already Rossellini's taste for long, mobile takes in long shot (rather than montage and close-up) gave evidence of his desire to relate individuals to the world around them; while the bleak pessimism of *Germany Year Zero* (about a boy in ravaged, postwar Berlin who commits suicide after killing his sick father, on the advice of his Nazi teacher) was both a final cry of horror at the pain and moral confusion wrought by war, and a precursor of the examinations of spiritual suffering and salvation that would mark the series of films made with Ingrid Bergman.

L'Amore, a two-part tribute to Anna Magnani, who plays a sophisticated woman trying to save a love-affair over the phone and a peasant who believes she has become pregnant by St Joseph, was followed by *The Machine That Kills*, a weird comedy about a lethal camera. Then Rossellini made *Stromboli* >**3**, first of five features with Bergman (their affair and marriage effectively alienated audiences world-wide). Potentially an overwrought melodrama, in which a Lithuanian exile suffers a fraught marriage to a peasant fisherman in order to escape a postwar displaced persons camp, the film mirrored the off-screen relationship between actress and director while, at the same time, depicting an individual's struggles

Seduction and betrayal in Rossellini's seminal neo-realist drama, *Rome, Open City*.

to come to terms with the harsh society in which she must live. Indeed, all their films together display a similar concern for blurring the lines between fiction, documentary and (auto)biography: in *Europa '51*, a woman's desire to help others following the suicide of her neglected son leads her husband to believe she is insane; in *Voyage to Italy* >**4**, an English couple about to divorce achieve an ambiguous temporary reconciliation (at a religious procession celebrating a miracle), reunited by a sense of solitude increased by their travels around the Naples region. Amazingly, Rossellini reveals his characters' emotions not by dialogue or drama (there are long stretches with little of either), but by observing their reactions to what they see: camera position and movement evokes the space that divides them from each other and from the world about them. Equally notably, although treating subjects charged with emotion, he avoids sentimentality by understating many of the narrative's potential climaxes; the result is calm, detached and lucid.

Fear, an almost *noir* melodrama in which a man's decision to punish his wife's minor infidelity with blackmail results in the breakdown of a marriage, signalled the end of Rossellini and Bergman's personal and creative relationship. Thereafter, with the exception of *The General della Rovere* (about a con-man who, agreeing to help the Nazis by pretending to be a dead Resistance fighter, discovers his own capacity for heroism), and *Era Notte a Roma* >**5** (the tale of three escaped POWs, English, American and Russian, given sanctuary by a woman whose lover dies as a result of the concealment), Rossellini concentrated largely on documentary and didactic historical reconstruction. (Often made for television, these films subtly deployed the Pancinor zoom lens, which he himself had invented.) The director's aim was nothing less than a history of the world, charting socio-political and intellectual progress through key figures like Garibaldi (*Viva l'Italia*), the Sun King (*The Rise to Power of Louis XIV* >**6**), *Socrates*, the scientist and philosopher *Blaise Pascal*, *Augustine of Hippo* and *The Messiah*. No attempt, however, was made to create conventional biopics: ideas rather than individuals were the focus of attention, and dialogue and images were composed with admirable clarity. With astonishing flair, Rossellini used decor, costume, colour and composition to reflect abstract ideas: thus, Louis XIV's method of maintaining monarchic power over a conniving nobility is made concrete in the absurdly extravagant fashions he encourages at court to render his rivals bankrupt, and in precise spatial arrangements symbolic of a world dominated by complex, carefully delineated hierarchies.

Following *The Messiah*, Rossellini planned to make a film on Marx; sadly, his death forestalled the project. While a number of his later films are so far from traditional, emotionally involving drama that they demand a huge intellectual commitment on the part of an audience, their clarity of argument and explanation, coupled with Rossellini's unassertive visual style, constitutes unusually accessible didactic cinema. Whether for his war trilogy, his work with Bergman or the educational films he made for TV, he deserves praise as one of cinema's most innovative and challenging artists.

Lineage

Unlike **De Sica**, **Fellini** and **Visconti**, Rossellini remained true to neo-realism, while transcending its more naive aspects; the films of **Godard**, **Rohmer**, Rivette, **Antonioni**, **Bertolucci**, the **Taviani brothers**, **Rosi** and Ermanno Olmi testify to his enormous influence.

Further reading

Peter Brunette's *Roberto Rossellini* (New York, 1987).

Viewing

1 **Rome, Open City**
Italy 1945/ w Aldo Fabrizi, Anna Magnani, Marcello Pagliero
2 **Paisa (Paisan)**
Italy 1946/ w Carmela Sazio, Robert Van Loon, Maria Michi
3 **Stromboli (Stromboli, Terra di Dio)**
Italy 1949/ w Ingrid Bergman, Mario Vitale, Renzo Cesana
4 **Voyage to Italy (Viaggio in Italia)**
Italy 1953/ w Ingrid Bergman, George Sanders, Leslie Daniels
5 **Era Notte a Roma (It Was Night in Rome)**
Italy 1960/ w Leo Genn, Giovanna Ralli, Serge Bondarchuk
6 **The Rise to Power of Louis XIV**
Italy 1966/ w Jean-Marie Patte, Raymond Jourdan, Silvagni

Robert Rossen

Born: 16th March 1908/New York, USA
Died: 18th February 1966/USA
Directing career: 1947-1964

Adversely affected by the HUAC blacklist, the directing career of Robert Rosen was inevitably uneven. Nevertheless, an interest in social and psychological realism and a writer's ear for dialogue resulted in a handful of memorable if flawed films.

Having worked for some years in the theatre, Rossen entered the movies as a writer for Warners; most of the films he scripted were in the crime and action genres, many of them – *Marked Woman*, Mervyn Le Roy's *They Won't Forget*, **Walsh**'s *The Roaring Twenties*, **Curtiz**'s *The Sea Wolf*, Anatole Litvak's *Out of the Fog*, and Lewis Milestone's *A Walk in the Sun* – characterised by a liberal social awareness inspired, perhaps, by his membership of the Communist Party. Finally, in 1947, he made his directing debut with *Johnny O'Clock*, a moody *noir* thriller with an impressively complex plot about a gambler wrongly suspected of murder. Rather better, *Body and Soul* (scripted by **Polonsky** and starring John Garfield) used an otherwise routine boxing story to present a corrosive picture of naivety corrupted by success and the dollar, and climaxed with an expertly shot final fight. But it was *All the King's Men* >1 that established Rossen as a talent to watch: about a Huey Long-style Southern demagogue whose idealist integrity diminishes according to the power he commands, the film was an immaculately executed example of low-key Hollywood realism; it made imaginative use of locations and revealed Rossen's superior handling of relatively unknown actors like Broderick Crawford and Mercedes McCambridge.

Unfortunately, the HUAC was calling, and after the Mexican-shot bullfight film *The Brave Bulls*, Rossen refused to cooperate at a 1951 hearing. After two years on the blacklist he agreed to name names, but his career suffered badly: European-made, *Mambo*, *Alexander the Great* and *Island in the Sun* were material unworthy of his particular talents. *They Came to Cordura*, a study of army honour and cowardice in 1916 Mexico, was fairly intriguing, but it was *The Hustler* >**2** which at last brought the director back to the fold. Superbly performed, it is a cynically scripted tale of rivalry, self-loathing and betrayal, set in the world of intensely ambitious and proud pool-hall sharks. Even finer however, and far more ambitious, was *Lilith* >**3**, a lyrical, sensual romance between a male nurse at a psychiatric hospital and a beautiful patient. A delicate, understated study in obsession (the nurse finally comes to ask for psychiatric help for himself), the film is at the same time an oblique updating of myth and a sensitive attempt to view the phenomenon of madness without resorting to hysteria; crucial to its success are Eugene Schufftan's lustrous monochrome images.

Seemingly having embarked, with these two last films, upon a second, more mature phase in his career, Rossen died before making another film. If his tougher, early genre pieces now seem a little dated in their earnest sociological moralising, *Lilith*, especially, survives as a poetic glimpse of what might have been a newly discovered sympathy for life's outsiders.

Lineage

Rossen's scripts and early work suggest comparison with **Polonsky**, **Losey**, **Huston** and Richard Brooks; *Johnny O'Clock* was admired by **Melville**, *Lilith* by several of the younger French directors.

Further reading

Alan Casty's *The Films of Robert Rossen* (New York, 1969).

Viewing

1 **All the King's Men**
US 1949/ w Broderick Crawford, John Ireland, Joanne Dru

2 **The Hustler**
US 1961/ w Paul Newman, George C. Scott, Piper Laurie, Jackie Gleason

3 **Lilith**
US 1964/ w Warren Beatty, Jean Seberg, Peter Fonda, Kim Hunter

Alan Rudolph

Born: 18th December 1943/Los Angeles, California, USA
Directing career: 1972-

One of the more eccentrically imaginative talents to emerge from America in recent years, Alan Rudolph makes movies that are hard to categorise in terms of genre and tone: while usually set in a recognisably real world, elements of fantasy are common; equally, they veer between comedy and romance, originality and indulgence.

Rudolph had already made several undistinguished low-budget films, including the hippy horror movie *Premonition*, before serving as assistant director to **Altman**, who produced Rudolph's first truly serious film, *Welcome to LA*. An occasionally stilted satire on the mating habits of various cool, sophisticated Angelenos loosely connected with a vain rock musician, the film nonetheless revealed a strong visual sense and a quirkily oblique attitude to narrative. Rather better was *Remember My Name* >**1**, inventively updating motifs from '40s 'women's pictures' to create a gripping psychological study of a man menaced by his vengeful ex-wife, recently released from prison; the film's freshness was partly due to its use of seedy suburban locations, partly to the casting against type of both Anthony Perkins and Geraldine Chaplin. Sadly, neither film was a commercial success, and for the next few years Rudolph was forced to direct movies originated by others –

Roadie (an amiable comedy about the music business), *Endangered Species* (an intriguing but garbled sci-fi conspiracy thriller with political and ecological overtones), and *Return Engagement* (a documentary record of a tour undertaken by notorious 'celebrities' J. Gordon Liddy and Timothy Leary) – in which the director could reveal little of his erratic but attractively idiosyncratic storytelling talent.

With *Choose Me* >**2**, however, his ability to create a vaguely unreal, self-enclosed world populated by vividly drawn eccentrics was allowed full rein. The film is a complex, comic, and often ambiguous roundelay, portraying the ways in which a group of loners gathered around a singles bar pursue their various dreams of romantic and sexual love. Although low-budget, it nevertheless made excellent, stylish use of studio sets to evoke both fantasy and a faintly formalised sense of emotional choreography. Similarly, after the routine and sometimes incoherent Country and Western saga *Songwriter*, *Trouble in Mind* >**3** employed the story of an ex-cop, just out of jail, who helps the young wife of a man naively involved in criminal activities, to create a bizarre blend of thriller, romantic fairy tale and surreal comedy. Again, the setting (Rain City) was a sly mix of fantasy and reality, timeless and magical, while Rudolph's attention was focussed less on events than on his self-obsessed, somewhat pitiable but finally sympathetic characters. Rather less original but equally attractive was *Made in Heaven*, about a youth killed in a car accident who falls for an unborn female angel and gets to live a second life as he searches for her back on earth.

The long-planned *The Moderns* >**4**, about expatriate American artists, art-dealers, forgers and intellectuals in '20s Paris, while seen by some as slight, indulgent and pretentious, was yet another distinctively personal, romantic work from a fascinating, unpredictable director. Indeed, Rudolph's work overall is a very welcome alternative to the pat routines of mainstream Hollywood.

Lineage

While *Welcome to LA* encouraged comparison with Rudolph's admitted mentor **Altman**, the diversity of his later work refutes facile parallels. Indeed, from *Choose Me* onwards, his idiosyncratically charming work is perhaps more reminiscent of **Demy** or **Ophüls**.

Viewing

1 **Remember My Name**
US 1978/ w Geraldine Chaplin, Anthony Perkins, Berry Berenson

2 **Choose Me**
1984/ w Keith Carradine, Genevieve Bujold, Lesley Ann Warren

3 **Trouble in Mind**
US 1985/ w Kris Kristofferson, Keith Carradine, Lori Singer

4 **The Moderns**
US 1988/ w Keith Carradine, Linda Fiorentino, Genevieve Bujold

Ken Russell

Born: 3rd July 1927/Southampton, England
Directing career: 1957-

The flamboyant subjectivity and aversion to realism that marked Henry Kenneth Alfred Russell as Britain's most successful film-maker in the late '60s and early '70s rapidly degenerated into sensationalist excess and fatuous hallucinatory fantasy. What was once a valuable antidote to constipated notions of good taste now seems a self-conscious and vain desire to shock and titillate.

A former dancer, actor and photographer, Russell broke into television after making several amateur shorts. His work for the small screen impressed with its fresh, visually striking approach to the lives of great artists: thus his 'documentaries' on Elgar, Debussy, Delius (*Song of Summer*) and Isadora Duncan rank amongst his best achievements, being less conventional biography than attempts to relate, through lyrical images, the artists' lives and psychic make-up to their work. In the mid-'60s he had made two surprisingly anonymous features (the slight seaside satire *French Dressing* and the semi-parodic spy thriller *Billion Dollar Brain*); only with a relatively sensitive version of Lawrence's *Women in Love* >**1** did he finally establish himself as a cinematic talent of some note, the film benefitting from Russell's eye for a striking image and his feel for the expressive qualities of landscape. In *The Music Lovers* >**2**, he allowed himself greater freedom, illustrating the music of Tchaikovsky (romantically viewed as a sexually tormented figure destroyed but inspired by his battles with a hypocritical, uncaring society) with feverish symbolism suggestive of the director's own fantasies. Equally controversial was the morbid, inventively designed *The Devils* >**3**, a rather overheated account of religious fanaticism in 17th-century France, replete with scenes of torture, sexually hysterical nuns, and fornicating priests. Already, style dominated at the expense of coherence and characterisation.

Having made his name with nudity, violence and insanity, he next turned to more modest subjects with the '20s musical *The Boy Friend* and *Savage Messiah*, a biopic of the sculptor Henri Gaudier Brezska. Both were dull, however, and for *Mahler*, *Tommy* (an all-singing version of The Who's absurdly pretentious rock-opera) and *Lisztomania* (which portrayed Liszt as an anachronistic pop-star libertine), Russell's direction became increasingly fantastical, sensationalist and grotesque, dismissive of documented facts in the biopics, and featuring facile, banal and vulgar symbolism.

Russell's first film in America, a biopic of *Valentino*, was no less misguided. It seemed as if Russell was now trapped within his own iconoclastic conventions: unbridled contempt for a world against which sexually or psychologically disturbed artists rail; outrageously overused cod-Freudian symbols; lurid fantasy. But *Altered States* suggested a change of heart. Its traditional tale of a scientist whose experiments in sensory deprivation lead him to regress beyond the primitive, produced an array of psychedelic special effects. Even more atypical was *Crimes of Passion* >**4**, its reasonably coherent plot depicting the encounter of a prostitute, a quiet suburban husband and an insane priest, and constituting a scabrous, salacious but finally hollow satire on American sexual mores. Upon returning to England, Russell reverted to his private onslaught on 'arty' subjects: *Gothic* (a fictionalised re-creation of the night when Byron, Shelley and Mary Godwin held a seance, thus inspiring the writing of *Frankenstein*), *Salome's Last Dance* (from Wilde) and *The Lair of the White Worm* (from Bram Stoker) all foundered in flatulent camp humour, inept acting and a dated stress on sexual decadence. Moreover, Russell's former ability to mount visually astonishing set-pieces had deserted him altogether.

Russell's importance lies in the way his example encouraged other British directors to abandon notions of realism and attempt more personal forms of film-making. His own career, however, has been marred by self-indulgence and an absurd, finally pointless desire to be regarded as a perpetually ageless *enfant terrible*.

Lineage

Russell's Romanticism would seem to place him in a tradition of British film-making which reached its zenith with **Michael Powell**. In rejecting the realist style, he anticipated figures like **Roeg**, and **Jarman** (who designed both *The Devils* and *Savage Messiah*).

Further reading

John Baxter's *An Appalling Talent: Ken Russell* (London, 1973).

Viewing

1 **Women in Love**
GB 1969/ w Oliver Reed, Alan Bates, Glenda Jackson, Jennie Linden

2 **The Music Lovers**
GB 1970/ w Richard Chamberlain, Glenda Jackson, Christopher Gable

3 **The Devils**
GB 1971/ w Oliver Reed, Vanessa Redgrave, Dudley Sutton

4 **Crimes of Passion**
US 1984/ w Kathleen Turner, Anthony Perkins, John Laughlin

Carlos Saura

Born: 4th January 1932/Huesca, Spain
Directing career: 1958-

It is perhaps ironic that Carlos Saura, the most famous Spanish director of recent years, has moved from allegorical portraits of post-Civil War Spain, made under the censorious Franco regime, to less political films, made since the advent of democracy. Despite its relative lack of social commitment, however, his later work is still imbued with a distinctly Spanish sense of tradition.

After film studies, following which he made the documentary *Cuenca*, Saura made his feature debut with a harsh realist study of delinquency fostered by poverty, *The Hooligans* (*Los Golfos*), using non-professional actors and indicting, by implication, the backward and repressive nature of contemporary Spain. In *La Caza* (*The Hunt*) >**1**, he examined the moral divisions of a country still haunted by the experience of Civil War, through the characters of three ex-Francoist soldiers who fall out during a day's shooting in a starkly photographed desert valley. Hypocrisy, violence and sexual neuroses recur time after time as the fruits of political, moral and religious repression: in *Peppermint Frappé*, a doctor, rejected by the woman of his dreams, fetishistically transforms his assistant to become her double, before killing the former; in *The Garden of Delights*, the family of an ex-Francoist businessman (left mute after a car accident) re-enact scenes from his life in order to help him recall the number of their Swiss bank account; and in *Ana and the Wolves*, an English governess falls prey to the three sons of a mother-dominated household, the young men respectively symbolic of military aggression, sexual violence and the Church. The past hangs heavily indeed over Saura's characters, with plots merging past and present, fantasy and reality to intriguing effect. Most memorably, the 8-year-old heroine of *Cría Cuervos* (*Raise Ravens*) >**2** refuses to believe that her mother and adulterous father are dead; besides being a delicate study of childhood confusion, the film is a haunting thesis on the way the past affects the future.

After Franco's death in 1975, Saura alternated films about social and political problems with more personally inspired art-movies. *Elisa My Love* concerned a daughter's visit to her father, who is writing his memoirs from her own viewpoint; *Blindfold* (*Los Ojos Vendados*) dealt with terrorism and torture, and *Deprisa, Deprisa (Fast, Fast)* >**3** followed the anarchic, apolitical actions of four doomed delinquents. With no Francoist censor, Saura could present his disenchanted view of contemporary Spain more directly: *Deprisa, Deprisa* holds the attention through its pacy linear narrative, its unsentimental naturalistic acting, and an almost documentary-style portrait of modern suburban life. At the same time, *Mama Cumple Cien Años* (*Mother Turns a Hundred*), a comedy in which birthday party guests symbolise recent changes in the new Spain, evidenced a continuing tendency to allegorise.

Saura's most memorable recent work has been in collaboration with the flamenco dancer and choreographer Antonio Gades: adapted from Lorca's play, the ballet *Blood Wedding* >**4** (elegantly shot in rehearsal) was a celebration of ritual tradition in art; far less satisfying, a flamenco version of *Carmen* blurred the distinction between performance and off-stage reality, while *El Amor Brujo* (*A Love Bewitched*), to music by De Falla, was vivid but superficial. Having won an international audience, however, Saura was able to film an epic account of the conquistador Lope de Aguirre's search for the legendary South American land of *El Dorado*.

Although Saura appears to have lost his once sharp political edge, he is unlikely ever to make films entirely unconcerned with Spain's troubled history: the Civil War and Franco's dictatorship have had a lasting effect on the people and its memories. Such is his craftsmanship, too, that in terms of performances and visual invention, he remains in the vanguard of European directors.

Lineage

A devotee of **Buñuel**, Saura may be compared with Spanish directors like Luis Berlanga, Victor Erice and Jaime Chávarri, the last two of whom, like Saura, have worked with producer Elías Querejeta. Many of Saura's films were made in collaboration with his once long-term companion, the actress Geraldine Chaplin.

Further reading

John Hopewell's *Out of the Past: Spanish Cinema After Franco* (London, 1986).

Viewing

1 **La Caza (The Hunt)**
Spain 1965/ w Alfredo Mayo, Ismael Merlo, Jose Maria Prada
2 **Cría Cuervos (Raise Ravens)**
Spain 1975/ w Geraldine Chaplin, Ana Torrent
3 **Deprisa, Deprisa (Fast, Fast)**
Spain 1980/ w Berta Socuellamos, Jose Antonio Valdelomar
4 **Blood Wedding (Bodas de Sangre)**
Spain 1981/ w Antonio Gades, Cristina Hoyos

John Sayles

Born: 28th September 1950/ Schenectady, New York, USA
Directing career: 1980-

Although John Thomas Sayles' most financially successful work for the cinema has been his unusually witty and literate scripts for a number of exploitation films made by **Corman**'s New World, he has also won a cult reputation as the director of several low-budget independent films, notable for their oblique attitude to genre and for their subtle blending of the personal and the political.

Having drifted through a variety of jobs, Sayles was already established as a novelist before scripting **Joe Dante**'s *Piranha* in 1978; further screenplay credits included Lewis Teague's *The Lady in Red* and *Alligator*, *Battle Beyond the Stars* (a pulp sci-fi rip-off of *Seven Samurai* and *The Magnificent Seven*), and Dante's *The Howling*, all noted for their affectionately tongue-in-cheek, parodic humour. In 1980, he made his own debut with *The Return of the Secaucus Seven*, which used the ten-years-after reunion of a group of '60s drop-out radicals to explore the sexual, social and political changes suffered by America over a decade. Turning his minimal budget to advantage, Sayles employed wit, low-key acting and naturalistic dialogue to convey a wide range of emotions with honesty and intelligence. Similarly noticeable for its integrity and its delicate balance between comedy and serious social drama, *Lianna* >**1** examined the effects – on herself, her family and friends – of a woman's painful decision to leave her husband and live with her lesbian lover; incisive in its portrayal of male pride, admirably devoid of voyeuristic eroticism or simplistic moralising, it was a text book lesson in how to film a 'problem drama'. Conversely, *Baby It's You*, made the same year on a larger budget, was lighter (if equally charming and sensitive) in its unsentimental account of a doomed but moving romance between a shy middle-class Jewish girl and a brash working-class Italian Romeo in '60s New Jersey.

Sayles' versatile talent was at its quirkiest in *The Brother from Another Planet* >**2**, a delightfully discursive riposte to *ET*, with a mute black humanoid alien, a fugitive slave from a distant corner of the galaxy, seeking sanctuary in Harlem; employing wit rather than special effects, Sayles confounds genre expectations to combine offbeat comedy (through shaggy-dog bar-room banter), suspense (the plot concerns the hero's special powers taking on a drugs-ring), and a subtle study of contemporary Harlem's social mores, with characters untainted by the usual movie stereotyping. Still more impressive, however, was *Matewan* >**3**, a superbly tense and stylishly shot dramatisation of the '20s coal wars, in which a mining township is menaced by ruthless, violent strikebreakers. Lucidly charting the clash between individualism and collective action, private need and political necessity, it gained emotional power, not to mention a mythic dimension, from Sayles' typically original, wholly appropriate decision to structure and shoot the authentically grim conflict in the style of a Western.

Perhaps unsurprisingly, the hostility of public and industry alike to both Westerns and political films ensured that *Matewan* received almost no publicity or release; altogether more popular, however, was *Eight Men Out*, a based-in-fact baseball drama (about the infamous 1919 Black Sox scandal) once again serving to expose the evil of capitalist exploitation. Indeed, the sheer variety of Sayles' material, and his ability to mould it to a private vision of American history, confirm him as an unusually ambitious writer-director whose work admirably defies categorisation.

Lineage

While the idiosyncratic versatility of Sayles, who takes minor acting roles in most of his films, makes it virtually impossible to trace influences (other than, perhaps, **Corman**), his directing debut certainly anticipated Lawrence Kasdan's *The Big Chill*.

Further reading

Sayles' novels include *Pride of the Bimbos* (Boston, 1975), *Union Dues* (Boston, 1977) and *The Anarchists' Convention* (Boston, 1979).

Viewing

1 **Lianna**
US 1983/ w Linda Griffiths, Jane Hallaren, Jon DeVries

2 **The Brother from Another Planet**
US 1984/ w Joe Morton, Darryl Edwards, Leonard Jackson

3 **Matewan**
US 1987/ w Chris Cooper, Will Oldham, Mary McDonnell

John Schlesinger

Born: 16th February 1926/London, England
Directing career: 1948-

Often acclaimed as one of the finest directors to emerge from the flurry of low-budget, social-conscience film-making in Britain in the early '60s, John Richard Schlesinger has seen his reputation take a plunge in recent years. Indeed, even his most lauded films for the most part seem, in retrospect, hollow and misconceived.

An occasional actor, Schlesinger began shooting amateur films in 1948, before making his name in the late '50s as a director of documentary shorts for television. In 1962, on the strength of the award-winning *Terminus* (a brief study of a day in the life of Waterloo Station) he made his feature debut, *A Kind of Loving*, in which a romance in the grimy industrial North of England ends in pregnancy, sterile marriage and disenchantment. Set in an equally patronisingly viewed society, the comedy *Billy Liar* >**1** contrasted a boy's heroic Walter Mitty-style dreams with the tedious reality of his middle-class life. Though obvious, the film was certainly livelier and less pretentious than *Darling*, a vacuous and modish satire on the egocentric obsessions of jet-set society as seen by an ambitious fashion model. She was played by the director's 'discovery', Julie Christie, who reappeared as Hardy's Bathsheba in his shallow, plodding but lavishly photographed version of *Far From the Madding Crowd*.

Such was Schlesinger's reputation that in 1969 he made his first American film, the Oscar-winning *Midnight Cowboy* >**2**. About the uneasy friendship that develops between a tubercular con-man and a naive Texan stud in a New York viewed as a schizophrenic combination of crumbling tenements and extravagant, orgiastic parties, the film benefitted from strong performances and its outsider's perception of a tough, vibrant but alienating city. But it was weakened both by a reluctance to confront the homosexual elements of its buddy-buddy relationship and by a bathetic ending. Still more contrived was *Sunday, Bloody Sunday*, which featured an implausible romantic triangle involving a businesswoman, a quiet Jewish doctor and a trendy bisexual designer in a stultifyingly middle-class London; despite a fine performance by Peter Finch as the repressed gay medic, the film's earnest sensitivity drained what might have been a fraught relationship of pain, passion and vitality. Thereafter, in fact, Schlesinger entered upon a steady decline: *Day of the Locust* was an overblown travesty of Nathanael West's novel about corruption, hypocrisy and hysteria in '30s Hollywood; a routine and drawn-out thriller, *Marathon Man* >3 was enlivened by a memorably unpleasant scene of unanaesthetized dental torture and occasionally superior location photography (New York and Paris); and the potentially interesting examination, in *Yanks*, of Anglo-American tensions in wartime Britain, became bogged down in cheap period nostalgia and cloying, maudlin romance. Whatever claims Schlesinger once had to intelligence and integrity in his often bleak accounts of complex relationships stifled by callous societies, he abandoned once and for all in the '80s. *Honky Tonk Freeway* was a dismally unamusing satire, *The Falcon and the Snowman* an inept, clichéd spy thriller, and *The Believers* a risible voodoo horror film set in New York. Only *Madame Sousatzka*, a sentimental, sporadically astute account of a music teacher's struggles to protect a young pupil from the money-minded vultures tempting him towards the concert platform, was greeted with any critical enthusiasm – largely thanks to the acting.

But Schlesinger, often praised for his work with performers, is equally likely to foster theatricality; he has little idea of pacing, while his pretensions to social comment seem dictated by currently fashionable attitudes. Thus, his work will probably date badly.

Lineage

Schlesinger attracted attention alongside **Anderson**, Karel Reisz and Tony Richardson; his later move away from realism may perhaps be traced to influential European film-makers like **Antonioni** and **Godard**. His own influence on other directors is surely minimal.

Viewing

1 **Billy Liar**
GB 1963/ w Tom Courtenay, Julie Christie, Mona Washbourne

2 **Midnight Cowboy**
US 1969/ w Jon Voight, Dustin Hoffman, Sylvia Miles

3 **Marathon Man**
US 1976/ w Dustin Hoffman, Laurence Olivier, Roy Scheider

Volker Schlöndorff

Born: 31st March 1939/Wiesbaden, Germany
Directing career: 1960-

Compared to his better known compatriots, Volker Schlöndorff may seem a mere craftsman with little artistic character. Beneath his films' often glossy veneer, however, lies an abiding interest in the relationship of rebels and outsiders to a repressive society.

After film studies in Paris, Schlöndorff gained experience in movie-making as an assistant to **Malle**, **Resnais** and, most notably, **Melville**; though he had made the short *Who Cares?* in 1960, it was not until 1966 that he directed his first feature, *Young Törless*. This psychologically astute study of the seductive nature of cruelty, set in a disciplinarian German boarding school at the turn of the century, was based on a book by Robert Musil and was the first of many successful literary adaptations by Schlöndorff; moreover, it illustrated his tendency to turn to the distant past to reflect on Germany's more recent history. In *Michael Kohlhaas*, a polished but passionless adaptation of Kleist's novel about a 16th-century horse dealer who wages war on the world about him, the relevance to contemporary social unrest was clear; in *The Sudden Fortune of the Poor People of Kombach* >1, about rural peasants who, in 1822, steal a tax-cart, only to be destroyed by their inability to cope with new-found wealth, he pointed both to the moral conservatism of the working classes and to the need for collective rather than individual rebellion. Schlöndorff's visual style was here starkly realist compared to his earlier work; indeed, firmly committed to an ideal of film as intelligent but popular entertainment, he has repeatedly relied on traditional forms of narrative while varying his visual style to suit the tone and scale of his material.

Summer Lightning, an ironically witty feminist account of a recently divorced woman's attempt to build a new life in a male-dominated society, both starred and was written by Schlöndorff's future wife and regular collaborator, Margarethe Von Trotta. In the late '70s she embarked upon a directing career of her own, her finest films being *The German Sisters*, *Friends and Husbands* and *Rosa Luxemburg*. Together, however, the couple directed *The Lost Honour of Katharina Blum* >**2**, a taut, angry but occasionally sentimental version of Heinrich Böll's scathing book, in which an innocent young woman is hounded by the right-wing press after she is discovered to have spent the night with a suspected terrorist; despite its portrait of a modern Germany infected by paranoia and prejudice, the film's success brought its makers widespread fame. Indeed, after the relatively muted *Coup de Grâce* (about a Russian aristocratic family's downfall in the face of Bolshevism), and a key role in the making of the compilation film, *Germany in Autumn*, which dealt with Germany's reaction to recent terrorist activity, Schlöndorff was able to film Günter Grass's *The Tin Drum* >**3**, an epic, personal history of Germany before and during World War II, seen through the eyes of a child who refuses to grow. In staying true to the book, the director misguidedly opted for realism; the result is a vivid but emotionally uninvolving series of grotesque tableaux.

Shot on location in Beirut and depicting a journalist unable to make a commitment either to his wife or to one of the factions in the Civil War, *Circle of Deceit* >**4** transcended the potentially formulaic nature of its plot by means of a complex, ironic script and an authentically menacing mood of social instability. Rather less interesting has been Schlöndorff's recent work in France and America: *Swann in Love*, condensed from Proust, was elegantly decorative but plodding; *Death of a Salesman* an over-reverent and theatrical rendition of Arthur Miller's play; and *A Gathering of Old Men* a worthy, well-acted but finally predictable drama about the continuance of racial prejudice and injustice in the Deep South.

While Schlöndorff's literary and social concerns remain the driving force behind much of his work, he recently seems to have lost the subtle blend of balance and passion evident in his best films. At the same time, however, he is the most conventional and accessible of modern German film-makers, and his attempts to mix politics with popular entertainment are deserving of attention.

Lineage

One may detect the influence of both **Malle** and **Melville** in Schlöndorff's work, which may perhaps most fruitfully be compared with that of his wife Margarethe Von Trotta and Reinhard Hauff.

Further reading

John Sandford's *The New German Cinema* (London, 1980).

Viewing

1 **The Sudden Fortune of the Poor People of Kombach**
W. Germany 1970/ w Reinhard Hauff, Rainer Werner Fassbinder, Margarethe Von Trotta

2 **The Lost Honour of Katharina Blum**
W. Germany 1975/ w Angela Winkler, Mario Adorf, Dieter Laser

3 **The Tin Drum**
W. Germany 1979/ w David Bennent, Angela Winkler, Mario Adorf

4 **Circle of Deceit**
W. Germany 1981/ w Bruno Ganz, Hanna Schygulla, Jerzy Skolimowski

Paul Schrader

Born: 22nd July 1946/Grand Rapids, Michigan, USA
Directing career: 1978-

The films of Paul Schrader are marked by schizophrenic tension: thematically, between repression and indulgence, spirit and flesh; stylistically, between art and entertainment. Indeed, few American directors have produced such an obsessive, personal body of work.

Crucially, in regard to the later development of his career, Schrader received a strict Calvinist upbringing, and only saw his first film at the age of 18. Fascinated by cinema, which had been condemned by Calvinists as tainted by 'worldliness', he became a movie critic, went to film school and finally made his entry into the industry as a scriptwriter, his credits including *The Yakuza* (for Sidney Pollack), *Obsession* (for **De Palma**) and, most successfully, *Taxi Driver* for **Scorsese**. By 1977 his reputation was already such that he was able to direct *Blue Collar* >**1** from his own formulaic but intelligent script, in which three lowly car-workers steal union funds only to discover that the union itself is corrupt and linked to the Mob; although basically a genre piece, the film was notable for its grittily unsentimental view of working-class life and for its attempt to merge melodrama with politics. Rather more ambitious, if widely neglected, was *Hardcore* >**2**. A harrowing, admittedly overblown, story of a staid and profoundly religious middle-American who leaves his quiet Michigan home-town to look for his missing daughter in a sleazy LA, the film was not only clearly rooted in its maker's own emotional ambivalence, but an effective *noir* allegory about an innocent's descent into hell. Significantly, sin is most garishly evoked by pornographic movie-making, the thin divide between puritanism and sensuality, anger and moral vengeance by the blood-red paper walls of a sex parlour.

If *Hardcore* was flawed by hysteria, *American Gigolo* >**3** was a misguidedly cold affair, about a high-class gigolo entrapped in a police case involving murder, political corruption and adultery. Schrader drew explicitly upon **Bresson**'s *Pickpocket* to suggest his hero's final redemption through love; sadly, the accent on glossy style and the actors' hollow posturing mitigated against meaning. Likewise, a remake of *Cat People*, which turned **Tourneur**'s poetic, ambiguous view of destructive sexuality to more literal ends and introduced an element of incest through the heroine's similarly cursed brother, buried its examination of repression and violent release beneath an emphasis on exotic, sophisticated eroticism.

Mishima >**4**, however, was altogether more intriguing in subject – the relationship of the Japanese writer's life to his work, his politics and the culture he both typified and railed against – and style: the film consisted, ambitiously, of three diverse but interwoven threads showing Mishima's early life in black and white, his last days in naturalistic colour, and three of his stories in sets notable for stylised artifice. As previously, the theme was of an individual's battle with destiny, while mood veered from cerebral contemplation to violent action. Schrader's recent work, however, has been less satisfying: *Light of Day* measured the gulf between a dissolute rock singer and her deeply religious mother, while a film about *Patty Hearst* attempted a dispassionate view of her once controversial role in criminal and terrorist activities. Although both movies were evidently the work of an intelligent film-maker, the one suffered from melodramatic predictability, the other from an apparent lack of moral commitment rare in Schrader's work.

The raw emotional power and intellectual ambitions that mark Schrader's best films sit uneasily with the emphatic visual gloss and weak characterisation of his lesser work. But his seriousness of purpose and willingness to explore his own anxiety through an essentially popular medium confirm him as a fascinating director.

Lineage

The influence of **Bresson** (who figures, alongside **Dreyer** and **Ozu**, in Schrader's book) is clear in his work; he may be compared with the equally troubled (Catholic) **Scorsese**, for whom – since *Taxi Driver* – he wrote *Raging Bull* and *The Last Temptation of Christ*. He writes occasionally in collaboration with his brother Leonard.

Further reading

Schrader's *Transcendental Style in Film: Ozu, Bresson, Dreyer* (Berkeley, 1972) illuminates some of his own preoccupations.

Viewing

1 **Blue Collar**
US 1978/ w Harvey Keitel, Richard Pryor, Yaphet Kotto
2 **Hardcore (The Hardcore Life)**
US 1979/ w George C. Scott, Peter Boyle, Season Hubley
3 **American Gigolo**
US 1979/ w Richard Gere, Lauren Hutton, Nina Van Pallandt
4 **Mishima (A Life in Four Chapters)**
US/Japan 1985/ w Ken Ogata, Masayuki Shionoya, Junkichi Orimoto

Martin Scorsese

Born: 17th November 1942/New York, USA
Directing career: 1963-

The most consistently invigorating American film-maker of recent years, Martin Scorsese has drawn upon his own Catholic anguish to invest various traditional Hollywood genres with rare tension and insight. If his later films lack the intensity of his finest work (to which Robert De Niro's magnificent, versatile acting seems to have been crucial), he nonetheless remains a uniquely challenging director, his energetic style reflecting the nervy, violent and tormentedly obsessive characters he depicts.

His passion for movies having developed during a sickly childhood, Scorsese abandoned his ambitions to become a priest. He began studying film at New York University, where he made several impressive shorts and, by 1969, he had completed his first, low budget feature, *Who's That Knocking At My Door?* A raw, highly personal account of adolescent confusion, inhibition and guilt set in New York's Little Italy, the film already evidenced the stylistic bravura and interest in male psychology (coupled with touches of misogyny) which would become regular elements of the director's work. His first commercial feature, *Boxcar Bertha* (a **Corman**-produced exploitation movie set during the '30s Depression, with a gang of dispossessed misfits – including a union organiser – becoming rebellious rural desperados) was equally promising; and *Mean Streets* >**1**, a vivid and often violent return to the sidewalks, bars and pool-rooms of Little Italy, with a petty mobster's loyalty to an irresponsible friend undermined by Catholic guilt, was memorable both for its authentic feel for Italian-American streetlife, and for a superb rock soundtrack that heightened the effect of its dynamic images.

After focussing, for once, on a female protagonist in *Alice Doesn't Live Here Anymore* (which effectively mixed the realism of the modern road-movie with the subject matter – a widow's attempt to build herself a new life – of a traditional weepie), Scorsese scored a controversial hit with *Taxi Driver* >**2**: a study of urban alienation in which a New York cabbie, driven by a fear of sexual inadequacy and a paranoid hatred of those he considers inferior, murders a pimp and his friends in a nightmarish bloodbath. Music, colour, and a restless, fluid camera contributed to a view of the city as a hell on earth, and mirrored the protagonist's growing insanity. Even better – because more objectively distanced – studies of male violence (the result of sexual insecurity and repression) were *New York, New York* >**3**, a lavish, stylised musical set in the '40s and '50s, depicting the tempestuous, competitive marriage of a singer and a selfish, immature and possessive jazz-saxophonist; and *Raging Bull* >**4**, a bleak biopic of boxing champ Jake La Motta, which contrasted his socially acceptable violence within the ring with the private, irrationally jealous brutality extended towards his wife and brother. Both films were dark, intimate, disturbing variations on classic Hollywood genres; they were distinguished by an emotional intensity provided by performances of astonishing immediacy, and by

The end of the road? Harvey Keitel discovers you can't mess with the Mob, in Scorsese's *Mean Streets*.

Scorsese's ability to achieve psychological realism through a virtuoso visual style involving slow-motion, Expressionist colour and lighting, rapid montage, and sweeping camera movements. At the same time, his polished technique created a superior, elegaic rock documentary in *The Last Waltz*, bidding farewell to The Band.

Perhaps Scorsese's most difficult movie to date, in that it lacked a single sympathetic character with whom audiences might identify, *King of Comedy* >**5** concerned the kidnapping of a TV chat show host by a pair of none-too-bright nonentities, who decide to trade his life against a few minutes on prime-time television. A sinister, surreally funny investigation of the absurd fantasies and hero-worship fostered by the media, the film's static camera and harsh, varnished colours effectively created a lonely world of deluded, self-regarding losers. The film was not a success and, in *After Hours* (a black screwball comedy characterized by tortuous twists in its nightmarish plot, in which a quiet computer programmer sets out for a date and nearly loses his life in an insane sequence of events in downtown Manhattan), and *The Color of Money* (a belated sequel to **Rossen**'s *The Hustler*, portraying the uneasy relationship between an ageing pool player and the naive young Turk he elects to educate and manage), the director employed his considerable techniques to more commercial and conventional ends. The result was a loss of emotional depth.

The Last Temptation of Christ >**6**, however, was a welcome if highly controversial return to form. This adaptation of Nikos Kazantzakis' novel sees Christ's progress to Calvary in unusually human terms that posit, as the ultimate temptation, his desire to shed Godliness and lead a normal family life. Scorsese was accused of blasphemy, despite the fact that the film, a heartfelt attempt to understand the torment of the Messiah's *emotional* life, climaxed in an affirmation of His divinity. Performed with conviction and inventively using Moroccan locations and a percussive score, its faults lay not in heresy but in a script whose dialogue sometimes lapsed into banality, and in the film medium's basic inability to illuminate the soul – which was, after all, Scorsese's subject.

A restless, unpredictable and provocative talent, Scorsese is by far the most mature and ambitious of the 'movie brats' who took Hollywood by storm in the '70s. If his films mirror his own anxieties in matters related to violence, sexuality, guilt, faith and doubt, they are simultaneously entertainments that reflect on contemporary society. Indeed, his ability to mix the confessional with the commercial to exciting, intelligent effect makes him one of modern cinema's most distinctive and versatile artists.

Lineage

A true cinephile, Scorsese may be seen as influenced by figures as diverse as **Minnelli**, **Nicholas Ray**, **Fuller**, **Kazan**, **Cassavetes**, **Powell**, **Bresson**, **Godard** and **Visconti**. Of his contemporaries it is most useful to compare him with **Schrader**, **Demme** and James Toback. He has appeared in small roles in several of his own films and to memorable effect in **Tavernier**'s *Round Midnight*.

Further reading

Mary Pat Kelly's *Martin Scorsese: The First Decade* (New York, 1980); David Thompson and Ian Christie's *Scorsese on Scorsese* (London, 1989).

Viewing

1 **Mean Streets**
US 1973/ w Harvey Keitel, Robert De Niro, Amy Robinson
2 **Taxi Driver**
US 1976/ w Robert De Niro, Cybill Shepherd, Jodie Foster
3 **New York, New York**
US 1977/ w Robert De Niro, Liza Minnelli, Lionel Stander
4 **Raging Bull**
US 1979/ w Robert De Niro, Cathy Moriarty, Joe Pesci
5 **King of Comedy**
US 1982/ w Robert De Niro, Jerry Lewis, Sandra Bernhard
6 **The Last Temptation of Christ**
US 1988/ w Willem Dafoe, Harvey Keitel, Barbara Hershey

Ridley Scott

Born: 30th November 1937/South Shields, England
Directing career: 1977-

Although the films Ridley Scott chooses to make suggest a director of considerable ambition, he is unlikely to be taken very seriously until he overcomes an inability to tell a story clearly or to create credible, vivid characters. Too concerned with the look of things, his work is often predictable, even incoherent.

Scott was already established as a director of flash, glossy commercials when he made his feature debut with *The Duellists*, a turgid if visually sumptuous adaptation of Joseph Conrad's story of an obsessive feud between two officers during the Napoleonic Wars. But it was the gory, unpleasant sci-fi horror film *Alien* >**1** which first suggested his box-office potential: by immersing the hackneyed Old Dark House-style plot (a space-ship is invaded by a physically repulsive, ferociously murderous monster) in sombre, shadowy visuals, Scott was almost able to conceal the fundamental obviousness of his shock-editing and the stereotypical nature of his two-dimensional characters. Still more extravagantly mounted was *Blade Runner* >**2**. Here, the evocation of a rainy, foggy 21st-century Los Angeles (a hi-tech metropolis in a state of terminal urban decay) took precedence over a sloppily structured narrative about a cop hunting down dangerous humanoid 'replicants'. At least Scott's penchant for visual overload (lashings of mood with a bountiful use of back-lighting, reminiscent of television ads) lent this futuristic world a bogus authenticity, but *Legend* (a ludicrously fey sub-Tolkien fantasy, about a Lord of Darkness who attempts to plunge a world of unicorns, elves and princesses into wintry night), became so bogged down in irrelevant trivia that the film collapsed under the weight of its own design.

Even when dealing with a recognisable location (contemporary New York) in the thriller *Someone to Watch Over Me* >**3**, Scott felt duty-bound to go overboard with lavish, up-market photography and decor, although at least the palatial apartment inhabited by the wealthy murder-witness with whom a married, blue-collar cop falls in love, served the dramatic purpose of suggesting a difference in class background. Again, however, despite fine performances which for once acknowledged the more painful aspects of adultery, the over-emphatic, picturesque style tended to dissipate suspense.

Scott is perhaps a victim of his own advertising background; an erratic, often clumsy storyteller, all too prone to settle for a cheap and facile visual coup. Blessed with an eye for dazzling designs, he has yet to learn to equate style with meaning.

Lineage

Scott may be compared with other British directors with a past in ads: his own brother Tony, **Parker**, Adrian Lyne and Hugh Hudson.

Viewing

1 **Alien**
US 1979/ w Tom Skerritt, Sigourney Weaver, John Hurt, Ian Holm
2 **Blade Runner**
US 1982/ w Harrison Ford, Rutger Hauer, Sean Young
3 **Someone to Watch Over Me**
US 1987/ w Tom Berenger, Mimi Rogers, Lorraine Bracco

Don Siegel

Born: 26th October 1912/Chicago, Illinois, USA
Directing career: 1945-

It is perhaps odd that Donald Siegel, one of America's finest action directors, remained true to the modest spirit of his early B-thrillers even when a succession of box-office hits in the late '60s at last brought him larger budgets and greater freedom. Such was his ability to transcend financial limitations, however, that the best of his early films were as taut, skilful and exciting as his celebrated series of collaborations with **Clint Eastwood**.

A graduate of Jesus College, Cambridge, Siegel first worked as film librarian at Warners, before becoming editor then head of the studio's montage department; in shooting the short time-lapse sequences for films like *The Roaring Twenties* and *Casablanca*, he became renowned for deft characterisation and narrative economy – qualities evident throughout his career. Finally, in 1946, after directing two Oscar-winning shorts (*Star in the Night* and *Hitler Lives?*), he made his feature debut with *The Verdict*, a slight but moody little thriller set in Victorian London and starring Sydney Greenstreet as a reluctantly retired Scotland Yard detective bent on deadly revenge: the first of Siegel's several rogue cops. More typical of his future work, however, was *The Big Steal*, which mixed dark comedy with expertly mounted action scenes (the entire movie is a chase, with an innocent hero pursued through Mexico by a corrupt army payroll officer). Throughout the '50s, Siegel alternated routine thrillers and Westerns with subtler work, most of which focussed on the social outsider, often shown as torn between his irrational impulses towards violence and a need for self-control.

In the tough, grittily realist *Riot in Cell Block 11* >**1**, the leader of a gang of prisoners holding warders hostage in a battle for better conditions, continually struggles against his own anger and brutality; *Invasion of the Body Snatchers* >**2**, a classic sci-fi allegory on '50s paranoia, focusses on the sole survivor of an alien attack on smalltown America which, aiming at conformism the world over, turns humans into cold, emotionless replicas of themselves; *Crime in the Streets*, featuring an impressively nervy performance from **John Cassavetes**, is a gripping study of juvenile delinquency; while *Baby Face Nelson* and *The Line-Up* >**3** portray, respectively, the gangster and two hired killers as psychotics in a hostile world. Never given to explicit liberal pleading, Siegel reveals the unsentimental sympathy he feels for his anti-heroes through his vivid characterisation, and rarely allows the often violent action to overshadow his people.

In the early '60s Siegel was forced to alternate feature films with work in television; indeed, after *Flaming Star* (a tough study of anti-Indian prejudice and Elvis Presley's finest vehicle) and *Hell Is For Heroes* (which viewed war heroism as psychopathic violence), he remade **Siodmak**'s *The Killers* >**4** as the first movie shot specifically for TV. A cool, clinical account of two gunmen who attempt to find out, in a series of narrative flashbacks, why they were hired to kill a man, it was deemed too violent for the small screen and released in cinemas; in fact, Siegel established his electric mood in the first scene as the pair bully the staff and inmates of a home for the blind, and thereafter *implied* rather than showed brutality. Later telefilms (*The Hanged Man*, *Stranger on the Run*) were equally ambitious but less well executed, and it was *Madigan*, a complex, hard-as-nails police thriller pitching a liberal

Clint Eastwood discusses a scene with his director and mentor Don Siegel, on location for *Dirty Harry*.

commissioner against a ruthlessly pragmatic cop resentful of red-tape, which saw Siegel successfully rejoin the feature film world.

With *Coogan's Bluff* (which contrasted an Arizona deputy's hunting methods, as he trails a criminal in New York's concrete canyons, with those of the city's Police Dept), Siegel began his fruitful collaboration with Clint Eastwood. *Two Mules for Sister Sara* was an uneven, sporadically amusing Western; *The Beguiled* (a Yankee soldier, wounded in the Civil War, seduces pupils and teachers at a secluded girls seminary, only to find that his deceptions have awakened a lethal desire for vengeance) was a relatively arty, sombre and ambitious excursion into Gothic nightmare. Most impressive of all, however, was *Dirty Harry* >**5**, a complex, disturbingly ambivalent study of a cop whose vigilante ethics and brutal methods bring him into angry conflict with his liberal superiors. Without concealing the man's bigotry, Siegel reveals an acute awareness of the contradictions by which society demands to be protected from crime but distrusts those it employs to do the job. Far less troubled, but similarly benefitting from the director's brisk, linear style of storytelling, fluid editing, and crisp, uncluttered visual sense, was *Charley Varrick* >**6** in which a criminal's triumphant battle against the Mob celebrates 'the last of the independents': a title perhaps befitting Siegel himself.

Thereafter, although professionally crafted, Siegel's films became more erratic. *The Black Windmill*, *Telefon*, *Rough Cut*, and *Jinxed!* (a troubled production scattered with scenes of delicious black comedy) suffered from uneven scripting; *The Shootist* >**7**, on the other hand, was a superbly lyrical, elegaic Western about an aged gunfighter coming to terms with cancer, and a moving tribute to its star John Wayne; while *Escape from Alcatraz*, with Eastwood as a convict who patiently tunnels his way out of the prison with a pair of nail-scissors, was an impressively austere, strangely meditative study of human indomitability. Both films, subtly shot and acted, suggested a mature mellowing of Siegel's rugged individualism.

Working with modest budgets and largely disreputable genres, Siegel nevertheless managed to stamp his artistic signature on a remarkably high proportion of his films. His presentation of violence was never gratuitous; neither did he sacrifice wit, character or narrative fluency to the demands of action. In his best work, intelligence is balanced with excitement and vitality.

Lineage

Marked by his years at Warners, Seigel may be seen as a successor to action directors like **Walsh** and **Hawks**, and one may compare him with figures like **Fuller** and **Aldrich**. He himself clearly influenced **Peckinpah** (his former assistant) and **Eastwood**.

Further reading

Alan Lovell's *Don Siegel* (London, 1977), Judith M. Kass's *The Hollywood Professionals, Vol 4* (New York, 1975).

Viewing

1 **Riot in Cell Block 11**
US 1954/ w Neville Brand, Emile Meyer, Leo Gordon
2 **Invasion of the Body Snatchers**
US 1956/ w Kevin McCarthy, Dana Wynter, Larry Gates
3 **The Line-Up**
US 1958/ w Eli Wallach, Robert Keith, Warner Anderson
4 **The Killers**
US 1964/ w Lee Marvin, John Cassavetes, Angie Dickinson, Ronald Reagan
5 **Dirty Harry**
US 1971/ w Clint Eastwood, Harry Guardino, Andy Robinson
6 **Charley Varrick**
US 1973/ w Walter Matthau, Joe Don Baker, Andy Robinson
7 **The Shootist**
US 1976/ w John Wayne, Lauren Bacall, Ron Howard, James Stewart

Robert Siodmak

Born: 8th August 1900/Memphis, Tennessee, USA
Died: 10th March 1973/Locarno, Switzerland
Directing career: 1929-1969

The reputation of Robert Siodmak rests on a number of thrillers made during a few brief years in the '40s. Although his work in Europe both before and after that period is now rarely seen, he remains an important, if underrated, figure in the development and exploration of the style now known as *film noir*.

Born to German-Jewish parents, Siodmak moved to Germany when a year old. After working in business and the theatre, he entered the movies as title-writer and editor. His directing debut, *People on Sunday*, was a charming, almost plotless romantic comedy notable for its realist, location-shot study of Berliners at play over a weekend, and for Siodmak's collaborators, who included Edgar G. Ulmer, **Wilder**, **Zinnemann** and the director's brother Curt, later a screenwriter of note. Siodmak went on to make several competent but unremarkable dramas, but with the rise of the Nazis in 1933, he fled to Paris to continue his career. In 1940 he was again forced to flee, and embarked upon a number of B-movies in Hollywood, most notably the stylish *Son of Dracula* and the memorably camp *Cobra Woman*. But only in 1944 did he find his true niche with *Phantom Lady* >**1**, a superbly atmospheric thriller about a secretary's search for a missing woman who can supply her boss, arrested for murder, with an alibi. Well performed and making excellent use of a shadowy Expressionism – virtually abstract in a virtuoso jazz-club scene where the heroine's flirtation with a crucial witness provokes him to an orgasmic climax of drumming – the film featured a psychotic killer and introduced both Siodmak's eloquent visual style and his fascination with such psychological themes as insanity, obsession, paranoia, loyalty and betrayal.

For the next six years, Siodmak's murky, morbidly fatalistic and expertly crafted thrillers focussed on a gallery of vividly drawn characters involved in deathly struggles: *Christmas Holiday* imaginatively cast Deanna Durbin and Gene Kelly against type as a singer-hostess and her murderously vengeful husband; in *The Suspect* and *Uncle Harry*, **Charles Laughton** and George Sanders, respectively, played shy innocents driven to murder by romantic infatuation and repressive families; *The Spiral Staircase* >**2** milked suspense from having a deaf mute stalked by a killer with a psychotic hatred of women with physical imperfections; while *The Dark Mirror* featured identical twins (both played by Olivia De Havilland), one normal, the other a homicidal schizophrenic. Similarly, when in the later '40s Siodmak turned to a slightly more realist form of *noir*, shooting, as was then fashionable, partly on location, he not only retained his *chiaroscuro* visual style but emphasised the psychological and emotional aspects of character and plot. *The Killers* >**3**, a multi-flashback heist-movie based very loosely on a story by Hemingway, has a boxer (Burt Lancaster in an impressive screen debut) become fatally involved in a daring robbery because of his obsession with the gang-leader's treacherous mistress; in *Cry of the City* >**4**, a cop hunting down the hoodlum he grew up with is visually interpreted as the negative mirror image of his prey; *Criss-Cross* repeats the blend of erotic entrapment and murderous deception of *The Killers*; and *The File on Thelma Jordon* concerns an honest District Attorney whose gullible, illicit submission to the seductive wiles of a murderess endangers his career, his marriage and his life. Time and again, the pitfalls of melodrama are avoided by finely judged performances and the director's astute, economic characterisation through visual means.

In the '50s Siodmak's career went into decline. After the glorious exuberance and tongue-in-cheek wit of *The Crimson Pirate*, which revealed Lancaster's acrobatic talent to graceful effect, Siodmak resumed his career in Europe; the subsequent films made in France and Germany were largely mediocre. But his late '40s crime films have rarely been bettered, and his work is ripe for reappraisal.

Lineage

Siodmak's *noir* thrillers often inspire mention of **Lang**, who saw destiny rather than individual psychology as a moving force. One might also compare Siodmak with **Hitchcock**, **Anthony Mann**, **Lewis**, **Fuller** and – perhaps more appropriately – **Carné**.

Further reading

Colin MacArthur's *Underworld USA* (London, 1972).

Viewing

1 **Phantom Lady**
US 1944/ w Ella Raines, Thomas Gomez, Franchot Tone

2 **The Spiral Staircase**
US 1945/ w Dorothy McGuire, George Brent, Ethel Barrymore

3 **The Killers**
US 1946/ w Burt Lancaster, Ava Gardner, Albert Dekker

4 **Cry of the City**
US 1948/ w Victor Mature, Richard Conte, Shelley Winters

Douglas Sirk

Born: 26th April 1900/Hamburg, Germany
Died: 14th January 1987/Lugano, Switzerland
Directing career: 1934-1959

It is ironic that during the '50s, when the former Hans Detlef Sierck was at his most successful in terms of audience appeal, he was virtually ignored by the critics. He is now seen, however, as a director of formidable intellect who, despite his background in classical and avant-garde theatre, achieved his best work in melodrama.

Having studied law, philosophy and art history, Sirk became deeply – and very successfully – involved in the German theatre, directing countless classics throughout the '20s. In 1934 he was taken on by Berlin's illustrious Ufa studios and, after shooting three shorts, directed his first feature (*April April*) in 1935. He soon revealed a lustrous, intensely emotional style, creating meaning and mood through lighting, composition, decor and music: in *Pillars of Society* (a study of bourgeois hypocrisy and greed adapted from Ibsen), repressed passions finally gather force in a cathartic, symbolic sea-storm, while in *To New Shores* >**1**, largely set in an Australian penal colony of the 19th century, the exotic scorched setting is an apt dramatic backdrop to the story of a woman who sacrifices her happiness to help a worthless lover.

Nazi influence increasing at Ufa, in 1937 Sirk fled Germany for France and Holland, where he made two films now forgotten. In 1939 he went to Hollywood at the invitation of Warners to make an American version of *To New Shores*. The film was never made and it was only three years later that he completed *Hitler's Madman*, his first American feature, about the reprisals taken against a Czech village after the assassination of the Nazi tyrant, Heydrich. Very few of Sirk's early American films were remarkable, however well-crafted and ambitious: *Summer Storm*, a sensitive adaptation of Chekov's *The Shooting Party*, was strong on atmosphere; *Sleep, My Love* was an elegant wife-in-peril psychological thriller in the tradition of **Cukor**'s *Gaslight*; and *Shockproof*, about the doomed love affair between a murderess and her parole officer, was an effective *noir* thriller, scripted by **Sam Fuller**. Only in 1950, when he signed a contract with Universal, did Sirk find his true niche: after a number of intractable assignments, he directed a trilogy of musicals (*Has Anybody Seen My Gal?*, *Meet Me at the Fair*, and *Take Me to Town* >**2**), laced with lively comedy, shot in pastel colours, and imbued with a nostalgia for the innocence of smalltown life of earlier years; crucially, however, the second features a plot involving political corruption, and the third ends in a virtuoso chase scene contrasting reality with a stage play. Such dark, subtle undercurrents rose to the surface in his later work.

With *All I Desire*, a sombre melodrama about a failed actress who returns to her husband and children, and becomes a victim of smalltown gossip about her former lover, Sirk for the first time examined the American Dream and found it wanting. Time and again in the melodramas that followed, he presented America as a haven for hypocrisy, class elitism and racial prejudice, material greed and moral complacency; and by framing his attack on affluent postwar society within melodramatic conventions (which imply that the course of true love be forever troubled), he was able to create a body of work at once politically subversive and emotionally devastating.

Rock Hudson and Jane Wyman, lit with characteristic perfection, in Sirk's bitter portrait of bourgeois mores, *All That Heaven Allows.*

In *All That Heaven Allows* >**3** (made after the astonishingly popular, insanely contrived *Magnificent Obsession*), he turned a conventional love story between a widow and her younger gardener into a study of the fall of American idealism and innocence, the references to Thoreau and lush images of nature contrasting with the claustrophobic, petty-minded snobbery of a country-club set. Indeed, the family, so often glamorised by Hollywood, is regarded as selfish and inhibiting, with the widow's teenage children horrified at the idea of another man tainting their dead father's hallowed memory. Similarly, in *Written on the Wind* >**4**, an archetypal Texan oil dynasty is beset by impotence, nymphomania, alcoholism, self-loathing and sibling jealousy, the poisonous products of excessive wealth and a patriarchal favouritism that climaxes in manslaughter. The sordid drama is both made palatable and intensified by Sirk's delirious use of gaudy, non-naturalistic colours and imaginative symbolism: a woman, mourning the death of her father and brother and the loss of her beloved, weeps over a model oil-derrick, an apt phallic symbol of material greed and masculine domination.

Sirk's last three melodramas were no less original in their use of colour, movement, decor and music to lend satirical edge and emotional power to potentially soapy material. In *The Tarnished Angels* >**5** (a superbly bleak version of Faulkner's novel *Pylon*, shot in lush monochrome), a group of stunt fliers mirror the irresponsibility, insecurity and self-destructive despair of Depression America; in *A Time to Love and a Time to Die*, based on a book by Erich Maria Remarque and filmed in Germany, the wartime love affair between a soldier on leave and a young girl blossoms because of, rather than despite, the devastation and death around them; and in *Imitation of Life* >**6**, the glossy rags-to-riches life of an actress – metaphorically distanced from reality – contrasts with the emotional misery of her black friend and servant whose daughter, passing for white and also an actress, is driven by the racism of American society to deny her own mother. Indeed, the maid's lavish funeral, paid for by the friends her employer never even knew she had, was an achingly moving and appropriate end to Sirk's Hollywood career; abandoning a project he had written with Ionesco, he retired from the cinema in 1959 and returned to Germany to resume his theatrical work.

Though it is widely held that Sirk worked in melodrama less from choice than from necessity, the genre allowed him to confront contemporary American life directly, and to do so with maximum emotional impact. By adapting the contrived and sumptuous artifice of melodrama's conventions to his own needs, he won over a large audience who might otherwise have felt alienated from his morally disenchanted and intellectually cynical view of America.

Lineage

Influenced by literary figures and an admirer of **Dreyer**, Sirk was a successor to **Griffith**, **Borzage**, **Leisen** and John M. Stahl, whose *Magnificent Obsession*, *Imitation of Life* and *When Tomorrow Comes* Sirk remade (the last as *Interlude*). Although (like **Minnelli** and **Ray** to whom he may be compared) he impressed **Godard** and other New Wave directors, only **Fassbinder** emulated him, remaking *All That Heaven Allows* as *Fear Eats the Soul*, while the first episodes of television's *Dallas* were indelibly marked by *Written on the Wind*.

Further reading

Douglas Sirk ed. John Halliday, Laura Mulvey (Edinburgh, 1972). Halliday's *Sirk on Sirk* (London, 1971) is an interview.

Viewing

1 **To New Shores (Zu Neuen Ufern)**
Germany 1937/ w Zarah Leander, Willy Birgel, Viktor Staal

2 **Take Me to Town**
US 1952/ w Sterling Hayden, Ann Sheridan, Philip Reed

3 **All That Heaven Allows**
US 1955/ w Jane Wyman, Rock Hudson, Agnes Moorehead

4 **Written on the Wind**
US 1956/ w Robert Stack, Rock Hudson, Lauren Bacall

5 **The Tarnished Angels**
US 1957/ w Dorothy Malone, Rock Hudson, Robert Stack

6 **Imitation of Life**
US 1958/ w Lana Turner, John Gavin, Juanita Moore

Victor Sjöström

Born: 20th September 1879/Silbodal, Sweden
Died: 3rd January 1960/Stockholm, Sweden
Directing career: 1912-1937

Widely regarded as a founding father of Swedish cinema, Victor David Sjöström was also one of the silent cinema's greatest directors. Though much of his work is now lost, what remains reveals an astonishing talent, with visual beauty, psychological subtlety and restrained performances lending the films a timeless power.

Having spent his early years in New York with a puritanical, tyrannical father, the young Sjöström returned to Sweden where he later became a successful theatrical actor and director. In 1912, he appeared in his first film, his contemporary Mauritz Stiller's *The Black Masks*; that same year he made his own directing debut, *The Gardener*. His earliest surviving work, *Ingeborg Holm* (about a woman suffering a mental breakdown when poverty forces her to send her children to work), was a study in grim social realism, while *Terje Vigen* (*A Man There Was*), based on Ibsen's poem about a Norwegian sailor who, during the Napoleonic Wars, finds that his family has died of starvation while he has been imprisoned by the British navy, introduced the director's abiding interest in the themes of revenge, sin and redemption, as well as his sense of the natural elements as an epic, menacing, mystically active force.

In *The Outlaw and His Wife* >**1**, a wealthy widow and an alleged sheep-stealer's love for each other eventually leads them to live away from society in a remote mountain landscape; their happiness is assured in a sunny summer idyll, until winter's arrival coincides with their death. Besides Sjöström's ability to convey emotional states through vividly shot landscapes, however, he also treated often melodramatic stories with rare restraint and (frequently taking a lead role himself) elicited naturalistic contributions from his actors. Nor were his films all sombre or realistic: *His Lordship's Last Will* was largely comic, *Masterman* a touching and psychologically acute portrait of a money-lender redeemed by his unrequited love for a young girl, *The Phantom Carriage* a fantasy parable, complete with virtuoso multi-exposures and complex flashbacks, in which a drunkard sees the error of his violent ways.

In 1923 Sjöström went to Hollywood. Sadly, most of his output for MGM (where he worked as Victor Seastrom) is lost, the Garbo movie, *The Divine Woman*, included. *He Who Gets Slapped* >**2**, however, adapted from Leonid Andreyev's play in which a scientist, cruelly betrayed by his patron and his wife, decides to live out his fear and humiliation in public by becoming a circus clown, is an acerbic, subtle study of masochistic suffering; it is also an astonishing example of Sjöström's ability to mix seedy realism, Expressionist metaphor and surreal fantasy through startlingly original camera-work: at the end, the circus ring is transformed into a spinning globe from which the hero's corpse is tossed towards the audience by his colleagues, grinning grotesquely in mute reproach. More conventional if no less powerful was a version of Nathaniel Hawthorne's *The Scarlet Letter*, in which the director's lyrical depiction of 17th-century rural New England, combined with a luminous performance by Lillian Gish as Hester Prynne (the innocent adulteress hounded by Puritan intolerance), produced an uncommonly sensitive literary adaptation reminiscent of some of Sjöström's Swedish work. But it is *The Wind* >**3** that remains his masterpiece, and one of the great films of all time. About a naive Virginian girl who travels West to live with relatives, only to find herself in a hostile, desert wilderness suffering an unwanted marriage, rape, and the guilt and insanity that follow the killing of her assailant, the film (shot on location in the Mojave Desert) escalates with inexorable logic from delicately detailed, semi-comic realism to full-blown melodrama; Sjöström's poetic symbolism – wind, sand, a rampant white stallion – serves to reveal the psychological fears of Gish's romantically deluded heroine, and lends a mythical dimension to the theme of Man's battle against dangerous, elemental forces.

After *The Wind* – too bleak and bizarre for audiences of the time – Sjöström made only two more Hollywood films (including the talkie

Confronted with the jealousy of Dorothy Cumming, Lillian Gish (right) discovers that life out west is less than rosy in Sjöström's remarkable *The Wind.*

A Lady to Love) before returning to Sweden. Thereafter, but for one last Swedish film, and *Under The Red Robe*, a visually elegant but otherwise unremarkable costume drama made for Alexander Korda in England in 1937, he restricted himself to acting, most notably as Professor Borg in **Bergman**'s *Wild Strawberries*. If his work in the sound cinema was negligible, in the silent years he was both an important innovator (most especially in his location filming), and an astute dramatist, endowed with an imaginative sense of how to portray passion, anxiety and despair in purely visual terms.

Lineage

A more sombre and penetrating artist than Stiller, Sjöström was a huge influence on later Swedish directors such as Alf Sjöberg and **Bergman**, not to mention **Dreyer**. In terms of his contributions to the development of film storytelling, he may perhaps be compared with **Griffith**, **Lang**, **Von Stroheim**, and **Murnau**.

Further reading

Graham Petrie's *Hollywood Destinies* (London, 1985), Peter Cowie's *Sweden 2* (London, 1970).

Viewing

1 **The Outlaw and His Wife**
Sweden 1918/ w Sjöström, Edith Erastoff

2 **He Who Gets Slapped**
US 1924/ w Lon Chaney, Norma Shearer, John Gilbert

3 **The Wind**
US 1928/ w Lillian Gish, Lars Hanson, Montagu Love

Jerzy Skolimowski

Born: 5th May 1938/Warsaw, Poland
Directing career: 1960-

If Jerzy Skolimowski seems, in recent years, to have succumbed to the same aimlessness that marks several of his film's heroes, he nevertheless remains one of the most distinctive and invigorating directors to have emerged from postwar Poland. Mixing a basically realistic vision of society with a surreal, anarchic wit, his work is restlessly inventive and insistently offbeat.

A poet, actor and ex-boxer, Skolimowski co-scripted **Wajda**'s *Innocent Sorcerers* and **Polanski**'s *Knife in the Water*, in which an emphasis on the generation gap in postwar Poland anticipated one of the dominant themes of his own work. His first feature *Rysopis* (*Identification Marks: None*), shot during his four years at Lodz film school, saw the director himself playing the alienated anti-hero, whose diffident wanderings during the last few hours before he joins the army revealed not only Skolimowski's ironic, cynical attitude towards the political optimism prevalent in his country, but also his fluid, agile camera style. Its more polished sequel, *Walkover* >**1** (with Skolimowski reviving the earlier film's central character as a smalltime boxer tempted to duck a fight), was still more visually distinctive, comprised of only 29 long, complex and dazzlingly energetic takes. In each, the thin plot (structured as a meandering, seemingly meaningless search for identity) explores the tensions between rebellion and conformism, both in society at large and within the individual, while *Barrier*, more consciously poetic, probes the gulf between romance and cynicism, its student protagonist's contempt, for an older generation absorbed in their memories of the war, partly mollified by his meeting with a girl.

Made in Belgium, *Le Départ* >**2** was an altogether more frantic and funny treatment of a similar theme, its hairdresser hero torn between his obsession for car racing (the zany, pacy plot deals with his efforts to find money to hire a Porsche) and the more mature, sexual fulfilment represented by his girlfriend. Although finally shallow, the film's frenetic narrative and mobile camera provided a stylish reflection of its hero's neurotic mania. Darker by far, *Hands Up!*, an anti-Stalinist allegory in which Poles of all types and generations are trapped in a railway carriage going nowhere, was banned by the Polish authorities, resulting in Skolimowski's decision to continue his career in the West.

After *The Adventures of Gerard*, a hectic and uneven spoof of Conan Doyle's Napoleonic novel, Skolimowski returned to the theme of an anguished, alienated outsider's sexual awakening with *Deep End* >**3**, in which a shy young swimming-pool attendant falls for a female colleague, his obsession ending, tragically, in the girl's death. Though dated, the film still impresses with its unexpected plot twists, its vivid gallery of eccentrics, and its imaginative use of seedy London locations. *King, Queen, Knave*, however, while lauded by some as a superior Nabokov adaptation, was a glossy and emotionally hollow black comedy about an incestuous sex triangle.

Adapted from a story by Robert Graves and concerning another sinister triangle (a married couple and a mysterious, possibly mad visitor who claims he can kill with his magical voice), *The Shout* was an intriguing but finally implausible, even pretentious fantasy. Rather more satisfying, and reminiscent of Skolimowski's early talent for discovering the bizarre within the real world, was *Moonlighting* >**4**, a wry comic parable inspired by the recent advent of martial law in Poland. Here, four Polish builders – only one of whom speaks English and knows of the political crisis at home – become entangled in an absurd travesty of normal labour relations while decorating their (unseen) boss's *pied-à-terre* in London. Skolimowski's sharp intelligence lies not only in the way he allows a complex web of conflicting motives to account for the foreman's concealment of news of Warsaw from his compatriots, but in the delightfully observed clashes between hostile English and uncomprehending Poles. Alas, *Success is the Best Revenge* was an altogether too disjointedly incoherent attempt to rework a similar theme, while *The Lightship* (in which psychotic hoods take over a ship captained by a pacifist) was a taut, charismatically performed but surprisingly conventional thriller.

If Skolimowski's work is for the most part visually exciting, it nonetheless frequently suffers from a lack of emotional depth. His sceptical intelligence is agile but erratic, while his black, bizarre sense of humour is most effectively displayed when he is interpreting a real, contemporary society, rather than a world more recognisable as a product of cinematic or literary conventions.

Lineage

Together with **Polanski**, Skolimowski was the most notable of the younger Polish directors that followed **Wajda** and Andrzej Munk. *Barrier* and *Le Départ* admitted to the influence of **Godard**; comparisons with **Antonioni** and early **Forman** may also be useful.

Further reading

Second Wave, ed. Ian Cameron (London, 1970)

Viewing

1 **Walkover**
Poland 1965/ w Skolimowski, Alexandra Zawieruszanka

2 **Le Départ**
Belgium 1967/ w Jean-Pierre Léaud, Catherine Duport, Paul Roland

3 **Deep End**
GB/W Germany 1970/ w John Moulder-Brown, Jane Asher, Diana Dors

4 **Moonlighting**
GB 1981/ w Jeremy Irons, Eugene Lipinski, Jiri Stanislav

Steven Spielberg

Born: 18th December 1947/ Cincinnati, Ohio, USA
Directing career: 1971-

In bringing a distinctly personal sensibility to the traditional genres of mass entertainment, Steven Spielberg rapidly became the most commercially successful director in cinema history. While it is impossible to deny either his Midas touch or his extraordinary technical proficiency, it has nonetheless become increasingly clear in recent years that he is perhaps more at home with sentimental 'family' fodder than with more sophisticated material.

A movie devotee from an early age, Spielberg was already an adept amateur film-maker in his teens. In 1969, *Amblin'*, his first professional short, so impressed Universal that he was given work as a director on various television series. Two years later, *Duel* >**1**, the first of his three impressive TV films (*Something Evil* was an unusually frightening supernatural mystery, *Savage* an imaginatively photographed if otherwise routine thriller), was so well received by critics that in Europe it gained a theatrical release. A taut, gripping road-movie in which a travelling salesman's saloon comes into conflict with a seemingly driverless, murderous truck, the film presaged a recurrent motif in Spielberg's early work: an Everyman character, plunged into chaos by an encounter with the extraordinary or the irrational. In his theatrical debut proper, *The Sugarland Express* (still perhaps his most unsentimentally humane film), a woman and her escaped convict husband kidnap a police officer and his car, to find that their flight has become the focus of inexplicably enormous media attention; while in *Jaws* >**2**, a calm coastal resort suddenly falls prey to an unemotional, apparently indestructible, man-eating Great White Shark. Astoundingly successful, *Jaws* made excellent use of razor-sharp editing and numerous red-herrings to increase tension; more crucially, it thrived on universal fears of the unseen and of dismemberment, simultaneously evoking mythic dimensions reminiscent of Melville's *Moby Dick*.

Similarly remarkable was *Close Encounters of the Third Kind* >**3**, an unusually thoughtful, optimistic and mystical addition to the alien-visitors sci-fi genre in which various ordinary humans, haunted by inexplicable visions after sighting UFOs, meet up with benevolent extra-terrestrials at a suitably dramatic and remote site in the

Drawing upon universal fears about the mysterious inhabitants of the sea, the enormously successful *Jaws* turned Spielberg into a major Hollywood director overnight.

Wyoming desert. While the special effects throughout were superb, Spielberg's depiction of the sightings' baleful influence on the family life of those 'inspired' by the UFOs kept the human element of his story well to the fore. Conversely, *1941*, a hectic slapstick epic about invasion paranoia in wartime Hollywood, was wrecked by its extravagant, mechanical interest in objects out of control, rather than in human actions and emotions: an indulgent and dismal triumph of technique over content. Equally shallow but infinitely more amusing, *Raiders of the Lost Ark* >**4** was a parody-cum-tribute to the old adventure serials of the '30s and '40s, in which Spielberg's expert sense of timing was coupled with his love of comic-strip fantasy to create confident, inventive entertainment.

ET: The Extra-Terrestrial >**5**, in which a cute alien stranded in Spielberg's beloved smalltown America is befriended and cared for by a young boy, was both the director's most successful film to date and the beginning of a disappointing artistic decline. If it offered enormous evidence of a talent adept at manipulating an audience's emotions, it simultaneously wallowed in cheap, maudlin sentimentality and suggested that cinema's boy wonder was perhaps regressing to a childish vision of the world, totally removed from reality. A saccharine episode for *The Twilight Zone* was similarly devoid of mature insights, while the sequel to *Raiders*, *Indiana Jones and the Temple of Doom*, was so wrapped up in its re-creation of a '30s world-view that it also reproduced that era's unthinking racism and sexism. In 1986, as if to compensate for this last misjudgement, Spielberg filmed *The Color Purple* >**6**, a version of Alice Walker's novel about the cruel physical and spiritual suffering, and final rebellion, of a young black woman, victim of male pride and white prejudice in the Deep South during the early part of the century. While clearly deeply felt, not to mention technically faultless, the film seemed simplistic and sanitised, not only in the perhaps inevitable underplaying of the book's lesbian content, but in the presentation of place (glowingly pastoral throughout) and people, with virtually every character, including the heroine's tyrant of an ex-husband, redeemed by the weepy resolution of the finale.

Nevertheless, after a flawed but largely faithful version of J.G. Ballard's *Empire of the Sun* (a young boy, interned in the Japanese prison camps in China during World War II, discovers that survival necessitates a self-centred, dog-eat-dog morality), it seems that Spielberg is again concerned to treat a more complex, chaotic world than his early '80s films would admit to. While the childrens' adventure films he produces, directed by colleagues, tend (with the odd exception) towards the maudlin and mindless, there is yet hope that his own work will mature and grow more ambitious in terms of emotions, rather than technique.

Lineage

An admirer of **Hitchcock**, **Disney**, **Lean** and '50s sci-fi, Spielberg has collaborated with other 'movie brats' like **Lucas**, **Milius** and **Coppola**. As producer, he has also worked with (and inspired) such figures as **Dante**, **Zemeckis**, Tobe Hooper, William Dear and Matthew Robbins; **Kaufman** and Lawrence Kasdan have been his screenwriters.

Further reading

Lynda Myles and Michael Pye's *The Movie Brats* (New York, 1979), Donald R Mott and Cheryl McAllister Saunders' *Steven Spielberg* (London, 1986).

Viewing

1 **Duel**
US 1971/ w Dennis Weaver, Jacqueline Scott, Eddie Firestone
2 **Jaws**
US 1974/ w Roy Scheider, Richard Dreyfuss, Robert Shaw
3 **Close Encounters of the Third Kind**
US 1977/ w Richard Dreyfuss, François Truffaut, Melinda Dillon
4 **Raiders of the Lost Ark**
US 1981/ w Harrison Ford, Karen Allen, Paul Freeman
5 **ET: The Extra-Terrestrial**
US 1982/ w Henry Thomas, Dee Wallace, Peter Coyote
6 **The Color Purple**
US 1986/ w Whoopi Goldberg, Danny Glover, Margaret Avery

George Stevens

Born: 18th December 1904/Oakland, California, USA
Died: 9th March 1975/Paris, France
Directing career: 1930-1970

The '50s films of George Cooper Stevens, widely regarded at that time as a major American artist, now seem misguidedly solemn and pompous. Whereas before the war he had proved to be a proficient craftsman with a talent for romantic comedy, his later films are flawed by ponderous pacing and a dry emphasis on tastefulness.

A former actor, Stevens' first work of note in film was as cameraman for Hal Roach on several Laurel and Hardy comedies. Allowed to direct a number of lowly two-reelers, he finally made his feature debut in 1933 with *The Cohens and Kellys in Trouble*; many B-comedies followed, and it was only when Katharine Hepburn suggested he direct her in *Alice Adams* >**1**, an adaptation of Booth Tarkington's novel about a girl from the wrong side of the tracks who dreams of scaling the social ladder, that he could reveal his love of Americana and his interest in the pernicious influence of class and money. More evident, however, were his films' generally craftsmanlike visual elegance and his handling of actors: Barbara Stanwyck in the romantic Western *Annie Oakley*, Astaire and Rogers in the classic musical *Swing Time*, Hepburn in the costume romance *Quality Street*, and Rogers and James Stewart in *Vivacious Lady*, a lively comedy in which an academic is afraid to tell his snobbish parents that he has married a showgirl. After the tongue-in-cheek military heroics of *Gunga Din*, both *Vigil in the Night* and *Penny Serenade* were mawkish melodramas, but *Woman of the Year* >**2** (a reactionary but witty comedy pairing, for the first time, Hepburn and Spencer Tracy as a career woman and the man who subdues her), *Talk of the Town* and *The More The Merrier* (about housing problems in Washington) made for polished, patchily amusing entertainment.

At the end of the war Stevens won praise for his documentary coverage of D-Day and the liberation of the concentration camps; indeed, his experience in Europe seemed to have a sobering effect on his subsequent work, and after the nostalgic and sentimental *I Remember Mama* (about a Norwegian immigrant family's life in San Francisco in the early 1900s),

Stevens' increasingly painstaking attitude to filming resulted in fewer and fewer films. *A Place in the Sun* (an adaptation of Theodore Dreiser's *An American Tragedy*, about a love triangle that crosses class barriers and results in death) was the first of the director's epic, portentous message-movies to deal with the American Dream. Just as its leaden romanticism overshadowed what little, simplistic political content remained, so in *Shane* >**3**, Stevens' meticulously picturesque visuals and his apparent desire to treat the Western as art drained an archetypal plot of all its potential vitality. *Giant* >**4**, too, suffered from a self-conscious perfectionism in its attempt to transcend rather than revel in the innate melodrama of its Texan oil-dynasty plot; indeed, each film was distinguished only by the performances of a starry cast. Stevens' taste for important, worthy subject matter, however, was not to be sated; after the exceedingly lengthy *The Diary of Anne Frank*, he turned his attention to Christ in the plodding, ludicrously star-cameoed *The Greatest Story Ever Told*. Unsurprisingly, the film pleased neither critics nor public, and after *The Only Game in Town* (a forgettable Las Vegas romance between a chorus girl and a gambler) he retired from film-making.

The victim of his own overweening ambition, Stevens lacked the probing intelligence and inventive flair that might have transformed his more prestigious later projects into great films. A minor, middlebrow talent, he was most successful on an artistic level when he concerned himself with lightweight entertainment.

Lineage

If Stevens' early work is less emotionally affecting than that of **Capra**, **Cukor** or, for that matter, Leo McCarey (for whom he worked as cameraman), his later films lack the insight and power of **Ray**, **Sirk**, **Minnelli** and **Anthony Mann**. In terms of both his ambitions and achievements, he may be compared with **Wyler** and **Zinnemann**.

Further reading

Donald Richie's *George Stevens: An American Romantic* (New York, 1970).

Viewing

1 **Alice Adams**
US 1935/ w Katharine Hepburn, Fred MacMurray, Fred Stone

2 **Woman of the Year**
US 1942/ w Katharine Hepburn, Spencer Tracy, Fay Bainter

3 **Shane**
US 1953/ w Alan Ladd, Jean Arthur, Van Heflin, Brandon De Wilde

4 **Giant**
US 1956/ w Elizabeth Taylor, Rock Hudson, James Dean

Oliver Stone

Born: 15th September 1946/New York, USA
Directing career: 1973-

In the late '80s, Oliver Stone has suddenly come to prominence as a tough, controversial director of supposedly liberal sympathies. A cool assessment of his career, however, reveals a more complex, and artistically rather incoherent, figure.

A Vietnam veteran, Stone wrote a number of unfilmed scripts before making his debut in 1973 with *Seizure*, about a writer of horror stories plagued and destroyed by nightmares. Indeed, both this and *The Hand*, a second banal excursion into the supernatural made in 1981, attracted far less attention than the scripts Stone wrote for **Parker**'s *Midnight Express*, **Milius**' *Conan the Barbarian*, **De Palma**'s *Scarface* and **Cimino**'s *Year of the Dragon* – the first and last of these provoking charges of racism in their inability to detach themselves from their protagonist's emotions. Similarly confused, in fact, was Stone's best film, *Salvador* >**1**, a tough, convincing and action-packed account of an American journalist's experiences of the civil war in El Salvador in 1980. Authentically brutal and raw, the film was an admittedly provocative picture of the role played by the US government in giving military aid to the right-wing regime and, by implication, to its death squads; at the same time, Stone's script, written with Richard Boyle, whose own adventures provided a factual basis for the film, refused to see its hero's indulgence in cheap drugs and sex as a less murderous but still pernicious example of American exploitation of the Third World.

Platoon >**2** was no less muddled, concentrating – through its story of a 19-year-old 'grunt' torn between two officers seen as, respectively, honourably professional and manically sadistic – on the way the Vietnam War affected American soldiers, rather than its effect on the Vietnamese. Indeed, the refusal to confront the political and ethical implications of America's presence in South East Asia meant that the movie's age-old 'war is hell' theme never entirely escaped a traditional glorification of military heroics. Equally, *Wall Street* >**3** appeared seduced by the very jet-set wealth and devious intrigues it purported to condemn: in many ways it was a transposition of *Platoon*'s plot to the concrete jungle of New York, its young, inexperienced broker tempted away from his *bona fide* working-class hero father by the Mephistophelean delights offered by a monstrous surrogate father – his ruthless company-trading boss. If, however, Stone's moral viewpoint was schizophrenic, dramatically the film was destroyed by its risible dependence on hackneyed melodramatic clichés, complete with an office prophet continually foreseeing doom and an inevitable hospital scene allowing the erring son to make peace with poppa and gain redemption.

Talk Radio (a meandering study of a chat-show host's various relationships with colleagues, ex-wife and hostile listeners, inspired by the real-life killing of Denver DJ Alan Berg) seemed almost pointless, while plans to film the musical *Evita* boded ill. If *Salvador* and *Platoon* testify to Stone's ability to wrench the heartstrings, *Wall Street* merely underlines the lack of moral consistency and narrative originality that runs through even his best work. Despite certain claims to authenticity – visual with the chaos of the war films, verbal in the endless financial jargon of *Wall Street* – it may be that, with hindsight, Stone will be remembered as a primitive entertainer rather than a 'committed' artist.

Lineage

An admirer of **Buñuel** and **Godard**, Stone may perhaps be considered a successor to **Fuller** and **Aldrich**: brash, unsubtle and none too wary of courting controversy. He may be tentatively likened to figures such as **Hill**, **Parker**, **De Palma**, even Sylvester Stallone; *Salvador* provokes comparison with Haskell Wexler's *Latino*, Roger Spottiswoode's *Under Fire* and Roland Joffe's *The Killing Fields*.

Viewing

1 **Salvador**
US 1986/ w James Woods, James Belushi, Michael Murphy

2 **Platoon**
US 1987/ w Charlie Sheen, Tom Berenger, Willem Dafoe

3 **Wall Street**
US 1987/ w Charlie Sheen, Michael Douglas, Martin Sheen, Daryl Hannah

Preston Sturges

Born: 29th August 1898/Chicago, Illinois, USA
Died: 6th August 1959/New York, USA
Directing career: 1940-1957

In one brief period – from 1940 to 1943 – Edmund P. Biden (better known by the name he received from his adoptive stepfather) made seven of the most hectically inventive comedies ever to satirise the American way of life. Raucous yet sophisticated, revelling in verbal absurdities, they remain supreme examples of the writer-director's craft.

Before finding work in the early '30s as a Hollywood script-writer, Sturges had already written several plays, besides being an eccentric inventor. But it was his contribution to films such as **Leisen**'s *Easy Living* and *Remember the Night* which established him as a comic writer, and encouraged him to begin directing himself. His debut, *The Great McGinty* >**1**, in which a tramp who earns the gratitude of a corrupt political entrepreneur (by voting 40 times in a local election) finally rises to become State Governor, was typical of his affectionate, irreverent attitude to American mores and of his frantic, wisecracking style. Words constituted a major element of Sturges' often absurdist wit: aphorisms, slang, ludicrous names (Kockenlocker, Ratsky-Watsky, Hackensacker), acid one-liners, delirious non-sequiturs and innuendos, all delivered at a breathless pace. Meanwhile, plots – often featuring mistaken identities and characters involved in deliberate pretence – spiral steadily into hectic, improbable chaos, while flailing at various sacred cows. *Christmas in July*, in which the hero's desire to get rich quick has him entering endless competitions, gleefully tilts at advertising; *The Lady Eve* provides a droll parody of courtship as a con-woman hoodwinks an old flame who had jilted her on learning about her dishonest life-style; in *Sullivan's Travels* >**2**, a movie director takes to the road as a tramp in order to gather research for his worthy film on injustice and poverty ('Brother Where Art Thou?'), only to learn that laughter is the greatest antidote to hardship; while *The Palm Beach Story* >**3**, a superbly complex farce involving a romantic rectangle, satirises the idle rich, though it reserves a special affection for the bibulous, eccentric, and irresistibly boisterous members of the 'Ale and Quail Club'.

With the exception of *Sullivan's Travels* (a somewhat contrived apologia for Sturges' chosen profession) and *The Great Moment* (an unusually serious biopic of the inventor of anaesthesia, littered with odd moments of slapstick), Sturges' work was admirably free of moralising, a quality perhaps most evident in two unusually subversive satires on the puritan ethics and cheap sentimentality of smalltown America. In *Hail the Conquering Hero* >**4**, a dumb cluck who was refused entry into the Marines (due to hay fever) is mistakenly assumed to be a war hero and elected mayor, while in *The Miracle of Morgan's Creek*, a girl who drunkenly gets herself married to (and pregnant by) a soldier she subsequently forgets, becomes the mother of sextuplets and wife of a chronically timid imbecile. In both, mother-worship, war-crazy jingoism and political corruption are mercilessly lampooned, while the director's garrulous gallery of regular supporting actors (Jimmy Conlin, Franklin Pangborn and, particularly, William Demarest) lend their own inimitable brand of irascibility and absurdity to the noisily escalating lunacy.

Sturges' decision to leave Paramount for Howard Hughes sadly brought this period of prolific invention to an end: of several projects he began under Hughes, only *Mad Wednesday*, a comeback by silent comedian Harold Lloyd, reached completion. At 20th Century-Fox, he finally returned to the fray with the black and unusually sophisticated *Unfaithfully Yours* >**5**, in which a conductor, convinced for no good reason that his wife is having an affair, indulges in dreams of revenge that vary according to the dramatic mood of the music he is conducting; even here, however, Sturges' penchant for slapstick results in a superbly choreographed scene in which the demented husband clumsily prepares to murder his wife. Then, after the uneven musical Western spoof *The Beautiful Blonde from Bashful Bend*, Sturges retired to France, where he ended his film-making career with the disappointing *The Diary of Major Thompson*.

Although almost all of Sturges' finest work was the fruit of his four years spent at Paramount, and his wit, primarily verbal rather than visual, was often highly topical, so timeless is the appeal of his films that his importance as a comic film-maker is guaranteed. Similarly, as a successful writer-director, he set an example for others such as **Huston**, **Wilder**, and Richard Brooks.

Lineage

While Sturges' slapstick looks back to silent comedy, his lurid, colloquial verbal wit compares with figures as diverse as **Wilder**, **Levinson** and the **Coen Brothers**, his brash satire with that of **Tashlin**.

Further reading

James Ursini's *The Fabulous Life and Times of Preston Sturges* (1973).

Viewing

1 **The Great McGinty**
US 1940/ w Brian Donlevy, Akim Tamiroff, Muriel Angelus
2 **Sullivan's Travels**
US 1941/ w Joel McCrea, Veronica Lake, William Demarest
3 **The Palm Beach Story**
US 1942/ w Claudette Colbert, Joel McCrea, Rudy Vallee
4 **Hail the Conquering Hero**
US 1944/ w Eddie Bracken, Ella Raines, William Demarest
5 **Unfaithfully Yours**
US 1948/ w Rex Harrison, Linda Darnell, Rudy Vallee

Hans-Jürgen Syberberg

Born: 8th December 1935/ Nossendorf, Pomerania, Germany
Directing career: 1965-

Highly distinctive and original among the German directors who rose to prominence during the '70s, Hans-Jürgen Syberberg is a flamboyantly eccentric film-maker with scant regard for most of his contemporaries. His subject – the continuing schizophrenia of German culture over the last century – matches the epic scale and complexity of his idiosyncratic visual and narrative style.

While Syberberg was still living in East Germany, a youthful meeting with Brecht allowed him to film The Berliner Ensemble on 8mm: an encounter that proved a decisive influence on the film-maker's mature work. By the early '60s he was working in Bavarian television, and between 1965 and 1969 he made several full length documentaries on actors such as Fritz Kortner and Romy Schneider. In 1968 he made his first feature, *Scarabea* (a controversial and apparently surreal adaptation of a story by Tolstoy), followed by *San Domingo* (a semi-documentary film on Munich's rebellious youth with a plot taken from Kleist). But it was *Ludwig – Requiem for a Virgin King* >**1** that first announced his mature style. A decidedly different biopic of the reclusive, visionary Bavarian monarch – who preferred building extravagant, fantastic castles and acting as a patron to Wagner over conventional political activities – the film consists of largely static tableaux in which dialogue and visuals stress the enduring conflict between Romanticism and rationality in German society. Ludwig (played by an adult and a child dressed as an adult) speaks of Brecht in the past tense and plays host to a rumba-dancing Hitler and a motor bike-riding Bismarck; a single seemingly eternal scene of the king falling asleep to the strains of Wagner climaxes in the falling of blatantly artificial snow; documentary shots of modern tourists in Ludwig's palaces serve as a backdrop to the action. Slow, baroque and grandiose, the effect is nevertheless witty and engrossing, both as a lucid analysis of a nation's psyche and as a visually stunning collage.

Ludwig was merely the beginning of Syberberg's epic journey through German history. It was followed by *Ludwig's Cook*, a guided tour of Ludwig's castles lent special depth by having the actor-narrator frequently slip into character as the eponymous kitchen-hand; and *Karl May*, a study of German imperialist Romanticism as embodied and envisioned by the popular adventure writer, in which Nazi-era actors played the majority of roles. *The Confessions of Winifred Wagner*, similarly, was an epic five-hour interview with the composer's daughter-in-law, unrepentant about her friendship with Hitler (who patronised the Bayreuth Festival which she organised), which provided a sombre insight into the relationship between art and politics; while *Hitler, A Film from Germany* >**2**, the final part of the trilogy started by *Ludwig* and *Karl May*, was a seven-hour essay on

Germany's abiding capacity for Nazism. Still more multi-layered than *Ludwig*, it suffered from a lack of clarity, although scenes such as Hitler rising garbed in a toga from Wagner's grave exert considerable power and demonstrate the director's rich visual imagination.

No less indulgent, ambitious or effective was *Parsifal* >**3**, a version of Wagner's opera shot entirely on a studio set contrived out of a giant model of the composer's death-mask; typical of Syberberg's vision, it blurred past and present, myth and history, theatre and film. Indeed, Syberberg seems to have taken Brecht's theories of staging to their absolute extreme, entirely forsaking the illusion of reality for a fusion of art forms that constitutes an intellectually demanding, but visually sumptuous, cinema of ideas. If his sense of self-importance is distressing, he nevertheless possesses a singular intelligence and wit.

Lineage

Besides Brecht, figures as varied as Georges Méliès, **Eisenstein**, **Welles**, **Godard** and **Warhol** may be seen as having possibly had an influence on Syberberg. Of his German contemporaries, Alexander Kluge and Jean-Marie Straub perhaps bear closest comparison.

Further reading

John Sandford's *New German Cinema* (London, 1980).

Viewing

1 **Ludwig – Requiem for a Virgin King**
W. Germany 1972/ w Harry Baer, Balthasar Thomas, Peter Kern
2 **Hitler, A Film from Germany**
W. Germany 1977/ w Heinz Schubert
3 **Parsifal**
W. Germany 1981/ w Michael Kutter, Edith Clever, Karin Krick

István Szabó

Born: **18th February 1938/Budapest, Hungary**
Directing career: 1961-

The best known Hungarian director of his generation, István Szabó is conspicuous for his ability to merge the personal with the political and for his excellent handling of actors. Though his more recent international co-productions have tended towards glossy costume drama, his intelligence and sensitivity remain much in evidence.

Szabó first attracted attention with his film-school diploma movie, *Concert*. After two shorts, he made his feature debut in 1964 with *The Age of Daydreaming*, a lyrical story of a young, idealistic television engineer's romantic obsession with a female colleague that simultaneously reflected the disillusionment of contemporary Hungarian society. Subsequent films also focussed on individuals (and a deftly delineated Budapest) to present an oblique account of Hungarian postwar history; it is a pity, however, that works like *Father* (an adolescent boy belatedly manages to free himself from his fantasies about his dead parent) and *25 Fireman's Street* (the problems of postwar society viewed through the eyes of the tenants of a condemned tenement) have been little seen in the West. Indeed, it was only with *Confidence* >**1** and *Mephisto* >**2** that Szabó's talent was finally revealed to a wide international audience. The former, though perhaps the less ambitious of the two, is the more perfectly realised: its story, largely set in a single room, of a man and a woman who fall in love when they are forced to pose as husband and wife during the Nazi occupation, serves as a subtle study of paranoia, distrust, and affection nurtured by isolation. Crucially, although the film mirrors the mood of a whole society oppressed by war, its emotional power derives from the intimate observation of its two seemingly incompatible central characters.

Szabó's first international co-production, *Mephisto* was more lavish, and occasionally fell prey to art-movie chic as it told of the political and moral compromises made by an ambitious actor in '30s Germany; nevertheless, thanks to a remarkable performance by Klaus Maria Brandauer, who effortlessly suggested the hollow soul of the man behind the Faustian mask – a figure whose inability to stop himself acting causes him to betray friends and family, and to become a puppet to the Nazis – the film was a convincingly bleak account of the seductive appeal of Fascism. Equally, in the overlong but impressively mounted *Colonel Redl* >**3**, Brandauer gave another fine performance as the railwayman's son whose steady climb to a position of power in military intelligence in the last years of the Hapsburg Empire entails that he conceal his Jewish origins and his bisexuality, and results in his eventual suicide when he becomes a scapegoat in a political intrigue that climaxes in the shooting of the Archduke Franz Ferdinand at Sarajevo. Again, Szabó illustrates the personal motivations that encourage political compromise with psychological subtlety; again, too, the visual sumptuousness is often reminiscent of decorative television costume drama, an impression reinforced by a meandering episodic narrative. Next, Brandauer starred again in *Hanussen*, about a clairvoyant's rise to fame at the end of World War I; visually handsome and as sensitively performed as ever, the film nevertheless occasionally gave the impression that Szabó was beginning to repeat himself.

While the themes of betrayal and compromise in Szabó's most recent work clearly relate to Hungarian society, his proficiency as a director ensures that his films have a universal relevance and appeal. Though they are rooted in historical reality, they are perhaps most effective as intimate, low-key melodrama.

Lineage

Younger than **Jancsó**, Zoltán Fábri and Károly Makk, Szabó may be compared to Hungarian film-makers like Márta Mészáros, Pál Gábor, István Gaál and Pál Sándor. He has confessed to an admiration for **Truffaut**, although the tone of his work perhaps bears a greater resemblance to that of **Malle**, **Wajda** and Krzysztof Zanussi.

Further reading

Graham Petrie's *History Must Answer to Man: The Contemporary Hungarian Cinema* (London, 1978).

Viewing

1 **Confidence**
Hungary 1979/ w Ildiko Bansagi, Peter Andorai, Karoly Csaki

2 **Mephisto**
Hungary/W. Germany 1981/ w Klaus Maria Brandauer, Ildiko Bansagi, Rolf Hoppe

3 **Colonel Redl**
Hungary/W. Germany 1984/ w Klaus Maria Brandauer, Hans-Christian Blech

Andrei Tarkovsky

Born: 4th April 1932/Zavroshne, USSR
Died: 29th December 1986/Paris, France
Directing career: 1959-1986

Widely considered to be one of the most profound film-makers of recent years, Andrei Arsenevich Tarkovsky was certainly possessed of an uncompromisingly personal vision, at once poetic and spiritual. His later films, however, deeply flawed by self-indulgence, tend towards obscurantism and a cold, intellectual aloofness that sits uneasily with his interest in humanity's quest for salvation.

The son of the poet Arseny Alexandrovich, Tarkovsky made two shorts while at film school: *There Will Be No Leave Tonight*, and the medium-length *The Steamroller and the Violin*, in which a boy, who is training as a musician, befriends a building labourer, who thus learns the value of art. His feature debut, *Ivan's Childhood* >**1**, was altogether more grim, its orphan hero revered by his adult superiors for his audacious forays as a spy behind German lines during World War II), finally caught and killed by the enemy; if the film's story was comparatively conventional, it nevertheless gave ample evidence of its director's lyrical visual sensibility, especially in its shots of

Where personal, historical and metaphysical matters intersect: Tarkovsky's *Mirror.*

tranquil water and misty forests, and of his quasi-mystical attitude towards both the natural world and the saint-like boy. Even more notable for its pervasive Christian symbolism was *Andrei Rublev* >**2**, a long, episodic epic about a 15th-century monk and icon painter who takes a vow of silence – his response to the horrific violence and tortures perpetrated in a still divided Russia laid waste by the Tartars. That vow is at last abandoned when he encounters a boy who casts a giant bell, enabled to do so by faith – the miracle of the achievement restores Rublev's own belief. A grim account of faith rediscovered in times of darkness, the film was impressive for its scale and historical authenticity; its release, however, was delayed by the Soviet authorities who insisted on cuts.

After *Solaris*, an unusually meditative but portentous sci-fi epic about scientists who, observing a remote planet from a run-down space station, find themselves visited by tangibly corporeal figures from their fantasies and memories, in *Mirror* >**3** Tarkovsky turned to autobiographical reminiscence. A highly fragmented, dreamlike blend of dramatic and documentary footage, the result was a sometimes visually arresting attempt to mix private and social history, but seemed often wilfully obscure and indulgent. Conversely, *Stalker* >**4** was a model of linear clarity, in which the odyssey of three men – Stalker, Writer and Scientist – through a gloomy and desolate forbidden Zone to a Room where, it is said, prayers are answered, serves as an overextended allegory on the difficulty of faith and the need for humility. Again, the film won acclaim for its unusual visual qualities, consisting of long takes and stark, highly formalised compositions initialy drained of colour; again, too, it was flawed by its strangely detached and cerebral tone, with stilted dialogue and weak characterisation turning the three pilgrims into inhuman, two-dimensional cyphers.

Made in Italy, *Nostalgia* was of interest chiefly in that its rather opaque tale, of a Russian musicologist's encounter with a suicidal Italian recluse widely believed mad, reflected on its maker's feelings about living and working away from his homeland; strangely, although the film implied that it was impossible for a Russian to be happy abroad, it met with official hostility, thus encouraging

Tarkovsky to remain in exile. *The Sacrifice* was made, therefore, in Sweden; about an actor whose fears of a nuclear war lead him to make a private pact with God that, in return for his own and his family's safety, he will give up his material possessions and his contact with humanity, the film suffers from a somewhat contrived religiosity and a morbid disenchantment with human aspiration and achievement. It may be that Tarkovsky's increasing pessimism was related not only to his reluctant exile from Russia but to his worsening health; within a year of the film's completion, he was dead from cancer.

While there is no doubt about Tarkovsky's seriousness or his ability to create austerely beautiful, even unearthly images, his lofty tone and taste for plodding, obscure narratives render much of his work curiously unappealing and unilluminating. It may be that his preoccupations were, finally, both too private and too cerebral ever to be communicated clearly and effectively through a medium as concerned with visual surfaces as film.

Lineage

An admirer of **Dovzhenko** and (together with **Konchalovsky**, an early collaborator) a former student of Mikhail Romm, Tarkovsky may be compared to **Dreyer**, **Bergman**, **Bresson**, **Antonioni** and **Herzog**. Among his Russian contemporaries, **Paradjanov**, Georgy Shengelaya, Larisa Shepitko and **Klimov** are perhaps closest in style.

Further reading

Mark Le Fanu's *The Cinema of Andrei Tarkovsky* (London, 1987); Tarkovsky's *Sculpting in Time* (London, 1986) is film-theory.

Viewing

1 **Ivan's Childhood**
USSR 1962/ w Nikolai Burlyaev, Valentin Zubkov, E. Zharikov

2 **Andrei Rublev**
USSR 1966/ w Anatoly Solonitsin, Ivan Lapikov, Nikolai Grinko

3 **Mirror**
USSR 1974/ w Margarita Terekhova, Philip Yankovsky, Ignat Daniltsev

4 **Stalker**
USSR 1979/ w Alexander Kaidanovsky, Anatoly Solonitsin, Nikolai Grinko

Frank Tashlin

Born: 19th February 1913/ Weehawken, New Jersey, USA
Died: 5th May 1972/Hollywood, California, USA
Directing career: 1935-1968

As satires on the media madness and mass consumerism that swept America in the '50s, Frank Tashlin's films were often incoherent, vague and marred by the very vulgarity they mocked. At the same time, however, they were distinguished by an inventive visual style carried over from his earlier animated work, as well as a sophisticated, modernist acknowledgement of their own artifice.

Tashlin first entered the movies during his teens as an errand-boy for animator Max Fleischer; by the end of the '30s he was recognised as a major talent in cartoon-making, having worked for Warners, Disney, MGM and Columbia as an animator, gag-writer and director, establishing a surreal, frenetic style that often parodied contemporary movies and fads. In the late '40s he turned his attention to writing feature comedies, including *The Paleface* and *Love Happy* (for Bob Hope and the Marx Brothers respectively), and in 1950 he made his feature-directing debut when Hope asked him to reshoot half of *The Lemon Drop Kid*. In *Son of Paleface* and *Susan Slept Here* Tashlin's love of verbal and visual innuendo was already evident, but it was in *Artists and Models* >**1**, *Hollywood or Bust* (starring Dean Martin and Jerry Lewis), *The Girl Can't Help It* >**2** and *Will Success Spoil Rock Hunter?* >**3** (starring Jayne Mansfield) that Tashlin developed and consolidated his own style.

Each of these movies gleefully satirised, through grotesque

exaggeration and caricature, current fashions (comic-strip books, violence on television, movie fanaticism, rock 'n' roll and advertising). If, however, Tashlin's acerbic humour was blunted by his inability to turn his brash, often sexist slapstick (usually centred on Lewis' imbecile naivety, or the effect of Mansfield's pneumatic physique on various males) into a cohesive plot, the films remain conspicuous for their garish cartoon-like colours and for the barrage of movie in-jokes: most memorably, *The Girl Can't Help It* (which has as its main characters a couple named Tom and Jerri) plagiarises **Cukor**'s *Born Yesterday* and spoofs gangster films, while including a prologue in which Tom Ewell introduces CinemaScope and De Luxe colour; similarly, *Rock Hunter* opens on a multiple image of Tony Randall playing the Fox fanfare on sundry instruments, before the image shrinks to the size of a black-and-white television screen.

As Tashlin's career progressed he relied increasingly on the gormless persona of Jerry Lewis, and though *Rock-A-Bye Baby*, *The Geisha Boy*, *Cinderfella*, *It's Only Money*, *Who's Minding the Store?* and *The Disorderly Orderly* continued to display the writer-director's taste for frantic action, self-referential gags and broad satire, they were often ruined by the maudlin pathos seemingly inherent in their eternally infantile star. Moreover, with TV advertising, sex and rock 'n' roll having outgrown their novelty status in the '60s, Tashlin appeared lost. His beloved junk culture was no longer a rich subject for satire and, after two listless vehicles for Doris Day (*The Glass Bottom Boat*, *Caprice*), and the irredeemably sexist Bob Hope comedy *The Private Navy of Sergeant O'Farrell*, he retired.

For all their cleverness and slapstick invention, Tashlin's films fall short of great comedy, partly because they lack logic and discipline, partly because he indulged his taste for visual gags at the expense of credible, likeable characters. Still, he remains fascinating as a rare example of an animator turned live-action director, and as an anarchic chronicler of '50s America.

Lineage

Tashlin's comedies are in the crazy satirical tradition of **Hawks**, **Sturges** and **Wilder**. Much admired by **Godard** and other French film-makers, he may perhaps be compared and contrasted with figures as diverse as **Blake Edwards**, **Mel Brooks**, **John Landis** and Russ Meyer, while he certainly influenced Jerry Lewis' own films as director.

Further reading

Frank Tashlin, ed. Claire Johnston and Paul Willemen (Edinburgh, 1973).

Viewing

1 **Artists and Models**
US 1955/ w Jerry Lewis, Dean Martin, Shirley MacLaine
2 **The Girl Can't Help It**
US 1956/ w Tom Ewell, Jayne Mansfield, Edmond O'Brien
3 **Will Success Spoil Rock Hunter?**
US 1957/ w Tony Randall, Jayne Mansfield, Betsy Drake

Jacques Tati

Born: 9th October 1908/Le Pecq, France
Died: 4th November 1982/Paris, France
Directing career: 1946-1973

Though a great mime and an imaginative formal innovator, Jacques Tatischeff was prone to simplistic social satire that ultimately reduced his film's comic force. Indeed, it is fascinating to note that in his attempts to reveal the way modern technology depersonalises human existence, he should have created a style as cold, neat and aloof in its dependence on technique as the society he was castigating.

A successful music-hall mime specialising in impressions of sportsmen during the '30s, Tati played several minor roles in films by René Clément and Claude Autant-Lara. In 1946 he made his own directing debut with the short *L'Ecole des Facteurs*, which he later expanded into the feature *Jour de Fête* >**1**. Set in a country village visited by a travelling fair, the film features Tati as a postman driven by the locals' insults to streamline his working methods according to American ideas of speed and efficiency. Tati's style was at once primarily visual, with little dialogue; unlike most silent comedians, however, he derived humour not from fantastic situations, but from a basically realistic observation of the small absurdities of human behaviour, forsaking close-ups in favour of long shots that emphasise both continuity of action and the postman's relationship to the world around him. Indeed, it is arguable that the protagonist of *Monsieur Hulot's Holiday* >**2** is not Hulot (Tati's faintly eccentric, archetypically middle-class Everyman, with pipe, overcoat, hat and awkward gait) but the calm seaside resort disrupted by his own unusually plausible brand of chaos. Tati's most perfectly realised, least obviously contrived film, it reveals his eye for visual detail and his ability to choreograph intricate and inventive running gags without ever falling prey to overstatement, hysteria or worn-out clichés.

With *Mon Oncle*, however, the writer-director first displayed a desire to be taken seriously as a social satirist, contrasting a nightmarishly soulless, mechanised modern house with a somewhat romanticised vision of traditional working-class life. The result – strangely passionless and bereft of rounded characters – was banal and largely unamusing: even Hulot seemed a mere cypher under Tati's detached gaze. Nine years in the making, *Playtime* >**3** was likewise remote, with Hulot removed to the sidelines and a garrulous group of female tourists (visiting a Paris seemingly built totally from concrete, steel and glass) portrayed with remarkably scant regard for individuality or emotion. Except for a virtuoso scene showing the systematic, if inadvertent, destruction of a restaurant, the film was so abstract in terms of photography and narrative, that humour took second place to the trite, reactionary moral message.

An enormously expensive failure, *Playtime* was followed by *Trafic*, an uneven satire on our fetishistic attitude towards, and dependence on cars. Again, Hulot was marginal to Tati's love-hate interest in things mechanical, while much of his humour, for all its formal difference from that of his contemporaries, seemed all too obvious. Finally, deep in debt, for Swedish television he made *Parade*, largely a record of his mime act filmed at a circus.

Had Tati allowed his vision of society to arise from comedy, rather than vice versa, his work might have seemed less precious. If his attempt to forge a visual style free of individual heroes theoretically offered audiences the opportunity to find humour wherever they chose, in practice such innovations resulted in a lack of human warmth and virtually non-existent characterisation.

Lineage

While Tati's debt to silent comedians like **Keaton**, Harold Lloyd, Harry Langdon and Max Linder is clear, one may also compare him with directors like **Clair**, **Antonioni** and **Bresson** (whom he greatly admired). He himself influenced Pierre Etaix, once his assistant.

Further reading

Penelope Gilliatt's *Jacques Tati* (London, 1976), Roy Armes' *French Cinema since 1946, Vol 1* (London, 1970).

Viewing

1 **Jour de Fête**
France 1949/ w Tati, Guy Decomble, Paul Frankeur

2 **Monsieur Hulot's Holiday**
France 1953/ w Tati, Nathalie Pascaud, Louis Perrault

3 **Playtime**
France 1967/ w Tati, Barbara Dennek, Jacqueline Lecomte

Bertrand Tavernier

Born: 25th April 1941/Lyons, France
Directing career: 1963-

Although in many respects Bertrand Tavernier is an old-fashioned film-maker, comfortable with the traditional virtues of narrative elegance and strong characterisation, he is one of the most steadily rewarding directors to have emerged from France since the '60s. While the variety of his subject matter suggests his versatility, his dynamic visual style and his concern with the way individuals react to society at large ensure a consistency from film to film.

Tavernier made his name as a critic for *Positif* and *Cahiers du Cinéma* before directing two shorts in 1963. During the late '60s he wrote a couple of scripts and worked as a film publicist, finally making his feature debut in 1972 with the impressive *The Watchmaker of St-Paul* >**1**, a Simenon adaptation about the effects of a murder case on the killer's father's political awareness; a subtly understated mix of social comment and psychological drama, it benefitted from a typically superb performance from Philippe Noiret, who would reappear in Tavernier's next two films. In *Que La Fête Commence!* (*Let Joy Reign Supreme!*), an historical costume epic of unusual integrity about sexual and political intrigues at the court of Philippe d'Orléans in 1719, he played the hedonistic regent; in *The Judge and the Assassin*, he gave an admirably complex, chilling performance as a magistrate attempting to judge whether a killer is really insane or only faking. Indeed, many of Tavernier's films feature performances of outstanding quality: in *Des Enfants Gâtés* (*Spoiled Children*) >**2**, Michel Piccoli excels as the director's *alter ego*, whose move away from home and family in order to facilitate the writing of a script drives him first into an affair with a neighbour then into a rent strike that reawakens both his creativity and his political commitment. Though the film transcends genre, such is Tavernier's ability to exact drama from everyday experience that it is witty, gripping *and* true to life.

Making excellent use of Glasgow and the Scottish Highlands, *Death Watch* >**3** was unusually sensitive sci-fi: set in the near future when terminal disease exists only in TV soap opera, a woman is told she is dying; she is befriended by a vagrant who, it turns out, is filming her every move with cameras fitted in his eyes. A sombre study of voyeurism and media exploitation, the film impressed through its unobtrusively fluid camera movements and its evocation of a world in which morality, rather than appearances, differs from our own. More conventional but no less intriguing, *Une Semaine de Vacances* (*A Week's Holiday*) examined a teacher confronting doubts about her career, while *Coup de Torchon* (*Clean Slate*) was a dark, witty portrait of an otherwise affable cop (Noiret again) driven to acts of murder by the unthinking racism of French colonials in '30s East Africa. Altogether more lyrical, *Sunday in the Country* was a lush, turn-of-the-century conversation piece, in which an elderly, unremarkable painter is visited by his children and grandchildren: evoking the joys and disappointments of memory through glowing photography and faultless performances, Tavernier not only pays homage to **Renoir** but, by analogy, acknowledges the essentially unadventurous, yet heartfelt, nature of his own work.

Like the documentary *Mississippi Blues*, *'Round Midnight* >**4** testified to his love of music and Americana. A romanticised but sincere and affecting tribute to jazz, it made atmospheric use of studio sets to re-create the '50s Paris jazz clubs, and was flawed only by minor inaccuracies and its implication that the French alone fully appreciated the music. Though it concerned a saxophonist's struggles against alcoholism, the images were again lavish, while Dexter Gordon was wisely allowed to be himself in a performance of enormous charm.

Tavernier's versatility was also evident in a dark medieval drama, *Béatrice*. If his films are not formally innovative, they retain a capacity to surprise with their insights into human behaviour and an occasional ability to disturb (as in *Death Watch* and *Coup de Torchon*). As such they offer provocative, intelligent entertainment that never patronises the audience.

Lineage

Like Claude Miller, Tavernier would seem to be influenced both by American directors (**Hitchcock**, **Hawks**), and by compatriots such as **Melville** (for whom he worked), **Truffaut** and **Malle**.

Further reading

None to speak of; though his own *30 Ans de Cinéma Americain* (co-written with J.-P. Coursodon) is highly regarded.

Viewing

1 **The Watchmaker of St-Paul**
France 1972/ w Philippe Noiret, Jean Rochefort, Jacques Denis

2 **Des Enfants Gâtés (Spoiled Children)**
France 1977/ w Michel Piccoli, Christine Pascal, Michel Aumont

3 **Death Watch (La Mort en Direct)**
GB 1980/ w Romy Schneider, Harvey Keitel, Harry Dean Stanton

4 **'Round Midnight**
France 1986/ w Dexter Gordon, François Cluzet, Gabrielle Haker

The Taviani Brothers

Vittorio: **Born:** 20th September 1929/ San Miniato, Italy
Paolo: **Born:** 8th November 1931/San Miniato, Italy
Directing career: 1954-

In steadily moving away from the stylistic tenets of neo-realism (their relationship to which they have compared to the love-hate a son feels for a father), Vittorio and Paolo Taviani have forged a cinema in which fable, fantasy, history and myth combine. While social and political realities still figure among their concerns, their increasingly formalised narratives and often surreal images spotlight metaphysical themes such as the roles played by cinema and language, tradition and memory, in the search for Utopia.

Inspired by **Rossellini**'s *Paisa*, the Tavianis founded a film club and wrote occasional movie criticism while studying at the University of Pisa. In 1954, collaborating with Cesare Zavattini, they made their directing debut with the documentary *San Miniato, July 44*, a short about a massacre perpetrated by retreating Nazis on their own Tuscan village. Having established their unusually close working method (they write each film together before taking it in turns to direct specific scenes), they continued in their documentary career until 1962, working in collaboration with the trade unionist Valentino Orsini, between periods spent assisting various film-makers including Joris Ivens and Rossellini. Their feature debut, *A Man for the Burning*, anticipated much of their later work in its story of collective action and self-sacrifice (a political idealist's attempts to arouse the Sicilian peasantry against their oppressive Mafia landlords results in his assassination), and in its undermining of conventional notions of realism through ironic comedy, fantasy and a theatrical, symbolic use of music and dance. Most of their early work was noted for an iconoclastic, even pessimistic attitude towards existing ideology. *I Fuorilegge del Matrimonio* questioned the Italian divorce laws; in *Subversives*, interlocking portraits of various Communist Party members refuted the idea that leftists were all dyed in the same wool; utopian, revolutionary action was seen as a troubled and on-going process, inevitably subject to setbacks, in *San Michele Aveva in Gallo*, which concerns the solitary, 10-year imprisonment of a radical intellectual who eventually commits suicide. At the same time, an increasing disdain for realism was evident in a growing involvement with symbolism, metaphor and highly stylised camerawork.

Allonsanfan was about a formerly revolutionary aristocrat whose reluctant participation in a half-hearted Sicilian peasant revolt in 1816 ends in his own death. It was an extravagant example of the Tavianis' ability to counterpoint their political pessimism with an operatic blend of lavish movement, lurid colours, music, dance and fantastic images. Still more remarkable was *Padre Padrone* >**1**, which took an archetypal neo-realist story – a Sardinian shepherd boy suffers unbearable economic, physical and spiritual hardships until he escapes into the army – and transformed it into a cruel, witty, Brechtian fable about the potential for individual growth, through language (the boy finally learns to read in the army), in the face of authoritarian patriarchy. At the beginning and end of the film, Gavino Ledda – whose autobiography serves as the plot – advises an actor on how to play him, and speaks directly to camera; despite this and other non-naturalistic devices, the film remains deeply moving, and won the brothers international renown.

The Meadow, about a young man returning to a country village romanticised by his memories, was an altogether more oblique view of political alienation; but in *The Night of San Lorenzo* >**2**, the Tavianis turned personal memory into gloriously resonant myth, as half the inhabitants of a Tuscan village disobey Nazi orders and escape into the fields, where they not only hear the destruction of the only world they know, but finally join with the Resistance in fighting the Fascists. Again, realism is held at bay by having the story seen – and embellished – through the wondrous eyes of a six-year-old girl, a source of dreamy, surreal, tragicomic fantasy.

Kaos >**3** was an equally idiosyncratic vision of peasant life, adapted from a handful of Pirandello's Sicilian stories and notable for having no meaning, moral, or final resolution: a woman finds her husband is a werewolf, a jar-mender mends a jar, a village is temporarily victorious in its battle with a landowner. The film's shifting moods and ambivalent symbols are indeed a reflection of the chaos of existence, but at the same time it is cinema itself which, through storytelling, imposes order. Even more direct a tribute to the Tavianis' chosen medium was *Good Morning, Babylon* >**4**, in which two Tuscan brothers – stonemasons whose family has decorated Italian cathedrals for centuries – travel to Hollywood where they find themselves work designing the elephants (symbols of memory) for the Babylonian set of **Griffith**'s *Intolerance*. For the Tavianis (who deny any autobiographical angle in the portrait of the brothers for whom separation means death), cinema is a new collective memory, a utopian pastime which, by its ability to record our present, makes possible our existence in the future. In their witty, lyrical, moving meditation on the way art gives life meaning and purpose, they pay tribute to, *and* create, a cinema that is at once mythic, philosophical and profoundly populist.

In recent years the Tavianis have proved themselves the most invariably imaginative of Italian film-makers, drawing on their private obsessions to make films that are touching, playful, wise and always joyously, authentically cinematic.

Lineage

In their epic, political interest in myth and memory the Tavianis are perhaps closer to Theodoros Angelopoulos than to such Italian contemporaries as **Bertolucci**, Marco Bellocchio and Ermanno Olmi. Though **Rossellini** was certainly an influence, one might also look at their work in relation to that of **Dovzhenko**.

Further reading

Peter Bondanella's *Italian Cinema: from Neo-realism to the Present* (New York, 1983).

Viewing

1 **Padre Padrone**
Italy 1977/ w Omero Antonutti, Saverio Marconi, Fabrizio Forte

2 **The Night of San Lorenzo (The Night of the Shooting Stars)**
Italy 1982/ w Omero Antonutti, Margarita Lozano, Claudio Bigagli

3 **Kaos**
Italy 1984/ w Margarita Lozano, Omero Antonutti, Claudia Bigagli

4 **Good Morning, Babylon**
Italy 1987/ w Vincent Spano, Joaquim de Almeida, Charles Dance

Jacques Tourneur

Born: 12th November 1904/Paris, France
Died: 19th December 1977/ Bergerac, France
Directing career: 1931-1965

Never a major director, Jacques Tourneur nonetheless possessed an unassertive and eloquent visual style that enabled him to transform decent scripts into superior films. Although much of his work was in the B-movie field, his subtle inventiveness and unerring taste frequently made for intelligent entertainment.

The son of silent director Maurice Tourneur, himself a much-lauded visual stylist, Jacques went to Hollywood in 1914 with his father, on whose films he worked as assistant and editor. In 1928 they returned to France where, in the early '30s, Jacques began a directing career of his own with a few minor films. But only upon his return to MGM, where he made a series of shorts, did he meet the man who would transform his career: as a second-unit director on *A Tale of Two Cities*, Tourneur worked with Val Lewton who, in the early '40s, established a special unit at RKO with the purpose of producing low-budget but high-quality horror movies. Tourneur, who had already shown some storytelling verve in his *Nick Carter, Master Detective*, was the director Lewton selected for his first three films: *Cat People* >**1**, about a woman believing she is cursed to kill when sexually aroused, revealed a rare ability to create tension through suggestive shadows and refined symbolism, while *I Walked with a Zombie* >**2**, transposing the basic story of *Jane Eyre* to a Caribbean island, belied its outrageous title with a strange and poetically shot tale of voodoo and spiritual possession. Both films were literate, moody and concise; and after *The Leopard Man* – a flawed but intelligent attempt to repeat *Cat People*'s success – Tourneur left Lewton to be entrusted with Gregory Peck's first major role (*Days of Glory*) and a relatively lavish costume-drama, the atmospheric psychological thriller *Experiment Perilous*.

Thereafter, Tourneur displayed a preference for Westerns and *noir* thrillers: in the former – *Canyon Passage*, *Stars in My Crown* and the excellent *Great Day in the Morning* – he generally avoided frantic action and violence to concentrate his visual talents on the massive beauty of the American landscape; while in *Out of the Past* (*Build My Gallows High*) >**3**, one of the most gripping, poetic and fatalistic *films noirs* ever made, he revealed himself equally at ease with complex flashbacks, shady interiors, and the haunted romanticism of Robert Mitchum's doomed, love-lorn private eye. In *Berlin Express* he made similarly fine use of Robert Ryan, a train and a ravaged postwar Germany, while *Easy Living* was an unusual excursion into moral cynicism, detailing a failing sports star's attempts to hold on to an ambitious, extravagant and promiscuous wife. At the same time, Tourneur could revel in the gaudy colours and ebullient action of undemanding swashbucklers: both *The Flame and the Arrow* (with a graceful, athletic Burt Lancaster) and *Anne of the Indies* were lively, tongue-in-cheek examples of the genre.

In the late '50s, Tourneur's assignments were more variable, and only *Nightfall* – an effectively paranoid *film noir* based on a novel by David Goodis – and *Night of the Demon* >**4** (an impressive, atmospheric study of Satanism and suggestibility, despite shots of an unconvincing monster inserted at the producers' insistence) proved worthy of his talents; even the presence of Price, Lorre, Karloff and Rathbone failed to ignite the *The Comedy of Terrors*. His other late film work (by this time he was also directing for television) was entirely negligible, and he retired in 1966.

Using shadows and unusual compositions, often with a telling detail in the foreground, Tourneur was adept at creating moods of mystery and suspense, both human and supernatural; he was also a gifted, succinct storyteller whose ability to turn even formular material into superior entertainment should not be neglected.

Lineage

It is likely that Tourneur inherited his father's visual talents, and that Lewton taught him the value of menace that is implied as opposed to shown. He may be compared with neglected 'B'-directors like **Brahm**, **Farrow** and **Lewis**, not to mention **Robert Wise**, a much more commercially successful Lewton graduate. **Schrader** and Taylor Hackford remade, respectively, *Cat People* and *Out of the Past.*

Further reading

Joel Siegel's *Val Lewton: The Reality of Terror* (London, 1972).

Viewing

1 **Cat People**
US 1942/ w Simone Simon, Kent Smith, Tom Conway
2 **I Walked with a Zombie**
US 1943/ w Frances Dee, Tom Conway, James Ellison
3 **Out of the Past (Build My Gallows High)**
US 1947/ w Robert Mitchum, Jane Greer, Kirk Douglas
4 **Night of the Demon (Curse of the Demon)**
GB 1958/ w Dana Andrews, Peggy Cummins, Niall MacGinnis

François Truffaut

Born: 6th February 1932/Paris, France
Died: 21st October 1984/Paris, France
Directing career: 1955-1983

The most commercially successful of the *Nouvelle Vague* directors, François Truffaut worked in a variety of genres and moods, often within a single film. And yet throughout his career, his thematic interests (the importance and pain of love, the relationship of life to art, the mysterious nature of women) remained constant.

Truffaut emerged from a difficult, near-delinquent childhood with a fanatical passion for cinema developed during his frequent truancy from school; after deserting from the army, he was taken under the wing of the celebrated film critic, André Bazin, who gave him work as a writer for *Cahiers du Cinéma* where besides making the acquaintance of **Godard**, **Rohmer**, **Chabrol** and Rivette, Truffaut formulated his polemical *politique des auteurs*. Indeed, he was a caustic, controversial critic, contemptuous of the stale literary tone of much contemporary French cinema, and in the late '50s set about making films himself. Of his three shorts (*Une Visite*, *Les Mistons*, and *Une Histoire d'Eau* – the last completed by Godard), only the second may be seen as anticipating his future work, with its bitter-sweet story of a doomed teenage romance observed by a group of mischievous boys. Eventually, however, having already served as assistant to **Rossellini** on three never-released films, he made his feature debut in 1959 with *Les Quatre Cents Coups* (*400 Blows*) >**1**, a partly autobiographical account of Antoine Doinel, a 13-year-old boy driven into petty crime by unfeeling parents and teachers. If the film's low-key realism was hardly iconoclastic, its passion, honesty and unsentimental warmth were palpable, especially in the scenes of the boy's lonely confinement in reform school. Much of its power, in fact, derives from the vividly naturalistic performance of the director's young *protégé* Jean-Pierre Léaud, who would repeat the same role in subsequent Antoine Doinel films, which over the next 20 years followed the shy, sexually gauche, self-regarding hero through unrequited adolescent love (the *Antoine and Colette* story in *Love at Twenty*), an encounter with an older woman (*Stolen Kisses*), marriage and infidelity (*Domicile Conjugale*) and divorce (*Love on the Run*). Just as during the cycle Doinel moved further away from Truffaut (becoming an amalgam of the director, his actor and pure fiction), so the films proceeded from realism to an increasingly whimsical, self-conscious, winsome irony that in retrospect seems all too indulgent of the immature, woman-obsessed, protagonist.

Far more subtle, if less obviously personal, were Truffaut's various experiments with genre. In his second feature, *Shoot the Pianist*, a distinctly European variation on the classic Hollywood crime movie, the story of a concert pianist-turned-café musician involved with gangsters allowed for alarmingly sudden, apparently haphazard switches in mood, suspense giving way to pathos via scenes of delightfully irrelevant comedy. Similarly, *Jules et Jim* >**2**, about a bizarre *ménage-à-trois* in the 1910s and 1920s, counterpointed a tale of unbridled amorous emotions with a detached, mocking voice-over. At this time, Truffaut's fluid, flexible editing and mobile camerawork were themselves a celebration of spontaneity, matched by his unpredictable range of subject-matter: *La Peau Douce* (*Silken Skin*) >**3** was a melancholy, touching account of adultery that finally accelerates towards a murder; *Fahrenheit 451* (his only English language film, and his first in colour) an uneven but ambitious version of Ray Bradbury's sci-fi novel about a repressive book-burning world; an adaptation of Cornell Woolrich's novel *The Bride Wore Black* features a woman consumed by a desire to punish her husband's killers, and was a strangely formal homage to Truffaut's hero, **Hitchcock**; and *Mississippi Mermaid* (again adapted from an Irish novel) was a languid romantic thriller that moves from simple mystery and suspense to an unexpected paean to *amour fou*.

With the exception of the Doinel films, Truffaut's work now displayed a new maturity, beginning with the tender, complex and moving assessment of the benefits and shortcomings of education in *L'Enfant Sauvage* >**4**, a lyrical account, taken from historical documents, of an 18th-century scientist's attempts to civilise a boy discovered roaming, speechless and wild, in a French forest; crucially, the enlightened Dr Itard, who comes to realise that he is learning as much as his pupil, was played by Truffaut himself. Equally poignant was *Les Deux Anglaises et le Continent* (*Anne and Muriel*) >**5**, a probing investigation of the bonds between life and literature (and film) framed as a doomed romantic triangle partly inspired by Proust and the Brontë Sisters. Then, after a raucous, comic hymn to murderous female independence and ingenuity in *Une Belle Fille Comme Moi*, Truffaut explored the gap between illusion and reality to deliciously witty effect in *Day for Night* (*La Nuit Américaine*) >**6**, a loving tribute to the chaotic, magical power of movie-making. Here, the unrepentant cinephile, despite his continuing focus on human relationships as his central theme, felt moved to ask, might films be more important than life?

After a two-year break, Truffaut returned to directing with the unprecedentedly dark *The Story of Adèle H*, an intense Gothic love story in which Victor Hugo's daughter travels the world in search of an unworthy lover, and ends her life hopelessly insane. Indeed, most of the director's later, highly variable work concerned romantic obsession; after a cute, maudlin account of childhood in *L'Argent de Poche* (*Small Change*) and an over-indulgent clinical study of a manic womaniser in *The Man Who Loved Women*, he returned, briefly, to form with *The Green Room* >**7**. Based on a Henry James story, its tale of a widower (Truffaut again) so obsessed by his memories of his dead wife, whom he worships in a private shrine, that he can no longer love the living and simply dies, is treated with delicate restraint; the sombre images never degenerate into sentimental, morbid melodrama, but achieve a serene, melancholy intensity of mood to match that of the protagonist. In his last three movies, however, his much-lauded simplicity seemed real rather than deceptive: *The Last Metro* was a superficial and complacently apolitical celebration of art, with a Parisian theatrical company struggling to survive the Nazi occupation; and the thrillers *The Woman Next Door* and *Finally Sunday!* – the first short on suspense as it charted the progress of adulterous *amour fou*, the second a slick but sloppily assembled *film noir* in which a secretary attempts to prove her boss innocent of murdering his wife – were but pale shadows of his earlier, more personal and imaginative

experiments in the genre. Then, tragically, at the age of 52, he died from cancer.

At his best, Truffaut's films displayed the gentle, romantic sensitivity of his beloved **Renoir**, revelling in the often absurd and surprising spontaneity of human behaviour. Frequently however, he was guilty of a cloying, bland humanism, his stylistic reserve, as it were, holding life's pain and chaos at arm's reach. Strangest of all, his work reveals a moral and artistic conservative, a far cry from the critically rebellious *enfant terrible* of the '50s.

Lineage

A fervent admirer of **Renoir**, **Vigo**, **Ophüls**, and **Hitchcock** (whom he interviewed for a now classic book) amongst many others, Truffaut was, in comparison to **Godard** (whose *À Bout de Souffle* he wrote), Rivette and **Rohmer**, a very conventional director: his influence on French mainstream cinema is consequently greater, most evident, perhaps, in the work of his former assistant Claude Miller. Truffaut may also be seen acting in **Spielberg**'s *Close Encounters of the Third Kind*.

Further reading

Annette Insdorf's *François Truffaut* (London, 1978), Don Allen's *Finally Truffaut* (London, 1985). *The Films in My Life* (London, 1980) is a collection of Truffaut's criticism.

Jean-Pierre Leaud and Kika Markham in Truffaut's lyrical, sadly neglected *Les Deux Anglaises et le Continent (Anne and Muriel).*

Viewing

1 **Les Quatre Cents Coups (400 Blows)**
France 1959/ w Jean-Pierre Léaud, Albert Rémy, Claire Maurier
2 **Jules et Jim**
France 1961/ w Jeanne Moreau, Oskar Werner, Henri Serre
3 **La Peau Douce (Silken Skin)**
France 1964/ w Jean Desailly, Françoise Dorleac, Nelly Benedetti
4 **L'Enfant Sauvage (The Wild Child)**
France 1969/ w Jean-Pierre Cargol, Truffaut, Jean Dasté
5 **Les Deux Anglaises et le Continent (Anne and Muriel)**
France 1971/ w Jean-Pierre Léaud, Kika Markham, Stacey Tendeter
6 **La Nuit Américaine (Day for Night)**
France 1973/ w Truffaut, Jacqueline Bisset, Jean-Pierre Léaud
7 **The Green Room**
France 1978/ w Truffaut, Nathalie Baye, Jean Dasté

Dziga Vertov

Born: 2nd January 1896/Byalistok, Poland
Died: 12th February 1954/Moscow, USSR
Directing career: 1918-1954

Though most of his work is now rarely screened, one need only see a single film by Vertov (born Denis Arkadievitch Kaufman) to recognise that he was one of cinema's greatest innovators. An ardent theorist and a militant proponent of new, revolutionary forms of film-making, he fully deserves his reputation as a pioneer documentarist, and also, perhaps, as one of film's earliest modernists.

The brother of Boris and Mikhail Kaufman (both of whom became fine cameramen), Vertov first took his pseudonym (roughly translated as spinning top) shortly before the 1917 Soviet Revolution, when he was already experimenting with sound-montage. Swept along by the enormous artistic fervour that accompanied the Bolshevik victory, in 1918 he was invited by Lev Kuleshov to work as writer, editor and supervisor on *Film Weekly*, the first Soviet newsreels. Almost immediately Vertov revealed an interest in the manipulation of actuality through montage and, over the next few years, in the compilation film *Anniversary of the Revolution*, in his experiences with the mobile agit-trains (which took news and propaganda to, and documented the lives of, the Russian masses), and in the newsreel series *Kino-Pravda* (*Cine-Truth*), he steadily refined his ideas and his technique. Hostile to fiction, he developed the theory of the camera-eye, arguing that the machine could observe and record things more clearly than the human eye; but at the same time as frequently using a hidden, candid camera – then innovative in itself – he experimented more and more with various editing techniques, which served both to make his films more visually invigorating, and to stress the participatory, and therefore revolutionary, role of the film-maker and his camera.

It was after *Soviet Toys* >**1** (the first Soviet animated film and a lively, satirical short on capitalism), *Kino-Eye*, and *A Sixth of the Earth* >**2** (which celebrated Russia's enormous variety and resources) that Vertov made his masterpiece, *The Man with the Movie Camera* >**3**. On one level, the film is a lyrical portrait of a day in the life of a Soviet city; on another, it is a stunning, avant-garde manifesto of film's capacity to record – and *transform* – reality. Split-screen, fast- and slow-motion, superimposition and subliminally swift montage are used not as mere trickery but as a hymn to the versatility of cinema; still more astonishing, Vertov literally (through animation) makes his camera walk on its tripod, and turns the entire film into a self-reflexive meditation on its own genesis by showing the cameraman and the editor at work, and a cinema audience watching scenes from the film itself. The final result is witty, exhilarating, and intellectually provocative.

With the advent of talkies, Vertov proved equally ambitious in his use of synchronised and non-synchronised sound; but after *Enthusiasm* and *Three Songs of Lenin*, he fell victim to the artistic conservatism of Stalinism, and made his last feature, *Lullaby*, in 1937. Thereafter, until his death, he was reduced to working on comparatively conventional newsreels, many in collaboration with Yelizaveta Svilova, his wife and long-term editor.

Vertov's importance as a founding father of documentary and an influential theorist – in terms of his analysis of the relationship between the camera, its subject and the spectator – is not merely historical. His finest films also remain exciting examples of the way in which cinematic artistry can transcend and revitalise the mere observation of everyday life and the demands of political propaganda.

Lineage

Himself influenced by Mayakovsky and Kuleshov, Vertov may be very favourably compared with **Eisenstein** or Pudovkin, while his style is far removed from **Dovzhenko**'s poeticism. His ideas sound echoes in Brecht, and his influence on documentarists such as Chris Marker, Jean Rouch and **Pennebaker**, not to mention **Godard** and Jean-Pierre Gorin (who collaborated as the Dziga Vertov Group), is enormous.

Further reading

Jay Leyda's *Kino* (London, 1960),

Erik Barnouw's *Documentary* (New York, 1974), Richard Meran Barsam's *Non-Fiction Film* (London, 1974). Some of Vertov's own theoretical writing can be found in *Cinema in Revolution* (London, 1973).

Viewing

1 **Soviet Toys**
USSR 1924
2 **A Sixth of the Earth**
USSR 1926
3 **The Man with the Movie Camera**
USSR 1929

King Vidor

Born: **8th February 1894/Galveston, Texas, USA**
Died: **1st November 1982/Paso Robles, California, USA**
Directing career: **1913-1959**

Although often naive, even crude, the films of King Wallis Vidor were frequently distinguished by their sheer energy and forceful visual style. While his work ranged widely, from light comedy and epic Westerns to sententious social and metaphysical melodramas, his abiding interest in man's battles with himself, with society and with nature provides his career with a clear thematic consistency.

Vidor grew up with movies, working as a ticket-collector and projectionist at a local nickelodeon before becoming a newsreel cameraman. Having directed a handful of shorts, he made his way to Hollywood, where he eventually set up his own studio. The ensuing films were none too successful and in 1922 he signed up with MGM; even so, only with *The Big Parade* >**1**, produced by Irving Thalberg when Vidor expressed his dislike of working on 'ephemeral' films, did he first achieve a major success. The initial film in a group of works meant to deal with 'wheat, steel and war', it was an epic, impressively mounted portrait of an ordinary doughboy's spiritual development during World War I, moving from a mood of patriotic hysteria to an awareness of the death, pain and isolation wrought by battle. Similarly, after a version of *La Bohème* (vividly acted by Lillian Gish), *The Crowd* >**2** charted the sentimental education of a young, Everyman-hero whose dreams of making it in the city are dashed by his inability to cope with the alienation and economic hardship of urban life. In terms of plot, the film is simplistic, but the images, which move from shots of the hero as one face in a sea of bored, anonymous desk-clerks, to a final scene in which he sits laughing in a packed theatre, eloquently argue the protagonist's need to accept his place, humbly, alongside the rest of humanity.

After two delightful comic vehicles for Marion Davies (*Show People* being a witty, sophisticated portrait of Hollywood's film community), Vidor greeted the advent of sound with the all-black, part-musical *Hallelujah*. A stylised, location-shot tale of an itinerant preacher plagued by sexual desires, it was flawed mainly by a naively patronising attitude to black life. Throughout the '30s, in fact, Vidor's career was curiously variable, ranging from his first Western (*Billy the Kid*), the maudlin boxing saga *The Champ*, and the exotically erotic South Seas hokum of *Bird of Paradise* to more serious material: *Our Daily Bread* (*The Crowd*'s rural sequel) was a politically muddled celebration of agrarian collectivism; *Stella Dallas* >**3** a compelling weepie about mother-love, disguised as a study of social inequality and class divisions; *The Citadel* an account of a doctor redeemed when his conscience forces him to help a disease-ridden Welsh mining community, rather than make his name in Harley Street administering to the rich and famous.

As Vidor's career progressed, his films became increasingly grand in terms of narrative scope and visual bravura. In the pioneering-adventure *Northwest Passage*, his ambivalent regard for Nature as a beautiful but hostile force is displayed in sumptuous landscape photography; *An American Romance*, a rags-to-riches tale of an immigrant miner-turned-industrial tycoon, was evidence of a continuing interest in steel as a metaphor for the indomitability of the human spirit; while *Duel in The Sun* >**4**, made for Selznick, was an absurdly overblown Western whose lurid colours, overheated passions (two brothers, one good, one bad, fall out over a half-breed Indian girl and their crippled, tyrannical father's ranch), and stylised performances achieved an almost operatic intensity. The production was so fraught that Vidor left the set in anger at the endless demands that he further glamorise the producer's wife, Jennifer Jones, and it was finally completed by other hands (**Von Sternberg**, **Dieterle** and Selznick himself included); but it remains an impressive, baroque folly, not least for the final scene in which the ill-starred lovers shoot each other before crawling over sun-baked rocks to die in a last embrace and enter the realm of myth.

No less bombastic was *The Fountainhead* >**5**, adapted from Ayn Rand's reactionary novel about a visionary architect's struggles against the apathy and mediocrity of the world around him. While as politically ambivalent – or confused – as ever, Vidor at least acknowledges his protagonist's aggressive contempt through a wild array of bizarre, hyperbolic images infused with phallic symbols. Similarly hysterical were the inferior *Beyond the Forest* and the torrid Deep South melodrama *Ruby Gentry* >**6**, both about frustrated desires, adultery and revenge. Thereafter, however, Vidor's films became ever less satisfying, from the patchily effective Western *Man Without a Star*, through an ambitious but lumbering version of *War and Peace*, to the uninspired Biblical epic *Solomon and Sheba*. He then retired from directing features, although during the '60s he made several documentary shorts and taught courses in film.

As the years passed, Vidor's films became both morally darker and more excessive in their depiction of tempestuous passion. If, however, much of his work lacks intellectual sophistication, his narrative and visual confidence, and conspicuous ambitions, tend to ensure (at least in his finest films) stirring entertainment.

Lineage

While Vidor's silent work may have been influenced by **Griffith**, **Flaherty** and **DeMille**, his later films are perhaps most usefully compared with the 'primitivism' of **Fuller**. His 1980 role in *Love and Money* may suggest an influence on James Toback, while **Oliver Stone** may be seen as Vidor's modern, as yet inferior, successor.

Further reading

Clive Denton's *The Hollywood Professionals*, Vol 5 (London, 1976), John Baxter's *King Vidor* (New York, 1976), *King Vidor on Filmmaking* (New York, 1972); *A Tree is a Tree* (New York, 1952) is Vidor's autobiography.

Viewing

1 **The Big Parade**
US 1925/ w John Gilbert, René Adorée, Hobart Bosworth

2 **The Crowd**
US 1928/ w James Murray, Eleanor Boardman, Bert Roach

3 **Stella Dallas**
US 1937/ w Barbara Stanwyck, John Boles, Anne Shirley

4 **Duel in the Sun**
US 1946/ w Jennifer Jones, Gregory Peck, Joseph Cotten

5 **The Fountainhead**
US 1949/ w Gary Cooper, Patricia Neal, Raymond Massey

6 **Ruby Gentry**
US 1952/ w Jennifer Jones, Charlton Heston, Karl Malden

Jean Vigo

Born: 26th April 1905/Paris, France
Died: 5th October 1934/Paris, France
Directing career: 1929-1934

Though he died at the age of 29, leaving only approximately three hours of film behind him, Jean Vigo remains to this day one of the most remarkable film-makers ever to have lived. None of his films were financially successful nor, at the time of release, did they receive the critical acclaim they deserved, but he was both a source of inspiration to countless later directors, and a superb example of the film-maker's

ability to transform mundane reality into pure poetry.

The son of a socialist/anarchist who went by the name of Miguel Almereyda, Vigo spent most of his early years in boarding schools; when his father, accused of treason, died in jail under mysterious and sinister circumstances, the teenage Jean set about trying to clear his name. By his early 20s he was already plagued by illness, but, having served as an assistant cameraman and been encouraged by Claude Autant-Lara and Germaine Dulac to pursue his film-making ambitions, he was finally able to make, with a camera bought with money supplied by his father-in-law, *A Propos de Nice* >**1**. Shot by **Dziga Vertov**'s brother Boris Kaufman, the film is an astonishingly imaginative and assured debut; ostensibly a silent, 40-minute documentary, it is, in fact, a savagely witty satire on a tourist bourgeoisie whose idle, futile lounging in the casinos along the beach is subtly juxtaposed with the community spirit of the working-class poor in the back-street slums. Vigo's method is at once lucid and surreal, his camera trickery mocking manic sun-worshippers, ancient militarists and nubile fashion-plates alike.

Though *Taris*, a celebration of

Dita Parlo and Jean Dasté, deeply in love but troubled by the demands of marriage, in Vigo's tender and masterly *L'Atalante*.

France's champion swimmer, was a mere 11 minutes long, it not only revealed Vigo's sheer love of film – with reverse and slow-motion and underwater shots – but offered him a major symbolic motif for his later, debut feature. First, however, he made the medium-length *Zéro de Conduite* >**2**, a poetic, characteristically surreal and anti-bourgeois fable (based partly on his own experiences of boarding school) about pupils rebelling against their petty-minded, hypocritical, and absurdly regimental teachers. Grotesque caricature – the headmaster is a midget, the governors literally dummies – ridicules the hierarchical adults (who are, nonetheless, never presented as wilfully cruel), while the boys' spontaneity, imaginativeness and easy camaraderie are conveyed in scenes of intense but never maudlin lyricism – perhaps most notably in a dormitory pillow-fight that becomes, through music played backwards and slow-motion, a ritual procession lent magic by the swirling of snowy-white feathers. Even so, for all its beauty, Vigo's film was banned, so vividly did its dreamlike fantasy-satire evoke a recognisable and regrettable situation.

With his one and only feature, the director – now seriously ailing – created one of the greatest masterpieces of all cinema. About the first troubled months in the marriage of a Seine barge skipper to a girl he has met in a small, dull, riverside village, *L'Atalante* >**3** is not only a remarkably honest account of the need to make compromises in affairs of the heart (the man, jealous and complacent, is loath to indulge his wife's understandable desire to see Paris, while she perhaps underestimates the rigour of his work-schedule), but a truly erotic rhapsody of images whose basis in everyday reality gives rise to a sensuous surrealism, the tone of which is astonishingly tender. When the wife eventually visits Paris, her husband, believing she has left him, searches for her image underwater, in the river – itself a symbol of life, passion, and the continuous need for change; and at night Vigo unites the pair, she in a hotel, he on the boat, through their dreams, alternating and finally superimposing shots of man and woman to create a scene that, perhaps more astutely than any other in film history, reveals that sexual need is as much emotional and mental as physical. The effect is electric, the entire film an intimate, witty, wise and extremely moving affirmation of human love.

Sadly, the Gaumont company interfered with the film, arguing that it needed to be 'popularised' and retitled; tragically, Vigo died from tuberculosis three weeks after its release, and years before it was restored to its original form. A martyr to his art, his greatness derives partly from his willingness and ability to invest so much of himself into his films. But he was also one of the most inventive, original and profoundly humane talents ever to grace the cinematic medium with his inspired, personal vision.

Lineage

While *A Propos de Nice* and Kaufman's presence on all Vigo's films suggest **Vertov**'s influence, and *Taris* and *Zéro de Conduite* a debt to Georges Méliès, it is more useful to compare him with **Renoir** and **Buñuel**. If his own influence on French cinema has been enormous (notably on **Clair**, **Cocteau**, **Carné**, **Franju**, **Truffaut**, **Godard**, **Rohmer**, **Malle** and, latterly, Léos Carax), it is also visible in figures such as **Bertolucci** (who pays homage in *Last Tango in Paris*) and **Anderson** (who remade *Zéro de Conduite* – ancestor of countless boarding school films – as *If...*).

Further reading

P.E. Sallès Gomès, *Jean Vigo* (London, 1972), John M Smith's *Jean Vigo* (London, 1972).

Viewing

1 **A Propos de Nice**
France 1929
2 **Zéro de Conduite**
France 1931/ w Louis Lefebvre, Gilbert Pruchon, Jean Dasté
3 **L'Atalante**
France 1934/ w Dita Parlo, Jean Dasté, Michel Simon

Luchino Visconti

Born: 2nd November 1906/Milan, Italy
Died: 17th March 1976/Rome, Italy
Directing career: 1942-1976

A Marxist aristocrat, Count Don Luchino Visconti di Morone was widely praised for both the realism and vaguely politicised tone of his early films, and the operatic sumptuousness of his later historical costume dramas. Throughout his career, however, style dominated content; all too often, the result was camp, decorative melodrama disguised as solemn, socially significant art.

Born to one of Italy's highest-ranking aristocratic families the young Visconti, after military service, set about developing his interest in art and horses. Having worked in the theatre as a set-designer, he then served as costume designer and assistant to **Renoir**, before making his debut in 1942 with *Ossessione* >**1**. Based on James M.

Cain's *The Postman Always Rings Twice*, its story about an adulterous romance that results in murder transposed to the Po Delta, the film revelled in a seedy provincial authenticity later seen as a precursor of neo-realism. Furthermore, its preoccupation with greed, deceit and lust, not to mention the presence of a probably homosexual character, ensured its suppression by the Fascists. *La Terra Trema*, an epic account of the hardship suffered by Sicilian fisherfolk, was even closer to neo-realism, shot on location with a cast of locals in place of actors. Its somewhat simplistic Marxist message, that the peasants' real enemy was not Nature but exploitative businessmen, was in fact less indicative of Visconti's future career than its long, elaborate takes and its use of a disintegrating family to mirror the social climate of Italy as a whole. Indeed, after the atypical comedy *Bellissima* (with Anna Magnani maudlin and loud as a working-class mother trying to turn her daughter into a child-star at Rome's satirically depicted Cinecittà studios), *Senso* >**2** paralleled the affair between an Austrian officer and a married Italian countess with the bourgeoisie's betrayal of the Italian revolutionary cause; more significantly, the film was Visconti's first excursion into full-blown melodrama, its realism restricted to a lavishly detailed reconstruction of the Risorgimento period, its colour, compositions, camera-movements, costumes and interior design all distinguished by a baroque, ornate extravagance.

White Nights, a studio-bound version of Dostoevsky's story about a romance between two lovers trapped in private fantasies, was equally overblown, while *Rocco and His Brothers* >**3**, about the disintegration, under economic, social and sexual pressures, of a Sicilian family forced to move to Milan, was Visconti's blackest, and greatest, film; as its episodic narrative steadily spiralled from low-key realism to powerhouse melodrama, its study of brutality, betrayal and brotherly rivalries benefitted enormously from its *noir*-style photography and urban locations. But *The Leopard* >**4** saw a return to plodding historical drama, observing an aristocratic family's reluctant but inevitable acquiescence to a son's romance with a middle-class girl, set against the backdrop of Garibaldi's unification of Italy; not only did the director seem less interested in the film's political elements than in the aesthetic qualities of a grandiose ball, but what little analysis there was of class conflict was clouded by his own elegaic identification with Burt Lancaster's kindly, indisputably honourable, sorrowing patriarch.

Worse, however, was to come: *Vaghe Stelle dell'Orsa* (*Sandra*) was an ambitious but deeply flawed Freudian family drama inspired partly by the Elektra myth; *The Stranger* a shallow, misguided and crassly 'filled-out' travesty of Camus' existentialist novel; *The Damned* a camp, ludicrously solemn munitions-dynasty melodrama set in a hysterically decadent Nazi Germany; and *Death in Venice* >**5** a turgid, hollow and indulgently bathetic version of Thomas Mann's novella, with an ageing composer suffering unrequited passion for an impossibly effete, effeminate teenager in a sailor suit: only the use of Mahler's music alleviated the effect of utter tedium. By now, Visconti's taste for long slow camera movements, elegant, cluttered decor and heavily theatrical performances had reached a nadir of spurious, middlebrow tastefulness; and *Ludwig*, a baroque and apolitical portrait of the mad, reclusive king of Bavaria, was little more than a romanticised study in neurotic homosexuality.

Conversation Piece >**6**, about a lonely, ageing professor both revolted and revitalised by the arrival in the flat below him of an incestuous group of vulgar, wealthy jet-setters, was something of a return to form: sombre, stately, relatively understated, and (with the exception of Helmut Berger as an angel of death figure) subtly performed. *The Innocent*, however, an obvious, heavily emphatic period piece about the double-standards that operate in relation to male and female infidelity, was merely innocuous. Typically lavish, it was the last film Visconti made before his death.

Also acclaimed as a director of

theatre and opera, Visconti adhered to a fundamentally static, art-director's form of cinema: opulently designed, with greater attention paid to surface values than to narrative pace, psychological depth, thematic complexity or moral insight. As such, his later, stodgier films may be seen as redundant exercises in aestheticism, and serve to call into doubt his earlier commitment to the tenets of neo-realism.

Lineage

Clearly influenced by his experiences with **Renoir**, Visconti, like **De Sica**, **Antonioni** and **Fellini**, abandoned neo-realism to forge a more personal style. His grandiose decorative sensibility, often applied to costume drama and literary subjects, may be compared with, or may have influenced, **Lean**, **Ivory**, **Coppola** and **Cimino**.

Further reading

Geoffrey Nowell-Smith's *Visconti* (London, 1973), Monica Stirling's *A Screen of Time: A Study of Luchino Visconti* (New York, 1979), Claretta Tonetti's *Luchino Visconti* (New York, 1983).

Viewing

1 **Ossessione**
Italy 1942/ w Clara Calamai, Massimo Girotti, Juan de Landa
2 **Senso**
Italy 1954/ w Alida Valli, Farley Granger, Massimo Girotti
3 **Rocco and His Brothers**
Italy 1960/ w Alain Delon, Renato Salvatori, Annie Girardot
4 **The Leopard**
Italy 1963/ w Burt Lancaster, Alain Delon, Claudia Cardinale
5 **Death in Venice**
Italy 1971/ w Dirk Bogarde, Silvana Mangano, Bjorn Andresen
6 **Conversation Piece (Gruppo di Famiglia in un Interno)**
Italy 1974/ w Burt Lancaster, Silvana Mangano, Helmut Berger

Josef Von Sternberg

Born: 29th May 1894/Vienna, Austria
Died: 22nd December 1969/ Hollywood, California, USA
Directing career: 1924-1953

Best known for the exotic, ironic melodramas he made with Marlene Dietrich, Jonas Sternberg was one of the most personal, ambitious and imaginative of early film-makers. Uninterested in naturalism, and fascinated by film's visual potential, he repeatedly revealed his cynical, detached attitude to the world by focussing attention on male-female relationships marked by sexual obsession, humiliation and cruel, casual betrayal, often by a contemptuous *femme fatale*.

Sternberg's childhood was spent in both Austria and America, where he developed an interest in the graphic arts. His initial encounter with cinema was as a lowly Hollywood editing assistant until, having attracted attention for his work on several army-training films during World War I, he became an assistant director. Then, in 1924, he made his own debut with *The Salvation Hunters*. An occasionally seedy melodrama about three 'derelicts', shot on location around the San Pedro mud banks, the film was at once acclaimed for its realism; even so, in retrospect its use of symbolism (memorably a dredger engaged in endless futile attempts to clear a harbour) and the visual care taken in a brothel scene anticipate Sternberg's later work. Of his subsequent silents, few remain (perhaps most regrettably lost is his second feature, *The Seagull*, made for **Chaplin** who suppressed its release). *Underworld* >**1**, the first of his many films made under contract to Paramount, is a seminal gangster thriller, less notable for action than for an almost fetishistic, elaborate visualisation of both a decadent hoodlums' party and a befeathered gangster's moll; while *The Last Command* >**2** was his first masterpiece, atypically complex in terms of plot but entirely personal in its ironic interest in role playing (a Tsarist general and a seemingly doomed Bolshevik actor who become deadly rivals during the 1917 revolution later meet in Hollywood as a down-and-out extra and a film-director, working on a movie-reconstruction of the conflict), and in its attribution of power to a seductive, beautiful woman, who inexorably changes *and* saves the lives of both men. But it was only after the likewise visually ornate *The Docks of New York*, and the stilted, plodding prison drama *Thunderbolt* (Sternberg's first talkie) that he began the series of Dietrich films for which he is best remembered.

Made in Germany at the request of Emil Jannings, who plays a staid elderly professor transformed and ruined by his obsessive, cuckolded love for flirtatious cabaret singer Lola-Lola, *The Blue Angel* >**3** was the first of Sternberg's seven, mutually beneficial collaborations with the hitherto unknown actress. The director supplied the films' basic conception (weak, masochistic males enthralled by an ambivalent, mysterious temptress whose occasional self-sacrifices fail to mask her mockery of the absurdity of romantic love and sexual infatuation); Dietrich supplied the aloof but sensuous charisma. All the films were embellished by Sternberg's brilliant, stylised compositions, which conjured up exotic erotic atmospheres, far removed from the mundane world of reality, through a shimmering play of light and shade upon smoke, veils, stonework, lattice frames, and drapes. *Morocco* was set in a luminously unreal, Arabic never-never land; *Dishonored*'s tale of Mata Hari-style spying unfolded in a shadowy Central Europe; *Shanghai Express* >**4** took place in a seething, war-torn China; *Blonde Venus* evoked an America polarised by sordid Depression landscapes and playboy luxury apartments. Finest of all, the flamboyant symbolism of *The Scarlet Empress* >**5**, in which Catherine the Great's rise to power is seen in terms of cunning sexual strategies, allowed for a delirious array of lavish boudoirs, grotesquely morbid statues, incense

Marlene Dietrich, *sans* gorilla suit, in Von Sternberg's visually resplendent *Blonde Venus.*

and cathedral candles, and white stallions thundering up wide palatial staircases. Eventually however, the partnership was bound to end, and after *The Devil Is a Woman*, set in a mythic Spain positively oozing mantillas, palm leaves, shawls and capes, and with forlorn hero Lionel Atwill bearing a distinct physical resemblance to the director, Dietrich and Sternberg went their separate ways.

Sternberg's other '30s films (versions of Theodore Dreiser's *An American Tragedy* and Dostoevsky's *Crime and Punishment*; *The King Steps Out* and *Sergeant Madden*) were altogether more uneven; an adaptation of Robert Graves' *I, Claudius*, made for Alexander Korda, met with countless production setbacks and was sadly never completed (what little remains can be seen in the documentary *The Epic That Never Was*). *The Shanghai Gesture* >**6**, was a superb, cynical melodrama in which a moralising, hypocritical American diplomat, a casino owner-cum-brothel madame – his ex-lover – and an Eastern voluptuary loyal to nothing but his own sensual needs, battle for the soul of the American's degenerate daughter. It was as extravagant, elaborate and brazenly metaphorical an account of erotic by-play as anything ever filmed, but the rest of the '40s saw Sternberg confounded first by the war, then by Howard Hughes, for whom he made the lumbering Cold War spy-romance *Jet Pilot* and the amiable comedy-thriller *Macao* (much of which was reshot by **Nicholas Ray**). Finally, he went to Japan where his penchant for symbolic artifice was allowed gloriously free rein: if *The Saga of Anatahan* >**7** was based on historical fact (Japanese sailors, unable to believe in Japan's defeat in World War II, turn on each other upon finding that they share the remote island on which they are stranded with a single, beautiful woman), Sternberg perversely but brilliantly translated it into a stylised, almost abstract study of masculine folly and feminine ambivalence. He did so by creating his hothouse latterday Eden in the studio and (ignoring the exact nuances of his actors' dialogue) revealing the significance of events with a commentary narrated by himself; he also contributed the photography.

Sternberg then retired from directing; though plagued by ill health he spent his last years writing an autobiography, teaching and visiting sundry festivals that, in mounting retrospectives in his honour, flattered his vain and arrogant estimation of his own worth. He was, nevertheless, a major director, whose abundant visual sensibility (often decried as camp aestheticism) served both as a means of exploring film's formal properties, and as the framework for his continuing inquisition into the destructive but, perhaps, ultimately redemptory nature of the human passion known as love.

Lineage

Both Sternberg's conceit and his love of visual detail have prompted comparisons with **Von Stroheim**; even so, his style was very different, and it is perhaps more illuminating to compare his obsession with love with the far less cynical **Ophüls** and **Borzage**; similarly, his interest in film's formal properties might be likened to that of figures as diverse as **Mamoulian**, **Minnelli**, **Powell** and **Sirk**. It is arguable that **Demy**'s *Lola*, **Fassbinder**'s film of the same name and the work of the Belgian Harry Kumel pay tribute to his influence.

Further reading

Andrew Sarris' *The Films of Josef von Sternberg* (New York, 1966), John Baxter's *The Cinema of Josef von Sternberg* (New York, 1971). Sternberg's *Fun in a Chinese Laundry* (New York, 1965) is a very provocative autobiography.

Viewing

1 **Underworld**
US 1927/ w George Bancroft, Evelyn Brent, Clive Brook

2 **The Last Command**
US 1928/ w Emil Jannings, William Powell, Evelyn Brent

3 **The Blue Angel**
Germany 1930/ w Marlene Dietrich, Emil Jannings, Kurt Gerron

4 **Shanghai Express**
US 1932/ w Marlene Dietrich, Clive Brook, Anna May Wong

5 **The Scarlet Empress**
US 1934/ w Marlene Dietrich, Sam Jaffe, John Lodge

6 **The Shanghai Gesture**
US 1941/ w Gene Tierney, Walter Huston, Ona Munson, Victor Mature

7 **The Saga of Anatahan**
Japan 1952/ w Akemi Negishi, Tadashi Suganuma, Kisaburo Sawamura

Erich Von Stroheim

Born: 22nd September 1885/Vienna, Austria
Died: 12th May 1957/Paris, France
Directing career: 1918-1933

Even though little of what remains of the films of Erich Oswald Stroheim now exists in a form he originally intended, it is still immediately evident that he was one of the very finest directors of the silent era. An obsessive perfectionist whose extravagance repeatedly brought him into conflict with producers, he was both a crucial figure in the development of cinematic naturalism and a superbly cynical moralist, whose insistence on sordid lust, avarice and hypocrisy (particularly among the idle rich) may also have contributed to the demise of his film-making career.

Despite his later pretensions to an aristocratic, military background, Stroheim was born to a middle-class Jewish merchant's family in Vienna. Emigrating to America at around the age of 20, he passed through a variety of lowly jobs before moving on to bit parts in the movies in 1914. Within a short while, he established himself as an actor for and military advisor to **Griffith** and John Emerson, working on *The Birth of a Nation* and *Intolerance* amongst other films; by 1917, his stiff posture, sardonic smile and cruel bullet-headed virility had landed him several roles as a Prussian officer, and won him a reputation as 'the man you love to hate'. Indeed, in his 1918 directing debut, *Blind Husbands*, he played an Austrian lieutenant, whose attempted seduction of the lonely wife of an American tourist is depicted in unusually sophisticated and erotic detail. The *Devil's Passkey* – now lost – was apparently an equally successful variation on the love-triangle theme; *Foolish Wives* >**1**, however, was Stroheim's first mature masterpiece. It focussed on a ruthlessly manipulative Russian, whose noble bearing and wealthy airs serve as a front for both his counterfeiting activities and his insatiable, possibly perverse sexual desires; the film was an acid comedy of manners whose moral thrust and psychological depth derive from Stroheim's witty, unprecedentedly precise observation of gestures; at the same time, this intimacy achieved an epic, universal dimension through a fetishistic, exact recreation of the casino, hotels and cafés of Monte Carlo, the indictment of individual evil thus embracing an entire, high-living society. So costly was his passion for verisimilitude, however, that producer Irving Thalberg stepped in to cut the film. Nor did the director fare any better with *Merry-Go-Round*, on which he was replaced halfway through shooting; at which point he left Universal for Goldwyn.

Unlike his earlier work, *Greed* >**2** was a distinctly American tale, an astonishingly epic, ten-hour adaptation of Frank Norris' realist novel *McTeague*; but, although Stroheim had abandoned the leisure-spots of Europe for the streets of San Francisco, his eye for minute, telling detail and moral laxity was as sharp as ever, with money again offered as the root of all evil. Shot on location (including a devastatingly bleak, ironic final scene in Death Valley, in which two former friends who have become deadly rivals since the winning of a lottery, die handcuffed together in the scorching desert), the film was a triumph of unusually subtle acting, fastidious compositions (an ill-fated wedding ceremony is shot with a funeral passing in the background), and black satire. Unfortunately, however, during the film's production the Goldwyn company became MGM, whose new executive (Thalberg again) reduced Stroheim's 42 reels to 10. Nonetheless, it remains a masterpiece.

As if to prove himself capable of compromise, Stroheim stayed at MGM to make the lavish if relatively innocuous Ruritanian romance *The Merry Widow*. Then, for *The Wedding March* >**3**, he reverted to a sumptuous visual extravagance, its two-part story, of a Hapsburg prince tempted away from his official bride-to-be by an innocent, pretty commoner, set in an immaculately re-created Vienna inspired by Stroheim's own boyhood memories. Grotesque satire was again to the fore in the unflattering depiction of the vain and avaricious members of the royal household; at the same time, a lyrical, even romantic side to Stroheim's moral pessimism manifested itself in love scenes set in luminous apple-orchards glowing with blossom, all the more effective for being counterpointed with outrageously hedonistic brothel-scenes. Once more, Stroheim's infatuation with the historical accuracy of architecture, costumes and props proved to be his undoing; the second, altogether blacker part of the film was mutilated and given a minimal release. Similarly, in *Queen Kelly* >**4**, a further doomed romance between a naive convent-girl and a jealous queen's wastrel lover, the sequences depicting the heroine's

Death in Death Valley: the inevitable outcome of human *Greed*, as imagined by Von Stroheim for what was intended as a 10-hour epic.

sordid, forced marriage (over her procuress aunt's deathbed) to a lecherous, crippled, elderly alcoholic were deemed so repulsive by the film's star and producer, Gloria Swanson, that Stroheim was fired before its completion, and a more conventional ending substituted. Even so, Stroheim's original conception is still evident in the subtle eroticism of the star-crossed lovers' courtship, in the balance of the intimate and epic, and, notably, in a scene where the queen, mad with anger, runs through the elegant corridors of her palace whipping her young rival.

Stroheim's directing career was almost over: his first sound film, *Walking on Broadway*, was largely reshot by other hands and never released. Thereafter he occasionally contributed to scripts (most memorably, perhaps, to **Browning**'s *The Devil Doll*), but for the most part he kept himself in work as an actor: his best roles were as a typically autocratic movie-director in *The Lost Squadron*, as a German prison-camp commander in **Renoir**'s *La Grande Illusion*, as Rommel in **Wilder**'s *Five Graves to Cairo*, and as Max, Swanson's butler, former husband and director in Wilder's *Sunset Boulevard*, which rather ambivalently includes an excerpt from *Queen Kelly*.

Stroheim's combination of naturalism and melodrama, not to mention his stately camera and editing styles, made a significant contribution to the progress of film language and technique. More importantly, his interest in the less salubrious aspects of both the individual psyche and society at large ensure that his films retain lasting sophistication and modernity.

Lineage

Stroheim's realism and moral complexity constitute a considerable advance on **Griffith**'s puritanical, 19th-century sensibility. In his pretensions to a European eroticism and wit he may be grouped with **Lubitsch** and **Von Sternberg**, while his influence on the future of film-making was immense.

Further reading

Joel Finler's *Stroheim* (London, 1967). Herman G. Weinberg's *Stroheim: A Pictorial Record of His Nine Films* (New York, 1975), *The Complete Greed* (1972) and *The Complete Wedding March* (1974) provide photographic reconstructions of his now irretrievably lost work.

Viewing

1 **Foolish Wives**
US 1921/ w Stroheim, Maude George, Mae Busch
2 **Greed**
US 1923/ w Gibson Gowland, Zasu Pitts, Jean Hersholt
3 **The Wedding March**
US 1926-28/ w Stroheim, Fay Wray, Maude George
4 **Queen Kelly**
US 1928/ w Gloria Swanson, Walter Byron, Seena Owen

Andrzej Wajda

Born: 6th March 1927/Suwalki, Poland
Directing career: 1950-

Arguably the finest, certainly the best known, Polish film-maker of his generation, Andrzej Wajda has repeatedly grappled with the problems of representing recent Polish history. Gradually moving away from a rather baroque, occasionally even Expressionist, style towards a more conventional naturalism, he has persistently taken issue with 'official' versions of events and ideology.

Having fought for the Resistance during the Second World War, Wajda attended the Lodz film school, where he directed several shorts; after assisting Aleksander Ford on *Five Boys from Barska Street*, he made his feature debut with *A Generation*, the first film in a loose trilogy that also included *Kanal* >**1** and *Ashes and Diamonds* >**2**. All three concerned the Polish experience of war (the first two portraying Resistance activity in occupied Warsaw; the last, set on the final day of the war, the killer of a communist party official), and were notable not only for their bleak imagery (the action of *Kanal* takes place largely in the city's sewers, while the protagonist of *Ashes and Diamonds* dies on a rubbish heap) but for their unromantic view of wartime heroism. Indeed, rather than accept the myth that to die fighting for one's country is purely a matter of glory, Wajda stressed his characters' confusion, fear and anxiety; and like them, Poland itself, trapped between Russia and Germany, was shown as searching for a sense of identity.

Though Wajda's subsequent work was comparatively minor, both *Lotna* (about Poland's battles against the invading Nazis in 1939) and *Innocent Sorcerers* (about the cynicism and disillusionment of contemporary youth) revealed a continuing interest in the effects of social and political change upon the individual. But only in *Everything for Sale* >**3** did he make a significant advance upon his early films: inspired by the death of actor Zbigniew Cybulski and measuring the effects of a similar death upon the cast, crew and director of a movie in mid-production, the film examined the relationship between illusion and reality and homed in on the often exploitative nature of artistic creativity. For some years, however, Wajda seemed to lose his way: *Hunting Flies* was a rare, none-too-successful excursion into satire, *Landscape After Battle* a return to the theme of war, *The Birchwood* and *The Wedding* solid but unremarkable and relatively apolitical literary adaptations.

For *Man of Marble* >**4**, Wajda abandoned his taste for allegory and symbolism to focus directly on the Stalinist legacy of postwar Poland. A young documentary film-maker decides to investigate the downfall of a bricklayer-hero of the '50s: her discovery that he is now missing, perhaps dead, and that his 'disgrace' centred on his loyal support for a friend framed in a '50s 'show-trial', allowed Wajda a sharp indictment of official corruption and media cover-up. It comes as no surprise that the film was initially banned. Likewise relevant in their blending of the personal and political were *Rough Treatment* (in which the emotional disintegration of a journalist coincides with his fall from political favour), *Man of Iron* >**5** (a sequel to *Man of Marble*, in which the documentarist's husband, clearly meant to call to mind Solidarity's Lech Walesa, is subjected to a smear campaign), and the French-made historical drama *Danton* >**6**, whose hero's opposition to Robespierre, when the French Revolution turns into the Reign of Terror, openly mirrored contemporary events in Wajda's homeland. At the same time, Wajda alternated these powerful, uncompromisingly political films with the rather less successful allegory *The Conductor*, two melancholy and nostalgic romances (*The Young Ladies of Wilko*, *A Chronicle of Love Affairs*), and yet another return to the Second World War (*A Love in Germany*), all distinguished by their sensitive depictions of human emotions, but all flawed by a certain predictability.

At his best, Wajda engages with politics and history with a commitment and intelligence that render his films both lucid and moving. But he is an erratic talent, and his lesser work (though worthy and proficient) can be academic and heavy-handed.

Lineage

A contemporary of Jerzy Kawalerowicz and the late Andrzej Munk, Wajda was instrumental in encouraging **Polanski** and **Skolimowski** to become film-makers. His influence may be discerned in the work of younger figures such as Krzysztof Zanussi, Agnieska Holland, and Krzysztof Kieslowski.

Further reading

Bolestaw Michatek's *The Cinema of Andrzej Wajda* (London, 1973).

Viewing

1 **Kanal (They Loved Life)**
Poland 1957/ w Wienczyslaw Glinski, Teresa Izewska, Emil Karewicz

2 **Ashes and Diamonds**
Poland 1958/ w Zbigniew Cybulski, Ewa Krzyzewska, Adam Pawlikowski

3 **Everything for Sale**
Poland 1968/ w Andrzej Lapicki, Beata Tyszkiewicz, Daniel Olbrychski

4 **Man of Marble**
Poland 1976/ w Krystyna Janda, Jerzy Radziwilowicz, Tadeusz Lomnicki

5 **Man of Iron**
Poland 1980/ w Jerzy Radziwilowicz, Krystyna Janda, Marian Opiana

6 **Danton**
France 1982/ w Gérard Depardieu, Wojciech Pszoniak, Patrice Chéreau

Raoul Walsh

Born: 11th March 1887/New York, USA
Died: 31st December 1980/ Hollywood, California, USA
Directing career: 1912-1964

Prolific and craftsmanlike, Raoul Walsh never aspired to profound artistry, contenting himself with the simple virtues of the fast-paced adventure film. Nevertheless, such was his intuitive story-telling ease and feel for dramatic locations that, given a strong script and a solid cast, his work was never less than gripping.

Walsh spent his early years travelling and working in a wide variety of jobs, finally entering movies as an actor at Biograph studios. There he assisted on, and appeared in, a number of films (including *The Birth of a Nation*) for **Griffith**, who despatched him to Mexico to shoot footage of Pancho Villa, later used in Walsh's directing debut *The Life of Villa*. Only in the '20s, however, did he finally make the grade as a top director, first with *The Thief of Bagdad* >**1**, Douglas Fairbanks' epic fantasy, then with the war-film *What Price Glory?*, which mixed raucous comedy and grim drama to enormously popular effect. No less intelligent was his version of Somerset Maugham's *Rain*, after which he was offered the chance to make the first talkie shot on location, *In Old Arizona*, (making which he lost his right eye), and to film the epic Western *The Big Trail* (with John Wayne) in the new 70mm Grandeur format. Neither was a hit, and his work of the '30s was atypically variable.

Finally, upon signing a contract with Warners in 1939, Walsh again hit his stride with a series of taut, tough thrillers. *The Roaring Twenties* >**2** was not only superb Cagney but one of the few gangster films to view the anti-hero from a social and historical perspective; *They Drive By Night* was a dark road-movie charting a clash between long-distance truckers and corrupt bosses; and *High Sierra* >**3**, despite a maudlin sub-plot, was a superior vehicle for Bogart's special blend of cynicism, professionalism and emotional vulnerability, here elegaically embodied as doomed desperado Roy 'Mad Dog' Earle, meeting his death in the eponymous grey cliffs that rank among Walsh's most memorably symbolic locations. At the same time, the director's versatility could be seen in the gentle period nostalgia for smalltown Americana he brought to *Strawberry Blonde*. But action remained his forte: his films with Errol Flynn – as Custer in *They Died with Their Boots On*, as a boxing champion in *Gentleman Jim*, as a Mountie in *Northern Pursuit* and, finest of all, as a platoon commander in *Objective Burma* >**4** – reveal his ability to milk suspense by visual rather than verbal means.

Pursued and *White Heat* >**5** (the first a Freudian, *noir*-tinged Western, the second a stark, brutal thriller about a psychopathic, mother-fixated gangster) confirmed Walsh's ability to cope with more complex material when necessary, but for the most part the '50s saw him working within the strict confines of robust action genres: nautical dramas (*Captain Horatio Hornblower*, *Blackbeard the Pirate*, *Sea Devils*), war films (*Battle Cry*, *The Naked and the Dead*), or Westerns (*Distant Drums* >**6**, *The Lawless Breed*, *The Tall Men*), often featuring relaxed performers like Gary Cooper, Rock Hudson, Clark Gable or Jane Russell. Conversely, *A Lion is in the Streets* was a largely impressive political drama, *The Revolt of Mamie Stover* a wry romantic comedy. In the 1960s, old and in failing health, he found it increasingly difficult to work on projects suited to his own particular talents, and only his last film, *A Distant Trumpet* – a stylish cavalry Western – was truly worthy of his efforts.

Walsh's direction was simple, direct and muscular, wary of self-consciously picturesque or poetic camera angles. Always a popular entertainer he was one of the more able, resilient and versatile Hollywood journeymen. Entirely lacking in pretensions, his confident, classical style, sense of humour, and overall adaptability ensured that much of his work has retained a greater vitality than that of many more prestigious directors.

Lineage

Initially influenced by **Griffith**, Walsh may be compared with figures like **Dwan**, **Hawks**, **Wellman** and Henry Hathaway.

Further reading

Kingsley Canham's *The Hollywood Professionals,* Vol 1 (London, 1973).

Viewing

1 **The Thief of Bagdad**
US 1924/ w Douglas Fairbanks, Julanne Johnson, Anna May Wong

2 **The Roaring Twenties**
US 1939/ w James Cagney, Humphrey Bogart, Gladys George

3 **High Sierra**
US 1941/ w Humphrey Bogart, Ida Lupino, Arthur Kennedy

4 **Objective Burma**
US 1945/ w Errol Flynn, William Prince, James Brown

5 **White Heat**
US 1949/ w James Cagney, Virginia Mayo, Edmond O'Brien

6 **Distant Drums**
US 1951/ w Gary Cooper, Mari Aldon, Richard Webb

Andy Warhol

Born: **6th August 1928/Pittsburgh, Pennsylvania, USA**
Died: **22nd February 1987/New York, USA**
Directing career: **1963-1973**

The importance of Andrew Warhol's cinema lies not in its content (which in terms of action is often minimal indeed) but in the way its (absence of) style provokes questions about the nature of the film medium itself. It is perhaps appropriate therefore that its relationship to mainstream cinema is also primarily conceptual.

Famous for his paintings of Campbell's Soup cans and his multiple silk-screen portraits of Marilyn Monroe, Warhol was already well established as a 'pop' artist when he began making films in 1963. As with his graphic art, the many films he made over the next few years were distinguished by their concern with surface appearances and their total abnegation of an authorial point of view: the camera, often static, was simply a passive recording device, directed at whatever caught Warhol's disinterested eye. Six hours long, *Sleep* showed a naked man in bed from a variety of angles; *Kiss* a number of couples kissing, each shot the length of a three-minute 16mm spool; *Empire* was a static, eight-hour record of the Empire State Building. Even when the adoption of sound enabled him to include dialogue, Warhol preferred raw, frequently tedious ad-libbing to structured narrative: in *Harlot*, transvestite Mario Montez sits eating bananas next to a woman with a cat on her lap, while the largely unintelligible soundtrack, barely relevant to what we are shown, is the off-screen banter of three of Warhol's friends; and in *Vinyl*, which like many of his films merely recorded the posing of various members of Warhol's 'Factory' coterie, when the camera falls over it is simply returned to its upright position; without the interruption of editing, continuity of action is preserved.

Just as Warhol neglected traditional, polished technique, so he ignored conventional plot in favour of meandering confessional monologues and camp role-playing by the 'superstars' (hangers-on, transvestites, junkies, artists, *et al*) who surrounded him. Sex loomed large both visually and verbally, as did a mimicry of old Hollywood stars. The twin-screen *Chelsea Girls* >**1** drily observed the attitudinising of figures like Marie Menken, Mary Woronov and Nico; *Bike Boy* >**2** documented a brief sexual encounter between an LA stud and Warhol regulars Viva, Ingrid Superstar and Brigid Polk; *Blue Movie* (*Fuck*) featured Viva and Louis Waldron improvising sex together; in *Lonesome Cowboys* >**3**, Viva and a host of gay men clad in camp cowboy garb assembled in an Arizona ghost-town to create a spaced-out, sometimes hilarious parody of Western clichés.

Shaken by the gun-wounds inflicted by an attempt on his life in 1967, Warhol became more reclusive, frequently leaving the job of direction to his long-term assistant/cameraman Paul Morrissey, he himself serving as producer. While the personalities and directionless life-styles depicted were carried over from earlier work, an increased emphasis on narrative and motivation, together with more conventional camerawork and editing, resulted in films with a far greater commercial potential. Hunky, inarticulate Joe Dallesandro became a lassitudinous sex-object, hustling for male customers to gain money for his wife's girlfriend's abortion in *Flesh*, trying to regain his drugs-destroyed sexual prowess in *Trash*, and acting out a seedy parody of *Sunset Boulevard* (with Sylvia Miles as the has-been movie queen) in *Heat*. Though sometimes witty, the films finally fail, both in terms of the conceptual rigour they lack, and as popular entertainment; Morrissey is too sloppy a film-maker to rival his mainstream counterparts. More provocatively amusing in its use of transvestites Holly Woodlawn, Candy Darling and Jackie Curtis to depict women whose dreams of stardom and happiness come to ruin was *Women in Revolt* >**4**, directed by Warhol himself. After the Paris-shot *L'Amour*, however, he retired completely from film-making, merely lending his name to Morrissey's gory horror spoofs *Flesh for Frankenstein* (made in 3-D) and *Blood for Dracula* and to Jed Johnson's grotesque TV-soap-opera parody, *Bad*.

While the sheer length and intentionally amateur quality of many of Warhol's early films make them almost unwatchable, they remain central to any discussion of what constitutes realism in film; although the unblinking camera observes people, rather than actors, in semi-documentary fashion, the question of 'reality' is complicated by the prevalence of role-playing. Morrissey, on the other hand, is of far less artistic or philosophical importance.

Lineage

While it is fruitful to compare Warhol with American underground film-makers like Kenneth Anger, Stan Brakhage, Michael Snow, and Shirley Clarke (among others), not to mention Europeans such as **Godard** and Jean-Marie Straub, his later work with Morrissey may be compared with that of semi-underground directors like George Kuchar, John Waters, Paul Bartel, and even Russ Meyer.

Further reading

Stephen Koch's *Stargazer: Andy Warhol and His Films* (New York, 1973).

Viewing

1 **Chelsea Girls**
US 1966/ w Mary Woronov, Ingrid Superstar, Gerard Malanga

2 **Bike Boy**
US 1967/ w Joe Spencer, Viva, Brigid Polk, Ingrid Superstar

3 **Lonesome Cowboys**
US 1968/ w Taylor Mead, Louis Waldron, Viva, Joe Dallessandro

4 **Women in Revolt (Sex)**
US 1972/ w Holly Woodlawn, Candy Darling, Jackie Curtis

Peter Weir

Born: 21st August 1944/Sydney, Australia
Directing career: 1967-

The best-known director to emerge from the New Australian Cinema of the '70s, Peter Weir has repeatedly proved himself an efficient, ambitious talent. But his pretensions would appear greater than his achievements: attempting to explore the irrational mysteries that underlie civilisation, and the gulf between primitive and modern cultures, he rarely rises above woolly generalisations.

Having already worked in television, Weir directed several vaguely experimental shorts before making his feature debut (and still arguably his best film), *The Cars That Ate Paris* >**1**, in 1974. A modest but highly imaginative comedy-thriller in which a car-crash victim, recuperating in a remote village, discovers that he is the prisoner of a community so dependent for their economy on scrap metal cannibalised from the vehicles they lure off a nearby highway that they will kill to preserve their secret, the film possesses a quirky black humour sadly lacking in Weir's later work. Rather more commercially successful, however, was *Picnic at Hanging Rock* >**2**, impressive enough for its languidly atmospheric portrait of a Victorian girls' boarding school, but wrecked by a lyrically voyeuristic attitude towards its romance-obsessed heroines, and by obfuscating, portentously symbolic hints at supernatural mystery, when a handful of girls go inexplicably missing during a picnic. Similarly concerned with the potentially malevolent powers of a pantheistic nature and the fragility of Western civilisation was *The Last Wave*. Here, a liberal white lawyer's investigations into an aboriginal tribal murder lead to muddled ethnography and murky speculations about the apocalypse, at last risibly suggested by a shot of an all too ordinary wave seen through a fish-eye lens.

Less ambitious but altogether more coherent, *Gallipoli* >**3** concerned two young Australians (one patriotically devoted to the British Empire, the other blindly isolationist) who join the army in 1916, only to die as cannon fodder in the disastrous Dardanelles campaign of the First World War; if its anti-British stance was a little obvious, Weir's handling of the chaotic war-scenes, and his evocation of the sheer geographical enormity of the Australian outback made for gripping, powerful visuals. When dealing, on the other hand, with the downfall of Sukarno's regime in 1965 Indonesia, as experienced by an Australian journalist and his American lover in *The Year of Living Dangerously*, Weir seemed unable to disentangle his complex web of political and moral issues: the movie was a conventional romance viewed against an ill-defined backdrop of threatening social upheaval. Likewise, *Witness* >**4** made much of its culture-clash theme (a city cop protecting a boy witness to a murder is forced to take cover in, and thus bring violence to, an Amish community whose old-fashioned, fundamentalist beliefs are defiantly pacifist), but despite its limpid visual lyricism, it offered implausible plot clichés, saccharine sentiment and a view of the Amish as simplistically idealised as it was well-meaning.

Weir's seemingly '60s-inspired passion for alternative, less technologically developed societies again manifested itself in a faithful, but maudlin and ambivalent, adaptation of Paul Theroux's *The Mosquito Coast*, in which an eccentric smalltime American inventor takes his family and his ice-making contraption to a Central American jungle, only to fall foul of Western mercenaries and missionaries and his own arrogant tendency towards megalomaniac tyranny. Again Weir's taste for exotica gave rise to occasionally vivid imagery, but the lack of a coherent moral perspective on the protagonist's doomily misanthropic, back-to-nature pronouncements weakened both the rambling narrative, and the political and ecological subtext.

Weir seems too wary of approaching his films intellectually to cope properly with the complex themes which attract him. If he is never less than a slick, proficient entertainer, the lack of depth in his work suggests that he may never be a great director.

Lineage

While it is useful to compare Weir with his compatriots such as Gillian Armstrong, Fred Schepisi, **Paul Cox** and Richard Lowenstein, one may perhaps also consider him in relation to American contemporaries, most notably **Spielberg** who, like Weir, once seemed interested in the effects of the irrational on modern civilisation.

Further reading

Brian MacFarlane's *Australian Cinema 1970-1985* (London, 1987).

Viewing

1 **The Cars That Ate Paris**
Australia 1974/ w Terry Camilleri, John Meillon, Melissa Jaffa

2 **Picnic at Hanging Rock**
Australia 1975/ w Anne Lambert, Rachel Roberts, Helen Morse

3 **Gallipoli**
Australia 1981/ w Mark Lee, Mel Gibson, Bill Kerr

4 **Witness**
US 1985/ w Harrison Ford, Kelly McGillis, Josef Sommer

Orson Welles

Born: 6th May 1916/Kenosha, Wisconsin, USA
Died: 10th October 1985/Hollywood, California, USA
Directing career: 1934-1985

It is almost tragically ironic that George Orson Welles, without a doubt one of the greatest film-makers ever, was forced to work for most of his career under the most adverse of conditions. Such were his genius and ambition that his films, years ahead of their time, still astonish by their inventiveness, stylistic virtuosity and freshness; while the widely held view that he never fulfilled his early promise fails to take account of the thematic and moral consistency of his work, not to say its restless experimentalism.

A former child prodigy adept at acting, painting and magic, Welles first came to prominence on the stage, having revealed an ability to play characters old beyond his years whilst a teenage actor at Dublin's Gate Theatre. He proved himself an innovative theatre director with various ambitious productions in New York (an all-black voodoo *Macbeth*, a modern-dress *Julius Caesar*, the now near-legendary staging of Marc Blitzstein's leftist *The Cradle Will Rock*). By 1938 his Mercury Theatre Group (formed in collaboration with John Houseman, later to become a distinguished film producer) had embarked on a series of experimental radio versions of various classics, whose fame was assured by the wide-spread panic induced by Welles' news bulletin-style adaptation of H.G. Wells' *The War of the Worlds*. By 1940 in fact, Welles had already dabbled in film, with a whimsically surreal home-movie (*Hearts of Age*) and the now lost farce, *Too Much Johnson*, made to accompany a play that never reached Broadway. But it was only when RKO, fired by the excitement aroused by *The War of the Worlds*, offered him a small budget and an unprecedented degree of artistic freedom that Welles was able to make his film-directing debut proper.

Having prepared and abandoned several projects (including a version of Conrad's *Heart of Darkness*), Welles finally completed *Citizen Kane* >**1** in 1941. A biopic of a newspaper tycoon (played by Welles himself and loosely based on William Randolph Hearst) told in flashbacks recounted by a handful of his acquaintances, the film made revolutionary use of a dazzling, eclectic array of visual, aural and narrative effects. It was photographed in deep-focus with low-key, *chiaroscuro* lighting; dense with quick, overlapping dialogue and virtuoso editing; structured as a labyrinthine, metaphysical mystery, whose secret was the final, essential unknowableness of human personality. Welles' witty, moving study of compromise, solitude and betrayal was both profoundly personal (much of Kane's early life paralleled the director's own youth) and universal in its political and philosophical relevance. But Hearst's press empire, incensed perhaps by the similarity of Kane's relationship with his talent-free opera-singing mistress to that of Hearst with actress Marion Davies, waged a bitter critical battle against the film; not only did its box-office suffer, but – more importantly – Welles would never again be allowed total artistic freedom in Hollywood.

Indeed, his next film, *The Magnificent Ambersons* >**2**, was cut and partly reshot by RKO while Welles was in Brazil shooting the documentary *It's All True* (which he was never allowed to finish). Nevertheless, *Ambersons* remains a mutilated masterpiece, a gently ironic, elegaic account of a wealthy American family's decline in the early days of mass industrialisation. Unlike *Kane*, the film is warmly romantic, its long takes and mobile camerawork (particularly at a superbly choreographed ball) evoking the elegance of a simpler more innocent age; while a happy ending shot in Welles' absence seems contrived, the film resonates with an aching sense of loss. Next, and similarly subject to studio

An empire built on paper: Charles Foster Kane (Orson Welles) and friend Jedediah Leland (Joseph Cotten) in *Citizen Kane*, Welles' stunning, complex feature debut about a Hearst-like press tycoon.

interference, *Journey Into Fear*, which Welles directed 'through' Norman Foster, was a stylish spy thriller which served to reveal both his versatility and (in his sinister Turkish police chief Colonel Haki) his love of playing ambiguous, larger-than-life characters.

By now bereft of his RKO contract, and unjustly regarded by the studios as a difficult and even profligate talent, Welles was moved to prove he could make more conventionally commercial films: *The Stranger* is an intelligent but comparatively straightforward political thriller about a Nazi hiding out in postwar, smalltown America. *The Lady from Shanghai* >**3**, however, is an outrageously baroque *film noir*, its plot (a naive Irish sailor gets caught up with a murderous *femme fatale* and her crippled, corrupt barrister husband) virtually incomprehensible, while its Expressionist images – all tilted angles, grotesque close-ups and bizarre reflections – create a treacherous, chaotic and confusing world. At once parody and a poetic, melancholy meditation on innocence all at sea in a society of human sharks, the film may also be seen as a wry commentary on Welles's own marriage to Rita Hayworth (whose famous hair he had shorn and dyed blonde for her role). Certainly, Columbia's Harry Cohn, irate at the way his glamorous star had been made to play a cold, heartless manipulator, delayed the film's release; and after a highly imaginative but all too obviously low-budget, elemental version of *Macbeth*, shot on *papier maché* sets at lowly Republic, Welles left America for a lengthy European exile, where his own projects were partly financed by his regular performances in other directors' films.

Shot piecemeal in several countries over four years, *Othello* >**4** was a miraculous triumph of mind over matter: obstacles were turned to imaginative advantage (perhaps most memorably a superb murder scene shot in a Turkish bath when actors' costumes failed to materialise), while the hallucinatory visual style was a vivid reflection of both the Moor's inner torment and Iago's malevolent jealousy, here rooted in sexual impotence. No less ambitious was *Mr Arkadin* (*Confidential Report*), a weird, frequently wonderful, semi-comic return to the dark mysteries of *Kane*, with a tycoon, claiming amnesia, hiring an opportunist adventurer to delve into his shady past in order that he might destroy all those who might bear witness to the sins of his youth. Best of all, however, was *Touch of Evil* >**5**, a deliriously nightmarish *noir* thriller made in America. (Its star, Charlton Heston, insisted that Welles direct). A complex, ironic examination of the relationship between the law and justice (Welles' bloated, bigoted cop Quinlan may be corrupt, but the Mexican he frames for murder is, it transpires, guilty), the film, set in a hellish bordertown, features narcotics, gang-rape, racism, prostitution and almost universal corruption. But, from the first remarkable travelling crane shot which follows a car until it finally explodes, to the finale set among monstrous oil-derricks, Welles transforms his sordid subject matter into a brilliantly stylised blend of melodrama and tragedy in which the flawed, doomed hero, finally, is not Quinlan but truth itself.

Poorly distributed, the film was a flop, and Welles returned to Europe. A version of Kafka's *The Trial* >**6** was distinctive in its inventive, Expressionist use of bizarre locations to evoke guilt-ridden hero K's sense of fear and alienation; *Chimes at Midnight* (*Falstaff*) >**7**, on the other hand, was a moving, nostalgic 'lament for Merrie England' with Welles plundering five Shakespeare plays to paint a loving portrait of Falstaff as an innocent dreamer who finally falls prey to Prince Hal's assumption of monarchic power. Despite its elegaic tone, the film avoids sentimentality; indeed, its epic battle scene is one of the most immediately physical and brutal ever filmed. Altogether more intimate, but imbued with an equally mature lyricism, was *The Immortal Story* >**8**, a miniaturist gem made for French television and taken from an Isak Dinesen (Karen Blixen) story about an ageing, Kane-like merchant in Macao who attempts to turn legend (in which an old man hires a sailor to impregnate a woman) into fact. An elegant, muted variation on Welles' abiding themes – the elusive nature of truth, the corruption that attends power – its visual subtlety mirrored the plot's deceptive simplicity.

Thereafter Welles returned to America to work on a number of films which he either never completed or never released: thus *The Deep* and *The Other Side of the Wind* took their place alongside an unfinished modern-day version of *Don Quixote*, started in 1958 and still tinkered with at regular intervals. Between his appearances in television commercials and chat-shows, however, he did release *F for Fake* >**9**, an effortlessly witty, highly original combination of re-edited found-footage (a documentary by François Reichenbach on art-forger Elmyr de Hory and bogus biographer Clifford Irving) and personal reminiscence on the relationship of charlatanism and authorship in art. At once discursive essay and mischievous joke, the film (Welles' last, apart from *Filming Othello*, a raconteur's account of that beleaguered production) was a singularly apposite swansong from a director of genius who had always taken film, but rarely himself, seriously.

To the end of his days Welles remained active, scripting and shooting fragments of films that would never – thanks largely to an unappreciative industry – be completed; just before he died, there were still hopes that he might make *King Lear* or a film about his '30s production of *The Cradle Will Rock*. He remains important not only for the authority, imagination and sheer bravado of his own work, but for the way he often inspired other directors with his performances (Robert Stevenson's *Jane Eyre*, **Reed**'s *The Third Man*, and Harry Kumel's *Malpertuis* are the most notable examples). But Welles' greatest achievement lies in the way he expanded the horizons of film, so that – whatever his source, Shakespeare or a low-brow thriller – philosophical, political and personal themes combined to create intelligent entertainment that was entirely cinematic.

Lineage

Himself an admirer of **Ford**, **Renoir** and the German Expressionists, Welles has been hugely influential on cinema (Houseman, **Robert Wise**, Mark Robson and Richard Wilson, not to mention the composer Bernard Herrmann, all worked on *Citizen Kane*). In later years, he was perhaps most closely connected with Henry Jaglom. Comparison, however, is impossible; he was, finally, unique and inimitable.

Further reading

James Naremore's *The Magic World of Orson Welles* (New York, 1978), Robert Carringer's *The Making of Citizen Kane* (London, 1985), Joseph McBride's *Orson Welles* (London, 1972); Barbara Leaming's *Orson Welles: A Biography* (New York 1986).

Viewing

1 **Citizen Kane**
US 1941/ w Welles, Joseph Cotten, Everett Sloane, Ray Collins

2 **The Magnificent Ambersons**
US 1942/ w Tim Holt, Joseph Cotten, Dolores Costello, Agnes Moorehead

3 **The Lady from Shanghai**
US 1946/ w Welles, Rita Hayworth, Everett Sloane, Glenn Anders

4 **Othello**
Italy 1952/ w Welles, Michael MacLiammoir, Suzanne Cloutier

5 **Touch of Evil**
US 1958/ w Welles, Charlton Heston, Janet Leigh, Akim Tamiroff

6 **The Trial**
France 1962/ w Anthony Perkins, Welles, Jeanne Moreau

7 **Chimes at Midnight (Falstaff)**
Spain 1966/ w Welles, Keith Baxter, John Gielgud, Jeanne Moreau

8 **The Immortal Story**
France 1968/ w Welles, Jeanne Moreau, Norman Eshley, Roger Coggio

9 **F For Fake (Fake!)**
France 1975/ w Welles, Oja Kodar, Clifford Irving, Elmyr de Hory

William Wellman

Born: 29th February 1896/Brookline, Massachusetts, USA
Died: 9th December 1975/Los Angeles, USA
Directing career: 1923-1958

During his prolific and uneven career, William Augustus Wellman – widely known as 'Wild Bill', due to his boisterous, hot-tempered behaviour – gained a reputation as a specialist in virile, action-packed adventure movies. But in retrospect, perhaps his best work was in the realms of screwball comedy and romantic melodrama.

Having distinguished himself in World War I as a pilot in the Lafayette Flying Corps, Wellman made a brief stab at a career in acting before deciding he preferred life behind the camera. Working his way up from messenger to assistant director, he began his directing career in 1923, for the most part making low-budget Westerns. Finally, in 1927, he was able to put his past experience to good use when the spectacular and authentic aerial footage he shot for the World War I epic *Wings* >**1** won the first ever Best Picture Oscar. Rather more dramatically intriguing, however, was *Beggars of Life* >**2**, a gripping if ultimately maudlin adventure about the dispossessed tramps of the mid-West, in which Wallace Beery's ingratiatingly hyperbolic hobo was overshadowed by Louise Brooks, in drag as a fugitive from the law. Indeed, for all his oft-noted interest in action, crime and violence, Wellman often gave way to excruciating sentimentality: despite James Cagney's fiery acting in *Public Enemy* >**3** (most memorable for his thrusting a grapefruit into his nagging moll's face over the breakfast table), the film is wrecked by the portrait of the hoodlum's good-living family, a simpering white-haired mother and a priggish war-hero brother.

Throughout the '30s Wellman was generally very busy, ranging from brisk tabloid-style crime dramas for Warners (*Night Nurse* is a better example, thanks to the presence of Barbara Stanwyck) to strenuous outdoors adventures (*Call of the Wild*, *Beau Geste*) and, finest of all, *A Star Is Born* >**4**, a gorgeous tragicomic melodrama outlining the destructive effects of a fickle Hollywood on a has-been, alcoholic matinee idol and his rising-star wife. Comedy was perhaps, in fact, the director's forte: certainly *Nothing Sacred* >**5** (about a young woman feigning terminal illness in order to win fame and fortune) and *Roxie Hart* (with a showgirl confessing to a murder she didn't commit in order to aid her career) are fast, furious and frequently very funny satires on American ambition. In contrast, the attack on lynch-mob ethics in *The Ox-Bow Incident*, a stolidly liberal Western, now seems contrived and simplistic, its artifice emphasised by all too obvious backdrops. Indeed, inconsistency is perhaps the hallmark of Wellman's career: if *The Story of GI Joe* was an engaging, seemingly sincere tribute to the courage of the ordinary American soldier, the political satire of *Magic Town* was compromised by Capraesque whimsy; while *Across the Wide Missouri* was a predictable pioneering epic enhanced by sumptuous location photography of Western landscapes; and in *Track of the Cat*, Wellman's experiments with bleached-out colour drained a potentially taut, intriguing thriller (about a backwoods farming family menaced by a cougar) of tension. Indeed, the '50s saw Wellman in decline, and after suffering production interference on *Lafayette Escadrille*, a final World War I flying drama, he retired from directing.

More variable than versatile, Wellman was a journeyman film-maker whose work's absence of thematic complexity mirrors his own apparent lack of moral commitment. At the same time, armed with a good cast and a superior script, he occasionally proved himself a minor but vigorously proficient entertainer.

Lineage

Wellman compares poorly with the superficially similar **Hawks** or even **Walsh**; slightly more fruitful comparison would be with **Wyler** or **Huston**. His lack of a clearly defined artistic personality would suggest that he has influenced few younger directors.

Further reading

A Short Time for Insanity (New York, 1974) is an autobiography.

Viewing

1 **Wings**
US 1927/Clara Bow, Charles 'Buddy' Rogers, Richard Arlen

2 **Beggars of Life**
US 1928/ w Wallace Beery, Louise Brooks, Richard Arlen
3 **The Public Enemy**
US 1931/ w James Cagney, Jean Harlow, Edward Woods
4 **A Star Is Born**
US 1937/ w Janet Gaynor, Fredric March, Adolphe Menjou
5 **Nothing Sacred**
US 1937/ w Carole Lombard, Fredric March, Walter Connolly

Wim Wenders

Born: **14th August 1945/Düsseldorf, Germany**
Directing career: 1967-

Preoccupied with his ambivalent feelings about Germany and America, Wilhelm Wenders has managed to turn a personal obsession into an intriguing and rewarding artistic career of strong cinematic and cultural relevance. Indeed, with **Fassbinder** dead, he now seems by far the most important of the film-makers who constituted, during the '70s, the flowering of talent known as the New German Cinema.

At film school in Munich, Wenders made several experimental, non-narrative shorts, notable mainly for the use of long takes and rock 'n' roll soundtracks and culminating in a diploma feature (*Summer in the City: Dedicated to the Kinks*) whose slim plot concerned an ex-convict trying to piece together his life through a series of journeys and desultory meetings. His first professional feature, an adaptation of Peter Handke's book *The Goalkeeper's Fear of the Penalty*, was in many ways a variation upon this abiding theme: as the footballer, having suddenly left a match without explanation, embarks upon a meandering odyssey that mirrors his own search for identity, Wenders allows meditative images of landscape, movement and silent, isolated individuals (rather than dialogue and plot) to suggest the psychological malaise infecting both his hero and modern Europe.

Similarly, after an anonymous version of Nathaniel Hawthorne's *The Scarlet Letter*, *Alice in the Cities* >**1** depicted the wanderings of a rootless, alienated photographer and a small, inquisitive girl in search of the latter's grandmother: the film, Wenders' warmest and wittiest, was both a portrait of Germany as a country whose desire to deny its recent history had entailed a whole-hearted acceptance of American culture (movies, cars, pin-ball machines and music), and a study in solitude broken down by the responsibilities of companionship. Of equal importance to the film's meaning, however, was its melancholy mood, established with great assurance by long, static shots of figures in a landscape.

Where *Wrong Movement*, based by Handke on Goethe's *Wilhelm Meister*, was rather too schematic and symbolic a road-movie, *Kings of the Road* >**2** featured a masterly consummation of Wenders' obsessions in a near plotless, intimate epic about two men (a recently divorced paediatrician and an itinerant cinema-projector repair man) whose travels along the East-West German border throw a gentle light on various themes: the undignified decline of commercial cinema; the baleful influence of America on Europe; the problems of living in the company of another man, away from women; the need for a sense of home. Detached yet compassionate, it was a subtle, honest film about the male psyche. No less remarkable, however, was a version of Patricia Highsmith's Ripley thrillers, *The American Friend* >**3**, a taut genre-piece in which an innocent German picture framer is lured into murderous crime by an expatriate American art-dealer. Though reworking familiar themes, the movie's visual and narrative style is *noir*: jagged editing, Expressionist colours and scenes featuring **Nicholas Ray** and **Sam Fuller** make it a respectful, but often barbed and ambivalent, homage to classic Hollywood.

Wenders' cinephilia led next to *Lightning Over Water* (*Nick's Movie*), a well-meaning but finally voyeuristic documentary, made in partnership with Ray, about the American director's struggles

Busy going nowhere: Hanns Zischler in Wim Wenders' assured study in cultural and psychological *ennui*, *Kings of the Road (Im Lauf der Zeit)*.

against cancer. Also shot in America, and beleaguered by countless production problems, *Hammett* – a glossy, self-consciously *noir*ish thriller hypothesising on the events that might have inspired the writing of Dashiel Hammett's *The Maltese Falcon* – suffered from a basic incoherence and Wenders' seeming awkwardness with Hollywood actors. Nor was *The State of Things*, made during a hiatus during *Hammett*'s production, and about a European film crew abandoned by their American financiers, free of flaws: not only did it climax in a scene of ludicrous contrivance (the director using a camera as a gun in an all too literal pun on the idea of 'shooting'), but it failed to overcome the problem of how to depict bored inertia in an interesting way. *Paris, Texas* >**4**, however, was something of a return to form. About a man who stumbles out of the wilderness after four years and tries to find a way to return his son to his now missing wife, it benefitted from Robbie Müller's superb photography of the desert and Los Angeles, and from Harry Dean Stanton's largely wordless but visually eloquent performance. It also gained a real mythical dimension through an astute use of Western conventions; sadly however, its ending (the hero drives into the sunset having left mother and son reunited) was both sexually reactionary and predicated on an endless, too verbally explicit confession scene.

After *Tokyo-Ga*, an intriguingly subjective documentary about Japan and **Ozu**, Wenders himself returned from exile to make *Wings of Desire* (*Skies Over Berlin*) >**5**, in which two invisible angels listen in to the anxious thoughts of Berliners, until one of the pair, falling in love with a trapeze artist, decides to trade in his immortality for the riches of an ephemeral, tactile, human life. In many ways, the film was a radical departure from realism, its almost documentary images of Berlin (shot with lavish, dreamlike lyricism by Henri Alekan) tethered to a thesis (rather than plot) based in metaphysical fantasy; equally, for once Wenders observed stasis rather than movement, while it was his camera that was in near perpetual motion. His themes, however, were much as before: loneliness, the shadow of history, the desire for human contact. The combination of such ideas with a more sumptuously, obliquely poetic style resulted in surprisingly uplifting, original cinema.

Wings of Desire would seem to suggest that Wenders may have finally come to terms with his emotional confusion about Germany and women. Whatever, he is a major European film-maker, deserving of praise both for his ability to reveal inner states of mind by means of images of landscape and movement, and for his ambitious, steadfast refusal to repeat himself and rest easy on his laurels.

Lineage

While Wenders' admiration for **Ray**, **Fuller**, **Ford**, **Hawks** and **Ozu** is much documented, one may also compare him with **Antonioni**, **Godard** or even Monte Hellman. One may perhaps discern his own influence in the films (some of which he produced) of **Jarmusch**, Chris Petit and Handke's *The Left Handed Woman*.

Further reading

John Sandford's *The New German Cinema* (London, 1980).

Viewing

1 **Alice in the Cities**
W. Germany 1973/ w Rüdiger Vogler, Yella Rottländer, Liza Kruezer
2 **Kings of the Road (Im Lauf der Zeit)**
W. Germany 1976/ w Rüdiger Vogler, Hanns Zischler, Liza Kreuzer
3 **The American Friend**
W. Germany 1977/ w Bruno Ganz, Dennis Hopper, Liza Kreuzer
4 **Paris, Texas**
USA 1984/ w Harry Dean Stanton, Nastassia Kinski, Dean Stockwell
5 **Wings of Desire (Der Himmel über Berlin)**
W. Germany 1987/ w Bruno Ganz, Solveig Dommartin, Otto Sander, Peter Falk

James Whale

Born: 22nd July 1889/Dudley, England
Died: 30th May 1957/Hollywood, California, USA
Directing career: 1930-1949

Most famous for the four horror films he made at Universal in the early '30s, James Whale is best regarded as an eccentric, erratic but highly original talent. Due to the current rarity of his non-horror work, however, his versatility is now often overlooked.

Whale initially made his name in the theatre, first as an actor and set-designer, then as a director. His London production of R.C. Sheriff's anti-war play *Journey's End* brought about an invitation to Hollywood where, after directing dialogue sequences for Howard Hughes' *Hells Angels*, he translated his greatest stage success on to film: set almost exclusively in the trenches of World War I, its lament for wasted youth was stilted and slow. After a further theatrical adaptation (the weepie, *Waterloo Bridge*), he found his feet with a version of Mary Shelley's *Frankenstein* >**1**, a remarkably successful horror movie that both established him as a major Universal director (he stayed with the studio until 1937) and revealed a distinctly cinematic talent. The film's lighting and sets were clearly inspired by Expressionism, although Whale's tone was lighter than that of his German counterparts, while the sympathy extended towards the monster (a childlike, unwittingly murderous victim, both of a scientist's ambitions and of a cruel lynch mob) was crucial to the film's emotional power. Whale, however, was an essentially ironic artist, and his subsequent work was memorable for its subtle, sophisticated, and often macabre wit. In *The Old Dark House* >**2**, the perilous predicament of a group of bright young things stranded in a Gothic mansion owned by a bizarre family of religious fanatics, gin-soaks and pyromaniacs is not only steeped in Gothic suspense, but allows Whale to parody horror conventions even as he invents them; *The Invisible Man* delights in malicious slapstick, absurd English stereotypes and superb special effects; while *The Bride of Frankenstein* >**3** is an hilarious sequel, with the monster (cunningly revived by means of a prologue featuring Mary Shelley herself, who is later revived as the monster's mate) meeting assorted unlikely characters, including a blind hermit and an impossibly unflappable mad scientist who miniaturises humans. Central to the success of each film was Whale's ability to elicit immaculately detailed performances from English actors: Karloff, **Laughton**, Elsa Lanchester and, most notably, Ernest Thesiger.

At the same time, however, the director's black humour and elegant, fluid visual style also embellished his work in other genres. *By Candlelight* was a frothy romantic farce about a valet pretending to be his aristocratic

Colin Clive and Elsa Lanchester as the good doctor and his latest creation in Whale's superbly witty *Bride of Frankenstein.*

boss in order to woo a princess; *One More River* an impeccably performed tale of divorce among the English upper-classes; *Remember Last Night?* a subtly satirical thriller in which a group of perennially drunken sophisticates attempt to solve a murder committed in their midsts. Finest of all, however, was the musical *Show Boat* >**4**; moving, majestic, witty and tender, it was exceptional both for its lyrical recreation of life on the Mississippi and for its magnificent singing (unforgettably, Helen Morgan's 'Bill' and Paul Robeson's astounding 'Ol' Man River').

Thereafter Whale's career began its steady decline. When *The Road Back* (a sequel to *All Quiet on the Western Front*) was cut by Universal, he left the studio; his subsequent films, charming and stylish but relatively minor, included a fond return to the world of theatre (*The Great Garrick*), a remake of Pagnol's *Fanny* (*Port of Seven Seas*), a swashbuckler (*The Man in the Iron Mask*), a jungle epic (*Green Hell*) and a war movie (*They Dare Not Love*). Versatility had turned to variability, and in 1941, Whale gave up film-making to concentrate on painting. In 1949, he attempted a comeback with a version of William Saroyan's *Hello Out There*, an episode for a compilation film that was never released, following which he occasionally worked again in theatre. Finally, in 1957, he was found dead in 'mysterious circumstances' in his swimming pool; a note suggested that illness may have prompted suicide.

If Whale's decline is hard to fathom (certain writers suggest that his homosexuality may have been a factor), his films of the early '30s were among the most consistently witty, inventive and stylish of the period. Very few directors managed to combine wit, self-parody, suspense and technical excellence so attractively.

Lineage

Whale's horror films are far less grotesque than **Browning**'s; though one may compare his versatility and wit with **Mamoulian**'s, Whale was ultimately, perhaps, quite unique in his eccentricity.

Viewing

1 **Frankenstein**
US 1931/ w Boris Karloff, Colin Clive, Mae Clarke
2 **The Old Dark House**
US 1932/ w Charles Laughton, Melvyn Douglas, Raymond Massey
3 **The Bride of Frankenstein**
US 1935/ w Boris Karloff, Colin Clive, Ernest Thesiger
4 **Show Boat**
USA 1936/ w Irene Dunne, Allan Jones, Charles Winninger, Paul Robeson

Billy Wilder

Born: 22nd June 1906/Sucha, Austria
Directing career: 1933-1981

While commercially and often critically successful, the films of Samuel Wilder have occasionally been charged with bad taste and vulgarity. More pertinent, however, to a proper appraisal of his career is that his work was perhaps over-dependent on dialogue for effect, and that his much-acclaimed cynicism is often undercut by a rather contrived, saccharine sentimentality.

Having worked as a journalist in Vienna and Berlin, Wilder came to cinema as a scriptwriter for Ufa, his first credit of any note being on **Siodmak**'s *People on Sunday*. In 1933 the rise of Hitler forced him to leave Germany for Paris, where he co-directed his first feature, *Mauvaise Grain*. He then emigrated to Hollywood where for a couple of years his scriptwriting work was stunted by his minimal knowledge of English. Only in 1937, when he signed up with Paramount and embarked upon a 13-year collaboration with the writer Charles Brackett, did his career really take off, the pair revealing a special talent for romantic comedy in movies like *Bluebeard's Eighth Wife* and *Ninotchka* (for **Lubitsch**), *Midnight*, *Arise My Love* and *Hold Back the Dawn* (for **Leisen**) and *Ball of Fire* (for **Hawks**). Finally, in 1942, Wilder made his American directing debut with *The Major and the Minor*, a farce whose vaguely risqué plot, about an army officer bemused by his own interest in a 12-year-old who, unbeknown to him, is a mature woman, perhaps ensured its success.

Wilder's early films were mostly notable for their acerbic, witty, hard-boiled dialogue and disenchanted view of sordid human frailty and vice: after a semi-comic war-thriller (*Five Graves to Cairo*), *Double Indemnity* >**1** rooted a murder in greed, deceit and adulterous lust; while in *The Lost Weekend* an alcoholic writer is so tormented by the need for drink that he even lies to his loved ones. In both films, Wilder's dependence on the bleak conventions of *film noir* tended to mask his fundamental lack of interest in film's capacity for revealing meaning through visuals, whereas in subsequent works like *The Emperor Waltz* and *A Foreign Affair*, his essentially academic, dialogue-oriented style was more evident.

Sunset Boulevard >**2**, an acidic satire on Hollywood, probing the mutually exploitative relationship between a has-been silent-movie queen who dreams of making a comeback and a penniless young writer who becomes her gigolo, might have been a more penetrating account of delusion and failure had Wilder allowed his characters a little more dignity. Indeed, so often were his creations merely mouthpieces for his barbed, venomous writing (rather than living, breathing, rounded human beings), that his cynicism seems largely hollow. His first film after the collapse of his partnership with Brackett, *Ace in the Hole* (*The Big Carnival*) >**3**, is an exception, all-embracing is its corrosive view of humanity; not only the ambitious tabloid reporter who deliberately delays a trapped pot-holer's rescue in order to further his career, but the public at large who descend like vultures to gape at tragedy in the making, are the victims of Wilder's unrelenting contempt. But later films – *Stalag 17* (with its dog-eat-dog account of life in a POW camp), *Sabrina* (a perverse romantic triangle), *The Seven Year Itch* (a male fantasy steeped in middle-aged misogynistic lechery), and *Love in the Afternoon* (an age-gap romance, and Wilder's first film with long-term co-writer I.A.L. Diamond) – combined a supposedly scabrous vision of social intercourse with a half-hearted romanticism that resulted in unconvincingly safe, sometimes maudlin, happy endings.

While *Some Like It Hot* >**4** was certainly funnier than most of Wilder's '50s films, its amiably frantic parody of gangster movies (after witnessing the St Valentine's Day Massacre, two musicians take to drag and hide out in an all-girl jazz band) suffered from offensive female stereotyping: as in *The Seven Year Itch*, Marilyn Monroe is merely a naive, brainless object of leering male desire, while Jack Lemmon's impersonation, in particular, is a grotesque vision of femininity. Altogether finer, despite another cop-out ending, *The Apartment* >**5** actually acknowledged the existence of emotional pain as an ambitious clerk (who, hoping for promotion, allows his home to be used by his superiors as an illicit love-nest) falls in love with his boss' mistress; the dark satire on office politics was considerably deepened by this rare interest in human feeling. Thereafter however, the '60s saw Wilder return to simple mockery: enlivened only by James Cagney's astonishing machine-gun staccato delivery of one-liners, *One, Two, Three* dealt in Cold War cliché; supposedly audacious in their nudging focus on sex, *Irma La Douce* and *Kiss Me, Stupid* were simultaneously crass, coy and cosy; and *The Fortune Cookie* (*Meet Whiplash Willie*) was a simplistic satire on shyster lawyers, rarely rising above a banal contrast between Walter Matthau's scheming opportunist and Lemmon's beleaguered innocent.

Wilder began the '70s promisingly with two of his very best films, both of which gave full rein to the romanticism which had often undermined his more pessimistic and cynical satires. In *The Private Life of Sherlock Holmes* >**6**, his tone was both respectful and affectionately parodic of Conan Doyle's original books, while a complex, imaginative, elegaic plot served not only to confront the detective's notorious misogyny head-on but to suggest reasons for his having become a cold, detached thinking-machine. *Avanti!* >**7** was no less lyrical, despite a potentially disastrous story in which a middle-aged couple come together over the bodies of their respective parents, themselves secret lovers who await burial in Italy; again the farcical nature of the situation is overshadowed by Wilder's evident commitment to his characters' subtly depicted emotional lives. His last three films, however, marked a distinct decline: *The Front Page* was a woefully brash, unnecessary remake of the classic Hecht-MacArthur comedy; *Fedora* a stilted return to the themes of *Sunset Boulevard*; and *Buddy Buddy* (about a would-be suicide forever intruding on an assassin) a redundant, unamusing remake of Edouard Molinaro's engaging black farce *L'Emmerdeur*.

Since then, Wilder appears to have retired from film-making. The priority he has given to writing over direction has resulted for the most part in films as frustrating (in their hints of what might have been) as they are flawed. Without doubt, he is a major writer; but only when he gave full rein *either* to his cynicism *or* to his romanticism, did his characters truly seem to come alive.

Lineage

Wilder may be compared with **Lubitsch** and with other predominantly comic writers-turned-directors like **Preston Sturges**, **Mankiewicz**, **Mazursky**, **Levinson** and **James L. Brooks**.

Further reading

Axel Madsen's *Billy Wilder* (London, 1969), Leland Poague's *The Hollywood Professionals,* Vol 7 (London, 1980). Maurice Zolotow's *Billy Wilder in Hollywood* (New York, 1977) is biographical.

Viewing

1 **Double Indemnity**
US 1944/ w Barbara Stanwyck, Fred MacMurray, Edward G. Robinson

2 **Sunset Boulevard**
US 1950/ w Gloria Swanson, William Holden, Erich Von Stroheim

3 **Ace in the Hole (The Big Carnival)**
US 1951/ w Kirk Douglas, Jan Sterling, Bob Arthur

4 **Some Like It Hot**
US 1959/ w Jack Lemmon, Tony Curtis,

Marilyn Monroe

5 **The Apartment**
US 1960/ w Jack Lemmon, Shirley MacLaine, Fred MacMurray

6 **The Private Life of Sherlock Holmes**
GB 1970/ w Robert Stephens, Colin Blakely, Geneviève Page

7 **Avanti!**
US/Italy 1972/ w Jack Lemmon, Juliet Mills, Clive Revill

Robert Wise

Born: 10th September 1914/ Winchester, Indiana, USA
Directing career: 1944-

While he never found a personal cinematic style or displayed a taste for any special theme or genre, Robert Wise made a number of films that may be described as superior entertainment. He was in fact a solid, conscientious craftsman and a fluent story-teller mercifully free of grandiose pretensions.

Wise began his film career in 1933 as an assistant editor at RKO. By the start of the '40s he had already graduated to editing ambitious productions such as **Dieterle**'s *The Hunchback of Nôtre Dame* and *All That Money Can Buy*, and **Welles**' *Citizen Kane* and *The Magnificent Ambersons* (the last re-cut in the director's absence). But it was while he was working for Val Lewton that he made his directing debut, taking over (when Gunther von Fritsch fell behind schedule) *The Curse of the Cat People* >**1**, an imaginative account of a childhood beset by solitude, fear and fantasy. No less atmospheric was *The Bodysnatchers*, a macabre Lewton movie set in an immaculately recreated Edinburgh of the 1830s, and by 1948, with the strangely *noir*-ish Western, *Blood on the Moon*, he was able to make his entry into A-features.

Over the next decade Wise proved a prolific director in many different genres, alternating routine programmers with films that transcended limitations of script and budget through taut pacing, strong performances and a seemingly intuitive sense of where best to place the camera. *The Set-Up* >**2** is a classic boxing drama, its tension deriving from Robert Ryan's ravaged dignity, the aligning of screen-time with real-time, and an authentically *noir* portrait of the seedy characters inhabiting the smalltime fight circuit. Further films of note included *The Day The Earth Stood Still* (an unusually intelligent sci-fi parable), *Executive Suite* (gripping boardroom intrigues), *Somebody Up There Likes Me* (a second boxing movie, with Paul Newman in fine, hungry form as Rocky Graziano), *I Want to Live* (an admirably full-blown, anti-capital punishment melodrama with Susan Hayward as a death-row victim protesting her innocence to the very end), and *Odds Against Tomorrow* (a downbeat heist-thriller, complete with an attack on the follies of racism, and an excellent use of New York locations). By now however, Wise was successful enough to become his own producer, and he embarked upon a series of more generously budgeted, prestige productions.

Co-directed with choreographer Jerome Robbins, his *West Side Story* foundered on miscasting and a schizophrenic commitment to both low-key street-realism and ultra-stylised gloss. Rather more satisfying was *The Haunting*, a return to the subtle psychological horror of his Lewton years, in which a house, reputedly inhabited by a poltergeist, steals the film from the group of neurotics and sceptics gathered therein. But by far Wise's greatest success was *The Sound of Music* >**3**: not only did he manage to avoid the worst, maudlin excesses prevalent in stories of similar sentimentality but, through sumptuous location photography and immaculate, fluid editing, his easy, classical professionalism ensured that the film seemed far shorter than it really was. Sadly, the same could not be said of the war film *The Sand Pebbles*, nor of *Star!*, a lightly likeable musical biopic of Gertrude Lawrence that vainly tried to repeat Julie Andrews' success in *The Sound of Music*. But *The Andromeda Strain* was gripping, superior sci-fi about boffins battling to isolate and destroy a deadly extra-terrestrial virus; and although *The Hindenburg* was a lumbering, if unusually polished, disaster epic *Audrey Rose* offered an intriguingly old-fashioned, gore-free supernatural thriller in which a 12-year-old girl is possessed by the soul of another killed in a car crash. Next, Wise turned his attention to hi-tech hardware in the mediocre *Star Trek: The Motion Picture*.

Wise's finest work reveals that technical proficiency, and sensitivity to performance, pace and setting may result in highly watchable, even memorable cinema. At the same time, his career as a whole offers evidence that cautious, anonymous professionalism is unlikely ever to be responsible for the creation of great art.

Lineage

Compared to other Lewton directors, Wise is less imaginative than **Tourneur**, more fluent than Mark Robson. While his style is very different, in terms of his modest, variable craftsmanship, he may be likened to figures like **Curtiz**, **Dieterle** and Henry Hathaway.

Viewing

1 **The Curse of the Cat People**
US 1944/ w Simone Simon, Kent Smith, Ann Carter
2 **The Set-Up**
US 1949/ w Robert Ryan, Audrey Totter, George Tobias
3 **The Sound of Music**
US 1965/ w Julie Andrews, Christopher Plummer, Eleanor Parker

Fred Wiseman

Born: 1st January 1930/Boston, Massachusetts, USA
Directing career: 1966-

A leading exponent of 'direct cinema', Frederick Wiseman differs from figures like **Pennebaker** and the Maysles Brothers in that he uses documentary not for individual portraiture but for a mammoth socio-political investigation of specific American institutions. If the dispassionate tone of much of his work sometimes suggests a rather woolly liberal reluctance to take sides or to analyse, there is no denying his ability to evoke a wider social context through the relentless, intimate observation of human behaviour.

Educated at Yale and Harvard, Wiseman worked for some years as a lawyer before revealing an interest in film as the producer of Shirley Clarke's *The Cool World*. His own directing debut, *The Titicut Follies* (about the treatment of inmates at a hospital for the criminally insane) introduced the fundamental elements of his style: black-and-white, hand-held camerawork, an absence of music and commentary, and an attempt to view events from a multiplicity of moral angles. At the same time, however, Wiseman warily denied any claims to objectivity by calling his films 'reality fictions' and stressing the fact that the structural organisation (through editing) of the enormous amount of footage originally shot served to indicate his own personal point of view. Be that as it may, by avoiding facile didacticism, his finest work painted a complex portrait of the oppressive workings of bureaucracy: in *High School*, a 'model' educational establishment is presented as a factory dedicated to the mass-production of entirely conformist human beings; *Law and Order* >**1** confronts the racism at the heart of Kansas City society by exposing police brutality; *Hospital* indicts not the medical staff but a bureaucratic system that favours the rich and neglects the poor; and *Basic Training* >**2**, observing the processes of military indoctrination practised at Fort Knox, gently extends its sympathies towards those soldiers who fail to make the grade.

As Wiseman's career progressed, he roamed farther afield in his attempt to record an entire natural history of American life; if *Juvenile Court* and *Welfare* (in which both claimants and social workers are regarded as victims of a society that thrives on the oppression and humiliation of the poor) signify no great advance on his early work, *Essene* was an account of monastery life, and *Primate* >**3** a harrowing, visually explicit indictment of forms of scientific research that rely on the maltreatment and vivisection of animals. After the similarly polemical *Meat*, however, Wiseman ventured abroad to observe American imperialism at work in *Canal Zone*, *Sinai Field Mission* and *Manoeuvre*; but his lack of analysis meant that complex political questions were largely evaded, while *Model* (about New York's fashion world) never addressed the issues of sexism, voyeurism and exploitation central to its subject.

Although Wiseman's films, exhaustive in terms of both detail and length, make for fascinating sociological records, their lack of an analytical (as opposed to descriptive) dimension is finally limiting; while his commitment to detached observation ensures a rare immediacy, it may also fall prey to inconsequentiality.

Lineage

Wiseman's methods align him with **Pennebaker**, Richard Leacock, and Albert and David Maysles, but his enduring interest in American institutions is echoed in the more subjective (and analytical) work of figures like Emile De Antonio and Allan Francovich.

Further reading

Thomas R. Atkins' *Frederick Wiseman* (New York, 1976), Richard Meran Barsam's *Nonfiction Film* (New York, 1973).

Viewing

1 **Law and Order**
US 1969
2 **Basic Training**
US 1971
3 **Primate**
US 1974

William Wyler

Born: 1st July 1902/Mulhouse, Alsace-Lorraine (then in Germany)
Died: 27th July 1981/Beverly Hills, California, USA
Directing career: 1925-1972

With his distinctive visual style and a taste for solemn material, Willy Wyler gained a reputation as a meticulous, serious artist. In retrospect, however, his often academic use of deep-focus, his dependence on rather bloodless versions of respectable theatrical and literary works, and his stodgy liberalism seem the product of an unadventurously middle-brow, if professionally skilful, sensibility.

Wyler first went to work in Universal's publicity department in New York after a meeting in Paris with Carl Laemmle (a distant relative) in the early '20s. Moving to Hollywood, he trained in a variety of jobs before making his directing debut, in 1925, with *Crook Buster*, first of some 40 two-reeler Westerns he made before turning to features a couple of years later. Only with the advent of sound, however, did he begin to make a reputation for himself: *A House Divided* was a dry adaptation of O'Neill's *Desire Under the Elms*, *Counselor-at-Law* a fine vehicle for John Barrymore, and *The Good Fairy* an amiable romantic comedy scripted by Preston **Sturges**. But in 1936 Wyler left Universal for Sam Goldwyn, whose similar taste for quality films not only enabled the director to make 'serious' movies like *These Three* >**1** (a bowdlerised heterosexual version of Lillian Hellman's lesbian drama *The Children's Hour*, measuring the effects of malicious smalltown gossip on two schoolteachers), and Sinclair Lewis' *Dodsworth*, but introduced Wyler to cameraman Gregg Toland (**Welles'** cinematographer on *Citizen Kane*) whose expert lighting technique allowed the pair to experiment with deep focus. Indeed, apart from the often intense performances induced by Wyler's painstaking perfectionism (which earned him the nickname '90-take Wyler'), the most notable aspect of his work is visual: while the stagey, stilted crime drama *Dead End* explores its single street set from a multitude of angles, in the Old South melodrama, *Jezebel* >**2**, and in *Wuthering Heights*, costume and decor take on a near-symbolic significance, with Bette Davis' dark dress, conspicuous in a sea of white gowns in the former's sumptuous ball scene, revealing her status as a social outsider.

After *The Westerner* (a rare return to his filmic origins), Wyler made what is arguably his finest film, an impeccably acted version of Somerset Maugham's *The Letter* >**3**, in which both Bette Davis' performance (as a woman whose illicit desires lead her to murder) and Tony Gaudio's luminous photography create a superbly steamy melodramatic mood of stifling and sensuous Malayan nights. In contrast, the extreme deep-focus of *The Little Foxes* >**4** seems deliberate and detached: the relationships and distances between the members of an internecine Deep South family, mirrored all too neatly in the way characters react on various visual planes, are presented in exceedingly schematic form. Indeed, Wyler's work was by now becoming almost academic in both its strained sobriety and its text-book use of deep-focus and long takes. *Mrs Miniver* was a turgid, albeit immensely successful, tribute to British pluck in times of war, while, after two documentaries made to uplift the Allies' morale, only *The Best Years of Our Lives* >**5** – an epic and moving realist study of the disenchantment and alienation experienced by returning war heroes, demonstrating Wyler's most adept use of deep-focus – revealed a real commitment to emotional content. Thereafter, leaving Goldwyn to set up a short-lived independent company, Wyler moved increasingly towards half-hearted eclecticism and hollow, grandiose spectacle.

The Heiress, based on Henry James' *Washington Square*, was at least blessed with fine performances by Montgomery Clift, Ralph Richardson and Olivia de Havilland, but it lacked the novelist's sharp sense of irony; *Detective Story* seemed wary of becoming a thriller, *Carrie* was dull and actorly, *Roman Holiday* so lame as to point up Wyler's poor comic sense. Worse, the Western, *Friendly Persuasion*, foundered in portentous pacifist moralising, while *The Big Country*'s routine ranch-war plot failed to match the sweep of Franz Planer's landscape photography; the interminable Roman epic *Ben-Hur* was notable only for its chariot race. The '60s saw Wyler decline still further: *The Loudest Whisper* was a more explicit if infinitely inferior remake of *These Three*, *The Collector* a stolid exercise in claustrophobic psychodrama, *Funny Girl* an elephantine costume musical tediously indulgent of Barbra Streisand, and *The Liberation of L.B. Jones* an uninvolving account of Southern racism.

Wyler's lack of artistic personality can be seen both in the absence of thematic consistency within his work, and in the cool detachment of his imagery, according to which characters may come to resemble pieces on a chess-board. Only when the actors display sufficient power to overcome the inflexible tyranny of his visual arrangements do his films take on any real life.

Lineage

Claims for Wyler's 'realism' now seem untenable, deep-focus being as contrived a stylistic mannerism as the montage he avoided. He can be seen as a vaguely liberal melodramatist (who may well have despised such a term), and is thus comparable with figures such as **Stevens**, **Zinnemann**, **Lean**, **Schlesinger** and **Attenborough**. He was much admired by, and perhaps an influence on, Laurence Olivier.

Further reading

Axel Madsen's *William Wyler* (New York, 1973).

Viewing

1 **These Three**
US 1936/ w Miriam Hopkins, Joel McCrea, Merle Oberon

2 **Jezebel**
US 1938/ w Bette Davis, Henry Fonda, George Brent

3 **The Letter**
US 1940/ w Bette Davis, Herbert Marshall, James Stephenson

4 **The Little Foxes**
US 1941/ w Bette Davis, Herbert Marshall, Teresa Wright

5 **The Best Years of Our Lives**
US 1946/ w Fredric March, Myrna Loy, Dana Andrews, Harold Russell

Peter Yates

Born: 24th July 1929/Aldershot, England
Directing career: 1962-

The most commercially successful British director to transplant to Hollywood in the last 20 years, Peter Yates is best known for his action movies. But his best work shows a greater interest in characters and their position in society; only when he engages with a film's human dimensions does he transcend mere narrative proficiency.

Before entering the movies as a dubbing assistant, Yates had worked in the theatre (as a RADA-trained actor and director), and in car-racing, as a manager and stunt-driver. After serving as an assistant to Tony Richardson, Jack Cardiff and others, he finally made his feature debut directing the Cliff Richard musical, *Summer Holiday*. Neither that, nor a version of the surreal fantasy comedy *One Way Pendulum*, were notable, but for the sometimes effectively low-key thriller *Robbery* (about the Great Train Robbery), he shot a car chase so well that an admiring Steve McQueen invited him to Hollywood to direct *Bullitt* >**1**. Again, as a cop-thriller the film was largely routine, but Yates' staging and editing of a lengthy car chase through the steep hilly streets of San Francisco was so virtuoso that it was a major success. Thus established in America he then made an innocuous study of casual romance in *John and Mary*, but the film's failure ensured that most of his subsequent work – *Murphy's War*, *The Hot Rock* (an amiably parodic heist-comedy about inept jewel thieves), the Streisand vehicle *For Pete's Sake*, and *Mother, Jugs and Speed* (a noisome, hectic black farce about rival ambulance companies) – focussed on broad comedy and action-packed set-pieces. Only *The Friends of Eddie Coyle* >**2**, an authentically bleak, understated thriller concerning betrayal and deception in Boston's underworld, with a vivid performance from Robert Mitchum as a small-time hood-turned-police-informant, revealed an ability to evoke the mores of an entire sub-culture through the subtly observed interplay of credible, never glamorised characters.

Though the underwater adventure, *The Deep*, was pure pap, its commercial success allowed Yates to make his finest film to date, *Breaking Away* >**3**. Written by Steve Tesich (also an immigrant), it was an often hilarious, always affecting account of the dilemmas facing four recent school-leavers in a small university town, one of whom is so obsessed with cycling that his admiration for the Italian team pushes him to learn the language, eat pasta, serenade his girlfriend with a Verdi aria, and re-name his cat Fellini (much to his working-class father's bemusement). On the surface, the film is merely an uplifting, witty, rites-of-passage comedy; delve beneath, however, and it reveals a rare study of class divisions in America while dealing with unemployment, student elitism, and teenage disillusionment. Likewise perceptive and original, though rather less coherent, was the Tesich-scripted *Eyewitness* (*The Janitor*) >**4**. Its quirky, romantic comedy-thriller plot (a Vietvet janitor claims to have witnessed a murder simply to win the affections of the television newscaster of his dreams) allows for offbeat characterisation, tenderly observed relationships, and taut suspense. Disappointingly, however, Yates' later work was less distinguished: *Krull* was visually spectacular but hollow sci-fi; *The Dresser* a hammy and woefully stagey version of Ronald Harwood's play about an ageing actor and his gay assistant, the latter portrayed with offensive camp; *Eleni* was a cliché-ridden blend of revenge-thriller and costume drama set in a picturesquely primitive Greek village during the Civil War; *Suspect* a contrived courtroom-cum-conspiracy thriller; and *The House on Carroll Street* a routine, if sometimes moody, thriller set in the paranoid, witch-hunting '50s.

Despite his professionalism Yates seems too often confounded by the quiet moments between action set-pieces; it is perhaps no accident that his finest work functions as an offbeat, outsider's view of modern American society. When dealing with more strictly formulaic genre material, he is at best a journeyman technician.

Lineage

It is hard to compare the erratic Yates with anybody; if he lacks

Russell's or **Roeg**'s idiosyncratic visions or **Boorman**'s ambitions, he is arguably more talented than other expatriates such as **Schlesinger**, **Parker**, Tony Richardson, and **Ridley Scott**.

Viewing

1 **Bullitt**
US 1968/ w Steve McQueen, Jacqueline Bisset, Robert Vaughn
2 **The Friends of Eddie Coyle**
US 1973/ w Robert Mitchum, Peter Boyle, Richard Jordan
3 **Breaking Away**
US 1979/ w Dennis Christopher, Dennis Quaid, Paul Dooley
4 **Eyewitness (The Janitor)**
US 1980/ w William Hurt, Sigourney Weaver, James Woods

Robert Zemeckis

Born: 14th May 1951/Chicago, Illinois, USA
Directing career: 1978-

One of the most successful young American film-makers of recent years, Robert Zemeckis is also one of the most talented. With no less than three of his first five films accounted as major hits, he looks set to become an influential figure in cinematic comedy.

After studying film at the University of Southern California and working as a cutter for TV commercials, Zemeckis attracted the attention of **John Milius** and **Steven Spielberg** with his script – written with Bob Gale, collaborator on his next two projects – for *I Wanna Hold Your Hand*, an amiable, inventive and raucously atmospheric satire on the lunacy of Beatlemania, which Spielberg agreed to produce. Still more frantic was the Zemeckis-Gale script for *1941*; unfortunately Spielberg's visual overkill and juvenile characterisations counteracted the film's attractively original premise. Far better was Zemeckis' similarly slapstick *Used Cars* >**1**, an often brilliant black comedy on American salesmanship strategies, focussing on the ludicrously mean-spirited business rivalries of two companies owned by twin brothers: if Zemeckis' unerring, breathless sense of pace ensured that the intricately planned gags came thick and fast, he never neglected the need for vividly offbeat characters (Gerrit Graham's omen-believer merely the most memorable of many) while his plot spiralled into populist fantasy. Inexplicably, the film was a commercial failure, but *Romancing the Stone*, an exotic adventure spoof about a staid writer of romantic novels suddenly finding herself plunged into a dangerous madcap whirl in darkest Colombia, was sufficiently funny and gripping – and close enough to Spielberg's *Raiders of the Lost Ark* – to put Zemeckis on the map.

But it was *Back to the Future* >**2** that confirmed his arrival as a major-league director. About a teenager transported back to the '50s by a crazed scientist's time machine, it centred on the boy's attempts both to fend off his own (still teenage) mother's advances and to bring his parents together so that he himself can be born. Again, the script was rewardingly complex, the direction fast and polished, and the comedy primarily visual. Indeed, motion is the crux of all Zemeckis' tall tales, and he was, perhaps, the obvious choice to make *Who Framed Roger Rabbit?* >**3**, a spoof *film noir* in which human characters (including an archetypally seedy, down-at-heel private eye) interact with cartoon characters, seen as a *real* minority working in the Hollywood studios and living in LA's Toontown neighbourhood, in a wild plot that embraces murder, blackmail, adultery and conspiracy. Technically astonishing (the Toons, thanks to Richard Williams' animation expertise, even cast shadows), the film was as vulgar, sophisticated, self-conscious (a *femme fatale* insists, 'I'm not really bad; it's just the way I'm drawn') and breathtakingly imaginative as Zemeckis' earlier work. As a tribute to the violent, grotesquely surreal humour of the Warner Brothers cartoons of the '40s and '50s, it was at once affectionate and sharply satirical, while as a modern example of unusually intelligent popular entertainment, it has had few peers.

Voluptuous Toon Jessica Rabbit – 'I'm not bad; I'm just drawn that way' – entrances bewildered gumshoe Eddie Valiant (Bob Hoskins) in Zemeckis' *Who Framed Roger Rabbit?*

Blessed with a sense of comic timing that is nowadays rare, Zemeckis has the ability to make the impossible both credible and emotionally involving. As a director of action comedy, he rarely opts for the obvious; and perhaps even more crucial to his development, almost every gag he stages is visual, and thus fundamentally cinematic.

Lineage

Zemeckis has spoken of his admiration for **Capra**, **Hitchcock** and **Wilder**, although Spielberg, who has produced all Zemeckis' films except *Romancing the Stone*, might also be seen as an influence. He may perhaps be compared with **Dante** and the **Coen Brothers**.

Viewing

1 **Used Cars**
US 1980/ w Jack Warden, Kurt Russell, Gerrit Graham

2 **Back to the Future**
US 1986/ w Michael J. Fox, Christopher Lloyd, Lea Thompson

3 **Who Framed Roger Rabbit?**
US 1988/ w Bob Hoskins, Christopher Lloyd, Joanna Cassidy

Fred Zinnemann

Born: 29th April 1907/Vienna, Austria
Directing career: 1934-

The films of Fred Zinnemann – once regarded as a serious moralist with a talent for social realism – have not aged well. Frequently slow, solemn and simplistic, they are the work of a director who appears to have equated artistry with neatness, objectivity with aloofness, and significance with decorative, humourless reverence.

Having served as an assistant cameraman on various films in Paris and Berlin (including **Siodmak**'s classic *People on Sunday*), in 1929 Zinnemann emigrated to Hollywood, where he worked in the same capacity for his compatriot Berthold Viertel, **Flaherty** and **Berkeley**. In 1934, with photographer Paul Strand, he co-directed *The Wave* (*Los Redes*), a semi-documentary feature on the lives of Mexican fishermen that gained him a contract with MGM directing shorts for the *Crime Does Not Pay* series. Only eight years later did he make his feature debut proper, with *The Kid Glove Killer*, a craftsmanlike, low-key drama about a police pharmacologist who solves a murder. This initiated a series of B-thrillers that came to an end in 1944 with *The Seventh Cross*, an anti-Nazi film about a concentration camp prisoner's escape through wartorn Germany. But it was the maudlin humanism of *The Search*, shot amongst the ruins of postwar Berlin, with Montgomery Clift tending to the needs of a child refugee, that first established Zinnemann as a sententious, supposedly realist film-maker; nor did *Act of Violence* or *The Men* >**1** fight shy of meanings: the first was an agreeably taut thriller in which a vengeful GI tracks down the officer who betrayed his pals in a POW camp, the second a melodrama set in a hospital ward full of disillusioned, paraplegic war-veterans. Admittedly, Zinnemann was adept with actors (*The Men* gave Brando his first screen role) but his tendency to a heavy-handed hammering-home of dramatic and moral points was already beginning to manifest itself.

High Noon >**2** was the turning point: a Western that displayed its maker's contempt for the genre's conventions, it concerned a sheriff whose failure to hire a posse, from the cowardly townsfolk he is hired to defend, was intended to mirror the treacherous mood of McCarthy's America; in the event, its paralleling of real-time and film-time and its stark high-contrast images seemed more gimmicky than meaningful. No less contrived or portentous, though considerably less gripping, was Zinnemann's subsequent series of adaptations of literary and theatrical works: Carson McCullers' *The Member of the Wedding* was stagey and overwhelmingly tasteful; James Jones' *From Here to Eternity* >**3** executed with such po-faced disdain for melodrama that any vitality originated solely from the acting; the Broadway musical, *Oklahoma!*, translated with wearisome pedantry. As Zinnemann's career moved increasingly into prestige productions, so his work became more ploddingly high-minded. *The Nun's Story*, perhaps the most excruciatingly obvious of the director's several movies dealing in a crisis of conscience, was relentlessly tedious in its desire to steer clear of poor taste; *The Sundowners*, with Robert Mitchum and Deborah Kerr struggling to make it as sheep-farmers in '20s Australia, was amiable but over-extended; *A Man for All Seasons*, taken from Robert Bolt's play about Sir Thomas More, seemed lumbering and superficial. By now, in fact, Zinnemann seemed to have slowed his films and his career down to a snail's pace, and over the next 16 years he made only three movies: *The Day of the Jackal*, a lifeless version of Frederick Forsyth's middlebrow best-seller about an assassination attempt on De Gaulle; *Julia*, about Lillian Hellman's affair with Dashiell Hammett and her friendship with a political activist in '30s Europe, which transformed the Nazi menace into the stuff of vapid costume-drama; and the lavish *Five Days One Summer*, a bloodless, picturesque romance set in the Swiss Alps during the '30s. Zinnemann's emphasis on pernickety good taste was now no longer fashionable, and he retired from directing.

However well-intentioned in their vaguely liberal leanings, Zinnemann's films suffer from his unimaginative, over-methodical tendency to make every point tidily explicit; since everything in his work exists on the surface, there are no subtle undercurrents or nuances left to uncover. The result is often exceedingly dull.

Lineage

Zinnemann exhibits none of the vitality or passion that is found in **Von Stroheim**, **Vidor** and **Flaherty** whom he much admired. Rather, he may be compared with **Wyler**, **Stevens**, **Lean** and **Attenborough**.

Viewing

1 **The Men**
US 1950/ w Marlon Brando, Teresa Wright, Everett Sloane

2 **High Noon**
US 1952/ w Gary Cooper, Grace Kelly, Lloyd Bridges, Katy Jurado

3 **From Here to Eternity**
US 1953/ w Burt Lancaster, Montgomery Clift, Deborah Kerr, Frank Sinatra

Glossary

THROUGHOUT THE FILM HANDBOOK clear, plain English has been used, and specialised technical terminology and critical jargon avoided wherever possible. The following glossary, therefore, is not so much an explanatory dictionary of stylistic and generic terms – most people, after all, know what a Western is – as a suggested alternative way of looking at films, in order that the entries on individual directors may be better placed in context.

The Main Genres

EPICS As much a style as a genre: films dealing primarily with history, myth and heroic figures, usually set in ancient times, though very often both dialogue and themes reflect the anxieties and preoccupations of the times in which they were made. All too frequently, historical accuracy and dramatic depth are sacrificed to colourful visual spectacle and pompous, grandiose sermonising, the latter quality perhaps most conspicuous in epics derived from the Bible. Other subjects popular in the genre are ancient Greece and Rome, and Dark Ages tales of Nordic warriors. The Western and the Japanese *samurai* film may both be seen as offshoots of the genre. Key directors: **Griffith**, **Gance**, **DeMille**, **Eisenstein**, **Kurosawa**, **Mann**, **Nicholas Ray**, **Stevens**; and in terms of style: **Leone**, **Visconti**, **Cimino**, **Coppola**, **Milius**, **Lean**, **Attenborough**.

HORROR Movies designed to provoke feelings of terror and/or revulsion in the spectator, often – but far from always – based in macabre fantasy, and thus frequently overlapping with science-fiction. The supernatural is a common element, but many hold that the genre connects with very real deep-seated human fears about death, sexuality, disease and evil. On a visual level, darkness is often predominant, while both narrative and editing tend to emphasise suspense; thus, suggested menace can be as effective as the explicit gore that has coloured most recent examples of the genre. Key directors: **Browning**, **Whale**, **Tourneur** (for producer Val Lewton), Terence Fisher, **Corman**, Mario Bava, **Romero**, **Cronenberg**, **Carpenter**, **Cohen**, Dario Argento, Lucio Fulci, **Lynch**, Tobe Hooper, Wes Craven.

MELODRAMA Now largely superseded by the television soap-opera, the film melodrama was also known as the weepie or women's film. Generally fulsome in its stress on love, emotional loss, illness and physical hardship, the genre frequently focusses on domestic divisions and tensions to paint a portrait of society that is at once subtly critical and sumptuously, even romantically stylised. While coincidence and contrivance are common, sentimentality does not necessarily preclude intelligence and irony: indeed, in the hands of a great film-maker, the melodrama's unrivalled emotional power may provide a devastatingly bleak critique of contemporary social – and even political – *mores*. Key directors: **Griffith**, **Von Sternberg**, **Von Stroheim**, **Borzage**, John Stahl, **Cukor**, **Leisen**, **Wyler**, **Ophüls**, **Mizoguchi**, **Rossellini**, **Buñuel**, **Powell**, **Vidor**, **Sirk**, **Nicholas Ray**, **Minnelli**, **Fassbinder**.

MESSAGE MOVIES Didactic form of melodrama in which a social, political or moral message is allowed to take precedence over demands of plot and characterisation. Seldom, in fact, truly enlightening or provocative, such films often tend towards bland liberal platitudes in approaching time-honoured issues like racial prejudice, war, poverty, inequality, injustice, insanity and unorthodox sexuality; the complacency of many examples of the sub-genre is evident from their frequent final acceptance of the status quo. Key directors: **Griffith**, **Chaplin**, **DeMille**, **Capra**, **De Sica**, **Kazan**, **Kramer**, **Zinnemann**, **Ashby**, **Attenborough**.

MUSICALS Arguably the most fantastic of all film genres, often rather fatuously dismissed as mere escapism. At its best the form is richly expressive of inner emotional realities, using song and dance, dialogue, colour, décor and camera movement in imaginative counterpoint to both plot and characters. Certainly, the genre is perhaps the one most suited to conveying sheer ecstatic abandon and – especially through dance – the complete compatibility of a couple in love. Key directors: **Mamoulian**, **Lubitsch**, **Berkeley**, **Clair**, **Minnelli**, **Powell**, **Donen**, Gene Kelly, **Sirk**, **Cukor**, Charles Walters, Charles Vidor, Walter Lang, **Wise**, Bob Fosse, **Demy**.

SCI-FI Generally speculative films based to a greater or lesser degree on fantasy. Various sub-genres exist (space travel, insane boffins and doctors, alien invasion, future dystopias), but the majority concern a world (or universe) in chaos, often to be restored to order by the forces of science. Another consequent motif is the uneasy balance between the benefits and dangers of experimentation (Faustian themes of aiming for too much knowledge, or playing God). Technological hardware and jargon are common in visuals and script, although many of the finest sci-fi films are grounded in – and thus potentially critical of – a recognisable contemporary reality; indeed, the societies and moral systems depicted often function as an only mildly distorted mirror-image of our own. The line dividing sci-films from horror is frequently very thin. Key directors: Georges Méliès, **Lang**, **Whale**, **Arnold**, Byron Haskin (for producer George Pal), **Corman**, **Kubrick**, **Cronenberg**, **Cohen**, **Lucas**, **Spielberg**, **Carpenter**, **Dante**, George Miller, **Gilliam**.

THRILLERS An all-embracing term covering a multitude of films whose main element is suspense, including horror, sci-fi, whodunnit and conspiracy mysteries, police, private-eye and gangster films. Pace and, in narrative terms, the withholding of crucial information are thus central to the films' effect on an audience. Violence, crime and death are staple elements, sometimes making for a dark and disturbing vision of the world, where nothing is quite what it seems; action set-pieces, particularly the chase, are also common. Key directors: **Lang**, **Hitchcock**, **Walsh**, **Welles**, **Siodmak**, **Dassin**, **Nicholas Ray**, **Clouzot**, **Lewis**, **Siegel**, **Melville**, **Chabrol**, **Polanski**, **Rosi**, **Costa-Gavras**, **Eastwood**, **Michael Mann**.

WAR MOVIES All too often degenerating, during times of war, into propaganda and facile notions of heroism, the genre has seemed, in practice, somewhat limited in scope, generally confining itself to a handful of themes: the importance of teamwork, the conflict of duty and cowardice, the madness and wastage of war, and the glorification of virile, selfless action. In many of the best examples, in fact, war is not the central focus of attention but a backdrop to more private conflicts, a metaphor for the threatening chaos of human existence, against which is pitted man's will to survive with personal moral integrity intact; often, the more contemplative, less action-packed films are finally the most effective. Key directors: **Griffith**, Lewis Milestone, **Borzage**, **Ford**, **Hawks**, **Walsh**, **Renoir**, **Rossellini**, **Powell**, **Aldrich**, **Fuller**, **Kubrick**, **Bergman**, **Coppola**, **Stone**.

WESTERNS *The* great American art-form, which transformed recent history into the stuff of myth. Ranging from the lowliest serial oaters (often complete with singing cowboys) to the most epic and poetic of masterpieces, the genre repeatedly treated themes that examined the confidence and doubts of a young nation fighting to assert itself: the triumph of civilisation over wilderness, the conflict between law and anarchy, word and gun, community and lone outsider, East and West, man and nature. Thus, its concerns are social, political, moral, and historical. The genre developed a rich array of formular situations – the establishment of a railroad or peaceful township, pioneering settlers battling against Indians or greedy cattle-barons, 'some things a man just can't ride around' – which gave ample scope for countless, and subtle, variations. Very few films are historically accurate, but the thematic and mythic wealth of the genre ensured that, for several decades, it was prolific, sturdy, and universally popular. Key directors: **Griffith**, **Dwan**, **DeMille**, **Walsh**, **Ford**, Joseph Kane, **Hawks**, **Lewis**, **Aldrich**, **Mann**, **Boetticher**, **Fuller**, **Nicholas Ray**, **John Sturges**, Delmer Daves, André de Toth, Henry Hathaway, Burt Kennedy, Andrew V. McLaglen, **Siegel**, **Penn**, **Peckinpah**, **Leone**, **Eastwood**.

Stylistic Terms

EXPRESSIONISM Originally an offshoot of the movement (in visual art, music, literature, theatre and architecture) that had arisen primarily in Germany in the 1910s. The mood was generally bleakly pessimistic, conjuring up a world of chaos, disintegration, *Angst* and madness; the method was the distortion, even exaggeration, of emotions through non-naturalistic means. In cinema, therefore, acting was wildly, grotesquely stylised; décor angular, fragmented and menacingly overbearing; camerawork tended towards looming shadows and topsy-turvy angles, depicting a world out of kilter. Characteristically, Hollywood diluted and adapted the style to its own purposes, most notably in horror movies and *film noir*. Key directors: Robert Wiene, **Lang**, **Murnau**, **Pabst**, E. A. Dupont.

FILM NOIR Not a genre but a style (though it is usually applied to crime-thrillers), *film noir* is primarily, but not exclusively, a question of visuals. Generally seen as having developed out of Expressionism, it makes use of dark, shadowy, *chiaroscuro* (high-contrast black-and-white) camerawork to evoke a menacing, hostile universe in which nothing is as it appears. Initially coming to the fore in the urban crime-thrillers of the '40s (its heyday lasting until the mid-'50s), it thrived on a mood of romantic fatalism and paranoia – emotions often explained with reference to the spiritual disillusionment and moral confusion of postwar America. Plots are complex, tortuous, downbeat, and often related in flashbacks which enable the doomed, flawed hero to explain or understand the reasons for his downfall: frequently, a misguided sexual obsession with a duplicitous *femme fatale* is a key factor. As such, this format was most commonly and fruitfully applied to the kind of hard-boiled fiction favoured by writers like Hammett, Chandler and James M. Cain (indeed, the term was coined by French critics after the crime novels published as *série noire*), though there are examples of *film noir* in other genres, including the melodrama, the Western, and sci-fi. Perhaps unsurprisingly, given its links with German Expressionism, some of its finest adherents were immigrant film-makers who had come to Hollywood from Europe, in several cases fleeing the Nazi menace. Key directors: **Huston**, **Lang**, **Siodmak**, **Welles**, **Wilder**, **Dassin**, **Dmytryk**, **Wise**, **Tourneur**, **Farrow**, **Rossen**, **Nicholas Ray**, Henry Hathaway, Richard Fleischer, **Aldrich**, **Mann**, **Fuller**, **Lewis**, **Losey**, **Preminger**, **Siegel**, **Melville**.

NEO-REALISM A rather nebulous, amorphous Italian movement that arose during the early '40s, partly inspired by the 'poetic realism' of French directors like **Renoir** and **Carné**, and undertaken in opposition to the middle-class 'white telephone' films favoured by the Fascists. As defined by influential scriptwriter Cesare Zavattini, the movement entailed the use of non-professional actors, location shooting, simple, usually working-class, human situations rather than contrived dramatic plots, and a socio-political consciousness that challenged the assumptions of the establishment and bourgeoisie. Poverty, injustice, and an emphasis on human brotherhood were common narrative motifs, which were in turn carried over into Hollywood's own relatively realist films of the postwar years, Britain's Free Cinema of the early '60s, and most other attempts to create alternative, socially-conscious forms of cinema. Although neo-realism proper died out in the early '50s, its legacy can be found in many subsequent Italian films, including comedies. Key directors: **Rossellini**, **De Sica**, **Visconti**, Alberto Lattuada,

Giuseppe De Santis, Pietro Germi, Carlo Lizzani; **Pasolini**, **Rosi**, Olmi, the **Taviani Brothers**.

SURREALISM Initially a French literary movement, evolved from Dada in the early '20s, which spread into most art-forms, cinema included; essentially opposed to conventional, bourgeois realism, and often intended to shock both by its random juxtaposition of images from the subconscious and by its emphasis on death, cruel violence and sexual desire (thus connecting with Freud's theory of dream symbolism). Its first manifestations in cinema were amongst the Paris-based avant-garde of the '20s. Its influence, however, has been enormous on all forms of cinema, including not only the independent underground film-makers, but more mainstream figures, particularly those working in comedy and fantasy. It may indeed be argued that screen comedians as diverse as **Keaton**, the Marx Brothers, W. C. Fields and Jerry Lewis have contributed (albeit probably unwittingly) to the cause of surrealism in film, while the movement's emphasis on *amour fou* (obsessive passion) finds a counterpart in many romantic Hollywood melodramas. Key directors: **Buñuel**, **Clair**, **Renoir**, **Vigo**, **Cocteau**, **Berkeley**, **Franju**, **Fellini**, **Resnais**, **Borowczyk**, Jacques Rivette, André Delvaux, **Blier**, Jan Švankmajer, **Herzog**, **Lynch**, **Gilliam**, **Greenaway**.

Film Books

THE FOLLOWING LIST is a selection of titles covering various aspects of cinema, including general film history and criticism, reference books and dictionaries of film, genre studies, and film theory. Books which deal specifically with individual film-makers are listed in the further reading section of the relevant entry.

Dictionaries and encyclopedias:

A BIOGRAPHICAL DICTIONARY OF THE CINEMA – Superbly written and stimulatingly, provocatively personalised: essential reading. David Thompson/ Secker and Warburg/1980.

THE INTERNATIONAL FILM ENCYCLOPEDIA – Fact-filled rather than critical, but highly useful. Ephraim Katz/ Macmillan/1982.

CINEMA: A CRITICAL DICTIONARY (2 vols) – Serious critical essays of variable quality and length by generally superior writers. ed. Richard Roud/Secker and Warburg/1980.

THE INTERNATIONAL DICTIONARY OF FILMS AND FILMMAKERS (4 vols) – Covers movies, directors, actors, and writers and production artists; often poorly, derivatively written but usefully wide ranging. ed. Christopher Lyon/ James Vinson/Macmillan/1984–86.

THE MOTION PICTURE ANNUAL – Published each year and covering every film released in the US (including foreign films) over the previous 12 months. Detailed synopses, full credits, and lively, opinionated critiques. ed. Jay Robert Nash & Stanley Ralph Ross/CineBooks/ annual.

THE MOTION PICTURE GUIDE (12 vols) – The ultimate reference resource, with thorough synopses, credits and unhurried, incisive critiques of over 60,000 movies. Prohibitively expensive, but any decent library should possess a set. ed. Jay Robert Nash & Stanley Ralph Ross/CineBooks/1985–88.

TV MOVIES AND VIDEO GUIDE – Exhaustive, low-brow thumbnail sketches of English-language and a few foreign movies. ed. Leonard Maltin/Penguin/ annual.

HALLIWELL'S FILM GUIDE – As above, but with credits; synopses and critiques are poor indeed. Leslie Halliwell/Collins/ various editions.

Genre:

THE ENCYCLOPEDIA OF WESTERN MOVIES – Exactly what it says; very intelligently compiled and written. ed. Phil Hardy/Octopus/1985.

THE BFI COMPANION TO THE WESTERN – Equally essential but rather more concerned with historical and cultural background. ed. Ed Buscombe/André Deutsch/BFI/1988.

THE ENCYCLOPEDIA OF SCIENCE FICTION MOVIES – Another exhaustive account of a genre. ed. Phil Hardy/ Octopus/1986.

THE AURUM FILM ENCYCLOPEDIA – HORROR – As above. ed. Phil Hardy/ Aurum/1985.

NIGHTMARE MOVIES – A CRITICAL HISTORY OF THE HORROR FILM, 1968–88 – Enthusiastic, knowledgeable defence of the modern horror film. Kim Newman/ Bloomsbury/1988.

HORROR MOVIES – Useful historical overview. Carlos Clarens/Panther/1971.

A HERITAGE OF HORROR – Pioneering study of English Gothic cinema from 1946 to 1972. David Pirie/Avon/1973.

FILM NOIR – Encyclopedic, uneven but largely sensible. ed. Alain Silver and Elizabeth Ward/Overlook/1979.

CRIME MOVIES – Historical study, strong on relating movies to social factors. Carlos Clarens/Secker and Warburg/1980.

THE HOLLYWOOD MUSICAL – Film by film history. ed. Clive Hirschhorn/ Octopus/1981.

THE EPIC FILM – Usefully compares movies with relevant history and literature. Derek Elley/Routledge and Kegan Paul/1984.

Directors:

THE AMERICAN CINEMA – Pioneering if now rather dated American auteurist study. Andrew Sarris/Dutton/1968.

KINGS OF THE Bs – Excellent pot-pourri of essays on Hollywood's lower echelons. ed. Todd McCarthy & Charles Flynn/ Dutton/1975.

GREAT FILM DIRECTORS – Uneven, safe but useful anthology of essays on 23 top directors. ed. Leo Braudy and Morris Dickstein/Oxford/1978.

THE MOVIE DIRECTORS STORY – Intelligent overview of the careers of 140 Hollywood film-makers. Joel W. Finler/ Octopus/1985.

INTERVIEWS WITH DIRECTORS – Exactly what it says. ed. Andrew Sarris/Avon/1969.

HOLLYWOOD DIRECTORS 1914–40 & 1941–76 (2 vols) – Articles by a wide array of American directors. ed. Richard Koszarski/ Oxford/1976.

Hollywood:

THE HOLLYWOOD STORY – Well-researched facts and figures stressing the collaborative and industrial nature of Tinseltown's output. Joel W. Finler/Octopus/1988.

ANATOMY OF THE MOVIES – Useful essays and statistics about modern Hollywood. ed. David Pirie/Windward/1981.

THE HOLLYWOOD FILM INDUSTRY – Largely theoretical: Hollywood as a social/cultural/economic phenomenon. ed. Paul Kerr/Routledge & Kegan Paul/BFI/1986.

THE HOLLYWOOD STUDIOS – Basic historical survey. Roy Pickard/Muller/1978.

THE MGM/WARNER BROTHERS/RKO/PARAMOUNT/UNIVERSAL/UNITED ARTISTS STORY (6 vols) – various/Octopus.

THE PARADE'S GONE BY – Pioneering study of silent Hollywood with many fine interviews. Kevin Brownlow/Secker and Warburg/1968.

Theory and criticism:

FILM THEORY AND CRITICISM – Variable anthology serving as useful introduction to different critical methods. ed. Gerald Mast & Marshall Cohen/New York/1985.

SIGNS AND MEANING IN THE CINEMA – Seminal, admirably lucid survey of montage theory, auteurism and semiology. Peter Wollen/Secker and Warburg/1972.

THEORIES OF FILM – Sensible round-up of diverse approaches to film criticism. Andrew Tudor/Secker and Warburg/1974.

FILM AS FILM – Basic but clear-eyed argument for a synthetic view of the movies. V. F. Perkins/Penguin/1972.

Film Information

THIS SECTION lists selected information sources for a further exploration of cinema: magazines; film institutes, archives, and film schools; festivals. The listing – inevitably, given the universal popularity of film, not comprehensive – is based on the latest information available at time of going to press, but will inevitably be subject to change. Where possible, the magazines listed are in English. Amendments and suggestions for inclusion should be sent to: The Film Handbook, Longman Group UK Limited, Longman House, Burnt Mill, Harlow, Essex CM20 2JE, UK.

UNITED KINGDOM

Magazines
MONTHLY FILM BULLETIN
British Film Institute,
21 Stephen Street,
London W1P 1PL
01 255 1444

SIGHT AND SOUND
British Film Institute,
21 Stephen Street,
London W1P 1PL
01 255 1444

SCREEN INTERNATIONAL
King Publications,
6–7 Great Chapel Street,
London W1
01 734 9452

AFTERIMAGE
1 Birnham Road,
London N4 3LJ

FILMS AND FILMING
248 High Street,
Croydon,
Surrey CR0 1NF

SCREEN
29 Old Compton Street,
London W1V 5PL
01 734 5455

FRAMEWORK
40A Topsfield Parade,
London N8 8QA

Institutions
BRITISH FILM INSTITUTE
21 Stephen Street,
London W1P 1PL
01 255 1444

NATIONAL FILM THEATRE
South Bank,
London SE1 8XT
01 928 3535

MUSEUM OF THE MOVING IMAGE
South Bank,
London SE1 8XT

NATIONAL FILM ARCHIVE
21 Stephen Street,
London W1P 1PL
01 255 1444

NATIONAL FILM SCHOOL
Station Road,
Beaconsfield
Bucks HP9 1LG
04946 71234

LONDON INTERNATIONAL FILM SCHOOL
24 Shelton Street
London WC2H 9HP
01 240 0168

Festivals
LONDON
National Film Theatre,
South Bank,
London SE1 8XT
01 928 3535

EDINBURGH
The Film House,
88 Lothian Road,
Edinburgh EH3 9BZ
031 228 2688

CAMBRIDGE
Arts Cinema,
Market Passage,
Cambridge CB2 3PF
0223 462666

TYNESIDE
Tyneside Cinema,
10–12 Pilgrim Street,
Newcastle-upon-Tyne
0632 321507

AUSTRALIA

Magazine
CINEMA PAPERS
43 Charles Street
Abbotsford 3067

Institutions
AUSTRALIAN FILM COMMISSION
8 West Street,
North Sydney,
New South Wales 2060
02 922 6855

NATIONAL FILM AND SOUND ARCHIVE
McCoy Circuit,
Acton,
Canberra ACT 2601

AUSTRALIAN FILM AND TELEVISION SCHOOL
Box 126, PO North Ryde,
New South Wales 2113

Festivals
MELBOURNE
GPO Box 2760EE,
Melbourne 3001

SYDNEY
Box 25, PO Glebe,
New South Wales 2037
02 660 3844

AUSTRIA

Institutions
MINISTRY FOR ART AND EDUCATION,
Section 4, Freyung 1,
A 1010 Vienna
0222 66200

ÖSTERREICHES FILMARCHIV
Rauhensteingasse 5,
A 1010 Vienna

ÖSTERREICHES FILMMUSEUM
Augustinerstrasse 1,
A 1010 Vienna

(Film School) HOCHSHULE FÜR MUSIK UND ANGEWANDE KUNST, ABTEILUNG FÜR FILM UND FERNSEHEN
Metternichgasse 12,
1 1030 Vienna

Festival
VIENNALE
Künstlerhaus, Karlsplatz 5
A 1010 Vienna
0222 56 9823

BELGIUM

Magazine
CINÉMA CINÉMA
Ministry of French Culture
Avenue de Cortenbur 158,
1040 Brussels

Institutions
MINISTRY OF EDUCATION AND CULTURE (CINEMA DEPT.)
7 quai du Commerce,
1000 Brussels
02 217 4190

CINEMATHÈQUE ROYALE
23 Rue Ravenstein,
1000 Brussels
02 513 4155

(Film School) INSTITUT DES ARTS DE DIFFUSION
Rue des Blancs Chevaux 38–40,
B 1348 Louvain-la-Neuve

(Film School) INSAS
Rue Théresienne 8,
B 100 Brussels

Festivals
ANTWERP
Filmhouse,
Lange Brilstraat 12,
Box 6, B 2000 Antwerp

BRUSSELS INTERNATIONAL FILM FESTIVAL
Palais des Congrès,
1030 Brussels

BRUSSELS FANTASY FILM FESTIVAL
Passage 44 Auditorium,
Boulevard du Jardin Botanique,
1000 Brussels

BRAZIL

Institutions
CONSUELHO NACIONAL DO CINEMA
Rua Visconde de Inhauma 58,
Rio de Janeiro
021 233 8329

CINEMATECA BRASILIERA
Caixa Postal 12900,
São Paulo

CINEMATECA DO MUSEU DE ARTE MODERNA
Caixa Postal 44,
20000 Rio de Janeiro

(Film School) ESCOLA SUPERIOR DE CINEMA
Pontificia Universidade Católica,
Av Brasil 2033,
Belo Horizonte,
Minas Gerais

ESCOLA SUPERIOR DE CINEMA,
Faculdade São Paulo

Festival
RIO DE JANEIRO
362 Rua Paissandu,
22210 Laranjeiras,
Rio de Janeiro

BULGARIA

Institutions
FILM BULGARIA
96 Rakovski Street,
1000 Sofia

BULGARSKA NACIONALNA FILMOTEKA
ul. Gourko 36,
1000 Sofia

Festival
VARNA WORLD ANIMATION FESTIVAL
International Film Festivals Office,
1 Bulgaria Square,
1414 Sofia

CANADA

Magazine
CINEMA CANADA
Box 398, Station Outremont,
Montreal H2V 4NF

Institutions
NATIONAL MOVING IMAGE AND SOUND ARCHIVES
395 Wellington Street,
Ottawa, Ontario K1A ON3

LA CINÉMATHÈQUE QUÉBECOISE
335 Boul. de Maisonneuve est,
Montreal, H2X 1KI
514 842 9763

ONTARIO FILM INSTITUTE
770 Don Mills Road,
Don Mills, Ontario M3C 1T3
416 429 4100

Festivals
MONTREAL
1455 Boul. de Maisonneuve ouest,
Montreal H3G 1M8

TORONTO
Suite 205, 69 Yorkville Avenue,
Toronto, Ontario M5R 1B8

CHINA

Magazine
CHINA SCREEN
25 Xin Wai Street,
Beijing

Institutions
CHINA FILM CORPORATION
25 Xin Wai Street,
Beijing,
2014316

CHINESE CINEMATHEQUE
25B Xin Wai Street,
Beijing,

CUBA

Magazine
CINE CUBANO
Calle 23, 1155,
Havana 4

Institution
CUBAN INSTITUTE OF ARTS AND THE FILM INDUSTRY
Calle 23, 1155,
Havana 4
34719

Festival
HAVANA
Calle 23, 1155,
Havana 4

CZECHOSLOVAKIA

Magazine
CZECHOSLOVAK FILM
28 Václavské Máměsti,
Prague 1

Institutions
CENTRAL MANAGEMENT OF CZECHOSLOVAK FILM
Jindřiška 34,
11206 Prague 1
02 223751

CZECHOSLOVAKIAN FILM ARCHIVE
Národni 40,
11000 Prague 1
260087

FACULTY OF FILM AND TELEVISION (FAMU)
Academy of Arts,
Smentanovo nábřeži 2,
Prague 1

Festival
KARLOVY VARY
Československý Film,
Jindřiška 34,
11206 Prague 1

DENMARK

Magazine
KOSMORAMA
The Danish Film Museum,
Store Søndervoldstraede,
DK 1419 Copenhagen K

Institutions
DANISH GOVERNMENT FILM OFFICE
Vestergade 27,
1419 Copenhagen K
01 132 686

DANISH FILM MUSEUM/DANISH FILM SCHOOL
Store Søndervoldstraede,
DK 1419 Copenhagen K

FRANCE

Magazines
CAHIERS DU CINÉMA
Éditions de l'Étoile,
9 passage de la Boule Blanche,
75012 Paris

POSITIF
Nouvelles Éditions Opta,
1 quai Conti,
75006 Paris

PREMIÈRE
23–25 rue de Berri,
75388 Paris

L'AVANT SCÈNE (CINÉMA)
16 rue des Quatre-Vents,
75006 Paris

Institutions
CENTRE NATIONAL DE LA CINÉMATOGRAPHE
12 rue de Lübeck,
75784 Paris
01 505 1440

CINÉMATHÈQUE FRANÇAISE
29 rue de Colisée,
75008 Paris

(Film School) FEMIS,
Palais de Tokyo,
2 rue de la Manutention,
75116 Paris

(Film School) CONSERVATOIRE LIBRE DU CINÉMA FRANÇAIS
16 rue de Delta,
75009 Paris

(Film School) INSTITUT SUPÉRIEUR DE CINÉMA, RADIO ET TÉLÉVISION
65 bd. Brune,
75014 Paris

Festivals
ANNECY ANIMATION FESTIVAL
4 passage des Clercs,
BP 399, 74013 Annecy

AVORIAZ FANTASY FILM FESTIVAL
33 avenue MacMahon,
75017 Paris

CANNES
71 rue de Faubourg St-Honoré
75008 Paris

CLERMONT-FERRAND FESTIVAL OF SHORT FILMS
26 rue des Jacobins,
63000 Clermont-Ferrand

FINLAND

Magazines
SPEKTRI
Box 142,
SF-00101 Helsinki

STILL
PO Box 432,
SF-33101 Tampere

Institution
(Archive) SUOMEN ELOKUVA-ARKISTO
Pursimiehenkatu 29–31,
SF-00150 Helsinki
171417

Festival
TAMPERE SHORT FILM FESTIVAL
PO Box 305,
SF-33101 Tampere

WEST GERMANY (GFR)

Magazine
KINO
Türkenstrasse 93,
8000 Munich 40

Institutions
MUNICH FILMMUSEUM
St Jakob-Platz 1,
8000 Munich
2332348

STIFTUNG DEUTSCHE KINEMATHEK/DEUTSCHE FILM- UND FERNSEHAKADEMIE
Pommernallee 1,
1000 Berlin 19
30307234

DEUTSCHES FILMMUSEUM/ DEUTSCHES INSTITUT FÜR FILMKUNDE
Schaumainkai 41,
6000 Frankfurt am Main 70
617045

ARSENAL KINO DER FREUNDE DER DEUTSCHEN KINEMATHEK
v Welserstrasse 25,
D-1000 Berlin 30
2136039

Festivals
BERLIN
Budapester Strasse 50,
1000 Berlin 30

MANNHEIM
Filmwochenbüro,
Collini-Center-Gallerie,
D-6800 Mannheim

MUNICH
Türkenstrasse 93,
8000 Munich 40

HOF
Postfach 1146,
D-8670 Hof

OBERHAUSEN SHORT FILM FESTIVAL
Westdeutsche Kurzfilmtage,
Grillostrasse 34,
4200 Oberhausen 1

EAST GERMANY (GDR)

Institutions
STAATLICHES FILMARCHIV DER DDR
Hausvogteiplatz 3–4,
1080 Berlin
2124324

(Film School) HOCHSCHULE FÜR FILM UND FERNSEHEN DER DDR
Karl Marx-Strasse 27,
1502 Potsdam-Babelsberg

Festivals
LEIPZIG DOCUMENTARY AND ANIMATION FESTIVAL
Chodowieckstrasse 32,
DDR 1055 Berlin

GREECE

Institution
TAINIOTHIKI TIS ELLADOS
1 Canari Street,
Athens 10674
3612046

HONG KONG

Magazine
FILM BIWEEKLY
Flat E,
14/F Tung Nam Building,
475–481 Hennessy Road,
Hong Kong

Festival
HONG KONG
Hong Kong Coliseum Annex Building,
Parking Deck Floor,
KCR Kowloon Station,
8 Cheong Wan Road,
Kowloon, HK

HUNGARY

Magazines
HUNGAROFILM BULLETIN
Báthori útca 10,
Budapest V

FILM KULTURA
Népstadion út. 97,
Budapest XIV

Institutions
CENTRAL BOARD OF HUNGARIAN CINEMATOGRAPHY
Szálai út. 10,
1054 Budapest

MAGYAR FILM INTÉZET
Budakészi út. 51b,
1021 Budapest
767106

INDIA

Magazine
CINEMA INDIA INTERNATIONAL
A-15 Anand Nagar,
Juhu Tara Road,
Bombay 400 049

Institutions
NATIONAL FILM DEVELOPMENT CORPORATION
1st Floor, 13–16 Regent Chambers,
208 Nariman Point,
Bombay 400 021

NATIONAL FILM ARCHIVE OF INDIA/FILM AND TELEVISION INSTITUTE OF INDIA
Law College Road,
Poona 411 004
51559

FILM AND TELEVISION INSTITUTE OF TAMIL NADU
Department of Information and Public Relations,
Adyar,
Madras 600 020

Festival
NEW DELHI/BOMBAY (alternate years)
Lok Nayak Bhawan,
Khan Market,
New Delhi 110 003

IRELAND

Institution
IRISH FILM BOARD
65 Pembroke Lane,
Dublin 2

Festival
CORK
38 MacCurtain Street
Cork

ISRAEL

Magazines
ISRAEL FILM CENTRE INFORMATION BULLETIN
Ministry of Commerce and Industry,
30 Agron Street,
Jerusalem,

CINEMATHEQUE
Minicipality Building,
Tel Aviv

Institutions
ISRAEL FILM ARCHIVE/ JERUSALEM CINEMATHEQUE
Hebron Road,
PO Box 8561,
Jerusalem 91083
724131

DEPARTMENT OF FILM AND TELEVISION
Tel Aviv University,
Tel Aviv

Festival
JERUSALEM
PO Box 8561,
Jerusalem 91083

ITALY

Magazines
BIANCO E NERO
Via Tuscolana 1524,
00173 Rome

CIAK SI GIRA
Ca. 50 Europa 5–7,
20122 Milan

Institutions
CINEMATECA ITALIANA
Via Palestro 16,
20121 Milan
799224

MUSEO NAZIONALE DEL CINEMA
Palazzo Chiablese,
Piazza San Giovanni 2,
10122 Torino
510370

CINETECA NAZIONALE
Via Tuscolana 1524
00173 Rome
746941

(Film School) CENTRO SPERIMENTALE DI CINEMATOGRAFIA
Via Tuscolana 1524,
00173 Rome

Festivals
TAORMINA
Via P.S. Mancini 12,
00196 Rome

VENICE
La Biennale,
Ca. Giustinian,
30100 Venice

PORDENONE FESTIVAL OF SILENT CINEMA
Cinemazero,
Viale Grigoletti 20,
33170 Pordenone

JAPAN

Institutions
JAPAN FILM LIBRARY COUNCIL/KAWAKITA MEMORIAL FILM INSTITUTE
Ginza-Hata Building,
4–5, 4-chome,
Ginza,
Chuo-ku,
Tokyo

NATIONAL FILMCENTER
7–6, 3-chome,
Kyobashi,
Chuo-ku
Tokyo

Festivals
TOKYO
3 Asano Building,
2–4–19 Ginza,
Chuo-ku,
Tokyo

HIROSHIMA ANIMATION FESTIVAL
1–1 Nakajima-cho,
Naka-ku
Hiroshima 730

LUXEMBOURG

Institutions
CINÉMATHÈQUE MUNICIPALE DE LA VILLE DE LUXEMBOURG
28 place Guillaume,
L 1648
Luxembourg
479 62644

MEXICO

Institutions
FILMOTECA DE LA UNIVERSIDAD NACIONAL AUTONOMA DE MEXICO
San Ildefonso 43,
06020 Mexico DF
522 4665

CINEMATECA MEXICANA
Museo Nacional de Antropologia,
Clazada M. Gandhi,
Mexico 6, DF

CINETECA NACIONAL
Av. Mexico-Coyoacán 389,
03330 Mexico
688 8814

DIRECCION GENERAL DE RADIO, TELEVISION Y CINEMATOGRAFICA
Guanajuato 125,
Col. Roma,
Mexico DF

NETHERLANDS

Magazines
SKOOP
Postbus 11377,
Amsterdam

SKRIEN
Postbus 318,
1000 AH Amsterdam

Institutions
STICHTING NEDERLANDS FILMMUSEUM
Vondelpark 3,
1071 AA Amsterdam
831646

AUDIOVISUAL ARCHIVE OF THE NETHERLANDS INFORMATION SERVICE
Baden Powellweg 5,
2583 KT The Hague

NEDERLANDSE FILM EN TELEVISIE ACADAMIE
De Lairessestraat 142,
1075 HL Amsterdam

Festival
ROTTERDAM
PO Box 21696,
3011 AR Rotterdam

NEW ZEALAND

Magazine
ONFILM
PO Box 6374,
Wellington

Institutions
NEW ZEALAND FILM COMMISSION
PO Box 11–546,
Wellington
04 859 754

NEW ZEALAND FILM ARCHIVE
PO Box 9544,
82 Tory Street,
Wellington
847647

Festivals
AUCKLAND
PO Box 1411,
Auckland

WELLINGTON
PO Box 9544,
Courtenay Place,
Wellington

NORWAY

Magazine
Z FILMTIDSSKRIFT
Wessels gt 4,
Oslo 1

Institution
NORSK FILMINSTITUTT
Militaerhospitalet,
Grev Wedels plass,
Postboks 482,
Sentrum,
0105 Oslo 1
42 87 40

POLAND

Magazines
POLISH FILM
Film Polski,
ul. Mazowiecka 6–8,
00–054 Warsaw

FILMOWY SERWIS PRASOWY
ul. Mazowiecka 6–8,
00–950 Warsaw

Institutions
FILMOTEKA POLSKA
ul. Pulawska 61,
00–975 Warsaw
455 074

(Film School) PAŃSWOWA WYSZA SZKOLA FILMOWA
im Leona Schillera, U1,
Targowa 61/63,
90 323 Łodz

Festival
CRACOW
Pl. Zwyciestwa 9,
PO Box 127,
0 950 Warsaw

PORTUGAL

Magazine
CINEMA NOVO
Apartado 78,
4002 Porto Codex

Institution
CINEMATECA PORTUGUESA
Rua Barata Salgueiro 39,
1200 Lisbon
548799

ROMANIA

Magazine
ROMANIAN FILM
25 Julius Fucik Street,
Bucharest

Institutions
ARCHIVA NATIONALA DE FILME
Bd. G.H. Gheorgiu dej 68/65,
Bucharest

(Film School) INSTITUTUL DE ARTĂ TEATRALĂ ŞI CINEMATOGRFICĂ
Str. Matei Voievod nr. 75–77,
sect 2 cod 73226, Bucharest

SPAIN

Magazines
CINEMA 2002
Ardemans 64,
Madrid 28

DIRIGIDO POR . . .
Rbla de Catalunya, 108 3.1.,
Barcelona 8

Institutions
FILMOTECA ESPAÑOLA
Carretera de la Dehesa de la Villa s/n,
28040 Madrid
449001

FILMOTECA DE LA GENERALITAT DE CATALUNYA
Diputacio 281,
08007 Barcelona
317 35 85

Festivals
SAN SEBASTIAN
Apartado Carreos,
397 Reina Regenta s/n,
20080 San Sebastian

SITGES FANTASY FILM FESTIVAL
Rambla Catalunya 81-Entre,
Barcelona 7

VALLADOLID
Apartado de Correos 646,
47006 Valladolid

SWEDEN

Magazines
CHAPLIN/SCANDINAVIAN FILM NEWS
Swedish Film Institute,
Box 27 126,
S-102 52 Stockholm 27

FILMHÄFTET
Box 16046,
S-750 16 Uppsala

Institutions
SWEDISH FILM INSTITUTE/CINEMATHEQUE
Filmhuset, Borgvägen,
Box 27 126,
S-102 52 Stockholm 27
665 1100

(Film School) DRAMATISKA INSTITUTET
Borgvägen,
Box 27 090,
S-102 51 Stockholm

Festival
GOTHENBERG
PO Box 7079,
S-402 32 Göteborg

SWITZERLAND

Magazines
CINÉ-BULLETIN
Clarastrasse 48,
Postfach 4005,
Basel

FILM-BULLETIN
Postfach 6887,
8023 Zurich

Institution
CINÉMATHÈQUE SUISSE
3 Allée Ernest Ansermet,
1003 Lausanne
237 406

Festival
LOCARNO
Via F. Balli 2,
Casella Postale 186,
6600 Locarno

TAIWAN

Magazine
FILM APPRECIATION
Film Library, 4th Floor,
7 Ch'ingtao East Road,
Taipei

Institution
FILM LIBRARY OF THE MOTION PICTURE DEVELOPMENT FOUNDATION
4th Floor,
7 Ch'ingtao East Road,
Taipei

Festival
TAIPEI
Film Library, 4th Floor,
7 Ch'ingtao East Road,
Taipei

THAILAND

Institution
NATIONAL FILM ARCHIVE OF THAILAND
4 Chao Fa Road,
Bangkok 10200

TURKEY
Magazine
FILM MARKET
Kuloğlu sok. 28/4,
Beyoğlu-Istanbul

Institution
SINEMA-TV ENSTITÜSÜ
80700 Kislaönü-Besiktas,
Istanbul
166 983031

Festival
ISTANBUL
Yildiz Kultur ve Sanat Merkezi,
80700 Besiktas,
Istanbul

USA

Magazines
AMERICAN FILM
30 E 54th Street
New York, NY 10022

FILM COMMENT
140 W 65th Street,
New York, NY 10023

FILM QUARTERLY
University of California Press,
Berkeley, Ca 94720

HOLLYWOOD REPORTER
6715 Sunset Boulevard,
Hollywood, Ca 90028

PREMIERE
2 Park Avenue,
New York, NY 10016

VARIETY
154 W 46th Street,
New York, NY 10036

Institutions
AMERICAN FILM INSTITUTE
John F. Kennedy Center for the Performing Arts,
Washington, DC 20566

LIBRARY OF CONGRESS
Motion Picture, Broadcasting and Recorded Sound Division,
Washington, DC 20540
202 287 5840

MUSEUM OF MODERN ART
Department of Film,
11 W 53rd Street,
New York, NY 10019
212 708 9602

GEORGE EASTMAN HOUSE/ INTERNATIONAL MUSEUM OF PHOTOGRAPHY
900 East Avenue,
Rochester, NY 14607
716 271 3361

ACADEMY OF MOTION PICTURE ARTS AND SCIENCES
8949 Wilshire Boulevard,
Beverley Hills, Ca 90211

PACIFIC FILM ARCHIVE
University Art Museum,
2625 Durant Avenue,
Berkeley, Ca 94720

UCLA FILM AND TELEVISION ARCHIVE
1438 Melnitz Hall,
University of California,
405 Hilgard Avenue,
Los Angeles, Ca 90024
213 206 8013

(Film Schools: information from) PETERSON'S GUIDES
228 Alexander Street,
Princeton, NJ 08540

Festivals
CHICAGO
415 North Dearborn Street,
Chicago, Ill 60610

NEW YORK
Film Society of Lincoln Center,
140 W 65th Street,
New York, NY 10023

SAN FRANCISCO
1560 Fillmore Street,
San Francisco, Ca 94115

USSR

Magazines
SOVIET FILM
Sovexportfilm,
14 Kalashny pereulok,
Moscow 103009

SOVYETSKI EKRAN
ul. Chasovaya 5–6,
Moscow A-319

Institutions
GOSFILMOFOND
Stantsia Byelye Stolby,
Moskovskaya Oblast
546 05 16

ALL-UNION STATE INSTITUTE OF CINEMATOGRAPHY
ulitsa Vilgelma Pika 3,
Moscow 129226

Festival
MOSCOW
Sovinterfest,
State Committee for Cinematography,
10 Khokhlovsky pereulak,
Moscow 109028

YUGOSLAVIA

Institutions
JUGOSLOVENSKA KINOTEKA
Knez Mihailova 19,
11000 Belgrade
622 555

(Film School) FAKULTET DRAMŠKIH UMETNOSTI
Ho Si Minova 20,
11070 Belgrade

Festivals
BELGRADE
Sava Center,
M Popovica 9,
11070 Belgrade

ZAGREB ANIMATION FESTIVAL
Nova Ves 18,
41000 Zagreb

Index

D

E

F

G

H

I

J

K

M

N

P

Q

R

S

U

V

W

Z